SECOND EDITION

Journalism

PUBLISHING ACROSS MEDIA

Janet Ewell, MA, MJE
Student Journalism Advocate
Huntington Beach, California

Michelle Balmeo, MJE
Journalism Adviser
West Albany High School
Albany, Oregon

Ellen Austin, M.Ed, MJE
Director of Journalism
The Harker School
San Jose, California

Randy Hamm, CJE
Bella Vista, Arkansas

Publisher
The Goodheart-Willcox Company, Inc.
Tinley Park, Illinois
www.g-w.com

Manufactured in the United States of America.

ISBN 978-1-63563-833-2

1 2 3 4 5 6 7 8 9 – 19 – 24 23 22 21 20 19

Cover image: The cover of *Journalism: Publishing Across Media* is comprised of photos taken by and featuring real student journalists. These students are acknowledged on page v. For a more detailed list of cover credits, see page 564.

Dedication

To the Journalism Education Association Listserv, which brought us all together and made each one of us a better adviser.

We would also like to extend a special thank you to the Los Angeles Times for its generous permission to reproduce examples of fine journalism from its pages and website.

About the Authors

Janet Ewell has advised award-winning newspapers at two Title One urban high schools. She is a Master Journalism Educator, a recipient of the Journalism Education Association Medal of Merit and the Columbia Scholastic Press Association's Gold Key. The University of Southern California Annenberg School for Communication honored her in 2008 for "Defense of the First Amendment and the rights of all California students."

She credits her background as a National Board Certified Teacher and as a Fellow of the South Basin Writing Project for much of her approach to teaching journalism.

She graduated from Brigham Young University and received her Masters from California State University Long Beach. She has been published in English Journal, Journalism Education Today, California Publisher, Dow-Jones Adviser and the Los Angeles Times, and has presented at multiple Journalism Education Association conventions and other journalism workshops.

Michelle Balmeo, Master Journalism Educator, has spent over a decade advising high school journalists, first in California and now in Albany, Oregon. In that time, her students have been multiple-time National Scholastic Press Association Pacemaker Award winners and Columbia Scholastic Press Association Crown Award winners. She guided her first staff through the transition from a print monthly newspaper to a monthly newsmagazine and news website that incorporated interactive and multimedia storytelling. Now at West Albany High School, she has helped a new group of students bring back a publication that died years ago and is guiding them through the process of building a multi-platform converged media program. Balmeo was a 2010 California Journalism Educator of the Year, High School Division, a 2011 Journalism Education Association Rising Star, and a 2014 Dow Jones News Fund Distinguished Adviser. She regularly presents at local and national conferences, contributes to the JEADigitalMedia.org website, and served as the Web Curriculum Leader and a Partner Project Lead for JEA.

Ellen Austin has taught journalism and advised student publications since 2000. She is currently the director of journalism at The Harker School in San Jose, where she advises the award-winning newspaper, news magazine, website and yearbook programs. Previously, Austin taught journalism for six years at Palo Alto High School, where she started the nationally recognized Viking sports magazine and website, and co-advised the broadcast program.

Austin has served on the Journalism Education Association national board of directors and the JEA (Northern California) regional board. Austin serves on the Student Press Law Center steering committee, and was its former chair. She was a JEA Rising Star honoree in 2006, the inaugural year of that award. She received the 2011 CAL-JEC Journalism Educator of the Year (High School Division) and was the Dow Jones News Fund 2012 National Journalism Teacher of the Year. She holds a Gold Key from the Columbia Scholastic Press Association. She is a presenter at state and national conventions, and teaches at several journalism workshops.

Austin holds an undergraduate degree in business from the University of Illinois (Urbana-Champaign) and a master's degree in secondary education from the University of Minnesota.

Randy Hamm advised The Kernal, the student paper at East High School in Bakersfield, California, for 21 years. The California Journalism Education Coalition named him High School Journalism Educator of the Year in 2006, the same year his students received a Pacemaker award from the National Scholastic Press Association. Hamm served for many years on the board of the Northern California Journalism Education Association. He lives with his wife Norma in Bella Vista, Arkansas.

Contributors

Goodheart-Willcox Publisher and the authors would like to thank the following individuals for the photographs, stories, and excerpts from online and printed student publications featured throughout the textbook. The cover of *Journalism: Publishing Across Media* is comprised of photos taken by and featuring real student journalists. We are proud to feature these photos, along with the many student-created pieces found inside the textbook, as examples of high-quality student journalism.

On the cover

Forrest Czarnecki
Conifer High School
Conifer, Colorado

Kyle Farrell
Lee County High School
Leesburg, Georgia

Nora Parisi
Woodrow Wilson High School
Washington D.C.

Ana Perez
Daniel Pearl Magnet School
Van Nuys, California

Inside the textbook

Tracy Anderson and **Colleen O'Brien**
The Communicator
Community High School
Ann Arbor, Michigan

Jonathan Dai and **Kacey Fang**
The Winged Post
The Harker School
San Jose, California

Shari Adwers and **Allison Dunn**
North Pointe
Gross Pointe North High School
Gross Pointe, Michigan

Emily Arnold and **Valorie King**
Buffalo
Haltom High School
Haltom City, Texas

Tasha Beaudoin
The Lancer
Thousand Oaks High School
Thousand Oaks, California

Forrest Czarnecki and **Leslie Thompson**
Conifer High School
Conifer, Colorado

Kellen Ochi and **Michelle Min**
Sage Hill High School
Newport Coast, California

Greg Anderson, Emily Cunningham and **Paige Paulsen**
Arapahoe Herald
Arapahoe High School
Centennial, Colorado

Eric Aboytes, Scotty Bara, Sam Borsos, Ami Drez, Kevin Dukovic, Jacob Lauing, Austin Poore, Allie Shorin, Grant Shorin, Ryan Stratheran, Chris Smith and **Brian Wilson**
Viking Magazine
Palo Alto High School
Palo Alto, California

Deanne Brown, Cindy Todd, Chris Bull, Hannah Kunz and **Casey Simmons**
The Featherduster and El Paisano
Westlake High School
Austin, Texas

David Doerr, Johanna Dakay and **Amanda Livingston**
The Eagle's Eye
W. Charles Akins High School
Austin, Texas

Erin Coggins and **Tori Caudill**
The Crimson Crier
Sparkman High School
Harvest, Alabama

Greg Gagliardi and **Joel Greenspan**
Eastside
Cherry Hill High School East
Cherry Hill, New Jersey

Hillary Blayney and **Anita Hodge**
The Register
Omaha Central High School
Omaha, Nebraska

Paul Kandell
The Paly Voice
Palo Alto High School
Palo Alto, California

Matthew LaPorte
The Howl
Southwest Career and Technical Academy
Henderson, Nevada

Rodney K. Lowe, Patricia Delacruz, Jonah Charlton and **Trinity Collins**
The Evanstonian
Evanston Township High School
Evanston, Illinois

Susan Massy and **Andy Wickoren**
The Northwest Passage
Shawnee Mission Northwest High School
Shawnee, Kansas

Amy Morgan and **Garrett Wilson**
Epic
Shawnee Mission West High School
Overland Park, Kansas

Sarah Nichols
Whitney High School Student Media
Whitney High School
Rocklin, California

Ana Perez
Daniel Pearl Magnet School
Van Nuys, California

Melissa Rife and **Ashley Potts**
Legend
Centreville High School
Clifton, Virginia

Kyle Farrell
Lee County High School
Sanford, North Carolina

Julia Satterthwaite
The Talon
Rochester High School
Rochester Hills, Michigan

Tracy Anne Sena and **Rachel Fung**
The Broadview
Convent of the Sacred Heart High School
San Francisco, California

Alexandra Stryker, Mary Brown, Christopher Martin, Nora Parisi and **Amber Primus**
Woodrow Wilson High School
Washington, D.C.

C. Dow Tate, Stefano Byer, Jake Crandall and **Danielle Norton**
The Harbinger and Hauberk
Shawnee Mission East High School
Prairie Village, Kansas

Sheldon Thibodeau
The Villager
Westport High School
Westport, Massachusetts

Mike Williams
The Roar
A&M Consolidated High School
College Station, Texas

Mitch Ziegler and **Jake Collins**
Pilot
Redondo Union High School
Redondo Beach, California

Julia Satterthwaite
El Estoque
Monta Vista High School
Cupertino, California

Alexandra Fernholz and **Dean Hume**
Lakota East Spark
Lakota East High School
Cincinnati, Ohio

Josie Pringle and **Lisa Stine**
Hornet Yearbook
Bryant High School
Bryant, Arkansas

Reviewers

Goodheart-Willcox Publisher and the authors would like to thank the following instructors who reviewed selected manuscript chapters and provided valuable input into the development of this textbook program.

Sarah Beth Badalamente
Journalism Teacher
Grand Ledge High School
Grand Ledge, Michigan

Claire Burke, CJE
Journalism Teacher
Charles E. Smith Jewish Day School
Rockville, Maryland

Linda Drake, MJE
Journalism Teacher
Chase County Jr.–Sr. High School
Cottonwood Falls, Kansas

Brad Froebel
Journalism Teacher
Klein Collins High School
Spring, Texas

Leah Glotzbach
Communications Department Chair
Episcopal School of Jacksonville
Jacksonville, Florida

Karen Hott
Journalism Teacher and Adviser
Broadneck High School
Annapolis, Maryland

Rachel Kidder
Journalism Adviser
Midlothian Heritage High School
Midlothian, Texas

David A. Ragsdale, CJE
Journalism Teacher
Clarke Central High School
Athens, Georgia

Robin Sawyer
Journalism Teacher
First Flight High School
Kill Devil Hills, North Carolina

Karen Slusher
Journalism Teacher
Eaglecrest High School
Centennial, Colorado

Debbie Smelley
Journalism Teacher
Starr's Mill High School
Fayetteville, Georgia

Mark Webber
Print Journalism, Online Media and CTE Instructor
Vidal M. Trevino School of Communications and Fine Arts
Laredo, Texas

Stan Zoller, MJE
Lecturer, Journalism
Lake Forest College
Lake Forest, Illinois

Brief Contents

Contents

Photo by Forrest Czarnecki, Conifer High School

Contents *(Continued)*

Courtesy of Ellen Austin

Chapter 8

Chapter 9

Chapter 10

Photo by Kellen Ochi, Courtesy of Michelle Min, Sage Hill School

Chapter 11

Contents *(Continued)*

Photo by Kyle Farrell, Lee County High School

Photo by Kyle Farrell, Lee County High School

Features

Journalism Style

Writers' Workshop

And Now...Closer to Home

(Continued)

Features *(Continued)*

And Now...Closer to Home *(Continued)*

For the Record

MEET THE PROFESSIONALS

CASE STUDY

To The Student

This text is not so much a textbook *about* journalism as it is a book about how to *do* journalism.

It is true you will find features that discuss our human hunger for news through thousands of years and our desire to be heard beyond the sound of our own voices. In the chapters on law and ethics, you will read about the close, and sometimes stormy, marriage between journalism and democracy.

But primarily this book contains what you first need to know in order to think, research, write, record and photograph, design and publish as a journalist, no matter what your current talents are, no matter what media you use to gather news and to publish it, or how you converse with your audience.

No one is born a proficient and ethical journalist. We grow as we practice the craft. This text provides basics, but basics you will revisit frequently even if you work as a journalist for decades: What is my job as a journalist? What should I cover? What legal protections do I enjoy as a citizen and as a journalist? Who do I trust as a source? How do I decide what to publish when it may help some and hurt others? When do I report all I know, and when do I remain respectfully silent?

Journalism is communication for a real audience who cares about—or can be made to care about— real events and issues. Here you will find chapters on reporting news, features stories, sports, reviews, and editorials and other opinion pieces. In each chapter the needs of your audience will influence your journalistic decisions.

Because we use words to think, journalism is at its heart about writing, no matter how many other modes of communication we employ. *Writers' Workshops* at the end of each chapter will help you hone your writing as a whetstone sharpens a knife. *Journalism Style* activities help you prepare your work for publication—and to be received with respect when it is published.

One commentator called journalism "twenty-first century English." So welcome to what can be a high point in your high school career, your best preparation for college work and perhaps the passion of a lifetime. Welcome to ***Journalism: Publishing Across Media***.

Janet Ewell

Michelle Balmeo

Ellen Austin

Randy Hamm

Chapter One

Bringing Information to an Audience

What does a journalist do?

Courtesy of Ellen Austin

G-WLEARNING.COM

While studying, look for the activity icon to:

- **Build** vocabulary terms with e-flash cards and matching activities.
- **Extend** learning with further discussion of relevant topics.
- **Reinforce** what you learn by completing style exercises, worksheets and end-of-chapter questions.

Visit the Journalism website: www.g-wlearning.com/journalism/

Chapter Objectives

After reading this chapter, you will be able to:

- Tell what a journalist does.
- Explain how journalism is different from other types of communication.
- List the journalistic skills, talents and abilities you already have.
- Discuss decisions a journalist makes because she knows her audience.
- Distinguish between the intended and the unintended audience.
- Tell how to learn about your audience.

Key Terms Build Vocab

accountable
content
context
implicit bias
intended audience
journalism
media
unintended audience

Before You Read...

Decoding is the translation of a message, such as a word, into terms that the reader can understand. Decoding occurs in the reader's mind. Locate the glossary of this text. Identify three words with which you are unfamiliar. Look at the letters that create each word and think about the sounds each one makes. Then, sound out the words by reading each letter from left to right. Practice saying the words aloud.

Introduction

"... were it left to me to decide whether we should have a government without newspapers, or newspapers without a government, I should not hesitate a moment to prefer the latter."

–Thomas Jefferson, third president of the United States

Journalism is so important to democracy that it is mentioned in the United States Constitution—the only profession mentioned there. In America, journalists enjoy certain specific legal privileges beyond the rights of other citizens.

So what is it journalists do that is so important? And what determines whether or not someone is a journalist? The answers to these questions are not simple because changes in technology have altered the ways in which a journalist works. We can say, however, that a journalist's core role is *to bring timely and accurate information and ideas to a mass audience*. Journalists are constrained by ethics and are held **accountable** (responsible) for their work. They also provide **context** (background and setting) for the news and help their audience make sense of events.

The journalist's audience includes readers, listeners and viewers who receive—and may help report—**content** (information and ideas). Content may be delivered through various **media**, including print, digital and broadcast (Figure 1.1).

Figure 1.1 News content may be delivered through print media, such as newspapers, and digital media, such as smartphones and tablet computers. Content may also be broadcast over television or radio networks. *How do you learn about news events?*

What exactly is journalism? No one definition suits everyone, and journalism changes as technology changes. For Thomas Jefferson in 1787, the chief news medium was a newspaper. In 1920, the first radio news program was broadcast. In 1948, television networks began to broadcast news. Beginning in 2011, more Americans got their news through the Internet than from any other source. Each new medium has allowed—and forced—journalism to change, but certain core ideas animate journalism in almost all media.

This definition of journalism works for many people: **Journalism** is a discipline of collecting, verifying, reporting and analyzing information regarding current events, including trends, issues and people, for a broad audience.

The phrase cloud in Figure 1.2 contains other definitions and other obligations of journalism.

We can have facts without thinking, but we cannot have thinking without facts.
one of the great interpreters between the government and the people
one of the great bulwarks of liberty
comfort the afflicted and afflict the comfortable
the first rough draft of history
inform the people
Journalism
freedom of expression
front door access to the truth
acta diurna
ensuring the government's accountability to the people
journalism is the discipline of gathering, writing and reporting the news
a public responsibility and a public trust
the duty of a journalist is to tell the truth
history in its first and best form, its vivid and most fascinating form
the press is the eye and ear and tongue of the people
full, fair, accurate
right to information
comment is free, but facts are sacred
those who practice journalism are journalists

Figure 1.2 *What do you think is journalism's most important role?*

Are You Already a Journalist?

You probably already have many skills and talents that are valuable to a journalist, but journalism may be different from the ways you already communicate. It is important for you to develop a strong sense of what journalism is and what it is not.

Do you communicate electronically through text messages, feeds, tweets, social sites or message services? Do you include pictures, video and sound files in these messages?

What text messaging shares with journalism:

- Each is meant to be read or viewed soon after it is created. Each is *timely*. Journalists strive to give fresh, new information accompanied by meaningful background information.
- People who send text messages usually know their audience (the people who will receive the messages). They know what their audience knows, is interested in, needs to have explained and needs or wants to learn.

Do you write research papers for your classes and make formal presentations that may include pictures, charts and video?

Characteristics that papers and presentations share with journalism:

- Your paper or presentation is only as strong as the information you have gathered.
- You identify your sources and make sure they are reliable.
- You have multiple sources.
- You make certain all your facts and quotations are accurate.
- Your paper and presentation are polished and proofread so that your ideas will be respected.
- You take the work through several drafts, using peer responders and proofreaders.

"Truth is stranger than fiction, but it is because fiction is obliged to stick to possibilities; truth isn't." –Mark Twain

Do you write songs, poems, stories or plays? Do you make videos or record music and publish these online?

Journalism uses many of the skills and tools of creative work:

- Both journalists and storytellers strive to portray vivid, interesting characters.
- They create narratives, pace their stories, create suspense, and use flashbacks and flash forwards.
- They control the tone of a story and the voice in which the story is told.

- They use multiple—and creative—points of view to tell a story.
- They use vivid and specific pictures of actions, people and settings.
- They compose, frame and crop images.
- They record and edit sound.
- They may use rhetorical devices such as metaphors, literary allusions, puns, alliteration and imagery.

YOUR TURN

Create an inventory (a list) of the talents and abilities you bring to journalism, based on the information in the section "Are You Already a Journalist?" Feel free to include abilities that you are just beginning to develop, as well as things you can do at a near-professional level.

Figure 1.3 Journalism is meant to communicate with a much larger audience than the average text message. *How might your text messaging experiences help you become a journalist?*

What Is Different About Journalism?

Look closely at these examples of communication to see how they resemble journalism but ultimately are NOT journalism.

Text Messaging

Suppose you send a text message to ten of your closest friends: "It's a party for Kristy's birthday. Meet at the south parking lot of Bella Terra Mall at 4:00 Saturday" (Figure 1.3).

Are you acting as a journalist?

Why This Is NOT Journalism

Journalism is meant to communicate to a mass audience. Your text is private communication; only a few people are meant to have access to this text. But if Kristy is a candidate for city council and your text announces the party to the whole city of 170,000, it may have become journalism.

The Principle

Journalism involves mass communication of reliable information that an audience wants or needs.

But Text Messaging Does Relate to Journalism Because–

Journalism, like your text message, decreases our isolation by informing us about other people, places, events and ideas and by helping us make sense of the world.

In addition, journalism strives for accuracy, just as your text message needs to be accurate. After all, if your text gives the wrong information and your audience arrives two hours early or goes to the wrong place, people will be mad and think you are untrustworthy. You would probably apologize and strive to be much more accurate in the future. You will be held accountable for your error. Journalists also strive for accuracy and are held accountable for what they write or broadcast.

How Your Experiences Texting May Help You Become a Journalist

- You may already have a strong desire to keep in touch with others and share information they want or need.
- You may already be good at identifying and understanding problems that affect you and others.
- People may count on you to be honest and accurate and to get the facts straight.

Social Networking

Figure 1.4 Imagine this conversation was recorded by one of the girls' younger brothers. *If he posts the video online, is this an act of journalism or a violation of privacy? Why?*

A student's older sister and her friends were talking about plastic surgery they would like to have. The student recorded video of the discussion and posted it online (Figure 1.4).

Was he acting as a journalist?

Why This Is NOT Journalism

Journalists are constrained by laws and ethics. This student was not acting ethically, or even within the law. It is probably safe to assume that these girls did not want or expect the world to hear what they said to a few of their closest friends in private, so publishing (posting) this video violated journalistic ethics—the rules and standards that journalists apply to questions about their own conduct and the work that they publish.

- The girls in the video had a reasonable expectation of privacy. This video violates that legal right.
- It appears that the maker of the video failed to identify himself as a journalist—someone who was involved in mass media—before recording the conversation. This is unethical.
- A journalist would carefully weigh the video's potential harm against the public's right and need to know about this conversation.

Recording and posting *this* video destroys trust between the recorder of the video and the subject.

The Principle

Journalists consider ethics and law as they gather news and before they publish.

But Social Networking Does Relate to Journalism Because–

A journalist always has his eyes and ears open. Teenagers and their interest in plastic surgery may be a great idea for a story. The article might include a description of what happens during plastic surgery and in the recovery process, information about laws and medical ethics regarding teens and plastic surgery, psychologists' opinions, and interviews with those who have had plastic surgery or are thinking about having it. The idea for the story may have come from what the journalist overheard.

Being a Good Listener May Help You Become a Journalist

- You may already listen respectfully to others to understand their interests and concerns—even when they are different from your own.
- You may already be skillful with audio and video recording equipment and with Internet publishing.

And Now... Closer to Home

Your Ethical Filter

In the case described on the previous page, publishing a recording of private conversation violates journalism's code of ethics and possibly the law. Before a journalist publishes anything, he or she should ask: "Who does this help? Who does this hurt?" Journalists should balance the public's right to know against the privacy rights of the individuals involved in the story. A journalist's desire to be the first to reveal something is never a justification for injuring others. You will read more about ethics in Chapter 4.

Research and Presentations

Your research topic in a literature class is "Stonehenge and the Arthurian Legend." After spending weeks gathering information from print and online sources, you have written a paper and prepared a formal presentation (Figure 1.5).

Were you acting as a journalist?

Why This Is NOT Journalism

A journalist remembers his audience at each step of the reporting, writing and publishing process. After all, if his first sentence is not interesting, it does not matter what his second sentence says because no one will read it. The same is true of his 13th sentence and his 14th.

When readers or viewers lose interest, they click on something else, change the channel or turn the page.

Figure 1.5 *How is this well-researched, formal presentation on Stonehenge related to journalism?*

The audience for a formal research paper is usually the teacher who assigns and grades it. Teachers read to the end of papers whether or not you have engaged their interest. And your classmates are captive until the bell rings.

The Principle

Journalists keep their audience in mind as they prepare stories. They strive to keep the viewer or reader interested throughout the piece.

But Presentations Do Relate to Journalism Because–

Like journalism, formal presentations require accuracy as well as careful proofreading. Your audiences for your journalism work—and for your class work—will be more likely to trust your information and ideas if you present them in finished form, carefully read, corrected and prepared for publication.

Journalists also use graphics, video and sound as well as words in their storytelling.

Doing Papers and Presentations Well May Help You Become a Journalist

- You may already be good at finding information and judging who or what is a reliable source.
- You may already be skillful with technology.
- You may already take pride in producing a polished and attractive work for publication.
- Your peers may already ask you to proofread or respond to their work.

YOUR TURN

Suppose you have been asked to give two presentations on the atomic bombings of Hiroshima and Nagasaki. The first presentation will be to a class of fourth graders, that is, 9- and 10-year-olds. The next presentation will be for a class of high school juniors and seniors.

Base your presentation on the information in the info box on the next page. Working with a partner or in a small group, create a Venn diagram comparing the two presentations.

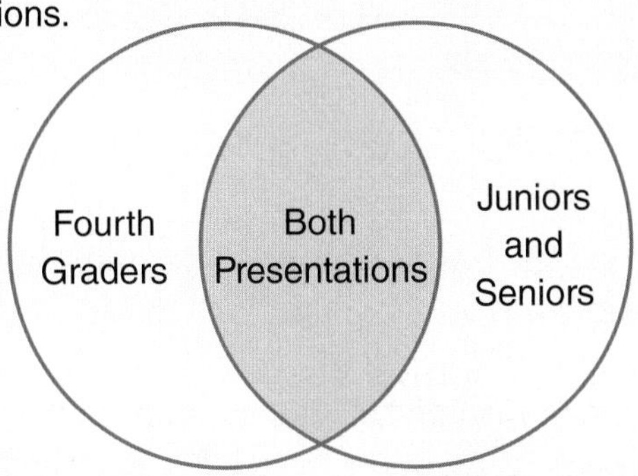

(Continued)

Your Turn *(Continued)*

The intersecting center of the Venn diagram should contain information that will be presented to both groups. On the right, put information and commentary that will be presented only to the high school students. On the left, include explanations, perspectives and information that you feel fourth graders should know, but that you do not feel are necessary for high school students.

Now imagine the visuals you will use with each presentation. Consider photographs, charts and maps. Note which you will use with each group on your Venn diagram.

Discuss your group's choices with at least one other group. Explain your choices. Your group's choices may be different from those of another group, but equally intelligent and thoughtful. In this exercise, a respectful discussion in which you listen to others and express your opinions is more important than coming to an agreement.

Atomic Bombings of Hiroshima and Nagasaki

In August 1945, the United States deployed atomic bombs over two Japanese cities, Hiroshima and Nagasaki. It was the first—and thus far the only—use of nuclear weapons in warfare.

The Allied powers had already defeated Germany, but despite extensive firebombing that had destroyed many Japanese cities, the Japanese continued to fight. In late July, the United States, together with the United Kingdom and China, issued the Potsdam Declaration. It called for Japan to surrender or face "prompt and utter destruction." When Japan rejected the declaration, U.S. President Harry Truman authorized the atomic bombing.

Little Boy, a uranium gun-type atomic bomb, was dropped on Hiroshima on August 6, destroying 90 percent of the city and immediately killing between 60,000 and 80,000 people. Fat Man, a plutonium implosion-type bomb, was dropped on Nagasaki on August 9 and killed 40,000 people. In the months following the bombings, many more people died from the effect of burns, radiation sickness and other injuries, compounded by illness. It has been estimated that the total death toll was 90,000 to 166,000 in Hiroshima and 60,000 to 80,000 in Nagasaki.

On August 15, just six days after the bombing of Nagasaki, Japan announced its surrender to the Allies. On September 2, the Japanese Instrument of Surrender was signed, formally ending World War II.

The role of the atomic bombings on Japan's surrender and their ethical justification are still being debated.

Self-Expression

Sometimes it is easier to write about something than to talk about it. Perhaps you keep a journal or write music to describe your experiences, ideas and feelings (Figure 1.6).

Are you acting as a journalist?

Figure 1.6 Methods of self expression, such as playing an instrument or writing in a journal prepare you to write and report well, but journalists concentrate on the experiences of others, not their own experiences.

Why This Is NOT Journalism

Journalists rarely are the subject of their own writing. They strive to avoid appearing in the story or video (except when necessary as interviewers). A journalist's strong personal reactions to a news event *may* be conveyed under certain circumstances through details, images or factual anecdotes, but not through a discussion of the journalist's emotions.

Factual material from a journal or diary may be incorporated into a journalistic blog or into a journalistic story, but the blog or story will focus on the event, not the reporter, and adhere to journalistic standards of verification, fairness and accountability.

The Principle

Journalists strive to write in an unbiased and accurate manner. They almost always use the objective point of view. In news stories, they write about events, not about their own reactions to them.

But Self-Expression Does Relate to Journalism Because–

Journalists often cover other people's intense emotions. Knowledge of your own emotions may help you understand theirs.

Music—how it is made, distributed, sold and classified—is part of American life. Journalists cover music. Experience in writing and performing music will make you better able to understand, evaluate and write about other musicians and lyricists.

Journaling is a powerful way to become a close observer and an interesting writer.

Journaling and Writing Music May Help You Become a Journalist

- You may already be a fluent writer. Good writing in any genre helps prepare you to write as a journalist.
- You may already record, edit and post sound or video files.
- You may already be a close observer of what goes on around you.
- You may already describe things well, including people, sounds, smells, tastes and movement.
- You may already capture dialogue accurately, including both what people say and the way they say it.

Creative Writing

You enjoy writing poetry and short stories (Figure 1.7). Some of your work has been published in a literary magazine.

Are you acting as a journalist?

Why This Is NOT Journalism

Journalists strive to report events as accurately as time and circumstances allow. Their editors fact check their reporting and challenge its accuracy and objectivity.

Creative writing blends fiction and nonfiction. At least one, if not all, of the major elements of literature—setting, action, character—is fictional (made up).

In addition, creative works often are written over a long period of time, while journalists often work against the clock—reporting, taping, writing, revising and publishing in a short span of time.

Also, creative writing, especially poetry, may *suggest* rather than *explain* ideas and experiences. A journalist's job is to make the difficult clear, including difficult ideas and unusual experiences.

Figure 1.7 Both creative writing and journalism are polished through response, revision and editing, but journalists often polish while working against a ticking clock.

The Principle

Journalists strive to be truthful and accurate.

But Creative Writing Does Relate to Journalism Because–

Journalists strive to perfect their work through several drafts, even if they are quickly written. Fiction writers already understand they need others to read their work. Fiction writers revise often, just as the good journalist does.

Editors are as essential to journalists as they are to creative writers.

In addition, journalists use almost every tool poets, public speakers and novelists use as they write and record stories.

Experience as a Creative Writer May Help You Become a Journalist

- You may already naturally use poetic tools such as metaphors, puns and personifications when you talk and write.
- You may already care enough about your writing, your photographs, your recordings or other creative work to revise until the work is of a high quality and ready to be published.

Quality journalism requires many skills, talents and abilities, which you will develop in your journalism courses and by publishing as a journalist in student media. As a journalist, you will have the opportunity to build on your strengths and learn new skills.

YOUR TURN

1. Which media, programs or apps are rarely used for journalism? Which are frequently used for journalism?
2. Some content is obviously journalistic—soccer results, for instance. Some content is almost never journalistic—your fight with your ex-best friend, for instance. How do *you* decide which content is journalistic and which is not? Give examples of both.

Who Is a Journalist?

Some forms of communication obviously are journalism and some obviously are not; but no definition is perfect in every situation, and many interesting questions remain. Journalism is morphing swiftly as freedoms and technology change and become available to more and more people. These changes often challenge traditional definitions of journalism and blur the lines between audience and reporters.

MEET THE PROFESSIONALS:

Jennifer George-Palilonis

"Good writing is the core of good journalism," writes multimedia journalist Jennifer George-Palilonis, but she adds, "There's a HUGE market for journalists who know programming languages and can build new products and conceptualize novel design ideas for how news and information will be distributed in the future. There's also a huge market for journalists who can think visually, carefully analyze large amounts of data, and expertly use social media as a reporting tool.

"Don't be afraid because things are changing so swiftly. This is an exciting time to be in journalism because there are so many things you can do with journalism skills. Journalism skills are more relevant in more fields than ever before because journalists know storytelling, they know how to check facts and do research and they understand how to make complicated information understandable to a general audience."

Jennifer George-Palilonis knew she wanted to be a writer from the time she was 14, but her high school journalism teacher "gave her the bug" for journalism. She worked for her school paper, the Dispatch, at Wayne High School in Fort Wayne, Indiana, and the school yearbook, the Sentry.

In college, she double-majored in writing and editing and in journalism graphics and worked in news design at two major papers, the Detroit Free Press and the Chicago Sun-Times. Graphic design allows her "to combine everything I love about journalism. I use all the same tools as any other reporter. I research, interview, write, and build a story using graphics."

She currently is George & Frances Ball Distinguished Professor of Multimedia at Ball State.

She values the variety of experiences available to journalists. "Someday (when I grow up), I'll be an investigative reporter!"

For instance, an on-camera reporter for a television station stands in front of Disneyland reporting on a new attraction and the long lines of people waiting to board it. The reporter is clearly a journalist. She or her anchor will probably mention the average attendance at the park on this date in other years, the usual length of the lines, and the temperature. She may compare the opening of this attraction to the opening of Space Mountain in 1977. In short, she reports for mass media and provides context for the information, which is as accurate as possible.

At the same time the reporter is broadcasting her story, a high school student with a yearly pass to Disneyland texts 10 of her friends: "I'm hot and tired and have a headache. I stood in line for two hours behind three crying children who wiped their noses on the back of their mother's knees. I finally got on the ride, but it just wasn't worth it. Come another day." This probably is not journalism (though it is interesting writing).

But what if 300 people are following her texts that day? Is she a journalist?

What if her texts are fed to the website of a convention held at the Anaheim Marriott near Disneyland, and 2,000 people check the website for updates? Is this journalism?

What if a major broadcast network quotes her in its story of the attraction's opening? Or runs her tweets down the margin of its Web page? Is she a journalist?

A professional print journalist is on assignment in a war zone. In an interview with a newscaster working from the United States, the professional journalist relates a personal experience, during which the tank she was riding in came under fire. In telling the story, she describes her own terror. Is she a journalist when she relates her own experience, or is she merely a source?

The same print journalist posts a journalistic blog about a child who was badly burned. As a result, a burn center in the United States volunteers to treat the child. Is she an unbiased journalist or an advocate for the child? What if she flies to the United States with the child and his father and follows the child's story for several months, translating for the father and comforting the child as he undergoes reconstructive surgery. She writes about the child's recovery for a news outlet, but she is clearly no longer an objective observer of the events. Is she still a journalist?

Because journalism is a living profession—it is being practiced even as you are reading this—the answers to these questions are open to discussion and interpretation, sometimes by the courts.

For the Record

A Citizen Journalist?

When Pakistani IT consultant Sohaib Athar tweeted from his home in Abbottabad before 2 a.m. on May 1, 2011, that he heard helicopters and an explosion, he was unknowingly reporting the U.S. Navy SEALs attack on Osama bin Laden, mastermind of the 9/11 attacks. His Twitter feed had about 750 followers. Was he a citizen journalist?

The night Osama bin Laden was killed, Sohaib Athar tweeted @ReallyVirtual:

- Helicopter hovering above Abbottabad at 1AM (is a rare event).
- Go away helicopter - before I take out my giant swatter :-/
- A huge window shaking bang here in Abbottabad Cantt. I hope its not the start of something nasty :-S
- ... all silent after the blast, but a friend heard it 6 km away too ... the helicopter is gone too.
- ... seems like my giant swatter worked!

His tweets were retweeted many times among people with slightly larger followings—generally in the thousands—including several journalists. Were they all acting as journalists? Were they broadcasting or publishing news?

More than five hours after Sohaib Athar tweeted about the sound of helicopters, blogger Chris Applegate pointed out that Athar appeared to have live-tweeted the raid without knowing it: "Wow. Turns out at least one person, @ReallyVirtual, inadvertently liveblogged the raid in Abbottabad earlier today."

Applegate may have been the first person to put Athar's tweets into the context of Osama bin Laden's death. Was he acting as a journalist? Was he the first journalist in this chain, or one of many?

The Audience: Who They Are, Why They Matter

These are recent headlines:

£6m Old Bailey trial halted after law lords' anonymity ruling

David Cameron sets out NHS reform plans

Schedule unveiled for curling series at Waterloo, Ont.

Would you use these headlines in your school's media? Would they pique your audience's interest and make them want to read or listen to the stories that follow?

If you answered no, it may be because they are bad headlines, but it is more likely that your school is not the intended audience for them. The **intended audience** consists of the people who are likely to read or view your publication. It also includes the people you *want* for readers or viewers, if only you can catch their attention.

The first two headlines came from The Guardian, a widely respected paper founded in 1821 in Manchester, England. The figure £6m means six million pounds, a large amount of money. Old Bailey is the popular name for the central criminal court in London. The House of Lords is the upper house of the British Parliament; "law lords" refers to its judiciary committee. It recently ruled that evidence cannot be given anonymously in a trial—that is the anonymity rule.

The NHS is not the National Honor Society (as most high school readers might expect) but the National Health Service in England.

The third headline, from the Toronto Star, is not about competitive hairdressing but about a 500-year-old sport played widely in Canada that involves four players on each side, ice, granite stones weighing roughly 40 pounds each and brooms (Figure 1.8).

If you do not have the background to understand Canadian and British terms, you will not understand these headlines; and you probably will not read the articles that follow.

The electronic messages you send to your friends may confuse your grandparents as much as these headlines confuse you because your grandparents are not the intended audience. But when a journalist publishes in mass media, his job is to be as clear as possible to his audience.

Figure 1.8 Can you identify this piece of sporting equipment? Can your friends? If not, a story about curling, or the curling stones pictured below, would not be the best choice for your high school newspaper.

Why the Audience Matters

Journalism involves hundreds of decisions. Some we make without even thinking about them (these are often the ones we most regret), some we make consciously, and some we make after much discussion with our peers and editors. But the more we know about the audience, the better the decisions will be.

Your audience influences what you cover (Figure 1.9). Do you cover calf roping?

Figure 1.9 Consider the audience before you chose the topic of your next story. *Do you want to write a story that will be of interest to the parents in this photograph? Their daughters? Both?*

Jazz? Religious holidays? Cafeteria food? Global warming? Terrorism? Body piercing? Campus clubs? Gay and lesbian issues? Prom? Tardy policies? Immigration? As a journalist you should ask, "What interests my audience?"

Your audience influences how prominently you cover a given topic. Is your lead story about Winter Formal or the planned closure of the senior parking lot? Which story deserves more time or space: the military death of an alumnus who graduated three years ago or the arrest of a custodian for stealing? Which story should have a picture with it: the winning junior varsity tennis team or the losing varsity baseball team? Knowledge of your audience should shape every edition or broadcast. As a journalist you should ask, "Which story is more important to the greater part of my audience?"

Your audience also influences how a story is put together. The administration just announced that the high school will compete in rowing for the first time in 30 years. What is your teaser, headline or lead? What comes next in the story: an explanation of why rowing was eliminated 30 years ago? What competitive rowing is? How to join the team? The costs to the district or to individuals? How to get into a scull without getting wet or embarrassed? As a journalist you should ask, "What does my audience want to know next?"

Your audience influences how you cover a topic. If a source uses a word that is common on your campus but that you would not use in front of the school board, do you repeat the exact quotation, ask him to say it another way or do you use an indirect quotation and paraphrase him? If you cover a service project by members of the Gay-Straight Alliance, which includes students who identify themselves as homosexuals and also students who identify themselves as heterosexuals, do you identify a student in the Alliance as either gay or straight? If you review a movie or book that depicts teenagers drinking, what words do you use to describe the drinking? As a journalist you should ask, "How can I be respectful to my audience, yet honest, as I cover this story?"

And Now... Closer to Home

Fahgettaboudit

Would your readers continue reading an article that begins: "In a city inhabited by bike thieves so crafty and notorious that many people are loath to leave a bike chained outside where it can be stolen or quickly stripped of parts, the bicycle lock company Kryptonite calls one of its locks the New York Fahgettaboudit."

This long and complex sentence is from The New York Times—a great paper written for an educated adult audience, an audience that is probably different from that of your publication. Would members of your audience be able to pronounce *Fahgettaboudit* (forget about it) and get the joke? Would they read to the end of the long sentence to get to the joke?

Your audience influences what words you use. If you write that a student has been *legally emancipated,* do you need to define the term for your audience? Can you refer to a student's odyssey and be sure your audience understands that you mean a long, difficult journey? What do you mean by PDA: "public displays of affection" or "personal data assistant"? Does "I Want to Hold Your Hand" remind your audience of a Beatles song? As a journalist you should ask, "Will this be clear to the greater part of my audience?"

If your audience influences almost all aspects of your stories—everything from what you cover to the words you use—you need to know a great deal about your audience.

Your Intended Audience

Your publication's mission statement may already describe your audience. It probably includes the students in your school, but it may be broader. Does it also include alumni? Neighbors? Junior high students who will enter your school? Administration and staff? Parents and community supporters? The whole community? (Visit the *Journalism* website to learn more about mission statements.)

Extend

Whoever they are, the people in your audience are not all exactly like you and your closest friends, and it is poor journalism to assume that they are. You are producing mass media for what is probably a diverse audience (Figure 1.10). If only 30 percent of the audience is both female and college-bound, your publication should not seem like a newsletter for college-bound girls. If 100 adults work at your school as teachers, administrators and support personnel but 1,900 students attend, do not publish "The Faculty News." If 27 percent of your audience are freshmen, do not write a junior-senior newsletter.

The students whose interests, voices and faces are excluded may feel marginalized, isolated or alienated by your publication. They certainly are unlikely to view or read it if it is not about them, their friends and their interests or about students who are in other ways like them.

Figure 1.10 *Is your school publication or broadcast meaningful to all segments of the school population?*

Journalism's duties include building a sense of community and increasing understanding among members of the community. If you are not aware of the great diversity in your audience, you may increase prejudice and misunderstandings instead of building a sense of community.

Your Unintended Audience

Everything you publish or broadcast has at least two audiences: the intended and the unintended. The unintended audience may be the larger of the two. Journalists need to be conscious of both.

Once something is published—literally "made public"—it is available for anyone to view or read and will remain available as long as a paper copy exists or as long as anyone, anywhere, retains an electronic

The Last Thing a Fish Discovers Is Water

It is natural for us to assume that everyone else is like us and to ignore many of those who are different.

When you were a very small child, you were probably oblivious to others' differences. Famously, little children play peacefully side by side with children who have disabilities, speak other languages, come from different ethnic heritages, or dress or eat differently.

Somewhere in elementary school or junior high school, this peaceful acceptance gives way to a self-centered assumption that whatever I am is "normal," and whoever is different is "weird." At this stage, the less someone is like us, the less empathy we feel for that person.

Eventually, immature students may cease even to see those who are not like themselves. People who are different become invisible to these students. When they think about them—if they think about them at all—it is as if they were furniture, not people.

By high school many students have matured and now recognize other people as interesting and valuable human beings, even those—or especially those—who are different from us.

copy. Removing something from a website or from your computer does not erase all copies of it. When we publish, our **unintended audience** is potentially all people for all time, including our future employers, as-yet-unborn children, political opponents and the people who offer scholarships to high school seniors.

Of course you are not obliged to make every headline, teaser, caption and reference clear to people who may be reading your work 25 years from now. But when you as a journalist decide what to publish, what to keep confidential and how you express yourself, you need to consider both the intended and the unintended audience.

YOUR TURN

1. Based on your understanding of your audience, list two topics that your publication should cover that you may not have covered to this point.
2. Based on your understanding of your audience, both intended and unintended, identify a topic that you and your peers would need to discuss fully before you decided whether or not to cover it. Explain your choice.

How Do You Learn About Your Audience?

Journalists need to be good researchers. They use three types of sources to gain information for stories: documents, direct observations and interviews. These same three tools will help you define your audience.

Documents

Documents (including electronic and online documents) can give a profile of your audience. Just as a photographic profile does not show everything about a person's appearance, statistical reports show only a brief outline of your audience. Nonetheless, such documents can be a first step to understanding who the people in your audience are.

Your district is required to publish statistics about the students and teachers and about your school's test scores. Called a school accountability report or a school report card, the information is available online at the district or school website, through sites such as GreatSchools or Ed-Data, or on paper from the district or school administration.

Different states and districts publish different information, but you should be able to find information about

- gender distribution (47 percent female, 53 percent male, for example);
- ethnicities;
- the percentage of students who qualify for free or reduced-price lunches (this statistic is often used as an indicator of students who are poor or at-risk educationally);
- the number of students who are enrolled in special education;
- the number who are learning English;

- the number enrolled in honors or AP (advanced placement) courses;
- the graduation rates;
- the number of students in each grade; and
- the faculty-to-student ratio.

What do you do with what you learn from the school's profile?

Compare it with the makeup of your journalism class or staff. Does your staff look like your school as a whole? What percentage of your journalism staff is learning English? Is male? Is enrolled in honors or AP courses? Is enrolled in special education? (You may be surprised by what you learn and also surprised by the strengths students in various programs may bring to your journalism staff.)

If you have previous editions of your school's electronic or print publication or tapes of broadcasts, look at the topics covered, the people pictured or portrayed, and the people quoted. How many adults were interviewed? How many freshmen and seniors? How many close friends of staff members have their names or faces in the publication?

What would someone assume your school population is like from viewing your broadcast or publication?

In addition to the school report card, you can find statistical information at the United States Census Bureau American FactFinder website (Figure 1.11). This site provides statistics by ZIP code, including

- the average household income;
- the number of people who live below the poverty line;
- the percentage who have graduated from high school;
- the percentage with college degrees;
- the percentage of residents with disabilities;

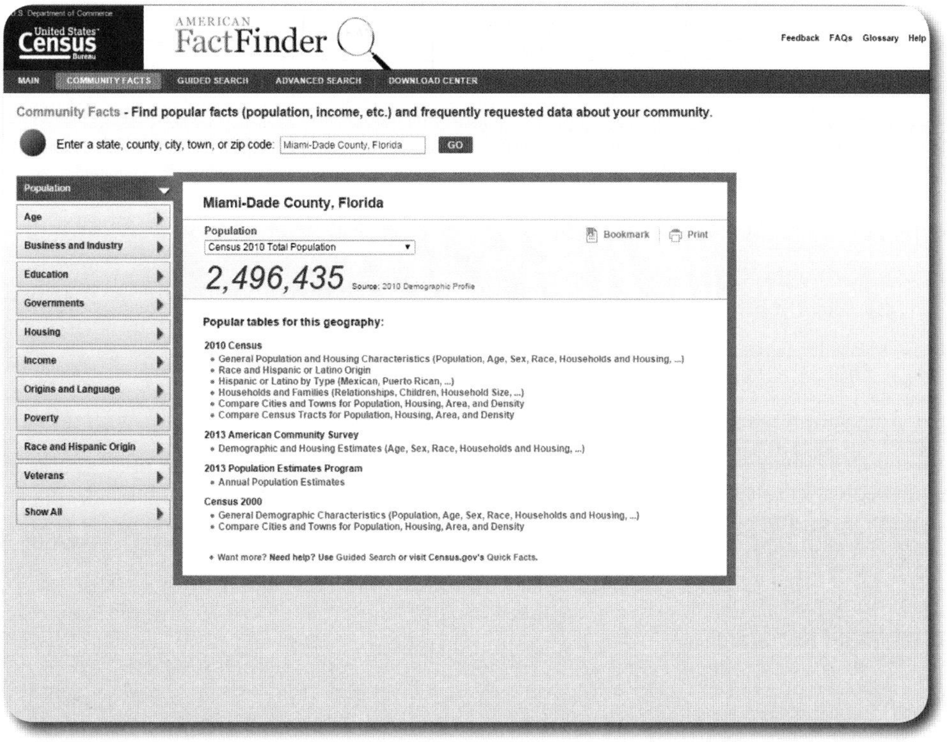

Figure 1.11 The U.S. Census Bureau American FactFinder website provides important statistical information for communities across the country. *According to the FactFinder website, how many people in your community are living below the poverty line?*

- the number who have served in the military (civilian veterans); and
- the average income per household and individual.

If your school's attendance area spans two ZIP codes, FactFinder will let you know, for instance, that the per capita yearly income in one ZIP code is $49,000 and the per capita income in another is $16,000. (Per capita income is income per person—per head; your *capit* is your head.)

If incomes are this varied, you may safely assume that while some of your audience will be interested in designer accessories and travel-learning to Australia during summer break, others will be concerned about job fairs and work permits. Make sure you do not talk to just one group.

Observation

Observation—evidence obtained with your own eyes, ears and nose—is a second powerful tool, at least as important as statistics. Statistics are valuable but clumsy, dividing your audience into large chunks. Most people are repulsed by the idea of being known not as an individual but only as a member of a subgroup—sorted by gender, ethnicity, financial status or year in school.

The Gray Areas

Journalists—both professional journalists and student journalists—wrestle with how to use statistics such as those found on the school report card and the Census Bureau FactFinder. They ask questions like these:

- If the school population is made up of three major ethnic groups, the green, the orange and the purple people, is it insulting to try to interview five green people, two orange people and three purple people just to match the school's demographic statistics? Is it insulting to interview or photograph someone because the journalists need one more green person with a disability to balance their coverage?
- The college-bound juniors and seniors seem to be the ones doing newsworthy things. Why would anyone be interested in a freshman with a 1.9 grade-point average?
- Can someone who is green and female cover a story that includes many purple males, or do you need a purple male to cover it?
- Is it better to become blind to color and not notice if someone is orange, green or purple? Or is this just another way of assuming everyone is like you?
- How do you avoid stereotyping people in your audience based on the statistical groups they belong to? Is it safe to assume that green students aren't interested in football but love lacrosse? That orange students like a certain kind of music? That purple students are all religious or conservative or angry about pollution?
- Is our job to entertain or to inform? Do we have a duty to inform the audience, even if the audience is not already interested? Freshmen may care principally about finding their lockers and working their locks, instead of preparing for college. Should more of our stories be about lockers and locks and fewer about academics?

These questions do not have easy answers. They cut to the heart of issues that trouble educators, politicians, lawmakers and citizens as well as journalists.

Clearly, high school students and the groups to which they belong are more complicated than any statistics can show. A softball team may have students from several ethnic or religious groups. Academic Decathlon may include students who are bilingual or trilingual in a variety of languages. Students may identify more strongly with their religious community than they do with their economic status. A type of music or a style of dress may make brothers and sisters out of people whose ethnicities or financial status make them appear very different.

To learn more about the people in your audience, you need to observe them carefully. Though you may find out about the statistical groups in your audience from the comfort of a chair with a computer on your lap, you need to leave your chair and go out where your audience is if you want to learn about the people.

Teenagers self-identify with others in ways that will never show up on the Census Bureau's statistics, and one student may have several identities. Students may identify themselves with groups in many observable ways.

What sorts of things should you look for to learn about your audience (Figure 1.12)?

Clothing, of course, may link people with subgroups, but even on campuses with uniforms or strict dress codes, an observant journalist can learn a great deal.

What kinds of shoes do people wear? What brands? Work boots? Cowboy boots? Athletic shoes? Flip-flops? Inexpensive or name brand? How clean are they?

How do people carry their books and school supplies between classes and after school? In a loose pile in their arms? In backpacks? Oversized purses? Athletic bags?

Jewelry, hairstyle, size of clothing and other grooming issues often signify a student's self-chosen identity. How long are the pants? The shorts? The bangs? The shirts? Is any clothing ironed?

How do students greet each other? Do they scream and then hug? Nod upward and say nothing? Bump knuckles? Slap or punch each other? Enter and leave a group without speaking? Speak loudly? Quietly?

Figure 1.12 *If these people were the intended audience of your publication or broadcast, what could you learn about them from this photo?*

Interviews

Interviews are the backbone of journalism and an essential tool for learning about people. Professional journalists estimate that they gain 75 to 80 percent of their information through interviews. Without interviews, journalists would be left to report stereotypes based on statistics or on their observation of superficial characteristics like skin color or how someone does his hair or how much fabric is in her jeans.

How do you plan, set up, and conduct an interview? Here are some basic tips. You will find detailed information in Chapter 9.

What to Ask

An interview can be as brief as one question or take several days. One or two survey questions asked of a sampling of your audience can give you useful information. Try asking one of these questions:

1. "What is coming through your earbuds?" The answers will tell you more about the musical tastes of your audience than if you asked them to name their favorite band or tell you what sort of music they like.
2. "Tell me a bit about what you were doing Sunday around noon." (Notice the question is really a gentle command—"Tell me a bit about…") This will let you know about the values, activities and demands on your audience. Were they with family? With friends? Studying? Worshipping? Working? What sports and recreation do they follow? Where do they go shopping or for amusement?
3. "Tell me two or three things you do most days after school." (This is another gentle command.) The answers will indicate how many of your audience work, how many watch younger children, how many play sports or skateboard or do things that you never imagined a teenager could do. Use a follow-up question if you need more information. If a student says, "I go home," ask, "What do you generally do once you are home? Can you do as you please, or do you need to do things for school or for your family? Tell me more."

Before you go out to interview people, write the question you will use in a reporter's notebook (Figure 1.13). Bring the notebook with you, even if you are doing audio or video interviews.

Finding People to Interview

It is easiest to talk to your friends. Don't!

You want a representative sample, so talk to every fifth person in line for lunch or three people from the middle row of the first classroom in each building or every 15th person who comes through the front entrance of the school (Figure 1.14). Make sure you talk to freshmen as well as seniors.

Ask, "Do you have a minute or two for a short interview?"

Figure 1.13 This journalist is preparing for a story about how students are utilizing the school library. By approaching every third student in the library—rather than just asking her friends—she is able to establish a representative sample.

Conducting the Interview

1. Pull out your reporter's notebook, the one with the question written in it.
2. Be serious and professional. Identify yourself and the purpose of the interview. "I'm on the staff of the Daily Thunderstorm, and I'd like to ask you a question or two so that we will know more about our readers'/viewers'/listeners' tastes and interests."
3. Don't be shy. The person you interview will very likely be flattered. Who else ever asks about her tastes and then listens closely to the answer?

4. If the person agrees to be interviewed, ask her name and year in school. Ask her to spell her name (first and last) and repeat back to her what you have written. Make corrections if necessary. (Two journalists working together can make this easier.)
5. Ask her the one question from your reporter's notebook. Ask follow-up questions if you need more information.
6. Record her answers carefully, asking her to repeat or spell anytime you are not sure you heard exactly what she said. You do not need to copy down whole sentences. Key words generally will do, but make sure they are accurate.
7. Thank her for talking with you.

The whole interview may have taken less than a minute.

Avoiding Implicit Bias

We each have blind spots, and one of the most common is to assume that everyone is like us and our friends. Even more subtle is our tendency to cover only people who are successful, powerful or attractive. Unless we consciously correct for our **implicit bias**, large parts of our audience become invisible to us, and we become invisible to them.

Strong journalists make conscious choices to overcome their implicit bias. They also monitor their publication to recognize and correct their blind spots.

How can you better prepare news that is valuable for your audiences? One strategy is to recruit members of underrepresented groups into your class or onto your staff, and then value and listen to them. Another is to assign reporters to cover underrepresented groups—and to break down stereotypes. Strong publications also consciously choose to include diverse students when they conduct interviews or take photos or shoot video. Your potential audience is diverse. As they recognize familiar faces, names and voices, they will be drawn to your work.

Where and how we publish is important. You should select the most appropriate journalistic format when presenting your content. To reach your audiences, know what types of media they consume: print, broadcast, online websites, podcasts, photo sharing sites, microblogs, other types of social media. Do they access their media from a newsstand, on tablets, phones or laptops? Your publication needs to have a presence where your audiences already are, perhaps to lead them to longer works published in a second type of media.

Also consider the journalistic format most appropriate to your content, or the story you have to tell. Breaking news should go out first in the fastest, most easily accessed format your audience uses. Stories full of action videos work well as broadcast news or imbedded in a robust webpage. Feature stories rich in audio make strong podcasts. In-depth coverage of a sports victory are most valued and best shared in print. A memorial for a deceased student has lasting impact in a print news magazine.

Chapter One

Review and Assessment

Recall Assess

1. What does a journalist do?
2. In what ways are the following like journalism? In what ways are they unlike journalism?
   A. *text messages*
   B. *videos on social networking sites*
   C. *research papers*
   D. *class presentations*
   E. *music videos*
   F. *journals and poetry*
   G. *fiction*
3. What kinds of journalistic decisions are influenced by the audience?
4. What is meant by *intended audience*?
5. What is meant by *unintended audience*?
6. What are three ways for journalists to learn about their audience?
7. Which type of source usually provides professional journalists with the most information?

Critical Thinking

1. What literary or artistic tools do journalists use that also are used in fiction writing and filmmaking? How is journalism different from these activities?
2. Should a student journalist do a story about something he overheard in the lunch line? Why or why not?
3. How could the skills, talents and abilities you have be applied to journalism?
4. Refer to the description of a journalist's core role at the beginning of this chapter. Find examples from professional journalism—newscasts, newspapers, news websites or newsmagazines—and explain how fulfill their job as news outlets.
5. Find examples from professional journalism that do *not* meet the criteria in question 4. Decide whether or not they are journalism and defend your answer. Defend your answer.
6. How can choosing the appropriate media format enable you to reach your audience?
7. How might an awareness of the *unintended audience* influence what you publish? Give a specific example.
8. Based on your understanding of your audience, tell which of these three stories should be the dominant story in your features section:
   A. introducing a new assistant principal
   B. vintage clothing shopping
   C. restaurant reviews for the night of Winter Formal
9. Describe three roadblocks a journalist might experience that would keep him or her from conducting interviews. Suggest possible strategies to overcome each roadblock.

Application

1. If you have previous editions of your school's electronic or print publication or tapes of broadcasts
   - list the topics the broadcast or publication covered. What segments of your audience are interested in the topic?
   - list the people pictured or portrayed. Identify the statistical group from which they come.
   - list or highlight the names of people who were quoted. Identify the statistical group from which they come. Are they students or adults?
2. Write a paragraph describing what a stranger would assume your school is like from reading your publication or viewing your broadcast.
3. Spend 15 minutes at two different locations observing one of the following personal characteristics:
   - clothing, shoes or jewelry
   - method of carrying books and school supplies
   - grooming or hairstyles
   - people's methods of greeting each other

   Identify and describe the people, places and objects objectively. Do you notice any patterns or groups? Estimate the number of students involved.
4. Write a paragraph describing each group you observed. Suggest news topics that might be of interest to each.

Chapter One

Journalism Style

Stylebooks

Every publication should have its own stylebook—its guide for common issues—and strive for consistency. For instance, is the youngest football team on your campus the

- Freshman Team;
- Freshmen Team;
- Freshmen's Team;
- freshman team; or
- freshmen team?

If you quote your principal, Avery Klineman, in the opening of a story, how do you refer to her later in the story?

- Klineman;
- Principal Klineman;
- Ms Klineman;
- Ms. Klineman;
- Mrs. Klineman; or
- principal Klineman?

Do you use contractions in news writing? In reviews? In sports? Columns? Editorials?

Once your publication decides how to handle these issues, the policy should be written in your style manual and applied consistently.

Most publications, including student publications, base their style on the guidelines in The Associated Press Stylebook and Briefing on Media Law, the standard used by professionals. Exceptions and additions to AP style are included in their publication's own stylebook. For spelling, the AP Stylebook in turn references Webster's New World College Dictionary.

AP style varies from the style you use in your other classes, which may be based on the Modern Language Association's MLA Handbook for Writers of Research Papers. For example, in AP style, the title of a novel is enclosed in quotation marks: "The Scarlet Letter." In MLA style, it is italicized: *The Scarlet Letter*.

Why all this concern about style?

Clarity is the first reason. Our writing should not call attention to itself or to us. Our audience should not need to figure out what we mean. Rather, our words should efficiently convey ideas, events, facts and images from our heads into the readers' heads. Like a good swimmer, our words create almost no splash and very little wake. Consistent style serves that end.

Trust is the second reason. As a journalist you belong to a community that values careful observation, accurate quotations, verified facts and opinions, and absolute honesty. Readers can see who most of your sources are and be able to trust you when they cannot see them.

Sloppiness in style suggests sloppiness in the rest of your work. Unfortunately, both you and your whole publication may be ridiculed as amateurish, childish, knee-jerk or unreliable if you call an assistant principal a vice principal or say the "freshmens danced the whole time," no matter how good the rest of your journalism is.

Try It!

Look in your publication's stylebook or create entries for your stylebook for each of the following issues. If you create entries or suggest changes to your publication's stylebook, refer to AP style. Discuss and defend your choices.

1. On your second reference to an adult, Sophie Lim, how do you refer to her? As Lim? Ms. Lim? AP style says to use just the last name, Lim. Should your style be different? Should it be Ms. Lim, Miss Lim, or Mrs. Lim?
2. Would you treat references to a rabbi, a nun, a judge or a physician differently?
3. How do you identify students with their year in school? Sophomore Taylor Cutter? Taylor Cutter, '23?
4. How do you identify buildings on your campus? Is it Smedley Hall? Smedley? The north gym or the North Gym?
5. What is the female version of your sports teams? Do you have Mushers and Lady Mushers? Musherettes? Men's Mushers and Women's Mushers? Boys Mushers and Girls Mushers? How do you avoid sexist language and still differentiate the records of the two track teams or two basketball teams?

Extend Your Knowledge

Style Exercises

To learn more about using the AP Stylebook and other stylebooks commonly used in broadcast and publication, visit the *Journalism* website.

Chapter One

Writers' Workshop

In this Writers' Workshop, you will:

- Practice close observation.
- Practice writing from the objective point of view.
- Learn the importance of reading your work aloud.
- Collaborate with other writers.
- Experiment with verb tenses.

This workshop, the first of many, will help you develop the power and flexibility you will use in journalism—and in all your writing.

Workshop 1.1

Observation and the Objective Point of View

At the beginning of Workshop 1.2, you will have from six to ten minutes to write your first entry. Your job will be to describe what you observed during the five minutes before you entered the journalism classroom. So be observant as you come to class and notice what you hear as well as what you see.

Though this may seem like a trivial exercise, it will become powerful as you learn to

- observe accurately;
- write under deadline;
- collaborate;
- read your work aloud; and
- respond to others who have done the same.

Mini-Lesson: The Objective Point of View

When you do your first writing for Workshop 1.2, you will try to put your reader in the scene, to allow the reader to experience what you observed coming to class. To do this, you want to take yourself out of the scene. Instead of writing:

> *As I came around the corner of the 200 building, I saw empty-handed students sauntering across the grass and other students hunching over a heaping armload of books. I saw other students leaning to their left, pulled down by the weight of their green and yellow athletic bags…*

you will write:

> *Empty-handed students saunter across the grass while others hunch over heaping armloads of books or lean to their left, pulled down by the weight of their green and yellow athletic bags slung from their shoulders…*

The text—now written from the objective point of view—is 13 words shorter and more interesting.

Rules for Writing Time

- Begin writing immediately, before class starts if possible.
- Write the whole time allotted to you, usually six to ten minutes.
- Keep writing, no matter how badly you spell or how slowly you write or type.
- No erasing—in Writers' Workshop there are no errors, just first drafts.
- If absolutely necessary, delete a small section by placing a line through it.
- No staring and thinking, waiting for genius to strike. Write!
- Save everything you write, all year, in a collection folder. You will use your earlier writing, reflect on it, and learn from it later. You will choose from among your earlier work as you learn writing and editing skills.

Workshop 1.2

Observing, Writing and Rereading

Mini-Lesson: The Importance of Rereading Your Own Work

After you have written for the allotted time, read what you have just written to yourself, with your lips moving, or read aloud into a voice recorder.

"Why in the world do I need to move my lips?" you may ask.

Good writing preserves the rhythms of speech. It has long and short sentences and falls smoothly from the tongue. If you visit any large newsroom, you will see writers looking at computer screens, moving their lips.

Reading to yourself is also great preparation for writing broadcast news. Text written for broadcast tends to be less formal and to use shorter sentences than text written for print. It relates only one idea per sentence, while written journalism uses more formal diction and longer sentences. But all journalistic sentences should be easy to read and easy to speak. (Please note: While broadcast language is less formal than copy written for print, it is not as informal as the way you usually speak or text.)

If you read your own work with your lips moving, you also will pay more attention to each word on your page or screen and learn things about your own writing. Good writers reread their work often as they write.

Apply It!

1. As you reread your work, put a small X in the margin next to any place in the text that makes you pause or stumble, but don't make a change. Keep reading. (If you are working on a screen, highlight that text.) After you have finished reading the whole piece, make any small changes you wish, inserting an additional word or crossing others out.
2. **Collaboration** Working with two or three other students, read your own work aloud and listen as others in your group do the same. Watch for any difficulty with the objective point of view. Choose the most interesting sentences from each writer's work. Form the best sentences and phrases from each writer into one paragraph, adding conjunctions or changing verb tenses as appropriate. Read the paragraph aloud. Save this paragraph.

Workshop 1.3

Playing With Tense

Mini-Lesson: Finding the Best Tense for Your Purpose—Simple Past and Simple Present

English has 12 basic verb tenses and as many as 30 tenses if you count those created with auxiliary verbs such as *could*. Each one serves a real purpose. Your task as a writer is to make sure you are using the tense that serves you best.

This means choosing a tense for an entire paragraph or section. It also means choosing the best tense for each phrase, clause and sentence.

For this lesson, you will concentrate on choosing between just two tenses, the simple present and the simple past. Once you have chosen to write in one tense, stay in that tense unless you have a compelling reason to change it. Can you find the tense shifts in this passage?

> *The campus security officer perched on her stool by the door to the building as softball players lugged gym bags the length of their bats. Smokers hustle from behind the handball courts while freshmen pull their wheeled backpacks.*

Here it is all in present tense:

> *The campus security officer perches on her stool by the door to the building as softball players lug gym bags the length of their bats. Smokers hustle from behind the handball courts while freshmen pull their wheeled backpacks.*

Here it is all in past tense:

> *The campus security officer perched on her stool by the door to the building as softball players lugged gym bags the length of their bats. Smokers hustled from behind the handball courts while freshmen pulled their wheeled backpacks.*

Which passage do you prefer? Can you suggest a type of writing or place in the writing where you would use the past-tense passage? Where would you use the present-tense passage?

Apply It!

1. Edit your passage, either your own or the one you did as a group, so it is all in the present tense, then all in the past tense. Which style do you prefer? When would you use each style?
2. Please see the *Journalism* website for more help honing your verbs.

Extend Your Knowledge Extend

As you have seen in this workshop, journalists show their work to others and seek their responses. Responding to a story involves more than just saying you like or dislike something. Visit the *Journalism* website to learn processes and techniques for giving and receiving responses effectively.

Chapter Two

News Values and Story Ideas

What do we cover?

Photo by Forrest Czarnecki, Conifer High School

G-WLEARNING.COM

While studying, look for the activity icon to:

- **Build** vocabulary terms with e-flash cards and matching activities.
- **Extend** learning with further discussion of relevant topics.
- **Reinforce** what you learn by completing style exercises, worksheets and end-of-chapter questions.

Visit the Journalism website: www.g-wlearning.com/journalism/

Chapter Objectives

After reading this chapter, you will be able to:

- List the seven news values that help you identify strong story ideas for your audience.
- Give examples of how a journalist can incorporate news values into a story to make it stronger.
- Find story ideas through beat reporting.
- Find story ideas from the professional press.
- Find story ideas through direct observation.
- Develop story ideas.
- Pitch story ideas to your producer or editor.

Key Terms Build Vocab

across the wire
beat
conflict
deadline
dominant story
enterprise stories
human interest
impact
lead story
local angle
news aggregator
news cycle
news peg
news value
oddity
pitch
prominence
proximity
put to bed
scoop
spike
stale
timeliness

Before You Read...

A sentence is a group of words that express a complete thought. In the English language, a complete sentence is structured, or built, to have a subject and a predicate. The subject is the person speaking, or the person, place or thing a sentence describes. The predicate describes the action or subject's state of being. Select three sentences in this chapter. Identify the subject and predicate in each. Exchange your sentences with a partner to check each other's work.

Introduction

"What you see is news, what you know is background, what you feel is opinion."

–Lester Markel, journalist

"What do you want to write about?"
"I dunno. Interesting stuff never happens around here."
"We've got 20 more minutes to fill.
Anything interesting in the announcements?"

Nothing is more important to a broadcast or publication than strong, relevant and interesting stories—stories that inform and engage the audience. The noted sports writer Bill Plaschke said that the most important concepts in journalism are

- ideas,
- ideas,
- ideas,
- reporting, and
- writing.

This is true whether you work for an online publication that streams school games live, a daily paper that reports the results of yesterday's school funding vote, a news show that is broadcast weekly, or a newsmagazine that comes out once a month. No matter what your media or your timing, strong stories make strong publications.

How do you find great story ideas for your broadcast or publication? The seven news values that you will learn about in the following paragraphs will guide you. Later in this chapter you will learn three ways to locate strong story ideas.

News Values

Whose job is it to come up with the story ideas? While it is possible for the editors to assign all the stories the staff reports, that is rarely the best way to produce a quality publication or broadcast.

Seeing What Others Miss

An experienced journalist could walk out of your classroom and locate three or four solid story ideas in less time than it takes you to get through the lunch line. Indeed, Bill Plaschke made that claim to a journalism class at the University of Southern California Annenberg School for Communication.

"They all laughed. Then two days later, I wrote a story about a 5-foot-4 poor, disabled kid from East L.A. who took two buses for two hours every day to come to football practice to carry water for the football team. It turns out, the coaches fed him and the equipment guys clothed him and they all cheered for him, made him their unofficial mascot. I wrote this story about a great team reaching down to help one of society's weaker members, and the USC writers came up to me later, all mad, and said, 'Man, we just thought he was some weird kid who kept showing up.'"

More often, a strong newsroom is a cooperative community, with everyone—from the editor-in-chief to the newest staff reporter—bringing story ideas to staff meetings. At staff meetings, story ideas are developed and then evaluated for their news values and their value to the particular audience.

What is it that makes a strong story? Your high school is like no other, so your high school publication or broadcast should be like no other. The news values help you choose from among the almost infinite number of possible stories you could cover, so that you find the right ones for your audience.

Seven News Values

What are the **news values**? Many journalists identify seven values: proximity, timeliness, impact, prominence, oddity, conflict and human interest. Most strong stories have at least two or three of these values.

Not only do these values help you determine whether or not a story is strong, they also influence which is the **dominant story**, or which story should receive the best position on the page, website or broadcast (Figure 2.1). The stronger the story, the more time or space it should receive. The values also influence how you start the story, how you tell the story and the tone, or manner of expression, of the story.

Proximity

How near is the story to your school? An unexpected power outage at noon on your campus is much more newsworthy than one at a nearby school or one in another state, even if the out-of-state outage covers a wider area and lasts longer, or if a transformer fire starts it. The story on

THURSDAY FEB. 22, 2018

EVANSTONIAN

1600 DODGE AVE. EVANSTON, IL. EVANSTON TOWNSHIP HIGH SCHOOL VOL. 101, ISSUE 7

Sophomores will be exposed to PSAT

BY MATTHEW BARBATO AND MARGO LEVITAN
Managing and Online-Executive Editors

Starting last school year, the Illinois State Board of Education required that all students take the SAT plus the writing component in 11th grade. This requirement marked a shift from the ACT to the SAT in the Illinois high school testing system, and ETHS is furthering this shift on Feb. 27 by administering the PSAT 10 to sophomores.

Juniors will not only take the SAT, but also the PSAT/NMSQT, in the fall. This serves two purposes: the first is to give students exposure to the format and content of the test, and the second is that the test is used to determine whether or not students qualify for various scholarships given out by the National Merit Scholarship Corporation.

This year, while not a state requirement, the ETHS administration has decided to administer the PSAT 10 to sophomores, giving students even earlier exposure to the SAT suite of assessments.

Pete Bavis, Assistant Superintendent for Curriculum and Instruction, said that beyond giving students the opportunity to familiarize themselves with the test. "The assessment system provides us with detailed information that can be used to modify the curriculum to support student achievement."

Get Woke, Stay Woke

Speaker Devea Williams, below, and dancers Jacline Baptise and Dominick Mcintosh, above, at the Black summit. *Photos by Litzy Segura*

Students find empowerment at summits

BY MEREDITH HERRICK
News Editor

A powerful speaker has just walked off-stage, and the student audience is cheering. At that moment, many ETHS students feel

no longer have a gender-segregated event brought students together in community," Hamilton said.

This year's slogan was "Get Woke, Stay Woke."

Your Voice".

"With the Latinx Identity, there are so many different kinds of people," Vizcarra said. "We want to include everyone and help students find their stories."

Courtesy of The Evanstonian, Evanston Township High School

Figure 2.1 The dominant photo catches the reader's eye first. *Is it difficult to tell which is intended to be the most important story?*

your campus has the greater news value because it has **proximity**, which means the event occurred close to your geographic location.

On occasion you can make distant stories local by finding a **local angle**, which is something about the story that is of interest primarily to your audience. When an earthquake and tsunami hit Japan in 2011, The Broadview, a publication from the Convent of the Sacred Heart in San Francisco, found the local angle by writing about the disaster's effects on one of its seven sister schools in Japan. An international story became local (Figure 2.2).

Caution: If you cannot find or develop a local angle, do not repackage what is already widely available from other sources. You are not a **news aggregator**—a person, agency or website that collects news stories for wide distribution but does no reporting and does not create original content. Without a new and local perspective, such aggregates or summaries make for very weak journalism.

Timeliness

Strong stories are about to happen, just happened, or are happening as you publish, broadcast or stream; they have **timeliness**. How recent is the event? Is the event in the very near future? The closer it is to the date or time you publish or broadcast, the more timely it is and the more prominence it should be given. Your **news cycle** (the period between editions, broadcasts or digital posting of stories) will control what is timely for your publication.

If you publish online, an earthquake report may be timely, as was this report in The Paly Voice, which was published before the professional press (Figure 2.3). If your publication does not come out for two more

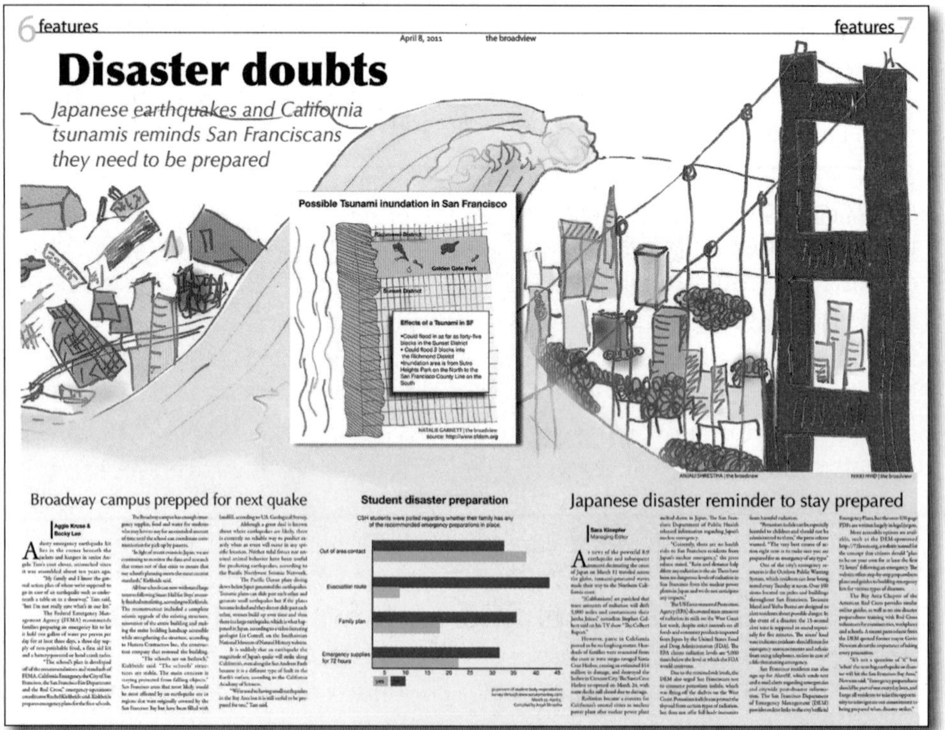

Figure 2.2 A story that takes place somewhere far away can be made relevant for your publication by finding a local angle. In this case, a distant disaster was used to remind the audience of disaster preparedness at home—just one way of giving the story proximity.

Courtesy of The Broadview, Convent of the Sacred Heart High School weeks, however, the same earthquake story may be **stale** (out of date) unless you find a timely angle. If the gym lights fell in the earthquake and the gyms are closed until the school board votes next week on funding to retrofit all the lights, the earthquake story is still timely.

Reporting and writing quickly will allow you to keep your publication or broadcast strong. The afternoon La Nueva Voz, a monthly newspaper, was being **put to bed** (being sent to the printer), a naval helicopter experienced technical difficulties and landed on the school's football field. Because the paper came out the next day, the picture and explanation were a **lead story** (the more dominant story) on the front page. If the paper had been published two days later, the story would have become stale and been pushed to an inside page, if it was published at all.

thePalyVoice

Home News Sports Opinion Multimedia Features A & E School Links Archives

LATEST We're on Facebook, fb.me/thepalyvoice, and Twitter, @thepalyvoic

Magnitude 5.6 earthquake hits Bay Area

by THE PALY VOICE
Published October 30, 2007

Tweet

A magnitude 5.6 earthquake struck the Bay Area today at 8:04 p.m. tonight. The earthquakes epicenter was about fives miles north of San Jose's Alum Rock according to US Geological Survey Earthquakes Hazards Program. So far, three aftershocks have occurred between 8:12 and 8:13, going from magnitudes 1.4 at 8:12:23, 1.3 at 8:12:48, and 1.5 at 8:12:55. The earthquake has been felt from as far away as the Santa Cruz Mountains to Stockton.

Tremors from this earthquake were felt in Palo Alto, bringing with it a warning of the need to be prepared for such events.

Many Paly students felt the tremor.

Tamar Ben-Shachar, a junior at Palo Alto High School was one such student.

"It caught me by surprise. I was doing my homework, and I so I ran to the doorframe. My little siblings screamed because they had never felt an earthquake before," Ben-Shachar said.

According to Barbara Cimino, manager of the Office of Emergency Services for Palo Alto, there are currently no reports of damages or injuries, and they are advising people to contact 911 only if there are problems.

Sophomore Abby LaPier was at Policy Debate in Room 220 at Paly when the earthquake occurred.

Courtesy of The Paly Voice, Palo Alto High School

Figure 2.3 Online publications, such as the one above, are often more able than print publications to publish timely stories. The news cycle is usually shorter for the online publications. *What are the news cycles for the various publications and broadcasts at your school?*

Impact

"So what?" If you can answer that question, you have defined the **impact** of your story. How does the story affect the lives of your audience? The strength of the story's effect or impression on your audience determines its impact.

Almost everyone will want to know if spring break is being eliminated because of extra snow days or if graduation and the end of the school year are being postponed because of flooding. These stories impact everyone in your school, and so they have news value, even if the snow has long melted and the water has receded before you publish.

How many students does the theme of the senior prom affect? Think about it: your audience may include seniors who have been planning their prom night for months and will spend hundreds of dollars on the evening, as well as freshmen and sophomores who are looking forward to their own senior prom. Your audience will also include many students from all four classes who simply do not care about the prom. You must know your audience to decide whether prom is your lead story. In the same issue, you may also cover the closure of a nearby skate park and a summer job fair. Which story will impact more of your audience? The story with the most impact should be your lead story.

Journalists recognize the impact of a story on their audience and report it in such a way that the audience understands the impact. Few students follow what goes on at your state capital; but when actions at the capital affect your community, it is a journalist's job not only to bring the news to the audience but also to help the audience understand the story's impact on their lives. The state budget may force your district to

For the Record

Deadlines, Spikes and Being Put to Bed

Historically, morning newspapers had a long news cycle—staffers had a full day to gather news and write stories before the paper was published. They "put the paper to bed" sometime around midnight. Everything had to be finalized and sent to the typesetters and then to the printing presses by 12:00 if the paper was to be on the customers' doorsteps or in the newsstands by 6:00 a.m. Any story received after midnight would go into the following edition or be **spiked**—literally impaled on a spike—if it was not fit to print or if it would be stale by the following day. A **deadline** was really a deadline, a term that comes from an Andersonville prison camp during the Civil War. If a man crossed a marked boundary—the deadline—he was shot dead. That is how journalists regard deadlines.

Afternoon papers in large cities could have much shorter news cycles, especially when several papers competed for the penny a New Yorker paid for each paper in the 19th and early 20th centuries. You may have seen old movies that show newsboys on city streets calling out the latest headlines. Each paper wanted to be first with the news, as an important story developed, a new edition of the front page would be written and a new plate made in the composing room to print it. This was sometimes done as often as every 20 minutes. Papers could go through five or six editions when a developing story was on the front page.

Radio news broadcasts also may have short news cycles. All-news stations ("all news, all the time") may have two news cycles in an hour. Several boast "You give us 22 minutes, we'll give you the world." Other stations broadcast news at the "top of the hour"—every hour on the hour. These stations can rewrite their lead stories for each broadcast as soon as they receive new information, and they break into their other programming when something important comes **across the wire**—from the wire services. Though news stations may employ reporters, especially for local coverage, many stories come from one of the wire services, such as Reuters, Associated Press (AP) or United Press International (UPI). The wire was originally a telegraph wire. Now it is the Internet.

Internet-based news sites and microblogging sites make the news cycle so short it is almost instantaneous, with several reports a minute coming in from scenes of natural disasters, war zones, political conventions, the Olympics or the Oscars or Emmys.

shorten the school year, or requirements for work permits may be changed. How would these events affect your campus? How does college tuition going up (it almost never goes down), affect recent alumni and seniors (Figure 2.4)? If immunization requirements are changed for the fall, how does the requirement to have the whooping cough vaccine affect your audience?

School board meetings may not seem as exciting as football games, but if the school board changes graduation requirements or considers a change in the district's cellphone policy, your publication or broadcast needs to tell your audience about it.

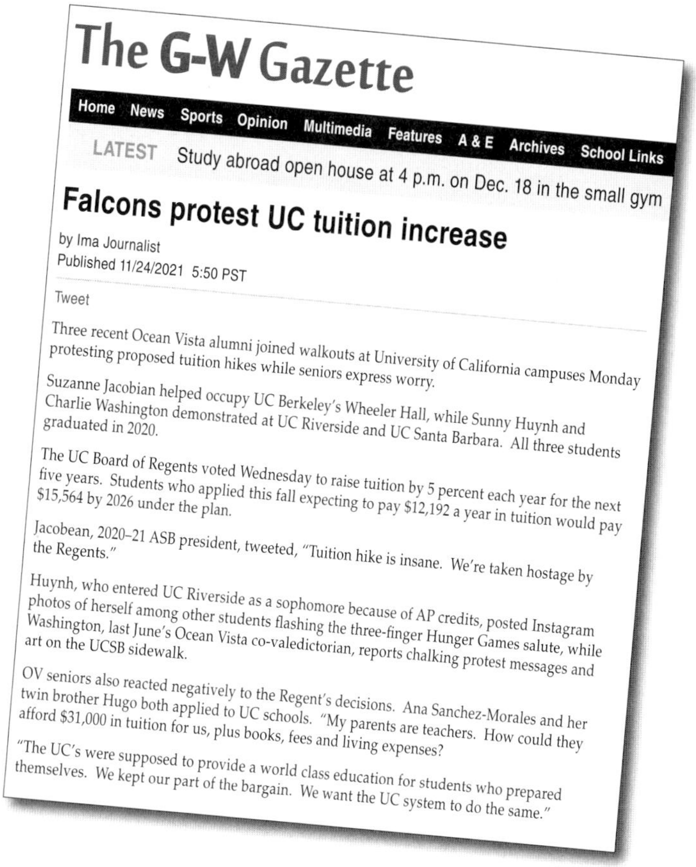
The G-W Gazette

Home News Sports Opinion Multimedia Features A & E Archives School Links

LATEST Study abroad open house at 4 p.m. on Dec. 18 in the small gym

Falcons protest UC tuition increase

by Ima Journalist
Published 11/24/2021 5:50 PST

Tweet

Three recent Ocean Vista alumni joined walkouts at University of California campuses Monday protesting proposed tuition hikes while seniors express worry.

Suzanne Jacobian helped occupy UC Berkeley's Wheeler Hall, while Sunny Huynh and Charlie Washington demonstrated at UC Riverside and UC Santa Barbara. All three students graduated in 2020.

The UC Board of Regents voted Wednesday to raise tuition by 5 percent each year for the next five years. Students who applied this fall expecting to pay $12,192 a year in tuition would pay $15,564 by 2026 under the plan.

Jacobean, 2020–21 ASB president, tweeted, "Tuition hike is insane. We're taken hostage by the Regents."

Huynh, who entered UC Riverside as a sophomore because of AP credits, posted Instagram photos of herself among other students flashing the three-finger Hunger Games salute, while Washington, last June's Ocean Vista co-valedictorian, reports chalking protest messages and art on the UCSB sidewalk.

OV seniors also reacted negatively to the Regent's decisions. Ana Sanchez-Morales and her twin brother Hugo both applied to UC schools. "My parents are teachers. How could they afford $31,000 in tuition for us, plus books, fees and living expenses?

"The UC's were supposed to provide a world class education for students who prepared themselves. We kept our part of the bargain. We want the UC system to do the same."

Figure 2.4 A distant story becomes a strong local one when you understand its impact on your audience and include the news value of prominence.

Prominence

If the people involved in the story are prominent (well-known), then the story is more newsworthy. **Prominence** is the quality of standing out, being conspicuous or being widely known. If the starting defensive lineman for the varsity football team is taking a course in American Sign Language at a community college, the story is more newsworthy than if a less well-known student is doing the same thing.

An article on the childhood of a local physician may not have great news value, unless he happens to be the son of author Kurt Vonnegut, Jr., whose "Cat's Cradle" is read by sophomores at your school and whose "Slaughterhouse-Five" is read by the seniors. Dr. Vonnegut's prominence makes a story about a local physician newsworthy (Figure 2.5).

the Villager

Team raises MS funds
page 8

Volume 25, Number 89 Thursday, April 14, 2011
Produced Tuesday thru Friday by the students of Westport High School, 19 Main Rd. Westport, MA 02790
25 cents

Town Crier
Today
Parent Conferences 6-8 p.m.
Sports
Friday
Baseball hosts Blue Hills at 3:30 p.m.
Softball at Blue Hills at 3:30 p.m.
Lacrosse hosts Upper Cape Cod at 3:30 p.m.
Boys' Tennis at Bishop Connolly at 3:30 p.m.
Girls' Tennis hosts Bishop Connolly at 3:30 p.m.
Track at Bristol-Plymouth at 3:30 p.m.
Other
Two job opportunities available. One is for females 17 or over interested in day care work. The other is for students 16-19 interested in environmental work. See guidance

The son of the late, iconic author Kurt Vonnegut Jr., Mark Vonnegut had a unique childhood growing up with his father.
--Vonnegut family

by Madlyn MacKillop

There was no ice nine in his

I was grown up."
He had many fond memories

mal."
He knew his father was a

Figure 2.5 A story becomes more prominent if a well-known individual is involved.

Courtesy of The Villager, Westport High School

If a popular student who graduated last year wins the Young Entrepreneur of the Year award for your city, his prominence probably makes for a good story. If, however, the award is won by a less well-known student who graduated four years ago, he probably does not have enough prominence to make the story worthwhile. If a high school senior runs for a seat on your school board, his prominence on your campus makes the story newsworthy, even though you may not choose to regularly comment on school board candidates (Figure 2.6 on the next page).

Figure 2.6 If your students are involved in cleaning up a distant disaster, the far away story becomes local.

Oddity

Oddity, the quality of being unusual, can by itself make something newsworthy. If you have many immigrant students in your community, a feature story on a brother and sister from Nicaragua would not have great news value. If, however, your community has few immigrants, a story about the close relationship between a newly arrived brother and sister would have news value because of the oddity. A student who rides a unicycle to school may make a good story because of both oddity and proximity.

Oddity may allow journalists to use a humorous tone, such as this article from National Public Radio. The "Morning Edition" show began each day with a slightly odd story, a feature called *Diversions*.

> *"A school in Ashland, Montana is looking for lunch. It seems to have wandered off. The school maintains a herd of bison. They provide meat for student lunches, but the animals are gone. The school's executive director says they may have run through a fence during the Memorial Day weekend thunderstorm. People in the area should be on the lookout for shaggy brown creatures with horns that taste great on a bun with ketchup and mustard."*

Conflict

Humans are interested in all kinds of **conflicts**—disagreements, arguments, contests, fights and rivalries. Suppose the school board is debating whether the auditorium tower should be torn down or repaired. People feel very strongly about the tower, but the budget is already stretched thin. Or suppose twin brothers wrestle each other on the junior varsity team. The conflicts make these stories newsworthy.

Sports stories in particular have built-in conflicts and so capture our attention with words such as *rivalry*, *contest*, *battle* and *victory* (Figure 2.7). After sports, politics probably provides the most opportunities to portray conflicts, both polite and vicious.

While every conflict has at least two sides, many have more than two sides. Even seemingly trivial matters assume greater news value when journalists report the

Figure 2.7 Sports events provide a source of conflict, which can attract readers' attention, to any story. *What conflicts at your school might you write about? How many sides are involved in the conflict?*

NOT A MINOR ISSUE

CCS sets the guidlines for league rules. Many of them make perfect sense, but others are somewhat controversial

by ERIC ABOYTES and RYAN STRATHERAN

Jamir Shepard ('20) was unable to play varsity football until age 15, despite having the skills and talent to do so.

Photo courtesy of Karen Ambrose Hickey

As Jamir Shepard ('20) comes down with his 2nd touchdown of the game against Milpitas High School, he knows even with his superior performance he will have to wait until maturity, and a statement of compliance sent by the principal to a Section Office for verification, then the requirement can be waived.

The process stated above is one that requires a lot to be done and many coaches and principals may not want to

man with little varsity experience, he acted as one of the team's standout players.

In the CCS Football Bylaws, it is not clear why this rule even exists. Although these rules are implemented throughout the whole section, the CCS may have these to prevent injuries.

Story by Eric Aboytes and Ryan Stratheran, Viking Magazine, Palo Alto High School position of all sides involved. The empty planters in front of your school may not have much news value, but if one group wants to take them out because they are ugly, another wants to fill them in with concrete to use as benches, but still another thinks that would only attract skateboarders looking for a place to grind, you have a major conflict or controversy. What if yet another group wants to replant them with white roses, but others want drought-resistant plants to conserve water? If those empty planters are a source of controversy or conflict, they have news value.

The news value of a story is stronger if your audience can express its opinion on the controversy. Provide links to an online survey where registered users of your site may vote, post comments or write to the editor. Even though the vote probably is not binding, asking people their opinions will engage your audience and strengthen your publication.

Human Interest

News stories with strong **human interest** cover people—usually ordinary people but almost always members of your community—and their problems, concerns, interests, backgrounds and achievements so that the reader's interest and perhaps emotion become involved. A human interest story may cover the student whose ballet career is threatened by a knee injury or the junior who runs his own computer repair business after school and on weekends. It could be about the senior arrested for protesting cruelty to lab animals, the sophomore who hopes his mother will soon be allowed to immigrate to this country after a 10-year separation from her son or the freshman who posts YouTube videos demonstrating dance moves.

Every member of your community has a story, probably more than one. Good reporting and good writing create strong human interest stories, which often give a human face to news events (Figure 2.8).

Figure 2.8 Human interest stories provide insight into your community and create a local angle for your story.

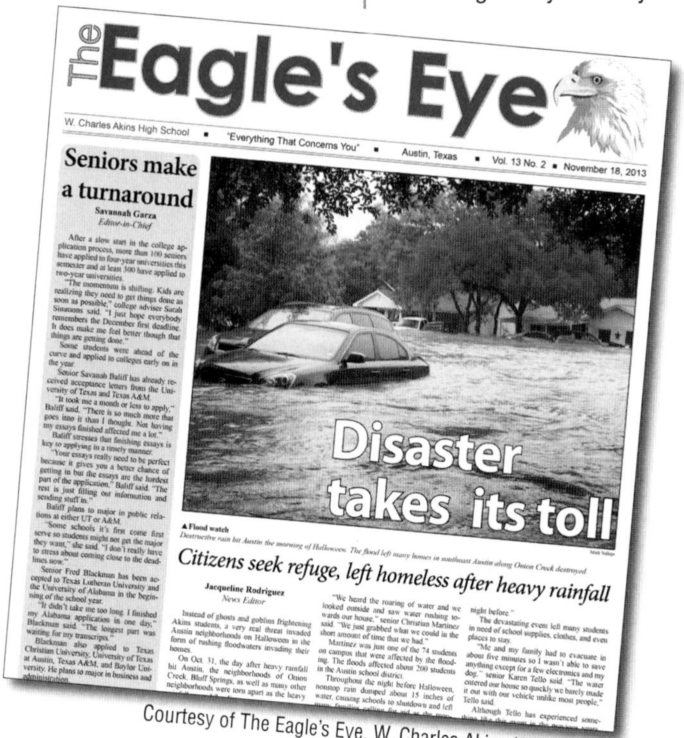
The Eagle's Eye
W. Charles Akins High School ▪ "Everything That Concerns You" ▪ Austin, Texas ▪ Vol. 13 No. 2 ▪ November 18, 2013

Seniors make a turnaround
Savannah Garza
Editor-in-Chief

Disaster takes its toll

Citizens seek refuge, left homeless after heavy rainfall
Jacqueline Rodriguez
News Editor

Courtesy of The Eagle's Eye, W. Charles Akins High School

Your Turn

1. Locate and then print out, summarize or clip seven stories from a variety of sections in the professional press. Each story should illustrate at least one of the seven news values. Identify the news value(s) in each story.
2. **Going Deeper.** Identify the major news values in four stories from one edition of any of your local or student media.

Incorporating News Values into Stories

A good journalist and a strong staff, working as a community, often discover ways to incorporate more than one news value into a story. Finding those additional news values is a skill that grows with practice.

If a power outage took place a week before you publish (so the story lacks timeliness) or it took place at a neighboring school (so it lacks proximity), the incident can still provide a **news peg** (a connection to a timely event that justifies a feature or soft news story) for a human interest story. For example, you might be able to do a story about a classmate from the Middle East whose first eight years of school took place in a village with no electricity for 23 hours each day: "When the October 23 power outage plunged parts of Puente Vista into darkness, Panthers wondered if learning would stop, but for Ali Mohammet, who arrived here in September from Iraq, learning in the dark seems natural."

You could also add impact to the power outage story by researching what would happen to cellphone towers if your area experienced a widespread power outage. Your audience might be surprised to know that their cellphones may not work during such a power outage (Figure 2.9).

You may discover you have ham radio operators on your campus who could provide disaster communication in the event of a power outage. That would add human interest or perhaps oddity to your new story. If a student was recently elected president of the campus ham radio club, that news story with very little impact could be "pegged" to the power-outage story and become a story with a high news value.

Figure 2.9 A cellphone tower may not be very interesting, but if it is damaged and the students at your school are unable to use their cellphones, you may have a story. *Why?*

If the National Collegiate Athletic Association is debating changes to the courses it considers college preparatory, you could find a local student whose eligibility to play college ball may be altered by the decision. If a story has impact, a good journalist can find and develop a local angle. World War II correspondent Ernie Pyle is reported to have said, "If you want to tell the story of a war, tell the story of one soldier."

If the citizens who want to preserve the auditorium tower include the governor's wife, you can add the element of prominence to the story. If the group includes four generations of a family, the youngest of which still attends your school, you may be able to add the element of oddity.

The student running his own computer business will experience conflict as he tries to balance time for homework and a social life. Perhaps a school requirement for fifteen hours of public service conflicts with the needs of his business. His story may become timelier if the county announces changes in its work permit policy. If he discovers the networking problem at a local church was caused by mice nesting in the server, you can add the element of oddity. How will the tone of the story change if you emphasize the oddity of the story? Would you use a pun on the two meanings of *mouse*? Mention church mice?

A word of caution: If you cannot identify one or more strong news values in your story, consider carefully whether the story idea is a good one.

Courtesy of the Los Angeles Times

Meet the Professionals:
Bill Plaschke

"Only in journalism can our words mean so much. Only in journalism can we use those words to change the world," Bill Plaschke told 3,000 student journalists at a Journalism Education Association convention.

Bill Plaschke, a sports columnist at the Los Angeles Times since 1996 and a regular panelist on the ESPN daily talk show "Around the Horn," has been nominated for a Pulitzer Prize and chosen as the Associated Press's National Sports Columnist of the Year five times. He has authored five books.

Plaschke says journalism is "one of the toughest businesses in the world, but one of the coolest businesses in the world, a business that still makes millions of dollars and reaches zillions of people."

Here's Bill talking about how he got started in journalism:

"Growing up in Louisville, Ky., I went from a tiny Catholic grade school to this giant public high school called Ballard. My parents weren't rich, I didn't know anybody, and I stuttered. My first three months, every day I would run home after school and sleep for two hours, I was so scared and depressed.

"I was sure of only two things in the entire world. I loved to write, and I loved sports. But what good was that? I didn't figure it out until one day at a basketball game, I noticed everyone in the stands chanting for the worst guy on the team to play. His name was Earl. 'We Want Earl!' Well, Earl was one of my first friends, one of the only people at school who would talk to me. I thought, 'This is fascinating, people cheering for the worst guy on the team, what was that like?' So I asked him. And then I wrote a story about it and turned it in to the school newspaper.

"And here came that miracle. Two days later, people were holding the paper and pointing at me as I walked the halls. Teachers were patting my back. Even the jocks were suddenly talking to me. And I realized this was not because of my background or athletic skill or coolness. I couldn't even talk without stuttering, remember? This was all because of my words. I thought, I can have this much effect on my world with just words? Wow.

"My words brought me through another tough situation, at my college, Southern Illinois University Edwardsville. It was, at the time, a small school with few facilities. I went there because we had just moved to Illinois and it was cheap. I lived in a church basement. I had no money, no connections, I had only my words.

"We had no gym at school, no football team and a basketball team that played in a local high school. Besides soccer, we didn't really have any big-time sports. So I didn't write about games. I wrote about people. The school's only competitive pool player, doing his homework in smoky taverns. The school's long-distance runner, trying to qualify for a marathon by running through cow pastures. I didn't write stars, because we had no stars. I wrote humans. That's how I learned of the simple power in their stories. That's why I still do that today."

For instance, if a staff writer wants to cover immigration, ask how many of the news values—proximity, timeliness, impact, prominence, oddity, conflict and human interest—this story has. Is there a local angle to give the story proximity? Has a recent change—or an impending change—made the story timely? Does it have impact on a significant number of people in your audience? Can you report on a local conflict or find a human interest angle, such as the teacher whose parents were undocumented Russian immigrants? Can you find a prominence or oddity angle? Though a writer's passion for a topic may help her to find great stories, passion is not a substitute for news values.

Great gizmos also are not a substitute for news values. Suppose someone is dying to use an interactive map on your website, voice-changing software on your broadcast or pictures inside of outline letters in the paper. Do not let the gizmo control the story. Use the tools that tell the story best and save those great gizmos for the right story.

Story Ideas

Are you developing a "nose for news"? If so, you may have already found many ideas for stories as you studied your audience in Chapter 1 and completed the Writers' Workshops associated with that chapter. Indeed, if you know your audience well and observe well, you will rarely have trouble finding stories.

Finding Story Ideas

Most strong student publications or broadcasts use a mix of three methods—beat reporting, information from the professional press and information from direct observation—to be sure they cover their community and inform and engage their audience.

Story Ideas from the Beat System

Beat reporters are journalists who regularly cover the same topics or news areas, such as the school board or track, which are called **beats** (Figure 2.10). Beat reporters know

- the people to talk to and how to reach them by phone, in person or electronically;
- when interesting events are scheduled to happen or when they might happen;
- the history of the beat;
- the big picture of the beat, as well as the details;
- the controversies or conflicts involved in the beat;
- the abbreviations, initials and slang of the beat; and
- where to go for clarification when they are confused about an aspect of their beat.

Beat reporters talk with people on their beat regularly, often once every news cycle.

Figure 2.10 Beat reporters become specialists and know who to talk to about politics that impact schools, non-high school sponsored sports, or extra curricular activities such as the art fair or robotics club. *Which beats need to be covered in your publication or broadcast?*

Warning! Beat reporting leads to dull stories, or no stories at all, if you assume your contacts (the people you usually talk with on your beat) will recognize strong story ideas and tell you about them. It is your job to recognize news, not theirs.

When you physically attend your beat's activities and meetings, you will discover story ideas. In addition, if your contacts know you and know you are interested in them, they will be more willing to talk to you. This is especially valuable when a conflict develops.

Beat reporters risk returning empty-handed if they only talk to the adults on the beat: the athletic director, club adviser, special education teacher or drama teacher. Cultivate student contacts: the athletes, members of the club, students enrolled in special education and cast members or student directors of a play. Talk to and listen to everyone on your beat. Your publication should be full of student voices, student names, student faces and student interests and concerns.

Beat reporting allows a good reporter to discover untold stories that do not necessarily come from breaking news events. These are called **enterprise stories**, or stories a reporter develops in addition to those assigned by an editor. In addition, a reporter who knows her sources may also learn of something before anyone else and **scoop**, or get ahead of, her competition, even in the professional media.

What beats should you have? Every school and every publication will have different beats. Here are some traditional beats:

- school site council
- school board and superintendent
- physical facilities
- security, crime and punishment
- school calendar
- academic counseling, scheduling and testing
- student government
- clubs and service organizations
- principal
- teachers union
- religion
- campus arts
- fall sports, winter sports, spring sports (It is best to have a reporter for each sport during the season.)

Your Turn

Based on the articles described below, what do you think the reporter's beat is?

1. The Wall Street Journal's Max Colchester wrote these stories:
   - Russia Dismisses Claims That Spy Poisoning Suspect Is Military Colonel
   - Credit Suisse Fined $77 Million Over 'Relationship Hires' in Asia
   - May Survives Confidence Vote but Brexit Path Still Unclear
   - Europe Goes Harder on Money Laundering With Record ING Fine
2. Tampa Bay Times' Tom Jones wrote these articles:
   - The Lightning is quietly prepping for another Cup run
   - Lightning journal: Alex Killorn's just puttin' on the Fitz
   - The magic has worn off. Time for the Bucs to start Jameis Winston
   - Bucs-Steelers: No wrong answer for Tampa Bay at quarterback
3. The Hollywood Reporter's Tatiana Siegel wrote these stories:
   - Inside the Marketing for Faith-Based 'Unbroken' Sequel
   - Toronto Wrap: Music-Themed Acquisitions Kept Market Humming ... Barely
   - Toronto: Neil Jordan's Psychological Thriller 'Greta' Nabbed by Focus for $4 Million
   - What's Driving the Boom in Nonfiction Filmmaking?

(Continued)

YOUR TURN *(Continued)*

4. Dallas Morning News' Sarah Blaskovich wrote these stories:
   - McDonald's announces change to burgers: no artificial flavors or preservatives
   - Snooze wakes up Dallas and Fort Worth brunch scene with 3 new restaurants
   - ChopShop is North Texas' newest 'better for you' restaurant, and it's now open in Plano
   - Do you live in one of D-FW's healthiest neighborhoods?
   - Dig in: 12 brand-new restaurants to check out in Dallas-Fort Worth
5. The New York Times' Hilary Howard wrote these stories:
   - Books about beauty
   - New sunscreens: Beauty spots
   - New lipsticks for summer
   - Tattoos
   - Here come the braids

A strong publication will include many of these traditional beats but also will look beyond this list. In Chapter 1 you identified members of your audience whose interests and activities have not been covered well in your publication in the past. These groups, which are potential beats, may include a minority ethnic group or minority religious group, a population learning English, a population with disabilities (see Chapter 4 for guidelines on covering issues of disability), students in foster care, rock climbers, belly dancers or students with after-school jobs.

Any population whose interests, lifestyles, situations, commitments or talents may cause them to become invisible to the rest of your community may deserve a beat. Strong beat reporting will not only cover a group's activities but also increase the group members' interest in your publication or broadcast.

Remember: Your publication should include the names of many students, and not the same ones over and over.

Story Ideas from Professional Media

Journalists are great readers. Why is reading so important when we have many ways to get news and many ways to tell a story?

At its heart, almost every form of journalism relies on strong writing, so you will need to read strong writing. Even if you plan to produce broadcast or visual media, you still need to read text-rich media such as newspapers and journalistic websites every day.

As you read professional media (and occasionally other high school publications), look for story ideas for your publication. Any story that catches your interest or the interest of your classmates may be a story idea for your publication. Summarize the stories and keep notes of the story ideas you find. The ability to summarize quickly, accurately and

And Now… Closer to Home

Dead Beat or Lively Beat? It's What You Make It

Beats will be as interesting or as dull as you make them. Here is an example of what an enterprising reporter can do with a new beat, in this case the school's physical plant.

1. The new reporter talks to the person who had the beat before her. He says it is a boring beat, but he does tell her which assistant principal is in charge of the physical facilities, the name of the head of the physical plant and the location of his office and the name of the lead custodian.
2. She introduces herself to each contact, but more importantly, she spends time with the contacts. In the first two months of the beat, she writes these notes in her reporter's notebook.

- The dance studio in the PE building is being turned into a science room. Do we still have a dance class? If not, when did it go away and why? Check counseling office and old yearbooks? Does this connect to larger issues such as physical fitness and obesity?
- The Asian custodian, a soft-spoken man about five feet tall, was a colonel in the Vietnamese army. He probably didn't pick up trash in Vietnam. What's his story? Who else around campus has a military background? Veterans Day is in November. Personality feature?
- Is anyone recycling the cans and bottles in the trash? Why/why not? Who gets the money?
- When does the custodian's day start? Use audio recorder. Sound of custodian opening the gate at 5:25, grating sounds, quiet campus, rain, ducks in the quad, cafeteria ladies laughing as they cook and the first students arriving. Why do they come so early?
- Toured and videotaped the crawlspace above the stage as the custodian changes the lights. Visited the "crouch space" under the stage, the furnace room, pool filtration room, loading docks, roofs, places students rarely go. Halloween story?
- Taped early Monday morning graffiti cleanup and vandalism repair. Rival high school's colors were spray painted on walls. Assistant principals came out and photographed the graffiti. What for?
  - If we run the story, are we giving the vandals what they want?
  - Will there be police action? How can I find out about it?
  - What is the difference between pranks and acts of vandalism?
- Many trucks come through the campus entrance by the weight room: Pepsi, Coke, Frito-Lay, a restaurant supplier, Sysco (what's that?). It would make a cool video to shoot 5 seconds of the side of each truck coming past the weight room. Or shoot all the stuff being off-loaded at the cafeteria and student store and then drop out every other frame and speed up the tape like an old-fashioned movie.
- How many bags of chips and bottles of Gatorade do we consume each week? How do I find out?

While her predecessor thought this was "a really boring beat," this journalist found a great beat with multiple strong story ideas.

thoroughly will help you often in journalism. Journalists frequently need to summarize events, information and ideas. Summarizing is also a good way to be sure you understood what you read or viewed.

At first it may be difficult to see how the stories from other media outlets can be developed into stories for your broadcast or publication, but you will develop that skill with practice. Do not be afraid to clip anything that interests you, that might interest others on your campus or that seems to relate to your audience. Note possible local angles as they occur to you (Figure 2.11).

Figure 2.11 The more you read, the more you are exposed to story ideas.

WEEKLY STORY IDEAS

If you don't read it, you cannot write it

Worksheets

Name	Ima Journalista
Date submitted	Friday, January 25, 2014
Title and source of article (name of publication, section, date)	"Family hopes genome test will help cure girl's mystery disease" Los Angeles Times First (A) Section, Monday, January 20, 2014
Summary in 3-5 sentences; include info after the jump	Lilly Grossman has an unnamed muscular weakness that requires she uses a wheelchair. She was junior class homecoming princess, has written a novel and blogs. In her novel, her heroine takes a pill and becomes "normal" and exacts revenge on all her tormenters. She hopes to attend UC Berkeley, which has an all-accessible campus, unlike her high school where an aide needs to open doors. She's had her genome sequenced but has not found a "cure."
Pitch your story to your editors. Be as specific as possible, , including angle, sources and subject	1. Is our campus accessible? What is it like to navigate RAHS in a wheelchair? Follow (name) the football player with the damaged knee in his wheelchair? **[Prominence, timely]** Or

YOUR TURN

1. Find story ideas from other publications or broadcasts that contain kernels of ideas for your publication or broadcast. Clip or print out the stories and summarize them in three or four sentences. Your summaries should reveal your intelligent reading of the stories.
2. **Going Deeper.** Suggest possible local stories derived from the professional stories. The more specific the suggestions, the better. Save your suggestions for a "Your Turn" exercise later in this chapter.

Story Ideas from Direct Observation

Your school publication or broadcast is by and about the students at your school. A stranger should be able to see, hear and "taste" your school as she views your broadcast or reads your publication. Your journalistic efforts, regardless of your media, should reflect what the students are talking about and worried about, what makes them excited and what makes them mad. The paper, post or broadcast should cover what students are buying, what they are listening to and what they are driving.

A school is made up of individuals, however, often several thousand individuals, and no two are talking and worrying about the same issues. So every member of the staff is needed, no matter what his or her job title, whether it is the business manager, graphics editor, staff writer or copy editor.

You all are the eyes and ears of the news organization. You should listen, especially to students you do not know well or who are different from you and your friends. Listen in the lunch line. Listen before the bell rings for your classes. Listen in the locker room and the restrooms.

As you listen, use your reporter's notebook to write down what people are talking about, even if you do not hear the whole conversation. Note who is talking or describe the people who are talking. Do you see any signs of emotion? Note actual phrases and any details you hear.

Not all of your observations will turn out to be kernels of great stories, but some will.

YOUR TURN

1. Make at least three entries in your reporter's notebook observing what students are talking about, are concerned about and are planning.
2. **Going Deeper.** Write the story ideas your observations suggest. Save your story ideas for another "Your Turn" exercise later in this chapter.

Developing Your Story Ideas

Not all of your observations or all of your articles from other publications can be turned into strong stories for your publication, but many of them hold more promise than you may realize. Staff meetings provide an opportunity to work as a community to develop story ideas (Figure 2.12 on the next page).

Those observations and articles can provoke fruitful discussions like this:

One reporter observed two sophomore football players on a game day, revved up and unable to concentrate in class.

Another staff member adds, "Yeah, there was a guy in my fifth period too who…"

Another says, "I heard the girls team members always braid each other's hair. It's like a good-luck thing."

"We could do a feature on pregame jitters and include the frosh-soph and JV players. We don't cover them enough."

"How about other traditions? Or superstitions?"

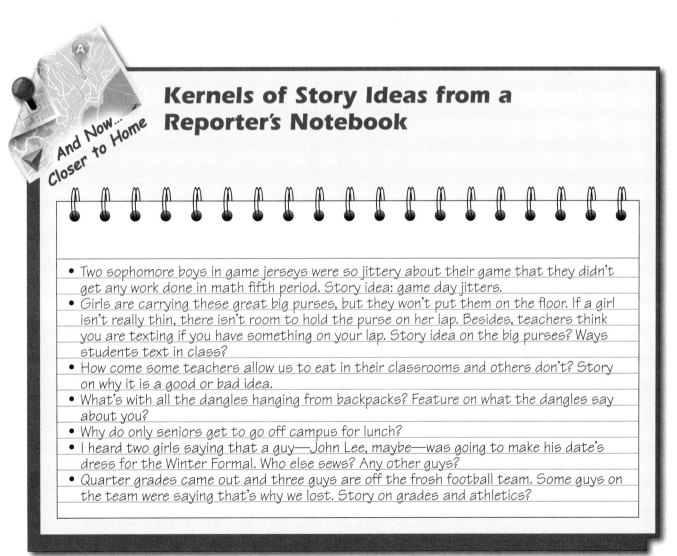

Kernels of Story Ideas from a Reporter's Notebook

- Two sophomore boys in game jerseys were so jittery about their game that they didn't get any work done in math fifth period. Story idea: game day jitters.
- Girls are carrying these great big purses, but they won't put them on the floor. If a girl isn't really thin, there isn't room to hold the purse on her lap. Besides, teachers think you are texting if you have something on your lap. Story idea on the big purses? Ways students text in class?
- How come some teachers allow us to eat in their classrooms and others don't? Story on why it is a good or bad idea.
- What's with all the dangles hanging from backpacks? Feature on what the dangles say about you?
- Why do only seniors get to go off campus for lunch?
- I heard two girls saying that a guy—John Lee, maybe—was going to make his date's dress for the Winter Formal. Who else sews? Any other guys?
- Quarter grades came out and three guys are off the frosh football team. Some guys on the team were saying that's why we lost. Story on grades and athletics?

Figure 2.12 The staff of a publication or broadcast often meet to discuss story ideas. *What talents and attitudes can make these meetings productive?*

A staff member says, "I printed out an article that says there may be millions of planets roaming free, but my science book says stars with planets may be rare and doesn't say anything about planets roaming free of stars. Are there other things in our books that just aren't true or may be out of date?"

"How about global warming? The AP bio text doesn't even mention it."

"My English teacher said our textbook left out a great deal about the Japanese relocation camps in its background to the poem 'Internment.'"

"My math teacher says there are mistakes in the text."

"Can we do a feature on 'Lies our textbooks tell us'?"

Another staffer heard someone was pregnant and going to drop out of school.

"Can we do a story on that?"

"How about a feature on a girl who leaves this campus for the School-Aged Mothers Program and one who stays on campus?"

"Does she have to take PE?"

"Do you know anyone who'd let you write about her?"

"Wouldn't that be giving her attention for doing something that is wrong?"

A first-year student reports a student thought a friend's Curious George purse is "so cute." Others mention a Winnie the Pooh backpack, a Spiderman lunch box used as a purse, Ninja Turtles shoelaces, a Barbie pencil case and a pencil case that looks like a stuffed animal giraffe. Someone suggests that "we are returning to childhood treasures." Someone notes most freshmen rarely risk being seen with such items.

A student clipped a story about a neo-Nazi being killed by his 10-year-old son. The parents had loaded guns in the house.

"Do we have neo-Nazis around here?"

"Or at school?"

"Do we have people with loaded guns in their homes? That seems more likely."

"What are the laws?"

"Is it different for a hunting rifle than for a handgun?"

"What do people here think about guns? Would they have them in their own homes?"

"There's a kid in my sixth period whose dad teaches gun safety classes for the National Rifle Association. I think he has earned some shooting medals."

Another student mentions the freshmen who spend hours grooming themselves before school, while seniors wander in at 7:59 in pajama bottoms and flip-flops or Ugg boots with a bed-head.

Story ideas from this discussion might include the following:

- a feature spread on students' childlike belongings with short interviews and photos
- an opinion column suggesting that the campus needs swing sets, so students can unwind
- an article on what is cool for freshmen, sophomores, juniors and seniors
- a spread on hair by class, freshmen, sophomores and so on
- a sports feature on the award-winning marksman
- an investigation of out-of-date textbooks and curriculum

These conversations do more than help new writers find story angles. They also build the writing community, raise ethical and legal issues that need to be discussed, develop a sense of the publication's audience and create a powerful bank of possible stories. While no idea is dismissed as worthless, the newer writers learn from their peers and the adviser about the paper's mission and audience. Good journalists keep notes of these ideas.

Your Turn

1. Listed below are possible story ideas resulting from the imaginary brainstorming session that you just read. Choose one or two of these ideas and develop a local angle for an upcoming broadcast or publication.
   - students' childlike belongings
   - opinion column advocating campus swing sets
   - how does "what's cool" change from class to class
   - sports feature on award-winning marksman
   - report on out-of-date and inaccurate textbooks
2. **Going Deeper.** What news values could each story have? List and explain the news values.

Pitching Your Story Ideas

The editors, who will have taken notes during the story idea discussions, choose which stories to develop based on the news values of proximity, timeliness, impact, prominence, oddity, conflict and human interest. They may then assign stories to the writers they believe will do the best job covering each particular story. Sometimes, but not always, the writer chosen to cover the story will be the person who originally suggested the idea for that story.

An enterprising journalist may not be content with just the stories he is assigned. In addition to the assigned story, he may want to work on an idea he has for a different story. After a little background work to be sure of the news values, he will need to **pitch** (describe in a persuasive way) his story to an editor. If the editor likes the idea, she may give him the time, the resources—such as cameras and microphones—and the support to pursue the story. In addition, she may meet with him periodically to help him focus his story. If the story is strong, she will give him time in the broadcast or space in the edition (Figure 2.13).

So how do you pitch a story so that your editor will accept it? You begin with preparation.

1. Read your source article thoroughly if you are pitching a story from the professional media. Do not go to your editor and say, "Hey, I found this neat article about Lap-Band surgery being approved for kids as young as 14. I want to write about it!" Rather, show your understanding of the article; for instance, "The LA Times wrote an article about Lap-Band surgery being considered for marketing to teens as young as 14, but many people think this is not a good idea."

Figure 2.13 Pitch your story idea to your editors if you think the story will be interesting, relevant, and newsworthy for your publication.

2. Develop a specific local angle. "One-third of teens are overweight, and the PE department has weight records for students here. We could see if we are above or below the national average. Also, I know two students who have lost a great deal of weight in the last year. I'd like to interview them about how they did it. I know a couple of local adults who have had the Lap-Band surgery. The article questions whether the Lap Band should be marketed to teens. If parents approve, teens can get the surgery now, but the new law will allow the company to market the surgery to teens. Perhaps we could do a survey to see if teens think it is a good idea to market a surgery to teenagers."
3. Be prepared to talk about the news values. For example:
   - Point out the local angle, the proximity: "I know people here involved in weight loss."
   - Mention the conflict: "Should this be marketed to teens?"
   - Show your editor the timeliness: "The Food and Drug Administration will be hearing arguments about it shortly."
   - Talk about impact: "If a third or more of teens here are obese, this must affect many of the families in our community."
   - Ask: "Could we do a human interest story on one of the people who lost weight? One person was willing to be interviewed and has 'before' pictures."

   The only two news values not mentioned here are oddity and prominence. The editor may tell you to go ahead with the story or tell you, "No, we covered the topic last spring." She is likely to suggest the angle she would like you to research.

Your Turn

Be enterprising! Choose one of the stories mentioned in this chapter or a story idea you came up with in a previous "Your Turn" exercise. Prepare to pitch this story idea to an editor. Include a thorough reading of the article if the idea comes from the professional press.

- Suggest specific angles. "We could write about girls who skateboard" is not very specific. Instead, you could say, "I know at least three girls who skate at the ramps and rails at the Quaker church on Magnolia."
- Be prepared to talk about the *specific* news values of the story idea. "We could do a human interest piece, or we could focus in on the conflicts between the male and female skaters. They are not always welcomed there. And there is a little oddity angle. I wonder if any of them compete?"

Chapter Two

Review and Assessment

Recall

1. Name the seven news values.
2. Explain proximity.
3. Explain timeliness.
4. Which news value is reflected in a story about the rivalry between two sports teams?
5. What are three main methods of obtaining story ideas for student publications and broadcasts?

Critical Thinking

1. Why is it important to consider news values when choosing stories to include in your publication or broadcast?
2. Search publications other than those from your own school to identify three stories that may have been developed by beat reporting. Identify the beat and explain why you think the stories were the result of beat reporting.
3. List beats that you think your publication or broadcast should have. Use the list in this chapter as your starting point, but add at least five more.
4. Examine the coverage in one local publication, preferably a news website, news broadcast, student publication or local newspaper. Using a table like the one shown below, identify the news values in six stories. In the first column, list the story's headline or write a *slug*—a one- or two-word description of the story. Place a + in the appropriate columns to identify the news values contained in each story. Is one news value more intense than the others? Highlight that one. Be prepared to explain your choices to your classmates.

Story	Proximity	Timeliness	Impact	Prominence	Oddity	Conflict	Human Interest
School security	+	+	+				

5. Working with a partner, write each key term from the chapter on a separate piece of paper. Take turns choosing terms. Describe each term for your partner using prior knowledge and experiences, comparisons, or formal and informal language until your partner correctly identifies the term you have chosen. Repeat until all of the terms are used.
6. Look at three or four editions of your publication (or another school's) and evaluate the stories in each to determine which of the traditional beats have been covered well and which ones have been neglected in each publication.

Application

1. Find three stories from the professional media that could become strong stories for your publication. Clip or print out the stories and accurately summarize each. Explain how you would adapt the stories for your publication. Access the *Journalism* website for a template like the one shown on page 49.
2. Carry your reporter's notebook (or a digital substitute) for 24 hours on a school day and record observations. Create three strong story ideas from your observations. Include the news values, your pitch to an editor and the source material from your reporter's notebook.
3. In a small group, read—either individually or aloud—four interesting articles you have chosen from the professional press. Brainstorm possible local angles for each one. Identify the news values in each localized story. Rank the story ideas for each example from the professional press according to how strong you feel the story idea is.
4. Imagine you are an editor and the other members of your group are reporters who are pitching their story ideas from their beats, direct observation or the professional press. Explain to your group members why their pitch is strong or weak. Then switch roles; you will pitch your story ideas and others will react as if they are the editor.

Chapter Two

Journalism Style

Look It Up!

Do you need hyphens in your review of a *cloak and dagger* movie? Do you call the female teacher who heads the English department the *chairman*? *Chairwoman*? If your Winter Formal theme is "Paris at Night," what do you capitalize in *the city of light*? If your debate team will compete at Fordham University, how many capitals do you need in *new york city*? If the ski team competed in the Catskills, how many capitals do you need in *new york state*?

Journalists don't guess, yet very few are walking databases of this kind of information. They look up what they are not absolutely sure of. Student journalists need to do the same thing—look it up.

Where do you look it up? That depends on your publication or broadcast's media and style. The most-used stylebook in journalism is *The Associated Press Stylebook and Briefing on Media Law*, available in print and online.

If you publish a news magazine, your staff leadership may have adopted *The Chicago Manual of Style*. If you publish online, you may use *The Yahoo! Style Guide: The Ultimate Sourcebook for Writing, Editing, and Creating Content for the Digital World*. If you are mainly a broadcast staff, you may use *Broadcast News and Writing Stylebook*. Other publications base their style on other resources that fit with their school's mission.

In addition to your stylebook, you should have copies of *Webster's New World College Dictionary*. All stylebooks and dictionaries should be the most recent edition possible.

Your publication should also have a stylebook that overrides the official, printed stylebook your staff adopted. For instance, the AP Stylebook allows the use of *chairwoman* and *chairman*, but your staff may have decided that your publication will use the gender-free *chair*, as in "The competition will be organized by the English department chair, Marlys Nelson." A publication's stylebook addresses issues that arise often in school life and carves out exceptions to the adopted stylebook.

In the next column is a short quiz to help you assess your knowledge of the correct usage, help you become familiar with AP style resources, and develop the "look it up" habit.

Journalism Style Quiz

Directions: On your own paper, number 1 through 28. Next to each number on your paper write any needed corrections for the line below with the corresponding number. If no corrections are needed, write "correct" next to the number.

1 Four fighting Irish forensics team
2 members, Seniors David Cassel and
3 Hector Martinez and Juniors Aisha
4 Chopra and Karen Carlyle, will
5 advance to the US Speech and
6 Debate Tournament in Dallas May 4—5.

7 Cassel, Martinez, Chopra, and
8 Carlyle were propeled to the national
9 competition when the fourensics team
10 brought home 5 gold medals from the
11 New York State forensic league state
12 championship tournament in Mineola,
13 NY, Apr. 12.

14 Sophamore Kanye Jackson's gold
15 added to the total

16 Senior David Cassel, a four year
17 veteran of John F Kennedy High
18 School forensics competitions
19 gathered a gold medal for his ten
20 minute original speach on the
21 importance of intrapersonal
22 communication in a society obsessed
23 with technology.

24 Senior, Hector Martinez captured
25 a gold metal with his policy debate
26 titled The Importance of Space
27 Exploration in an Age of National
28 Debt.

Chapter Two

Writers' Workshop

In this Writers' Workshop you will:

- Use participial phrases to enrich sentences.
- Experiment with the wording and placement of participial phrases.
- Use triplets to add impact to your writing.

Workshop 2.1

The "ing" That Describes

Mini-Lesson: Using Present Participial Phrases to Modify

A present participle is the "ing" form of a verb: drip/*dripping*, pound/*pounding*, dance/*dancing*. When you use a present participle with the *to be* form of a verb, you create the progressive form of the verb: He is *dripping*. Her heart *will be pounding*. They *have been dancing*. Without the *to be* verb, the participle becomes an adjective, which is the participle form we will be using in this workshop.

Participial phrases such as *hair dripping*, *heart pounding* or *feet dancing* can be used to modify the noun or pronoun that is the subject or object of a sentence or clause. They can make an active sentence even more active.

Start with a strong verb—in this case, *kicks*. Create a simple Subject/Verb/Object (SVO) sentence. Use the simple present or simple past tense of the verb. Your sentence should look something like this: *The soccer player kicks the ball toward the goal*.

Participial phrases can be inserted at several places in the sentence, but put them between the subject and the verb for now. Your sentence should look something like this: *The soccer player, hair dripping, heart pounding, feet dancing, kicks the ball toward the goal.*

Apply It!

Follow the step-by-step instructions below to enrich your own sentence.

1. Think of an active verb that you can picture. Write an SVO sentence using that verb.
2. Now list at least four participial phases to describe the subject of your sentence.
3. Read your phrases aloud, but to yourself.
4. Choose your three best phrases and insert them between the subject and the verb.
5. **Collaboration and Editing**. Read your sentence aloud to a partner. Do you and your partner agree about the order of the participial phrases in the sentence? Where do you want to put your strongest, freshest, most interesting participial phrase?

Mini-Lesson: Where to Put the Participial Phrases

Experiment by moving the participial phrases to different places in your sentence. Try them at the beginning of the sentence, before the subject: *His hair dripping, his heart pounding, his feet dancing, the soccer player kicks the ball toward the goal*. The reader's attention will now focus on the dripping hair because it is the opening element of a sentence. Is this where you want the reader's attention?

Beginning your sentence with a participial phrase lengthens the time it takes your reader to get to the *who* and the *what* of the sentence. Participial phrases create a left-branching sentence when placed before the subject. Left-branching sentences often slow down your reader. Journalists use them very sparingly.

Now try the participial phrases at the end of the sentence: *The soccer player kicks the ball toward the goal, his hair dripping, his heart pounding, his feet dancing*.

The last element of the sentence lingers in the reader's mind. It is the second most important part of the sentence. Do you like the idea of the dancing feet remaining in the reader's mind?

Apply It!

Follow these step-by-step instructions to experiment with participial phrases.

1. Pick one of the nouns below and add a strong action verb and an object, making an SVO sentence.

   airplane

   boat

   horse

   car

   sword (or *knife*)

   wolf (or other animal)

Example: Using the noun *needle*, you could write: *The needle hemmed the dress.*

2. Now improve the two nouns in your sentence a little. Make them more specific by modifying them: *Her flashing needle hemmed my prom dress.*
3. Create at least four participles or participial phrases to modify the subject of your sentence.

Examples:

darting in and out of the crisp satin

puncturing the cloth

drawing closed the sutures

pulling the scarlet thread

4. Choose the three best phrases from the four or more phrases you created. Write several versions of your sentence with these participial phrases. Experiment with the order of the phrases and their location. For instance, try it this way: *Her flashing needle, puncturing the cloth, drawing closed the sutures, pulling the scarlet thread, hemmed my prom dress*. Or: *Her flashing needle hemmed my prom dress, puncturing the cloth, pulling the scarlet thread, drawing closed the sutures.*

The core SVO sentence remains the same, but the participial phrases foreshadow the possibility that this will be a bloody prom night. Is there a vampire in the audience?

Workshop 2.2

Congratulations! It's Triplets!

Mini-Lesson: Using Three Specifics or Three Modifiers

There is something about three. Three little pigs. Three wishes. Three chances to spin straw into gold.

We write with threes: "… one nation
under God,
indivisible,
with liberty and justice for all."

Abraham Lincoln described America at Gettysburg as "government
of the people,
by the people,
for the people…"

In the Declaration of Independence, Thomas Jefferson's prose talks about
"life,
liberty and
the pursuit of happiness."

President Barack Obama used this principle of three when he wanted Americans to remember the 9/11 attacks as he announced the death of Osama bin Laden. He said, "On that day,
no matter where we came from,
what God we prayed to,
or what race or ethnicity we were,
we were united as one American family."

Apply It!

Almost every part of speech can be used effectively as triplets. Try triplet prepositional phrases, using this as your sentence: *We played hide-and-go-seek.*

Now describe where you played the game.

Example:

in the basement

in the attic and

in the garage

Mini-Lesson: Triplet Verbs

Triplet verbs have a long and dignified history. In 47 B.C.E. when Julius Caesar had conquered the city of Zela (now Zile, in Turkey), he is reported to have penned this perfect *tricolon*, a form of triplet, using three verbs: "Veni, vidi, vici—I came, I saw, I conquered."

A less dignified verb triplet might be: *He danced, sang and generally made a fool of himself.*

Notice that the triplet verbs can be parallel, as in the example above, but they can also zoom, create a sequence, or ascend or descend in importance or gravity.

Zooming: *He located where the mosquito had bitten him, clawed at it with his nails and did not stop until pink-white plasma tinted with blood oozed from the sore.*

Sequential: *He grabbed the gallon jug of milk from the fridge, twisted off the cap and began to gulp.*

Ascending: *We pledge our lives, our liberty and our sacred honor.*

Descending: *We live to learn, love and die.*

Apply It!

Use the sentence frame below to answer the question "What do you live for?"

Example: *I live to complain, criticize and correct.*

I live to _____, _____ and _____.

Extend Your Knowledge

Extend

Visit the *Journalism* website for additional examples and practice.

Chapter Three

Media Law

May we cover that?

Courtesy of Ellen Austin

G-WLEARNING.COM

While studying, look for the activity icon to:

- **Build** vocabulary terms with e-flash cards and matching activities.
- **Extend** learning with further discussion of relevant topics.
- **Reinforce** what you learn by completing style exercises, worksheets and end-of-chapter questions.

Visit the Journalism website:
www.g-wlearning.com/journalism/

Chapter Objectives

After reading this chapter, you will be able to:

- Name the privileges given the press by the Founding Fathers.
- Discuss the privileges given the student press under the Tinker and Hazelwood standards.
- Describe the limitations on student journalists under the law.
- Explain the difference between prior restraint and prior review.
- Describe shield laws and their application to student journalists.
- Describe other privileges traditionally given to journalists.
- Describe how to use the sunshine laws and the Freedom of Information Act.
- Define libel and slander and tell how they relate to the student press.
- Define invasion of privacy and how it relates to the student press.
- Describe FERPA and how it relates to the student press.
- Discuss how copyright laws may protect the work of the student press.
- Identify copyright violations and explain how to avoid them.

Key Terms Build Vocab

copyright
copyright infringement
court-recognized privileges
defamation
fair use
freedom of information laws
intellectual property
liability
libel
press credentials
press package
prior restraint
prior review
public forum
shield laws
slander
subpoena
sunshine laws
underground publication

Before You Read...

Practicing silent reading is a good way to improve your understanding and vocabulary. It is a helpful first step to building the confidence to read aloud in a group. Form small groups and sit together while you each begin reading the chapter silently. After silently reading a few pages, begin taking turns reading aloud. When you have finished reading the chapter, reflect on your experience. Did you find that silent reading helped build your confidence and prepare you for reading aloud?

Introduction

"If a person goes to a country and finds the newspapers filled with nothing but good news, there are good men in jail."

–Daniel P. Moynihan, former U.S. senator

Imagine you are a general who has just led your people in a rebellion against a tyrant. The tyrant had limited your liberty, taken your money and property, and had used hired soldiers from another country to hold on to his power.

It has been a long struggle, starting with protests and boycotts, then warfare, town by town. Citizens said they backed the revolution but then switched their loyalty to the tyrant when his army was back in control. Other rebel military commanders seemed more interested in their reputations than in helping you win the war. Your closest advisers turned against you, and one became a spy and traitor. Civilian leaders worried about their own religious or geographic group, their "tribe," rather than the fight against the tyrant. They withheld money and supplies, so your soldiers nearly starved. Your troops sometimes ran from battle, killed their own officers, took bribes from the enemy, or deserted the army.

Now the tyrant is finally gone and you have been given power as the head of the new government, though you are so broke you need to borrow money to travel to the capital. Now the hard part begins: establishing a democracy.

How will you handle your newfound power? Rate yourself from 1 to 5, with 1 being "not at all likely" and 5 being "very likely," on what you will do.

Now that you have power:

1. How likely are you to use your power to make money for yourself?
2. How likely are you to keep your military title and its power?
3. How likely are you to use your power to help people who supported you or who come from the same "tribe," that is, the same religious, economic, social or geographic background as you?
4. How likely are you to use your power and influence to punish your rivals and enemies?
5. How likely are you to want to give orders (as you did in the military), rather than let the people debate and vote?
6. How likely are you to want the military to keep power over the civilian government?
7. How likely are you to limit the rights of common citizens?
8. How likely are you to want what you do and say to be kept private, away from the eyes and ears of the common citizens?

Add up your points. If your total score is...

- between 8 and 16: You are an exceptionally trustworthy person and people can count on you to do what is right, whether anyone is watching you or not.
- between 17 and 24: You have excellent self-control, but someone should check up on you.

(Continued)

- between 25 and 32: You probably will be corrupted by power. You need to be watched!
- between 33 and 40: You love power more than almost anything else. You may be a great general, but you need to be watched constantly.

Now rate the other former rebels—the civilian leaders, soldiers and military commanders—who are now in power with you:

1. How likely are they to use their power to make money for themselves?
2. How likely are they to keep their military or civilian titles and power?
3. How likely are they to use their power to help people who supported them or who come from the same "tribe"?
4. How likely are they to use their power and influence to punish their rivals and enemies?
5. How likely are they to want to give orders, rather than let the people debate and vote?
6. How likely are they to want their faction (either military or civilian) to predominate?
7. How likely are they to limit the rights of common citizens?
8. How likely are they to want what they do and say to be kept private, away from the eyes and ears of the common citizens?

Add up the points. If your total score is...

- between 8 and 16: You think most people are trustworthy when given power and you can count on them to do what is right even if no one is watching.
- between 17 and 24: You think most people have excellent self-control, but someone should check up on the people in power.
- between 25 and 32: You think most people will be corrupted by power. They need to be watched!
- between 33 and 40: You think most people love power more than almost anything else. They need to be watched constantly.

Did you guess that the general was George Washington (Figure 3.1) and the war was the American fight for independence from Britain? And did you know that the first president, who presided over the Constitutional Convention without expressing his opinion on any of the other debates, did speak up on one issue? He spoke in favor of the amendments that limited the power of the government over the individual. He spoke in favor of the Bill of Rights.

Figure 3.1 George Washington addresses the Continental Congress after they appointed him Commander in Chief of the colonies' forces in 1775.

If you rated yourself between 8 and 16, you may be as trustworthy as our Founding Father George Washington. You would probably do what is right for your country even if no one could observe your actions or had any power over you. But if you thought that you or other people were less trustworthy than General Washington, then you understand why it took over four years from the time the Constitution was written until it was finally accepted. People were afraid that a distant, federal government would become too powerful. The new states did not approve the Constitution until the first 10 amendments—the Bill of Rights—were added. These amendments were added in part to make sure that the distant, federal government would remain the servant of the people.

The First Amendment and Journalists

The First Amendment

Congress shall make no law respecting an establishment of religion, or prohibiting the free exercise thereof; or abridging the freedom of speech, or of the press; or the right of the people peaceably to assemble, and to petition the Government for a redress of grievances.

The First Amendment deals directly with journalism. Journalism is the only profession singled out for protection in the Bill of Rights.

Journalists are the people who watch and report what those in power do. A free press allows the people to observe and debate the actions and policies of those whom they have elected as well as the actions of others in power in the society.

The foundation of press laws, including copyright law, can also be seen in Article I, Section 8 of the U.S. Constitution, which protects the progress of science and "useful" arts by "securing for limited Times to Authors and Inventors the exclusive Right to their respective Writings and Discoveries." In subsequent years, copyright press laws received further protections.

The Bill of Rights was originally meant to restrain the federal government and applied only to laws passed by the United States Congress. The First Amendment, for instance, did not originally keep states and towns from establishing religion. Some towns did have established religions. The Bill of Rights was originally meant to restrain the distant, federal government.

In 1925 the Supreme Court ruled that the First Amendment applied to all state and local governments as well as the federal government. No level of government could pass laws that restrained First Amendment rights of the people of the United States, including freedom of the press.

The Tinker Case and Student First Amendment Rights

But what about school districts? Are they government? Are they restrained by the First Amendment? Do students have First Amendment rights? That was decided in 1969 by the Supreme Court in *Tinker v. Des Moines*. Justice Abe Fortas wrote, "It can hardly be argued that either students or teachers shed their constitutional rights to freedom of speech or expression at the schoolhouse gate."

Students do have First Amendment rights, and public school districts, part of the government, are restrained by the First Amendment. In 1965 three students—Mary Beth Tinker, 13, John F. Tinker, 15, and Christopher Eckhart, 16—had worn black armbands to school as a silent protest against the deaths in the Vietnam War and in support of the Christmas Truce called for by Senator Robert F. Kennedy (Figure 3.2). The Des Moines Independent Community School District required the students to remove the armbands or be suspended. The students chose suspension. Justice Fortas, four years later, wrote that the school's desire "to avoid the discomfort and unpleasantness that always accompany an unpopular viewpoint" was not a strong enough reason to limit the students' First Amendment rights.

Figure 3.2 Mary Beth and John Tinker hold the armbands that led to their suspension from school in 1965.

GRANGER

As with all rights, student First Amendment rights were not without limitations. The Tinker case

- does not allow student free speech to create "a substantial disruption or a material interference with school activities." Shouting "Fire!" in a crowded gymnasium would not be protected, nor would advocating that everyone march out of fourth-period class. Both would create a substantial disruption. However, distributing an underground (nonschool) student paper on a public school campus, even if it advocates burning report cards after they are mailed out, would be protected. Though school officials may worry about a substantial disruption, unless a substantial disruption actually occurred, the student speech is protected.
- applies to public high schools and junior high schools but not to elementary schools and not to private schools, since private school administrators are not arms of the government. Their decisions are not First Amendment violations because the First Amendment restrains the *government*.

YOUR TURN

The five rights mentioned in the First Amendment are often interlinked. A decision about one may affect another. The Tinker case was about free speech, but it also affects the press. Though the First Amendment provides for freedom of religion and freedom of assembly, laws limit prayer in school, and certain groups—notably gangs—may be forbidden to assemble on a street corner. What other laws limit any of the five freedoms in the First Amendment—religion, speech, press, assembly and petitioning the government? Create a list. Do you agree with them?

A later case, the Bethel case in 1986, further limited student speech. Student speech that is considered vulgar or obscene is not protected by the Tinker ruling. Under Bethel, images would also be classified as a type of speech in most cases. Except for student speech that would create a substantial disruption or material interference with school activities and speech that is held to be obscene or vulgar, student First Amendment rights under Tinker duplicate those given to all other citizens.

What does the Tinker standard mean to student journalists? The California Education Code, section 48907, expresses it clearly, saying students have the "right to exercise freedom of speech and of the press ... whether or not [the activities] are support financially by the school." The Tinker standard does not apply in cases of obscenity, libel, slander *and* when the materials lead students to "create a clear and present danger of the commission of unlawful acts on school premises or the violation of lawful school regulations, or the substantial disruption of the orderly operation of the school."

"Student editors of official school publications shall be responsible for assigning and editing the news, editorial, and feature content of their publications subject to the limitations of this section."

"There shall be no prior restraint of material prepared for official school publications" except in cases of obscenity, libel and a clear and present danger of substantial disruption.

For the full text of California's education code, see the *Journalism* website. **Extend**

The Hazelwood Case and Its Limitations on Student Expression

Student rights to free expression, however, were further limited under certain circumstances by the *Hazelwood School District v. Kuhlmeier* decision in 1987. In 1983 students at Hazelwood East High School in Missouri had written articles about teenage pregnancy and about the effect of divorce on teenagers (Figure 3.3). The principal removed the articles from the paper because he thought the articles were inappropriate for high school students and because he was afraid the unnamed students who were interviewed for the story could be identified by the readers.

The Supreme Court, which ruled on the case four years later, decided the principal did have the right to censor a student paper—and also the yearbooks, school magazines, radio and television broadcasts and other publications—under certain circumstances. Why was an arm of the government, the principal, allowed to censor the student press?

The Hazelwood East paper was not a **public forum**, that is, a publication where the student editors have the authority to make their own content decisions. The adviser, not the students, decided what was published, though the students researched and wrote the stories. Because the paper was not a public forum, the administration could censor the paper for educational reasons, the Supreme Court held. The educational reason should "reasonably relate to legitimate pedagogical (educational) concerns."

- Material could be censored if it was "ungrammatical, poorly written, inadequately researched, biased or prejudiced, vulgar or profane, or unsuitable for immature audiences" or if it advocated "conduct otherwise inconsistent with the shared values of the civilized social order."

Student Press Law Center

Figure 3.3 The spring 1987 edition of the Student Press Law Center report depicted the *Hazelwood School District v. Kuhlmeier* case as it moved to the Supreme Court. *Who do you think the right side of the cartoon represents? The left side?*

- "In addition, a school must be able to take into account the emotional maturity of the intended audience in determining whether to disseminate student speech on potentially sensitive topics, which might range from the existence of Santa Claus in an elementary school setting to the particulars of teenage sexual activity in a high school setting."

Because the adviser to the student paper, not the student editors, was thought to have the ultimate authority over what went into the paper, the paper was not a public forum and was not covered under the Tinker standard, which was meant to protect the students' rights, not the teachers' rights.

Though the Hazelwood case came after the Tinker case, many student publications are not governed by the Hazelwood restrictions (Figure 3.4). Is your publication protected by Tinker, or is it further restricted under the Hazelwood standard? You are *not* under Hazelwood if any of the following apply:

- You publish at a public high school in a state with laws to protect the student press: Arkansas, California, Colorado, Illinois, Iowa, Kansas, Maryland, Massachusetts, Nevada, North Dakota, Oregon, Rhode Island, Vermont or Washington.
- You publish in a public high school where regulations protect the student press: District of Columbia or Pennsylvania.

Extend

- Your school district has designated the student press as "public forums" for student free expression. The school district has limited prior restraint to cases of libel, obscenity or material that encourages students to break the law, violate school rules or substantially disrupt the school day. See "Model School District Publication Policies" on the *Journalism* website.
- Your school publication has a written policy that states it is a "public forum." The school has limited prior restraint to cases of libel, obscenity or material that encourages students to break the law, violate school rules or substantially disrupt the school day. See "Model School Publication Policies" on the *Journalism* website.
- You have an established tradition of publishing or broadcasting with the student leaders making the editorial and content decisions.
- You publish an **underground publication**, a publication edited and run by students without support from the school and not prepared during the school day.

Figure 3.4 All public schools are governed by the Tinker decision, but only some may use the Hazelwood standard to further limit student press freedom. *Where does your school fall?*

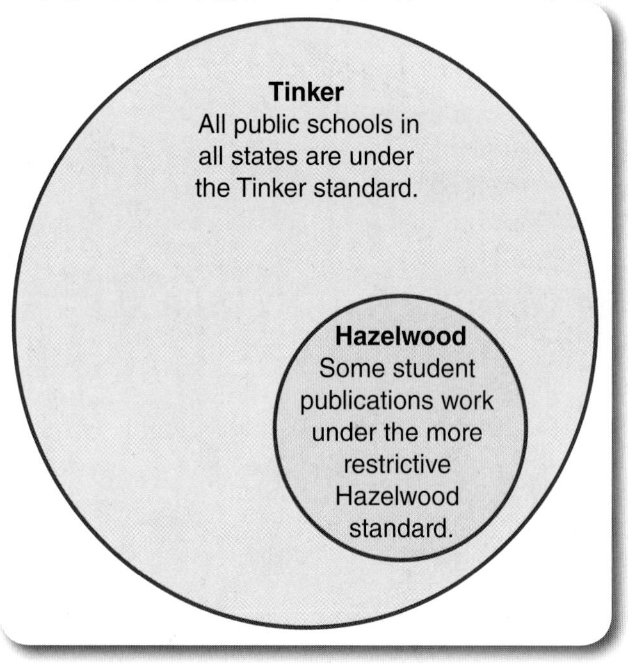
Tinker
All public schools in all states are under the Tinker standard.
Hazelwood
Some student publications work under the more restrictive Hazelwood standard.

Prior Review

Administrative oversight of student media may take two forms: prior review and prior restraint. **Prior review** means an official with the school district reviews the publication before it is broadcast, distributed or posted online. For instance, if an assistant principal wishes to review yearbook photos to check for students wearing gang insignia or flashing gang signs, that would be prior review. It may be legal even under the Tinker standard.

As the term implies, prior review takes place before publication or broadcast and is done by a representative of the administration. A policy that prohibits or avoids prior review of course may still permit review of a work *after* publication. Students may still be held accountable for the quality of their work and their adherence to standards of journalism ethics and good writing practices through grades and through disciplinary measures.

Prior review has its downsides for both the administration and the students who publish or broadcast.

Negative Implications for the School Administration

The administration may assume **liability**, legal responsibility, for the publication or broadcast if they review it prior to publication. The general theory of legal liability is that any person who could have and should have prevented an injury can be held responsible for it. In 2009 a Seattle school newspaper, The Roosevelt News, referred to the alleged owners of property located across from the high school as "slum lords." The brothers named in the article—one of whom denied owning the property—sued the school district (not the school paper) for **defamation**, or harm to their reputations. The court ruled in 2011 that since the students controlled the content, and the administration did not screen the paper prior to publication, the school district could not be held responsible. This case joins a growing body of legal opinion that holds that schools and universities can best protect themselves by allowing student control of student publications.

Prior review by administrators undermines several important educational goals, including the development of

- critical thinking. All authentic writing and all student leadership involves students making multiple decisions based on sound instruction by a knowledgeable adviser. Just as a student athlete, not the coach and certainly not the administration, makes free throws during basketball games, so students should use their training to make decisions and then bear the responsibility for their decisions.
- an understanding of the role of a free press in society. For its audience and producers, the successes and shortcoming of the student press provide valuable lessons in such 21st century literacy skills as recognizing objectivity, judging the reliability of sources, exercising the power of research and writing, evaluating ethics and realizing the audience's ability to hold the press accountable.

Students who know that their work will be reviewed before publication are likely to shy away from controversial issues, to self-censor, thereby denying administration a valuable window into the concerns of their students.

Underground newspapers and other forms of publication, often Internet based, arise more often when students feel their interests and voices are absent from other student publications. A strong student press under a knowledgeable adviser provides greater opportunity for students to learn about journalistic standards, ethics and law than do underground publications which may not adhere to—or even know about—these matters.

Negative Implications for the Students

- Prior review increases the time required before publication, making some stories stale before they are seen or read.
- Prior review decreases the publication or broadcast's credibility with its audience.
- Prior review decreases the publication or broadcast's ability to serve as a public watchdog.
- Prior review causes the students to concentrate on what their reviewing administrator will approve rather than the news values of the stories and what their audience needs to know.

Prior Restraint

Prior restraint means that the administration censors (forbids) the students to include certain elements in their student publication or broadcast. This is legal if you publish in a Hazelwood state *and also* in a district that allows such restraint *and also* for a publication that does not have a policy or tradition of student control.

Under these conditions, administrators may censor student work done in connection with a school journalism class or club if it

- could "associate the school with anything other than neutrality on matters of political controversy";
- advocates drug or alcohol use, irresponsible sex or "conduct otherwise inconsistent with the shared values of a civilized social order";
- is vulgar, profane or unsuitable for immature audiences;
- is biased or prejudiced;
- is inadequately researched;
- is poorly written; or
- presents any other problem that "reasonably relates to legitimate pedagogical (educational) concerns."

Your Turn

1. Do you publish in a state that is under the Hazelwood or Tinker standard?
2. What does your district's publication policy say?
3. Does your publication have a tradition as a free and open forum for student expression?

(Continued)

YOUR TURN *(Continued)*

4. **Going Deeper.** You have been given the opportunity to address your administration or your school board about its publication policies. What would you say to the school board members? Would you congratulate them on their policies and practices, or would you wish to change their minds? How would you approach them to convince them of your point of view? What arguments would you use?

What If You Attend a Private School?

Private school administrators are not arms of the government, so they are not restrained by the First Amendment. Nonetheless, strong student journalism is often produced by students who control the content of the student media at their private schools. Why are they able to do this? Just because administrators *may* censor does not mean that they *must*. (This is true of public school administrators, also.) Many private school administrators are deeply committed to the free flow of ideas that makes good citizens and critical thinkers. In addition, many parochial schools (schools supported by a church) recognize that the First Amendment, which protects the free press, also protects the free exercise of religion. Doing damage to one does damage to the other.

Alumni and public opinion also may influence a private school's policies and may secure First Amendment rights for the student press. Schools may create written policies protecting the student press that also serve to shield the school from legal obligations for the content of the student press.

In addition, the law may support the student press. School policies stated in brochures and course catalogs may create an obligation for the school to avoid censoring student expression. Some states have laws, most notably California's Leonard Law, securing First Amendment rights to all students in private or public schools.

What About Underground Publications?

Underground newspapers and other publications are student publications that do not use school resources and are not affiliated with the school. They are student publications only in the sense that students produce them and they may be distributed on school property. Underground publications are exempt from the Hazelwood standard. They are not subject to prior review. They may therefore use stronger language and explore more controversial topics in ways not available to officially sanctioned papers. However, they are still subject to legal action for the same reasons as any other publication produced by adults or students: libel or slander, copyright infringement, invasion of privacy and for violation of laws related to obscenity. These laws are complicated and subject to the interpretations of the courts. Underground journalists will want to research these laws thoroughly before including R- or X-rated material in their publications.

Underground publications also may not cause a disruption to the school day, part of the Tinker standard. Recent rulings have held that they should not advocate, encourage or glorify violence; sex between unmarried minors; or illicit drug use. Courts have upheld punishment for students publishing in underground papers who have provided instructions for hacking school computers, recipes for desserts containing illegal substances and for telling students to perform disruptive acts such as wearing banned T-shirts or urinating on the floor. Advertising drug paraphernalia is also not protected speech in an underground paper aimed at a high school audience.

Underground journalists have the right to distribute their paper, even if it contains advertising, at public schools in a manner that does not cause a substantial disruption to the school day. If the school has a written policy concerning the distribution of materials at school, the creators of the underground publication should understand the policy.

Though the students who produce the underground publication are exercising their First Amendment rights independent of the school, the school may attempt to punish the students for the content of the underground paper. Though the courts may overturn the punishment, court cases tend to move slowly.

YOUR TURN

1. Are there conditions or locations in which you would consider working for an underground publication? If so, what sort of content would you want the publication to have? What would be the positive aspects of doing so? What would be the negative aspects?

(Continued)

YOUR TURN *(Continued)*

2. **Going Deeper.** An underground newspaper is exploring what it can and cannot do and has come to you for legal advice. (That may be different from ethical advice.) What would you tell them and why if they asked you about
   - using language that some may consider obscene;
   - publishing a link to a recipe for brownies with marijuana; or
   - hacking into the guidance counselor's emails?

Shield Laws

The law generally recognizes that journalists cannot do their job if the public thinks of them as arms of the government or private investigators for government officials. For that reason, journalists enjoy certain privileges that the general public does not. Journalists may refuse to give evidence to the police or other officials and may refuse to testify about what they have learned as a journalist, refuse to give their notes and images to officials and refuse to identify confidential sources, even in situations where a private citizen would be required to provide evidence or testimony.

As with any rights, these are not absolute, and each year reporters face **subpoenas** (court orders) for their materials. Some serve jail time if the courts override their claims of privilege and demand the reporter's photos or notes.

Shield laws are laws that protect journalists from official demands for their journalistic research and images. They vary from state to state. Some states, such as Delaware, define a journalist as someone who earns his principal livelihood, his living, from journalism. Student journalists may not be shielded from subpoena under the Delaware shield law, while in other states they may be included as journalists. However, an additional source of protection may come from **court-recognized privileges**, journalists' privileges recognized by the courts and usually based on the First Amendment. These also vary from state to state and from situation to situation. If you receive a subpoena for your journalistic materials, you should contact a media lawyer or the Student Press Law Center immediately to learn your rights and responsibilities under the law in your state.

YOUR TURN

Once it was easy to define who was a journalist. Journalists were people who worked for newspapers, newsmagazines or broadcasters. Now many people publish online. How do you define which ones are journalists and should be protected by the shield laws?

MEET THE PROFESSIONALS:

Mark Goodman

Mark Goodman, who headed the Student Press Law Center for over 22 years, grew up in rural Missouri in a family that taught him to stand up for what was right. At one point in his childhood, his family subscribed to eight different newspapers, "leading me to conclude that journalism was important and they were a little bit nuts."

He earned a degree in journalism from the University of Missouri—Columbia and a law degree from Duke. While studying law, he realized that his own earlier ignorance of the law, and the bad advice of teachers, had misled him as a high school journalist and also again in college.

Goodman said, "When in high school, I created an underground newspaper—really a single-page flier about a school policy under debate at the school—in which I offered my take on the topic. (The student newspaper never covered that kind of thing.) I was showing it to a teacher on the morning I planned to distribute and she said to me, 'You can't distribute that at school.' It had nothing to do with the mild content of my leaflet but rather her mistaken belief that students didn't have the right to distribute independent publications at school. I said, 'Oh' in response and accepted what she said. I remember being disappointed, but it never occurred to me that she was wrong.

"Then while a journalism student in college, I was just beginning to report a story that involved a confidential source who was involved in a criminal enterprise. My professor, who edited the magazine, urged me to speak to the media law professor, a lawyer, about the legal implications of my reporting. He basically scared the heck out of me and said if I published the story, I should be prepared to go to jail to protect my source. I chickened out and dropped the story.

"A year or two later when I was in law school I realized that the chances a prosecutor would attempt to send a college student journalist to jail for uncovering a crime ring were slim to none. I was angry at the law professor for not putting my legal protections or lack thereof in context or not attempting to help me find ways to do my job as a journalist, instead of just scaring me away from it. I thought at that time I wanted to be the kind of lawyer that didn't do to clients what he's done to me. When the SPLC job came along, it all just fit together."

Goodman became the eighth director of the Student Press Law Center. He edited the second edition of Law of the Student Press, published by the SPLC. By 2007 the SPLC's website received about 60,000 visits a month. It responds to over 2,500 requests for help each year from high school and college journalists.

Goodman said, "Our shared values of editorial independence, commitment to the truth and serving as a watchdog of those in power will not survive if we produce a generation of First Amendment illiterates."

Traditional Privileges

In addition to legal protections, journalists traditionally enjoy privileges not shared by the general public because journalists are considered the eyes and ears of the general public. The privilege you may know best is a seat in the announcer's box at your school's football games next to members of the professional press. You can view the game from the best seats in the stadium while compiling statistics and reporting the action for your publication or broadcast. In addition, your photographers, videographers and sound reporters are probably allowed on the sidelines—where the shoulder pads "thunk" into each other—while the general public is kept farther away.

By securing **press credentials**, usually a card with your picture and name and the name of your publication, you may gain access to political leaders, celebrities, events and legal or governmental proceedings. Seats at trials are often reserved for the press. Press photographers often are allowed closer to events than the general public. Some press passes also come with parking permits.

Generally the organization controlling the event will issue its own press passes. Generic press passes, sometimes available online for a "membership fee," will not take the place of press credentials issued by the sports team, venue or league, the charity, the political party or the event you wish to cover. A good first step is to register with your local and national political parties as a member of the press. You may need government-sponsored identification such as a driver's license or passport in addition to a student ID. Once you have one set of press credentials, it is easier to get another set. Find the press desk at museums, government offices and entertainment venues; present your ID and other credentials and ask for a press pass.

As a courtesy, you may wish to send links to your story or photos or clips from your publication to the media affairs office of the local organizations and events you cover. A feature story about a sophomore's challenging audition for an all-city youth orchestra, even if the sophomore is not selected or the process seems grueling, may later help you hear about and gain access to newsworthy events surrounding the youth orchestra. If your writing, recording and photography are fair, balanced and strong, you will probably be welcomed back.

Freedom of Information Act—Everyone's Right

The Freedom of Information Act (FOIA) and sunshine laws, also known as *open meeting laws*, are frequently used by journalists to gain information from all levels of government and to gain access to meetings. These laws, however, are rights available to everyone. The FOIA and sunshine laws are federal and state laws based on the belief that the citizens own the government and the government does not have the right to decide what the citizens can see. Together they allow public access to government records and most government meetings. Of course certain information, such as battle plans during a war, should be kept secret, but most of what the government does should be subject to public view, kept out of darkness, in the sunshine.

Freedom of information laws say that all records generated by a public body are open to the public unless they are specifically exempted by law. **Sunshine laws** say meetings of public officials should be open to the public. School districts in most cases are obliged to protect a limited number of student records under FERPA (see page 80), and they may discuss personnel issues and pending lawsuits in private; but all other matters are to be handled in the "sunshine." Sunshine laws and freedom of information laws vary from state to state, while the federal FOIA applies throughout the nation.

In most cases, public agencies and public officials will allow you to attend meetings and will help you access public records if you identify yourself as a journalist and share with them your interest in attending their meetings or in searching specific records. You may need to show them the appropriate sections of sunshine or freedom of information laws that indicate the meetings or records should be available to the public.

In other cases, you may need to write an FOIA letter stating specifically what records you are looking for, addressed to the agency of the government that has the records. State your request clearly. For example, if you want to know how many animals are euthanized each year, research which agency is responsible for animal care. Is it a state or a county agency? Is it part of the health department? Who keeps the records, the health department or the shelter where lost and stray animals are housed?

Once you find where the records are kept, be as specific as possible. Ask for the records for only one or two years, perhaps not the most recent but two previous years, as statistics are not always immediately available for the current year. Specify which kinds of animals you are interested in. Only dogs and cats? Horses? All animals? Remember, the more information you ask for or the more copies the agency will have to make, the longer it may take and the more data you will need to read.

If an agency does not have a report containing the information you would like to see, they may not be able to help you, or they may indicate to you that you will need to examine the records yourself. If you want to know how many large-breed dogs or how many pit bulls were put down, you may need to go through 3,000 records yourself to compile the statistic.

When you write to an agency for information, write Freedom of Information Act Request on the outside of the envelope. The laws specify the amount of time an agency has to respond to an FOIA request, so it is important that the agency sees that you are requesting information. Often the information will come within that time limit, but other times you will receive a response telling you that they need additional time to search through their records or they need additional clarification concerning what you want. You will need to plan ahead. If you want to do a story on how much local districts spend on girls sports and how much they spend on boys sports, plan the story several months in advance so that you can be sure to receive all the information you requested.

You may be charged a fee for photocopying or printing out information, though the fee should only reflect the agency's printing costs. Sometimes journalists, including student journalists, are excused from the copying fees others may be charged.

Laws That Limit Rights and Privileges

Though the First Amendment recognizes their important role, journalists are not above the law. Laws that you need to understand as a journalist include those concerning libel and slander; invasion of privacy; the records the school must not publish under FERPA; and copyright law.

Libel

Libel is publishing anything—words, pictures or symbols—that harms another person's reputation or harms an organization's ability to conduct its affairs in a community. This includes the reputation of corporations, churches, schools and businesses as well as individuals. **Slander** is the spoken version of libel. Both slander and libel can result in a defamation of character lawsuit, a suit based on the damage you have done to a person or an organization. In addition, if you publish someone else's libelous statement, for instance in a letter to the editor, you may expose your publication to a lawsuit.

There are four protections against being successfully sued for libel: truth, consent, privilege and opinion.

Truth

If what you say is true, you cannot be sued for defamation of character. If it is true, it is not libel. Ethical publications verify every fact they publish, but they verify and then reverify anything that might harm someone's reputation.

The more likely your story is to hurt someone, the more sources you should have and the more certain you should be that what you publish or broadcast is accurate and fair. Be sure to talk to all sides, obtain and read all pertinent documents, and take and keep accurate notes. These steps may protect you and your paper from a successful libel suit, even if you publish something that turns out not to be true.

Consent

If the person whose reputation is damaged has given you specific and clear consent to publish the information that damages her reputation, you also are protected. However, journalists, especially student journalists,

For the Record

The Zenger Case

Truth has not always been a good defense against libel, but it has been an American principle since 1735, well before there was a United States of America. Editor John Peter Zenger was charged with "seditious libel" for criticizing the British-appointed governor in The New York Weekly Journal. His defense never denied what he wrote but argued that what he wrote was all truthful. The American jury acquitted Zenger, which means he was cleared of all legal charges.

need to consider their subject's youth and all the other people whose reputations may be damaged, including the parents and siblings of the person providing consent. A student may sign a waiver when he tells you about his ability to shoplift, but the reputations of his parents and his younger sister may be injured if you publish his account.

Privilege

You may also be protected if you report what you learn from a public document such as a police report and you pass on an error in the document. If a police report states that the driver of the car that struck a freshman in a crosswalk was Jesse Smith, 24, but the police report was wrong and it was really Jeffrey Smith, 24, then Jesse Smith may *not* successfully sue you for libel so long as you

- got your information from an official, public record;
- have tried to be fair and balanced in your reporting; and
- have identified your official source: "According to the Garden City police report, Jesse Smith, 24, was traveling southbound on Westminster in a blue Suburban."

Opinion

An opinion cannot be libelous. If you write in an opinion piece that "Principal Blackburn's policy that we cannot wear plain, colored T-shirts

Secret Identities

What if you do not publish the person's name? If you do not identify someone, you cannot libel him, right? But legal dangers remain when you publish statements about—or attributed to—an unnamed person.

1. You may reveal who the person is, even without a name. The courts hold 25 is the magic number. If you identify someone simply as "a sophomore" and there are well over 25 sophomores at your school, you may have concealed his or her identity. But if you identify someone as "a sophomore cheerleader" and there are fewer than 25 sophomore cheerleaders, you may be libeling at least one cheerleader, your source.
2. You may libel an innocent person. Suppose you quote an unnamed advanced placement chemistry student: "American teachers are too soft on their students. Here you seem afraid to study and memorize. We all cheat on tests." You may have libeled AP chemistry students who have studied outside of the United States. Because you may be liable if you print someone else's libelous statement, you also may have libeled all AP chemistry students, who are all accused of cheating in the quotation you have published.
3. You may identify the wrong person with a pseudonym. Susan Quinonez, for instance, may be libeled if you report on the arrest of someone you are calling "Suzie Q." Always tell your reader when you are using a false name. It is sometimes done like this: "Suzie Q (not her real name) told of her frightening night in the county jail."

is the silliest rule he has ever made," you cannot be successfully sued for libel because there is no way to prove the truth or falsehood of your opinion about the degree of silliness of a school policy.

However, if you state, "In my opinion, he established the ruling because he owns stock in Hollister," you may be guilty of libel. It is possible to prove whether or not the principal owns stock in Hollister, and it is also possible to show whether other schools, without investments in shirt companies, have made similar rulings. A person can prove the truth or falsehood of your statement, so it is not protected as an opinion. Note that "in my opinion" does not provide you with protection. Neither does the word *alleged*. Reserve the adjective *alleged* for reporting on an indictment, an arrest or a statement by a public official connected with a case.

One form of opinion is satire. If an editorial page cartoon shows the superintendent of schools dressed as a Mary Poppins-type nanny and the football players as bawling infants with pacifiers and ruffled bonnets, the cartoon is probably protected as opinion. The test is whether a reasonable person would think you are accusing the football team of using pacifiers or the superintendent of schools of flying with an umbrella.

Invasion of Privacy

You invade someone's privacy if you gather news or images without consent

- where people have a reasonable expectation of privacy, for instance, in the restroom at school, in a home, at a small private party, in a medical office, in many religious settings or in a school counselor's office.
- on private property, that is, a place where the general public does not go without invitation or permission *and* you do not have the owner's consent. Private homes, private clubs and private offices would generally be off-limits without permission.
- on public property that is privately owned, if you do not leave when you are asked to do so. Privately owned public property includes buildings or land where the public is usually allowed to go such as stores, private schools, amusement parks or restaurants. If you are asked to leave, do so.

If you obtain information through electronic surveillance that allows you to see or hear what a person could not see or hear from public property, such as a sidewalk, you are invading privacy.

You invade someone's privacy if you misrepresent yourself to gain access to space or information. You may not pretend to be a cable repairman to gain access to private space. You may not pretend to be from the library or police department to gain information. You may, however, go "undercover" wherever the public is allowed to go. You may, for example, research how hard it is for someone with visible tattoos to get a job at the local mall by posing as a job seeker and donning temporary ink. You have the right to apply, whether you are serious about getting the job or not.

You invade someone's privacy if you take pictures, record sound or gather news inappropriately, even if you do not publish or air what you obtain. In addition, you invade someone's privacy if you use her image or voice to promote the sale of a commercial product or service without her consent.

You invade someone's privacy if you reveal information about a person's medical condition, sexual conduct or school records without his consent. However, if the person is a well-known public figure or public official, the information may be considered newsworthy and you may be able to publish it without consent.

You do *not* invade someone's privacy

- when you print the names of minors, as long as the names are lawfully obtained and truthfully reported.
- if you use private documents, images or sound recordings that were given to you. You must not engage in unlawful conduct or encourage or aid someone else to do so. However, if someone sends you a copy of the softball coach's email to a parent, promising to play her daughter more, and you have not hacked her email account nor encouraged anyone else to do so, you may consider using this information, which came "over the transom." *Over the transom* is an old term for information thrown into a newsroom anonymously and without the newsman requesting it. Of course you need to question the motives of the person who sent you the hacked email and question whether or not it is really what it seems to be. You need to investigate further, but you have not violated anyone's privacy by reading the supposed email. If you find further convincing evidence, you may use the email in your reporting.

FERPA

FERPA, the Family Educational Rights and Privacy Act, is a 1974 federal law that requires school districts to give parents, and students over 18, access to their educational records. It also forbids the school from releasing to others any records directly related to a student if the records are "centrally maintained" by the school and used in making decisions that affect the life of the student and include the student's name. Information that a school may safely release without violating FERPA includes students' names, addresses, phone numbers, honors, awards and other basic demographics. Security videos, teacher emails about students, individual test scores, parking violations and a student's record as an employee of the school district may also be released without violating FERPA.

The Department of Education administers this law and may withhold federal funding if the school district does not comply. As of the time this book was printed, FERPA was nearly 45 years old and no district had ever lost funding under FERPA. The Department of Education had written fewer than 200 letters concerning FERPA violations. Individuals may not sue school districts for violation of FERPA. Instead, they need to report problems to the Department of Education.

And Now... Closer to Home

What Does FERPA Mean to Student Journalists?

Though it is sometimes cited as a reason to keep information from the press or to limit what may be published, posted or broadcast, FERPA should have little impact on the student press. Journalists may request—and receive under the federal Freedom of Information Act—a broad range of information, even though "centrally maintained" records that are used to make decisions that affect the life of the student (and that also include the student's name) may be unavailable.

In addition, the student press in almost all cases is not an official arm of the school district. FERPA restrains the school district from revealing "centrally maintained" records, but the student press is not the school district. In 1992, the Department of Education wrote, "FERPA was not intended to apply to campus newspapers or to records maintained by campus newspapers."

Information that is in a "centrally maintained" student file but also available elsewhere may not be protected under FERPA. If a student's name appears on the principal's honor roll, you may safely report that the student has a GPA above 3.75, even though that information is usually maintained in files protected by FERPA. If a student involved in a school fight has already received an interdistrict transfer following fights on another campus, you may report that, even though his disciplinary record may be kept in a file protected by FERPA. The Department of Education wrote in 2006:

> *FERPA applies to the disclosure of tangible records and of information derived from tangible records. FERPA does not protect the confidentiality of information in general, and, therefore, does not apply to the disclosure of information derived from a source other than education records, even if education records exist which contain that information. As a general rule, information that is obtained through personal knowledge or observation and not from an education record is not protected from disclosure under FERPA.*

Your Turn

1. How would you explain FERPA to an administrator who did not want to give your publication the names of scholarship recipients? Cite FERPA in your explanation.
2. **Going Deeper.** What would you say to administrators who ask you to remove names from all photos in your online edition, citing FERPA?

Copyright Laws

Copyright laws in the U.S. date back to the country's founding and were included in the Constitution. The Copyright Act of 1790 further established this important press law—protecting original works such as books, maps and charts for 14 years. Copyright laws say that if you do creative work—write a story, compose a song, invent an app or a device—the result of this creativity is your **intellectual property**. Various press laws protect an intellectual property owner's rights. These laws concern copyrights, trademarks, patents and, in some states, trade secrets.

Copyright laws are press laws that protect your work as a journalist. They also limit the ways you can use the work of others. A **copyright** is your right to own your creative work, just as you may own a car. No one else should profit from your car or your work, sell your car or your work, use your car or your work, or alter your car or work and use it, unless you specifically give them permission to do so. The copyright holder has the exclusive right to reproduce, adapt, distribute, display or perform the work (Figure 3.5).

It is illegal to use copyrighted material without permission. **Copyright infringement** is the theft of intellectual property. Car theft is still car theft even if you put a sticker in the window of the stolen car that says "Stolen from Gus Vlaxos." Copyright infringement is still copyright infringement even if you give credit to the original writer, photographer or artist.

Figure 3.5 This thief is not only stealing a journalist's physical property (the laptop), but he may be stealing her intellectual property as well.

What Kinds of Works May Be Copyrighted?

To be copyrighted, works must show creativity and be "fixed," that is, put on paper or in video or in digital files. If a work exists only in the creator's mind, it cannot be copyrighted.

Copyrights may protect literary works, including song lyrics; sound recordings, including music; musical compositions and works of art and architecture.

What Kinds of Works May Not Be Copyrighted?

Some works, by themselves, are not protected by copyright. They are not sufficiently creative to receive protection. These include slogans; titles and names; individual words and short phrases; designs; instructions and lists of ingredients; familiar symbols, such as those used to indicate roadside rest areas and facts, ideas and statistics.

Nike's phrase "Just Do It" cannot be copyrighted, and you may use the words. However, if you use the same typeface as Nike and include the Nike "swoosh," you will probably violate copyright law because the logo and phrase together are sufficiently creative to be protected by copyright law and perhaps trademark law (Figure 3.6).

Figure 3.6 Using Nike's "swoosh" along with the phrase "Just Do It" will likely violate copyright law. *Can you think of any other logo and slogan combinations that would be protected by copyright or trademark law?*

A Time magazine article on drug violence will hold a copyright on the exact words (as a literary work) and images (as artwork) in the article, but the facts, quotations from sources, statistics and ideas in the article are not copyrighted and other writers may use them freely. Of course, ethical use involves giving credit to the source of your information.

In addition, trademark law protects some images, usually those associated with products. Another fast-food provider could not use McDonald's golden arches on its restaurant. That use might confuse the consumer and damage McDonald's business. In addition, decorating the inside cover of your literary magazine in golden arches would also probably violate McDonald's trademark by diluting, or weakening its value. Trademarks sometimes are indicated by a superscript ™ or ® next to the name.

Protecting Your Work Through Law

Who owns the work you do for your school publication or broadcast? That depends. Since you are not paid (except perhaps with a grade), you—not the publication or the school—probably retain the ownership of your work, even though you may have used school equipment to create it. The creativity and hard work were yours. The publication has the right to use the work, but you probably retain all future rights.

You can be sure who holds the copyright by signing a written agreement with your publication. (See "Copyright Agreement" on the *Journalism* website.)

Extend

Creative work is protected by copyright press law as soon as it is put into a fixed form. You do not need to include a copyright notice, though if you do so, you will make it easier for others to contact you for permission to use part of your work. Include the symbol ©, your name and the date. You do not need to register your work with the U.S. Copyright Office, but you may wish to do so. Unless you register with the Copyright Office, you may not sue anyone for infringing on your copyright; that is, using your work without your permission. You may register your work later, if you wish.

While the individual contributors own the individual copyrights, it is probably best for the publication or academic department or school to own the copyright on a complete work, such as a yearbook, newspaper edition, broadcast or literary magazine. This will allow the copyright owner—the journalism department, for instance—to send a "cease and desist" letter or file suit if, for instance, someone posts your literary magazine or yearbook on the Internet without permission.

Respecting Others' Copyrights

What can you do if you want to use a creative work that you believe may be under the protection of copyright or trademark press laws? There are several options:

1. Ask to use it. If you want to print and post online the lovely graphic of how to tie a double Windsor knot in a necktie, find out who owns the copyright and ask permission in writing. Just giving credit for the work is not enough. You need the copyright owner's permission to use his or her creative work. Do not try to get permission at the last minute. These matters often take time. (It is notoriously difficult to get permission to use recorded music or even the lyrics and charts from music.) You may, however, link to other websites without first asking permission. You do not need to ask permission to send your viewers and readers to the site with the great instructions for tying a double Windsor knot.
2. Pay the copyright holder for the use. If you want to remix a popular song, voice over your own version of the lyrics and use it as theme music for your broadcast, you will owe the composer or author of the song a fee for the use of the creative work you adapt. You will also owe the recording artist for the public use of the recording. The copy you bought or downloaded for your private use does not come with permission to use it in public performance.
3. Use art, music or written works that are made available through a website such as Creative Commons. Works there are available for public use if you credit the copyright holder. But please note, some owners will allow you to use their work but not alter it. Others will allow you to use their work, but not for commercial purposes. Be sure to note exactly what is and what is not allowed for each work you wish to use, and be sure to credit the copyright holder.
4. Use images and information prepared for the press. If you want pictures of Bert and Ernie, find the Press section of the copyright holder's website, in this case SesameWorkshop.org. You may request specific images or download **press packages** or press kits (material the company has prepared for the use of the press) from the site. These usually contain good quality images that will reproduce well. Include credit for the image and Sesame Street's copyright mark. Organizations frequently specify how their images may be used.

5. Under certain circumstances copyrighted materials may be used without consent if the use falls under a **fair use** exemption. The media rely on fair use exemptions so they can convey information about—and comment on—works that may be copyrighted. Fair use may include news reporting, criticism and reviews, and commentary.

Fair use for commentary, reporting and for criticism and reviews should use only a small sample of the work. The sample should not lessen the commercial value of the work or dilute the brand. You may use 15 seconds of a film to illustrate the quality of the dialogue in a film you are reviewing. You may reproduce one frame of a comic strip if you are reporting its creator's retirement, but you may not use the whole comic strip. You may show a Joe Camel advertisement from a national magazine to show the effect of advertising on teens, but you may not put Joe Camel on the senior T-shirts. That would not be either reporting or commentary. You may sample a small portion of a song for a review of the album, but you may not play the whole song under fair use. You may quote the first lines of the senior class's favorite 10 songs, but you may not reprint all the lyrics.

Parody (satirical or humorous imitation) is also considered a fair use exemption, but make sure the parody is obvious. It must be easy for the audience to see that you are commenting on the original. Include a disclaimer if there is any doubt that what you are doing is satire. Use the briefest or smallest possible amount of the original to remind the audience of what you are parodying.

Obtaining Permission to Use Copyrighted Material

You want to do the right thing, that is, ask the owner or creator for permission to use his or her work in your publication or broadcast. Look for the copyright symbol followed by the name of the copyright holder; for example, ©2019 by Darcy May. All rights reserved.

This information is often at the bottom of the page, at the end of the article or on the back of the title page. You can also search the database of the U.S. Copyright Office in Washington, which is available online.

If you want permission to use something you have found online, search for a Contact Us button.

Leave plenty of time to obtain permission. You may call first to verify contact information for the copyright holder. Write to the copyright holder with the following information:

- State your name, address and telephone number; the name of the publication; and the expected date of publication.
- Say that the request is for a nonprofit student publication.
- Tell exactly what you want to use. It helps to include a sketch of your page or module so the copyright holder knows how the work is to be included.
- Politely mention your deadlines.

Chapter Three

Review and Assessment

Recall Assess

1. What are the five freedoms in the First Amendment?
2. Who (or what) was restrained by the First Amendment when the Constitution was ratified?
3. In what landmark Supreme Court decision do you find this sentence: "It can hardly be argued that either students or teachers shed their constitutional rights to freedom of speech or expression at the schoolhouse gate"? Which Supreme Court justice wrote it?
4. How did Mary Beth Tinker, John Tinker and Chris Eckhart shape the development of student journalism?
5. How do prior review and prior restraint differ?
6. What are freedom of information laws, and why are they important for journalists?
7. What are sunshine laws, and why are they important for journalists?
8. What is the difference between libel and slander?
9. What is fair use and what guidelines must you follow when applying this press law in your publication?

Critical Thinking

1. In what ways are student journalists different from adult journalists under the Tinker standard?
2. In what ways are student journalists different from adult journalists under the Bethel decision?
3. In what ways are student journalists different from adult journalists under the Hazelwood standard?
4. Explain important press laws, including copyright law and the fair use exemption. Why do you think the Founding Fathers included press laws in the U.S. Constitution?
5. You are reporting on a truck drivers' strike and its effect on local businesses. You are photographing and interviewing people near the food court of a local shopping mall. Mall security tells you to leave, that you may not photograph or interview people there. Are you legally required to leave?
6. Create a presentation comparing and contrasting prior review and prior restraint. What do these terms mean? Then research your state's press laws to determine which applies to your publication. Share your presentation with the class. Discuss the pros and cons of each approach with your classmates.
7. Who owns the images and stories you create for your publication? Which press law applies here?

Application

1. Do you publish in a state that is under the Hazelwood standard? If you answered yes, what restraints and freedoms are outlined in your school board's publication policy? Does your publication or broadcast have a policy or a tradition of being a public forum?
2. What reporter's privileges do you enjoy in your state under the state's shield laws? (Hint: You can research your state's shield laws on the Internet. Use *shield law* or *reporter's privilege* as search terms along with the name of your state. The Reporters Committee for Freedom of the Press and the Student Press Law Center also have state-by-state resources.)
3. Secure press credentials from a local organization, institution or agency.
4. Create a practice Freedom of Information Act letter to a local or state agency. Identify the agency that has the information you would like to see and specify precisely what you are looking for. You may use an automatic FOIA letter generator such as the one found on the National Freedom of Information Coalition site or at the Student Press Law Center site.
5. What kinds of student records kept at your school or in your district must be kept confidential by the district because of FERPA?

Chapter Three

Journalism Style

How to Proofread

Proofreading is the final check before your work is uploaded to a Web page, imported into a document, sent to the printer or otherwise released into the world to live on its own without you nearby to explain it. All alone, it will represent you—and your publication.

Good proofreading, which may also be called *copy editing*, protects the hard work you put into your reporting. If your work has been proofread well, your ideas may be respected. You may appear intelligent and mature. Your audience may trust your publication. Guess what happens if your work is poorly proofread?

Is proofreading hard? Read this passage aloud and see if you can spot the three errors.

> *Though at first glance proofreading and reading look like the same thing, in in reality they are very different. Readers consume text in huge bites, one idea after another, and their brains actively predict and fill in the small words their eyes may miss. When a reader becomes a proofreader, he changes hats or approaches text in a very different way. While readers gobble ideas, a proofreader—nibbling at pages, layouts, columns and cutlines need to look at words, punctuation marks and sentences one at a time.*

Did you spot the errors? The spelling and grammar checker embedded in a standard word processing program noticed only one of them, and it marked one correct word as an error.

Proofreading is so difficult, only a human can do it! To proofread your own work, follow these steps:

- Wait until your responders and editor have seen your copy several times and fact checked your work. You cannot write and revise a story while proofreading.
- Stay away from your work for five minutes or, better yet, three days. The time away may allow you to forget what you wanted to say. Then you can read what you actually wrote.
- Pay attention to the squiggly red and green lines of spelling and grammar checkers. Know what you got wrong and why you are right in some cases, even if Bill Gates thinks you got it wrong.
- Print out your copy. You will notice different things on a printed page as compared to a computer screen.
- Change the font or the font size. Again, you will notice different things.
- Move your lips while you read, saying every word. Sure, you may look like a first grader, but you will also look like many professional reporters.
- Put the tip of your pen under each word as you say it. (Use the tip of a pencil's eraser on a computer screen.)
- Know your own pet mistakes—the ones that you make over and over. Do you often forget to type the *r* on *your*? Do you spell *surprise* with a *z*? In a spare reporter's notebook, keep a list of mistakes you frequently make. This is your "demon book," in which you keep words and expressions that give you trouble. Monitor your writing for those mistakes.

I have spell-checkers. Why should I spend so much time on spelling?

Spell-checkers are not everywhere. They are not on pens, paintbrushes, aerosol cans or on many programs used to microblog, post to the Web, create a design or perform engineering functions. Spell-checkers cannot read your mind either. They do not know whether you mean *teeth* or *teethes*.

Try It!

Bring in a computer file of a sample of writing that you completed at least several days earlier, for this class or another. Something that is about 200 words long should work well. Proofread your own work using the bulleted suggestions above.

Extend Your Knowledge

Style Exercises

Though all reporters must proofread their own work before handing it off to another, everyone needs a proofreader who can do the job just as well. Visit the *Journalism* website to learn about eight common errors and how to spot them. On the website, you can also try team activities for practicing and improving proofreading skills.

Chapter Three

Writers' Workshop

In this Writers' Workshop you will:

- Discover the power of writing short.
- Cut away unnecessary words.

Workshop 3.1

The Power of Short

Mini-Lesson: Discovering the Power of Short Writing

You are offered more written words in a day than your ancestors saw in a lifetime. No wonder you are attracted to short, dense expressions: T-shirt slogans, tweets, headlines and taglines.

Each of the following slogans or sentences packs a great deal into a few words. With your group, list the ideas, sensations, images or story elements—such as plot, character, setting—that each creates in your mind.

1. On a magnetic sign stuck to the side of a car: **Charo Chicken: Fast, Fresh, Flame-broiled.**
2. On a T-shirt: **Don't mess with Texas.**
3. On a World War II poster of a female factory worker: **We Can Do It!**
4. Attributed to Hemingway: **For Sale: Baby shoes, never worn.**
5. Attributed to Blaise Pascal, in French: **If I had more time, I would have written a shorter letter.**
6. Augusto Monterroso: **When he awoke, the dinosaur was still there.**
7. On a T-shirt: **Stop Plate Tectonics!**
8. Motto of the City of Hope Cancer Hospital: **We live to cure cancer.**
9. Old farmer standing by his wife's grave: **I really loved her. I nearly told her.**

Choose your favorites and study each. Discuss with your group or class how each communicates so much in so few words.

Apply It!

1. Try writing your own short work in the same form as two of the examples above. For instance, another version of number five might be "If I were not so short, I would not store my junk boxes on top of the wall units."
2. Read your sentences aloud to your partner or group. Revise as appropriate. Publish your group's best efforts electronically or on a wall.
3. For your next class, find at least three dense sentences or slogans of less than 15 words that appeal to you. Be prepared to discuss what they communicate to you and how they create ideas with few words.

Workshop 3.2

Shorten in the Middle

Mini-Lesson: Clearing the Underbrush

Most of us speak more than we write, and our oral habits spill out through our fingers and thumbs. As we speak, we repeat the same idea several ways until we see understanding on our listeners' faces. We include filler words to allow our brains to catch up to our mouths—and to keep family from interrupting while we silently compose the rest of our comment.

Spoken language might look like this: "He was, you know, kind of nerdy-like with this goofy laugh, kind of a whoop, and he wore his pants pulled way up too high and gathered with this belt and with his T-shirt tucked into his pants. No one thought he was cool or anything until he invented the first real hang glider."

Written language trims every unnecessary word, so 54 words becomes this: "We knew he wasn't cool, with his whooping laugh and T-shirts tucked into pants gathered waist-high—until he invented the hang glider." That is 22 words in 133 characters, short enough to tweet.

Which would you rather read?

You may have been told to write the way you talk. Better advice would be to draft the way you talk, then edit the way you tweet to remove the underbrush. Strong writers improve their work by cutting at least 10 percent off their finished work without removing content. Beginning writers should plan on cutting 20 percent.

What do you cut?

1. Remove any expressions that clutter your solid verbs and nouns. If you use these phrases to fill time, or to intensify adjectives and adverbs, you generally are safe eliminating them: *sort of*, *kind of*, *a lot of*, *like*, *really*, *literally*. For example, "She had on a really classy dress" can become "She wore a classy dress." (Notice the colloquial "had on" becomes the shorter and clearer "wore.")
2. Replace wordy expressions with shorter versions.

Instead of	Try
prior to	before
following (or following on)	after
at the same time as, simultaneously with	as
is able to, has the opportunity to, is in a position to	can
is going to, is about to	will
it is possible that, there is a chance that	may, might, can, could
on the occasion of, in a situation in which	when
in regard to, concerning the matter of	about
it is necessary that (or for), it is important that	must, should
is aware of, has knowledge of	knows

3. Use the simplest form of the verb. "He was taking a nap when…" is probably better as "He was napping when…" or "He slept as…"
4. Avoid redundant expressions such as "free gift" (if it is not free, it is not a gift) and "new innovation" (*innovation* means "new").

Apply It!

1. With your partner or in a group, read each of the wordy expressions in this mini-lesson aloud. When there is a wordy and a clean example, read both.
2. Which wordy expressions do you use? Choose five and create two sentences for each, one full of underbrush and one clean.
3. Alone or with your group, check a student publication (either your own or one posted online) for wordiness or colloquial usage. Clip, copy or print the passage that needs to be trimmed. Read it aloud to your group and experiment with revisions, reading each proposed revision aloud. Count the words in the original passage and in your revised passage. Is your version at least 10 percent shorter?
4. Look for wasted words in something you have written that is at least 150 words long. It can be something you have written for a class or to friends. Revise it as if every character counted. (It does!) Can you shrink it by 10 percent? By 20 percent? Share your revised work with your response group.

Extend Your Knowledge Extend

Which of these sentences creates the stronger image in your mind?

- Precipitation is in the forecast for tonight.
- Tonight, expect rain followed by sleet.

Rain and *sleet* are concrete words; they describe things we can see, hear, taste, smell or touch. *Precipitation* is a more abstract term for any water vapor that condenses and falls toward the ground. Abstract terms (such as *cold*) are useful, but concrete terms (such as *ice-covered*) are more likely to grab your audience's attention. Visit the *Journalism* website to learn how you can use concrete language to make your journalistic writing more powerful.

Chapter Four

Media Ethics

Should we cover that?

Courtesy of Ellen Austin

G-WLEARNING.COM

While studying, look for the activity icon to:

- **Build** vocabulary terms with e-flash cards and matching activities.
- **Extend** learning with further discussion of relevant topics.
- **Reinforce** what you learn by completing style exercises, worksheets and end-of-chapter questions.

Visit the Journalism website: www.g-wlearning.com/journalism/

Chapter Objectives

After reading this chapter, you will be able to:

- Describe the purpose of a code of ethics.
- List the ABCs of journalism and describe their importance.
- Explain the importance of and procedure for corrections and retractions.
- Describe the conditions under which it is ethical to go undercover.
- Explain why a journalist should use extra consideration when dealing with high school students as sources and subjects.
- Describe situations in which it might be ethical to grant a source or subject anonymity.
- Explain why it is important to separate the news department from the business department.
- Describe a typical story flow and the way it protects journalistic integrity.
- Describe the dangers of writing breaking news or working under a tight deadline.

Key Terms Build Vocab

attribution
balanced reporting
code of ethics
credibility
firewall
gatekeeper
photo illustration
retraction
scrutiny
story flow
transparent
unbiased

Before You Read...

Accuracy is particularly important when working as a journalist. This includes using correct spellings in your work. The spelling of English words often follows set rules or patterns. Being able to use those spelling rules or patterns helps to spell words accurately. Listen to your instructor read key terms aloud and write them in your notebook. Make an effort to spell them correctly without checking your textbook. When you have finished, review your work for accuracy. Identify any spelling patterns or rules you may have used.

Introduction

"Each story ... must present a full, fair and accurate account...These are our bywords—full, fair, accurate."

–Richard Cole, journalism educator

Some activities are clearly illegal:

- Taking a teacher's cellphone to investigate a rumor of "sex texting" is theft.
- Publishing a medical record that indicates the principal is HIV positive, then writing that this "report brings into question the principal's morals" may be both invasion of privacy and libel.
- Bugging the counselor's office may break several laws and is an invasion of privacy.
- Broadcasting reports from two girls saying a PE teacher, now on leave, made sexual advances toward them may be slander. (But share the information with your adviser and save the digital file for use if the allegations become public or charges are filed.)
- Using the Beatles' "Hey Jude" as you report your victory over St. Simon and Jude's volleyball team violates copyright law unless you have permission to use the music.

In these cases, it should not be hard to decide what your publication will do, and what it will not do. But other ethical decisions are more difficult. Sometimes an action is legal, but still violates journalism ethics. A rare few activities may be ethical but put you in opposition to the law.

Ethical Dilemmas

When you sense something is wrong, or at least not quite right, you need more than a feeling in your gut to convince others. You need reasons and language to prove that an unethical situation has taken place (Figure 4.1). Journalists must decide what to report and how to report it. This can lead to ethical dilemmas as you determine the difference between responsible and irresponsible media action. What would you say in the following situations? Do they represent responsible or irresponsible media action?

Figure 4.1 Different ethical dilemmas may come up as you prepare your publication or broadcast.

- Your sports photographer wants to publish a "joke" picture of a 125-pound football player apparently bench-pressing 220 pounds, which is cropped so you cannot see his buddies holding up the weight. The photographer says, "It's funny, and everyone will know it is a joke."
- When you interview the athletic director about the funds that go toward male and female sports, she tells you she wants to read the story before you publish it.
- A reporter pitches a story about her best friend who was raped under the influence of a date-rape drug.
- A reporter wants to go undercover and buy cigarettes to expose a nearby donut store that some say sells cigarettes to minors.
- Your business manager suggests you cover the opening of a nearby bowling alley and arcade "so they will advertise with us."
- An administrator asks you to give teachers at your school 12 inches in each issue to write guest columns.

A **code of ethics**—a written set of guidelines for ethical behavior—will help you make your decisions and will provide you with the language to explain your position to others.

However, the most difficult decisions are not between right and wrong but among conflicting goods or the lesser of several evils. Consider the following situations:

1. You want to write a story about how students use the time allotted for silent reading and what they do while the announcements are read. The student reporters are planning to stick their heads into classrooms during the announcements and reading time and record what is going on. As a courtesy, do you give teachers warning in advance? Do you ask for their permission first? Do you see any problems with this method of reporting or with the story?
2. You are covering issues of bullying on your campus after a student in a nearby state committed suicide. The professional press is covering it as an issue of homophobia. You wish to create a **photo illustration** (a staged photograph) of bullying on your campus. Several students have volunteered to play the parts of the student being bullied and the bullies if you digitally blur their faces in the picture. You intend to label the image as a photo illustration. What problems might there be in doing this?
3. One of your teachers, who was quoted in a sports feature story, tells you she was never interviewed for the piece. Another student claims he was misquoted. What should you do? What should your publication do? What should your adviser do?

Journalistic ethics will give you both the principles and the language you need to think about, discuss and make decisions concerning each of the scenarios above. Each scenario is based on a real ethical dilemma faced by high school publications.

Codes of Ethics

Codes of ethics and their cousins—codes of conduct, codes of chivalry, codes of honor, statements of principles, professional oaths and ethical guidelines—are resources for ethical decision making on principles of right and wrong. They are most often developed by people who have been given extraordinary power or extraordinary access to information or to people when they are especially vulnerable. Many professions, from archaeologists (World Archaeological Congress Codes of Ethics) to zookeepers (Association of Zoos and Aquariums Code of Professional Ethics), have codes of ethics to help them make difficult decisions.

Codes of ethics are almost always written by members of the group the codes guide, not by someone outside the group. These codes are founded on the belief that the media must earn and keep the public's trust. For no other group is the public's trust more important—and more difficult to keep—than it is for journalists.

The Code of Ethics developed by the Society of Professional Journalists (SPJ) is one of several ethical codes related to journalism. Other codes include the following:

- National Scholastic Press Association Code of Ethics for High School Journalists
- National Press Photographers Association Code of Ethics
- Radio Television Digital News Association Code of Ethics; Social Media and Blogging Guidelines; Guidelines for Covering Breaking News; and Guidelines for Avoiding Conflict of Interest
- American Association of Newspaper Editors Statement of Principles
- Journalism Education Association Advisers Code of Ethics
- Society for News Design Code of Ethical Standards
- National Public Radio Ethics Handbook

Your Turn

1. Discuss groups of people, ancient or modern, who have had extraordinary power or access and who have created codes of ethics for themselves. These may include medical professionals, knights and samurai, law enforcement officials, and builders and engineers. With members of your group, research the code of ethics or similar guidelines for four such groups. Read the code to determine:
   - the responsibilities the group believes it has;
   - to whom the group feels it is responsible; and
   - what dangers or temptations the members are to avoid.

   Share the most interesting code with your group or class.

(Continued)

YOUR TURN *(Continued)*

2. **Going Deeper.** Research and compare two journalism-related codes of ethics concerning the three points mentioned on the previous page. What is the most striking difference between the codes?
3. While most codes of ethics are written by members of an organization, several publications have codes of ethics for their employees. The New York Times and the Los Angeles Times both have these, while MSNBC News has Social Media/Blogging/Online Publishing Guidelines. Is it appropriate for a publication—the employer—to create such a code? Why or why not?

With very few exceptions, the Society of Professional Journalists Code of Ethics serves student journalists just as it serves professional journalists. Founded in 1909, the SPJ is the cornerstone for ethical journalism in the U.S. and the SPJ Code of Ethics should serve as the foundation by which your publication operates. It is important for you to understand the SPJ Code of Ethics and adhere to it. As a journalist, you will frequently be asked to make ethical decisions, sometimes many in a day. You may also be asked to explain and defend your decisions to your peers, your editors and to your audience. The SPJ Code of Ethics will aid you in these situations.

The preamble to the SPJ Code of Ethics discusses journalism's most important responsibilities as well as what journalists owe the public, their audience (Figure 4.2). The body of the code discusses journalistic responsibilities in more detail. As you read the code, you will see that journalists must consider many groups in addition to their audience, including the following:

- their subjects, or the people they report on
- their sources, or the people who give them information
- their advertisers
- their publication or broadcast and the other people who work there
- the profession of journalism

The most difficult decisions a journalist faces involve conflicts between responsibility to the public and responsibilities to one or more of these other individuals or groups.

Figure 4.2 The Society of Professional Journalists Code of Ethics acts as a guideline for both professional and student journalists faced with ethical dilemmas.

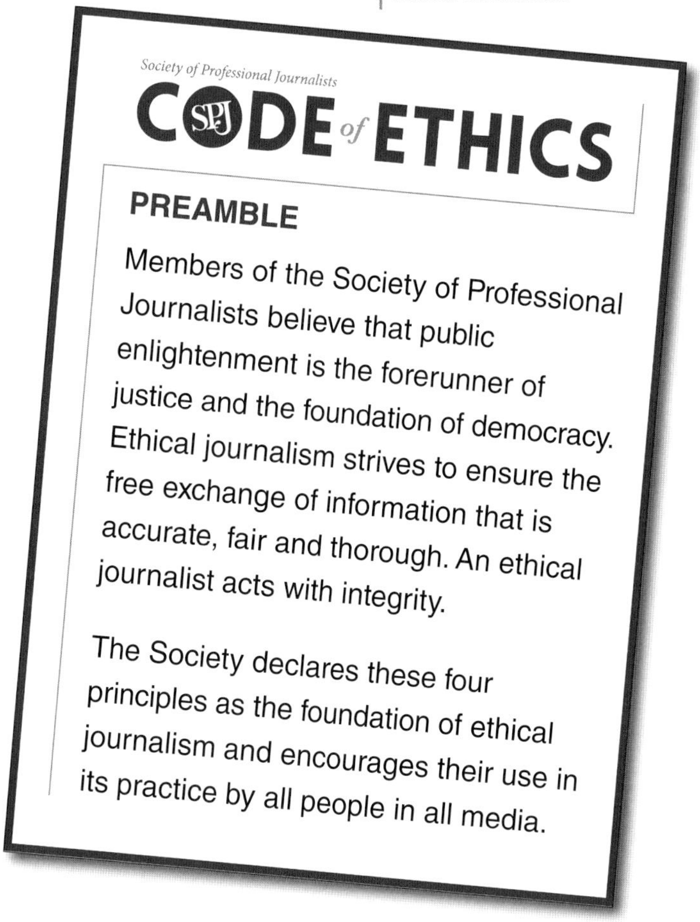
Society of Professional Journalists

CODE of ETHICS

PREAMBLE

Members of the Society of Professional Journalists believe that public enlightenment is the forerunner of justice and the foundation of democracy. Ethical journalism strives to ensure the free exchange of information that is accurate, fair and thorough. An ethical journalist acts with integrity.

The Society declares these four principles as the foundation of ethical journalism and encourages their use in its practice by all people in all media.

YOUR TURN

Study the Code of Ethics preamble and answer the following questions.

1. What is the forerunner of justice and the foundation of democracy?
2. Find the full SPJ Code of Ethics online. What four principles does the SPJ see as the foundation of ethical journalism?

In this chapter, you will study key principles from the Society of Professional Journalists Code of Ethics. You will see these principles highlighted in blue throughout the chapter, followed by explanation, discussion, and examples of those principles being put into action. These principles represent the foundation of journalistic ethics. Learning about each principle will help you evaluate whether certain situations demonstrate responsible or irresponsible media action.

What You Owe Your Audience

"Journalists should be honest and courageous in gathering, reporting and interpreting information."

Journalists are protected by the Constitution and paid by their readers (either directly or through publishers or advertisers) to seek the truth and report it as accurately and truthfully as possible. As a journalist, your side of the bargain is to be courageous as the public's eyes and ears and to be accurate, balanced and concise as you write. Concise writing contains specific and accurate information and avoids generalities or clichés. Your audience's trust is your most important asset.

Seek Truth and Report It

"Recognize a special obligation to serve as watchdogs over public affairs and government. Seek to ensure that the public's business is conducted in the open, and that government records are open to all.

Be vigilant and courageous about holding those with power accountable. Give voice to the voiceless"

If you are doing your job as a journalist and acting responsibly, you are reporting on the government in all its forms because the government does the public's business. You also report any other business that affects the public. This will probably include your local school board and your city, including parks and recreation, police and safety and the courts, as well as state and national business that affects your school and your audience.

"Boldly tell the story of the diversity and magnitude of the human experience. Seek sources whose voices we seldom hear."

As a journalist, you spot trends and explain events to the public. Sometimes the trends you follow will be less than earthshaking, such as baggy pants or skintight jeans. Others will be more serious, such as who is dropping out of school or who is making military commitments. Other trends you may track are youth employment—or unemployment—or fewer students being admitted to college and more students needing five or seven years to graduate from college.

Good journalism also provides context to what otherwise might seem like random events. What was behind the fight in the cafeteria? Why is a public skate park opening or closing? Are other facilities in the community closing or opening? Are more facilities being offered for senior citizens and fewer for young people? If citizens know the context of the decision—who is making the decision and why—they may have more power. Journalism can make democracy possible.

You go places your audience rarely goes, and you see things the public rarely sees—or notices. You also listen to people who would not

Handout via REUTERS

Meet the Professionals:
Daniel Pearl

Daniel Pearl was an American-Israeli journalist who was abducted by Pakistani militants and beheaded by al-Qaida Islamic militants in Pakistan in 2002, just four months after the 9/11 attacks on the World Trade Center in New York and the Pentagon in Washington. The photo shown here was taken by Daniel's captors. They have him holding a newspaper to prove he was both alive and in captivity on the date the paper was printed.

A journalist since his student days, Pearl co-founded the student newspaper at Stanford University, the Stanford Commentary. Just five years after graduating, he was hired by The Wall Street Journal, working first in Atlanta, then Washington and London, and serving as a Middle East correspondent. He became The Wall Street Journal's South Asia bureau chief, based in Mumbai. He was known for his uncompromising objectivity and his tenacious reporting. He uncovered that the United States had mistakenly bombed a Sudanese pharmaceutical plant, believing it to be a weapons factory. He was also known for his belief in tolerance and the importance of communication.

Pearl began retracing the steps of the al-Qaida-linked "shoe bomber," who had attempted to blow up an American Airlines flight from Paris to Miami with explosives packed in his shoe. The shoe bomber had been recruited and trained as a terrorist in Pakistan and Afghanistan. Pearl was kidnapped in Karachi, Pakistan, while attempting to interview the head of a fundamentalist Islamic group.

For weeks after the kidnapping, millions of people around the world, including heads of state, religious leaders, members of the press and friends worked to secure Daniel's freedom; but his captors made demands that could not be met. In February they posted videos of his beheading on YouTube.

Three months later Daniel's widow gave birth to their son.

In 2010 President Barack Obama signed into law the Daniel Pearl Freedom of the Press Act, which provides grants to promote freedom of the press worldwide and requires the U.S. Department of State to include a description of the status of freedom of the press in its annual Country Reports on Human Rights Practices, which it submits to Congress.

otherwise be heard, even if their opinions are unpopular or different from your own. You cover how football players tape up before a game and what injuries they are trying to prevent. You cover how the custodians change the lights 45 feet above the floor in the gym and how the school board, or the superintendent, decides which programs to cut.

Seeking the truth may uncover heartwarming stories, such as an assistant principal who stays late on Mondays and Wednesdays to coach a basketball team made up of students who have disabilities. You may learn that an alumna, a successful software developer, donated 48 tablet computers to the ESL (English as a second language) department.

But seeking the truth is not always easy or fun. Sometimes seeking the truth will uncover facts that make people uncomfortable or facts they would rather not discuss. For instance, maybe the president of the Football Boosters has been charged with embezzling $29,000. Perhaps the school's boys soccer team is 100 percent Hispanic and the boys tennis team is 100 percent Asian.

Not everyone will welcome the kind of **scrutiny** (close examination) you bring. Some may make it hard for you to research your story. The federal and state Freedom of Information acts were written for such cases. Others will tell you that you are making your school or community look bad, that negative news distracts students from their studies, or that you will be hurting innocent family members if you report the charges against the president of the booster club. They may tell you that the news you are reporting is too negative for students. While you should give due consideration to each of these opinions, journalists need to act independently and make many important decisions based on ethical grounds.

Before you abandon a story, examine your reasons. Do you have a sound journalistic or ethical reason for turning away from the story? Would your reporting hurt your audience? Remember, the public should be able to trust you to seek truth and report it to them.

The ABCs of Journalism

To keep the audience's trust, journalists act responsibly and follow higher standards than may be regularly required of high school students. This is true as they research and write for their publication or broadcast and as they relate to the people around them. It is important to always follow the ABCs of journalism—be accurate, balanced and concise. Journalists who do not follow these guidelines are demonstrating irresponsible media action.

Be Accurate

Big truths are made from little truths, so it is important to be accurate (That is the *A* in the ABCs of good writing.) This is true whether you are reporting a happy story about students winning prizes or a more serious story about teachers losing their teaching positions and class sizes increasing.

> *"Journalists should take responsibility for the accuracy of their work. Verify information before releasing it. Use original sources whenever possible."*

Get the names right. Ask the person you interview how to spell his name. Write it down. Spell it back to him. Most people will be flattered, not annoyed, that you care about their names.

Get the details right. Do not guess or assume. Know whether you are facing north or south in the gym. Use a compass. Know the correct name of the league in which your school competes. Know how the other team's coach spells her name. If you do not know, find out before you publish. Call the athletic director at your school or at the competitor's school. Do not assume an accident at Graham and Rancho Road was on Graham Street. It may have been on Graham Place. Check a map.

Quotations are especially tricky. If possible, read the quotation back to your source after you write it down. Record the conversation with a tape or digital recorder as a backup to your notes if your subject is willing to be recorded. If in doubt, call your source to confirm what he said before you publish. Never try to write a quotation from memory, especially while you are composing the story.

Accuracy is essential to strong reporting. Responsible journalists get the details right. Do not guess or make up anything. Doing so represents irresponsible media action. Journalism requires shoe leather and sturdy fingers and thumbs for all the phoning, texting and emailing you do to verify everything.

Intentionally misleading the public is never acceptable. Journalists and photojournalists who do so end up unemployed and sometimes unemployable.

> *"Acknowledge mistakes and correct them promptly and prominently. Explain corrections and clarification carefully and clearly."*

One small factual error may cause your audience to dismiss everything else you do. If you write that Kerry Mays took first place in the high school division of Laguna Beach's Sawdust Art Festival last week with her three-dimensional work "Collage," you may think you have checked all the facts.

But the one fact you forgot to check is how to spell the winner's first name. She is *Keri* Mays, not *Kerry*. This is an error in fact, not a typographical error. People will notice a two-letter error and doubt your accuracy on seven facts you got right and everything else you report. They may dismiss all the hard work done by you and the rest of the staff as "a bunch of kids pretending to be journalists" as a result of this small inaccuracy.

> *"Respond quickly to questions about accuracy, clarity and fairness."*

Make it easy for your audience to report your errors and other problems to you. Allow members of your community to comment on your online stories and include a link for them to email comments to the reporter or editor. Along with options for *commenting, liking, forwarding, tweeting* and *sharing* online stories, insert a button allowing your reader to *report an error* or provide an email address where they can contact you. Provide a phone number or an email address for your print editions or broadcasts. Allow students to proofread the caption of their club's yearbook picture and the information associated with their senior pictures before you print. If you publish a literary magazine, let the author see the proofs before you publish.

When you do discover an error, discuss with your newsroom leaders and peers why you and your publication or broadcast made the error. Make a plan to avoid similar errors in the future. Often the editors need to revise their **story flow** (process for creating and editing stories) so that they will catch such errors in the future. In a typical story flow, the reporter does background reporting, shares notes and tells the editor what the story is in 30 words or less. The editor assigns the appropriate multimedia team, sketches a possible story package and sidebars and assigns deadlines. Reporting, recording and photographing are done by assigned staff members. Others may be responsible for writing, creating graphics, choosing photographs and editing audio and video.

Responses are then sought from peers and the team. This stage may make use of blogging and wikis. The reporter revises the story, the editor reviews progress, the reporter revises again and the editor requests more changes. The reporter revises once more and the copy editor edits the copy. He or she may send it back to the writer or confer with the reporter. The reporter verifies all facts and quotations. At any point in this story flow, an error can easily be made.

If an error in fact is made, print a retraction as soon as possible. A **retraction** identifies the error and provides the correct information. Generally, you should not repeat the error in the correction. A retraction might look like this:

> *In the Arts and Entertainment article "Five take firsts at Sawdust Festival" we misspelled Keri Mays' name. We regret the error.*

Figure 4.3 A crack and peel sticker can be used to correct errors in a yearbook, as shown here. *In what other publications might you use a crack and peel sticker?*

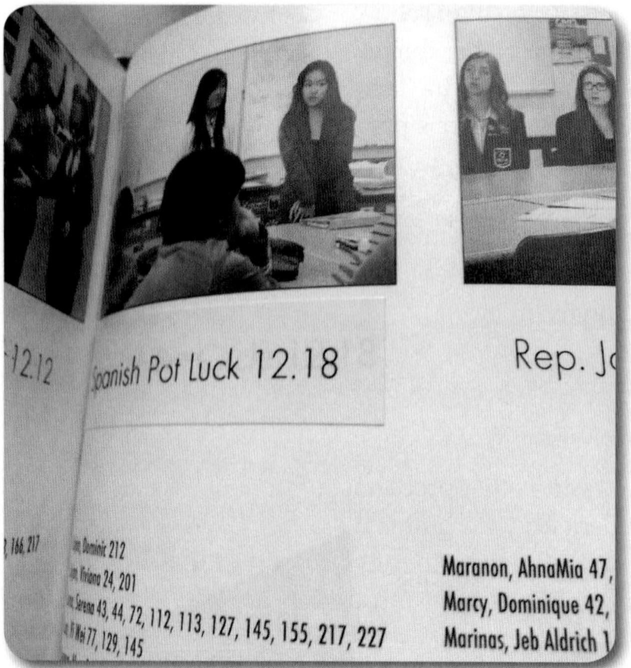

Courtesy of Matthew LaPorte

If you publish a glossy magazine, a literary magazine or a yearbook, use crack and peel stickers printed with the corrected image and/or text (Figure 4.3). You may need to contact all those who purchased your publication to offer them the correction.

It is easier to print a retraction to an error in a print edition than it is to retract a tweet, yet it is so much easier to make a mistake online because of the swiftness with which you can post information. In addition, you may have less peer review and editorial oversight.

If you need to correct an electronic message such as a tweet, text message, mass email or Facebook posting, you have a problem. The error has already been re-tweeted, linked to and re-sent. That error spreads like ink in water, and it is rare that a retraction travels as far and wide as the message it is trying to correct.

It may not be fair to hold students to an adult standard of accuracy, but if students are to claim the privileges and protections of being journalists, they need to earn and maintain the public's trust. For both adult and student journalists, the public's trust is journalism's only real asset.

Be Balanced

You owe your audience **balanced reporting**. (*Balanced reporting* is the *B* of the ABCs of good writing.)You tell more than one side of a story and you are fair to each side. Another way of being balanced is to be **unbiased**, or impartial, meaning that you strive to keep your personal feelings and opinions out of your reporting and your writing. You should also be **transparent**, letting the audience know if there is even a hint of conflict of interest. Publishing a story that is unbalanced or biased is an example of an irresponsible media action.

You decide to be balanced when you decide what to cover. Imagine a publication that covered the mountain region of Tibet, where Buddhist monks have burned themselves to death to protest the brutal and repressive Chinese regime. If the whole magazine spread or broadcast was about the beautiful mountains, the quaint costumes, the ancient monasteries and the great Chinese food, it would sound like publicity from the tourism board rather than trustworthy journalism. The publication would lose the readers' trust because of its lack of balance.

You can earn or lose your readers' trust with the most basic decisions, even the stories you pitch or the stories you are assigned. Are you covering the stories that most affect your viewers' lives or most interest them? Which story gets more coverage in your paper, Winter Formal or the district's cuts to bus service?

If the more affluent students have always come to school in cars, they may be more interested in Winter Formal, but for those who relied on the now-discontinued bus, the bus story may be important news. If you lead with Winter Formal, you are making a statement about what and who is important, whether you intend to or not. Much of your audience may no longer trust you to cover their important concerns.

When you cover the cuts to bus service, balanced reporting requires that you talk to all (or almost all) sides of the controversy. If you interview five students who report they now walk 45 minutes each way to school or ride in the back of a pick-up to school, you are still only covering one side of the story. Talk to members of the school board or the superintendent for another perspective.

Why was bus service cut? Have you asked members of the school board or the superintendent? If they blame state budget cuts, have you talked to your local state representative? Were gasoline prices to blame?

Is there an upside to the problem? For instance, have students who now have two 45-minute walks each day lost weight? Does a cross-country runner jog home every day in 14 minutes? What do the PE teachers think?

How about the bus drivers? Are they now part-time employees? Did they lose their jobs?

Though journalists strive to cover all sides, not all sides deserve equal attention. Balance does not require you to quote the man who thought all the buses had been abducted by a UFO looking for spare parts. Nor does balance demand that you give the same amount of space or time to the superintendent and to the bus driver.

Balance does require that you treat each position fairly. Journalists report what people say but allow their audience to decide the merits of each point of view. You should be unbiased in your reporting and writing. Do not favor one position over another. For instance, use *said* for each quotation, not *whined, complained, argued, pointed out, protested, explained* or *asserted*.

"Avoid conflicts of interest, real or perceived."

You should not cover a story in which you have personal bias or even a personal interest. That would strain your readers' trust. If your mother is one of the bus drivers whose hours were cut, or if you are now walking an hour and a half to school each day, you should tell your editor and the editor should take you off the story. You may be able to write about your experience in an opinion piece in the editorial section or in a column. A news or feature story, however, needs to be covered by a reporter who is objective and appears objective to the audience. You also must guard against making the news while you cover it. If you are photographing and making audio recordings of trash-talking on the basketball court, you are reporting the news. If two groups initiate a trash-talking contest because you and your equipment are there, and the contest escalates into a physical fight, you are influencing the news and so may have a conflict of interest. As much as is humanly possible, you should record, not create, events.

When you write commentary, your opinion should be clear. When you cover the news, your opinion should be absent. Do not insert commentary into news. You generally should not publish or broadcast commentary on issues you also cover as a reporter.

"Disclose unavoidable conflicts."

If every reporter on your staff is now walking an extra hour and a half to school each day, you can and should still cover the bus story. But you need to be transparent about your connections to the story. Inform your audience that the photographer and a reporter on the story are among those who previously rode the bus. You could say something like, "Reporter Kitt Fox and photographer Neda Focus, who both contributed to this story, were bus riders." You need to guard against any appearance of bias in your reporting.

Be Concise

You owe your audience concise writing. (*Concise* is the C in the ABCs of good writing.) Journalistic style demands precision and brevity. The audience should not need to trudge through a swamp of words to reach a small island of meaning. But concise writing is not just a matter of sentence structure and vocabulary. Concise writing demands accuracy.

Figure 4.4 Writing concise stories begins with getting the facts and making sure you include them in your notes.

If you have not prepared your notes well, your writing will wander around in passive sentences meant to hide what you did not find out. You will start sentences with *there are* and use words like *many* or—worse yet—*a lot of*. You will also risk inaccuracy.

Consider this lead paragraph from a poorly reported news story: "There are many teachers who have been fired due to budget cuts."

If the reporter had done her job, she would have known that it is not "many" but six teachers, or 10 percent of the staff (Figure 4.4). She would know the names of those who are leaving and what they taught, if the information has been made public. She should at least report that the 10 percent will come from among the teachers most recently hired by the district, with special categories of teachers left untouched. She should know whether they are leaving immediately, at the end of the semester, or at the end of the school year. If they are to leave in the middle of the school year, she should have found out what will happen to their classes.

If teachers lost their jobs because of a reduction in funds, do not say they were fired. If they have been reassigned to another school, do not say they lost their jobs.

When you have reported well, your audience can read that

> *Six teachers will leave GCHS February 6, at the beginning of the second semester, causing hundreds of schedule changes as their students are absorbed into other classes.*
>
> *Three will lose their jobs because of the January 1 state budget revision, which cut funding to schools, while another three will move to other GCUHSD campuses. History teacher Raymond Huizar, English and ELD teacher Mai Tran McDuff and PE teacher Philip Cutrell, who each were hired in the last year, will lose their jobs. Cutrell will continue to coach JV baseball. Moving to other campuses are...*

Copy Editing, Revising and Rewriting

A strong copy editor is the final check for accuracy, balance and fairness. Good copy editing avoids embarrassing or harmful mistakes. While the copy editor may correct some issues, the writer is often responsible for rewriting troublesome copy.

Copy editors focus on language as it will appear on the page. Accuracy includes grammatical accuracy, spelling and punctuation. Has the writer followed your publication's style? How has the writer referred to a principal on the first reference? In the following references? How does your style print the name of a book or movie? How do you refer to the teams made up primarily of females, such as their swim team? Your publication may have decided to follow the Associated Press Stylebook, the Broadcast News and Writing Stylebook or another standard. Issues unique to your high school should be addressed in your publication's stylebook, no matter which style you follow.

Extend

Copy editors note these issues and mark copy using standard copy editing marks or *proofreading marks*, which are widely used and understood. These marks go in the line of text where the change is needed and in the margin to offer more details. For example, a caret (^) marks where text should be added. The new text is then written in the margin. Either the writer or the copy editor will make the changes the copy editor identifies.

Copy editors also may identify language that is not efficient and economical and needs revision. For instance, *There were two sprinters who took home second place ribbons, Junior Sailor Gonzales and Junior Annie Chin* (17 words) can be revised to read *Juniors Sailor Gonzales and Annie Chin each sprinted to second place.* (11 words.) Generally wordy or fluffy prose will be sent back to the writer for revision, sometimes with the copy editor's suggestions.

Strong copy editing will also fact check statistics, addresses, names and their spelling, titles and dates, as well as quotations from other printed work and other cultural references. Copy editors may insert the corrected information or ask the writer to research further and rewrite the troublesome passage.

Copy editors look for language that reveals bias and language that could inadvertently convey double meanings. The writer will need to rewrite these passages. Copy editors may also challenge the balance in the story, suggesting the need for additional sources. The writer is then responsible to report further and rewrite the story.

What You Do and Do *Not* Owe Your Subjects and Sources

Your subjects are the people and institutions you cover in your stories, including those whom you mention but who are not the main subject of your reporting. Your sources are the people and institutions from whom you gather your information. It is sometimes difficult to draw a clear line between who is a source and who is a subject.

You owe your sources and subjects fair, balanced and unbiased reporting whether you like them or not, and whether you agree with them or not. Your audience also expects this of you.

The Chance to Respond

> *"Diligently seek subjects of news coverage to allow them to respond to criticism or allegations of wrongdoing."*

You owe your subjects and sources a chance to respond before you publish anything negative about them. If they choose not to respond, you

Your Mission Statement to the Rescue: For, By and About Students

Your publication or broadcast's mission statement will help guide you through many ethical dilemmas.

If someone or something distracts your publication from its mission, reread your mission statement. It will help you make ethical decisions and explain your decisions to others.

If faculty members want to write a 12-inch column in each edition of your paper, you can politely point out that your mission statement says your paper is "by, for and about the students" of your high school. If the football coach wants you to remove from the yearbook picture the names of people who quit football, remind him that your mission is to make an accurate history of the year. You cannot leave names off the picture if the people are in the picture. You can, however, discuss other ways to cover a winning season.

owe your audience an explanation. You should state that your subject or source refused to comment, did not return your phone calls or simply directed you to their press releases. Your audience needs to know that you tried multiple times in good faith to contact the subject or source and to hear their side of the issue. For example, if a student brings you a school salad with a human hair in it, you need to tell the cafeteria supervisor what you found and ask for her comment. That is only fair, and your audience needs to know you are fair. Freedom of the press does not grant the right to make sneak attacks on people in your publication or broadcast.

Respect and Courtesy

> *"Balance the public's need for information against potential harm or discomfort. Pursuit of the news is not a license for arrogance or undue intrusiveness."*

You owe everyone good manners. Speak to each person as if he is the most important person on the planet and you can hardly wait to find out what he can teach you. Politely request access to classrooms and to students who are in class, but only if such access is necessary. Avoid humor that may be cruel—it is easy to be funny at another's expense. Guard against arrogance as you use social media sites and microblogs such as Twitter.

> *"Avoid undercover or other surreptitious methods of gathering information unless traditional, open methods will not yield information vital to the public."*

Let your sources know you are a journalist. Never trick a subject into thinking you are someone you are not. If you gather story ideas from social media, identify yourself as a journalist as soon as you begin reporting a story. Make contact outside social media with each source or subject. Verify all identities in the physical world, outside the social media or microblogging site, before you quote anyone. It is wise to keep all your personal interactions in a different account than the one you use for your journalism activities.

Going undercover should be done only when there is no other means available to get important information on a story of great significance. When you go undercover, you will forever lose the trust of the people on whom you report. If you get and use information through such misrepresentation, you need to tell your audience what you did and how and why you did it, or you will lose their trust as well. Remember that if you break the law while you are undercover as a reporter, you have still broken the law. If you publish what you have done, you have confessed to a crime.

"Avoid stereotyping. Journalists should examine the ways their values and experiences may shape their reporting."

You owe your subjects coverage as individuals, not merely as members of a stereotypical group. Do not reinforce stereotypes such as the dumb jock, the Asian braniac, the fluffy-headed cheerleader or the inspirational person with a disability. If you are reporting well, what you publish and what you do will help combat the public's stereotypes of teenagers rather than enforce them.

"Recognize that private people have a greater right to control information about themselves than do public figures and others who seek power, influence or attention. Weigh the consequences of publishing or broadcasting personal information."

You owe your subjects, if they are not public figures, as much privacy as possible as you seek the truth and report it. You recognize that you can cause harm to your subjects and sources. If three students report seeing a fire in the grass during third period and all report roughly the same thing, you do not need to explain that Anna Kleinstuck was going to the restroom from a special education classroom, Jeremy Bouchan was standing outside his Spanish classroom because he had been punching at another student during presentation practice or that Inga Blackrock uses a wheelchair and leaves class early to avoid the crowded hallways. Unless their private lives are essential to your story, you simply report their names, their year in school and what they said.

Compassion and Consideration

You owe your subjects, especially children and those dealing with tragedy or grief, compassion and consideration. Have a standard, written policy for dealing with deaths in your school community. Decide in advance whether your headlines will say the student died (which is

Covering Issues of Disability

If a disability is not relevant to the story, do not mention it. Think of the disability as you would a person's race or ethnicity. You would only identify a person as Haitian-American if it was important to the story. Mention a disability only if it is important to the story. A disability is a characteristic of the person, but it does not define him or her any more than ethnicity, height, primary language, religion, gender or taste in jeans defines a person. It is also not a source of shame, so it should be mentioned if it is relevant. See "Covering Issues of Disability" on the *Journalism* website.

Extend

Associated Press style) or that he passed away. How do you cover a death? With a news story? An obituary? Do you give more coverage to a prominent student than to a student who is new to your school? How do you handle suicides? To ignore a death may be the most unkind treatment of all.

If you are covering a student's death some days after it occurred, you may wish to inform those close to the student that her name and picture will appear in your broadcast or on your front page so that they can prepare themselves for the coverage.

> *"Show compassion for those who may be affected by news coverage. Use heightened sensitivity when dealing with juveniles, victims of sex crimes, and sources or subjects who are inexperienced or unable to give consent. Consider cultural differences in approach and treatment."*

Though high school students can legally give consent to publish information about themselves, they are also entitled to extra consideration. In some important ways they are still children. They probably are not able to foresee all the consequences of publishing confidential information. But what you publish or broadcast will be available to everyone with an Internet search engine, including colleges, future in-laws and voters—long after high school. Once a story is published electronically, even in PDF, it cannot be completely removed from the Internet as long as a copy exists on any computer or in any cloud.

For instance, a student may give you permission to use his story and his name for an article about computer hacking, sexually transmitted disease or underage online gambling. However, he may not have thought carefully about the difficulties this information may cause him as he tries to get a job working with children, a security clearance for the military or a bond to work in the financial industry. You and your editors may decide not to publish his name—or his story—to protect him, even though he is willing to have the information published.

Your Turn

1. In what ways are high school students "juveniles," as mentioned in the SPJ Code of Ethics, and therefore entitled to more compassion as you report?
2. **Going Deeper.** When you interview high school students, they are clearly adults in some ways. For instance, they have the rights of an adult to express their opinions or relate what they have witnessed or done. But they are also "inexperienced sources or subjects." Describe two imaginary situations in which you, as a responsible journalist, will exercise special sensitivity when working with high school students.

Student journalists often cover issues that affect juveniles—their fellow students. They must balance the responsibility to "show compassion for those who may be affected by news coverage" with the public's right to know. For instance, consider the story about the president of the Football Boosters being charged with embezzling $29,000. It is quite likely that a relative of the president attends your school, perhaps a son or grandson. If you cover the theft, will you be hurting the student? If you do not cover the theft, are you failing to inform your audience concerning information important to them? Is protecting the student more important than informing your audience of a theft that will affect a large athletic program?

There are few easy answers. However, several factors may influence your decision.

Has the embezzlement already been reported in the professional press? If so, your reporting may add more depth and a local angle to the professional story. Does this suggest you should cover it? Or that you should not cover it?

Is it already being discussed as gossip? If so, your fair and objective reporting may dispel misunderstandings and lessen, rather than increase, the family's discomfort.

Have charges been filed? If not, you are probably speculating, not reporting the news. The charges, the court action, the verdict and any out-of-court settlement are all news.

Though you have a responsibility to seek truth and report it, you do not have a license to injure others if the injury can be avoided while still pursuing the truth. Treating your sources and subjects with respect is good, unbiased journalism. It is the ethical thing to do, and it will help you or the next journalist to gather information in the future.

What You Do *Not* Owe Your Sources and Subjects

Though you owe your sources and subjects accurate, fair, unbiased reporting and ethical—and sometimes compassionate—treatment, there are many things you do not owe them except under the most extraordinary circumstances. These include money, control of the story, the right to review your work or anonymity. After consulting with others, including your editors, your adviser, your editorial board or perhaps an online journalism community, you may decide to offer special treatment to a source, but this should be done only if you can show that the situation is an exception to the SPJ Code of Ethics and the guidelines discussed here.

Money

> *"Be wary of sources offering information for favors or money; do not pay for access to news. Identify content provided by outside sources, whether paid or not."*

You do not owe your sources or subjects money. An ethical journalist, especially in this country, is wary when someone wants money for information.

Control of the Story

> *"Refuse gifts, favors, fees, free travel and special treatment, and avoid political and other outside activities that may compromise integrity or impartiality, or may damage credibility."*

You do not owe your sources control over what you write, publish and broadcast. Sources may attempt to negotiate with you in many ways as they seek to obtain—or avoid—press coverage. They may also negotiate for favorable treatment for their cause.

A volunteer at the police department may tell you, "If you cover the Christmas Craft Faire at my kids' grade school, I'll make sure you know when someone is arrested for the vandalism at your high school." Your answer, of course, is *no*. If you foolishly promise coverage of the Christmas Craft Faire but then do not cover it, you may be sued for breach of promise. Even if you are not sued, you certainly will lose a source's trust.

Instead, you may tell your source, "The editors assign the stories, but I will be happy to forward a flyer or press package to our editors if you send me a copy." Make sure your potential source knows you have made no promise beyond forwarding the information.

Though it is possible that the source will refuse to talk to you, it is just as likely that he will give you whatever information he has. If you treat him fairly, he may remain a source longer than if you "trade favors." It is also possible he did not have—or cannot share—significant information in the first place and was simply negotiating to place his story in your publication or broadcast.

Sources may also attempt to use the press to embarrass or take revenge on someone else. A member of the prom committee comes to you saying, "Millie's Formal Wear promised us we could borrow tuxedos for the prom assembly, but when we went to pick them up, they wanted a $200 deposit before we could take them. We nearly didn't get the clothes for the assembly. Will you cover what happened?"

Be wary. The core news values of proximity, timeliness, impact, prominence, oddity, conflict and human interest should control what your cover. You need to question why the source wishes to have the story told, especially when a source comes to you. Revenge may be a motive, but the press is not a hit man for hire.

The Right to Review

A source may allow you to interview him only if he gets to see what you write before it is printed so that he can review it "for accuracy." But prior review often becomes prior restraint. You do not owe your sources or subjects the right to review what you have written or recorded before you publish or broadcast.

You should give your sources and subjects an opportunity to respond to criticism and information that contradicts what they have said. You may even read short sections of your story to them to verify that you are accurate. But you do not owe them control over how they are portrayed or what you broadcast.

If a source says she will not talk to you unless you promise that she may review the story, you may reply, "I would like to have your phone number so that I can verify facts and quotations with you and seek further clarification, if that is all right with you." That response may assure her that you are an accurate and fair journalist. She may decide to give you the information you seek.

If she refuses to talk to you unless you give her prior review, you may tell her that you will publish that she "refused comment." Sometimes a source will decide it is better to risk an interview rather than to refuse comment.

However, there will be times when you may promise to limit an interview to certain subjects. For instance, let's assume that a student at your school was just signed to act in a made-for-television movie. The student is reluctant to talk to you, however, because her sister has been arrested for a hit-and-run accident. You can agree to talk only about her acting career and not about her family life. Stick to your promise, but at the end of the interview, if you feel you have established a good relationship with your subject, you may give the young actor a chance to broaden the interview. If she does not respond readily, respect your promise and do not press for more information about her family life.

Anonymity

> *"Identify sources clearly. The public is entitled to as much information as possible to judge the reliability and motivations of sources.*
>
> *Consider sources' motives before promising anonymity. Reserve anonymity for sources who may face danger, retribution or other harm, and have information that cannot be obtained elsewhere. Explain why anonymity was granted."*

Sources may ask you to grant them anonymity. Granting anonymity is different from using an anonymous source. An anonymous source is a source whose identity you do not know. Granting anonymity means you know who your source is, but you will not reveal the name in your publication or broadcast.

Figure 4.5 A source may try to influence what you write or insist on the right to review your draft of the story. You need to refuse these requests, but if you do so diplomatically, you may persuade the source to give you information without any qualifications.

You do not owe your sources anonymity in exchange for information. Though giving you "off the record" information may imply that the source is doing you a favor, the reality may be that the source wants the information published without risk to himself (Figure 4.5).

When a source offers to share information with you "off the record," your first reaction should be to politely close your reporter's notebook and tell him that you will need to discuss the matter with the leadership of the paper. Ask, "Would you like to tell me a little more about the information you are offering me?" A promise of anonymity should be given only rarely and then only after discussion with your editors.

Such promises have multiple dangers for you and your publication, including the following:

- suit for breach of promise if the source's identity is disclosed after you promised anonymity
- pressure from others to reveal the source or subject. Your school's administration, law enforcement, or those mentioned in the article may demand the person's identity and perhaps *subpoena* your notes or images and digital files. A subpoena is a court order demanding that you turn over your materials. Though shield laws may protect you, you may risk time in jail while the matter is going through the courts. One possible compromise you may offer your source—if you and your editors decide to promise anonymity—is to specify that you will not reveal his identity *unless* you are subpoenaed to do so. This compromise protects your source from anyone who does not have a court order forcing you to share your notes. It also keeps you from having to decide between being sued for breach of promise and being jailed for contempt of court.
- suit for libel from someone who appears to be your source but is not. If you try to disguise your source's identity, you may unintentionally suggest another person is your source.
- loss of your readers' trust. They also may suspect that you have made up the source and the quotations and information. Always explain to your viewers or readers why you are protecting the identity of a subject or source.

What about using information from an anonymous source? If you receive information "over the transom," meaning that neither you nor anyone else in your newsroom knows its source, then you may treat the information as a story idea but not a verified fact. A transom was a window above a door in 19th and early 20th century office buildings. Writings tossed "over the transom" were truly anonymous.

If information cannot be tracked back to a source, you may search for three other sources that support what you heard "over the transom." If you find other strong, on-the-record sources and evidence, you may cover the story, but the anonymous source should not count as one of your reliable sources. The story must be strong enough to print without the anonymously supplied information. Always consider the possibility that the "over-the-transom" information is false or misleading.

On rare occasions, you may make the decision with your editors to grant anonymity for a source. You and your editors might do this when

- you have verified the source's **credibility**, that is, both his knowledge of the subject and his ability and desire to give truthful information;
- you have verified as many details as possible with sources you can quote;
- the information is available from no other source;
- the story is of great significance and your source's information is vital to the story; and
- there is a compelling reason to protect the source.

Your Turn

1. You talk to a source who tells you about the abuse he suffered in a county foster home. He wishes to remain anonymous. How would you verify his credibility? Under what circumstances would you print his comments?
2. **Going Deeper.** Whom would you talk with to balance this source's claims? Who needs to be given a chance to answer the criticism he made?

> *"Explain ethical choices and processes to audiences. Encourage a civil dialogue with the public about journalistic practices, coverage and news content."*

If you decide to include an anonymous source or disguise the identity of a source, your audience deserves an explanation. Explain your choice and why you think it is ethical.

Remember that your adviser, who is a school district employee, may be asked by her administration to reveal a source of information. She will need to comply with the request. She should not know anything you have promised to keep concealed. Student leaders, not the adviser, need to decide whether to offer anonymity.

You do not need to protect anonymity at the cost of someone's life. If you learn that someone is in danger from himself or from others, your adviser should know and should report the danger to someone who can help. You may also feel the need to contact authorities directly. You are a human being first, a journalist second, and you will not want to live the next 70 years knowing you could have protected someone and you did not.

A young journalist may seem easy to manipulate or bully. But journalists and their editors who follow a strict code such as the SPJ Code of Ethics will find protection from sources and subjects who try to sell information, control what is published, use the press for private purposes and avoid taking responsibility for information they provide.

What You Do and Do *Not* Owe Your Advertisers

You owe your advertisers a broadcast, yearbook, paper, magazine or website that attracts eyes and ears. Otherwise no one will see their advertisement. Essentially, you owe your advertisers strong journalism.

You also owe them the truth about when you will publish their ad, where it will appear in the publication and what your circulation or audience numbers are. The circulation can be determined by the number of hits your online edition receives, the number of viewers or listeners of your broadcast, the number of papers you distribute (but you probably should not count any that remained stacked in the back of classrooms) or the number of magazines and yearbooks you sell.

If you design an ad, you owe your advertiser an accurate, legal and ethical ad. You need to make sure you do not illegally use an image or audio that is copyrighted or that implies someone pictured in the ad is endorsing the product. Ask the advertiser to get permission or get permission yourself before you include such images.

Figure 4.6 Publications owe their advertisers good service, but not influence over news and content. *How do you respond if an advertiser expects to influence your content?*

There are also many things you do not owe your advertisers. Your advertisers should not have control over your journalistic content (Figure 4.6). Remember that your audience's trust is your most important asset. If your audience suspects that advertising money has bought or sold news, you will lose their trust as well as their eyes and ears. Those eyes and ears are what your advertisers are paying for.

> *"Deny favored treatment to advertisers, donors or any other special interests, and resist internal and external pressure to influence coverage."*

A **firewall**, a figurative wall that protects journalists from influences that would harm their ability to act independently, must separate the business department and the rest of your publication or broadcast. The separation must be clear to your audience so that you can maintain their trust. Your advertisers should not influence what you cover or how you cover it. Your business department should never suggest to advertisers that they can influence coverage. If you do mention an advertiser in your journalistic coverage, you owe your audience full disclosure. If you are covering a link between sleep deprivation and obesity and quote a trainer at a nearby health club, let your audience know "South Coast Club is a sponsor of our morning broadcast."

> *"Distinguish news from advertising and shun hybrids that blur the lines between the two. Prominently label sponsored content."*

If an advertiser wants to place an ad that mimics a news item, they should clearly label it as advertising and ensure that it does not look or sound like your news coverage. Design elements such as the font should set an ad apart from your journalistic content. Your viewers and listeners should be able to tell immediately that they are listening to or reading an advertising segment, not news. Many broadcasts do not allow on-air journalists to read ads for this reason.

You, not the advertisers, determine what is acceptable in your publication or broadcast. It is a good idea to establish guidelines for advertising in your policies manual before a controversy arises. Do you accept ads (and paid dedications) that show a high school senior as a beautiful—and nude—baby? Will you accept ads for candidates for the school board? For restaurants that serve alcohol? From religious groups? For R-rated movies? For tattoo parlors? For tanning salons? Ads that contain hate speech? Though you cannot make all decisions in advance, your policy manual should clearly define your audience and provide you with guidance for making these ethical and business decisions.

What Do You Owe Your Publication and the Journalism Profession?

You owe it to your publication and to the profession of journalism as a whole to represent true and honest reporting in everything you write. Fabrication and plagiarism damage the profession of journalism and the public's trust in your publication. Never fabricate anything. Not a quotation. Not a source. Not a fact. Not an experience. Do not pretend to have talked with anyone, seen anything, attended anything, or tasted, smelled or heard anything that you did not. These fabrications betray the profession of journalism as well as the public's trust.

When a journalist betrays the public, he damages more than himself and his own credibility. He damages his publication, and he damages the profession of journalism. The publication or broadcast that employs him may need months or even years to regain the public's trust. Restoring trust usually includes the following:

- a full investigation into the extent of the violation. That means examining all the work the unethical journalist has done for that publication. His previous employers may also examine that journalist's work.
- an examination of how and why the ethical violation occurred
- scrutiny of the editors who allowed the unethical work to be published or broadcast
- a full and detailed report to the public of all those involved and all the stories, photos or broadcasts involved, which is published prominently in the same media where the ethical breaches occurred
- the firing or resignation of the journalist and perhaps the resignation of editors. It is doubtful that the offending journalist will ever work again in the profession of journalism or be admitted to any other profession that values the public's trust.

For the Record

Stephen Glass

Neville Elder/Corbis Historical/Getty Images

The movie "Shattered Glass" portrays Stephen Glass' career as a serial liar who wrote fiction and passed it off as journalism, managing to get his lies past the fact checkers and editors at several major magazines. A journalist at Forbes magazine uncovered his lies and brought them to the attention of Glass' editor at The New Republic. After conducting his own investigation, the editor fired Glass.

In the years following the end of his journalism career, Glass has earned a law degree and passed bar exams in at least two states, but he was refused a license to practice law in New York and California. The State Bar of California opposed his application, saying law and journalism "share common core values—trust, candor, veracity, honor, respect for others. He violated every one of them."

High school publications and broadcasts will need to follow a similar path to restore the public's trust if ethical breaches occur. Policies should clearly state what the consequences of a breach of ethics will be both for those responsible and for staff members who knew about it and did not report it. Consequences may include

- being stripped of leadership positions;
- losing the right to publish in the future;
- being dropped from the staff;
- being dropped from the class;
- a failing grade and unsatisfactory citizenship and work habits marks; and
- loss of high school honor society membership, including journalism honor societies such as Quill and Scroll.

Your Turn

1. One of your teachers, who was quoted in a sports feature story, tells you she was never interviewed for the piece. Another student claims he was misquoted. What should you do? What should your publication do? What should your adviser do?

(Continued)

YOUR TURN *(Continued)*

2. **Going Deeper.** What is your responsibility if you suspect that a fellow journalist on your publication is plagiarizing or making up information and passing it off as research? What is your responsibility if you suspect it is being done at a neighboring school? In the local press?

> *"Provide context. Take special care not to misrepresent or oversimplify in promoting, previewing or summarizing a story."*

Never knowingly distort the truth in what you write or put into a video, in a photograph, in how a photograph is cropped, in a quotation, in a chart or in a headline or tease.

> *"Never deliberately distort facts or context, including visual information. Clearly label illustrations and re-enactments."*

If you miss a photo opportunity, do not ask for a "do-over." Avoid staged photographs and rehearsed videos. If a staged photo is necessary—to show how to tie a necktie or pin a corsage, for example—make sure the audience knows it is staged.

> *"Never plagiarize. Always attribute."*

Do not steal another person's work and pass it off as your own. That is plagiarism, and plagiarism is a serious ethical violation, even though using words and research from someone else may not violate copyright law in all cases. Plagiarism is, however, easy to avoid.

The difference between plagiarism and honest use is **attribution**, or saying where you got information or a description. Give credit to the source. Use quotation marks so your reader knows what you wrote and what you are using from another's work. A good rule of thumb is to attribute all facts that you did not gather and verify yourself. Use quotation marks anytime you use more than three words of another person's prose.

Look at these paragraphs from the middle of an article about a garbage truck's collision with a wrong-way SUV on a nearby freeway.

> *According to the San Fernando Times, "the impact hurled dark green plastic garbage sacks down onto homes adjacent to the 22 Freeway like bombs. The sacks exploded on impact and spread trash across almost a half mile of the backyards on the north side of Elsie Street, which backs up to the freeway."*
>
> *Freshman Brandon Lyon returned home from school to find trash sticking to his parents' patio. He told La Voz Nueva, "It was disgusting. It was like someone had*

glued bits of trash bag and garbage—kitchen garbage, gardening waste, even dog droppings—onto our patio window and screen and the ceiling of the patio. Some of it I washed off with a garden hose on high pressure, but some of it didn't come off until my dad got a ladder and scraped it off."

Without those six little words "according to the San Fernando Times" and those two little quotation marks, the first paragraph of the story is plagiarized. With those little marks and the six words of attribution, the story is strong journalism, localizing a story from the professional media with vivid sources from the high school community.

If you discover that almost everything in your story is attributed to another source, you will need to find a local angle and do more reporting to generate original content. But do not try to trick your audience—or your editor, peers or adviser—into believing you have gone somewhere and interviewed someone when you have not. Do not pass off someone else's observation as your own. Using someone else's journalism and pretending that you did the interview or made the observation goes beyond plagiarism. It is lying.

Who Is Responsible for Guarding Against Ethical Breaches?

Extend

"Journalists should expose unethical conduct in journalism, including within their organizations.

They should abide by the same high standards they expect of others."

Who is responsible for guarding against ethical breaches? The short answer is this: Everyone is responsible, starting with the person gathering the news. The reporter must be both honest and well-informed about ethics and law. However, both ethics and law are too important to leave to just one person.

While all members of the journalist's community must guard the publication or broadcast's integrity, newsroom leaders have a *direct* responsibility to guard that integrity. These leaders are **gatekeepers**, that is, people who have the power to send a story back for additional work, who may alter it before it is broadcast or published or who may spike (or kill) a story, that is, withhold it from publication (Figure 4.7). These gatekeepers usually include the editor-in-chief, editorial board, content editors, copy editor and online editor.

Figure 4.7 The term "to spike" a story comes from an actual spike kept in the newsroom on which editors could place stories to be deleted.

Chapter Four

Review and Assessment

Recall Assess

1. What is the purpose of a code of ethics?
2. What is a journalist's—or a publication or broadcast's—most important asset?
3. Describe the ABCs of journalism and explain why they are important as foundations of journalistic ethics.
4. When is it acceptable to go undercover?
5. In what ways are high school students entitled to the protection journalists give juveniles? In what ways are they like adults?
6. What is the difference between granting anonymity to a source and using an anonymous source?
7. Under what conditions may you grant a source anonymity in your publication or broadcast? What are the hazards of doing so?
8. What legal issues should you keep in mind as you design ads for print or broadcast?
9. What are the consequences of plagiarism, both for the journalist and the publication?
10. Journalists must be able to distinguish between responsible and irresponsible media actions. Mark each of these statements as True, False or Sometimes. If your answer is "Sometimes," explain why.
    A. It is acceptable to promise that you will publish something in exchange for information.
    B. It is acceptable to read a quotation back to a source for review.
    C. It is acceptable to give your source a copy of the story before it is published.
    D. It is acceptable to tell someone if he or a loved one will be in the news before the news is broadcast.
    E. You may publish advertising that looks or sounds like a news story in your publication or broadcast.
    F. You do not need to attribute facts.

Critical Thinking

1. Look again at the ethical dilemmas described on page 5. For each situation, consider the foundation of journalistic ethics and determine which sections of the SPJ Code of Ethics or which principles in this chapter you would use to make a decision and defend your position.
2. Create a list of 10 fictional scenarios, five of which represent responsible media action and five of which represent irresponsible media action. Exchange your list with a classmate. Identify which scenarios demonstrate responsible and irresponsible media actions.

Application

1. Go to a website such as the Committee to Protect Journalists and research one journalist who was jailed for his or her journalism in the past 18 months. Create a report to present to your peers.
2. Locate a retraction or correction from three different media, including the medium in which you expect to publish or broadcast. What are the strengths and weaknesses of each retraction or correction?
3. Create a checklist of local "words that injure," that is, words that are used on your campus that are biased or sexist and should be avoided by your publication.
4. Use a successful story you have published or broadcast to create a display board that shows your newsroom's story flow. Include all steps, from the story idea to the final product. Include the story assignment, background notes, pages from a reporter's notebook, sketches of the story, drafts and revisions of the text as the writer received responses from peers, counsel from the content editor and suggestions from the copy editor.
5. Exchange a story you have written with one of your classmate's. Copy edit each other's work using proofreading marks. Be sure to identify any passages that you feel would benefit from revising or rewriting. What did you learn from this exercise?

Chapter Four

Journalism Style

Composition Titles

Each time you refer to a composition—something a person wrote, programmed, filmed or created artistically—you need to indicate to your audience that it is a composition. This is frequently done by putting the composition's title within quotation marks and capitalizing the important words.

Quotation Marks

Most journalistic publications use quotation marks, not italics or underlining, to enclose the titles of books, computer games, movies, plays, poems, songs and albums, television programs and episodes, speeches and paintings.

- "The White Album" by the Beatles
- "Mona Lisa" by Leonardo da Vinci
- "Tetris" by Alexey Pajitnov

But do not use quotation marks or any other punctuation when writing about these:

Exceptions—No Quotation Marks Around These	
Names of sacred books—Bible, Tanakh, Quran, Book of Mormon	Standard reference books—Encyclopedia Britannica, American Heritage Dictionary, National Geographic Atlas of the World
Names of magazines and newspapers—The New York Times, People	Handbooks and textbooks—Diagnostic and Statistical Manual of Mental Disorders
Software titles—Windows Vista, InDesign, Photoshop	Names of websites—Creative Commons, Google

Try It!

Which of these composition titles require quotation marks? Write those titles on a separate piece of paper. Punctuate as necessary.

1. The Wizard of Oz (the movie)
2. Merriam-Webster's Collegiate Dictionary
3. Microsoft Office Excel (computer program)
4. Led Zeppelin (band)
5. Stairway to Heaven (album)
6. Newsweek (magazine)
7. Super Mario Bros. Deluxe (computer game)
8. I Have a Dream (speech)

Capitalization

Always capitalize the principal words of a title: nouns, pronouns, verbs, adjectives and adverbs.

Always capitalize the first and last words.

But unless they are the first or last word of the title, do not capitalize articles (the words *a*, *an* and *the*).

- "The Hobbit" but "To the Lighthouse"

Conjunctions of three letters or fewer are not capitalized unless they are the first or last word of a title.

- "And Then There Were Three" but "Franny and Zooey"
- "As the World Turns" but "Gently as a Dove"

Prepositions of three letters or fewer are not capitalized unless they are the first or last word of a title.

- "Of Mice and Men" but "Anne of Green Gables"
- "Gone With the Wind"

The word *the* is not always part of the title, nor is the word *show*.

- I read it in the Los Angeles Times. (Remember, names of newspapers are not enclosed in quotation marks.)
- He hopes to report for The New York Times.
- He spent his summer watching "The Simpsons," the "Today" show and "The Tonight Show."

If in doubt, check the masthead of the paper, the composition's Web page (which *may* be helpful) or how The New York Times prints it.

Try It!

Some of these titles are incorrectly capitalized. Write the correct version on a separate sheet of paper.

1. Crime and Punishment
2. One for his Lordship, and one for the Road
3. A Child is Born
4. Nothin' But Good Times Ahead
5. Much Ado about Nothing

Extend Your Knowledge Style Exercises

Visit the *Journalism* website to find out where to put the punctuation when you are using quotation marks. Also, learn how composition titles are treated in a headline.

Chapter Four

Writers' Workshop

In this Writers' Workshop you will:

- Learn to recognize and avoid forms of *to be* verbs.
- Learn to recognize passive constructions and use them sparingly.

Your words, phrases and sentences should impel your audience forward as surely as strong wind propels a sailing craft. For example:

> Sailing craft slice through water as graceful as sea birds, their sails arced full of the propelling air. But when all wind dies, the craft wallows at the mercy of the sea, its sails empty and sagging, its rudder useless. It is becalmed.

This Writers' Workshop focuses on avoiding the verb *to be*, which lacks almost all forward momentum and risks becalming your writing—at which point, your audience may abandon ship!

Workshop 4.1

Put Your Writing on a *To Be*-Free Diet

Though strong writers do sometimes use *to be* verbs—and they are almost indispensable when you are asking questions—in this Writers' Workshop you will avoid any form of *to be*.

Mini-Lesson: If the To Be *Verb Joins Two Nouns*

Sometimes a *to be* verb joins two nouns in a sentence: *Their mascot is a chubby bear. He jiggles his tummy and dances on the sidelines*. (15 words) You can use *to be*-free substitutes to combine these two sentences.

***To be*-free substitutes**:

- Use an appositive: *Their mascot, a chubby bear, jiggles his tummy and dances on the sidelines.* (13 words)
- Use an adjective: *Their chubby bear mascot jiggles his tummy and dances on the sidelines.* (12 words)

A noun phrase following a *to be* verb may be long or complex: *Eileen Collins was the first female space shuttle commander and has logged 38 days, 8 hours and 10 minutes in outer space. She will speak in the amphitheater at noon Thursday.* (31 words) A *to be*-free substitute may use both an appositive and a subordinate clause.

***To be*-free substitute**:

- *Eileen Collins, the first female space shuttle commander, who logged 38 days, 8 hours and 10 minutes in outer space, will speak in the amphitheater at noon Thursday.* (28 words)

Apply It!

Working with a partner, create several sets of two sentences in which the first uses a *to be* verb. Rewrite them, combining the first sentence with the second and eliminating the *to be* verb. Include at least one *to be*-free sentence that uses an appositive, one that uses an adjective, and one that includes both an appositive and a subordinate clause.

Mini-Lesson: If the To Be *Verb Joins a Noun and an Adjective*

When *to be* verbs join a noun and an adjective, use any of the techniques that work in the examples above—appositives, adjectives and subordinate clauses. In addition, you may use noun phrases.

Example: *Students are lethargic after lunch. They doze during fifth period.* (10 words)

***To be*-free substitutes:**

- Use a noun phrase: *Students, lethargic after lunch, doze during fifth period.* (8 words)
- If the two sentences do not have the same subject, then writers need a little more agility. *Students are already lethargic after lunch. Hot classrooms make them sleepy during fifth period* (14 words) In this case, writers can use a noun phrase: *Hot classrooms make students, already lethargic after lunch, sleepy during fifth period.* (12 words)
- Auxiliary verbs plus *to be* verbs pose additional challenges. *Spring can be a depressing season for some people. Calls to the Melrose County Suicide Prevention Hotline spike in late March and April.* (23 words) The *to be*-free substitute could include an appositive: *Spring, a depressing season for some, brings a spike in calls to the Melrose County Suicide Prevention Hotline.* (18 words)

Apply It!

With a partner, create a variety of sentence pairs where one of the sentences includes a *to be* verb joining a noun to an adjective or a noun to a noun. Trade your sentences with another group, then rewrite both your sentence pairs and theirs as *to be*-free sentences. Read them aloud and compare methods. Ask your response group which versions are clearer. Which have the most momentum?

Mini-Lesson: If the To Be *Verb Forms Part of a Progressive Tense*

When a *to be* verb is part of a progressive form (*She is running the club*), use the simple form of the verb instead (*She runs the club*). Though the progressive form is sometimes better (*is running for office*, for instance, as opposed to *runs for office*), it often is longer and likely to bog down your sentence. Compare the length of these sentences with simple verbs with the sentences that contain the verb's progressive form.

With *To Be*	Without *To Be*
She is avoiding all her ex-boyfriends.	She avoids all her ex-boyfriends.
He was texting her all evening.	He texted her all evening.
She has been wearing makeup since she was 12.	She has worn makeup since she was 12.

Apply It!

Highlight progressive verb forms in a student publication, either your own or from another school. (Present progressive verbs are a mainstay of breaking news leads. You probably will not be able to eliminate them from leads, so look for sentences further into the story.) Rewrite these sentences with the simple form of the verb in the same tense. Which progressive forms were necessary to convey meaning and which ones could be rewritten using the simple form of the verb? Discuss your conclusions with your response group.

Mini-Lesson: If the To Be *Verb Uses Passive Voice*

Passive forms focus on what happened to someone or something, not on who did it. Sometimes this is appropriate: *President John F. Kennedy was assassinated this morning.*

However, passive sentences often make for awkward writing. Compare the passive and the active versions of these sentences.

Passive	Active
All the glories of an early Pacific sunset were enjoyed.	Prom-goers enjoyed all the glories of the early Pacific sunset.
When he is talking to me, I learn a great deal.	When I talk with him, I learn a great deal.
With fewer games and shorter practice hours, academic subjects could be kept up and we would not have to cram so hard for finals.	With fewer games and shorter practices, we could keep up with our classes and not need to cram for finals.

Apply It!

1. Locate at least six passive constructions among the *to be* sentences in professional publications. Within your group, make sure everyone can identify passive constructions.
2. Look in a student publication for passive constructions. Are they more or less common than in the professional press? Is the passive form the best form in some or all of these sentences? Explain why.

Extend Your Knowledge Extend

Visit the *Journalism* website for the following:

1. Learn to identify *to be* verbs in all their forms.
2. Practice changing passive voice to active voice.

Chapter Five

Writing Breaking News and Developing Stories

Is it timely?

G-WLEARNING.COM

While studying, look for the activity icon to:

- **Build** vocabulary terms with e-flash cards and matching activities.
- **Extend** learning with further discussion of relevant topics.
- **Reinforce** what you learn by completing style exercises, worksheets and end-of-chapter questions.

Visit the Journalism website: www.g-wlearning.com/journalism/

Chapter Objectives

After reading this chapter, you will be able to:

- Name the five W's and use each of them.
- Identify special considerations when writing the *why* of a news story.
- Identify and discuss breaking news and developing stories.
- Tell how the news cycle influences how a story is covered.
- Identify and use inverted pyramid form.
- Identify journalists' function as gatekeepers.
- Use the questions the audience would ask as you report.
- Explain why it is important to avoid editorializing.
- Identify steps necessary to maintain accuracy in breaking and developing news stories.

Key Terms Build Vocab

add value
breaking news story
dateline
developing story
editorializing
five W's
five W's lead
folo story
hard news
inverted pyramid
jump line
lead
signature line
soft news
summary lead
tag

Before You Read...

Strong listening skills are critical for a journalist. *Informative listening* is used when specific information or instructions are needed. Ask a classmate to give you directions on how to find the school cafeteria. Take notes as the directions are given. If necessary, ask the person to slow down or repeat a step. Summarize your notes and retell the directions to your classmate to confirm your understanding. Use your prior knowledge of the school's layout to follow the directions you were given.

Introduction

"Literature is the art of writing something that will be read twice; journalism, what will be grasped at once ..."

–Cyril Connolly, English author, editor and critic

Nora Ephron (Figure 5.1) fell in love with journalism in high school. The American journalist, essayist, playwright, screenwriter (she was nominated for three Oscars), novelist, producer, director and blogger told about her first day in journalism class:

> *The teacher who changed my life was my journalism teacher, whose name was Charles Simms. ... I had already decided that I was going to be a journalist. I didn't know why exactly, except that I had seen a lot of Superman comics. Lois Lane and all of those major literary characters like that, but Mr. Simms got up the first day of class, and he went to the blackboard, and he wrote "Who, what, where, why, when, and how," which are the six things that have to be in the lead of any newspaper story. Then he did what most journalism teachers do, which is that he dictated a set of facts to us, and then we were all meant to write the lead that was supposed to have "who, what, where, why, when, and how" in it.*
>
> *He dictated a set of facts that went something like, "The principal of Beverly Hills High School announced today that the faculty of the high school will travel to Sacramento, Thursday, for a colloquium in new teaching methods. Speaking there will be Margaret Mead, the anthropologist, and two other people." So we all sat down at our typewriters, and we all kind of inverted that and wrote, "Margaret Mead and X and Y will address the faculty in Sacramento, Thursday, at a colloquium on new teaching methods, the principal announced today." Something like that.*
>
> *We were very proud of ourselves, and we gave it to Mr. Simms, and he just riffled through them and tore them into tiny bits and threw them in the trash, and he said, "The lead to this story is: There will be no school Thursday!" and it was this great epiphany moment for me. It was this, "Oh my God, it is about the point! It is about figuring out what the point is." And I just fell in love with journalism at that moment.*

Figure 5.1 Journalist Nora Ephron was nominated three times for the Academy Award for Best Writing. Her nominated screenplays were for the movies "Silkwood," "When Harry Met Sally" and "Sleepless in Seattle."

A Journalist's Job

Ephron was right. A journalist's job is to figure out the point, and not just any point, but the point that her audience, in this case, the students of Beverly Hills High School, needs or wants to hear. Finding the *so what* is the heart of a journalist's job.

The *so what* of Ephron's story would have been different if her audience had been Sacramento taxi drivers, car rental agencies, and restaurant and hotel owners. The lead to that story might have been *Seventeen thousand California teachers will descend on Sacramento Wednesday evening for meetings Thursday in the capitol rotunda. Their arrival will place unusual demands on the hospitality industry.*

Although Ephron's journalism teacher put six things on the board, most journalists today talk about the **five W's**—who, what, when, where and why. (You will learn about the sixth term, *how*, later in the chapter.) The five W's dominate breaking news stories. A **breaking news story** communicates new information about unexpected events as they occur or shortly afterward. In such stories, the opening sentences (the **lead**, also spelled lede) convey the five W's—who, what, when, where and why—or as much of that information as is available. The rest of a breaking news story is told in **inverted pyramid** form, with the most important information first and less important items toward the bottom of the story.

Developing stories relate new information about a breaking story as it becomes available. These developing stories may also be called **folo stories**, or follow-up, stories. Like breaking news stories, developing stories use **five W's leads**, which are also called **summary leads**. The new information is placed at the top of the story, with a new headline. As more information becomes available, the information from the update is put above the previous summary lead or folded into it. Sometimes—but not always—the freshest information is near the top of the pyramid. Other times it will be placed appropriately within the inverted pyramid.

Your News Cycle

Your news cycle (the amount of time between the publication or broadcast of one edition and the next edition) may influence the type of story you write, even more than the content of the story. It may also influence the journalistic format you choose to present your content.

For instance, suppose the principal announces at a faculty meeting that the band teacher will be moving to the district office to become the fine arts administrator. You have a breaking news story if you microblog or post to a website that has an RSS feed to most of your audience. Your publication can be the first to deliver the news, as it breaks. On your website, you can publish a more complete story starting with a five W's lead and using inverted pyramid form to relate new information and its implications.

If you broadcast the story the next morning, many students may have already heard the news. It is now a developing story. Reactions from students and alumni could add to the original breaking news. Your audience will expect you to answer their questions and thus **add value** to the five W's

For the Record

Why the Funny Spelling?

When news was transmitted by telegraph, one letter at a time, journalists needed a way to distinguish copy—the actual words meant to appear in a newspaper—from the instructions to the editor. So if a reporter wanted a new lead, but did not want the editor to print that there was a new lead in the crime story, he would write *New lede*.

Other odd spellings used to mark instructions to the editor include

- hed for headline;
- dek for deck (another term for headline);
- graf for paragraph; and
- tk for "more to come."

The reporter would also mark the end of the story with *30* or *###.* No one knows why.

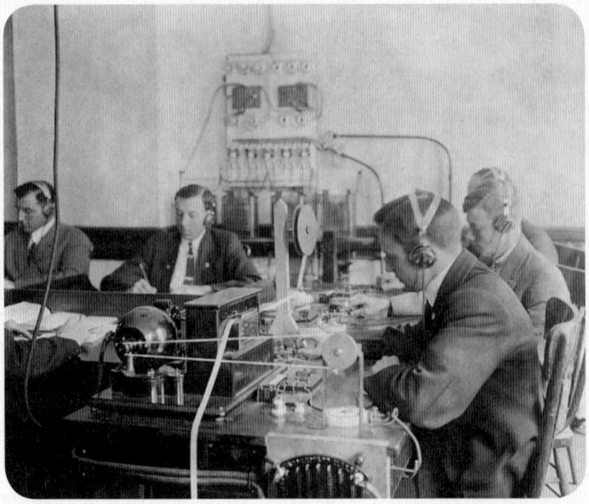

lead. If the breaking news lead was *Band director Stacy Harris will leave HTHS this July to become fine arts administrator for the district*, your audience may want to know:

- Will someone else in the district replace her as band director?
- Will her student teacher be considered for the position?
- How will they choose the person to direct the band?
- Will we still have band camp?
- Will the class schedule change?
- Who gets to choose the new director?

As a reporter, you will ask these questions for your audience. You may not learn much. Your principal may say only that her replacement will be chosen this summer, but at least your audience will know they have all the information that is available. *"A committee will be formed this June to interview candidates for the position," principal Hardy Goodfellow said.*

If you have a longer news cycle—for instance, if you publish a weekly newsmagazine—you can add value to the basic information your audience already received by giving a context for the move. It is no longer a breaking or developing news story. It has become general news and will be stale (out of date) if you try to handle it as a breaking news story. (Stale news, like stale food, is not appetizing.)

In general, the shorter your news cycle, the more often you will report breaking news. The longer your news cycle, the more often you will produce general news or feature content.

Your Turn

1. Identify the news cycle of the student news outlets for which you write. Examine three past issues or broadcasts. How many breaking news or developing news stories are in the three editions? Should there be more or fewer, based on your news cycle?
2. **Going Deeper.** How can you add another form of media to increase your opportunities to cover breaking news?

For the Record

Hard and Soft: Not Just Two Ways to Boil an Egg

Journalists and people who talk about or teach journalism need words to describe journalism and how it is done. But no two days are exactly the same for a journalist, no two stories demand exactly the same treatment, no two audiences or two forms of media need and want the same news presented in the same manner. So the labels we use to describe stories are helpful, but they are never fully accurate.

Hard and soft news are labels used by sociologist Gaye Tuchman in 1973, though the expressions had been used in journalism classes and newsrooms long before that. In this system, **hard news** was about politics, economics, war, fires, earthquakes or murders. **Soft news** was about entertainment, fashion, celebrities, human interest stories, tourism and unusual or odd events.

Hard news was timely. It needed to be covered immediately—as it happened, if possible. Soft news—the 10th anniversary of your school's mascot or fight song, for instance—could be prepared days or even weeks ahead and was often placed near the end of the broadcast or in its own section of the paper. Soft news could be shortened or published a day later than planned, if breaking hard news demanded more space in the paper. If there was a bank robbery or a fire, the soft article about the couple who had been married 75 years could wait for the next edition.

The prejudice seems to be that hard news was real news while soft news was for fluffier minds. (The categories we create often tell more about us than they do about journalism.) A quick glance at publications or broadcasts in 1973—and today—shows that large numbers of the stories do not fit in either category. For instance not all entertainment stories are soft or fluffy—a 1988 strike in the entertainment industry cost Californians $500 million. Not all war stories are hard news—stories that follow the rehabilitation of a 5-year-old Afghan boy who lost his leg in a mortar attack also defy this category system.

Hard or soft are not the only ways to sort the news. Other researchers rated stories from 1 to 7, with 7 being the hardest news (a declaration of war, for instance) and a 1 being a story about the design of a celebrity's wedding dress.

In 2010 researchers suggested that the category general news join hard news and soft news. A general news story does not need to be reported immediately, but it is important. For instance, if a recent report says 57 percent of graduates from your high school who enrolled in community colleges dropped out by December, you have a general news story. It is important in all the ways hard news stories are important, but it does not demand immediate attention.

Your publication or broadcast will have its own mix of hard, general and soft news stories. Indeed, many feature stories could be classified as soft news because they are triggered by an event.

YOUR TURN

1. Examine a recent issue, Web page or broadcast from student media. First identify the news stories (as opposed to features, reviews, columns and opinion pieces). Which news stories are hard news? Which are general news? Soft news? How many fit in each category?

   Now look at the news coverage of two professional news publications: broadcast, print newspaper, print newsmagazine or web publication. Which news stories are hard news? Which are general news? Which are soft? How many fit in each category?
2. **Going Deeper.** Count the number of stories that are hard news or breaking news and the number of stories that are soft news or general news in several publications in at least three formats, such as Web-based news, broadcast news, newspapers, newsmagazines or microblogs such as Twitter. Which has the highest percentage of hard news or breaking news? You may wish to work with a partner or small group.

   Share your findings and draw preliminary conclusions:
   - Which medium is most likely to provide space for soft news?
   - For general news?
   - Does every news organization need hard news to engage its audience?

Five W's Leads

Each element of a five W's story is crucial for a journalist. If you have not carefully and accurately answered each one of them—checking people's job titles and name spellings and dates as you report the story—you have not finished reporting the story. Indeed, the five W's are the hallmark of good reporting.

You *do* need these five pieces of information in breaking stories, though the pressure of deadlines and the rush to inform your audience may force you to publish before all information is available. You may broadcast when the *who* is still unknown, but you must indicate that you made an effort to get that information. This information simply may not be available: *The names of those still stranded on the damaged ski lift have not been released*. This is quite different from saying: *I haven't bothered to ask who the stranded skiers are.*

You may report before the *why* has been determined. *The cause of the damage to the gondola is under investigation*. This says you have asked about a cause and officials have said, "We are still investigating the cause. But right now, the safety of those people is our first concern." (That quotation may be useful later in the story.) This is quite different from implying, "I was in such a hurry to push Send that I didn't think about why it happened."

The five W's—all of them—help define what journalism is and separate journalists from many other observers. In addition, journalists seek the most reliable version of each of the five W's from credible sources. They are suspicious of—and do not report—"what everyone is saying."

They rely on specific sources—the police, the mountain search and rescue captain, a skier who had just left the gondola before it stopped. They also tell their audience when part of the information is not available instead of guessing or repeating gossip as fact.

Journalists need to guard against guessing, especially on the air or in breaking news in print. It is a strong human impulse to want to make sense of what we see, but once we have attached ourselves to an explanation, we may be unable to observe or report facts that do not agree with our assumption. Learn to write what the facts *are*. Be slow to tell your audience what the facts *mean* (Figure 5.2).

As the story develops, you may consider reporting what credible observers and officials think, but those opinions must be clearly labeled so that your audience will know you are documenting the speculation, not necessarily providing the facts. *Officials believe that as many as 28 people may be on the lifts. Police have not ruled out sabotage. A summertime fire in the 9,000 foot warming hut was allegedly linked to a disgruntled former employee, though no charges were ever filed, a police spokesman said.*

Solid reporting gives you reliable information for each of the five W's. But gathering that information is just a starting point for a journalist. There are many decisions left to be made. As Nora Ephron pointed out when she wrote about her teacher Charles Simms, the journalist's job is to figure out the *so what* for the audience and craft the lead so the audience sees what the point is for them. When you write a five W's lead, you find and use the most active, interesting version of the *who, what, when, where* and *why* that the story and your media allow.

Who

The *who* in a lead can be who did it—this one is usually the strongest. It can also be who had it done to them, or who reported it. The *who* is underlined in each of the following five W's leads.

> *Band director Stacy Harris will leave HTHS this July to become fine arts administrator for the district.*

Figure 5.2 When she unpacks her groceries, Irmatrude might assume she forgot to buy sausage. However, the first explanation is not always the best.

For the Record

What's All the Fuss About Leads?

If your lead is not strong, nothing else you write matters. If it is not clear and inviting, if it does not invite your audience to click, scroll down, read the next paragraph or keep listening, then no one will see the rest of your work.

If your lead is weak, your audience will move on before they get to the next paragraph. Only your grandmother will read to the end. A strong lead anchors the whole article. Though a well-crafted lead looks like it was easy to write, leads require solid reporting, clear writing and a great deal of rewriting. But good leads are worth all the work.

Some thought we had seen the end of the five W's toward the end of the last millennium (1996, for instance). Narrative leads (leads with anecdotes and dialogue, controversial statements, action and telling details) were replacing five W's leads across most sections of the newspapers and in many newsmagazines. Everyone loves a story, and those leads promise stories. Narrative leads infiltrated the front page of major newspapers. News broadcasts sounded more like neighbors talking and less like authoritative sources of the five W's.

What changed? We did, when we went online.

Online we discovered a flood of information that now seems as natural as air and water. While we once waited for the news on TV, on the radio or in the paper, we now are awash in more information—and disinformation—than we can hope to digest.

We need to know which sources will give us information we want. We want the most important part of the story first, so we can stop reading when we lose interest without missing the crux of the matter. We want efficiency.

We want journalists to become gatekeepers again, the people who pick and choose from among all the data, stories, statements and information available and who present to us what they think is most important. We want them to make sense of all the data and the many opinions we hear. We want them to find the facts. We want them to help us decide what we should be worrying about and talking about and keeping an eye on. And of course we want to gripe about what they do and how they do it.

Five W's leads and the inverted pyramid do all these things. The five W's and the inverted pyramid have made a comeback in Web-based journalism and in print publications that write for people immersed in the Web. Some have said that journalism is the new English, and all modern people need to learn to write as journalists do.

Wombats, playing without five players who were detained by Harbor police earlier in the day on suspicion of drug possession, lost to Lobos 57-0 at Pioneer Stadium Friday.

Community college tuition will increase 25 percent next fall if the November ballot measure 101 is not passed, according to a report issued Wednesday by the Government Accounting Office.

Unless all your audience will immediately recognize the name of the *who* in your sentence (Stacy Harris, for instance), put an identifier before her name: *band director Stacy Harris.* (Identifiers do not need capitals; only titles do.)

If the name is not familiar to most of your audience and not important to your story, consider moving the name out of the lead. Replace it with an identifier: *A scientist at the Jet Propulsion Laboratory said* ... or *a cafeteria worker was injured* or *a 2013 alum donated*. This works well for plural nouns, too: *Maintenance workers pulled bleachers from the swimming pool Monday morning after vandals broke into the pool area over the weekend.*

If the identifier is in the first paragraph, the name may belong in the second paragraph, as in this second graf: *Head custodian Richard Wright and his assistant Eugene Campobello tied ropes on the partially submerged bleachers and lifted them out with the help of a backhoe that was positioned on the other side of the pool wall.*

People love to read about themselves and their experiences. Whenever possible, make the *who* about your audience. Tell them how the story relates to them.

> *Lobos will be left out in the cold starting December 10 as the district closes the gym to refinish the floors in preparation for the state basketball championship to be held here January 4.*

> *Matadors will break in another band director, their third in less than three years, when band teacher Stacy Harris moves to the district office this June.*

What

Use active, strong verbs to tell what happened—or better yet, what is happening or will happen.

> *The varsity Wombats <u>lost</u> to Lobos 57-0. (*not *were beaten by)*

> *Half of all HTHS graduates <u>abandon</u> community college by Christmas, according to data published on the state Department of Education website. (*not *do not* or *did not finish their first semester)*

> *Band director Stacy Harris <u>will leave</u> HTHS this July to become fine arts administrator for the district. (*not *has been appointed* or *is leaving)*

Find a future angle to a story if possible. A dull lead, in the past tense, may do little more than repeat the information everyone heard over the public address system during sixth period.

> *Senior Angela Suarez was elected homecoming queen in noontime elections Wednesday, according to Associated Student Body president Fernando Lim.*

A stronger lead finds a future angle:

Homecoming Queen Angela Suarez will perch on the back seat of a red 1957 Corvette as she enters Vernal Stadium with her court at halftime Friday night.

When

The *when* can be the star of a lead: *Flood waters will crest at noon Thursday*. More often it is a supporting element, providing context for a story. But context is essential, so *when* must not be left out, even when it does not star.

If your media allow instantaneous postings or broadcasts from the scene, the present tense is compelling.

Paramedics are loading referee Schnurr Bart into an ambulance after an on-field collision with members of the visiting team.

A moment later, you may be able to add more information, which of course would appear above your earlier message if you are microblogging but would appear below it if an online editor is posting your reports.

Bart is on a stretcher, wearing a white plastic cervical collar from his ears to his shoulders, but he is waving at the players.

Filmed footage or sound bites may use the present tense even through the film is hours old.

Flames are licking at the trees surrounding this Wildwood home above Lake Ediza. Firefighters were able to save the structure.

For most media, the strongest *when* is in the future—and the future tense.

The cafeteria <u>will be</u> shuttered <u>every Friday beginning in January</u> to save money, school district public affairs spokesman Mo Peace said after Tuesday's school board meeting. Cold box lunches prepared at the main district kitchens <u>will be</u> distributed from the food carts.

If a future tense angle on the story does not work, the more recent the past tense, the better. In this story from the Los Angeles Times, one element happened more than five billion years ago; one element, the research, happened in the last five years; and one happened that day, Wednesday, when an online scientific journal published the results of the research. The time element focuses on Wednesday and the astronomer who was interviewed Wednesday.

> *A newly discovered cluster of galaxies, more than 5 billion light years from Earth, creates new stars at an "unmatched" pace of more than 700 per year, said Michael McDonald, a Hubble fellow at MIT and lead author of a paper detailing the cluster's properties, published online Wednesday in the journal Nature.*

In your story, avoid *today, tonight* or *tomorrow* except in a direct quotation. *Flood waters will crest shortly before dawn Thursday* is more precise than *"Flood waters will crest tomorrow," Mayor Noah Mark said*. Your readers may pick up your story on Friday and expect the flood waters to crest on Saturday.

The Los Angeles Times article on the productive galaxies was published Wednesday, August 15, 2012. The online journal Nature also published the story on August 15, 2012, probably shortly after midnight, but the news article uses *Wednesday*, rather than *today* or *August 15, 2012.*

Where

Where, like *when*, may be the star of the lead, or it may play an essential but supporting role. A hurricane warning for another state is clearly different from one for your school attendance area. The location makes all the difference. In some stories the *where* is so important that a map accompanies the story, such as this one about a collapsed roadway (Figure 5.3).

Where is essential to provide context, whether it stars in the story or not. The words indicating *where* are underlined in the following leads.

> *Russian activists have sued Madonna for millions of dollars, claiming they were offended by her support for gay rights during a recent concert in St. Petersburg. (tweeted by NPR, National Public Radio)*

> *The Zoological Park in Cuba's capital, Havana, is busy preparing for a delivery that it hopes will transform its fortunes: 146 wild animals, donated by the government of Namibia. (broadcast by the BBC, British Broadcasting Corporation)*

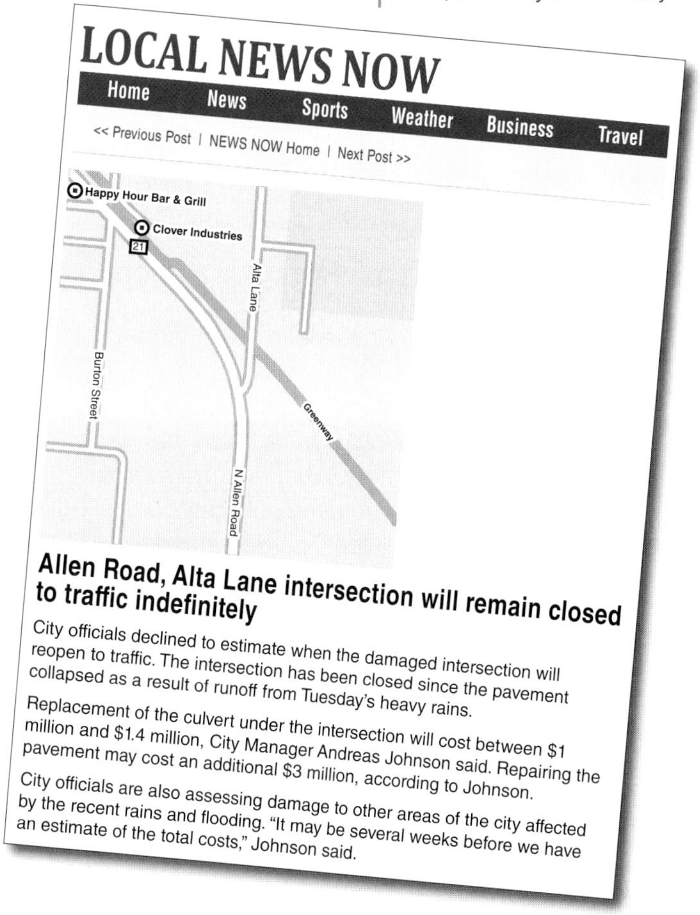

Allen Road, Alta Lane intersection will remain closed to traffic indefinitely

City officials declined to estimate when the damaged intersection will reopen to traffic. The intersection has been closed since the pavement collapsed as a result of runoff from Tuesday's heavy rains.

Replacement of the culvert under the intersection will cost between $1 million and $1.4 million, City Manager Andreas Johnson said. Repairing the pavement may cost an additional $3 million, according to Johnson.

City officials are also assessing damage to other areas of the city affected by the recent rains and flooding. "It may be several weeks before we have an estimate of the total costs," Johnson said.

Figure 5.3 Even if it is not the star of the lead, the where of a story is often a critical component. *Can you identify the* who, what, when, *and* why *in this story?*

SACRAMENTO—California farmworkers would receive the same overtime pay benefits enjoyed by workers in other industries under a measure approved by the state Senate on Monday and sent to Gov. Jerry Brown. (Los Angeles Times)

In this story, the where is indicated by the capitalized dateline, SACRAMENTO, placed after the headline and byline and before the text.

Why

The *why* is important to readers. We hunger for explanations. We want to understand, we want to judge (and complain), we want assurance that the same trouble will not strike us. Though essential, *why* may be the most difficult to determine, especially in breaking news.

The *why* may tell the purpose of an act, the cause of an act or simply how we know about the act. The *why* element in each of the following news leads is underlined. Without the *why*, the leads are considerably less interesting.

Band director Stacy Harris will leave HTHS this July to become fine arts administrator for the district.

Wombats, playing without five players who were detained by Harbor police earlier in the day on suspicion of drug possession, lost to the Lobos 57-0 at Pioneer Stadium.

Datelines, Signature Lines and Tags

In the lead about farm-worker protection legislation, SACRAMENTO in all caps is the **dateline**, the place from which the reporter filed the story. When reporters write or record their stories from the publication's home, no dateline is listed. The Sacramento Bee carried a similar story but used no dateline, since Sacramento is the publication's home.

If a reporter from a Los Angeles paper had written the story from Los Angeles, she would have had to indicate in the lead where the story took place but would have used no dateline.

In broadcasts, on-air reporters may follow the same pattern in their **signature lines** or **tags** (their identification at the end of their report). When a reporter is filing a story from the station's base location, the sign-off is probably something like this: "Ruxandra Guidi, 89.3, KPCC." But when the reporter is on the scene of the news event, his sign-off may include "John Burnett, National Public Radio, South Sudan," or the host of the show may close with "That is NPR's John Burnett. He has been reporting from South Sudan."

Oddly enough, datelines almost always tell the place but not always the date. Other publications may include both the date and the source, such as the Associated Press wire service. The dateline might look like this:

SACRAMENTO (AP) June 15

> *Community college tuition will increase 25 percent next fall if the November ballot measure 101 is not passed, according to a report issued by the Government Accounting Office.*

> *Lobos will be left out in the cold starting December 10 as the district closes the gym to refinish the floors in preparation for the state basketball championship to be held here January 4.*

Sometimes the *why* is hard to determine and the best the lead can do is give the source of the information.

> *Half of all HTHS graduates abandon community college by Christmas according to data published on the state Department of Education website.*

A longer news article could look at possible explanations. (See Chapters 8 and 9 for more about research.) Later you may research past statistics, create a timeline and ask educators at the colleges for possible explanations. But if you are reporting on deadline and the data from the website does not give an explanation, it is better simply to credit a source for the information than to give a *why* that is only speculation.

What Happened to *How*?

Some stories have five W's plus an H for *how*. The *how* may be essential for some stories, even breaking news stories. How did the people survive the flood? On the roof of a school bus. How did we lose the game? Our starting forward was injured in the first four minutes of play.

In other stories the *how* may require more information than is available as a story breaks. The cause may be still under investigation. Your audience will need to wait until more is known. For instance, if you report a robbery from a well-guarded and securely locked art museum, your audience will want you to solve the mystery for them. *How* was the theft accomplished? But that information may simply be unavailable as yet.

If you let your audience know the *how* is still unknown, and if you broadcast or publish frequently or you update stories on your site, your audience may check back with you to see if you now can tell them the *how*, creating traffic to your media.

How also tells how something went wrong and may be part of a breaking or developing story, such as how a car skidded on the ice or how the soccer team lost to the worst team in the league.

How sometimes tells how breaking news was revealed—by an investigation your publication did, by a criminal's confession or by the release of statistics.

But *how* is not in every breaking news story or even every developing one. Its place may be in general news or in features where *how* may be the point of a story: How does a blind man photograph hummingbirds? How do the fire sprinklers in the chemistry lab's ceiling know when to spray water?

In breaking news the *how* may also be implied by one of the W's, such as the *what—The family survived the flood* *by clinging to a capsized boat for two hours.*

Sometimes *how* is just omitted.

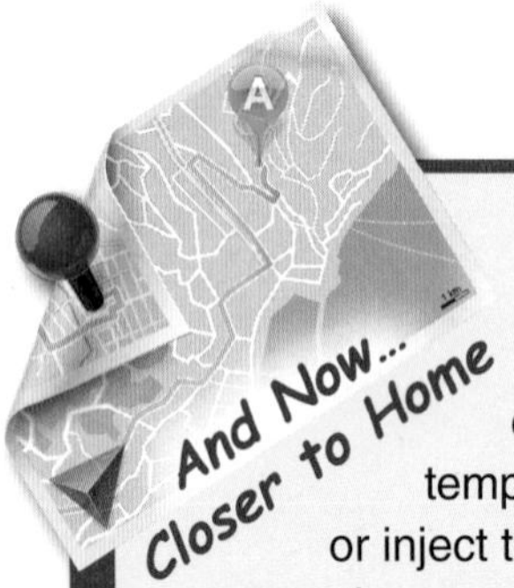

Why Not to Have *Why*

More than any other element of the five W's, *why* tempts journalists to speculate or inject their own opinions. Careful reporting, careful thinking, and careful writing and rewriting of the *why* element are hallmarks of sound journalism. Breaking news often does not give the reporter time to report, think, and write and rewrite well.

Journalists avoid jumping to conclusions. They rarely say one thing *causes* another. Rather, they say that one act *follows* another. Avoid saying: *Two freshmen attempted suicide because of a fight with three other girls on Facebook*. If strong evidence tends to link the fight and the attempted suicides, the ethical way to report it would be to write: *Two freshmen attempted suicide following a fight with three other girls on Facebook.*

It is almost impossible to assign a single cause to any result, even simple mechanical acts. Try proving that flipping a light switch causes the light to go on. The best most of us can do is to show that every time we flip the switch, the light goes on—one act follows the other. It takes a discussion of electrons flowing in wires, and of infinite resistance and zero resistance, to come close to proving that your hand on the switch causes the bulbs to give light or to stay dark.

Human activities are immensely more complicated than light switches, so if you say one thing caused another you risk jumping to conclusions. Unless you have an authoritative source giving a cause—in which case you attribute the information to that source—it is best to say simply that one thing *follows* another. So this five W's lead avoids diagnosing the referee's injuries or giving their cause:

Referee Schnurr Bart is being transported to the Regional Medical Center following a 7:43 p.m. collision with members of the visiting team during the first quarter of the Lobos-Wombats football game at Wolfman Stadium.

It is possible the visiting team creamed the referee, either accidentally or on purpose. It is also possible a member of the home team tripped Schnurr Bart. It is possible that he was blinded by your photographer's strobe lights. It is possible that he just wanted to ride in an ambulance.

There may also be multiple causes. The referee may have suffered a mild seizure or a small stroke during the game, so he was not able to get out of the way of play as he usually would.

If you cannot quote a reliable source who gives the cause, you may decide reporting a cause is too complicated for a breaking news report. Simply report that the cause is under investigation or has yet to be determined. Or report that game footage will be examined for a possible violation, according to head referee Foley Burns.

Your Turn

1. Examine three issues of student media or three broadcasts for five W's leads. Identify each of the five W's in three of the leads. Which element is the hardest to include in a summary lead, based on what you have read?
2. **Going Deeper.** Have the five W's leads been used appropriately, or would other types of leads have worked better on some stories? Should five W's leads have been used on more stories?

How Long Should a Lead Be?

How long a lead should be depends on how you communicate with your audience. Suppose you are working on a story about Jaime Martinez, the starting pitcher for your school's baseball team. The five W's and an H would look like this:

- Who: junior starting pitcher Jaime Martinez, an all-league player
- What: may be well enough to pitch, according to his doctor
- When: in eight weeks, when the season opens, against the Vikings
- Where: on the pitcher's mound, for the SHS team, at the Lobos' field
- Why: rotator cuff surgery in August following a motocross accident in late June; on Friday his doctor gave him the go-ahead to work out with the team
- How: six hours a week of physical therapy for five months

Print, online or broadcast leads can be derived from your five W's and an H, but how you utilize this information when writing your lead will vary depending on what type of media you use. For example, print leads often contain all of the five W's, while broadcast leads rarely do. The length of the lead will depend on whether it is meant to be heard or to be read.

Leads Meant to Be Heard

If your lead is meant to be heard—for instance, on the radio, in a podcast or on television—it may be several sentences long, but each sentence should contain only one, or at the most two, ideas. The lead should consist of simple, direct sentences written in a conversational tone. Our ears simply do not absorb the flood of information packed into long, elaborate leads. Figure 5.4 on the next page shows a broadcast lead for the Jaime Martinez story.

Leads Meant to Be Read

Leads meant to be read by the audience, in print or on a screen, pack more information into each sentence but are shorter overall than broadcast leads. The sentences tend to be longer, but there are fewer of them.

The lead in Figure 5.5, written to be read in print or online, uses almost 20 percent fewer words than the broadcast story and only three sentences instead of five—easier on the eyes, a little harder on the brain.

Oilers will probably have their starting pitcher back on the mound by opening day.
SPORTS COVERAGE
NEWS

Who, What, When, Where: 14 words, one sentence
The tone is casual, much like a conversation. This is a simple subject-verb sentence. It focuses on the school's team, the Oilers, and uses the future tense.

Junior Jaime Martinez damaged his left shoulder in motocross competition last June and had surgery to repair his rotator cuff in August. He wore his pitching arm in a sling for eight weeks.
SPORTS COVERAGE
NEWS

Jaime Martinez's name is introduced in the second sentence after he was identified in the first as the starting pitcher. This is delayed identification and works well in broadcast when the *who's* name is not instantly recognizable. Sentence length varies here. A 22-word sentence is followed by an 11-word sentence.

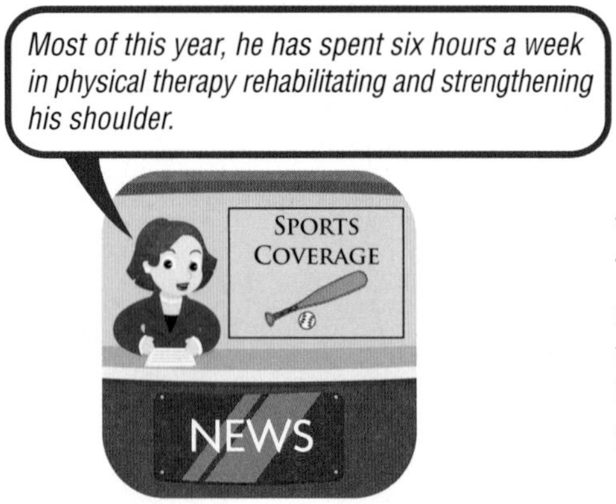

Most of this year, he has spent six hours a week in physical therapy rehabilitating and strengthening his shoulder.
SPORTS COVERAGE
NEWS

Why and How: 19 words, one sentence
This is the first sentence to start with a phrase: *Most of this year*. Every other sentence starts with the main noun, followed by the main verb. Use an introductory phrase rarely, and only to maintain a casual tone.

Friday, his doctor gave him the go-ahead to take the mound March 5.
SPORTS COVERAGE
NEWS

One more simple subject-verb sentence, 13 words. In this lead, the five W's and an H take a total of 79 words in five sentences.

Figure 5.4 Concise, direct sentences are easier for people to comprehend than lengthy, information-packed sentences.

The Goodheart Times

Oiler pitcher Jaime Martinez may be fit to pitch by the March 5 opener against the Vikings, his doctor said.

The junior's status was in doubt after the all-league player injured his shoulder in a summertime motocross accident that required rotator cuff surgery on his pitching arm. He spent six months on the disabled list and was in physical therapy six hours a week.

Who, What, When, Where and Why:
20 words, one sentence
The tone is less chatty, more efficient than a broadcast story. Martinez is fully identified in the lead. Eyes can take in more information than ears. The verb *may be fit* implies that conflict and suspense will be in the story and draws many readers, not just die-hard baseball fans.

44 words, two sentences
The sentences are longer, more complex, with information packed into prepositional phrases and a subordinate clause: that required rotator cuff surgery on his pitching arm.

The five W's and an H are packed into three sentences, 64 words.

Figure 5.5 Print or online stories can include more information than one shared in a television broadcast. *What information would you want to read in the next two paragraphs of this story?*

The broadcast story may contain only the information in the lead. It may be enriched by stills or video of Martinez pitching last year, competing in motocross, wearing his arm in a sling at Halloween. It may include a slide show of his physical therapy, followed by video of preseason training.

The online or print story could include more information that answers the questions the readers would like to ask:

- Will coach let him start?
- How many innings can he pitch?
- Who was set to start if Martinez had not been cleared to play?
- How does the other pitcher feel about Martinez coming back?
- Has he begun spring training? And how does he look?
- Has he lost his speed?
- Will this mess up his chances to play college ball? Professional ball?
- What will this do to the season and our chances of being league champs again?

Online Leads

The first sentence of an online lead may be shorter than its print counterpart, with one or more elements moved into later sentences. Online publications have only a few seconds to capture a reader's interest before the reader may decide to move on to something else, so online leads need to be easily read with clear subjects and powerful verbs. The reader may get no farther than those two elements.

The subject and the verb of an online lead must not be buried under less important clauses and phrases. Even adjectives are sparse. Those can come later in the lead. Though that is especially important in digital publishing, it is also good advice for five W's leads in print publications.

A compelling lead uses the few seconds it has its readers' eyes to tell them what the story is about and why it is important. It calls out, "More interesting things are to come. Keep reading!"

Practical Limits to the Length of the Lead

Though the sentences in print leads may be longer than broadcast leads or online leads, there are practical limits to the length of a strong lead. The Wall Street Journal, writing for educated business people with an appetite for precise details, may publish 48-word leads, but most readers of student publications would need a marking pencil and a map to find their way through such writing. In the following examples, the most significant *who* is underlined, the *what* is double underlined.

The Wall Street Journal printed this lead:

> *Two U.S. congressmen said in a letter to Wal-Mart Stores Inc.'s chief executive Tuesday that they have obtained internal company documents that suggest the company's Mexico affiliate may have engaged in "questionable" financial behavior such as tax evasion and money laundering, in addition to prior allegations of bribery.* (48 words)

The science section of the Los Angeles Times also counts on intelligent, patient readers:

> *A newly discovered cluster of galaxies, more than 5 billion light years from Earth, creates new stars at an "unmatched" pace of more than 700 per year, said Michael McDonald, a Hubble fellow at MIT and lead author of a paper detailing the cluster's properties, published online Wednesday in the journal Nature.* (52 words)

These are probably too long for most student publications.

Some publications written for more general audiences are comfortable with leads of up to 35 words, if they are clear, though beyond 35 words, editors become nervous. Here are two print leads you have read in this chapter:

> *Lobos will be left out in the cold starting December 10 as the district closes the gym to refinish the floors in preparation for the state basketball championship to be held here January 4.* (34 words)

> *Referee Schnurr Bart is being transported to the Regional Medical Center following a 7:43 p.m. collision with members of the visiting team during the first quarter of the Lobos-Wombats football game at Wolfman Stadium.* (34 words)

Some journalists suggest leads for the general public ought to be under 20 words. Others suggest if you can read it aloud in one (natural) breath, the lead is probably OK.

There is nothing wrong with using more than one sentence to write a lead—a lead may be several sentences long—but the first sentence needs to be especially compelling and clear.

YOUR TURN

1. Reread the two long leads about the gym floors and the injured referee. Identify and write down the who, what, when, where, why and possibly the how. Can you identify the *so what* in these leads?

   Which of the five W's comes first? Which comes second?
2. **Going Deeper.** Would readers of your publication read a 35-word lead? How long are the news leads in your three most recent editions?

What Comes First?

The most significant element (often a *who*) comes first, followed almost immediately by a strong and compelling verb, a verb strong enough to stand on its own, without modifying adverbs.

To every rule of journalism there are exceptions, especially if the exceptions contribute to style and clarity. Remember the lead *There will be no school Thursday*. But generally leads start with the most significant element, which is followed by the most compelling verb.

In these examples from this chapter, the most significant element, a noun (sometimes with modifiers), is underlined. The verb—following closely—is double underlined.

1. *Seventeen thousand California teachers will descend…*
2. *Band director Stacy Harris will leave…*
3. *Community college tuition will increase…*
4. *Lobos will be left out in the cold…*
5. *Varsity Wombats lost to Lobos…*
6. *Half of all HTHS graduates abandon community college…*
7. *Paramedics are loading referee Schnurr Bart…* **(If Schnurr had been a well-known or popular figure, the lead might have read** *Schnurr Bart is being loaded into an ambulance after…*)
8. *Oilers will probably have their starting pitcher back on the mound…* **(broadcast)**
9. *Oiler pitcher Jaime Martinez may be fit to pitch…* **(print or online edition)**
10. *Wombats, playing without five players who were detained by Harbor police earlier in the day on suspicion of drug possession, lost...*

In most of these leads, the most significant element carries additional information, usually in the form of adjectives, but almost all of the information further identifies the noun: *band director* Stacy Harris, *Oiler pitcher* Jaime Martinez.

Identification is different from description. Descriptions often invite editorializing and are rare in leads. The adjectives in each of these phrases are describers, not identifiers, and should be avoided: *wildly popular Stacy Harris, towering giant Jaime Martinez*. Think of an identifying adjective as a backpack, which the most significant element in the lead carries.

Occasionally that first, important element is further identified with a prepositional phrase: *half of all HTHS graduates*. Think of prepositional phrases as athletic bags. The athletic bags may carry the *where* or *when*, but they ride on the significant element.

Only the last lead listed on the preceding page burdens the main element with phrases or clauses: *playing without five players who were detained by Harbor police earlier in the day on suspicion of drug possession*. Think of these clunking constructions as rolling backpacks. They are all pulled behind the element, never pushed ahead of it. They come after the noun they modify. That means they may obscure the connection between the most significant element and its verb.

The most significant element can become so overloaded with modifiers—adjectives, prepositional phrases and clauses—that it cannot be recognized or connected to the verb. Broadcast leads shuck off most of the identifiers and modifiers, leaving them for later sentences, while the Wall Street Journal and the science section of the Los Angeles Times count on the reader to find the noun under all the baggage. You and your editors will decide what is appropriate for your media and your audience.

All other elements of the lead—the rest of the five W's—follow the most important element and the verb. Prepositional phrases attached to the main verb may tell how, why, where or when, but they should come *after* the most significant element and verb. The verb lets very little come between it and that significant noun. Other phrases, clauses and appositives may add further information, but they also generally follow the verb.

So how long can a lead be? Only as long as it can be clear and interesting to your audience in your media. Generally…

- The most important element and the verb stay close.
- The most important element and the verb come first in the sentence.
- The most important element should not tote or pull more luggage than it can gracefully carry.

Writing clear leads takes time and skill, and a great deal of rewriting. Clear leads demand good, thorough reporting. A journalist may need to make follow-up calls to sources to get all the information right as the shape of the lead develops during rewriting.

The Inverted Pyramid

Inverted pyramid form follows naturally from a five W's lead and is normal for breaking news and developing stories. Your readers or listeners get the most important facts in the lead, the first few sentences. If that is all they read or hear, they have the gist of the story. Motivated readers will read farther, scroll down or click through to get more details or to find answers to their questions (Figure 5.6).

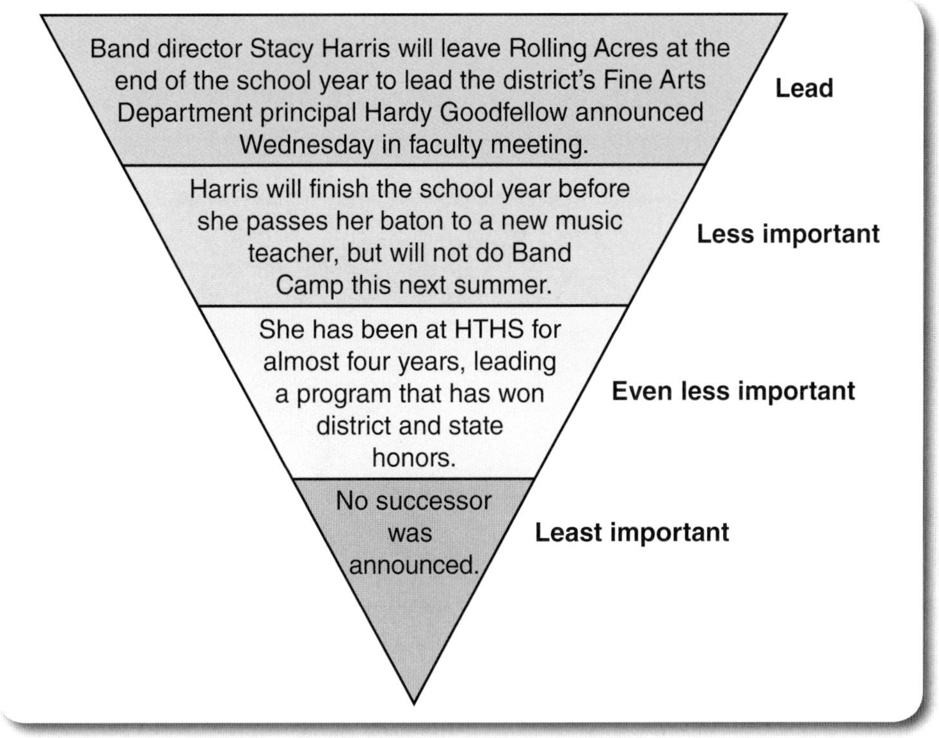
Band director Stacy Harris will leave Rolling Acres at the end of the school year to lead the district's Fine Arts Department principal Hardy Goodfellow announced Wednesday in faculty meeting.
Lead
Harris will finish the school year before she passes her baton to a new music teacher, but will not do Band Camp this next summer.
Less important
She has been at HTHS for almost four years, leading a program that has won district and state honors.
Even less important
No successor was announced.
Least important

Figure 5.6 Inverted pyramid form helps journalists organize information, the most important information followed by less crucial details. The writer's map worksheets on the *Journalism* website can help you perfect your use of the inverted pyramid style when writing breaking or developing stories.

Worksheets

The paragraphs following the lead contain increasingly less crucial information, so the reader is free to move on to another story after he has learned what he wants to know. He does not need to make the jump from the front page to page AA5 to read to the end, even though the jump line requests that he "See LL Cool J, Page AA5." (A **jump line**, shown in Figure 5.7, is a line of type that directs the reader to the page where the story is continued.) Online readers do not need to click through or scroll down or follow the URL (Web address) to the full text. They may quit reading at the ninth inch of your 12-inch story.

Of course reporters want their work read, so each paragraph tries to focus clearly on details about one or more of the five W's or perhaps the H. Unclear writing derails readers. Clear and interesting writing invites the reader further into the story.

For example, early on a Wednesday morning, rapper LL Cool J (Figure 5.8) discovered an intruder in his home. The story was reported and written Wednesday by Andrew Blankstein and Richard Winton (Figure 5.9 on page 145). It was printed in the Thursday edition of the Los Angeles Times. By the time the paper was put to bed Wednesday night, the story was almost 24 hours old, but it had been posted and then updated online six times.

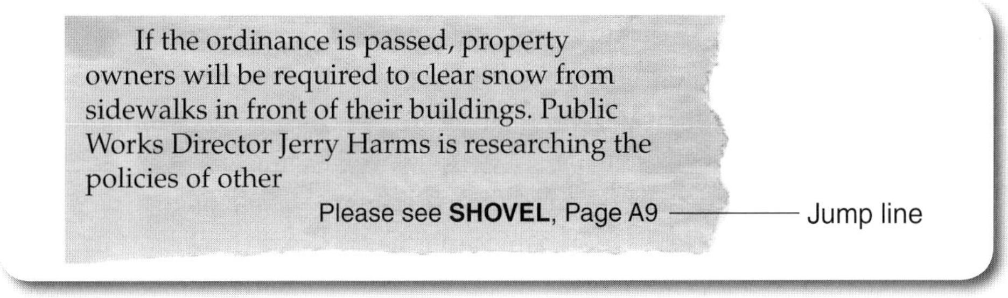
If the ordinance is passed, property owners will be required to clear snow from sidewalks in front of their buildings. Public Works Director Jerry Harms is researching the policies of other

Please see **SHOVEL**, Page A9
Jump line

Figure 5.7 *How likely are you to follow an article's jump line? Do you always read the article in its entirety, or do you assume that you've already gathered the most crucial information by reading the beginning?*

For the Record

What Is a Pyramid Doing, Standing on Its Point?

A right-side up pyramid has a broad base and tapers up to a point. A century or two ago most writing—storytelling, scientific writing, letters and journalism—was organized like this pyramid. It would start slowly at the pointed top of the pyramid with the setting, background, description, history and details. Near the end of the writing, the reader finally got to the broad part of the pyramid—the action, the conclusions, the exciting stuff, the most important news. This style assumed that people had such an appetite for news that they would sit down and read all the way to the end to get to the point.

Journalism in the 19th century turned that pyramid on its head, inverting it, with the most important stuff coming first, the details and background following afterward, and the least significant details coming at the end. The inverted pyramid, as it has been used for over a century and a half, works today because people are busy. It also works because people expect to pick and choose what they read, paying attention only to what interests them. (Very few people read every word of each edition of The New York Times.)

Inverted pyramid form is not used for every news story, but it is essential to breaking news. Its philosophy—start with the most interesting stuff, let the reader decide, do not waste people's time—lies behind almost all journalistic writing, including columns, news, features and reviews, and almost all media used for news.

Figure 5.8 Actor and rapper LL Cool J

Solid reporting and a well-organized inverted pyramid helped the two reporters create a clear, interesting breaking news story. The story seems to have three principal sources: LL Cool J's representative, police reports and announcements, and perhaps court and prison records.

Developing Stories

Developing stories call for a new post or story as new information becomes available. Microblogging or social media sites may announce the new development—*LL Cool J's burglar, hospitalized with broken ribs, jaw and nose, is identified by police*—with an embedded link to your story. Do not give away all you know in the Twitter message or Facebook post. The best tweets will create curiosity about what you have to say in your story. You want to drive traffic to your story on your site.

After you have written your initial breaking news story, new information will require a new headline and lead. Sometimes new information is placed at the top of the existing story, though this can become confusing to the reader who needs to read through several paragraphs to get to the five W's of the story.

Print story: LL Cool J fights, detains home intruder	Use of the Five W's
A man who allegedly broke into actor-rapper LL Cool J's home suffered a broken nose and jaw at the performer's hands Wednesday morning after what police sources describe as a 'knock-down, drag-out' fight.	The five W's lead is careful not to jump to conclusions and so concentrates on what happened to the intruder, not what LL Cool J did. **Who:** intruder **What:** suffered a broken nose and jaw **When:** Wednesday morning **Where:** performer's home **Why:** the intruder allegedly broke into the performer's home **How:** at the performer's hand in a knock-down, drag-out fight
LL Cool J, who rose to fame with the aptly named hit song "Mama Said Knock You Out" and portrays a special agent on the CBS drama "NCIS Los Angeles," proved life imitates art and nabbed the burglar inside his expansive Studio City house.	This paragraph further identifies the rapper and the location, Studio City. It also focuses on the humor of the situation—the intruder obviously picked the wrong house to burglarize. The reader is willing to read more.
When Los Angeles police arrived at the Blairwood Drive home around 1 a.m. Wednesday, LL Cool J had detained the battered and bruised suspect. The man was later identified as Jonathan Kirby, 56, a transient with a lengthy arrest record for thefts, fights and drugs, officials said.	The street—but not the house number—further specifies the location. The intruder's name and biographical details go here—certainly not in the lead. These are less crucial details, but they may answer the readers' unspoken questions. "Was this a deranged fan? An acquaintance of LL Cool J's?"
The next paragraphs give more details about the charges against Kirby, where LL Cool J was when he heard noise in his kitchen, that the intruder attacked first and that he suffered broken ribs in addition to a broken nose and jaw. LL Cool J was not injured.	Readers may want a detailed account of the fight—a video would be even better—but no further details of the fight seem to be available.
After the jump, we read that the actor's representative said he acted to protect his family. The last three paragraphs tell where the intruder was born, his previous arrests and incarceration and the police's suspicion that he had broken into other homes in the area.	The information decreases in importance. Some of these details could be cut without losing anything of great significance to the story.

Figure 5.9 The left-hand column above contains the first three paragraphs and descriptions of the following paragraphs from the *print story* reported by Andrew Blankstein and Richard Winton in the Los Angeles Times. The right-hand column explains how the writers used the 5 W's and the inverted pyramid to craft their story.

Remember, not all your readers have been following the story from the beginning. After each update, reread your entire story and consider carefully if the lead is clear and compelling to someone viewing the story for the first time. Is information prioritized from the most important to the least in inverted pyramid style? The lead and at least the first few paragraphs may need to be reworked for clarity. Paragraphs may need to be moved around.

The Los Angeles Times published the first versions of the LL Cool J story on its website, LATimes.com, 19 hours before the print edition of the story was available. The LA Times updated the story six times in the first 37 hours after LL Cool J thwarted the burglary (Figure 5.10 on the next page).

Figure 5.10 The timeline of events and how they were reported by the LA Times.

Time	LA Times Postings in Response to LL Cool J Event	The Stories
1:00 a.m. Wednesday	1. Police are called to LL Cool J's house. They arrest an intruder.	
11:32 a.m. Wednesday	**2. The first story is posted online.** Journalists learn of the event from a police report. The report is the principal source of information for this first post.	***LL Cool J burglary suspect is transient; LAPD seeks his name*** *The Los Angeles Police Department is trying to learn more about the transient who alleged (sic) burglarized the home of actor-rapper LL Cool J.* *Officials don't know the name of the suspect, who suffered a broken nose and jaw in what police sources described as a "knock-down, drag- out" fight.* *Los Angeles police were called to the star's home in the 12000 block of Blairwood Drive about 1 a.m. Wednesday, officials said. LL Cool J was holding the suspect when officers arrived, officials said.* (The next two paragraphs report that the police were waiting to interview the suspect at the hospital and that LL Cool J was upstairs when he heard the suspect.)
2:23 p.m. Wednesday	**3. The online story is updated** when a written statement from LL Cool J's representative is released. A new lead answers several questions readers may have. (The "manager" is referred to as a "representative" in later posts.) There is a new second paragraph, giving *who*, *what* and *when*. *Where* is in the first paragraph.	***LL Cool J and family 'safe' after burglary attempt, thankful for concern.*** *LL Cool J and his family are safe and cooperating with the police who are investigating an attempted burglary at his Studio City home Wednesday morning, according to a statement released by his manager.* *The rapper and actor, who stars in the CBS drama "NCIS: Los Angeles," thwarted a burglar who tried to break in about 1 a.m.* (The rest of this story repeats paragraphs from the 11:32 a.m. post, but in different order.)
4:04 p.m. Wednesday	**4. The online story is updated again** an hour and forty-one minutes later when the police release the name of the intruder. The lead focuses on the new information, but the story is clear to someone learning about the break-in for the first time. It has *who*, *what*, *when* and *where*. The identification of the suspect, since Kirby is not well-known, is delayed to the second paragraph. This paragraph may suggest the *why*.	***LL Cool J's alleged burglar has lengthy arrest record, police say*** *The transient who tried to break into the Studio City home of LL Cool J early Wednesday morning has a lengthy criminal record in Orange and Los Angeles counties, law enforcement sources say.* *Jonathan Kirby, 56, was arrested on suspicion of burglary and may also face a battery charge, police said.* (The remaining paragraphs repeat information from earlier stories, rearranged and edited slightly.)

(Continued)

Time	LA Times Postings in Response to LL Cool J Event	The Stories
10:21 p.m. Wednesday	**5. The story written for Thursday morning's print edition is posted online.** Over six hours have passed since the last online update. Only the headline is different from the print edition's, which reads "LL Cool J fights, detains home intruder." All the information from the previous posts has been arranged in inverted pyramid order. The writing is tighter than in the online posts.	***LL Cool J has 'knock-down, drag-out' fight with home intruder.*** (The entire print-edition story follows, identical to what will be in the paper the next morning. The rapper's song "Mama Said Knock You Out" is juxtaposed to the intruder's fate, proving that "life imitates art." LL Cool J's representative's statement has been moved down the story to the fourth paragraph from the bottom.)
5:30 a.m. Thursday	**6. The online story is changed**. The story now has a different headline from both the print edition and last night's 10:21 online edition. (Perhaps a new online editor reworked the lead and rearranged the paragraphs.) The lead has been shortened by 12 words and the *how* of the story removed, perhaps to accommodate the way people read on the web. This paragraph has been moved from near the bottom to third from the top.	***LL Cool J 'safe' after violent confrontation with burglar at his home.*** *The man who allegedly broke into actor-rapper LL Cool J's home suffered a broken nose and jaw at the action star's hands Wednesday morning ~~after what police sources described as a "knock-down, drag-out" fight.~~* (The struck-out text did not appear in the post.) *"LL Cool J, and his family, are safe and thank everyone for their thoughts and concern," his representative said. "As a father, husband and citizen, he is committed to keeping his family safe and is cooperating with the authorities on this private matter."*
11:45 a.m. Thursday	**7. Another update is posted online roughly six hours later** when reporters learned no charges were to be filed against LL Cool J. The first two paragraphs of the previous post have been removed. The rest of the post begins at the third paragraph of the print edition version of the story and as posted on LATimes.com at 10:21 p.m. Wednesday and 5:30 a.m. Thursday.	***LL Cool J acted in self-defense during fight, detectives believe*** *LL Cool J isn't expected to face any criminal charges during (sic) a violent confrontation with a burglar at his home this week.* *The alleged burglar suffered a broken nose and jaw at the action star's hands Wednesday morning. But law enforcement sources say detectives believe the actor acted in self-defense.*
2:19 p.m. Thursday	**8. The story is updated online** when the intruder is charged that evening. The charges are explained in two paragraphs. The lead from the former post has been removed. The rest of the story is identical to the previous post.	***LL Cool J burglary suspect faces up to 38 years in prison*** *The transient who allegedly broke into the home of LL Cool J, resulting in a violent confrontation with the star, was charged Thursday by prosecutors.* *Jonathan Kirby, 56, was charged with residential burglary with a person present, which in combination with his criminal history could result in significant prison time. Kirby, who is facing his third strike for serious or violent felony, faces a possible maximum sentence of 38 years in state prison.*

Though the five W's frame this story, the readers' potential questions have driven the reporting. The reporters have asked the questions the readers might want to ask.

- Was the intruder someone LL Cool J knew?
- Was the rapper or anyone who lives with him hurt?
- What kind of a person is the intruder?
- What is going to happen to him?
- Was LL Cool J doing anything wrong?
- Is he in trouble for hurting the intruder?

Avoid Editorializing

Editorializing is inserting your opinions into news coverage. You should not do this in either news or feature coverage. A journalist's job is to present the facts and let the audience form their own opinions.

In many cases, editorializing is unintentional. We simply do not recognize our own prejudices. Constant vigilance helps us to remove editorializing from our work. Your editor, who serves as the readers' representative, should also help you to recognize and remove editorializing.

A well-written story may leave some members of your audience thinking, "That loser sure got what he deserved when he broke into LL Cool J's house!" Other parts of your audience may think, "As bulked out as LL Cool J is, he didn't have to beat the guy up. He's 56 years old, for heaven's sake. He could have just put a chokehold on him or sat on him. Broken jaw and nose? My gosh!"

Guard against your opinion sneaking into your reporting, perhaps without your notice. Make sure you describe people and events in neutral

Breaking and Developing News Checklist

To assure accuracy, check

Everyone's name:

- Make sure it's not a made-up name or another person's name.
- Is it spelled correctly?

Every title:

- Is he an *assistant coach* or the *JV coach*?

The time and date:

- If police are arresting students for curfew violation, there may be a big difference between 10:57 p.m. and 11 p.m.

Every location:

- Check the address.
- Check the map. Half of Denni Street may be in La Palma, half in Cypress.

Your *why*:

- Have you announced that one thing caused another before it is known for certain?

To avoid editorializing, ask

Who deserves a chance to defend himself before I publish this?

Is there another side to this story or point of view?

Do any descriptions contain editorializing?

Do any verbs and nouns suggest I favor one side over another?

words. LL Cool J is "a rapper." The intruder is a "transient." "He has a criminal record." Do *not* write: *bulked-out actor and rapper LL Cool J (for Ladies Love Cool James)* or *professional criminal and ex-con Jonathan Kirby.*

"Knock-down, drag-out" fight seems to be quoted from the police. There are quotes around it, so we know that the reporters did not describe the fight—one they did not see—in those terms.

The verbs we choose often reveal our prejudices. Choose neutral words. If you write that citizens *complain, gripe, protest* or *shout* in a city council meeting, you appear to have passed judgment on them. The neutral language is *expressed concern about.*

You may add details so your readers can make their own judgments.

> *Fourteen people spoke against the proposed skate park and four spoke in favor of it.*

Do not make assumptions about anyone's guilt or innocence.

By avoiding even the most subtle editorializing, you may maintain the respect of both sides in a controversy. By presenting the facts and staying neutral, you are paying your audience a high compliment. You trust them to make up their own minds.

Creating a Stringbook

A stringbook is a portfolio showing the types of reporting, photography and multimedia reporting you have done, as well as your experience in design. It should represent your most professional work in a wide variety of journalism.

Historically, a stringer was a journalist who did articles for several publications but was a full-time employee of none. His stringbook showed a potential employer what he could do. Journalists who are paid by assignment are now often called correspondents or contributors. Today, professional journalists favor digital stringbooks.

A strong stringbook communicates your abilities and experiences when you apply to be on the staff of a high school, college publication or professional publication, or for admission to journalism programs of study. It can help you earn scholarships and recognition. Your stringbook may determine part of your grade in a journalism course.

Throughout this textbook you will see *Application* exercises marked with this icon: S. The pieces you write for these exercises should go in your stringbook. Since the work represents you, you will want to revise your piece after it is graded to reflect what you learned from your adviser's evaluation.

You should also include your published work in your stringbook. Label each piece as either an *Application Exercise* or *Published Work.* Include evidence of publication and the date of publication for each published item.

When you have published several stories in one type of journalism, breaking news for instance, you may wish to take out your earlier, weaker pieces and leave in only your best work. Once this course is complete, your application exercises may be removed from your stringbook and kept or discarded, as your adviser suggests.

Stringbooks can be a powerful tool for reflection. You can chart your own growth in various types of journalism and recognize the challenges you are now ready to undertake.

Chapter Five

Review and Assessment

Recall

1. Name the five W's and explain why they are important in news reporting.
2. Where do the most important pieces of information go in an inverted pyramid form?
3. How does your news cycle influence the kind of story you will write?
4. How can you add value to a news story?
5. What is the difference between breaking and developing news?
6. What is editorializing and why should you avoid it?
7. What should you check in order to assure accuracy in news stories?
8. How are leads written for print, online or broadcast the same? How do they differ?

Critical Thinking

1. Why do you need to identify the source in breaking news stories?
2. Under what conditions may the *why* be left out of a breaking or developing story? How should this omission be handled?
3. Under what conditions may the *how* be left out of a breaking story? Is your answer different if the question is about a developing news story?
4. How might your news cycle influence the journalistic format you choose to present your content?
5. Describe how journalists function as gatekeepers. Do you think this role is important today?

Application

1. Read the following lead and create a chart showing the five W's and an H for the story.

   From the Los Angeles Times:

   Headline: Lawmakers pass timber tax in a last-minute scramble

   Deck: The bill would put a 1% levy on lumber sales and limit firms' liability in wildfires.

   By Chris Megerian and Anthony York

   Lead: SACRAMENTO – A proposed tax on timber came back from the dead early Saturday, passing after Gov. Jerry Brown's aides muscled votes in the final minutes of a legislative session that stretched past midnight.

2. Working with a partner, create a five W's chart and then a five W's lead from the information below. Consider the media for which you are writing: broadcast, online or print.

   Airlines for America is the trade organization for airlines in the United States.

   Airlines for America released an estimate Thursday of how many people will fly on U.S.-based airlines this summer.

   The number is up 1 percent from a year earlier but still far below the total from 2018.

   Almost as many Americans will fly this summer as flew in 2019.

   Most airline seats will be sold.

   Airports will be crowded.

   Passenger totals have been improving each year for four years.

3. Using the breaking news writing map on the Journalism website, write a breaking or developing story, using imagined details, for the following scenarios.

   A. The city has decided to make the street in front of your school a one-way street, it was announced Friday. The change will take place next month.

   B. An explosion in the parking lot of your school has put the school into lockdown.

4. Review a police department's crime blotter or a fire department or 911 dispatch log.

   A. Choose three incidents and write a breaking news lead for each.

   B. Choose one of the incidents. Using the breaking news story writing map as a guide, interview the watch commander or public information officer. Consult maps and other sources. Write the story using the writing map.

Chapter Five

Journalism Style

Attribution

Journalistic writing is full of sources, and almost all need some form of attribution, that is, identification of the source of the information. In almost all cases, journalists should attribute (identify the source of) their information. Most often, they do so by using the terms *according to* and *said*.

Reporters avoid using language that seems to editorialize, that is, evaluate the value or reliability of the quotation. So *claimed*, *gushed*, *argued*, *alleged*, *asserted*, *whimpered*, *responded*, or even *added* are not replacements for the more neutral terms *according to* and *said*. While *according to* and *said* may seem repetitious to the writer, they are nearly invisible to readers and listeners. They simply connect information with a source and otherwise disappear.

> What does *not* need attribution?
> - What the reporter witnesses herself: *Nearly 100 Martindale High School students picketed the district office Thursday after school.*
> - What is generally known by most readers: *Martindale High School is overcrowded, with academic classes held in the cafeteria, in the unused auto shop, on the stage of the auditorium, in the PE weight room and in aged computer labs.*

According To

Generally you should reserve *according to* for attributing written material. Besides books, written sources may include websites, press releases, newspapers, broadcasts and government documents.

> *"AP news reports must attribute facts not gathered or confirmed on our own, whether the pickup is from a newspaper, website, broadcaster or blog," according to The Associated Press Stylebook.*

If you use *according to* when you attribute a quotation to a person you heard speak, it may suggest you doubt the speaker is telling the truth: *"It's just a smear campaign, cooked up by my opponent," according to candidate Wiley Coyote."None of it is true," he added.*

Said

Use *person said* when you quote someone you interviewed or someone you heard speak. The most basic form of attribution follows this pattern: *"Juniors and sophomores may choose whether to transfer to Mimosa Valley High when it opens next fall, but freshmen will be asked to go to the high school that serves the area where they live," Mimosa Unified School District Superintendent Chuck Cannibal said.*

Only rarely will *said* come before the name of the speaker. Reserve *said speaker* for when you need to further identify a person after you have given his name. For instance: *"I don't like the policy. Everyone in my family has gone to Martindale. Now we are being split up," said junior Joao Mucci, whose freshman sister Thais is scheduled to transfer to Mimosa Valley.*

Try It!

What is the most appropriate form of attribution for each of these quotations?

1. "All the profits from the dance will go to Habitat for Humanity." Source of quotation: Shellsea White. She is a senior and on the dance committee.
2. "Volunteers donated over 1 million hours of work to Texas Habitat for Humanity in 2013." Source of information: Habitat Texas Annual Report.
3. "While spring tends to produce more tornadoes, they're not uncommon in fall. On Nov. 17, a late season tornado outbreak that struck seven Midwestern states became the most active tornado day of 2013 with a total of 74 tornadoes." Source of quotation: press release from nws.noaa.gov.
4. "I learned more than how to hammer nails. I learned about teamwork and community." Source of quotation: Ben Bigler, who helped repair two houses in Taft and one in Waco after last year's tornadoes damaged broad swaths of the area.

Extend Your Knowledge — Style Exercises

The default position is to put the attribution after the quotation: *"I like the new lunch menu," John Smith said*. Sometimes, however, the attribution should be placed before the quotation or within it. Visit the *Journalism* website to learn more about placement of attributions.

Chapter Five

Writers' Workshop

In this Writers' Workshop you will:

- Craft breaking news leads using the most significant or interesting part of the story.
- Find a colorful verb or phrase to draw in your audience.
- Use the appropriate verb tense.
- Include the appropriate time element.
- Experiment with word order in your lead.

Workshop 5.1

Finding the Right Lead

Mini-Lesson: Asking the Right Questions

Great news leads seem almost inevitable, as if they could have written themselves, but journalists will tell you they struggle to find the right lead and then to choose the right words.

They start with four questions:

1. What is the most significant or interesting part of the story for my audience?
2. Who did it, said it or experienced it?
3. Is there a colorful verb or phrase to lead my audience into the story?
4. What is the most appropriate verb tense?

The story of Little Red Riding Hood is gory enough for any crime beat. Ask

1. What is most significant or interesting for my audience? The cute red hood? The fresh bread? Little Red's conversation with the ersatz Granny in the nightgown? Probably not. The most significant part is that the woodsman slit open the wolf's carcass and Granny emerged alive.
2. Who did it, said it or experienced it? That could be either the woodsman or Granny. Each *who* has strengths.
3. Is there a colorful verb or phrase to lead my audience into the story? *Emerged* and *slit* are strong verbs. You might write: *Granny has emerged alive from the wolf's still-warm carcass* or *The woodsman slit open the still-warm carcass to release Granny, unharmed.* Active verbs are better than passive verbs. *Emerged* is stronger than *was released*.
4. What is the most appropriate verb tense to entice the audience into the story? Some tenses are more interesting than others. Present and future tenses are usually the strongest. Use present progressive tense (*is recovering*) or, better, future tense (*will return home*). Next best is present perfect (*has been rescued, has slain*). In some circumstances the simple past tense is the best choice for something that happened recently (*emerged from the belly of a wolf this afternoon*).

The answers to the four questions may suggest very different leads.

> *Granny Hood is recovering at home in Northwoods after escaping from the belly of the dead Big Bad Wolf, who was slain by a woodsman's ax this morning.*

> *Granny Hood will recover at her daughter's home in Southwoods.*

If Granny is the subject, the sentence may be passive (and therefore less interesting):

> *Granny Hood was rescued by a woodsman.*

The strongest lead may use the past tense:

> *Granny Hood, 84, emerged alive from the still-warm carcass of Big Bad Wolf after woodsman Johann Chopper, 17, slew the animal with his ax and slit open its belly in rural Northwoods this afternoon.*

Apply It!

Use the four questions in this mini-lesson to create compelling leads for three nursery rhymes, fables or fairy tales, such as

- Little Bo Peep;
- Cinderella;
- Peter, Peter Pumpkin Eater;
- Rapunzel;
- The Fox and the Grapes.

Share your leads with your group, receive response and revise to create the strongest leads possible.

The Time Element

Unless the *when* is the focus of the story, its default position is near the end of a breaking news lead, as in the Granny Hood lead, on the preceding page.

Breaking news in any media may use a specific time: *6 a.m., this afternoon*.

Print journalism tends also to use the day of the week—*Thursday, last Tuesday*—in addition to *today*, but avoids *yesterday* and *tomorrow*. If the event is more than one week in the future or past, use the date (*February 12* rather than *next Monday*).

In electronic media, if a time stamp is clearly shown (such as *Story revised 7 minutes ago* or *Posted 7:02 a.m.*), it is safe to use *today* or *yesterday*; but remember, the time element of the story needs to be revised before midnight. If a story is updated as it develops, you may also need to revise the time element.

Live broadcasts may skip the time element: *Victorious Lady Broncos are celebrating their double-overtime win over South High School.* They may also use *last night*, *tomorrow* or *yesterday*. But if a broadcast is embedded in a Web page, the time element needs to be treated like any other time element in electronic or print publishing.

Mini-Lesson: Putting Things in the Best Order

A strong breaking news lead should be easy to read and generally no longer than you can read in one breath, yet it should contain most or all of the five W's. Think of the five W's as little magnetic word strips, such as people put on their refrigerators. You may select different words and phrases and rearrange them many times before you find the lead that seems inevitable, natural and obviously the right one.

The default and usually the best arrangement is to put the *who* (the subject) first and the *what* (the verb) next. Though you may modify the *who*, all other information goes after the verb, ending with the time element.

Apply It!

With your response group, try various versions of your fairy tale or nursery rhyme leads. For example:

- Begin the lead with two or three different "most significant parts of the story."
- Find five verbs you could use with your favorite two "most significant elements."
- Add a prepositional phrase to the *who* and the *what* to tell where, when, why or how. Prepositional phrases will go after the verb. *Johann Chopper slew the wolf in hand-to-jaw combat.*
- Now try communicating the same information as adjectives. *Hand-to-jaw combat between Chopper and Wolf lasted over an hour.*
- Attach a subordinate clause to an important noun. *The wolf, who had been terrorizing residents of Northwoods for over a year, was pronounced dead at the scene.*
- Try the same information as an appositive. *The wolf, terror of Northwoods for over a year, died at the scene.*
- Divide the lead into two sentences. *A local woodsman, Johann Chopper, struggled with Big Bad Wolf in hand-to-jaw combat. The wolf, who had been terrorizing the Northwoods community for over a year, died at the scene.*
- Try the lead in broadcast style, with only one idea per sentence. *The Big Bad Wolf is dead tonight. Johann Chopper, 17, a woodsman, slew the wolf. They fought in fierce hand-to-jaw combat for more than an hour. The wolf has been terrorizing the Northwoods community for more than a year. He was pronounced dead at the scene.*
- Try online style, keeping the first sentence of the lead within 20 words but still giving the audience a strong *who* and *what*. *A 17-year-old woodsman slew Big Bad Wolf, terror of Northwoods, today in an hour of hand-to-jaw combat.*

If you stumble over a phrase or run out of breath, edit that section for smoothness or shorten the sentence. Do the same if anything is unclear or otherwise awkward.

Publish your revised leads digitally or in your classroom.

Extend Your Knowledge Extend

Visit the *Journalism* website for additional information and practice in writing strong leads.

Chapter Six

Writing General News Stories

It's news, but it's not breaking.

Courtesy of Ellen Austin

G-WLEARNING.COM

While studying, look for the activity icon to:

- **Build** vocabulary terms with e-flash cards and matching activities.
- **Extend** learning with further discussion of relevant topics.
- **Reinforce** what you learn by completing style exercises, worksheets and end-of-chapter questions.

Visit the Journalism website: www.g-wlearning.com/journalism/

Chapter Objectives

After reading this chapter, you will be able to:

- Tell how general news stories differ from breaking news stories.
- Explain how an audience's potential questions guide reporting.
- Develop a focus for your story.
- Identify the expanded role of *why*, *how* and *so what* in five W's leads for general news stories.
- Discuss creative writing techniques that may be used to develop narrative leads.
- Tell how writing a narrative lead differs from writing fiction.
- Describe nut grafs and their purpose.
- Describe the importance of the closing in general news stories.
- Describe five ways to organize, or give shape to, a story.
- Describe brights and their purpose.

Key Terms Build Vocab

brights
general news
narrative lead
nut graf
punch list
sidebar

Before You Read...

When writing, you must be able to relate the sounds of the English language to letters of the alphabet. As your instructor presents a lesson, listen carefully to the sounds of the language. Listen for the vowel sounds of *a*, *e*, *i*, *o* and *u*, as well as the other letters, called consonants. Take notes to record the sounds you heard.

Introduction

"Put it before them briefly so they will read it, clearly so they will appreciate it, picturesquely so they will remember it and, above all, accurately so they will be guided by its light."

–Joseph Pulitzer, American publisher

Not all news stories are breaking or developing stories, and not all news stories start with a summary lead or end with the least important details. **General news** stories *are* news stories—they have strong timeliness and impact—but they do not necessarily involve an unexpected and immediate event. General news stories may not give a journalist an adrenaline rush as does breaking news, yet they can be immensely satisfying as you bring important information to your audience, information the audience may use to change the world. If writing breaking news is like doing emergency room surgery, then writing general news is like practicing family medicine.

General news gives the reporter more choices and different responsibilities than breaking news. Compared to breaking or developing news, general news stories need

- more reporting;
- more sources—and judgment about the credibility of the sources;
- more first-person reporting, including interviews, observation, photography, sound and video recording;
- more news judgment to find a focus for the story;
- more creativity in the lead, followed by the **nut graf**, the paragraph that includes any of the five W's not covered in the introductory paragraphs and tells why the story matters;
- creativity in the closing—it is as important as the opening;
- more skill to find a shape for the story;
- more types of writing in the story—straight reporting, analysis, narration, description, even poetic language; and
- more explanation of complicated issues in language your audience can follow.

A writing map can help you organize your information and draft your story. You will find a general news story writing map on the *Journalism* website.

Worksheets

Reporting for General News Stories

Your editor has assigned you and a partner two stories to be covered as general news. One is about a block wall near your campus, painted black. At the top of the wall is written: "Before I die..." Boxes of chalk hang from the wall (Figure 6.1).

The other is about a U.S. Senate report, published in The New York Times. The report condemns for-profit colleges, which, according to the Times, took $32 billion in taxpayer funds but "the majority of students leave without a degree, half of those within four months."

Neither of these two potential stories contains an event that would make breaking news, though each will still be fresh when you next publish, post or broadcast. The block wall story has proximity and

Figure 6.1 The first Before I Die wall was created by artist Candy Chang in New Orleans after losing a loved one. The wall pictured is located in Louisville, Kentucky and is just one of the hundreds of walls that have been created in communities all over the world.

timeliness, both core news values. As a reporter, you will look for human interest, conflict, oddity or prominence angles. The for-profit colleges story is timely because of the recent release of the report. As a reporter, you will look for further news values, especially impact, proximity and conflict, but also human interest, oddity or prominence.

The Block Wall Story

Because you are your audience's eyes and ears, going where they are not able to go, you will seek information the audience will want. Before you head out with your notebook, sound recorder, camera and video recorder, you and your editor meet to generate questions your audience may want answered. These are the questions you will ask as you report:

1. Who painted the wall black and put out the chalk?
2. Why?
3. What sorts of things are people writing on the wall?
4. Why do they write there?
5. Who owns the wall?
6. Has anyone objected to the wall?
7. How do they keep inappropriate comments and gang insignia off the wall—or do they need to?
8. How long does each chalk comment last?
9. Is anyone recording the comments before they fade?
10. Are images of the wall being posted anywhere online?

Figure 6.2 Conducting interviews with people at the scene can help you get answers to your questions. *What questions would your audience want you to ask?*

When you arrive at the wall, you see one person writing on it. At the top of the wall you see the words "Before I die…" apparently written in white paint. As you spend time at the wall, several other people write on it. (It is rare for a reporter to arrive at one perfect moment. Some of good reporting is just hanging out at the right spot.)

One person writing on the wall is an elderly gentleman, perhaps foreign-born. The other two look like students. You photograph some of the comments and the wall itself. You interview each of the three people, getting their names and contact information, in case you need to get in touch with them for more information, clarification or to check your notes for accuracy (Figure 6.2). Many of your questions to your interviewees are really gentle commands—to tell you more, to explain, to tell you why. (More information about interviews is in Chapter 9.)

You: I see you are chalking something on the wall. Tell me about it, please.

Student One: It just seems like a neat thing to do, to think about what we want to do before we die. It's more important, kinda, to think about this than the stuff we talk about in school most of the time.

You: Tell me about what you are writing, please.

Student One: (*answers*)

You: Why did you write on the wall?

Student One: (*answers*)

You: Do you know who put up the wall?

Student One: No. I just noticed it Wednesday. I walk by here all the time, but it wasn't there before.

Student Two: This is my second time here—I erased what I wrote yesterday and wrote something different.

You: What did you write today?

Student Two: I wrote that I want my family to be together again in one place, and happy to be together.

You: Tell me about that.

Student Two: (*answers*)

You: What did you write yesterday, that you erased?

Student Two: I wrote about wanting to take a road trip with some guys I've known since grade school. You know, to surf the Pacific Coast. But when I thought about it last night, it didn't seem like the most important thing.

You: Why did you write on the wall?

Student Two: (*answers*)

You: Do you know who put up the wall?

Student Two: No. Carla here (indicates Student One with a tilt of his head) just told me about it.

You speak to the older gentleman: (Lucky you, you are bilingual and are able to approach him respectfully in what you guess is his first language. Most of the interview is in English, though.) I see you are writing on the wall. Can you tell me about it?

Older Gentleman: I was walking by here today and saw so many people writing things on the wall. Many of them are very wise for such young people. They write about family and education and making good choices.

You: You are much older than the students who are writing here today. I'd like to know what you have written.

Older Gentleman (reads): Before I die, I would like to see my homeland at peace, and free. All of it. I would like to see where my parents are buried.

You: Why did you write on the wall?

Older Gentleman: (*answers*)

You now have great sound, good photographs and pretty good video. You also have the answer to questions three and four from your list. You still need the answers to eight more questions.

You tackle them, starting with who probably owns the wall. You check an aerial map of the neighborhood and hunt down the owner.

You ask him about the wall and find out he is allowing a friend to use it, a friend whose 22-year-old daughter committed suicide last June. The city has told the owner of the wall that it can be used this way for only two more weeks, but he is appealing that ruling to the city council.

You contact the father and meet him at the wall. Every few days he photographs the comments and posts them on a page the family created as a memorial to his daughter. It has become part of an anti-suicide campaign.

The father washes the wall off every two or three days, but so far, almost all of the comments have been respectful. "Just one or two jerks, but that's life, isn't it? After losing a daughter to suicide, a little bad language doesn't seem that big a deal. You know what I mean?"

To be fair, you need to hear from the city officials who, you are told, have asked that the wall no longer be used. Reporting that they want the writing removed may portray them in a negative light, so they need an

Five Ways to Approach a Story

(From the Planet Money Team on National Public Radio)

1. Find the person who does the thing.
2. Find the person who is strangely affected.
3. Tell the history.
4. Explain.
5. Solve a mystery.

opportunity to be heard. You call the city zoning office to find out about their request that the wall be repainted in two weeks. Have there been complaints? What is the law? What is the city's position on the wall? Are they negotiating or trying to accommodate the wall?

When your editor sees your notes, he suggests you contact a suicide prevention expert to ask if the wall will be helpful in preventing suicides. (Chapter 8 will tell you how to locate experts.)

The For-Profit Colleges Story

Before you head out to report, you read the New York Times story in full as well as a similar story in your nearest metropolitan paper. You find a wealth of information on ProPublica.org, a nonprofit investigative journalism site (Figure 6.3).

You note that in the NY Times story the report was praised by Democrats but criticized by the Association of Private Sector Colleges and Universities. This suggests a conflict, and a conflict means you need to contact people from several sides of the conflict.

With the help of your editor, you generate questions the reader might like to know:

1. Which colleges near here are for-profit? Are any of them mentioned in the Senate report?
2. What is the difference between a for-profit college and a private college?
3. What sorts of degrees do these colleges grant?
4. What are the advantages of the for-profit colleges? Why don't their students go to the state-owned community colleges or the state universities?
5. Which colleges do members of your community—current students or recent graduates—attend or consider attending?
6. Are the for-profit colleges online, brick-and-mortar or both?
7. How hard is the class work?
8. Do some students complete the training and get good jobs?
9. Why do some students drop out?
10. Do students still have to repay government financial aid even if they drop out?
11. Are members of your community hurt by these schools?
12. Are members of your community helped by these schools?

Figure 6.3 The *Our Investigations* tab on ProPublica's website allows you to read articles on the same topic and compare perspectives. *How can comparing perspectives from different sources increase the depth of your reporting?*

Courtesy of ProPublica / propublica.org

You begin your research online but come away confused. Sites praise the for-profit schools, saying they are more "flexible in meeting the needs of the learner" and "perform a valuable service to the country." But some of the sites praising the for-profit colleges have advertisements down the right-hand side for the for-profit colleges. Does this make the information on the site unreliable? You decide not to quote from the websites without first identifying and interviewing the people in charge of the site.

In contrast, the NY Times story and ProPublica's infographic say a two-year degree from a for-profit school costs over four times as much as one from a public community college, while the for-profit colleges spend much less on each student. You click through to find the same information in the Senate report, so you write down what is in the Senate report but continue to use the ProPublica site for further research. (See Chapter 8 for information on evaluating websites.)

You head for a college counselor at your school, who explains the difference between public schools, non-profit schools and for-profit schools to you. You ask which schools cited in the report are in your area, but he says he does not know. You ask if he knows who from your school has attended for-profit schools, but he declines to give you that information, citing privacy concerns.

Back on your computer, you search ProPublica again and find a link to the Senate report. In a section headed "Institutions Examined," you read the names of the for-profits. Some advertise locally and have campuses near you.

You still have questions and as yet, not much of a story. You decide to put a face on the problem. You use social media to ask for members of your community who considered going to a for-profit college such as (and here you list the nearby ones) or actually attended one. Or perhaps they know someone who has. By the next morning, you have names and contact information for nine local people who have experiences with the for-profits.

You try to arrange face-to-face interviews and discover that only five of the people really went to one of the colleges you are covering. Four of the five had negative experiences, dropped out and were left with debt. One successfully completed a program and got a job in her field, which she loves, but she tells you she owes more money in student loans than she makes in a year at her new job.

As you talk with each person face-to-face and record the interview, you ask questions 4, 7, 8, 9, 10 and 11 from the list you generated when you were first assigned the story.

Journalists need to be fair and balanced in their stories. That means contacting sources on each side of the story (Figure 6.4). There may be more than two sides. Anyone who is criticized in a story or even shown in a negative light needs to be given a chance to respond before the story is published.

Figure 6.4 A phone interview can be a good alternative to a face-to-face interview if your source is unable to meet in person.

You call the recruitment office at three nearby for-profit colleges and ask for interviews. One recruiting officer tells you: "Lots and lots of our graduates are working in their fields. Hundreds from this campus alone." He declines to give you names, citing privacy concerns.

"Students still have to decide whether or not to do the work when they take [our] classes, but we stand by to help any student who asks for help. We have great counselors and a great staff.

"We take more than our share of low-income students. Some of them are better prepared than others.

"Online courses are not for everyone, so we have options. You can take an online course, a traditional classroom course or a hybrid with some online components and some in person."

At another school, a public affairs officer tells you, "This college was not one of the ones cited in the Senate study. We are fully accredited and we stand by our record of placing students in rewarding careers." You check the Senate list for the school's name.

You take up the third school's invitation to come and see what they do, videotaping classes and labs.

Finding a Focus for Your General News Story

You are looking at piles of information—reporter's notebooks, sound files, photos, videos, websites and printouts from websites (Figure 6.5). What do you do with all of it?

Finding the focus of your story is difficult, perhaps the most difficult part of a reporter's writing process. But focusing your story is crucial. A good focus helps you write swiftly and well and helps you craft your lead. But if you do not focus the story well, what you write may not be read or viewed. You may not even be able to write it.

There is no magic formula to finding a focus. No fill-in-the-blank forms. No five W's to guide you. However, a good editor or writing group and a few questions may help you focus.

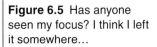

Figure 6.5 Has anyone seen my focus? I think I left it somewhere...

Review your material, then set aside your notes, photos and files for a moment and ask yourself, or have your responders or editor ask you, "What is this story about?"

Try to answer that question in one sentence, usually a sentence with a subject, a verb and a direct object. It may take several tries, but one of those answers will provide a focus to your story. Your editor or response group may help you find it.

The focus for the block wall story may be

- a family tries to help people realize how precious life is;
- a wall helps people think about what is really important;
- LLHS students record their dreams; or
- chalkboard paint from several companies can turn a block wall into a chalkboard.

You decide on the second focus statement, that the story is about a wall that helps people think about what is really important. The first statement focuses too much on the girl who committed suicide, whom your audience did not know and who has no other connection to your community. She should be mentioned, but she will not be the focus. The third statement is too general to focus the story. The fourth one might make a good sidebar, an "explainer" alongside the main story.

The focus of the for-profit colleges story may be

- seniors face dangers choosing a college;
- good grades and good skills prepare students for college success; or
- local students give a face to the national controversy about for-profit colleges.

You decide on the third focus, the local face to a national story, but you save "seniors face dangers" as a future story idea.

Figure 6.6 Assembled by the maestro, or editor, each team member plays an important role in producing the story.

The Maestro Concept

Another way to find a focus involves team storytelling and the Maestro Concept. After preliminary research, you describe to your editor in a few words what the story will be about and suggest a lead and a headline. The maestro—usually the editor—assembles a team that includes page designers, photographers and video and sound engineers, as your media platforms allow (Figure 6.6). Together you map out a package that is organized by these questions:

- Why should the audience care?
- What does the audience want to know first, second and third?

Extend

For more information about the Maestro Concept, access the *Journalism* website.

Drafting the Lead

General news stories may use an almost infinite variety of leads. Two of the most common are variations on the five W's lead and **narrative leads**, a type of feature lead. (See Chapter 10 for more on feature leads.) Narrative leads use storytelling techniques to engage the reader, followed by a nut graf that completes the five W's. Though narrative leads read like fiction, they must be accurate and truthful.

Sidebars: Great Stories, Slightly out of the Focus

A **sidebar** is a story set outside—usually alongside—the main story. It goes along with the main story but does not belong in it, and it is shorter than the main story. It may explain something in the news story or give background, even historical, information that would clog the flow of the news story. A sidebar may be another news story or, more commonly, a feature story. It may be just a bullet list of items, such as the five signs of seasonal affective disorder (SAD) as a sidebar to a story on beating the midwinter blahs. It may contain statistics, charts or graphs, polls or poll results, quotations, pictures, links to other sites or Twitter trends related to the news story.

Potential sidebars to the chalkboard wall story include

- other local and digital spaces for public comment (feature);
- famous places for public art and comment, including Duke University's graffiti wall (feature), the Berlin Wall (history) and the Freedom of Speech Wall in Charlottesville, Virginia (feature);
- a report of the city zoning commission hearing about the wall (news); or
- an "explainer," a how-to article on turning exterior and interior walls into chalkboards (feature).

A sidebar is connected to the main story by a news peg, a reference in the sidebar to the general news event. The news peg comes near the lead and might look like one of these:

- The chalk wall across from LLHS is not the only place in Centerville that welcomes public comment.
- The chalk wall across from LLHS is part of a long tradition of public comments.
- If the chalk wall near LLHS makes you want more places to write, try these techniques to turn plain surfaces into chalk.

THE WALL

Continued from Page 3

For Travonne Cherish, a senior at LLHS, "It just seems like a neat thing to do, to think about what we want to do before we die. It's more important, kinda, to think about this than the stuff we talk about in school most of the time."

For Jackson Silverman, a computer programming student at Central Valley Community College, the wall invoked some personal reflection. "This is my second time here. I erased what I wrote yesterday and wrote something different." His first message had been about "wanting to take a road trip with some guys I've known since grade school. You know, to surf the Pacific Coast. But when I thought about it last night, it didn't seem like the most important thing."

His new message reflects a deeper concern. His sister's divorce has caused a rift in the family. "I want my family to be together again in one place, and happy to be together."

The writing is on the wall

The chalk wall across from LLHS is part of a long tradition of public comments. Sometimes the practice is tolerated by local authorities, sometimes not. Public places that encourage personal reflection and expression include:

– The graffiti wall at Duke University in Durham, N.C.
– Freedom of Speech Wall in Charlottesville, Va.
– Freedom of Expression Tunnel at North Carolina State University in Raleigh, N.C.

Five W's Leads, Plus More

Five W's leads, used in breaking news, also work well for many general news stories, though the emphasis may be different. While breaking news needs to urgently communicate *who, what* and *when*, general news may focus more on the *so what*, the *why* and the *how*.

In the following lead, the *so what* (underlined here) is prominent:

> *SAN JOSE—Apple Inc. won an overwhelming victory over rival Samsung Electronics Co. in a widely watched federal patent battle, a decision that some worry could stymie competition in the fast-moving markets for smartphones and computer tablets. (Los Angeles Times)*

Note that broadcast and many print publications would have broken this lead into at least two sentences:

> *SAN JOSE—Apple Inc. won an overwhelming victory over rival Samsung Electronics Co. in a federal patent battle.*
>
> *Some worry the decision in the widely watched case could stymie competition in the fast-moving markets for smartphones and computer tablets.*

How to Write a Great Lead

Write 10 or 15 bad ones.

Write three pretty good ones.

Write them in your head as you finish your reporting and as you walk to classes.

Write them on the back pages of your reporter's notebooks. Try several as you draft your article.

Write them last, after you have finished the rest of the story. Write them when you first sit down at a keyboard.

Read them aloud to your editor or writing group. Rewrite them. Move the five W's elements around. Move clauses around. Move sentences around. Change the tense from past to present, or from present to past, as in the story about the murdered 14-year-old girl.

Replace each verb with a stronger one. Make each detail more specific, based on your close observations. Is he smoking a cigarette or a Camel? Is he wearing a jacket or a Seattle Mariners' windbreaker? Is she fidgeting or picking at her fingernail polish?

You may not come up with a great lead for every story, but you will know that the lead you have is the best possible lead.

Remember, if your audience does not like your lead, it does not matter what else you write.

Here is a *why* lead:

> *In a policy shift brought on by scrutiny of the disastrous 2009 Station fire, the U.S. Forest Service will begin nighttime helicopter missions to battle blazes in the Angeles National Forest and other federal lands in Southern California. (Los Angeles Times)*

Here is the same lead rewritten as two sentences:

> *The U.S. Forest Service will begin nighttime helicopter missions to battle blazes in the Angeles National Forest and other federal lands in Southern California.*
>
> *The policy shift was brought on by scrutiny of the disastrous 2009 Station fire.*

The Los Angeles Times is modestly congratulating itself in this article. It was the LA Times itself that had supplied the "scrutiny" mentioned in the lead. The LA Times reported extensively on the Forest Service's ban on flights to drop water on forest fires during the night, a ban that may have cost the Forest Service control of the earlier Station fire and lead to the death of two firefighters. The source of the scrutiny is identified in the fourth paragraph of the story when it reports: *The reversal in tactics grew out of Times reports and subsequent congressional inquiries into the Forest Service's initial response to the Station fire. ... Two firefighters died in the flames*. Good news reporting can save forests—and human lives.

Figure 6.7 An accompanying image of the match allows the reader to quickly establish the *who* of the story.

The *how* is dominant in this tennis story, "Touch sets the tone for Serena" (Figure 6.7). The nut graf comes in the third paragraph.

> *WIMBLEDON, England—It was a gentle drop shot that finally made Serena Williams raise her arms in almost-triumph Saturday in the Wimbledon championship match against Agnieszka Radwanska.*
>
> *Williams had dominated most of the tournament with her percussive serve. She hit 24 aces in one match, 23 in another and a record-setting 102 in the tournament.*
>
> *But that drop shot, on a break point in the seventh game of the final set, it was the winner. It allowed Williams to feel free in her final service game and it helped send her to a fifth Wimbledon championship and 14th major title with her 6-1, 5-7, 6-2 win. (Los Angeles Times)*

When writing a general news story, beginning with a five W's lead is a good start. You can also follow a writing map to complete your story. A writing map is an often-used form that allows you to properly organize and structure your story.

Extend

Your Turn

1. Find three news leads in the professional media that include most of the five W's and either *how* or *so what* in the headline, caption and lead. Underline and mark any of the five W's plus the *how* or *so what*.
2. **Going Deeper.** Using a table such as the one below, identify which W comes first, second, and so on for each of the news leads.

First	*Who:* Apple Inc.
Second	*What:* won an overwhelming victory over rival Samsung Electronics Co.
Third	*Where:* in a widely watched federal patent battle
Fourth	*So what:* a decision that some worry could stymie competition in the fast-moving markets for smartphones and computer tablets

What generalizations can you make about five W's general news leads that include *how* or *so what*? What is left out? In what order is the information presented? Compare your conclusions with that of your group.

Narrative Leads

Is the lead in the tennis story "Touch sets the tone for Serena" really a five W's lead? It extends over three paragraphs. The score and Williams' win, arguably the most important *what* of the story, are delayed until the nut graph of the third paragraph, while the *how* is explained in the first 73 words that include character and description of the crucial shot, the gentle drop shot.

This lead may actually be a narrative lead, sometimes called a soft lead. There are no clear criteria that always separate narrative leads from five W's leads.

General news stories may delay the five W's in favor of narrative writing. The narrative lead pulls the reader into what otherwise might be a less interesting but still important news story, perhaps one full of statistics, facts or legal matters. The narrative portion of the lead makes the readers care about the information they find in the nut graph.

A narrative lead can also give the audience the sense of actually observing an event that may have been covered in a bare five W's fashion in breaking news. It puts a face on a story that otherwise might exhaust the audience's attention—or compassion. Narrative leads may use almost any of the skills of a fiction writer to

- set a scene—the real one, of course;
- introduce a character—a real one, of course;
- create suspense—but only with actual events;
- portray conflict—a real one, of course;
- describe the action or the event—accurately, of course.

Narrative leads sound a great deal like creative writing. Journalists use the same skills but with one twist. A fiction writer can make up a detail anytime one is needed. A journalist relies on great reporting and great powers of observation. A journalist must be certain every word is true. Every observation, every detail, every action must be observed firsthand or learned from a reliable source.

Never make up a single detail. Not what your character wore, said, did or owned. Not what was in the room. Not what happened. Not how someone reacted. Only close observation and strong interviewing can give you those details. Strong journalism writing may look a bit like fiction writing, but the demand for truth makes it more challenging. To make up even the slightest detail risks the trust of your audience and fellow journalists and is an ethical breach.

Coming to Terms With the Short and the Long of Leads

While breaking or developing stories use five W's leads—almost always in the form of a one-sentence paragraph—general news stories offer more choices. Here are some of them, from the shortest to the longest:

- Five W's leads, also called summary leads, are still a mainstay.
- When you add a *so what* or develop the *why* in a summary lead, the single-sentence lead often grows to over 30 words. Broadcast news and many student publications in print and online choose to break such long leads into two or more sentences, sometimes two or more paragraphs, but they are still summary leads.
- When you add *how* to a summary lead, vivid descriptive language can stretch the lead even longer. The *who*, *where*, and *when* may be in the first paragraph and the *how* in the second, but you may not finish the *what*, *why*, or *so what* of the lead until the nut graf, where the five W's are completed and the audience learns why the story is important and why they should care.
- Narrative leads, a type of feature lead, contain anecdotes, settings, characters, quotations and more detailed descriptions, often from first-person observation. These may extend over multiple paragraphs, depending on the length of the story and the medium in which it appears. Newsmagazines, for instance, use narrative leads more often than shorter-form media such as broadcasts. A narrative lead is followed by a nut graph that gives the five W's of the story and tells why it is important.

These two narrative leads are the result of strong reporting as well as the techniques of storytelling.

1. The full story appeared in the Los Angeles Times.

   Primary headline: On the trail to a new life

   Read-out: (See Chapter 7 for more about headlines, including read-outs.) More than 60 horses were found starving in the Central Valley in the last year. One's training to be a packhorse.

   Byline: Diana Marcum

> *HUNTINGTON LAKE, Calif. – Comanche has one pale blue eye, one deep brown and a prancing gait that has cowboy Morgan Austin suspecting this mystery horse once paraded around an arena.*
>
> *Until two weeks ago Comanche wouldn't let anyone in the saddle. It took Morgan, 17, two months of talking to him "real quiet-like," slipping on a saddle blanket, then the saddle, before he could hoist his own lanky frame on the brown-and-white quarter horse.*
>
> *Now, on a day when the sky is pale with heat and ragged breaths of wind kick up thick, sticky dust, Comanche and Morgan lead the way down a boulder-strewn Sierra trail.*

The hundred words in the lead describe two characters—a horse and his boy—a relationship, a conflict and a setting. The news story that follows is not about Comanche; it is about the cost of a bad economy and droughts on both animals and people. But Comanche and Morgan put a human—and animal—face on the story that otherwise might be all grim statistics and facts.

2. This story also appeared in the Los Angeles Times.

   Kicker, in small type above the headline: Hundreds of women and girls are killed every year in Mexico state, known as Edomex. One woman who lost her daughter, 14, puts her life at risk to press her case.

   Headline: Seeking justice for Mexico state's female victims

   Byline: Tracy Wilkinson

> *ECATEPEC, Mexico – At 14, Jessica Lucero had already lived a hard life. A stint in rehab, dropping out of school, making her way, day in, day out, in a terribly violent, desperately poor neighborhood.*
>
> *But things were looking up. She had stayed clean and was planning to resume studies. She dreamed of becoming a forensic pathologist.*

The headline and kicker let us know this is a murder drama. The past tense helps create the suspense, which builds in the next two paragraphs:

> *Then, in June, Jessica was raped by a man she later identified as a notorious neighbor, a known drug pusher. Jessica's reaction was to do something that few people twice her age have ever dared. She went to the authorities and denounced the crime.*
>
> *Not 30 days later, she was killed, beaten to death with a small boulder. The force of the blow was so strong that her skull left a dint in the ground that would remain for days.*

Jessica is the focus of the lead, a face we can care about among the grim statistics: 200 to 300 girls and women are killed each year in this Mexican state. Suspense, character, action—all pull the reader into the story, which is about the larger issues of government corruption and crimes against women.

YOUR TURN

1. Find three narrative leads used in general news stories in the professional media.
2. **Going Deeper.** What literary techniques, such as suspense, characterization, details or literary devices, does the writer use in each of the three narrative leads?

The Nut Graf

The nut graf is the paragraph that tells the story in a nutshell, much like a five W's lead. It follows a narrative lead and provides a transition from the lead to the body of the story. It tells why the story is important (Figure 6.8). It also provides any of the five W's plus an H and perhaps the *so what* that were not already included in the main headline, read-out or kicker, and narrative lead.

A nut graf signals, "This is a news story, though it starts with a feature lead." The nut graf lets your reader know the article is not a personality profile of a horse or a murder victim. Rather the horse and the murder victim are the face of the larger story. The nut graf tells the audience what that larger story is.

Figure 6.8 Remember how important a nut is to a squirrel, and you will also recall the importance of a strong nut graf in your story.

For the Record

The Name of the Dog

Journalists tell of a diligent young reporter being trained by a hard-to-please editor (is there any other kind?). The reporter wrote about a fire that had burned three houses. He had everyone's name spelled right in each family, the number on the fire engines, the time the blaze was reported, every detail he thought his editor might demand. He'd filled a complete reporter's notebook, both sides of every page. What did his editor say, when he saw all this great reporting?

"Did you get the name of the dog?"

Like many jokes, this story contains an important truth. Strong reporting matters. Details matter. The name of the dog may be the very piece of information you need.

Roy Peter Clark wrote about getting the name of the dog after the 2001 attack on the World Trade Center. He is the vice president and senior scholar at Poynter Institute (http://www.poynter.org), a leading resource for journalists.

The Name of the Dog

by Roy Peter Clark, http://www.poynter.org
Published Sep. 2, 2002 3:46 pm
Updated Mar. 2, 2011 11:46 am

One of my favorite survivor stories out of the World Trade Center disaster is this gem from the AP: "Mike Hingson, who is blind, made his way to safety from the 78th floor of the World Trade Center during the terrorist attacks thanks to Roselle, his 3-year-old yellow Labrador guide dog."

We learn from Hingson that "Roselle did a good job. She stayed focused. We stayed to the side. We smelled a lot of jet fuel on the way down … Some people had a lot of problems breathing."

For about 20 years now, teachers at Poynter have been preaching this lesson: "Get the name of the dog." Never was that lesson more important than in the coverage of disasters in which dogs are used for rescue and security.

The Poynter adage is meant to stand for a wider truth: that powerful writing depends upon detail. Sol Stein calls the effect "Particularity." Writes Stein, "It is not just detail that distinguishes good writing, it is detail that individualizes. I call it 'particularity.' Once you're used to spotting it–and spotting its absence–you will have one of the best possible means of improving your writing markedly."

An excellent story distributed by Knight Ridder describes the plight of more than 300 dogs working at ground zero: "Lacerated paws. Burns. Dehydration. Overheating. Irritated eyes. Stress." Halfway through the story, the writer achieves particularity:

"'It's just hazardous to the Nth degree,' said Erick Robertson, 36, who drove from Oakhurst, Calif., near Yosemite, to offer the services of his independently trained search dog, Porkchop. Since Sunday, they have worked about eight hours a day.

"Wednesday morning, Robertson knelt by Porkchop's side as the year-old Australian shepherd got a checkup. Puncture wounds–suffered when a police dog bit him in the back–were tender to the touch. The dog's gentle green eyes were red from the acrid dust. And he was favoring one leg, which doctors tended to after carefully snipping away three layers of bandages and dog boots.

"When Porkchop catches the scent of human remains, he signals his master either with three barks or a motion that resembles a sneeze. Robertson said his dog has been making as many as a dozen recoveries per shift.

"'I'm very proud of him. He's 100 percent out there,' Robertson said, nuzzling Porkchop as the exhausted, dehydrated dog received fluids intravenously. 'It just blows me away.'"

Of course, the name of the dog says as much about the human namer as it does about the beast. Consider the difference between "Roselle" and "Porkchop."

In covering a story with so many characters and so broad a landscape, journalists would do well to remember the power of the particular: the color of the rosary beads, a family photograph recovered from the rubble, the name of the dog.

If the first two and a half paragraphs of the sports story "Touch sets the tone for Serena" may be seen as a narrative lead explaining *how*, then this is the nut graf of the story, where the reader learns *what*:

> *It allowed Williams to feel free in her final service game and it helped send her to a fifth Wimbledon championship and 14th major title with her 6-1, 5-7, 6-2 win. (Los Angeles Times)*

The first five paragraphs of "On the trail to a new life" are a narrative lead about Comanche and Morgan. The sixth paragraph is the nut graf with *who, what, when, where* and *why*:

> *The number of abandoned horses has more than doubled nationwide in the last five years, according to rescue groups. But in the Central Valley, where banks foreclosed on homes and ranches at one of the highest rates in the country, the numbers are even harsher. (Los Angeles Times)*

In "Seeking justice for Mexico state's female victims" the first five paragraphs tell of the life and death of a 14-year-old girl. The fifth paragraph is the nut graf with *who, what, when, where* and a compelling *so what*—the man who was until recently in charge of the state will be the country's next president:

> *And with that, Jessica became one of hundreds of women and girls killed every year in Mexico state, a region of 15 million people governed until recently by the man who will be the next president of Mexico. (Los Angeles Times)*

YOUR TURN

Write a narrative lead for the block wall story. (You will need to create details, since you have not actually reported this story.) Then create a nut graf to follow your lead. Place labels in the margin of your paragraphs to identify the nut graf and each of the five W's and an H, which may be in the narrative lead or in the nut graf.

Do the same for the for-profit colleges story.

Crafting the Closing

Unlike breaking news stories, general news stories are designed to be listened to or read from the first word to the last. National Public Radio

Six Leads to Avoid

A lead should say, "Look here! I promise you wonderful stuff if you read on." It should invite and entice the audience further into the story. Certain kinds of leads turn your audience away, even slam the door in their faces.

Noun-Only Leads

Verbs carry action, suspense and meaning. Nouns state topics. Avoid noun-only leads, especially one-word leads, like "Finals!"

The one-word lead labels the piece the way you label a filing cabinet drawer. The lead names the topic and shuts the drawer, as if you were saying to your audience, "Nothing interesting in here."

Advertising Leads

Though some strong writing uses a question as a lead, good leads should not sound like the start of a commercial or even an infomercial. Guard against talking down to you audience. If you can imagine an elementary school teacher asking the question, it probably is not a good lead.

- How would you like a new car?
- Do you know anyone with a drinking problem?
- How will you spend your holidays?
- Do you worry about your skin?
- Would you like $60,000 for college?

Leads That Think They Are Headlines

What *not* to do: Sullivan, Martinez to head WASC Committee

Lead: History teacher Sullivan and math teacher Martinez will lead the WASC team studying Coyote Hills High School to renew its accreditation, according to principal Otto Smith.

Lead language is different from headline language. Leads use complete sentences. They avoid jargon and insider language, such as WASC. Leads identify people clearly, in this case with last names and positions.

Copycat Leads

A good lead does more than simply repeat what is already in the headline. Here is an example of what *not* to do.

Headline: Fall Follies postponed until spring
Read-out: Scheduling conflict cited.
Lead: The Fall Follies have been postponed until sometime in the spring because of a scheduling conflict with club week and homecoming, assistant principal Cal Ender said Friday.

Leads That Start With a Quotation

Though dialogue can portray character, set a scene, show conflict and catch the reader's eye or ear, it can be dangerous in a lead. Sources rarely sum up a story, yet quoting a source in a lead suggests that the source just did.

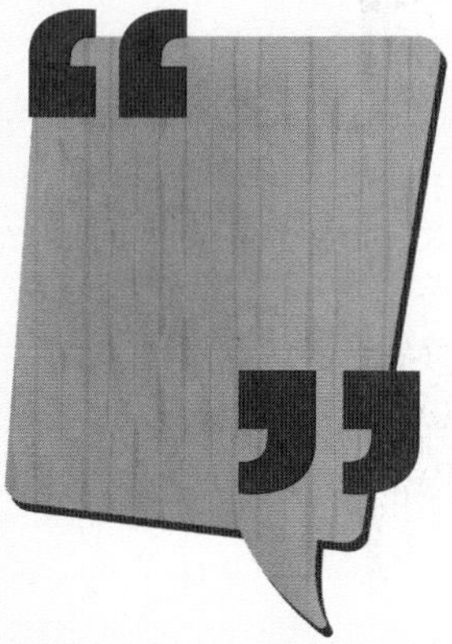

In addition, most quotes need to be set up—the reader needs to know something about the speaker, whom he is talking to, the context and perhaps the situation. That information needs to come before the quotation in most cases.

Leads That Order the Audience

Most of us prefer not to be ordered around by our media, so avoid leads that seem to be a command.

- Imagine being queen for a day.
- Prepare for finals with calendaring apps.
- Invest your time wisely ...

Figure 6.9 A great story keeps readers hooked until the end. *What techniques can both fiction writers and journalists use to keep the audience engaged?*

calls its best stories "driveway moments." Those are stories so good that people listening to the broadcast in their cars keep the radio on after they have arrived in their driveways, just to listen until the end. That is what journalists strive to do, pull their audience paragraph by paragraph to the end of the story (Figure 6.9). Endings are so important that some writers say they use their second-best lead as their closing.

The closing should give readers a sense of completion. They should know they have come to the end of the article. The cadence—the rhythm of the words—and word choice may create that sense of completion. The story of Serena Williams' fifth Wimbledon championship, a story that also covers her sister Venus' achievements, ends with this paragraph:

> *Five seems to be the luckiest number of all for the sisters.*

The closing often returns to the narrative lead, but this time looking forward. "On the trail to a new life," which started with the horse Comanche, ends with this:

> *If Comanche proves himself, he'll be entrusted with carrying strangers into the wilderness. Every summer, on trips somewhere in the High Sierra, he'll be a dead-broke, bombproof testament to second chances.*

The closing may reemphasize the *so what* of the nut graf. "Seeking justice for Mexico state's female victims" ends where it began, with Jessica's death, this time portraying her mother's desire for justice and the dangers she endures.

> *"There isn't a neighbor or friend who doesn't warn me we will get killed for going ahead with this," Cruz Perez (Jessica's mother) said. "They ask me, what could I possibly gain? But if you don't do it, it won't stop. I don't want there to be another mother like me."*

Finding a Shape for the Story

There are almost as many shapes for a story as there are general news stories, but each story has at least one organizing principle. You should be able to tell your editor what that principle is. Good news stories are never a jumble like the bottom of a gym bag, but their structure is different from other types of writing you may do in school.

Some, like the New York Times story on the Senate's report about for-profit colleges, rely on clear, compelling prose and additional important information to draw the reader to the end of the article. Others use stories and quotes to give life to each piece of information. Many stories use both techniques. The purpose of the writing often indicates the organization.

Analysis Writing

Analysis writing takes apart a complicated issue and lays it before the audience so that the audience can make up its own mind. Analysis writing often starts with a five W's lead with a prominent *so what* to attract a general audience. This lead is from the New York Times story about a Senate report on the practices of for-profit colleges. (The *so what* is underlined in the lead, below.)

The New York Times' readers are generally well-educated and informed, so the vocabulary is high and the lead is long—a whopping 86 words long, with 44 words in the first sentence. Though the two sentences are crammed with information, the lead attempts to be clear. Did it succeed?

> *Wrapping up a two-year investigation of for-profit colleges, Senator Tom Harkin will issue a final report on Monday—a voluminous, hard-hitting indictment of almost every aspect of the industry, filled with troubling statistics and anecdotes drawn from internal documents of the 30 companies investigated.*
>
> *According to the report, which was posted online in advance, taxpayers spent $32 billion in the most recent year on companies that operate for-profit colleges, but the majority of students they enroll leave without a degree, half of those within four months.*

The next four paragraphs outline contrasting views of the study, providing balance. The Senate study is strongly critical of for-profit colleges, so the reporter allows an industry spokesman to answer the charges. If people are shown in a negative light, journalists offer them a chance to defend themselves before the criticism is published.

- Quote from Senator Harkin: "These practices are not the exception—they are the norm."
- Quote from the Association of Private Sector Colleges and Universities: The report is "the result of a flawed process that has unfairly targeted private-sector schools and their students."
- The next paragraph summarizes the Democrats' argument for greater regulation of this industry and the Republicans' argument that for-profits are part of "a healthy free-market alternative."
- Next, the NY Times reports the Republican attack on the study and its authors.

The next 15 paragraphs summarize individual findings in the Harkin report. Each paragraph focuses on a different abuse. One paragraph says that almost 10 times more people work to recruit students than are employed helping them get jobs after they graduate.

> *Enrolling students, and getting their federal financial aid, is the heart of the business, and in 2010, the report found, the colleges studied had a total of 32,496 recruiters, compared with 3,512 career-services staff members.*

The reader is drawn on from one abuse to the next.

> *On average, the Harkin report found, associate-degree and certificate programs at for-profit colleges cost about four times as much as those at community colleges and public universities.*

Each paragraph strives to be clear and compelling. Even a NY Times reader turns to another story if the prose is not clear.

Narrative Writing

General news may also use both "hard news" elements—facts, quotations from expert sources, statistics and analysis—and narrative elements to make the information real and memorable to the audience. The proportions of these elements, the way they are mixed and the order in which they are presented is unique to each story, but there are general patterns.

Meet the Professionals:

Roy Peter Clark

Roy Peter Clark's passion for journalism began when he was a child growing up outside New York City in the 1950s, the golden age of baseball. "Every day I wanted to read everything I could about my favorite sports team—the New York Yankees—and my favorite players—Mickey Mantle, Whitey Ford and Yogi Berra. It was from the sports pages that I learned storytelling and colorful language.

"Those pages led me to a life of reading and writing and taught me how to live inside the English language," Clark said. In college he was managing editor of the Providence College newspaper, The Cowl, and editor of the literary journal. His career as a journalist includes a 29-part serial narrative, "Three Little Words," about one family's experience with AIDS, published in the St. Petersburg Times.

Clark serves as a writing coach to many thousands, from schoolchildren to Pulitzer Prize winners, and has written more than 16 books. He is a senior scholar and vice president at the Poynter Institute for Media Studies, whose mission is "to ensure that our communities have access to excellent journalism—the kind of journalism that enables us to participate fully and effectively in our democracy." He is the founder of the National Writers Workshop.

One pattern frequently used in news stories is SEE:

1. Say it.
2. Explain it.
3. Evidence (or examples) are provided, such as a quotation or vivid scene. This may be a sound or video recording or a written account, depending on your medium—radio, TV, print or a combination of these online.

In "Touch sets the tone for Serena," Diane Pucin writes:

> *The victory was the first major for the 30-year-old Williams since she won here in 2010.* (That was the Say it.)
>
> *Shortly after that title, Williams suffered severe cuts on both feet after stepping on glass in a Munich restaurant. She eventually needed two foot surgeries and also suffered a pulmonary embolism, a problem so severe that she ended up in a Los Angeles hospital and, she said, briefly feared for her life and for a longer time for her tennis future.* (That was the Explain it.)
>
> *"There was a moment," Williams said, "I remember I was on the couch and I didn't leave for two days. I was praying like I can't take any more. I've endured enough, let me be able to get through this.*
>
> *"I didn't give up. ... I had the blood clot, I had lung problems, I had two foot surgeries. It was a lot. I felt like I didn't do anything to bring on that."* (That was the Evidence—a powerful quotation that captured a scene and explained the conflict that was resolved on the courts of Wimbledon.)

Another pattern is to start with the narrative element followed by an expert source or statistic. The expert source supports the story and puts it in a larger context.

In "Seeking justice for Mexico state's female victims" David Mancera is part of the narrative, a vivid character. Tracy Wilkinson writes:

> *The dead women and girls of the state of Mexico, which abuts Mexico City, have as their voice and champion a fireplug of a man named David Mancera.*
>
> *Part political activist, part social worker, and a bit of a gadfly, Mancera carries a spiral notebook filled with the scrawled names and circumstances of recent slayings of women.*
>
> *"Just last week," he starts:*
>
> *Yuridia Valente, 22. Raped, strangled, single shot to the head.*
>
> *Fernanda Esparza, 19. Killed, allegedly by a boyfriend who killed his previous girlfriend three years earlier.*

The next five paragraphs tell more about the murdered women and about Mancera.

> *A Mexican watchdog group, the National Citizens' Observatory of Female Murders, said in a report this year that "a lack of investigation, prosecution and punishment" in Mexico state has led to a climate of impunity. It estimated that of 1,003 slayings of women during the Peña Nieto term (the man who would become Mexico's president), roughly half were unsolved and largely uninvestigated.* (This is the expert source.)

When we read fiction, we read to the end to learn the murderer's identity or how the hero destroys the weapon in its hardened silo or whether the lovers live happily ever after. A journalist writing general news or writing analysis of complicated, newsworthy issues has a harder job than a fiction writer. Not only does she need to be absolutely accurate, but she must also pull her reader along from one paragraph to the next by the strength of her writing. The information must be so compelling, the stories so vivid and the writing so clear that we do not want to stop.

Working from a Punch List

Other types of writing can be organized around a **punch list**, a to-do list of the most important points to include. *Punch list* is a term used in construction, where it means a list of tasks that need to be finished in a limited time. When journalists talk about a punch list, they are thinking of a story as if they were building a house or a mall or a skyscraper.

Working from a punch list, the journalist writes swiftly, incorporating each item on the punch list and inserting transitions between them, asking "What does my audience want to know next, or need to know next?" to help organize the information.

The journalist rereads the story frequently, often with her lips moving. When the story has been drafted, the editor reads it. Both the journalist and the editor look for any awkward or unclear wording that would cause a reader to look away (Figure 6.10). Both hone the transitions that link one paragraph to the next, that connect one item on the punch list to the next. Both arrange the material until the story flows so logically that the reader does not need to reread or to pause. The story should advance so smoothly that the reader does not even reach for a cup of coffee until the end.

Or, the story is rearranged until the deadline forces the reporter to push Send.

Chronologically, Geographically or by the Sources

Some stories are organized chronologically—first this happened, then that happened. Others are arranged geographically—first, a story or fact from nearby, then one from a neighboring city or the state, finally

Figure 6.10 Journalists and their editors work as a team to shape stories and make sure they flow smoothly from beginning to end.

an analysis linking national trends to local events. You can also arrange stories by sources. Report as much as you need from what one witness said, then move to the next witness, then to an expert source, then to the police spokesperson's comments.

Jumping around among sources, between locations or in time may confuse your audience, and confused people click on something else or turn the page.

YOUR TURN

1. Find three general news stories of at least eight paragraphs each from the professional press. Read the stories to determine the organizing principle: analysis, narrative, punch list, chronological or geographic. Mark the news stories and share your findings with your group or class.
2. **Going Deeper.** Find two examples of SEE (Say it, Explain it, give Evidence or Examples) being used as an organizing principle inside one or more stories, such as the three you selected from professional media. Underline the *Say it*. Highlight the *Explain it* in one color and the *Evidence* or *Examples* in another.
3. Find two examples of a Maestro question (what does my audience want or need to know next?) being used to organize sections of one or more stories.

It's Not All Bad News: Writing Brights

News is often bad news. No one needs to know—or is very interested in—a story about LL Cool J getting all four of his kids to sleep by 8:30 p.m. or reports that say everything is just terrific at for-profit colleges, all horses are asleep in their stalls and no one was killed last night.

But a steady diet of grim news and serious concerns can get heavy for your audience. Patronizing adults may criticize student journalists as "muckrakers" if they report concerns more serious than prom color schemes. Brights are one way to lighten the news diet.

Brights are short news stories whose primary news value is oddity. The story—as the journalist tells it—is funny or quirky or bizarre. Including a bright in your publication can be a valuable tool when you want to entertain your audience. Brights are often about human foibles, but a bright is not the place for satire. A bright's humor comes with a smile and a shrug, not a sting and an "Ouch."

Consider this bright, from National Public Radio's "Morning Edition." The story probably originated from another news source, but "Morning Edition" recognized its oddity and turned it into a bright.

> *Patrons of a public library in Port Chester, New York can continue reading in the bathroom. The Journal-News says the library will soon use toilet paper that features advertisements. Bryan and Jordan Silverman of Rye Brook developed the product. They contend it reaches a truly captive audience. Among other features, the toilet paper ads may include coupon codes that can be read by the cell phones that people will, of course, have in their hands.*

This bright, written for radio, is 75 words long and takes 29 seconds to read. In print most brights are under 300 words.

Brights require slightly odd material. The reporter needs an eye for oddity and the ear of a storyteller. The story does not have to be local, though proximity would add another news value.

To write a bright, start with a short lead—either a five W's lead or a feature lead—with a light tone. Do not give away your ending, though you may hint at it.

The next sentences give the necessary background information in the clearest possible fashion. This is the place for delayed identification. In print stories, quotes from the people involved work well. In the toilet paper story, "Morning Edition" could not resist the comment about "a truly captive audience," but not all brights will have humor in this middle section.

Your Turn

Journalism may be responsible for the continued popularity of several short words.

See if you can name the journalistic expression often used to replace the italicized words in each of these sentences.

1. The *man who was thought to have planned the crime* was arrested.
2. The *investigation* into the accounting *irregularities* will continue.
3. The decline in robins is caused *in large part* by the warmer weather.
4. Less popular books will be *identified and removed* from the library.

The last sentence is extremely important, almost a punch line. It is meant to create a smile, or a shrug and a smile. In the toilet paper story, the shrug comes because the listener may indeed know someone who takes her phone into a stall or reads in the bathroom.

This next bright may be filed under "stupid criminal stories," but it probably appeals to anyone who has had a bad haircut.

> *When most people get a bad haircut, they usually just hide until their hair grows out. But one woman in Richland, Wash., used a different strategy. She returned to the salon and demanded her money back — at the point of a gun. Police say she then shot out the back window of her stylist's car. The stylist was not in the car. Finally, she went to a different salon, told them she had a bad haircut and asked for a trim. No word on whether the hair repair was done before she was arrested.*

And one last bright for dog owners who think dogs should be, well, dogs.

> *An Italian city has passed a tough new law banning the mistreatment of dogs. The city council in Turin says people must walk their pets at least three times a day. If they fail, they can be fined the equivalent of $650. The new law also bars people from dyeing their pets' fur or from docking dogs' tails. A daily newspaper in Turin says it is now illegal to "turn one's dog into a ridiculous fluffy toy."*

Dogs, haircuts, cellphones in the bathroom scanning toilet paper: the oddity of the story suits it for a *potential* bright. Clear, tight writing *makes* it a bright.

Chapter Six

Review and Assessment

Recall

Assess

1. How do general news stories differ from breaking news stories?
2. How do the audience's potential questions guide reporting?
3. Why is it important for a general news story to have a good focus?
4. What are sidebars and why are they used?
5. The five W's, plus *how* and *so what*, appear in leads for both breaking and general news stories. Which are more likely to be emphasized in general news stories? Why?
6. What is a nut graf? What is its purpose?
7. Why is a good closing important for general news stories?
8. What are five ways to organize, or give shape to, a general news story?
9. What is the SEE method of narrative writing?
10. What are brights and what is their purpose?

Critical Thinking

1. List several questions you can ask yourself to find a focus for a general news story.
2. Describe how a general news story's lead might be different from a breaking news story's lead.
3. Describe the similarities and differences between fiction writing and journalistic writing.
4. What topics would generally be inappropriate for a bright? What topics might make good brights?

Application

1. Two walk-on coaches (not faculty members) will not be returning to coach next year because of "performance issues," according to your school's administration. Their firing has been controversial and publicly discussed in your community. Identify the people you should contact in order to be impartial when you report this story.
2. S Choose a national or regional story. Create a sidebar for that story that is aimed at your audience.
3. Choose a national and a regional story. Circle each item that should be fact checked before printing. How would you verify each fact?
4. S Your school is about to form a new sports team for competition. (Sculling? Rodeo? Skiing? Surfing? Curling? You choose.) List the questions your audience would want answered about this additional sport. Then research the sport at the high school level and write an imaginary general news story, beginning with a five W's (and *how* or *so what*) lead. Structure the story using strong transitions, varying sentence lengths and patterns and connecting words, letting your writing answer the questions your audience would ask.
5. S Choose a proposed law, regulation or policy at your school, in your community or in the news. Propose general news stories using each of the following approaches, as if you were pitching the story to an editor:
   1. Find the person who does the thing.
   2. Find the person who is strangely affected.
   3. Tell the history.
   4. Explain.
   5. Solve a mystery.
   6. Attend a public meeting such as your parks department, planning commission, school site council or PTSA. Identify one issue discussed. Use the general news story writing map on the Journalism website, take notes, interview people involved and research background, then write a general news story on the issue.

Chapter Six

Journalism Style

Direct Quotations: Using What Your Sources Tell You

If you place quotation marks around something, it should be *exactly* what the source said or wrote. A quotation mark is a reporter's certification of accuracy. "I heard this, or read it, and I am telling you exactly what was said."

Do not change words in a quotation, but do use standard spelling. If a source says, "He's not gonna tell you," write: *"He's not going to tell you."*

Quoting Complete Sentences

When quoting a complete sentence, begin with a quotation mark and a capital letter. Place punctuation inside the closing quotation marks.

"He's not going to tell you," she said.

She asked, "Did he tell you?"

Longer quotations may be presented as a block of text. To introduce a block quotation, end the preceding sentence with a colon. The block quotation should begin on its own line, indented, and does not require quotation marks.

Ellipses, Parentheses and Snippets

Some quotations are too long or contain unnecessary information. Use an ellipsis (one space, three periods and one space) to show that something has been removed from within the quotation.

If you need to remove something from the beginning or end of a quotation, embed the quote in your own sentence, as a snippet. A snippet is not a complete sentence, but your words provide what the snippet lacks to make an intelligent sentence.

You want to quote from a scholarly paper, "Helping or Hovering," about college students and over-involved parents, referred to here as helicopter parents because they hover. You find this information:

Specifically, we found that helicopter parenting behaviors were related to higher levels of depression and decreased satisfaction with life. Our results extend previous research that found increased use of prescription drugs for depression among college students who reported helicopter parenting.

You need to get the word count down, so you embed the most important information in your own sentence as a snippet and use an ellipsis to indicate what you have edited out. You use parentheses to show you added a word for clarity.

The study found helicopter parenting was "related to higher levels of depression and decreased satisfaction with life ... (and) increased use of prescription drugs for depression."

When you embed a snippet in your own sentence, you sometimes need to make a change for grammatical reasons. When you change anything, it no longer can go inside the quotation marks.

Use snippets and ellipses with great care. These edits should never change the meaning of the original quotation.

Try It!

Suggest edits using snippets, ellipses and perhaps parentheses that do not change the meaning of the following sentences but are shorter than the full quotation.

1. "I was kinda anti the idea of late-start days at first, but they are a good chance to talk with my teachers when I need help," Jason Carmack said.
2. "When I get out of school late, I'm late to my job at my uncle's dry cleaning shop on 43rd and Park so it messes up his schedule, too," Geraldo Calderon said.
3. You report that your state's senator quoted the whole of the First Amendment from memory late in a press conference. Properly punctuate, capitalize and indent the following:

   Late in the press conference the senator quoted from memory the First Amendment Congress shall make no law respecting an establishment of religion, or prohibiting the free exercise thereof; or abridging the freedom of speech, or of the press; or the right of the people peaceably to assemble, and to petition the Government for a redress of grievances

Extend Your Knowledge — Style Exercises

Each speaker's quoted words should be given a separate paragraph, no matter how short the comments. Go to the *Journalism* website to see examples and to learn how to punctuate quotations that extend for more than one paragraph.

Chapter Six

Writers' Workshop

In this Writers' Workshop you will:

- Learn one accepted pattern for general news stories.
- Identify the interviews and observations that should come from the news scene.
- Identify the information that should come from research and reporting.
- Create a fictitious general news story based on the pattern.

Workshop 6.1

News Patterns

It may seem like cheating, but news stories follow predictable patterns, patterns that allow you to report and write swiftly. They also help your audience read swiftly. You are free to break a pattern any time the story requires it, but the patterns serve you.

Mini-Lesson: Familiarity Breeds...Efficiency

Different media and different sections of publications use different patterns. The pattern used in the story below (the right-hand column of the table was described by Nanette Asimov of the San Francisco Chronicle.

The story pretends to report on the events in the limerick "Two Cats of Kilkenny," the origin of the expression "To fight like Kilkenny cats."

There once were two cats of Kilkenny

Each thought there was one cat too many

So they fought and they fit

And they scratched and they bit

Till (excepting their nails

And the tips of their tails)

Instead of two cats there weren't any!

Apply It!

1. Count the sources used in the Cats of Kilkenny story told in the table below. Include first-person observation, research and interviewing.
2. Choose a nursery rhyme, a fairy tale, a folk story or an urban myth and write a news story about it using the pattern described in the table that follows.
3. Look at the reporting you manufactured for the story. Make a list of the interviewing, researching and observations you needed to write.

Extend Your Knowledge Extend

If you do prewriting—that is, gathering and then sifting the information you have gathered—before you begin to type, your writing will give the reader interesting and clear information. Strong prewriting will allow you to pitch your enterprise stories to an editor and will allow an editor to decide if you are ready for a Maestro Concept meeting. Visit the *Journalism* website for a planning chart that will help you prewrite stories.

Paragraph	The Pattern	The Example: Cats of Kilkenny
1	A five W's lead that shines a flashlight on the story.	*Two Irish cats fought to the death yesterday in the town center of Kilkenny after several hours of mad-dogging and insults, according to bystanders.*
2	More details. *Don't pack too much into the lead.*	*Local magistrates reported finding only eight sets of claws and two tail tips at the scene of the fight.*
3	Strong quote. *Be sure to interview bystanders, witnesses and affected parties.*	*"Oh, they were going at it since early morning, saying the most awful things about each other and their mothers, then staring at each other. Then head-butting. Finally, that awful fight. It ruined my business all day. No one could get to my shop," local baker James Streehan said.*

(Continued)

Paragraph	The Pattern	The Example: Cats of Kilkenny
4	Larger context, why the story matters. *Be sure to check public records to see trends, give context.*	*Reports of assaults and battery, aggravated assault and murder have all declined in recent years in Kilkenny County, as they have across the Republic of Ireland, but the Cat-Irish population seems to be the exception.*
5	Summary of arguments to come. *When you summarize both (or all) points of view here, no one point of view seems favored.*	*Local residents gathering in front of the Pumphouse Pub said the cat fights are becoming increasingly more disruptive to civil order and forcing business away from the area near Kilkenny Castle, but leaders of the Cat-Irish Association said the fight was a tragedy for their community and that local reaction was an example of species stereotyping.*
6	Supporting quotes, in backwards order. This quote should support the last point of view in the summary. *Be sure to get at least two strong quotes from each side.*	*"Our community is in mourning for the loss of these two toms, barely into their prime. Adding insult to injury, some in Kilkenny want to punish all us cats instead of addressing the unemployment, poverty and catnip abuse that especially affects the Cat-Irish population," said Purry Motor Mouth of the Cat-Irish Betterment Society.*
7	Transition and second supporting quote for the same side, one that supports the first. *Use a transition to avoid using two quotes back to back.*	*Those who knew the two deceased cats also cite societal pressures. "I knew both of those boys, and sweeter cats you will never find. Oh, they could purr! But you see, they couldn't find work and living on the dole is no way for a young cat to thrive. They took to the catnip and made bad decisions. I blame the economy, I do," Father Thomas O'Halloran of Saint Gertrude's Parish said.*
8	Transition to signal we are now hearing from the other side and a supporting quote from the other side.	*But others call for stronger enforcement by the Garda, the police, of local laws to protect the broader community and tourism along The Parade and to the Black Abbey. "We need to do something about the violence. It may be just a cat fight, but it is driving away business. Why didn't the Garda come when they first started yowling this morning? Haul them away for disturbing the peace, I say. A few days in a cat kennel might teach them some manners," waitress Siobhan Scanlan said.*
9	Second supporting quote for the same side, one that supports the first. *Notice you do not need to make any comment about the arguments.*	*Local residents say the cat fights are changing their neighborhood. "I love cats as much as the next person, but I could not do my shopping here this morning for all the fighting, cats ricocheting across Parliament Street, hissing at each other. Then all the blood and just claws and tails left at the end. I walked clear down to the Market Cross to do my errands just to avoid the violence," local resident Bruno Duggan said.*
Next, use one or more of the following, if you have room.		
10	Real-time color—an anecdote or an example.	*While the Garda hosed down the crime scene outside, pub-goers watched from inside the Pumphouse, their dogs, a Jack Russell terrier, a rangy wolfhound and a "pure-bred mutt" named Charlie, sitting patiently at their feet.*
Or: 10	The past—what history can give the reader more understanding?	*Parliament Street is no stranger to violence. Cromwell's men battered down the south wall of Kilkenny Castle at the head of the street during the English Civil War in 1650. In 1922, during the Irish Civil War, the Republicans took the castle, and the Free Staters laid siege to it for two days.*
Or: 10	The future—what is the next step? What will the story look like in the future?	*The Garda Council will meet Thursday to discuss the police response to the violence.*
Finish the story.		
11	The kicker—a short, high-impact sentence, a telling quote, something that brings the reader back to the beginning.	*As dusk fell, a thin gray tabby carried a mewling kitten in her mouth across Parliament Street and toward the castle, perhaps looking for a place to raise her children.*

Chapter Seven

Writing Headlines and Captions

Why will they read it?

G-WLEARNING.COM

While studying, look for the activity icon to:

- **Build** vocabulary terms with e-flash cards and matching activities.
- **Extend** learning with further discussion of relevant topics.
- **Reinforce** what you learn by completing style exercises, worksheets and end-of-chapter questions.

Visit the Journalism website:
www.g-wlearning.com/journalism/

Chapter Objectives

After reading this chapter, you will be able to:

- Describe the main purpose of teasers, headlines and captions.
- Describe summary, narrative and descriptive headlines, and tell where each is used.
- Create broadcast teasers that attract and hold your audience's attention.
- Create informative print headlines that fit in limited space by using hammer heads, kickers and drop heads.
- Explain the importance of the first 55 characters for digital headlines.
- Discuss common journalistic techniques for writing efficient summary headlines.
- Discuss the danger of ambiguity and the importance of clarity in headlines, especially summary and narrative headlines.
- Describe literary devices employed in crafting descriptive headlines and the forms the headlines take.
- Explain how to craft search engine optimized headlines to attract traffic to your site.
- Describe the three elements of a strong caption.

Key Terms Build Vocab

catch line
descriptive headline
display font
drop head
hammer head
headlinese
kicker
main deck
narrative headline
read-out
search engine optimized (SEO)
spider
summary headline
teaser

Before You Read...

With a partner, read an article in an online publication, listen to an investigative journalism podcast or watch a local broadcast. Write down any words or concepts you do not understand. Ask your classmate or your instructor for clarification as needed. Then discuss the main ideas presented.

Introduction

"Never forget that if you don't hit a newspaper reader between the eyes with your first sentence, there is no need of writing a second one."

–Arthur Brisbane, American newspaper editor

Imagine you are up to your elbows in a large lake and quite comfortable. Someone comes by to offer you a drink of water. With water all around, what could tempt you to take it?

Your audience is up to its earbuds in information. The very air we breathe is full of it. We can connect to NASA, the stock market, the World Cup, March Madness and 257 of our closest friends while standing in a lunch line. Information tweets, tumbles, pings and downloads into our pockets and purses, onto wrists or eyeglasses. An ocean more is a click or two away.

As a journalist, you are offering a drink of news to an audience immersed in information. How can you tempt them to take it? The long answer, of course, is that you provide reliable information they want and need. You provide context, analysis or perhaps a local angle. But in the short run, how do you get your audience to take the first sip?

The job of print and digital headlines and of broadcast teasers as well as captions is to tempt readers to take a sip of your work. The best of these grab your audience and pull them into the story (Figure 7.1). They also direct search engines to your page.

Your audience will read, listen to or view your work when the headlines, teasers or captions are fresh, trustworthy and enticing. Strong captions, teasers and headlines

- promise information the audience needs or wants. They entice the audience into your story.
- use fresh, efficient and specific language. Every word and every character needs to be active, interesting and essential. Your readers do not want to wade through all this: *The Central School District Education Association and the Central School District's superintendent's office are discussing adjustments to the school calendar for the last 10 weeks of this year because of the days school was closed last week.* But they may like: *District and teachers' union grapple over year-end calendar* or *End-of-year calendar up in the air.*
- are accurate and fair. You do not use the word *grapple* unless the union and the district are struggling with the decision. Strong headlines do not frighten the audience into reading the story: *School in July?* They do not overstate the case: *Graduation threatened by rescheduling*. Of course you must never misspell a name or get a fact wrong in a headline, teaser or caption. Your audience's trust is your most valuable asset.

In addition, your headlines may be repackaged for search engines, social networks, feeds, aggregators, news alerts and mobile devices. The headline needs to make sense without its accompanying pictures, text or layout. If your headline has a digital future, it needs to be written for search engines to find.

Announcer: *Will Tuesday's snow change your graduation plans? District officials are negotiating with the teachers' union over the revised calendar. Story at noon.*

A teaser tells your broadcast listeners or viewers something is coming that they want to know.

Paying later for snow days now

District and teachers' union grapple over year-end calendar, graduation dates

A headline tells the reader, "This is important. This is interesting."

CHANGE OF PLANS—Senior Jamie Granger checks vacation plans she may need to scrap when the district revises the spring semester calendar. Last week's late snowstorm may shorten spring break or push back graduation. Granger has already ordered her graduation announcements.

A strong caption and a strong photo bring the readers into your writing.

Figure 7.1 Strong teasers, headlines and captions make your audience want to know more about a story.

Headlines

Strong headlines demand the skill of a haiku poet, the news sense of a seasoned journalist, the vocabulary of a crossword puzzle fanatic and the accuracy of a surgeon.

Headlines come in several flavors. A **summary headline** briefly summarizes the five W's of a news story. A **narrative headline** signals news, analysis or feature content. A **descriptive headline** balances the need to inform with the need to provoke interest or controversy (Figure 7.2, on the next page).

	Summary Headline	Narrative Headline	Descriptive Headline
What it looks like	Complete, compact sentences, often written in headlinese—an abbreviated style summing up the most important elements of the story.	Complete sentences written in standard, sometimes conversational, English.	Phrases, clauses, single words. Descriptive headlines often contain multiple layers of meaning, wordplay, a variation on a quotation or a vivid scene from the story.
Where it is used	Print media: in newspapers and newsmagazines; often on front page or first page of a news, sports or business section. Also in briefs. Digital media: on Web pages and for the small screen of a mobile device. Broadcast media: rarely used.	Print media: in newspaper and newsmagazines; may be on first page of news or on inside and in other sections. Digital media: on some Web pages and on mobile devices if the headline has fewer than 55 characters. Broadcast media: use this headline most often.	Print media: used sparingly on the front page of newspapers but important in newsmagazines. Digital media: used only when technological work-arounds make the story visible to a search engine. Broadcast media: may use these with a vivid or moving sound bite to give the audience a taste of an upcoming story.
The type of story it signals	• breaking news • general news	• general news • news in folo and continuing stories • news analysis • features • columns • editorials	• news or feature packages • news in continuing stories • features • sports • columns • editorials

Figure 7.2 Craft your headlines to suit your stories and your media.

Your Turn

1. Identify each of these headlines as summary, narrative or descriptive. Be prepared to defend your position to your group or class. There may be more than one right answer.
    - The crazy world of contortion (from a BBC story about really bendy people)
    - Glendale district says its online tracking is for safety (from a Los Angeles Times story about a school district that hired a company to monitor students' social media posts)
    - US poverty rate holds steady (from a Los Angeles Times business section article on a Census Bureau report)
    - Jury convicts man found stuck in air duct after bank robbery (from a Chicago Tribune story about a robber who might have escaped if he had a smaller waist and a larger IQ)

(Continued)

YOUR TURN *(Continued)*

- Can Emotional Intelligence Be Taught? (from a New York Times article on the importance of emotional skills—such as recognizing and responding appropriately to other people's anger, frustration or embarrassment—to success in school)
- 10 things you need to know about Trader Joe's (from an Austin American-Statesman article on the Southern California retailer opening a store in the Texas capital)

2. **Going Deeper.** Headlines should indicate both the content and the tone of the story. Stories with impact, timeliness and proximity are usually associated with the most serious tone. Oddity and human interest stories often take on a less serious tone, that is, a less serious attitude toward the subject, writer or audience. Based on the headlines in question 1, rate how serious you expect the story to be, with a 6 for the most serious and a 1 for the least serious story. Try to create a general rule about which kind of headline (summary, narrative or descriptive) should be written for the most serious stories and the least serious stories you cover.

Headlines Work in Tight Quarters

Whether you are working in print, broadcast or online media, your publication may have only one chance to capture your readers' attention. Headlines serve to introduce the audience swiftly to the story. "Audience, this is a story you will really want to know. Story, this is your audience." Yet headline writers work under tight constraints. Often time is short. Almost always space and word count are limited (Figure 7.3).

Though the journalist who writes the story may suggest a headline, an editor will carefully read the story while imagining the audience's needs and interests. Then the editor creates the headline that will be most helpful to the readers while still being absolutely accurate.

Broadcast Headlines

Broadcast headlines (also called **teasers**, teases or tasters) are brief summaries, usually under 48 words and in complete sentences, that are meant to attract and hold the audience's attention. They refer to the news stories that are coming: "New workplace rules may hinder teen employment. But first we bring you our top story." They may be heard at the beginning of a broadcast, just before a break, earlier in the day or on social media.

Figure 7.3 A good headline can be golden for a story, but headline writers have limited time and space.

A second type of teaser is more like a descriptive headline. It is vague and is meant to leave the audience wondering—and curious enough to tune in: "The end of the Scantron test? Story at noon."

Your Turn

1. Watch a newscast to find four teasers. Record each teaser or write it down as accurately as possible. How many words long is each teaser?
2. **Going Deeper.** Do the teasers fairly represent the story that will follow, both in content and tone? Do any appeal to the listeners' emotions? Their fears? What guidelines do you suggest for your publication or broadcast to keep your listeners' trust while also exciting their interest?

And Now... Closer to Home

Five Do's and Five Don'ts for Strong Teasers

DO

- ✓ Promise your audience something they want to know: *After weather, five great things to do with a formal dress after the prom*.
- ✓ Deliver what you promised, and more. Do not just give your audience five things to do; give them five solid suggestions and two wacky ways. And include sound files of the oohs and aahs from the young patients at a children's hospital opening a box of prom dresses, tiaras and glittery shoes, or the clacking of high heels along a hospital corridor.
- ✓ Find the focus of the story, the *so what*, before you create the teaser or produce the story. If you have discovered why your audience should care, writing the teaser will be easy.
- ✓ Plan, write and record teasers early, while you are still at the interesting location, even before you write the story. The tease and the story will work together and your tease will have access to the best audio and visual files.
- ✓ Collaborate with editors, videographers, writers and sound people as you create a tease. Something as important as a tease should not be something you think of all alone.

DON'T

- ✗ Appeal to your audience's fears unless there is a real danger. Avoid teasers such as *Pool chemicals used at Centerville High contain known cancer-causing agents! Film at noon.* You will lose your audience's trust if your big announcement is that high concentrations of chlorine bleach are dangerous.
- ✗ Give away the story. *Oilers accelerated in the last five minutes of play, burning up the Mariners 76 to 64. Story after the break.* Instead, make your audience curious: *Down by 15, the Oilers charge through the last five minutes of play. Story after the break.* Even if your audience knows the score, they will want to hear about the miracle that occurred in the last five minutes of play.
- ✗ Start teases with *If you*, as in: *If you ever played with a Barbie, you will want to …* That beginning just gave over half of your audience—the non-Barbie-playing half—permission to ignore your story.
- ✗ Use breathless adjectives: *fantastic*, *huge*, *unbelievable*, *heartbreaking*, *astonishing*. Only use adjectives that are honest and provable.
- ✗ Hype silly stuff, or your story will be known as the stupid broadcast. If you tease the overflowing toilets, it will be remembered as the toilet broadcast. If such stories have news value, cover them; but do not tease them to your audience.

Print Headlines

Page designers sometimes have the freedom to combine fonts, text and visual elements on a page—or substantial part of a page—that is as wide open as an artist's canvas (Figure 7.4). (See Chapter 15, Designing with Purpose for more about display headlines.)

However, more often print headlines are constrained physically by

- the width of the story. If the story is one column wide, the headline must also fit in that space (Figure 7.5). A word cannot be divided so that part of it is on one line and the rest is on the next. The entire word must fit on one line.
- the importance of the story. The more important the story, the bigger the font for the headline (and the more prominent its position on a page), so fewer words will fit into the space. Ironically, more important stories tend to have fewer words in their headlines (Figure 7.6).
- your publication's stylebook. Your stylebook outlines the capitalization styles you will use and when to use each style (Figure 7.7).
- your publication's headline fonts. Most publications use several fonts in different weights and styles. The kind of story or the tone of the story may indicate which headline styles or fonts should be used. Some take more room, and a few need more white space (blank space) around the font. The white space leaves less room for words in the headline (Figure 7.8).

NORTH POINTE
GROSSE POINTE NORTH HIGH SCHOOL
SINCE 1968
FRIDAY, APRIL 12, 2013

FANDOM
Take a glimpse into the lives of those who are obsessed and eternally in love with musicians One Direction, Ed Sheeran and Justin Bieber in this in-depth feature.
PAGE 7

A Caffeinated Existence
Some students use it to get them through the day – but adverse health effects and dependency can result.

END OF THIRD QUARTER
Friday, April 12

MINI COLLEGE NIGHT
Tuesday, April 16 at 7:30 p.m. in the cafeteria.

CLASS OF 2013 ICE CREAM SOCIAL
Monday, April 22 at 6 p.m. in the cafeteria and Cooper's Square.

HALF-DAY
Tuesday, April 23, 10:55 a.m. dismissal.

BOYS LACROSSE
Saturday, April 13 at 2 p.m. against Ligget.

GIRLS LACROSSE
Saturday, April 13 at 10:30 a.m. against Regina at home.

BOYS GOLF
Thursday, April 18 at 3 p.m. against South

Teachers, District hammer out new contract

By the numbers
30 meetings over 3 months
March 25
new contract took effect
62% of teachers voted

Dartmouth decision spurs debate over AP classes' value

Courtesy of North Pointe, Grosse Point North High School

Figure 7.4 The combination of art and text work together to form a visually interesting headline.

In addition, you may use **display fonts**. These large fonts add graphic interest to the design of the letters (Figure 7.9). Use such fonts thoughtfully. The font that is fine for the headline *Mailing your stuff to your college digs* may be inappropriate for an article about opening day of baseball or a news story about choosing a casket for a child. Display fonts are most often used in feature or news packages that are laid out in the style of a magazine page. See Chapter 15 for more about news and feature packages.

Figure 7.5 In print publications, headline size is determined by column width.

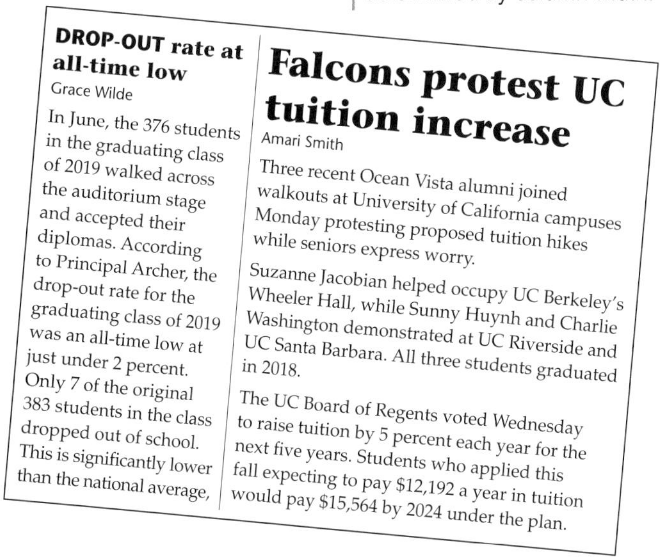
DROP-OUT rate at all-time low
Grace Wilde

In June, the 376 students in the graduating class of 2019 walked across the auditorium stage and accepted their diplomas. According to Principal Archer, the drop-out rate for the graduating class of 2019 was an all-time low at just under 2 percent. Only 7 of the original 383 students in the class dropped out of school. This is significantly lower than the national average,

Falcons protest UC tuition increase
Amari Smith

Three recent Ocean Vista alumni joined walkouts at University of California campuses Monday protesting proposed tuition hikes while seniors express worry.

Suzanne Jacobian helped occupy UC Berkeley's Wheeler Hall, while Sunny Huynh and Charlie Washington demonstrated at UC Riverside and UC Santa Barbara. All three students graduated in 2018.

The UC Board of Regents voted Wednesday to raise tuition by 5 percent each year for the next five years. Students who applied this fall expecting to pay $12,192 a year in tuition would pay $15,564 by 2024 under the plan.

Hammering, Kicking and Dropping for More Room in Print

Headlines are often referred to as decks. The primary headline is the **main deck**.

ONLINE UPDATES ON WWW.ADN.COM

■ 21 PAGES: Coverage of Tuesday's attack on the nation inside. See sections A, B, C and E.

State Final Edition

50 cents

Anchorage Daily News

ALASKA'S NEWSPAPER

www.adn.com

Wednesday, September 12, 2001

TERROR

Thousands feared dead as hijacked jets topple World Trade Center towers

■ CATASTROPHE: Other planes strike Pentagon, crash near Pittsburgh; government suspects Osama bin Laden.

Anchorage looks for answers after East Coast devastation

Courtesy of Anchorage Daily News

Figure 7.6 When paired with the powerful image of the World Trade Center attacks of 9/11, only a single-word headline is necessary.

Adding other decks—subsidiary headlines—above or below the main deck expands what you can communicate. Suppose this summary headline is the main deck of a news story.

Navy helicopter lands on Centerville High track

You have the opportunity to add more information in several ways.

Drop heads, also called **read-outs**, are subsidiary headlines that add more information below the main deck. A drop head is usually in a different font than the main head. It can be as wide as the main deck, or it can fit in a narrower space, such as one column width on a three-column story. Drop heads are narrative, while the main deck is a summary headline.

Navy helicopter lands on track
Mechanical trouble brought the Seahawk down on the empty Centerville football field, but it left under its own power

Kickers also add information to the main deck. Kickers go above the main deck and are usually half the point size of the main deck. For example, if the headline is in a 30-point font, the kicker is in a 15-point font. Kickers are usually less than half the length of the main deck and are often underlined.

Figure 7.7 Capitalization styles vary among publications.

Man bites dog	In down-style headlines, only the first word and proper nouns are capitalized, as in a sentence.
Man Bites Dog	In up-style headlines, every word is capitalized. Up style requires a bit more space.
MAN BITES DOG	Headlines written entirely in caps (capital letters) take up the most room, are more difficult to read quickly and are generally reserved for short words. They are good for emphasis, but use them sparingly.

Headline Fonts	
Man Bites Dog	A sans-serif font lacks the small "bird beaks" (serifs) at the beginning and end of each stroke of the letter. *Sans serif* means "without serif."
Man Bites Dog	This sans-serif font has a shadow effect.
Man Bites Dog	A condensed font may be used to fit a narrow column.
Man Bites Dog	A bold or heavy font may be used for emphasis.
MAN BITES DOG	Half-height capitals or small capitals are often used in subsidiary headlines.
Man Bites Dog	Serif fonts are typically used for body copy, but they may also be used for headlines.
Man Bites Dog	Spacing between letters and words differs from one font to another.
Man Bites Dog	Italic fonts slant to the right.
Man Bites Dog	A bold italic font takes more room than regular italic but has more emphasis.
Man Bites Dog	Fancy fonts are best reserved for feature stories.

Figure 7.8 These are examples of the many fonts that may be used for headlines. *Does your publication use the fonts that best express the nature of the story and the nature of your publication?*

Emergency Landing

Navy Helicopter Lands on Track

Hammer heads, also called barkers, are big and bold, centered and sometimes in all capital letters. They are used with news analysis and feature stories more than with breaking news stories.

COMING TO TAKE YOU AWAY?

The recent emergency helicopter landing on the track highlights the military's deep roots in the Centerville area.

The hammer head is often a descriptive headline with multiple layers of meaning, meant to intrigue the reader rather than communicate the most important or breaking news. In this case, the hammer head could be read in its most literal meaning. Did the helicopter land to take someone away? It also contains an allusion to a line in the Beatles song "Magical Mystery Tour." This suggests an adventure or something vaguely menacing, perhaps appropriate if the article is a news analysis or feature about the impact, both good and bad, of the military on your community.

The hammer head is in a large size and bold font. The main deck is narrative, in a smaller font, and it explains the story. Use hammer heads sparingly, no more than one on a page. They often introduce news packages or feature spreads.

Figure 7.9 Display fonts, such as those below can increase a headline's visual interest, but may not be appropriate for all stories.

Man Bites Dog

MAN BITES DOG

Your Turn

1. Access the front page of at least two print newspapers. They may be in a language different from your own. (You can find many at Newseum.org/todaysfrontpages.) Print out or otherwise capture the pages and identify the headline styles. Note any up-style or down-style headlines, all-capital heads, display fonts, read-outs, kickers and hammer heads.
2. **Going Deeper.** Examine several front pages from different print newspapers. They may be in several different languages, and you may find them online. Print out or otherwise capture the pages and identify the headline styles you find on the page.
   - Which front pages make it easy to find the most important story and the second most important story? What different headline styles do they use to direct your eye?
   - How many headline styles on one page are too many for your taste?
   - Do headline styles contribute to your impression of how interesting the paper is?
   - Do headline styles contribute to your impression of how trustworthy the paper is?

Digital Headlines

Headlines written for digital distribution also need to work in tight spaces, but in different kinds of tight spaces than print headlines. On several kinds of devices, only the first 55 characters—or fewer—may appear on a small screen. After 55 characters, your audience needs to specifically click or tap your story to read more, so the first characters need to be clear and interesting. If you have more than 55 characters, your headline is likely to be shortened—perhaps beyond recognition.

In addition, search engines will take your audience to your page only if the search engine finds key terms displayed prominently. *Prominently* usually means in the headline.

Summary Headlines

Subject-verb headlines demand attention, communicate efficiently

News, particularly breaking news, reports a *who* doing a *what*. Journalists write strong summary news headlines by identifying the most interesting and important *who* and *what* in the story, then summarizing the information in a brief sentence made of short words suitable for headlines. The headline may summarize the lead, but it never simply duplicates it.

This example from the BBC tells of workers at the Louvre Museum in Paris who refuse to go to work because of increasingly violent gangs of pickpockets. (In British English, *staff* is a plural and *organized* is spelled with an *s*.)

(Main deck) ***Paris Louvre shuts as staff strike over pickpockets*** (8 words)

(Read-out) *One of the world's most visited museums, the Louvre in Paris, did not open on Wednesday because of a protest by staff over pickpockets.*

(Lead) *Staff at the museum said thieves, some of them children, were targeting both employees and tourists.*

Two hundred workers took part in a strike organised by the SUD union, according to AFP news agency.

Notice the subject, the *who*, is *Paris Louvre* and the active verb, the *what*, is *shuts* in the main deck. The eight-word headline is followed by a 24-word read-out further identifying the *where* (the Paris Louvre) as one of the world's most visited museums and giving the *when*, Wednesday. The reader will have questions. Who are the thieves? Are they bothering just the staff or tourists, too? The 34-word lead answers those questions.

Your Turn

1. Identify the *who* and the *what* (the subject and the verb) in each of these headlines.
   - Judge frees death row inmate
   - North Korea raises global alarm
   - State Republicans push for tax reform
   - Long shot beats odds, sends Hawks soaring
2. **Going Deeper.** Locate five strong summary headlines in journalistic publications. Read the story that follows.
   - Would you describe the stories that follow the headline as breaking news, analysis or another sort of journalism such as a column, editorial or feature?
   - Identify the verbs and rate them from 1 to 5 (with 1 being boring, 5 being hyperexciting).
   - Do the same two activities (above) for sports journalism.
   - Do sports headlines differ from the headlines in the rest of the publication? Why?

Headlines Simplify Verbs

Summary headlines in particular try to compact the most significant information into the shortest possible, clear sentence. To do this, they rely on certain headline writing conventions, sometimes called **headlinese** because it can sound like a dialect of English and not standard English.

The heading above would be worded *Verbs Are Simplified in Headlines* if this were an ordinary, non-journalism textbook. But in summary headlines, forms of the verb *to be* are often eliminated. Headline writers avoid empty words—every letter must carry maximum meaning—so they rarely use *is, are, will be, was* or *were*. Forms of *to have* are also rare in headlinese.

Headlines tend to use the simple present tense, even though the story happened in the past. In the Los Angeles Times headlines *Disney adopts theme park age policy* and *Jury indicts former CALPERS leaders*, both *adopts* and *indicts* are present tense verbs, though the stories report actions that were completed in the past.

Though headlines usually stick to the present tense, there are exceptions to the rule, such as these from the Los Angeles Times:

- historical stories—*District rebuilt bell tower 90 years ago this month*
- obituaries—*Critic lived by rule of thumbs* (for film critic Roger Ebert)
- stories where background information is revealed—*Driver was on lam at time of crash*

Future tense in summary headlines is indicated by an infinitive (the word *to* plus the root form of the verb). Avoid *will* in summary headlines.

Doctor to get prison for illegal prescriptions

Trial to take new path

Health costs to rise

Progressive forms, the "ing" forms, of the verb are also relatively rare in summary headlines because they take up more space than the simple form, but developing stories may use the present progressive tense.

Imperial County betting future on renewable energy

Note the *to be* verb is eliminated. The headline does not say: *County is betting on renewable energy.*

Strong, Short Words Create Interest

Not only does each word in a headline need to be concise and active, it frequently also needs to be short. Short words help listeners understand a teaser even though they hear it only once. In print headlines, short words are not only easy to read, but they also can fit in one column in a large font.

Even when the layout allows for longer words, journalists use a vocabulary of short words. Some of the words are local or specific to a topic. For instance, Duke University basketball coach Michael William (Mike) Krzyzewski's name—even when you follow print headline practice of using only last names—would not fit in a single column unless you used a very tiny font, but "Coach K" does. Of course you do not put names in headlines unless your audience recognizes them easily.

Headlinese substitutes short words for longer words whenever possible. Figure 7.10 lists a few headline words commonly used to replace longer, multisyllabic nouns, verbs and adjectives.

Writing Short Headlines

Use ...	Instead of ...
accord (n)	agreement
aid (n/v)	assistance/to assist
ax (v)	to eliminate, remove, destroy
back (v)	to support, speak in favor of, assist
ban, also bar (n/v)	prohibition, exclusion/to prohibit, exclude
bid (n)	attempt
blast (n)	explosion
blast (v)	to criticize
boost (n/v)	help/to incentivize, invest in
call (for) (n/v)	demand/to demand
coup (n)	revolution, change in government
curb (n/v)	restraint/to limit, restrain
deal (n)	agreement
drama (n)	tense situation, dramatic action
drive (n)	campaign, effort
envoy (n)	diplomat
fear (n/v)	anxious expectations/to worry about
hail (v)	to celebrate, acclaim
hinder (v)	to make something more difficult or impossible
key (adj)	essential, vital
link (n/v)	connection/to connect
loom (v)	to approach (refers to something threatening)
mob (n/v)	mafia, uncontrolled crowd/to gather in large numbers
ordeal (n)	unpleasant or dangerous experience
pact (n)	agreement, treaty, contract
plea (n/v)	strong request/to ask fervently
poll (n/v)	election, public survey/to survey for opinions
plunge (v)	to drop dramatically
probe (n/v)	investigation/to investigate
quiz (v)	to interrogate
row (n)	argument, disagreement
slam (v)	to criticize severely
soar (v)	to increase dramatically
talks (n)	discussions, negotiations
toll (n)	number of people killed or amount of devastation
urge (v)	to strongly recommend

Figure 7.10 Headlinese favors short words over long ones.

What to Avoid in Print Headlines

Headline writing is hard. Shun these uses that would compromise clarity, efficiency or your readers' trust (Figure 7.11).

Beware Ambiguity!

It is best for at least two sets of eyes to see a headline before your audience does, to see how it reads to someone completely new to the story. The headlinese of summary headlines creates extra challenges. Words that can be both verbs and nouns—as well as adjectives—invite multiple interpretations. For instance, in the headline *Town urges curb cuts*

Figure 7.11 Your headlines will have more impact if you follow the guidelines below.

When writing headlines ...	Instead of this ...	Write this ...
Avoid contractions, unless they are in direct quotations.	*Goodfellow won't run*	*Goodfellow will not run*
Avoid names. Check with a diverse group of potential readers before using a name in a headline. If the name is not likely to be immediately recognizable, use a job title or other descriptor.	*Broadwater and Billings to debate Wednesday*	*Mayor, challenger to debate Wednesday*
Do not use simplified spellings.	*nite, thru, lite, bcuz, u*	*night, through, light, because, you*
Use active voice whenever possible.	*Students entertained by hometown band Stargazer*	*Stargazer plays for hometown audience*
Avoid clichés like the plague! Clichés creep in when reporting and writing are weak or the story has not found a focus. Do not expect a great headline on a poor story.	*'Tis the season for pumpkins, candy and service projects*	*Central High teens launch kid safety campaign*
Do not editorialize.	*Union rejects outrageous offer*	*Union rejects controversial offer*
Avoid breaking a line of type in a way that interrupts sentence flow or obscures meaning. Rewrite the headline if necessary.	*Smythe to* *ride at* *state rodeo* *final Friday*	*Sophomore* *calf roper* *to compete* *at state*
Avoid parroting the lead or the read-out (drop head) in the headline.	(Main deck) *Sophomore watches in horror as freeway footbridge collapses in front of him* (read-out) *Sophomore Jamie Welsh watched in horror as the freeway footbridge collapsed this morning.* (lead) *Sophomore Jamie Welsh was horrified when the freeway overpass leading to Central High School collapsed just as he was about to cross it.*	(Main deck) *Sophomore watches in horror as freeway footbridge collapses in front of him* (read-out) *Jamie Welsh, 15, narrowly escapes injury as the concrete and steel overpass buckles at 8:37, dropping debris—and his skateboard—onto the traffic below.* (lead) *Officials say they do not know why the 57-year-old overpass collapsed onto the freeway this morning. But sophomore Jamie Welsh reports having just reached the top of the steps on the west end when ...*

And Now... Closer to Home

Other Shorteners for Print Headlines

- No period is needed to mark the end of a sentence: *Judge declares mistrial*
- When a headline contains two sentences, use a semicolon and a single space: *Graffiti cleanup mandated; parolees to complete work by June*
- No articles are needed in a summary headline: ~~*The*~~ *Mayor to dedicate* ~~*the*~~ *High School for* ~~*the*~~ *Performing Arts*
- The word *and* is replaced by a comma in summary headlines: *G-8 teams up on Syria, taxes* (Los Angeles Times)
- Direct quotations are marked by a single quotation mark at each end: *Mayor 'embarrassed and saddened' by son's arrest*
- Use a colon instead of the word *said: Mayor: 'No arrests' expected in fraud*
- Or use an em dash, a dash as wide as the letter *m*: *FBI—'Person of interest in custody'*
- Use numerals, not words, even at the beginning of a deck: *3 injured in crosswalk hit-and-run*

is the subject the town, or is it the town's urges? Is the verb *urges* or *curb*? Does this headline mean that the city is asking for cuts in street curbs to allow wheelchair access or that the town's irresistible instincts restrain its ability to trim its budget?

Ambiguity can create embarrassingly funny headlines—funny for the reader, embarrassing for the publication. Richard Lederer's "Anguished English" recounts these:

Doctor testifies in horse suit

Hershey bars protest

Grandmother of eight makes hole in one

Town to drop school bus when overpass is ready

Your Turn

1. Columbia Journalism Review's regular feature "The Lower Case: Headlines that editors probably wish they could take back" publishes headline bloopers from the professional press. Find and share with your group or class several ambiguous headlines from "The Lower Case" at the Columbia Journalism Review website.
2. **Going Deeper.** Rewrite each ambiguous headline twice, once so it clearly conveys one meaning and once so it clearly conveys another. For instance, *Doctor testifies in horse suit* could be rewritten *Clad in horse costume, doctor testifies in trial* or *Doctor testifies in Del Mar Racetrack breach of contract suit*. Is the ambiguous headline shorter than your clear headlines?

Brevity vs. Clarity: When to Use Proper Names, Abbreviations or Acronyms

Use a proper name or nickname in headlines only if it is well enough known to be recognized by your audience immediately. Otherwise use a job title, such as *county commissioner*, or a descriptor, such as *bystander* or *competitor*. Neither a listener nor a reader should need to pause to figure out what person you mean. Generally, use only the last name when you do include a name in a headline. (But see the discussion of SEO headlines, page 207.)

Also avoid abbreviations and acronyms (words made of the first letters of a phrase) unless they are immediately recognizable by your audience. Abbreviations such as FBI, NBA and CIA are generally safe, as are the acronyms SCUBA, NASA, AIDS and NATO. Others depend on your audience and the context. If you attend a STEM (Science, Technology, Engineering and Math) high school or have an IB (International Baccalaureate) program or many AP (advanced placement) classes at your school, you should be able to use these abbreviations in your headlines without explanation.

When you are not certain if a proper name, an abbreviation or an acronym is widely understood, check with diverse potential readers, not just the other people on your publication staff, before you use it in a headline. If an abbreviation or acronym is relatively unknown, avoid it in headlines and write it out in the first reference in your story. Remember: If in doubt, write it out.

You may use a shortened name for your school's sports teams and, by inference, members of your school community. The University of Southern California's team, the Trojans, fits in a headline better than the pre-1912 team name, the Fighting Methodists. By inference, USC students may be referred to as Trojans. When space in a single-column headline is tight, *Trojans* can be replaced by *USC*. Note that would not work if your audience followed football in the Southeastern Conference. There, USC is the University of South Carolina.

Your Turn

1. List acronyms or abbreviations that would be clear to your audience but that might be unclear in a publication for another state or in a business publication.
2. **Going Deeper.** Scan the AP Stylebook, including the Social Media section, for common abbreviations or acronyms that do not require periods. Should your publication's stylebook add any abbreviations that are commonly known locally, for instance those related to high school sports or educational practices and institutions in your area?

Narrative Headlines

Storytelling headlines tell you why, and why you should care

Though summary headlines work well for breaking news and other timely stories, many other strong news stories are less timely but offer context for events or explain their impact. Narrative headlines signal this in-depth sort of journalism. In addition, columns and feature stories use narrative headlines. Broadcast news relies heavily on narrative leads, even in breaking stories.

Narrative headlines are complete sentences, usually in the present tense, but with no period at the end. They may use *to be* verbs, *and*, and the articles *the*, *a* and *an*, and they may include *says*. Narrative style, when used in the headline of a print news story, suggests that the reporting will include anecdotes and storytelling as well as facts and breaking news.

Compare these headlines, both published about the same time on the same subject. A summary headline provides the facts:

Ban on shark fins takes effect Monday
(NBC Los Angeles website)

A narrative headline promises more:

With shark fin ban, a slice of Asian culture ends in California (Los Angeles Times)

The Los Angeles Times narrative headline is followed by over 850 words of solid, interesting reporting on the impact of the new law, rewarding the reader who is enticed by the narrative headline.

A story that begins as breaking news with a summary head may later use a narrative headline in a folo story—a story written days or even weeks after the breaking news event as the story develops.

This breaking news story from the Los Angeles Times has a summary headline.

Two transients arrested in Hollywood stabbing

Several days later, in a folo story, the headline is narrative.

Suspect in Hollywood stabbing has a long record

The language is still efficient and brief, the tone serious, but the presence of the article *a* and *has* suggests this is a continuing story providing context to the earlier arrest.

In broadcasts, the tone may be even more narrative:

The suspect arrested last week in a Hollywood stabbing has a long police record.

A summary headline in a print news story, *Hepatitis B campaign focuses on Asians* (Los Angeles Times), becomes a broadcaster's *The Asian-American community here in the Southland is the focus of a new hepatitis B campaign.*

In print, *Formula One's Tire Fiasco Recalls the Sport's Sometimes Lethal Past* (New York Times) becomes a more narrative headline for a broadcast story: *The tire fiasco at last Saturday's Formula One race recalls the sport's deadly past.*

Descriptive Headlines

Engaging their attention, their curiosity, their emotions

Descriptive headlines, unlike narrative and summary headlines, are not always complete sentences. While they lose the impact of a specific *who* and a strong verb, they may use tools from creative writing. Descriptive headlines may include suspense, plot, literary and pop culture allusions and figurative language, as well as words and images that evoke emotions. These headlines work well for feature stories and packages as well as news packages and columns. They are especially common in newsmagazines. News broadcasts may use these as teasers: *A blind photographer. Learn how she does it. Stay tuned.*

Descriptive headlines lack the urgency of summary or narrative headlines. They suggest the story's news value may be human interest, oddity, proximity or conflict rather than timeliness, impact or prominence.

This headline from the Los Angeles Times suggests a strong plot with conflicts, villains, rescues and suspense.

(main deck) *Activists to the rescue*

(read-out) *Volunteers duel with the government and with 'kill buyers' who seek wild horses for slaughter*

Though all headlines need to communicate, descriptive headlines may be at their strongest when they intrigue the audience as well as communicate. The headline from the Monta Vista High School (Cupertino, California) El Estoque plays off the common expression "time after time" or perhaps the 1984 song by the same name (Figure 7.12).

Interrogative Headlines

Interrogative headlines are narrative headlines that ask a question. The story that follows is most often an explainer, a story that provides information and analysis. Generally avoid question headlines except for explainers.

- *Will block scheduling cut down on tardies?*
- *Will Centerville's move to 5A competition doom its athletes' dreams of playing college ball?*
- *Do AP students do better in college writing?*

SPECIAL REPORT

CRIME after CRIME

Every year 5,900 jaywalkers are killed. A person committing piracy can spend up to five years in prison and lose $250,000. Drivers with provisional licenses can have their licenses legally revoked by a judge and also be fined $50 the first time they're caught.

Certain crimes are so regularly committed by our population that we consider them minor and continue to perform them, time after time. But as commonplace as they may be, these crimes still have legal consequences.

When it comes down to it, we must ask ourselves what makes committing these crimes more acceptable than others — and where do we draw the line between what's petty and what's serious?

25 April 10, 2013

SPECIAL REPORT

THE EVERYDAY CRIMINAL

Though illegal and ethically questionable, piracy remains rampant among high school students

by **Yuna Lee** and **Angela Wang**

Senior Larry Xu likes watching movies in his free time — more frequently when he is bored. Either way, it's free.

Xu pirates two things: software and media. He downloaded Adobe Creative Suite, which costs around $2,000, along with regular updates. Xu also torrents television shows and movies on a weekly basis.

His reasoning? The service providers will not lose profit if he is never going to buy the product anyway. He believes that as long as consumers uphold this mentality, the fault is on the companies and their incapability to correctly market their product to make it affordable or available to their consumers.

"There is no limit to how much I should download," Xu said. "Downloading one episode of a show or downloading three seasons of a show — I don't really see a difference if I'm not going to purchase them anyway ... I'm aware of the consequences of being found out and possibly being fined, but there's a very low probability of something like that actually happening. I honestly don't feel any guilt whatsoever for doing it."

At MVHS, 63 percent of 345 survey respondents have admitted to participating in Internet piracy. However, students are not oblivious. 74 percent said they are aware of the consequences of Internet piracy.

THEY'RE TRYING TO MAKE THE SITUATION LOOK WORSE THAN IT ACTUALLY IT IS.

senior **Larry Xu**

Junior Sophie Min presents a similar justification. She pirates music, through a Youtube to MP3 converter, only on the occasion that she cannot afford or does not have access to it. And even if she

EL ESTOQUE 26

Courtesy of El Estoque, Monta Vista High School

Figure 7.12 Creative descriptive headlines draw your audience into the story.

Descriptive headlines may focus on a compelling detail rather than the *who, what, when, where* and *why* of the story. Examples from the Los Angeles Times include:

Clashing accounts of sisters' fatal shooting

"Like a huge blowtorch" (a witness's account of a brush fire)

If It Is Not a Sentence, What Is It?

Descriptive headlines rely heavily on two grammatical constructions: the gerund phrase and the noun phrase.

Gerund phrases use the "ing" form of a verb as a noun. They may suggest action because of their origins in the verb. Gerunds may take an object, but the *who* is generally missing. Perhaps the gerund is used because the name of the rescuer is not well-known, as in the example below. The drop head below the main deck is a complete sentence telling the *who* and *what* of a story that happened several weeks before.

(main deck) *Using his instincts to save a life*

(drop head) *Conner Reeves says he helped a fellow surfer who was face down in the water.*

The caption to an accompanying photo identifies Conner as a 16-year-old member of the Edison High School Surf Team.

And Now... Closer to Home

Repetition Warning!

Headlines of any sort can become dull if they are repetitive. Too many gerunds in headlines (and captions) make your readers' eyes glaze over. So do too many similar noun phrases.

Any device can be overused. Variations on these common sayings are about as fresh and interesting as week-old chewing gum:

- 'Tis the season
- versus (as in *Congress versus the patent trolls*)
- Springing forward
- Falling back
- Practice makes perfect
- Oh the places you'll go (for senior post-graduation plans)

Clichés may sometimes make strong, fresh headlines, but they should be used no more often than you get a tetanus shot. Once every 10 years should be fine.

Noun phrases lack the power granted to strong verbs. Descriptive headlines that use noun phrases suggest a story is static, even historical, as in a personality profile or obituary. The following example is from the Los Angeles Times.

(kicker) *Al Fritz, 1924–2013*
(main deck) *Godfather of the Sting-Ray bicycle*

Descriptive headlines allow the headline writer to create multiple layers of meaning and use wordplay when the tone of the story invites

And Now... Closer to Home

To Pun or Not to Pun: That Is the Question

Some tips about wordplay:

- Make sure the headline communicates to someone who does not "get" the pun or literary reference. Even if you have never heard of the play "Hamlet," or are not familiar with some of the play's more well-known lines, you probably understood that this sidebar is about when to use a pun.
- The more the pun obscures the meaning of the headline, the more likely it is that you should abandon it. The best puns are invisible until they are discovered, like clean glass. Once they are discovered, they add another layer of meaning to the headline.
- It is rarely acceptable to pun on a given or family name, though nicknames are sometimes fair game.
- Make sure the tone of the wordplay matches the tone of the story. Puns, for instance, range from groaners such as *Cone of silence* (about ice cream cones) to truly inspired puns such as this one from Seattle's KOMO News: *Man stumbles upon reptile near sewer, offers gator aid*.

it. Such wordplay abounds in descriptive heads but is rarer in narrative headlines and almost nonexistent in summary heads.

Wordplay, including puns, appears in these Los Angeles Times headlines:

> *Device maker's recovery faces a hang-up* (about stock shares of BlackBerry, a phone maker, plummeting 28 percent)
>
> *A cone of silence?* (about a law that would restrict when ice cream trucks could play their jingles)
>
> *Track skills run in the family* (about a track star whose parents were athletes)

Your Turn

1. Skim over several years of one or more student publications or several weeks of a professional publication. (Many school publications are posted online, and Newseum is a good source for professional publications.) Note the types of headlines: summary, narrative or descriptive.
2. **Going Deeper.** Do you see a pattern in how these types of headlines are used? Did you find any overused forms, such as gerunds or repetitive types of wordplay? Save examples. With a group, make a list of what you would like to avoid in your publication.

Search Engine Optimized Headlines

Headlines matter more than ever on the Web

You have done a great spread on the Quonset Kitchen Store, an award-winning food bank run by the International Club on your campus. It is housed in a Quonset hut on the north end of campus. When you publish the story in your newsmagazine, students and staff read it, talk about it and even compliment you. It is on your Web page, where you are getting some traffic but not as much as you had hoped. The pages are archived as PDFs at a national site. But almost no one seems to be reading it online, certainly not people outside your high school community.

To make matters worse, the next week a major news outlet in your area runs a story on the lack of local food pantries and never mentions your school's food bank, let alone your article. Of course that story fails to link to your publication.

What is wrong?

Search engines do not understand what a page is generally about. Instead, they look for exact words on the page, a few synonyms and relevant links. If the search engine does not find the words *food bank* on your page, it cannot guess that your page is about a food bank.

Search engines are also notoriously unable to catch wordplay and references to YouTube memes. They miss irony entirely.

If your headline is written only for human eyes—eyes that are looking at photos and graphics—your work may be invisible on the Web and meaningless on a cellphone. Your clever headline, *A half circle of caring*, is beautiful in print. It ties together your text and dominant graphic of the semicircular Quonset hut. But the headline is mute in the digital world because it is not **search engine optimized (SEO)**.

Using Headlines to Attract Spiders

SEO headlines need to include relevant proper names—both first and last—as well as geographic names (this is contrary to what you do when writing print headlines) and keywords. If you cannot fit all these into a headline, make sure they are prominent elsewhere in your article.

Keywords make your article visible online. Think about how people search for information digitally. They usually type three or four search terms into a search engine such as Google or Bing, perhaps *food bank, Centerville* and *high school*, or they may try *food pantry* and *Buchanan County*. Maybe they type in the name of the club adviser, *America Suarez,* plus *International Club* and *award*.

The work of finding relevant pages, pages that match the query, belongs to the search engine's **spider**, a program that crawls through millions of Web pages looking at the URLs, the headlines, the text of stories, the captions and the infographics. The spider also notices the number of links between one site and another (Figure 7.13).

When someone queries *food bank, high school, Centerville, International Club*, the spider displays the links to all the pages it thinks are relevant to those search terms. (Search engines also consider what they know about who is searching, such as where you live and what searches you usually perform. You may not get identical results when you search on a desktop computer at school and on your laptop while on your way home.) Your goal is for your article to appear on the first page of the spider's results.

How does the search engine rank pages? That is an ever-changing company secret, more closely guarded than the recipe for Coca-Cola. There are literally hundreds of factors, but at least three are important to your article's ranking.

1. How often the search terms are found on your page. If your text mentions *food bank* only once, your page may rank lower than if you use the term four times. The spider does not know you mean *food bank* when you refer to a *community commodity resource*, a *free neighborhood bodega*, a *mini food distribution center*, or a *tiny, free market*.
2. How relevant or important the search term is on your page. If Centerville High School is mentioned only once—in the disclaimer at the bottom of the page—it will not seem especially relevant to your

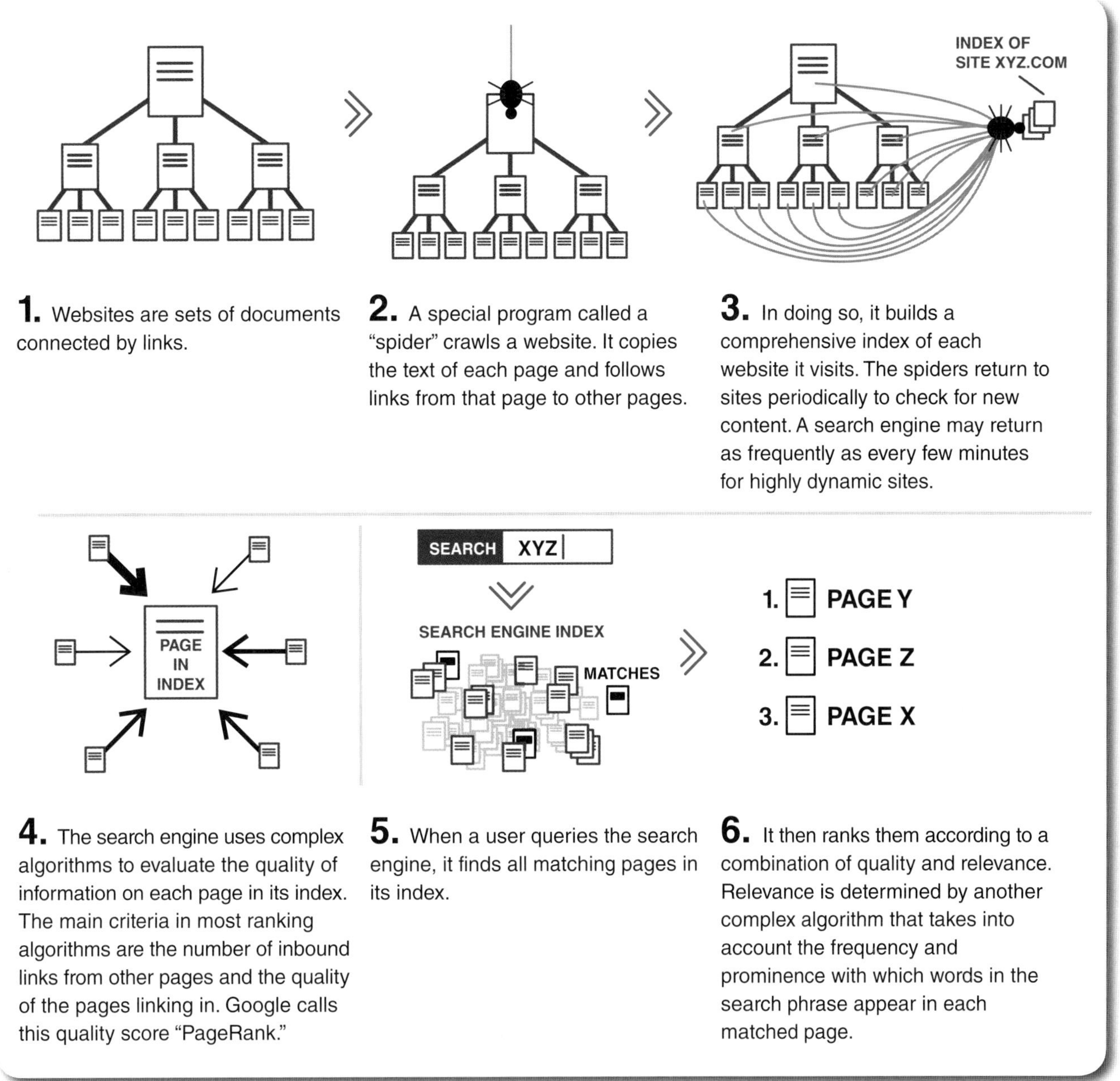
INDEX OF
SITE XYZ.COM
1. Websites are sets of documents connected by links.
2. A special program called a "spider" crawls a website. It copies the text of each page and follows links from that page to other pages.
3. In doing so, it builds a comprehensive index of each website it visits. The spiders return to sites periodically to check for new content. A search engine may return as frequently as every few minutes for highly dynamic sites.
PAGE
IN
INDEX
SEARCH
XYZ
SEARCH ENGINE INDEX
MATCHES
1. PAGE Y
2. PAGE Z
3. PAGE X
4. The search engine uses complex algorithms to evaluate the quality of information on each page in its index. The main criteria in most ranking algorithms are the number of inbound links from other pages and the quality of the pages linking in. Google calls this quality score "PageRank."
5. When a user queries the search engine, it finds all matching pages in its index.
6. It then ranks them according to a combination of quality and relevance. Relevance is determined by another complex algorithm that takes into account the frequency and prominence with which words in the search phrase appear in each matched page.

Courtesy of Poynter News University's e-learning course: Writing Online Headlines: SEO and Beyond

Figure 7.13 Understanding how a search engine works will help you create a strong headline that can be found easily using a keyword search.

story, so be sure the most likely search terms are used frequently and prominently. The most prominent places on your page are

- the headline.
- the URL, that is, the Web address, which should include your publication's name (Figure 7.14). Better yet, it should include the school name also, such as "Centerville High School Courier." News site URLs usually include the story's section, the date and the slug (one- or two-word description of the story). These attract spiders.

3. How reliable your site is. The spider determines this by looking for links to your page. In effect, it wants to know how often other pages are referring to your site as a source and how many times you link to reliable sources. The more links, the more reliable your site seems.

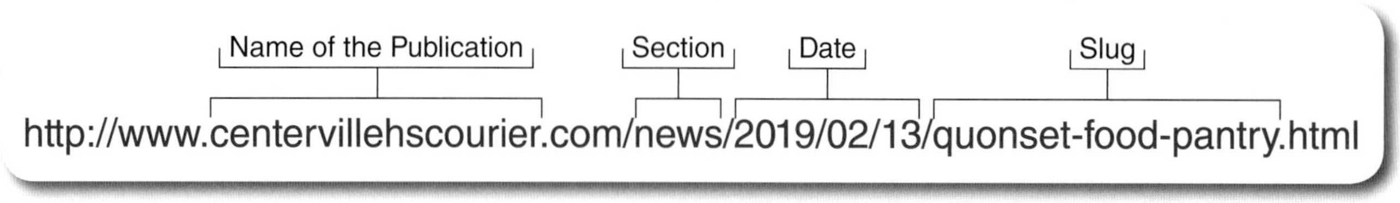

Figure 7.14 An appropriate URL will attract search engine spiders.

Notice what the spider did *not* look at: Your dominant graphic in the shape of a half circle gets no attention. The spider probably also did not look at the photos. If graphics or photos are necessary to explain a headline, the headline will make little sense when viewed on a cellphone or in a search engine's results. Therefore Web headlines rarely depend on pictures for clarity. For instance, *To the Pointe* next to a picture of a ballerina is obviously about a dancer. Without the picture, it looks like a typo.

To make your work visible digitally, you need to rewrite the headline using the most likely search terms (or at least the title that goes into your URL). It might read like this: *Centerville High School food bank aids Buchanan County*. Include other search terms in the drop head: *International Club adviser America Suarez has guided the award-winning club for a decade, feeding dozens of needy families each week.* Including these terms will make your story visible digitally in several ways.

- The short headline (without the drop head) will transfer well to a cellphone screen. Headlines longer than 55 characters are trimmed in many programs, and only the first half dozen or so words fit on some screens.
- The headline tells what the story is about, even on a cellphone. Those interested will read more.
- Search engines looking for *Buchanan County*, *food bank*, *Centerville High School* will find your story. So will engines looking for *America Suarez*, *International Club*, *award* and *needy families*. Depending on how many other documents include each of those terms, your page may show up on the first page of search results.

The Spiders Need to Find Your Publication As Well As the Article

As you put your school newsmagazine on the Web, you may need to rethink decisions that worked well in print but that hide your publication from spiders. Everyone at your school knows the mascot is a Buccaneer and the newsmagazine is called The Buccaneer. But your out-of-town audience searched for Centerville High School student newspaper. For some reason, you mentioned Centerville High School by name only once on your website—on the home page.

To make matters worse, you have named your news section "The Buccaneers' Spyglass," the Community and Arts section "The Buccaneers' Band" and your sports section "The Buccaneers' Battles." That would not be a problem in print, but those terms show up in the URL of your pages, and they mean nothing to a search engine.

A spider would see very little in the following URL to connect it to the most common search terms. (The number 1019 means the story was posted online in October 2019.)

http://www.buccaneer.com/1019/spyglass/Sophomore-watches-in-horror-as-freeway-footbridge-collapses-in-front-of-him/

But the spider is much more likely to find this URL.

http://www.centerville-hs_buccaneer.com/1019/news/lake-park-overpass-burlingame-beltway

This URL is 87 characters long. Since spiders generally read from left to right, the word *Beltway* may not be found.

Choosing the Right Words

A digital media headline writer needs to predict what search terms others will use, but choosing the right words is not merely a matter of luck.

- Use common words. *Needy* is better than *indigent*. *Award* is better than *accolade*. Sometimes two or three terms seem equally attractive. For instance, the International Club members talk about both their *food bank* and their *food pantry*. Which is the more commonly used term and should go in your headline? To find out, type each option into a search engine such as Google. Go with the term that generates the most hits: *food bank*.
- Write out words that might be abbreviated in print headlines, such as the name of your school. *Centerville High School* is better than *CHS*. *Buchanan County* is better than *Buck County*.
- Use both first and last names, even though you generally use only the last name in a print headline. If your retiring principal is Philippa Spielberg, few in your audience would really expect to find her with just *Spielberg* as a search term.
- Try not to get lost in the crowd. If you are using only common words in your headline, how do you keep your page from being shuffled to the 39th page of the search results? If there is something that sets your story apart from all other stories about food banks in Buchanan County, something that might be used as a search term, make sure to display it prominently. If there is a sign over the door of the Quonset hut reading "Quonset Kitchen Store," you will want the spider to find it for the person who uses it as a search term. Try *Quonset Kitchen Store: Food bank aids Buchanan County* (still under 55 characters). The drop head could read: *Centerville High School's International Club feeds the needy, wins award*.
- Think about how a wider audience may search. One of your jobs when you write for the Web is to interpret your local traditions for a wider audience. Terms that are familiar to locals may obscure what a stranger is hoping to find on your Web pages. Think about this headline from earlier in this chapter: *Sophomore watches in horror as freeway footbridge collapses in front of him.* You have a great story, but your word choices may make it difficult for a national audience to find it. Locally, you call it a *footbridge*. A wider audience types in *Lake Park Pedestrian Overpass*. You call it the *freeway*. Your wider audience types in *Burlingame Beltway*.

"But It's So Boring"

If you think SEO headlines are boring, you are not alone. The New York Times wrote this headline in 2006:

This Boring Headline Is Written for Google

Some headline writers have tried to make peace with Internet headlines. Just as they learned to craft strong headlines in narrow columns, they are learning to write for both people and search engines.

Others are trying technological work-arounds. The New York Times, for instance, sometimes writes a display head using wit or wordplay for the print edition front page—and for human consumption on their Internet site—and a boring, Google friendly headline in its URL. When the story jumps to an inside page, the NYT also uses a second SEO headline, getting another chance to utilize key terms. It does the same things inside its website.

The BBC News also often writes two headlines. A shorter headline appears on the site's front page, while a longer one appears on the story's page and therefore in search engine results.

Many platforms allow you to add keywords in the text, image or video box where you post parts of the story. Use all the proper nouns in the story as keywords, as well as the name of your school. If your school has a long name, such as Rancho Capistrano del Obispo, enter *Rancho*, *Capistrano* and *Obispo* as three separate keywords so searchers do not need to use the full name. If your video shows a referee's questionable call at a volleyball match, your headline for the video may be *Watch the heartbreaking final 15 seconds of Division One Play*, but you could insert the keywords *questionable*, *out-of-bounds call*, and *referee Nadia Faire* as well as the names of both schools and the players' names in the boxes. Make full use of the keywords for each box.

Figure 7.15 The caption for the photo below answers your initial questions about the image while also capturing your interest in the story.

NICHOLAS WINTON, with one of the children he rescued from the Nazis.

Captions

Look at Figure 7.15.

- What do you look at first? What questions do you have?
- What do you look at second?
- Third?
- Fourth?
- Fifth?

If you are like most people, one of the first five things you looked at was the main picture, the black and white photo of a man and a child in clothing that is long out of date. Something in the picture does not seem quite right. The man looks happy, but the child is somber and holding some sort of document. The child is turned away from the man and does not look at him. Are they relatives?

If you are like most people, you also read the caption shortly after you looked at the picture, hoping that the caption and the picture together would answer your questions and tell a story. That is what good captions do. They complete the job the photo began when it caught your eye. They inform the reader, answer her questions and tell a story. Though this caption is only one line long, the picture and the caption together pull the reader into a compelling narrative, full of danger and emotion. The caption hooks the reader in 12 words.

Each picture you publish needs a caption or a cutline. Technically, a caption is a headline or other material that appears above the picture, and a cutline is the material placed below the picture, or sometimes beside it. However, the terms are often used interchangeably, and your publication's style will dictate where each element goes.

Captions have three elements: the catch line, descriptive text and the credit. Though there are an almost infinite number of variations, captions tend to follow a set pattern. To maintain consistency, your publication should have a style sheet that specifies your styles and when each should be used.

The First Element: The Catch Line Begins the Caption

The **catch line** is meant to catch the audience, much as a headline pulls the audience into a story. If the catch line is interesting, your reader is likely to read the rest of the caption and perhaps the rest of the story (Figure 7.16).

Catch lines are set apart from the rest of the caption graphically. They may be in a different typeface than the rest of the caption or in bold or half-height caps, in a larger font, a different font such as a sans serif font, or on a shaded background. A catch line may start with a drop capital. In some cases catch lines are on a separate line.

In the absence of a strong catch line, the first word of the caption may be given the same treatment as a catch line to preserve consistency. It may be printed in half-height caps or in bold, for instance. Clearly that does not work well if the first word is *A* or *The.* Avoid these empty words. Names make strong beginnings for these simple captions.

A catch line should never state what is already obvious from the picture. The caption should add to the picture and begin to tell a story. The caption to the photo in Figure 7.15 should NOT read: *Looking pensive, a child sits on the arm of Nicholas Winton, who helped children leave Czechoslovakia in 1939*. That caption sits there like a lump of cold oatmeal. It has no emotion, no action, no story. We can already see the child

IN STEP AND IN TUNE, the Crimson Knights Marching Band trombone section displays the precision that earned the band a slot at the All-State competition in March.

Figure 7.16 Catch lines lure readers to your caption. Keep catch lines short—no more than five words.

is pensive and sitting on the arm of a man. The caption is longer than the effective one, but the only new information it adds to the picture is that Nicholas Winton helped children leave Czechoslovakia in 1939.

Catch lines tempt young journalists to editorialize. We cannot know why the child is looking sad. Perhaps he is cold and tired. We should not write, "Missing his family, a young Czech refugee sits on the arm …" unless we have interviewed the child. Then it is best to use a quote: "I was missing my mother and sister when they took that picture."

Do not use catch lines such as *having a good time*, *hoping for a home run* and *smiling at a friend* unless the people in the photo told you that is what they were doing.

Most gerunds—the "ing" form of a verb used as a noun—either state the obvious or editorialize. Use this form only if you have solid background information that adds to or explains the picture: *Fighting like Tinkerbell against Principal Lynn Black's Captain Hook, Assistant Principal Leon White fences his way down the aisle during the homecoming assembly.*

The Second Element: Descriptive Text Comes Next

The next sentence (or the continuation of the sentence you started as the catch line) should be written in a font that is clearly different from the body copy. Your audience should never wonder where a caption ends and the body text of the story begins. The caption font may be sans serif (body copy is usually in a serif font), a different size or simply surrounded by more white space.

Good Reporting Makes for Good Captions

The more information the reporter or photographer records about each photo, the easier it is to write a strong caption. The digital device you use to shoot photos probably has a microphone. Use it to record identifying information and quotes from the subjects of your photos, either to use later as sound elements on a Web page or for your own information as you write captions.

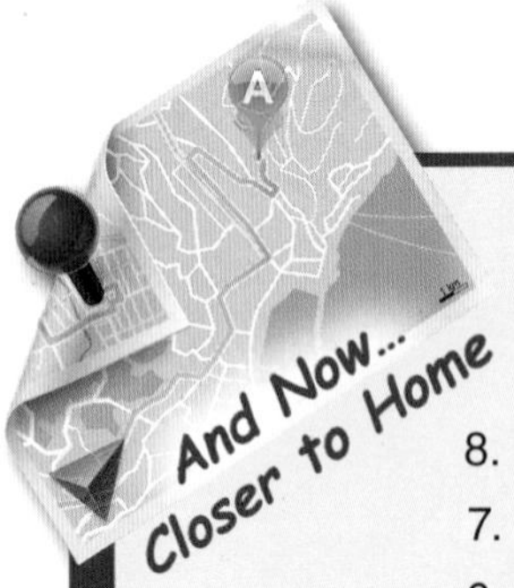

Runners-Up for the Most-Obvious-Gerund-Used-in-a-Catch-Line Award

8. Posing for the camera
7. Smiling for the camera
6. Running down the field
5. Working diligently
4. Walking through the halls
3. Lining up for lunch
2. Showing off their picture-perfect smiles

And the winner is …

1. *Dancing the night away!* for being all at once an obvious gerund, inaccurate and a cliché.

Accuracy Is First Priority

There is never a good time to misidentify someone in your publication, but mistaken identity in a photo caption is especially bad. Be absolutely accurate. If possible, have your subjects spell their names into your microphone or for your reporter's notebook. Do not guess someone's name or assume last spring's yearbook got it right. If you did not get identification information when you took the picture, track down the people in the picture and verify their names. Be sure to spell all proper nouns correctly, too.

Include Essential Details

It is rare that a caption is longer than two sentences, but what if you have a great deal of information? What is essential and what should be left out?

Suppose you have great picture of the Filipino Club dancing at your International Week assembly that was held in the North gym Friday morning, March 2 at Centerville High School (Figure 7.17). You know the names of the performers, the name of the club, that they dance in and out of poles while the poles smacked the floor in time to the music, that they practiced after school and Saturdays to prepare for the assembly.

If you reported well, the caption can explain clearly and specifically what is in the photo. Use the five W's but leave out the W's that are obvious from the picture or are already clear from the headline of the accompanying article. You should not describe what is obvious.

This is what should be in your reporter's notebook for Figure 7.17:

- Who: Rochelle Fuentes, Amiel Moro and Martin Supangco are the dancing members of the Filipino Club at Centerville High School. Bambi Jolejole, Crystal Veraga, and Anthony and Josh Carigma on the sticks. Amihan Macaraeg and Annie Dimaguiba wait to jump in.
- What: Dance the traditional tinikling barefooted while avoiding bamboo poles that rhythmically bang onto the floor and into each other. The music accelerates as the dance progresses.
- When: March 2, International Week assembly, Friday morning.
- Where: North gym, Centerville High School.
- Why: To demonstrate their love for the Filipino culture.
- How: Practice every Saturday and after school for the last month.

Essentials include the names of all the people in the photo unless you are working with a shot of a large group. People read local media to see their own names and other familiar names and faces.

Identify people by what they are doing if possible or from the left (if they are more or less in a line) or clockwise from the left if the individuals are more scattered. Avoid writing the words *clockwise from left to right* and *from left to right*. The extra words take up too much space. Many publications routinely leave out *from left* unless the picture and caption require special clarification.

Figure 7.17 This group shot raises questions in the viewers' minds and requires many identifications.

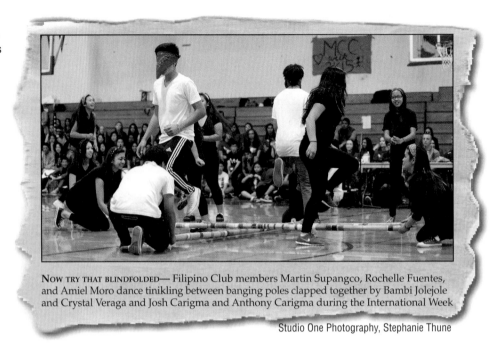

Now try that blindfolded— Filipino Club members Martin Supangco, Rochelle Fuentes, and Amiel Moro dance tinikling between banging poles clapped together by Bambi Jolejole and Crystal Veraga and Josh Carigma and Anthony Carigma during the International Week

Studio One Photography, Stephanie Thune

Filipino Club is essential, too, if it is not already identified prominently in the headline, deck or lead.

Specifics make good copy, so find out that this is not just a traditional dance, it is *tinikling* and include the name. *Banging poles* suggest conflict, or at least suspense, so those words should be included also.

Leave out whatever happened outside of the photo. If you write that the dancers practiced after school and on Saturdays, it will look like you are padding the caption, a sure sign that you did not do good reporting.

But be sure to explain anything that will strike the audience as odd or raise questions in their minds, such as the bandanas in Figure 7.17. You ask why some of them dance with blindfolds on. "Because we can," one answers, and explains his uncles in the Philippines wear blindfolds. They are so good at tinikling that they can do it blindfolded.

Leave out *in the North gym*. It is obvious from the photo that the location is a gym. Everyone at Centerville High will know that is where you have assemblies, and distant viewers do not care if it is the north or south gym.

If you are writing the caption for the Centerville High student publication or Web page, leave out *at Centerville High School*.

In the morning can also go. It does not help tell the story or answer your audience's most probable questions.

Writing the Caption's First Sentence

The first sentence of the caption is written in present tense, as if the events in the photo are going on as you read the caption. (Head shots—close-up portraits showing only head and shoulders—may use the past tense.) The sentence should explain the point of the photo, clarify the photo or finish telling the story the photo began. Verbs should be active and interesting. The first five to seven words of a caption—including the catch line—need to capture your readers' interest, so names may not be the best beginning.

As you did when you wrote the catch line, avoid stating the obvious. Especially if you are publishing a color photo, you do not need to say *in colorful costumes* or *wearing red bandanas over their eyes*.

As you did when you wrote the catch line, avoid editorializing. Your main verb phrase should not be *astonishes the audience*—unless, of course, the audience rose up as one and shouted, "We are astonished!" You may report *a foot-stomping, standing ovation* but either be accurate and specific, or be quiet.

Match the tone of the caption to the subject of the photo. *Remembering their heritage* may work well for a Memorial Day article, but it is too somber for a photo of tinikling. You may say *students party out the old year* if your picture was taken late on December 31, but the tone is wrong if your picture shows a shofar being sounded early in the morning of Rosh Hashanah, which is the Jewish New Year and a time of serious reflection.

Though a caption may include a conversational tone or wordplay in its catch line, all subjects in the picture should be treated with respect. Captions are not the place for teasing, good-natured or otherwise.

If possible, the caption should provide whatever the photo has not communicated, including missing essential five W's, as well as sounds and other sensory impressions.

> **NOW TRY THAT BLINDFOLDED**—*Filipino Club members Martin Supangco, Rochelle Fuentes, and Amiel Moro dance tinikling between banging poles clapped together by Bambi Jolejole and Crystal Veraga and Josh Carigma and Anthony Carigma during the International Week assembly Friday morning, with Amihan Macaraeg and Annie Dimaguiba waiting to jump in.*

Expanding the Caption?

Not all captions need a second sentence. If a second sentence is not needed, do not put it in.

Second sentences may use the past tense and emphasize the *how* and *why*. Use a second sentence only if you have specific, interesting information.

Quotations make good second sentences if they add to the story. "I got my ankles smacked all the time when I first danced blindfolded, but my uncles in Antipolo do it, so I kept practicing," Supangco said.

The second sentence also allows you to explain how you took the photo. If you used a fisheye lens or photographed through a microscope, explain that to your audience in the second sentence. If you publish a photo from a security camera, tell your audience the source. If the unusual angle comes because the fire department lifted you up in its Snorkel, tell your readers.

If the subjects in the photo are reenacting an event, explain it to your audience in the second sentence. But if the audience is likely to be misled by the photo, put that information near the beginning of the first sentence, "In this reenactment ..."

Figure 7.18 This image's credit line can be found flush right, beneath the photo.

The Third Element: Giving Credit Where Credit Is Due

The third element of any caption is the credit line. Publication styles vary, but often the photo credit is flush right, directly under the photo in a font that is big enough to read but smaller than the font used in the article (Figure 7.18).

The photo credit should tell who took the photo or owns the photo and indicate if that person is part of your staff. Remember that giving someone credit for a photo does not give you an excuse to steal it. If you did not take the picture yourself, you need to pay for the image, get express written permission from the owner to use it, or get the image from a source that intends to circulate it for free. Such sources might include a publicity department or Creative Commons. Abide by any restrictions your source places on the photo.

Figure 7.19 The two stand-alone photos in this package are all that is needed to tell the story of a bear who was found roaming a California neighborhood.

Photographs by IRFAN KHAN Los Angeles Times

A bear in suburbia

A tranquilized bear is inspected by I. Banks, above, a California Fish and Wildlife warden. The bear roamed through a Sun Valley neighborhood for more than an hour on Wednesday morning. At right, Fish and Wildlife warden J.C. Healy and LAPD officers search for the bear after it had been struck by a tranquilizer dart.

Courtesy of the Los Angeles Times

Stand-Alone Photos

Photos may stand independent of a story, as in this front-page package of two photos with a three-sentence caption (Figure 7.19). The caption may be a little longer in this case, like a brief, freestanding news story. It has the demanding job of communicating all of the important five W's.

In this example, the first sentence explains the photo—and lets the audience know the bear is not dead, only tranquilized. The second sentence gives four of the five W's. The last sentence suggests the narrative: the game warden and police officers searched for the anesthetized bear.

Other stand-alone photos may refer to the story, or to a related story, on an inside page. Notice that the *when* of the five W's has been left out in the example in Figure 7.20, but it is not essential to this timely feature story. The time element is prominent in the lead of the story on page AA6. The second sentence of this two-sentence caption explains the *why*. Note the wordplay on *platform*.

CHRISTINA HOUSE For The Times
NEW PLATFORM FOR THEATER
Members of the Watts Village Theater Company perform at a Blue Line station in Watts, reciting poems about growing up in the area. The troupe aimed to draw people to light rail and the neighborhood. AA6

Photo by Christina House for the Los Angeles Times

Figure 7.20 Strong photography and strong reporting—usually by the photographer—makes for strong stand-alone photos.

Infographics

Infographics use visuals such as photos, drawings, charts, maps and diagrams to present complex information. They replace many lines of body text, but they are little more than decoration unless they have captions. In Figure 7.21, the main caption is above the infographic (because the infographic appears above the article) and the catch line How Oscar votes are counted serves as a headline for the caption. The five numbered captions and the final, bold caption in the lower right explain what the infographic is illustrating.

Notice the credits come in two parts. Flush left, the word Source serves the same purpose a phrase such as "according to information received by the Times" would serve in the text. Flush right are the names of the two Los Angeles Times graphic artists, Len De Groot and Javier Zarricina, who created the infographic. Their names are done in the same style as photo bylines and are, in effect, their bylines.

Figure 7.21 Infographics are appealing and informative visuals that may be used to explain complex information.

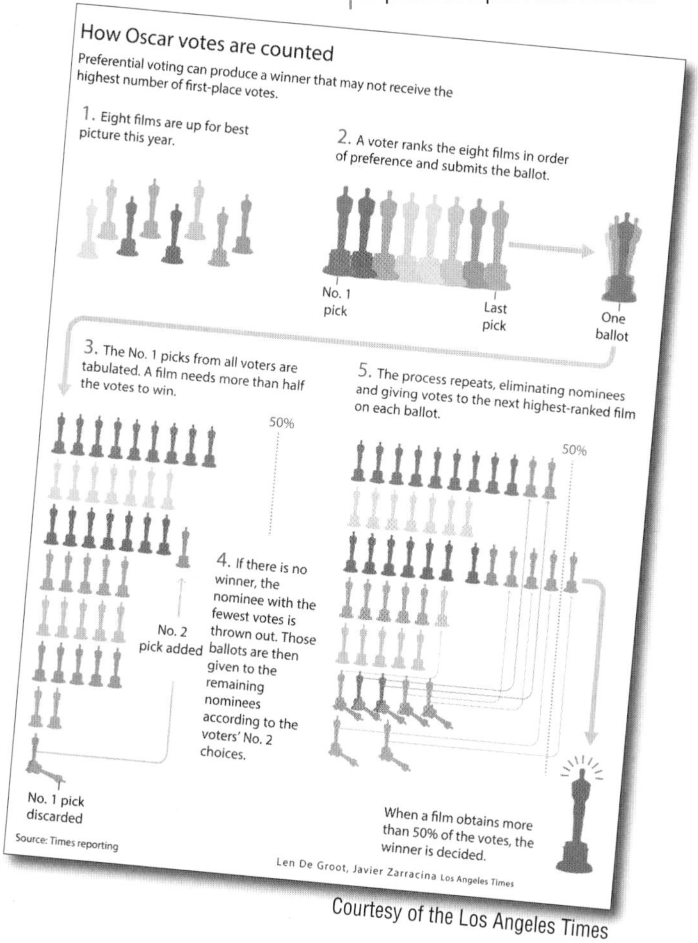
How Oscar votes are counted
Preferential voting can produce a winner that may not receive the highest number of first-place votes.
1. Eight films are up for best picture this year.
2. A voter ranks the eight films in order of preference and submits the ballot.
No. 1 pick
Last pick
One ballot
3. The No. 1 picks from all voters are tabulated. A film needs more than half the votes to win.
50%
4. If there is no winner, the nominee with the fewest votes is thrown out. Those ballots are then given to the remaining nominees according to the voters' No. 2 choices.
No. 2 pick added
No. 1 pick discarded
5. The process repeats, eliminating nominees and giving votes to the next highest-ranked film on each ballot.
50%
When a film obtains more than 50% of the votes, the winner is decided.
Source: Times reporting
Len De Groot, Javier Zarracina Los Angeles Times

Courtesy of the Los Angeles Times

Chapter Seven

Review and Assessment

Recall

1. What is the main purpose of a teaser? Of a headline? A caption?
2. The length of a headline is restrained by space or time. Give an example of how a print, a broadcast and a digital headline's size is limited.
3. List three techniques for keeping summary headlines brief.
4. Which type of stories rely heavily on summary headlines? On descriptive headlines?
5. List at least three types of stories where a narrative headline is appropriate.
6. Make a sketch of a headline with a hammer head, another with a kicker, another with a drop head or read-out. You may use nonsense words or X's.
7. What are two grammatical forms frequently used in descriptive headlines?
8. What are three literary devices often employed in crafting descriptive headlines?
9. When you write headlines for the small screen of portable digital devices, you need to include the most important information in a small number of words. How many characters generally appear on a small screen?
10. In SEO headlines, certain types of words will attract spiders. Describe two.
11. What are the three elements of a strong caption?

Critical Thinking

1. In the early days of broadcast journalism, radio and television news stories used summary headlines and the announcers "read the news." Modern newscasts use narrative headlines for most stories to make them seem like casual conversations. As the type of headline has changed, the role of the newscaster has changed. What characteristics and talents do modern newscasters need that earlier newscasters—the ones who simply "read the news"—did not need?
2. Headlinese may be unfamiliar to some of your readers, yet you will probably need to write for limited spaces. Which headline conventions will work for your readers? Which ones do you need to avoid?
3. What other ways do you have to communicate to your audience in limited spaces in the media in which you work? Which abbreviations, symbols and contractions are acceptable and which do you wish to avoid? Are some appropriate in tweets or other microblogs but not acceptable in Web-based or print stories?
4. How can you attract spiders and still write interesting headlines, such as descriptive headlines?

Application

1. Choose three print stories. Create teasers for each that are appropriate for your broadcast format.
2. Choose three pictures from your publication or from your photo files. For each picture, record information that could be used in a caption, such as photographer's name, where and when it was taken, what action is shown, why the audience should care, and the name and school year of each person in the photo. Use accurate information where possible, making up details that may be unavailable. Highlight and identify any details that are fictional.
3. Using the information you have from question 2, craft a strong catch line for the photo. Pay particular attention to your answer to "Why should the audience care?" Print the catch line in the font style your publication uses. Seek responses from your group and revise as appropriate.
4. Using the same photo, information and catch line, craft a one-sentence descriptive caption, including the names and years in school for all people in the photo. Make sure it adds any information the audience needs to understand the photo. Add a byline for the photographer.

Chapter Seven

Journalism Style

Paraphrases

Strong quotations are easy on the eyes and ears. They break up long blocks of type or long narratives in the reporter's voice. They give the reader a feeling of "being there" or really getting to know someone. They lend authority to the reporting and draw the reader into the story.

Great quotes come when someone important says something important or when someone unique says something unique.

Unfortunately, great quotations are rare. The worst are bland repetitions of your lead or so full of oral usages (such as "kinda," "OMG," "uh," "really," "umm" and "like") and maybe profanity that you would need to perform major surgery to make them worthy of print or broadcast.

If a direct quotation is unsuitable, you may need to paraphrase it (reword it while keeping the same meaning). You can edit paraphrases to avoid profanity, tighten language and avoid awkward asides. If your source does not speak standard English, you can avoid printing or recording language that might seem to demean someone. You can avoid ellipses and parentheses that scar edited quotations and make them as graceful as Frankenstein's monster.

But paraphrases sacrifice the freshness and authenticity of a direct quotation. You no longer have the quotation marks that say, "These are his exact words." Your reader now needs to trust you that you understood and reported the information accurately and fairly.

For instance, you are reporting on the police who arrive in your school parking lot the minute a school dance ends. Many parents express concern. You record a parent, Ernie Joe Clampet, saying, "Who do those cops think they are? Coming into the school parking lot at 11:01 and bullying the kids who were waiting for their folks to pick them up. My Amber was terrified. I don't want them bullying my girl. And I couldn't get to where I was to pick her up because of all the police cars."

Quoting Mr. Clampet might embarrass Amber while not strengthening your story. And he does not say anything that is worth 58 words in your story.

Instead, you paraphrase and write: *Parents complained that the police were intimidating the students. Ernie Joe Clampet, who came to pick up his sophomore daughter, Amber, reports that he could not get to the door of the gym because of the police cars.*

Bullying or "Bullying"?

It is tempting to write *Parents complained that the police were "bullying" the students*, because *bullying* is a strong and interesting word. But unless more than one parent used the word, it would be inaccurate in this sentence. You need to be accurate.

Also, if you put quotation marks around the word "bullying," it may suggest that you are using the word ironically. Think carefully before you put quotation marks around single words or phrases. The more common the word or phrase, the more it will seem that you are being ironic.

Try It!

Paraphrase or quote snippets from this interview for a section of your story about the negative aspects of helping in a Mexican orphanage over spring break. Try to do so in about 40 words.

I thought it was going to be, like, all wonderful when we went there. I mean, I thought they'd be grateful and happy that we came, right? But about an hour before we got to the orphanage the youth minister made us take our watches and jewelry and cell phone and put them in a lock box, and then he locked the box in the trunk of his car under the floor mat. I guess last time a bunch of stuff got stolen and the kid who did it got put in jail.

The bathrooms there were horrible. They were dirty and stinky and we had to go outside to wash our hands. Some of the kids were nice but some of the boys were really wild and mean. One kept throwing dust at us and running away.

Extend Your Knowledge

Style Exercises

Visit the *Journalism* website for more practice in paraphrasing.

Chapter Seven

Writers' Workshop

In this Writers' Workshop you will:

- Identify and rewrite headlines that could be libelous or contain editorializing.

Workshop 7.1

Avoiding Libel and Editorializing in Large Type

Mini-Lesson: What You Don't Know About Yourself Can Hurt Your Publication

News is always someone's summary of events, and every summary leaves some things out while trying to make sense of what is left. Headlines are summaries of those summaries. Headline writers must therefore make many judgments, judgments that may reveal the headline writer's values and prejudices.

As personal opinions seep into headlines, they cause the two most serious errors a publication can commit: libel and editorializing. Since many people read only the headlines of many stories, these errors, even if unconscious, will scream. In some cases the errors are so damaging that someone sues your publication for libel. In many other cases the audience loses faith in your objectivity and dismisses you as biased.

> Even if a story is fair and accurate, a libelous headline can skew the audience's impressions. In a study done at New Mexico State University, 40 students were divided into four groups. Each group read one of four versions of a news story about a man charged with robbing a grocery store. The students who read an article with a libelous headline but an accurate story were almost as likely to think the man was guilty as students who read an article in which both the headline and story were libelous.

Here are five ways you can shield your publication as you write headlines:

1. Don't jump to conclusions. The news story says the environmental science class found rat droppings inside the back entry to the school kitchen and around the outdoor dumpster. If you publish a headline that reads *Rats found in kitchen*, you have jumped to conclusions twice, once that the science class's research was credible and accurate and again when you say rats were found. A better headline would be *Science class reports rat droppings in kitchen*. An honest read-out below the headline, if it is in the story somewhere, would read *Samples from back of kitchen could have been tracked in from trash bins*.
2. Don't use a quote without attribution as a headline. Your district is studying the number of tests given during class time and will consider limiting tests in favor of more learning time. A chemistry teacher and an art teacher spoke in favor of fewer tests. If you use what one said as a headline without attribution, *Tests waste learning time*, you imply that the study is done and the conclusion is in. If you include attribution, you have a more honest headline, though it might be better as a read-out below a summary head.

Teachers: Tests waste learning time

District to study frequent testing's impact on instructional time

3. Don't take sides. If you have strong feelings about a matter, take extra care to be objective or ask someone else to write the headline. For instance, if a news source published *President X is trying to silence his critics by claiming other presidents used similar tactic*, the headline would be an editorial on the news page in extra-large type. The news source's opinions have seeped into his headline. Clearly he agrees with the critics and did not believe the president's statement. How do we know this?
   A. He writes that the reason the president made the statement was to counter something his critics had said. If the story shows that his statement was in response to a criticism in a debate or a press conference, then that assertion would be accurate and fair. Otherwise, unless the president identified his statement as a rebuttal of his critics' comments, do not jump to conclusions. (See point 4.)

B. He writes that the president's statement was meant to silence someone, a very un-American thing to do. It shows the president in a bad light.

C. He suggests the president's statement is contrary to fact or contrary to majority opinion when he uses the word *claiming*. Remember *said* is the proper word in almost all cases.

The same headline without editorializing might read *President X: 'Other presidents used similar tactics.' Critics disagree.*

4. Don't assume one thing caused another. Your football team had another miserable year and you just learned someone else will coach next year. Was the coach removed? Was it because of the losing season? Causation is generally complicated and difficult to prove. Do not write a headline based on what you assume caused the change. *Football coach removed because of losing season.* That would be acceptable only if you had a quote from the athletic director specifically stating the bad season caused the coach's removal. A better headline, one that leaves the reader to make the connections you cannot prove, would be *Football coach removed after losing season*.

5. Choose each word carefully for meaning and tone.

A. Be especially careful when you associate someone with a crime. Murder is different from manslaughter. *Knight sought in foe's murder* could be libel. *Knight sought in foe's death* could be a solid headline. If murder charges are filed, you may use *murder*.

B. Be especially careful when you associate someone with misconduct or what you construe to be misconduct. *School board candidate acted in porn films* may be libel if she in fact was an extra in one film that received an X rating. (Ratings are usually given after a film is completed.) *School board candidate was extra in X-rated film* could be a solid headline, if the story is newsworthy and your publication has given her a chance to respond.

C. Be especially careful to avoid sexist or racist comments. *Sob sisters' defense frees accused arsonist* implies the women who defended the accused were too easily swayed by emotion and suggests women have weaker intellects. *Emotional appeal by victims helps accused arsonist win acquittal* may be a solid headline, if it is accurate.

D. Be especially careful as you choose verbs. In *Midnight curfew rids Main Street of teens*, the word *rids* carries with it the idea of removing a pest and suggests Main Street is better off without teens. Instead, write *Teens leave Main Street for new midnight curfew.*

E. Be especially careful in controversies. In *Bus drivers to strike despite district's best offer*, the word *despite* means *in spite of* and suggests the drivers are being unreasonable.

F. Beware of adjectives. In *Radical group to buy local church building*, the adjective *radical* should be avoided. *Radical* may mean a labor union to one person and an evangelical church to another. Instead, be specific. *Aryan Nation to buy local church building*. (It is acceptable to describe the group's beliefs in the article and let the audience decide if they are radical. *The group, whose website says they fight "to safeguard the existence of our race, the purity of our blood, and the sustenance of our children," has been identified as a white supremacist organization by the U.S. Department of Justice.*

Apply It!

1. Working with a partner, locate 10 headlines from your own publications, from the professional press or other outlets that could be improved by avoiding editorializing and libel. You are free to use special interest publications such as those from union, trade, religious, ethnic or political groups. Find at least one violation of each of the five principles discussed in point 5. Clip or print the story and headline and note the source. Note why the headline needs improvement.
2. Rewrite eight of the headlines so they are free of potential libel and editorializing.

Extend Your Knowledge

Extend

You have learned the importance of keeping headlines free of libel and personal comments. Headlines also need to fit the available space, communicate clearly to the audience as well as to search engines, and be interesting and absolutely accurate. Visit the *Journalism* website to find out how to choose the best words for summary, narrative and descriptive headlines.

Chapter Eight

Researching and Evaluating Sources

How do we know that?

Photo by Forrest Czarnecki, Conifer High School

G-WLEARNING.COM

While studying, look for the activity icon to:

- **Build** vocabulary terms with e-flash cards and matching activities.
- **Extend** learning with further discussion of relevant topics.
- **Reinforce** what you learn by completing style exercises, worksheets and end-of-chapter questions.

Visit the Journalism website: www.g-wlearning.com/journalism/

Chapter Objectives

After reading this chapter, you will be able to:

- Describe the purpose and methods of preliminary research.
- Describe three ways to organize information gathered during your research.
- Collaborate with an editor during preliminary research.
- Discuss what to do with information you cannot use immediately.
- Describe the purpose and methods of deeper research.
- Explain how to conduct a survey.
- Discuss the strengths and weaknesses of reporters' first-person observations, primary sources and secondary sources as well as the dangers of hearsay.
- Explain the importance of triangulating, that is, finding corroborating evidence from three different sources.
- Describe how to evaluate Internet sources for preliminary research, for deeper research and for research on controversial issues.

Key Terms Build Vocab

advocacy site
affiliation
credentials
first-person observation
"has legs"
hearsay
impartiality
metasite
primary source
secondary source
unreliable source

Before You Read...

In *inductive reasoning*, an argument is made to prove a conclusion. Join in a shared, informal classroom discussion about evaluating and confirming the validity of your sources. Use what you've learned in this chapter, prior research experience and inductive reasoning to form an argument about the best methods for evaluating sources that proves a conclusion.

Introduction

"'Google' is not a synonym for 'research.'"

–Dan Brown, American author

How to write a boring story:

The editor tells a reporter, "The football teams and the cheerleaders are giving the bus driver a surprise retirement party by her bus Thursday. Cover it." (Figure 8.1)

The reporter texts a football player, who tells her the party is at 3:00 in the parking lot by the gym. She shows up with a camera, finds out the bus driver's name and gets a picture of Mrs. Winterset smiling and eating cake with some of the team. She snaps another of her at the wheel of the bus, a tiny, erect woman in jeans and a plaid blouse, a trace of gray in her ponytail, reaching out to turn the big, horizontal steering wheel.

"How many years have you driven the bus for the school district?" the reporter asks.

"Sixteen."

The bus driver's first name is Evalyn. E-v-a-l-y-n. W-i-n-t-e-r-s-e-t.

Her reporting done, the journalist types out a lead. *School bus driver Evalyn Winterset, who will retire this June after driving the bus for the Central Valley School District for 16 years, was honored Thursday by the cheer squad and football teams with cake and punch in front of the gym.*

The photos of people eating cake have too many backs in them. The best shot is the one of Winterset at the wheel of the bus. It was posed, so it really is not a news photo, but it is the best one. The reporter decides to call it a portrait.

The story could run as a brief, without the photo, or the picture could be a stand-alone photo with the lead as a caption.

But any way the story is run, it is boring. B-o-r-i-n-g.

What went wrong? Is it just an uninteresting story? The reporter was accurate. She got the facts straight, and the spelling. She went to the event with a camera. She took pictures. Why is the story boring?

Figure 8.1 Strong reporting—both interviewing and research—reveals what may have been invisible, even in a common yellow school bus or its driver.

It is boring because the reporter failed to do research. She failed to be curious and skeptical. She failed to collaborate with her editor. Research, curiosity, skepticism and collaboration are essential tools of journalism. They can turn a brief with a weak picture into a significant story, the kind people read, talk about, clip and link to.

Journalists think about their research in two phases: preliminary research and deeper research. These overlap, but they have different purposes. Preliminary research is done to inform you and your editors, while deeper research is meant to inform your audience.

Preliminary Research

Preliminary research helps you determine the scope of the story, whom you should interview and what you should ask. Its purpose is to prepare you to collaborate with your editor and decide on a direction for the story.

You begin your preliminary research when you collect story ideas. You have seen the school calendar or viewed articles in other media, talked to sources on your beat or heard what people are discussing. None of this, of course, is news worth broadcasting or publishing, not yet. Journalists do not tell people what they already know, nor do they report "news" based on rumor or gossip.

Your first job is to learn how the story idea might become an interesting, credible story. Preliminary research will help you

- discover the scope of the story;
- prepare intelligent interview questions;
- find avenues for further research; and
- find potential angles for the story.

Sometimes preliminary research can be done without leaving your newsroom, but it does require you to access and organize a great deal of information. You will want to create a collection folder, a list of questions and a list of potential sources for each story.

- The collection folder can be physical, digital or both. You collect relevant and interesting clippings, Web addresses, and social media and microblogging posts in this folder. You may not know yet exactly what the story is about—that is why it is a great story idea—so you are not yet sure what and who will be important and what is merely background. You are collecting and filing information that may prove useful (Figure 8.2).

Figure 8.2 Do not worry if your collection folder gets large. Well-researched stories may have nine pieces of information in the folder for every one that makes it into the news, but all research will help you write well, now or later.

Figure 8.3 Keep a paper or computer file of people you may need to contact. *Where should you keep your list of contacts and how should it be organized?*

- Your question list goes into a separate document or a fresh reporter's notebook. During preliminary research, your curiosity should be on overdrive, like a superactive child's. When questions occur to you, jot them down where you can refer to them easily. Do not worry if you find yourself writing the same question more than once. That is a sign the question is important. Your readers may want an answer to that question.
- Your list of sources and their contact information also deserves a separate notebook, folder or document (Figure 8.3). This list also needs to be easily accessible. The stronger the preliminary research, the more people you will have on your list. Jot down any contact information—phone numbers, email addresses, websites—along with a few words about who the people are and what you would like to ask them.

YOUR TURN

You hear a rumor that there were so many problems at the homecoming dance in the school gym that next month's Halloween dance and carnival may be canceled.

1. Begin an imaginary collection folder, question list and list of sources, both human and written or digital, that will help you determine if the rumor contains truth. Were there more problems than normal at the homecoming dance? Is the activity in danger of cancellation? Make sure you name at least three items for your imaginary collection folder, at least three questions and at least three possible sources.
2. **Going Deeper.** If you learn that the dance is going forward, or you learn the dance has been canceled, what should you do with your preliminary research? Name at least two possibilities.

Collaboration

After preliminary research, when your collection folder is well-stocked and your questions and contacts documents contain interesting possibilities, you are ready to talk with an editor or senior writer about your story. This is an editorial collaboration meeting, a meeting in which you discuss what you already know so that you can decide what you should do next (Figure 8.4).

Your editor will first decide if the story **"has legs"**— if the story has sources and information to make it potentially reliable, interesting and significant. If it does, you and your editor will decide the direction for the story. Remember, an editor's primary job is to represent the audience. The editor will help you focus on what the audience wants or needs to learn.

You should not leave your collaboration meeting until you have a clear understanding of the questions your story will seek to answer. If your preliminary research is strong, the difficult job will be to decide which sources, questions and information are *not* important and should be set aside. The remaining research questions will guide your deeper research and help you identify the people you should interview.

Collaboration meetings may also decide

- when the story is due;
- how much space or time it will get in your publication, broadcast or website;
- how much of your time and energy the story should take;
- whether it is a straight news story or a feature story with a news peg;
- the tone of the story; or
- if the story needs sound files, art, pictures or videos.

Figure 8.4 A collaboration meeting focuses on the story, but it may also be a chance for your editor to teach you and help you grow as a journalist.

Check It Out

Preliminary research may start with just a rumor, a student's blog, a tweet, something written on the mirror in the school bathroom, or something you overhear in the lunch line or see on social media. But none of these sources are good enough to quote, or even believe, until you check them out. They are hearsay—what you hear someone say but do not know to be true.

The watchword, or motto, of the City News Bureau in Chicago still holds true: "If your mother tells you she loves you, check it out—with two sources."

Unreliable sources, that is, sources that you cannot trust enough to quote in a story, *may* be absolutely accurate. But a journalist will need at least two independent sources to verify—or at least corroborate—what the source said. Two reliable sources and one unreliable source, taken together, can triangulate into something of importance to your audience. Three points of view create a stable triangle if they support each other.

It is tempting to tweet the third-quarter score from the lobby of the gym, based on a buddy's text message from inside the gym. Scooping—being the first one with a story—is an adrenaline rush. But people forget who got it first. They remember who got it wrong.

Pull out your press credential, walk into the gym and check out the official scoreboard yourself. Make sure it really is the end of the third quarter. Then tweet.

If a rumor is widespread or widely retweeted, it does not become more reliable. Juicy errors are spread faster and wider than careful truths. An unverified piece of information that is re-sent 2,000 times is still unverified.

If you need to issue a correction to something you wrote, remember you need to distribute the correction at least as widely and as often as your error.

Your editor may assemble a maestro team for your story—a photographer, a visual designer, an editor, and you the writer—to plan a package. See the *Journalism* website for more information about the Maestro Concept.

Extend

Your editor will almost never give you the resources—time, space and team support—to follow all the leads your research reveals, but your preliminary research need not go to waste (Figure 8.5).

Deeper Research

You use deeper research to uncover information your audience will want or need in order to understand the story. Deeper research provides new information or verifies things the audience already suspects. Information from your research provides context for the story.

Your audience should be able to see that you have read primary documents, records and financial statements, and that you have talked to well-informed people. You frequently tell your audience what your sources are so that they can judge if the sources are reliable and appropriate. Provide links to your sources whenever possible.

You concentrate your research on finding answers to the questions you and your editor think are most important for this story. You are preparing to answer your readers' questions, including "Why should I care?" In addition, you watch for information that could be presented as a chart, diagram, map, checklist, comparison chart, bio box or timeline along with your article's text.

Research can be done through numerous media, such as the Internet, books, financial statements and public documents. The Journalist's Toolbox, reference books, research databases, the Freedom of Information Act and surveys deserve special mention.

Your Turn

Find and clip or print out three stories of over 100 words each, either news or feature stories, from a variety of media—newsmagazines, newspapers, news websites that accompany broadcasts, or investigative journalism sites such as ProPublica and the Center for Investigative Reporting.

1. Highlight information in the story that appears to come from research (not from interviews, things the reporter observed or experienced, press conferences or press releases). How many sources does the story seem to have? Remember, research may be shown in even small details.
2. Use another color to highlight information from interviews.
3. If sources are identified, underline the attribution. If no source is given, imagine what the source might be. Do all the sources appear to be reliable? Share your clippings and conclusions with the class or your group.
4. **Going Deeper.** Grade each article on its use of sources. The more sources, the higher the grade. The more attribution, the higher the grade. Which media or media source appears to have done the most research?

Figure 8.5 **Three Things to Do With All That "Extra" Information**

Write an enterprise story

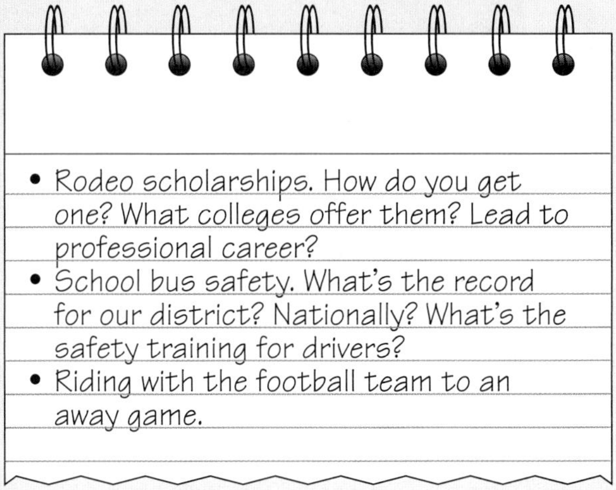
• Rodeo scholarships. How do you get one? What colleges offer them? Lead to professional career?
• School bus safety. What's the record for our district? Nationally? What's the safety training for drivers?
• Riding with the football team to an away game.

Add the information to your list of potential enterprise stories—the stories you develop on your own that may reveal patterns, influences, trends or ideas that get lost in the rush to cover timely stories.

Enterprise stories are the ones you pull out when you have a slow news day. Or you may publish them in a different medium or for another publication, such as a community paper, radio program, website or print magazine. Many journalists find their enterprise stories to be the most personally rewarding.

Write a reporter's blog

by Zack Cooper Posted Oct. 9
Members of the Mariners football team came to school today wearing T-shirts emblazoned with coach Gene Eagle's picture above the motto ...
Read Post

Is the Eagle in trouble?
by Zack Cooper Posted Oct. 5
After Friday night's game, Football Boosters Club president Ralph Cramer said, "It's clear that coach Eagle can't bring this team together. He should be replaced." That sentiment was voiced ...
Read Post

Do not confuse a reporter's blog with the sort of blog anyone with an Internet connection can publish. A reporter's blog is not the place to spread rumors or grind axes. Do not put anything in a reporter's blog that you would not put in your publication or broadcast if you had the space and time. Keep it separate from any personal blogs you write.

Be sure your reporter's blog maintains the same high standards of accuracy and fairness as your school publications. Check your facts before you push Send. (See Chapter 12 for more about blogs.)

If your reporting casts people or organizations in a negative light, give them a chance to tell you their side of the story before you publish.

Save the material as background for another story

The material may help you later, especially if you are assigned a beat. But saving these treasures is not enough. You need to be able to find them again when you want them.

Label, date and store your work, both the digital files and the paper files and notebooks. The clearly labeled reporter's notebooks can go in a shoe box or a drawer, with the newest one in front. It is OK if they still have empty pages. Organization is more important to you than saving paper.

Back up your digital files in one searchable place. Consider cloud storage, but keep a digital backup. For journalists, information is wealth. Treat your information like money: take good care of it and keep track of where it is.

Case Study Evalyn Winterset

The boring story at the beginning of this chapter could be different with research, curiosity and collaboration. Preliminary research can reveal a wealth of information and several interesting angles on the "retirement party and cake" story.

The Assignment

Your editor tells you to cover the bus driver's surprise retirement party given by the football team and cheer squad. You ask the editor for the driver's name and the place and time of the party.

Then you ask what the editor knows about the story. You ask for her source, the football player who told your editor about the surprise party. Your editor adds, "Mrs. Winterset drives the team bus for the away games. When we were in grade school, she drove our bus, the Star Route bus. Her own kids all went to South Valley High." South Valley is a neighboring school.

Preliminary Research

In addition to texting your editor's source, the football player, you check several other sources.

The first is the archive of your paper. If your archive has been digitized, a search for the bus driver's last name will take less than a minute. *Winterset* is reasonably uncommon, so you do not need to go through hundreds of entries. In the archives you find two mentions, one from eight years ago. A Jared Winterset of South Valley High beat out someone from your school in steer wrestling. It mentions Winterset was all-state champion and will go to college in Idaho on a rodeo scholarship.

The second mention is a sports story from 17 months ago, about the football team's victory in the invitational finals. The team bus did not return to your campus until after midnight because of unexpected snowfall in the elevations just above you. The reporter quotes bus driver Evalyn Winterset, who drove the team bus: "The guys were great. We just took it nice and slow and everything turned out fine." You make a note to talk to your sports editor, who wrote that story.

You search your local newspaper's website for Winterset's name. You do the same for the major paper in your state and the school district's public affairs releases. You check for her page on social media. Now that you know enough to recognize all the variations of her name, including E. L. Watson Winterset, you enter her various names and your location into search engines and see what else you can find.

You use social media, being careful to identify yourself as a reporter, to ask why the team is honoring her. Some of the answers are pretty general—she's always smiling and upbeat—but comments soon center around a "blizzard on the trip back from football finals." You schedule time for face-to-face and phone interviews to verify what you found on social media and to learn more. You make a note to check for photos, videos or text messages about the late-night trip. You make a note to yourself: "Is there something there to Storify—can I collect all the texts and microblogs, such as tweets, that went out on that trip?"

From your preliminary research online, you know Winterset is the mother of eight sons, all involved in rodeo, who attended five different Intermountain West colleges. She has run several half-marathons and at least one marathon. She graduated from a state university in January with a teaching credential in elementary education.

From social media, you have learned that on the trip home from the football finals, state troopers shut down the route just in front of her. The players were afraid they would have to turn around and go back down the hill, tired and dirty, and spend the night. Instead, the troopers waved the bus through and Winterset drove slowly through the higher elevations in the dark, down the center of the two-lane road. You see posts about sliding "a little," about getting "stuck once" or "maybe twice" and then something about kitty litter. You make a note: "Find out about kitty litter."

Because of good preliminary research, all done while sitting in the journalism room, you have several possible directions for the story. Your curiosity has kicked in, and you have many questions for further research. How did Winterset complete college while working and raising all those kids? Is she retiring to become a teacher in the fall? Where? How did her sons get involved in rodeo? Does she live on a ranch? Why was she allowed to take the bus over Route 47 in the snow when the troopers had closed the road? Was that risky? What did she do to earn the football players' respect? What's with the kitty litter?

Collaboration

You now know enough to collaborate intelligently with your editor. You and your editor discuss the issues you are curious about and what you think your audience will want to know. Core news values guide your discussion.

The retirement is *timely*. The story has *proximity*. People who rode the Star Route bus are likely to remember her, so she may be *prominent*. Eight sons involved in rodeo may give this story an *oddity* or *human interest* value. If Winterset is struggling to get a teaching job, that could be *conflict*. Completing college while driving a bus and raising eight sons may show conflict, too. There is probably a good "woman versus nature" story in how she was able to take the bus over Route 47 after state troopers had closed the road.

The editor helps you define your task before she sends you out to conduct interviews and do more research. She could tell you to keep the story short but to get good pictures for a slide show on your website. She could ask for a still photo and information for a strong and compelling caption. She could direct you to research the news angle—what Winterset will do next—or to pursue a longer feature story, perhaps about the rodeo family, though her sons attended another school. Perhaps the editor will want a story about Winterset's marathon runs and college.

After some discussion, you two decide the story will answer the question: "Why does the football team respect and even love Mrs. Winterset?" One of your research questions will be "What happened during the snowy trip home from the invitational finals?"

Your editor may decide to assemble a team and design a package.

What About Wikipedia?

Use it if you wish, but as an unverified source. Do not quote it.

A wiki is a website that is developed by anyone from among a community of users. Teachers build and run educational wikis. Fans build and run wikis about actors and soccer players. Vinyl record collectors, orchid growers and poodle breeders all build and run wikis for—and with—members of their online communities.

Wikipedia is an encyclopedia built and run as a wiki. Unlike a traditional encyclopedia, where editors invite scholars and experts to write articles, anyone may write, edit, change or even vandalize the articles. (The original work can be restored when a reader—a member of the community—discovers the vandalism. Vandals are generally banned from their communities.)

At any one moment, an expert may be improving an entry, an informed citizen may be updating it, a hoaxer may be posting ridiculous untruths and a hater may be replacing someone's moderate, objective writing with unfounded accusations. An enthusiastic but poorly informed person can write or edit an entry as easily as a college professor.

Wikipedia works surprisingly well. It often provides a high-quality overview of a topic and the most up-to-date information available on any number of topics. Strong Wikipedia articles have links to other online sources, parenthetical citations and dozens of endnotes referring to books and online sources. These may link you to expert analyses and primary sources that you *can* quote in your reporting.

So use Wikipedia as an unverified source. Like postings on social media and gossip in the lunch line, it can indicate the scope of the story. Consult it during your preliminary research, but remember that everything you learn there needs to be verified through other sources before you trust it and certainly before you include it in your reporting.

Journalist's Toolbox

The Journalist's Toolbox, presented by the Society of Professional Journalists, is a valuable, free online resource (Figure 8.6). It is a **metasite**, a website that is a directory to other websites. Search there for links to sites on almost all subjects of public interest, including facts, statistics, experts, original research, explanations and authoritative sources. Knowing how to use this resource may also give you an advantage as you research for other classes.

Clicking on the Federal Government category, for instance, retrieves a list of sites for information about the census, government spending, tools to help journalists cover government, and numerous other sites that provide information and statistics.

Your Turn

Explore three sites you find through the Journalist's Toolbox. Find one useful page or link on each of the three sites. Give your group or class a guided tour of what you found and how you found it. Explain what sort of information is available there and how it might be helpful to you as a journalist. Avoid duplicates among your group, if possible.

Reference Books

Not all information journalists need is free and online. Professional publications and broadcasts maintain a considerable library of reference books, such as stylebooks, dictionaries (including specialized types such as dictionaries of quotations), atlases, timelines of history, almanacs, Guinness World Records, and specialized reference works, such as books on plants, birds, rocks, Olympic records and local history. School publications should consider yearbooks as reference books, too. They are very likely to contain the most complete history of your school.

Figure 8.6 Like any craftsmen, journalists need a kit of tools. The Journalist's Toolbox is a good first stop for many kinds of research. *What would you put in a tool box created specifically for reporters covering high schools and high school students?*

Research Databases

Professional publications pay to access resources—larger publications have librarians and libraries—and consider the cost of the subscriptions to these research tools as part of the price of gathering news. Most student publications use a library to access subscription databases, including their school library and the libraries at colleges and universities, some of which are open to all users. College students may have access to these research tools online.

NewsBank and LexisNexis are important online databases for journalists. Both include media stories from major publications. They allow you to access the work of other journalists from across the English-language press. Reading others' work will help you write better, and the articles will suggest expert sources and give you additional information.

Your Turn

1. Find out what sources are available through your school library, at the public library or through a nearby university library. Can you access these databases?
    - ProQuest Newsstand (articles published in the professional press)
    - LexisNexis Academic (newspapers, legal and business information)
    - Communications & Mass Media (scholarly database for research on media topics)
    - CQ Researcher (background information on national issues)

(Continued)

YOUR TURN *(Continued)*

2. **Going Deeper.** Choose one of these topics or another one that may be of interest to your audience. Use one of the databases available through your library to find two interesting articles on the topic. Share them with your group or class.
   - bullying
   - climate change
   - gun control
   - immigration
   - obesity
   - race and ethnicity
   - science and technology
   - workplace equality (or women and work)

Freedom of Information Act

Student journalists also may utilize the Freedom of Information Act, discussed in Chapter 3, to obtain information from government agencies. The focused questions you and your editor developed will help you write intelligent and effective requests for information. The National Freedom of Information Coalition (NFOIC) can help you write your letters (Figure 8.7).

Figure 8.7 The NFOIC provides sample letters that you can use as templates when drafting state or federal Freedom of Information Act (FOIA) requests.

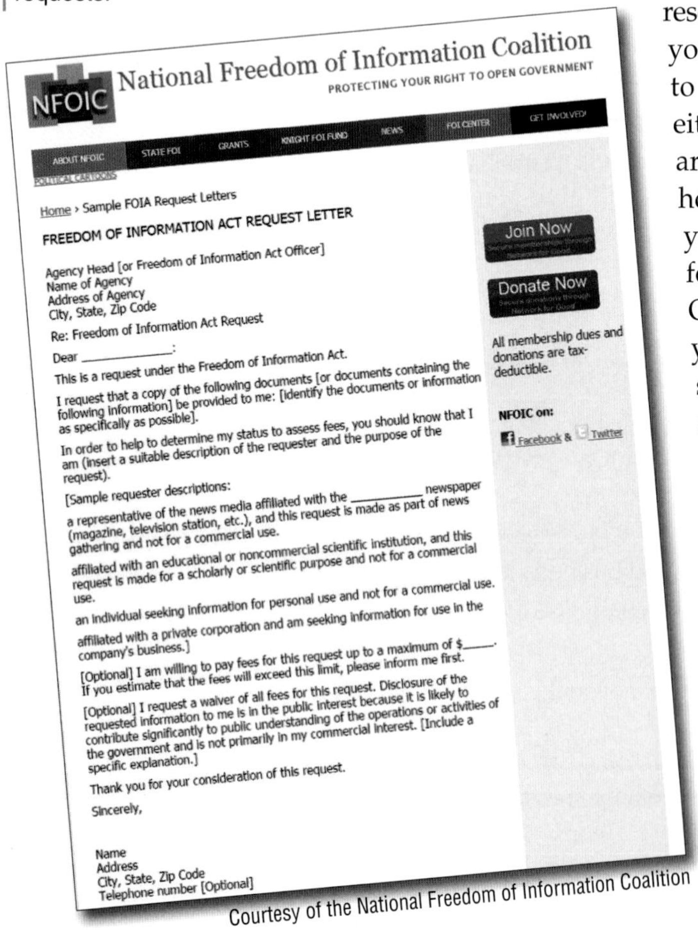
NFOIC National Freedom of Information Coalition
PROTECTING YOUR RIGHT TO OPEN GOVERNMENT

ABOUT NFOIC | STATE FOI | GRANTS | KNIGHT FOI FUND | NEWS | FOI CENTER | GET INVOLVED!

POLITICAL CARTOONS

Home › Sample FOIA Request Letters

FREEDOM OF INFORMATION ACT REQUEST LETTER

Agency Head [or Freedom of Information Act Officer]
Name of Agency
Address of Agency
City, State, Zip Code

Re: Freedom of Information Act Request

Dear ____________:

This is a request under the Freedom of Information Act.

I request that a copy of the following documents [or documents containing the following information] be provided to me: [identify the documents or information as specifically as possible].

In order to help to determine my status to assess fees, you should know that I am (insert a suitable description of the requester and the purpose of the request).

[Sample requester descriptions:

a representative of the news media affiliated with the __________ newspaper (magazine, television station, etc.), and this request is made as part of news gathering and not for a commercial use.

affiliated with an educational or noncommercial scientific institution, and this request is made for a scholarly or scientific purpose and not for a commercial use.

an individual seeking information for personal use and not for a commercial use.

affiliated with a private corporation and am seeking information for use in the company's business.]

[Optional] I am willing to pay fees for this request up to a maximum of $_____. If you estimate that the fees will exceed this limit, please inform me first.

[Optional] I request a waiver of all fees for this request. Disclosure of the requested information to me is in the public interest because it is likely to contribute significantly to public understanding of the operations or activities of the government and is not primarily in my commercial interest. [Include a specific explanation.]

Thank you for your consideration of this request.

Sincerely,

Name
Address
City, State, Zip Code
Telephone number [Optional]

Join Now

Donate Now

All membership dues and donations are tax-deductible.

NFOIC on:

Facebook & Twitter

Courtesy of the National Freedom of Information Coalition

Surveys and Polls

Surveys can be a strong form of original research and a good way to interest and involve your audience. A well-done survey allows you to produce strong evidence and may be either a primary or secondary source. Surveys are only reliable if you are transparent about how you conducted your survey and whom you surveyed. Then your audience can decide for itself how valuable your information is. Online surveys tell what some members of your audience think, while school-based surveys can give you more information about your whole school population.

If you design your survey well, it will provide data to help you answer your research questions. If you design it poorly, you risk being snowed under a literal pile of survey forms and a figurative pile of data you do not know how to use (Figure 8.8).

After an anti-drunk driving campaign at your school, you hear a student say, "I wish someone would show that film to my father." In a staff meeting discussing story ideas, several people agree that they have a drinking problem—and the problem is that their parents drink. Others agree they have a drug problem—their parents use drugs. Someone says, "Yeah. It's a dirty little secret. We know about drugs. We know they are preaching to the wrong people."

Figure 8.8 Think carefully about how you want to design your survey. A poorly designed survey can bury you with useless data.

You decide to do a survey to learn how many students feel this way. Results of the survey will be used in an article. You decide to administer the survey, with the teachers' permission, in all the sophomore English classes plus English as a New Language Level 3 to get a representative sampling and maintain the integrity of the poll. You ask that all responses be anonymous, both to increase the accuracy of your data and to protect the students' privacy.

What questions will you ask in your survey? That depends on what you think your audience will want to know, that is, your research questions. Those research questions can help you narrow the questions you ask on your survey.

Many possible questions occur to you. How many students have felt unsafe driving with a parent who is under the influence of alcohol or drugs? Do you want to know how many students think that their parents have drinking or drug use problems? What do you mean by *problem*? What do you mean by *parents*? What about stepparents or foster parents? Grandparents or guardians? Will you include only parents who have custody? How many students have lived through a divorce or separation or no longer live with a parent because of drug or alcohol abuse? Do their experiences with their parents' drug or alcohol abuse make them think they are more inclined to abuse drugs or alcohol themselves, or less so?

The questions you choose for the survey need to be so clear that they give you the information you and your audience want. They need to provide answers you can process to give your audience information. They should not swamp you with information you cannot sort or analyze.

"Do your parents have a drinking problem?" is probably too broad a question, unless your research question is to find out what the students think of their parents' drinking. More carefully worded questions may give you more usable data.

One good survey question might be: "Have you ever felt unsafe driving with a parent, either a birth parent or an adult with whom you are living, because the adult had been drinking?"

____ Never

____ A few times

____ Frequently

When you receive the responses, you can process that information and tell your audience that XX percent of the students at Atlantic Station High School report having felt unsafe riding in a vehicle because a parent or guardian had been drinking.

Conducting a poll is another way of gathering information. A poll usually consists of a single multiple-choice question, while a survey asks multiple questions in a variety of formats.

Evaluating Sources

Not all sources are equally valuable or equally reliable, so journalists need to be skeptical and ask many questions about the accuracy and reliability of information before they publish it. This is as true for preliminary and deeper research as it is for interviews. Remember, "If your mother tells you she loves you, check it out with two sources."

You cannot serve as the eyes and ears of your audience if someone has pulled the wool over your eyes or if you have simply accepted one source's version of events. While only a small percentage of sources purposely lie, almost everyone has a limited point of view, and many people may be muddled about their own experiences. Some people want to control information to protect their careers or interests. Some seek fame or profit through the press or want the press to punish their enemies for them. People have agendas. We tend to see events through the lens of our agendas. No one source can be guaranteed to give your audience the full truth. Two, or better three, sources are more likely to give you a reliable perspective, a triangulation on the truth.

The more quickly a story is published, the easier it is for misrepresentations, errors or lies to sneak into it. Though the public will tolerate some errors in exchange for immediate coverage of unfolding stories, reporters risk their reputations if they do not evaluate sources before they publish or broadcast. If errors slip into minute-by-minute coverage, they need to be corrected as soon as possible and in a transparent manner, that is, in the most open and honest manner possible. The greater the time after the event, the more thoroughly sources should be verified and evaluated before they are quoted or believed.

Imagine a chain with many links. The first link is anchored onto the actual events you are reporting. That link represents sources that experienced the story—the witnesses or victims, for instance. The second link represents reports made from contact with the witnesses or victims. The third and many of the following links stand for analysis and interpretation of the event. Each link has its strength and its weakness, but each is connected to the news event either directly or through other links in the chain. The chain ends, at least for the moment, with the news broadcast or published story (Figure 8.9 on page 240).

In addition to these sources, other links may float around the same general area, disconnected from the chain. These represent **hearsay**, or rumors, gossip or other unverified information.

Primary Sources: The First Links in Reporting

Primary sources are those who experience an event firsthand or have firsthand knowledge in other ways. These generally fall into two

CASE STUDY Deeper Research for the Winterset Case Study

You and your editor decide Evalyn Winterset is important to the football team because of their nighttime trip in the snow. Consider the questions you and your audience may have. Your research should try to answer some—but not all—of these questions.

You wonder if the loaded bus's great weight makes the bus safer or more dangerous than a passenger car in snow. How about its high center of gravity? Its large tires? You check the National Highway Traffic Safety Administration's website for information on handling a school bus in snowy conditions.

You wonder about the kitty litter several people have mentioned, so you search for "school bus," "kitty litter" and "snow" in your favorite Internet search engine.

You wonder what the trip was like, so you search tweets, photos, videos and other archived messages from players that night to see what happened. You consider using a program such as Storify to put them together in a timeline and create a narrative of the snowy trip.

You wonder how long the team would have needed to wait before Route 47 was open again. You search the online archives of your state's department of transportation for the road closures on that date and when traffic was next allowed to drive through the area.

How far would they have had to drive, either that night or the next morning, to find an open road home?

You wonder if November 23 is early for so much snow, so you check for state snow records, perhaps at the National Oceanic and Atmospheric Administration (NOAA) website.

You wonder whether the storm was really a blizzard or just a heavy snowfall? And what is the difference? You check the Associated Press Stylebook and find that a blizzard has winds of 35 miles per hour or more. You check NOAA's "Past weather information" link, click on your location and select November 23 to learn whether the storm was a heavy snowfall or a blizzard.

You wonder if Winterset was either commended or reprimanded for driving on a road that was closed to other traffic. You check the press releases of the school district for Winterset's name.

You wonder if the trip was in the news or if the snowstorm got coverage. You check the websites of the local and regional news organizations for mention of either the snow or the bus trip.

You want to see what other journalists have written about snow, school buses and safety, so you use a library's subscription databases. You choose Newspapers or LexisNexis, both sources that index news publications. You search for "school bus," "snow" and "safety," and you find almost 3,000 articles. You cannot read them all, so you skim through the titles, blue hyperlinks that take you to either an abstract (a summary) or to the full text of the article.

The hyperlinked headlines for the next five articles seem irrelevant, but the seventh, from The (Harrisburg, Pennsylvania) Patriot-News, reports on a "roadeo." "School bus operators demonstrate skills to earn shot at state title." You wonder, "Do we have a bus operators' roadeo here? Was Winterset in one?" If you cannot find anything on the Internet for your state, you make a note to call the school district's transportation coordinator. Even if it is not important for the Winterset story, a roadeo would make a great story idea.

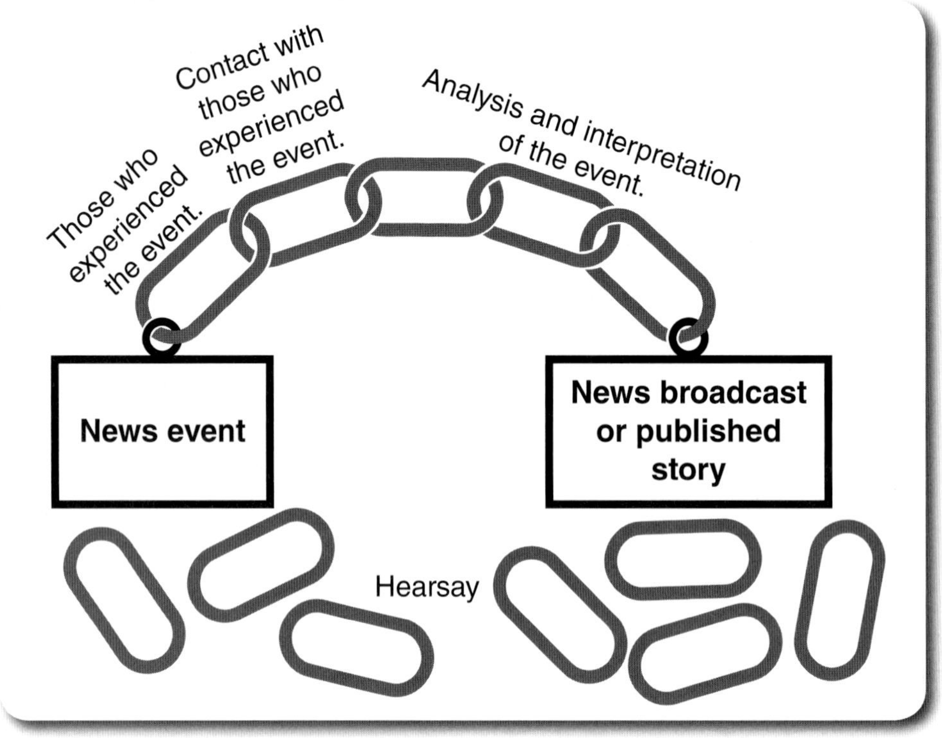

Figure 8.9 Journalists verify the strength of each source before they publish. If you cannot connect information to a reliable source through an unbroken and verifiable chain, it is hearsay and you may not use it.

categories: witnesses and experts. In addition, documents made near the time of an event, such as wills, transcripts, minutes of meetings and police reports, are considered primary sources (Figure 8.10). Images and sound recordings—if unaltered—may also be primary sources.

You should verify the identity of your primary sources. This is especially true for those who communicate with you electronically. Face-to-face or telephone interviews help you verify what was posted on the Internet. Ask yourself, "Could this be a hoax?"

However, breaking news sometimes requires you to report what people are posting rather than what you have verified. You should make this plain to your audience. As a journalist, you report: *A writer identifying himself as Elmer Fudd posted this image on Facebook, saying it shows the size of the hailstones pelting El Paso County.* As a journalist, you would not tell your audience that it *is* a picture of the hailstones until you had verified your source and the image. If you learn the picture is a hoax, notify your audience as soon as your medium allows.

As you interview primary sources, you need to consider factors that might color their judgment. Are they stressed emotionally? What was their part or their friend's part in the incident? Might they be trying to hide something or make someone else look bad? Do their past experiences or situations color how they see events?

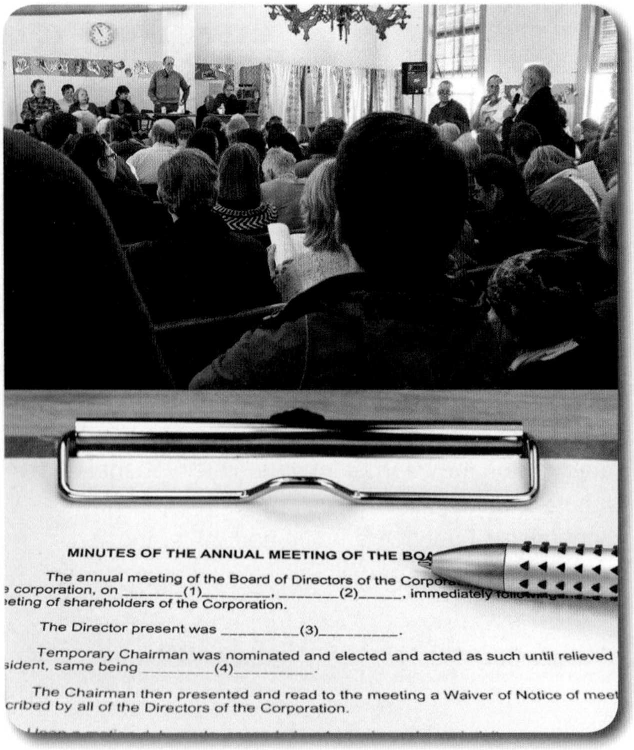

The annual meeting of the Board of Directors of the
The Director present was ______(3)______.
Temporary Chairman was nominated and elected and acted as such until relieved
The Chairman then presented and read to the meeting a Waiver of Notice of
by all of the Directors of the Corporation.

Figure 8.10 The audience attending a meeting can be primary sources. The official minutes of the meeting are also a primary source. *What are the strengths and weaknesses of each?*

Experts are considered primary sources if they have established a professional reputation for their knowledge of the field. Many are authors of papers and books. Often they are associated with universities, think tanks or research institutes that have recognized their expertise and scholarship. If the Centers for Disease Control and Prevention identifies a person as an expert in tropical diseases, you generally do not need to make sure he really knows about tropical diseases.

Because the expert has made a study of the topic or a closely related field and knows the current research done by others, because the expert's opinions are generally respected by others in her field, and because her professional reputation and perhaps livelihood would be marred by unfair or inaccurate statements, her comments are valued as primary sources.

Before you seek out expert opinion, be certain of your experts'

- identity;
- **credentials**, that is, academic degrees or professional experience or honors (an expert in defusing bombs might not be an expert on gun laws);
- **affiliations** (what organizations recognize him as an expert or what learned groups does he belong to?); and
- **impartiality** (she should have no personal or professional connection with the story).

Even experts disagree. It does not hurt to ask more than one and report each point of view.

First-Person Observation, *Sometimes* the First Link in the Chain

When journalists witness events as they unfold and then transmit words, images or sounds to their audience, they are providing **first-person observations**. These valuable and interesting accounts may form the first link of the chain, but they have severe limitations. As a practical matter

- Journalists simply are not able to get to the scene of many significant stories.

Seeing Through Your Personal Lens

Many students may witness a scuffle in the bleachers during a pep assembly but report it differently.

- To one observer, the scuffle in the bleachers shows bullying. "These skinny freshmen were trying to get past these big seniors sitting near the top..."
- To another, it shows the poor judgment of the administration. "The bleachers are way too crowded when they don't open up the other side. These guys were climbing over some people to get to the only open seats when..."
- To another, it shows the stupidity of freshmen or anti-immigrant tension or sexual harassment.

Each observer is being honest but is speaking through the lens of his experience or agenda.

- Journalists' observations, like everyone else's, may be manipulated or colored by danger, emotions or stress.
- Journalists rarely can experience their small parts of a story at the same time they also see the larger picture. Journalists embedded with ground troops, for instance, may have difficulty seeing the progress of the whole war.

Secondary Sources: The Links That Clip Onto the Primary Sources

Secondary sources are people and documents that interpret the evidence from primary sources. Your audience is hungry to understand events. The more troubling the event, the greater their hunger for understanding. A journalist's job includes this interpretation of the evidence from primary sources. Sports fans, for instance, do not just want a final score or even a play-by-play account. They want analysis from sports reporters and former players saying why someone lost, why someone won, how long it has been since a similar loss happened and

MEET THE PROFESSIONALS:

Working Like a Professional—Morgan Jones, 18

When a gunman killed 12 people and wounded 70 others in an Aurora, Colorado, movie theater, Morgan Jones' minute-by-minute postings on Reddit scooped the national and local press and became the go-to source for the traditional news media. (Reddit is a news aggregating bulletin board with user-generated content, either links or texts.)

Jones, who had served as online editor of his school paper, the RJ Voice, and producer for RJ Radio at Regis Jesuit High School in Aurora, first heard about the shootings from a 30-second-old Facebook post on the local NBC affiliate's page: "We're investigating shootings at a movie theater." A Facebook user had posted a link to the Aurora Police Department's scanner.

Jones and a friend listened to the police scanner and realized, "Oh my gosh, this a big thing.

"I just thought it needed to be chronicled," Jones said. He posted a link to the Facebook story on Reddit and added 13 more posts as the story unfolded through the dark hours of the morning. His posts quote primary sources and link to others, creating a timeline for the unfolding story. When later posts revealed errors in earlier ones, he crossed out—but did not remove—the errors in order to maintain maximum transparency.

Witnesses and victims began adding their reports and images, making Reddit the fastest way to get essential news. Reddit proved more informative than local news or official sources.

Jones' training as a high school journalist served him well. "To report something in that level of detail, you have to make decisions quickly. In the live broadcasts I did in high school, the decisions were in the span of minutes. That helped for sure.

"Behind every tragic event, there are people. Focus on the people behind it. Don't sensationalize. Report the facts. Maintain reverence and a solemn attitude. Remember that they are people and they have families and kids and loved ones," said Jones.

what the athlete or team must do to emerge victorious from the next contest. Audiences also look to journalists to interpret economics, politics, war, medical findings, scientific findings, entertainment, fashion and even weather.

Journalists may feel pressure to supply the audience with analysis before they have enough evidence to do so. This leads to speculation and errors, in fact, some of which live long after other evidence has painted a different picture. The longer the time that elapses between an event and the analysis, the easier it is to locate, judge and assemble primary sources and expert commentary. Fair, balanced and accurate reporting means journalists must sometimes simply report the primary evidence and say they will continue to follow the story.

In addition to journalists, scholars, politicians, religious leaders, educators, economists, pundits and private citizens all interpret primary sources to provide context and organization to chaotic events. Some will issue statements and provide analyses for the benefit of the public. Others, who want to control news, hope the media will disseminate their analyses. Politicians often strive to control the "spin" on events, talking to the public through the press.

While analysis may provide valuable context to primary documents, it may also introduce errors. Some may be errors in fact, but others arise because some sources or events are emphasized while other parts are left out. Journalists should use caution when they use or quote secondary sources. It is a good idea to check the primary sources that your secondary sources used. An error repeated 4,000 times is still an error.

Hearsay: Not Part of the Chain

Hearsay, or unverified information, is to journalism what gossip is to conversation—interesting but unreliable and potentially dangerous. Hearsay includes reported facts, statistics, quotations, events and even ideas that cannot be connected to a verifiable and reliable source. Responsible journalists never use hearsay as a source.

However, you may investigate claims you receive, even if you receive them through hearsay. Think of them as story ideas. If they are strong or important story ideas, do more research. The more important or the more serious the claim, the more sources you need and the stronger the evidence must be before you publish. Hearsay, like gossip, tends to focus on the most negative interpretation of facts.

Look for independent confirmation from reliable, primary sources or try to link the hearsay back to its source, if there is one.

If you find a reliable source for the information, you may find that the original story is different from the hearsay. The information may have been transmitted many times by people who do not understand the ethics of journalism, who tell stories they have heard as if *they* were part of the story or who have filtered the story through their own perceptions.

Case Study: A Case Study in Hearsay

The Tip

Person A: Mr. White has porno magazines in his office.
The journalist (you): Tell me what you saw.
Person A: Oh, this friend of mine was in his office and he said he saw them piled in the drawer of his desk.
You: How do I reach your friend?
(Person A gives Person B's contact information.)

Preliminary Research

You talk to Person B: Person A tells me you saw some inappropriate materials in a science teacher's desk.
Person B: Yeah. Mr. White's.
You: Tell me what you saw.
Person B: Well, I didn't see it myself, but my friend did.
You: How do I reach him?
(Person B gives Person C's contact information.)
You talk to Person C: Person B tells me you saw some inappropriate materials in a science teacher's desk.
Person C: This friend of mine said Mr. White ...
(You track down sources.)
Person G: Well, yeah. I was in his office to talk about my grade. He had a whole stack of them on this little bookcase.
You: Tell me more about what you saw.
Person G: I saw these magazines. These chicks were all posing, wearing oil and not much else. The magazines were all bright colored and glossy, like, you know, porn magazines.
You: Did you see the name of the magazine?
Person G: Nope. Well, maybe it had a big M and F on the front.
You: When did you see the magazines?
Person G: A while ago. At the end of last semester, just before finals.
You: Did anyone else see them?
Person G: No one was with me. I just went into his office after school to talk about my grade.
You: Did you tell anyone, like an adult, about what you saw?
Person G: No. Not really. Just some of my friends.

Right now, you have no story, just one person's months-old report of something that he says he saw. The source may be unreliable. He may have a grudge against a teacher because of a grading issue.

To pursue the story, you need to obtain more evidence and give Mr. White a chance to respond to the accusations, but those steps seem inappropriate because

- this may reveal a serious crime, one that will soon involve the police;
- interviewing Mr. White in his office may be unwise, since you are asking him to deny doing something for which he could be fired (journalists need to protect their own physical safety);
- written or electronic communication may lead to the destruction of the evidence a school administrator might want to see; and
- snooping in the teacher's office is both illegal and unethical.

Collaboration

Researching hearsay can be dark business. This accusation is serious and may involve student safety. You consult your editor, and the two of you decide to talk with your adult adviser.

You read your notes to the adviser. She listens to all your notes and says, "So let me summarize what I just heard. Person G saw a glossy magazine with a picture of a girl in a thong bikini, her body oiled, on the top of a bookcase in Mr. White's office, and you think he reads pornography and has a lot of porn.

(Continued)

CASE STUDY A Case Study in Hearsay (continued)

"Let me see what I can learn."

Note: When you take such a story to your adviser, you are not only seeking journalistic wisdom, you are acting appropriately when you suspect ongoing criminal activity. Journalists do not withhold information from the police when doing so would put lives in danger. Your adviser is one of your links to law enforcement and is also mandated in many states to report anything that would endanger students.

Finding the Truth

The next day, your adviser shows you a framed picture from the front cover of Muscle and Fitness Hers, a glossy and brightly colored publication. The cover features a well-oiled female bodybuilder clad in a turquoise bikini. The picture is signed, "To Uncle Mike, who started my feet on this incredible journey. Love, Angelica."

Your adviser says she borrowed the picture from Mr. White. She adds, "White runs an ultra-fitness training center with his brother, Angelica's father, out of a small industrial space. Check out their website."

The website shows ferociously buff men and women swinging on trapezes and jumping in and out of huge truck tires, then flipping the tires over. Angelica is featured for winning CrossFit competitions, and the science teacher and his brother are profiled as the owners on the "About Us" tab.

"It might be a good story idea," she says.

It might also clarify a rumor.

Evaluating Internet Sources

The Internet is not merely another source of information. It is an alternate information universe where you need every source-evaluating skill you already have, plus a few more.

On the Internet you can find both reliable and unreliable information, by people and organizations that could themselves be reliable or unreliable. Sites may be created to sell products or disseminate knowledge, to aid researchers and students or to argue for a point of view, to subtly influence your thinking or to perpetrate outright lies, hoaxes and frauds.

In this alternate universe, gossip and lies can be copied, forwarded, tweeted, linked to and liked a thousand times in just a few minutes—and still be untrue.

To research effectively on the Internet, you need to know why you are looking and what you are looking for.

Do You Need General Knowledge?

- Are you doing preliminary research to discover the scope of a story?
- Are you seeking background knowledge to prepare for an interview?

Many "hits," the different sites your search engine displays, can give you satisfactory preliminary information. Wikis and sites designed for children may give you good general surveys of a topic, for instance what tinikling is. Read at least three so you can triangulate—have three points of view—since no one source is likely to be completely impartial and absolutely correct. For instance, if you need general knowledge about a refugee community in your area, you may find a site that recounts the wars and politics in their home country, a site that asks for contributions to help the people in their old country and a site that suggests the refugee community is struggling to adapt to your community because of deep-seated differences with American culture. One of the sites may seem to be a little prejudiced against the immigrants, one may seem to tug at your emotions a bit too much to be trusted and one may tell you more about the old country's history than you really need to know. But by looking at three sources, you have established a bit about the refugees' backgrounds, perhaps what they care about and what they may struggle with. None of the sources you viewed could have done that job reliably by itself.

While doing background research, feel free to look at sites that clearly are not objective. A band's own website can be a good source for preliminary research on the group. Commercial sites may also be acceptable. Searching for images and video may help you also. But do not count as three different sources—a solid triangulation—three sites that seem to quote each other, repeat the same information or link to each other a great deal. You are looking for three points of view, not three sites with the same point of view.

Be a little skeptical as you search and evaluate websites. Your skeptical side questions the reliability of sources—including sites—rather than agreeing or disagreeing with what the source tells you. Ask:

- Who created this site? Why?
- Why do they say what they say?
- Who is their audience?
- How do they pay to maintain the site?
- Does the information here conflict with information on other sites? Does it conflict with common sense?
- Does the information on this site appear to be a "cut-and-paste" version of other sites? (Don't count three cut-and-paste sites as three points of view as you triangulate. Count all three as one point of view.)

Journalists strive to be fair and objective. Remember, unreliable sources can be right and reliable sources can be wrong.

Your Turn

1. Choose a topic about which you want general knowledge, for instance, a sport, a music group, a specialized tool or a vacation destination. Clear your topic with your adviser, then find three sites that would be acceptable sources for background research. Save or print at least one page from each site and answer the questions listed above for each. Share your information with your group or class.

(Continued)

YOUR TURN *(Continued)*

2. **Going Deeper.** Examine the sites you found and try to identify the sources of the information used on each. Do you find any of the following?
   - information identical to another site—evidence that someone, somewhere has been cutting and pasting
   - images (and the identification of the images) that are published elsewhere
   - primary documents: original research, photos taken by the author of the site, first-person observations
   - links to sources of information

   Which sites appear most reliable?

Do You Need Specific Information?

To answer the research questions you and your editor created, you may need specific facts, figures, descriptions or dates. If you are looking for the number of physical education credits each state requires for graduation, type "number of years of PE required in high school" into a search engine. You will probably get in excess of 42 million hits. Triangulation, looking at three or more sources, is still a good policy. But which three will be reliable and helpful?

Skip the ads and look at the first page or two of hits. Many search engines, including Google, consider how often other sites have linked to a site when they assign rankings. Valuable or interesting sites sometimes rise to the first few pages.

Look for sites that give all or most of the following information. (But remember, some unreliable sites give this too.)

- author's name (Organizations sometimes are authors.)
- author's title, position, expertise or education
- author's contact information, often an email address
- organization associated with the page or site
- date the page was created or updated

YOUR TURN

1. Choose a specific piece of information for which you will search (for instance, the amount of money or number of injuries involved in a sport or the person who invented, designed or created something you find interesting). Clear your topic with your adviser, then find three sites that seem to provide the information you are seeking. Save or print the home page and at least one other page from each site. Evaluate the sites based on the questions listed above. Share your information with your group or class.

(Continued)

YOUR TURN *(Continued)*

2. **Going Deeper.** Evaluate each of the sites you have chosen based on the criteria in this chapter. Give each a rank of 1 through 5, with 1 being hearsay and 5 being a very reliable source. Explain your ranking to your group or class.

Do You Need to Hear Arguments About a Controversy?

People, organizations, even governments host sites and publish on the Internet to convince others of their point of view or to gain business or votes. Journalists use these **advocacy sites** for information and to understand a variety of viewpoints. Rarely are there only two sides to a controversy, so journalists visit—and evaluate—many sites.

And Now... Closer to Home

Ten Questions Your Skeptical Side Should Ask

If you are looking on the Internet for specific information rather than a general overview, you need to be even more critical. Consider these questions:

1. Would I seek out this author as an expert source on this subject, based on his description on the website? Does his title, education, position or other expertise make him a reliable source?
2. Is the organization that sponsors the site respected and well-known?
3. What sort of organization is it? Is it a nonprofit (often .org)? A corporation (often .com)? A governmental agency (often .gov)? A university (often .edu)?
4. Would I contact this organization by phone for reliable information?
5. What is the organization's purpose for maintaining this page? To inform? To persuade? To sell something?
6. What is the organization's reason for maintaining the site? For public relations? To share knowledge? To increase its prestige? To inform the public, perhaps as mandated by law?
7. What prejudices or agendas might this site have?
8. Does the site provide links to primary sources, other trustworthy sites and peer-reviewed or adjudicated (judged) documents? (Scholars and scientists publish their findings in books and journals that use several experts in the field to review the work for the quality of the research before it is published. Only work that meets high standards will be published in peer-reviewed or adjudicated publications.)
9. Is the site up-to-date? (You don't need the PE requirements from 1990.)
10. Does information on the site conflict with information on other respected sites? Does it go against common sense? If it does, does the site give reasons and evidence for its position?

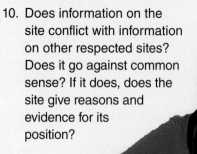

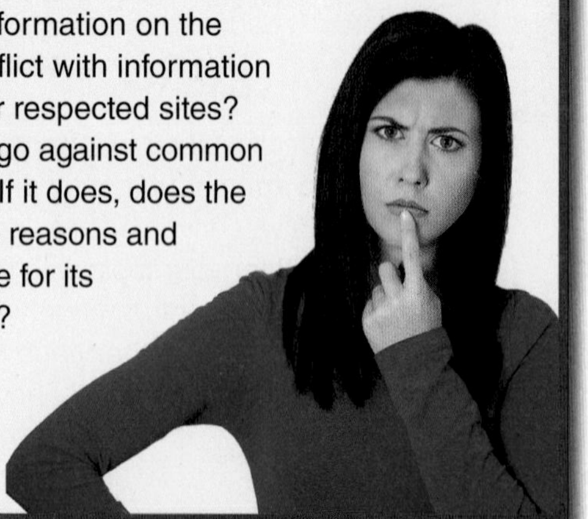

To judge advocacy sites, you need to use all the tools you used to evaluate websites during your preliminary research and during your search for specific information, plus a few more. You may need to judge the strength of the website's content as well as the credentials of the author and owner of the site.

It is weak journalism to mention strong, reliable sites for one side of an argument and sites that are little more than ranting for the other side. It is also weak journalism to give all points of view equal time or space in your story. The people who think the superintendent mismanaged school funds should get about as much time or space as those who think a poor economy has hurt all investments. But the group that thinks radioactive aliens from Krypton have taken the money probably does not deserve equal consideration.

And Now... Closer to Home

Who Is Saying This? Identifying the Sponsors of Advocacy Sites

Reliable sites are transparent about their identity and interests; they let you know who they are and what their purpose is. They allow you to see their biases. If the site is run by the Knights of Responsible Governance, you should be able to learn from the site who the knights are and what interests they represent.

If the site does not give you enough information, several sources will help you identify the owner of a site.

- Start with the Journalist's Toolbox category "Check Domain Names." It lists multiple sites that help you find a site's owner.
- What about the IP address? An IP (Internet Protocol) address is a string of numbers separated by periods that identifies each computer and other devices connected to the Internet. There are websites that list the physical location (city, state, etc.) associated with an IP address. (But they may show the location of the Internet service provider rather than the location of the person using the computer. Be aware, also, that IP addresses can be spoofed or otherwise disguised.)

Reliable sites generally are well proofread. Bad grammar, poor capitalization or inconsistent tone may indicate carelessness, ignorance and perhaps that the site is the work of one person acting alone, without the skills or resources to edit her work before she publishes.

Reliable sites contain accurate information. If facts, figures, dates and quotations are used without hyperlinks, or the hyperlinks are broken or connect to equally non-transparent and un-proofread sites, journalists attempt to verify that information through primary sources. An untruth repeated 27 times on 27 sites is still an untruth. Though any site may contain errors in fact, errors are corrected promptly on reliable sites. A pattern of errors undermines the site's value.

Reliable sites are moderate. They do not make sweeping generalizations (*all women are insecure; all the new residents are money-grubbers*). They do not use highly emotional language (*the new tax will destroy our local culture and murder our future*) or portray their opponents as irrational, satanic or untrustworthy. The frequent use of absolutes, such as the words *all, never, always, no one* and *everyone*, may indicate lack of moderation.

Chapter Eight

Review and Assessment

Recall

1. Name four ways preliminary research will help you develop a story.
2. Identify three files or documents you should create as you begin your preliminary research.
3. What things do you need to decide as you collaborate with your editor after your preliminary research is finished?
4. Name three things you could do with the preliminary research that will not be used in the story you are working on.
5. Are preliminary and deeper research done for the same purpose? Explain your answer.
6. As a student journalist, how can you access subscription databases?
7. What characteristics should you look for when evaluating the reliability of an Internet source? How can you confirm the validity of the information you find?
8. Identify and explain the links in the chain of sources from eyewitness to published accounts.
9. What should you do when you learn that a source in breaking news reports has been inaccurate or untruthful?
10. How can triangulating help you maintain balance and accuracy in your reporting?

Critical Thinking

1. Identify three media you can use in preliminary research.
2. Where would you search to find the number of children who have not been vaccinated against meningitis in your city or area?
3. Where would you search to read newspaper articles published in five major cities on metal detectors in schools?
4. What are the advantages and drawbacks when journalists provide first-person observations?
5. Why is skepticism an important part of reporting?
6. If an expert provides analysis for the story you are covering, would she be a primary or secondary source? Why?
7. What characteristics should you look for when evaluating the reliability of an Internet source?
8. If the term you entered in a search engine has generated a large number of hits, how can you narrow down the number of sites you look at?

Application

Choose at least three strong story ideas and demonstrate your ability to research the story. Clearly label the source for each piece of information you collect so that you can write an accurate attribution.

1. For one of the story ideas, do two of the following. In each case, copy or download the information and tell what you learned from it.
   - A. Find three appropriate sources of background information on the topic.
   - B. Search for three professional journalistic articles related to the topic.
   - C. Search public records for at least two items that pertain to the story.
2. Synthesize the information gleaned from your research and write a first draft of your story.
3. For one of the story ideas:
   - A. Identify information you would like to have from a government agency. Create a Freedom of Information Act request letter.
   - B. Create three questions for an online or pen-and-ink survey of your student body. Word the questions carefully to get information that would answer a research question. Explain what you would need to do with the data to publish your findings for your audience.
   - C. Identify an expert to interview for one of the stories. Explain why the expert's credentials and affiliation make her an appropriate choice. Draft an email requesting an interview and write out three questions to ask the expert.

Chapter Eight

Journalism Style

Brand Names and Trademarks: Do Not Say It Unless You Mean It!

Trademarks are brand names or symbols that are owned by a manufacturer and are protected by law. Trademarks become diluted—they lose their value to the manufacturer and their meaning to all of us—when they are used to identify another manufacturer's product that is similar to the trademarked item. Using trademarked names when you are not sure of the manufacturer is always wrong and sometimes can result in lawsuits.

For instance, Jell-O is the trademarked name of a brand of gelatin dessert. *Her baby brother was spiking his hair with his green Jell-O* is acceptable only if you know it was Jell-O from Kraft Foods. If you are not sure, write: *Her baby brother was spiking his hair with his green gelatin*.

As a journalist, you should use the generic name unless you are sure of the brand. If you have verified that the product in your story comes from the company that owns the trademark, you may use the trademarked name.

Notice that the generic name, gelatin or gelatin dessert, is not capitalized, but the trademarked name, Jell-O, is. Check the AP Stylebook's Food Guidelines to find out how the name is capitalized. It is Jell-O, not Jello.

Try It!

1. In the sample passage below, the writer used many trademarked names. Use the AP Stylebook to determine which words should be capitalized and to verify spelling.
2. Find the generic term for each trademarked name and replace the trademarked name with the generic one where appropriate.

Spa envy sends local resident to emergency room when rented loader crashes through fence

It started as a peaceful Saturday, according to Redda S. Beete, 56, who had been soaking in her backyard jacuzzi eating oreos and milk from a green pyrex cereal bowl. Muzak played from her easy listening station, and an ice-filled glass of 7up sat within arm's reach on the astroturf to her left. Just inside the door, in her family room, a xeroxed copy of her late husband's obituary was scotch-taped to the table by each chair, and a box of kleenex lay next to her ouija board in preparation for a séance planned for that evening. Brownies cooled on the kitchen counter.

Shortly after 3 p.m. backyard neighbor Vinny Verde, 33, shattered the peace—and her fence—when he started the diesel engine of a bobcat loader he rented to excavate for his own Jacuzzi. Verde, a construction worker who told police he was familiar with large earthmoving equipment, was new to skid-steer loaders.

Beete, who fell while trying to escape the bobcat lurching toward her spa, was taken to Queen of Angels Hospital and released with an ace bandage on her ankle and a band-aid on her forehead in time to host her husband's séance.

3. Search in the printed AP Stylebook or AP Stylebook online for five more trademarked names that are familiar to you. Write the generic name for each product.

Extend Your Knowledge — Style Exercises

Visit the *Journalism* website to learn more about trademarked names and how to use them correctly and effectively in your stories.

Chapter Eight

Writers' Workshop

In this Writers' Workshop you will:

- Write journalistic paragraphs of one or two sentences.
- Find one focus per paragraph and sentence.

Workshop 8.1

Hurrah for the One-Sentence Paragraph!

Mini-Lesson: Are They Really That Short?

Journalists have practical reasons for using very short paragraphs.

In print publications, paragraphs of more than one—or occasionally two—sentences become long blocks of grey type in the narrow news columns. A 40-word lead, normal length for the Los Angeles Times, fills up a solid inch.

Both in print and online, journalists give their audience many entry points into their stories. Those entry points include the main and subsidiary headlines, pictures, graphics and cutlines, but each paragraph of the story may also be an entry point. Paragraphs beginning with quotations are especially attractive to the eye (though they rarely make good leads).

Apply It!

1. Count the sentences in each paragraph of four or five stories from professional print and online publications. What is the average paragraph length?
2. Look at your journalistic work or work from other student publications. If possible, work from a digital document. Count the sentences in each paragraph. What is the average paragraph length?
3. Divide a student story, preferably your own, into one-sentence paragraphs. Read the story with a partner or small group. What did you notice about your work?

Mini-Lesson: Short Sharpens the Focus

If you are like most writers, you found that many of your sentences—and therefore your paragraphs—in the Apply It! exercise above seemed rather weak. They may not contain a complete thought worthy to stand on its own.

Journalists learn to write—or to revise—so that each paragraph has a mission. Look at the excerpt (in the table below and on the next page) from a general news story about a vote on Laura's Law, which would allow county courts to order treatment for people with serious mental illness. All but four of the paragraphs are one sentence long.

Los Angeles County supervisors vote to implement Laura's Law

Paragraph	Mission
Los Angeles County leaders voted Tuesday to fully implement Laura's Law, a state law that allows counties to pursue court-ordered outpatient treatment for people with serious mental illness.	**Who** voted, for **what**, **when**, **where** and **why** it is significant
The law was recently adopted by San Francisco and Orange counties. Los Angeles County launched a small program soon after Laura's Law took effect in 2003, but the county's current program is purely voluntary.	Provides the larger context for the action
The supervisors voted 4 to 0, with Don Knabe absent, to expand the existing outpatient treatment program from 20 to 300 slots and to create a team tasked with reaching out to potential patients and managing the court filing process when necessary.	More details about the lead and the law
The vote, which will expand funding for outpatient treatment in the county, will allow a family member, treatment provider or law enforcement officer to ask a court to order someone to undergo treatment. Patients, however, can't be forced to take medication.	More about the law: • Who can ask a court to order treatment • What the law cannot order
The annual cost of the expanded program will be a little under $10 million, but that is expected to be primarily covered by state mental health funds and Medi-Cal.	How much will it cost?

(Continued)

Los Angeles County supervisors vote to implement Laura's Law *(Continued)*

Paragraph	Mission
Laura's Law has been praised by advocates who say it gives a new tool to family members of adults with severe untreated mental illness. But it has also drawn opposition from civil liberties advocates and others who say court-ordered treatment infringes on patients' rights.	Summary of conflicts about the law and who is on each side. (This is the key to being fair. Both sides are mentioned before either has its say.)
Both sides voiced their views to the supervisors Tuesday.	Sets up the quotations to follow
Brittney Weissman, executive director of the National Alliance on Mental Illness' Los Angeles chapter, told the supervisors: "Laura's Law helps very ill individuals – who often don't recognize that they're sick – get well and stay in the community so that they can later continue in treatment on their own."	Arguments for the law and who raised them
Others, such as Mark-Anthony Johnson of local advocacy group Dignity and Power Now, cautioned the supervisors that the move could further criminalize those with mental illness.	Arguments against the law and who raised them
Johnson said Laura's Law "plays into the fear that folks with mental health conditions are violent people." And he expressed concerns that people of color would be disproportionately targeted for court-ordered treatment.	More arguments against the law

In narrative leads, each paragraph also has a mission. Look at the first three paragraphs—and sentences—of the LA Times story "Das Booter" in the table below. The headline, kicker, read-out, picture and caption gave the news (in case any soccer fan had missed it), but the game story pulls readers onward with sharply focused one-sentence paragraphs.

Kicker: World Cup Final
Germany 1, Argentina 0

Headline: Das Booter

Read-out: Second-half sub Goetze kicks Germany to its first championship since 1990, with an extra-time goal that will live for all time in World Cup annals

By Kevin Baxter

Apply It!

1. Working with a partner, choose a general news article from the professional press. Number the paragraphs. Working independently, write the mission of each paragraph. Compare your results with your partner's.
2. Examine a journalistic piece that was written by another student. Number the paragraphs and write the mission of each paragraph. Discuss what you found with members of your group. Imagine you were asked to give a response on the piece to the student writer before publication. Being as helpful as possible; suggest ways to improve the piece.
3. Choose two stories from the student press, either from your school or from another school. Rewrite the stories so that each paragraph has a mission. If you need more information than the story provides, supply the missing information with fiction, but place all *made-up information in italics*.
4. Discuss with your writing group or class what you learned as you rewrote the articles.

Extend Your Knowledge Extend

Visit the *Journalism* website for additional practice in writing short, tightly focused paragraphs.

Das Booter

Paragraph	Mission
Rio De Janeiro—When the final whistle sounded, Mario Goetze disappeared under a dog pile of German teammates in the middle of the field.	What the winner did. This sets the scene and introduces a character.
Argentina's Lionel Messi, meanwhile, ran his left hand over his face and hair, sidestepped the celebration and joined his teammates, many of whom were in tears, at the other end of the field.	What the loser did. Another character and a conflict and emotion.
The gap between winners and loser has rarely been both as wide and as narrow as it was Sunday after the World Cup final, with Goetze's goal 23 minutes into extra time giving Germany a title it has been chasing for 24 years, while denying Messi the one prize he hasn't won.	**What** happened, **who** did it, **when** it happened, **where** and **why** the result was significant. This is the narrative lead nut graf.

Chapter Nine

Interviews and Attributions

Whom do we ask? How do we quote them?

Photo by Kellen Ochi, Courtesy of Michelle Min, Sage Hill School

G-WLEARNING.com

While studying, look for the activity icon to:

- **Build** vocabulary terms with e-flash cards and matching activities.
- **Extend** learning with further discussion of relevant topics.
- **Reinforce** what you learn by completing style exercises, worksheets and end-of-chapter questions.

Visit the Journalism website: www.g-wlearning.com/journalism/

Chapter Objectives

After reading this chapter, you will be able to:

- List three sorts of information reporters may seek from interviewees.
- Explain the importance of both paper notes and sound recordings from interviews.
- Explain how to select and locate people to interview.
- Discuss what kinds of questions to use during interviews.
- Explain how to schedule an interview.
- Choose safe and effective places for interviews.
- Discuss how to handle requests to avoid certain topics during interviews.
- Describe how to present yourself at an interview.
- Discuss the importance of listening and asking follow-up questions.
- Discuss the importance of verifying information you receive in an interview.
- Discuss ways of handling unverified or contradictory information from interviews.
- Name the functions of quotations in an article or opinion piece.
- Describe the characteristics of strong quotations and what kinds of quotes to avoid.
- Explain how to handle partial quotes, snippets and paraphrases.

Key Terms Build Vocab

ambush journalism	follow-up question	paraphrase
direct quotation	indirect quotation	snippet

Before You Read...

Hearing is a physical process. It requires you to pay attention to the sounds and patterns of spoken language. These include the vowel sounds of *a*, *e*, *i*, *o* and *u*, as well the other letters, which are called consonants. Note when you hear words during class that are unfamiliar. Listen for familiar letter sounds that can help you try spelling the words. Review your list with a classmate or the instructor to confirm spellings. Then, locate the definition of each new word in a dictionary or glossary.

Introduction

"The people must know before they can act, and there is no educator to compare with the press."

–Ida B. Wells, American journalist

You are the eyes and ears for your audience. You meet people your audience might like to meet. You ask the questions the audience would like to ask. You bring back sound files and written records and then select the information and quotations your audience most needs and wants to hear.

Interviews

Experts say that 75 to 80 percent of news comes from interviews, that is, from talking to participants and experts in the field. When a reporter has not witnessed or experienced newsworthy events or done extensive research herself, she should talk to the people who have (Figure 9.1). Those conversations are interviews.

Good reporting is based on these interviews. Strong stories have

- **direct quotations**, the actual words of the sources—witnesses, participants or experts—plus attribution. *"I hate it when the band has to march behind the mounted police's parade unit. All those dancing horses leave poopy surprises for us to march around. Without getting out of step or losing the beat, of course," said sousaphone player Marcie Diaz.*
- **indirect quotations** from witnesses, participants or experts, plus attribution. Indirect quotations use some of the source's words, but the words are embedded in the reporter's sentence. *Their least favorite parade position is behind horse units that "leave poopy surprises" the band must avoid while not missing a beat, said sousaphone player Marcie Diaz.*
- **paraphrases**, which report the views of a witness, participant or expert, plus attribution. Paraphrases use the reporter's words but accurately represent the speaker's meaning. *Band members prefer not to march directly behind the horse unit because it is difficult to play well and avoid the horses' droppings, according to sousaphone player Marcie Diaz.*
- sound files or video files from witnesses, participants or experts, plus identification of the speaker.

Your Turn

1. Clip, print or listen to five news or feature stories from various sections of professional publications or broadcasts. Avoid duplicating those used by classmates. Print transcripts of the broadcasts, if possible. Highlight direct and indirect quotations and their attributions. In the margin, identify the speaker as a witness, participant or expert. How many sources are used in each story? What percent of the story is highlighted? Save these clippings for a later Your Turn exercise.
2. **Going Deeper.** Repeat the same process with stories from your school's publication or broadcast. How do they compare with the professional stories?

Figure 9.1 Interviews with the people who participate in events are essential to good journalism. In addition, strong quotations can hold your audience's interest.

Some things look easy when an expert does them—pole vaulting, for instance—but seem scary to a beginner. Interviewing is like that. Student journalists may avoid interviews, get by with email or text messages or try to put stories together without them. However, interviewing is much too important to avoid.

It is normal to be nervous about interviews. Both you and your interviewee may be nervous. But with preparation, a few essential attitudes and techniques and some practice, interviews can become powerful sources for your stories.

It is important to decide what you need from your source before you schedule an interview. Your research questions, the ones you and your editor discussed at your first collaboration, will guide your interviews. Though the best interviews may reveal surprises, you and your editors establish a purpose for each interview and create questions to help you find the information you need. You may be seeking the interviewee's

- knowledge, either his expert knowledge or his first-person experience;
- opinions or feelings about an issue; or
- personal story so you can feature the interviewee in an article.

And Now... Closer to Home

Paper or Digital?

You should come away from an interview with both sound files and written notes. One serves as the backup to the other. Once you have secured permission to record an interview, position the mic (microphone) or the recorder, turn it on and then ignore it. Your interviewee may be able to do the same, especially if you are a good listener.

If you are interviewing a source on a phone that does not have the capacity to record, you can still record the interview, if you have obtained permission, by securing a digital voice recorder with rubber bands to the back of the phone.

Whatever method you use to record the interview, make sure you are comfortable with your equipment and that it works well before you begin your interview.

Your written notes of the interview are the easiest to scan for information, especially if you are writing on deadline. The sound files serve as backup to verify the accuracy of both your subject's words and the context, including the previous and following questions and what you asked to get that answer. Using a source's answers without the context may misrepresent what she said.

If you are writing for broadcast or will incorporate sound files into online stories, your written record of the interview helps you locate the two or three sections from your interview you wish to use. If the interview is strong enough, you may post the entire interview or large sections of it on your publication's website and link to it in your story.

Figure 9.2 Your editor may suggest people to interview for a story. Keep clear and complete records of all contact information.

Where to Begin

A successful interview starts when the story idea is assigned. Discuss the assignment briefly with your editor (Figure 9.2). The editor may suggest someone who would make a good source. You may think of others as you develop a research plan.

Complete your preliminary research before you begin interviews. If you ask an expert on heat-related illness for information already on his website, you risk looking unprepared and perhaps foolish. However, if you are seeking sound files for a broadcast or Web story, you may ask your heat expert to tell *your audience* the four most important precautions they should take, even if the information is also on his website.

If you are interviewing a member of your community who is going to the International Paralympic Games, you should already know what her sport is, what competitions she has won and what country she will represent. (Do not assume it is the United States.) However, if you are seeking sound files, ask her to identify herself. "Please tell me *for our audience* what your name is, what sports you compete in and what country you will represent at the Paralympic Games."

Whom to Ask

Of course you will ask participants in the event you are covering, plus others close to them or the event. If you are writing about the Paralympic athlete, you will interview her. You may also interview other athletes, her coaches and family.

When you need an expert source—someone with academic credentials or significant experience—contact a university. Universities commonly make their research and teaching staff members available to the press and public. Many universities will have a "faculty experts guide," sometimes for the whole university, sometimes for each department, on their websites (Figure 9.3). Others will list "experts available."

Figure 9.3 Many colleges and universities, such as the University of Florida, have an online database of faculty members who may be interviewed as expert sources.

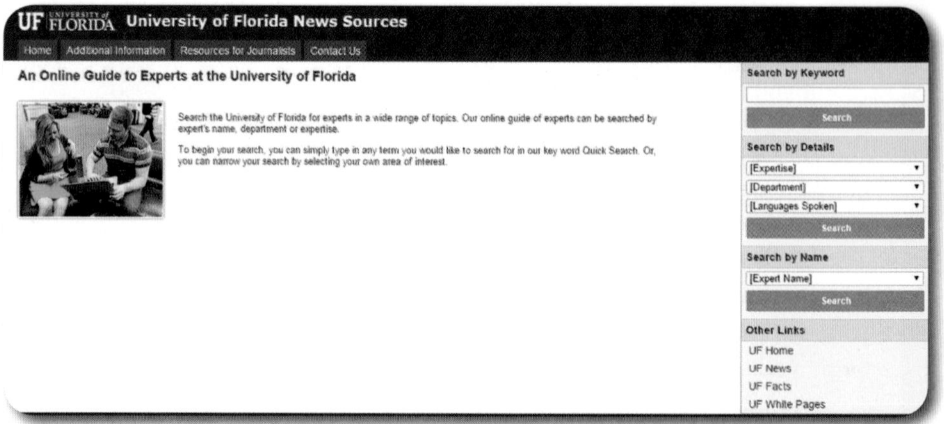

Courtesy of University of Florida Media Relations

For instance, if you want an expert opinion on whether high schools should have defibrillators on the field during August football practice, you can find several by searching online for "expert university heat exhaustion." You should find press releases, contact lists and university Web pages. To ask your particular question about defibrillators, look for a Contact link or look on the university's faculty directory for the expert's contact information. Do not confine your search only to a local university.

YOUR TURN

Locate an expert on sports psychology, stress management, sleep disorders, acne or another topic of your choice. Find the expert's contact information. Share the information you found and how you obtained it with your group or class.

After you have read the expert's published comments, prepare your questions to get the information you need. (You'll learn more about interview questions later in this chapter.) When you get the expert on the phone, you will have a clear goal in mind for the interview. If you are writing about safety and high school sports, you might ask, "Should we have a defibrillator on the field during football practices? Should our school be doing anything else?"

You may schedule an interview using email or through a department secretary. It is good practice to let your sources know your deadline so that they know how soon you would like your reply. "I'm researching a story for Friday morning's broadcast." It is also good practice to contact more than one expert, in case the first one does not get back to you in time.

Who Else Can Help You Tell the Story?

Stories are not all told through expert opinions, and strong journalists are storytellers. Sometimes with the help of their editors and writing community, they seek sources who can add a fresh and interesting perspective. Mardi Gras in New Orleans, for instance, gets extensive coverage. It is hard to say anything new about it. But the street cleaners who arrive Wednesday morning with skip loaders to clean up tons of beads and trash may give your best interviews. Theirs may be a fresh perspective on what could be a stale story.

One way to find fresh angles on worn-out but still important stories is to ask, "Who is affected by this? Who helps to make this happen?" These questions may lead you to a new point of view.

Case Study: Football Two-a-Days

A football player in a neighboring state has died during preseason practice in hot weather. The preliminary autopsy report indicates cardiac arrest—his heart stopped. Heat may have been a factor. You and your editor decide what questions the readers want answered: Could such a death happen here? How rigorous are the two-a-day practices? What safeguards are in place to protect players at our school? Should anything more be done to increase safety?

You have done your preliminary research, so you know the usual advice—drink water, seek shade, rest. You know the first aid for heat emergencies. The athletic director has shown you the district policies, including the requirement that all coaches be trained in first aid and CPR.

You have discussed with your editor the purpose of each interview and created interview questions designed to match that purpose.

You are ready to interview participants and witnesses. Whom do you talk to and what are you seeking from each person? There are several possibilities, including

- coaches. You are looking for expert knowledge and first-person experiences: What safeguards are in place? Have they had heat-related emergencies? What would they do if an athlete collapsed on the field? Could their policies and practices have saved the athlete who died in the neighboring state? What equipment do they have on the field in case of such an emergency? Is there something more they would like to have? Is there anyone else you should talk to about this?
- athletes and parents. You are looking for their opinions and feelings as well as experiences. Do the coaches watch out for the athletes? Do they follow the district policies? Do the athletes feel pressured to keep practicing, even if they want shade, water or rest? Have they seen or experienced heat-related illness? Does the death in the neighboring state cause the athletes or parents concern about two-a-days? Is there something they would like to see changed to protect the athletes? Are there other safeguards the school should put in place? Is there anyone else you should talk to about this?

You return to your newsroom with your notes, wondering where to go with the story. You've seen the giant jugs of ice and water. None of the players or coaches seems concerned about the policies, equipment or safety.

You and your editor collaborate and decide to focus on one question: Could better policies or equipment at our school prevent a death similar to the one in the news? To answer that question, you need to ask several others. Should we have other equipment? Specifically, should we have an automated external defibrillator, an AED, on the field?

Those are good questions to ask an unbiased expert in the field. To be unbiased, the expert should have no connection with the school, the district or the students.

You find a sports physiologist at a private and prestigious university through the university's website and arrange an interview.

You: Thank you for allowing me to interview you. I'm a student journalist at Bull Head High School in Lakeview and I'm writing about August football practice. We are following up on our school's athletic policies after the death of the football player last week in Vernality. I've read your writings on the University of Fieldstone website and I'd like to ask you a few questions, if you have a moment.

Expert: Sure. How can I help you?

You: Would you be comfortable with me recording our conversation?

Expert: That's fine.

(Continued)

CASE STUDY FOOTBALL TWO-A-DAYS (CONTINUED)

You: The coaches seem to be following most of the advice on your website, and the athletes report they are frequently sent to the water barrel. They stop morning practice at 11:30 and don't begin sunset practice until 5:00. But when I asked the coaches what they would do if a player collapsed in the heat, they pointed to ice in the water barrel and their cellphones. Should they have other first-aid equipment on the field?

Expert: *(gives his response)*

You: Specifically, I wonder if the school should provide an AED—an automated external defibrillator—to take out onto the football field.

Expert: *(gives his response)*

You: Let me read back to you what I just wrote. *(You repeat to him what you just heard, checking for accuracy.)*

Expert: That's about right.

You: Could you please explain heatstroke in terms that would be easy for an intelligent 10-year-old to understand?

Expert: *(He does.)*

You: Thank you very much for your time. Is there anything else I should have asked you?

Expert: *(Gives his response. This may be the most informative part of the interview.)*

You: May I email you if I need to clarify anything?

Expert: Yes. Use this email address ...

You: Thank you again for your time.

YOUR TURN

When President John F. Kennedy was assassinated in 1963, his body was honored in the Rotunda of the U.S. Capitol, where most reporters and cameramen vied to tell the same story. Their coverage is not often remembered, but Jimmy Breslin's is. He interviewed the man who dug Kennedy's grave for the New York Herald Tribune in November 1963. Search online for "Digging JFK Grave Was His Honor," to read Breslin's article.

1. What parts of this memorable piece of writing came from first-person observations? What parts came from interviews?
2. **Going Deeper.** Try to reconstruct the questions Breslin asked Clifton Pollard to get the information in the story.

What to Ask, What to Pack

An interview should be a conversation between you and your interviewee, but it is a conversation with prompts—your prewritten questions will remind you of what you need or want to ask. After you do your background research and before you go to your interview, you develop interview questions based on your goals for the interview. Your editors can help you prepare the questions.

Use your reporter's notebook to write down the questions you hope to have answered. Your goals for the interview will indicate the sorts of

MEET THE PROFESSIONALS:

Jimmy Breslin

Breslin described himself as a "street reporter," but his fans and readers know he earned a Pulitzer Prize and wrote columns and commentary, documentaries, novels and biographies in an almost seven-decade-long career that began as a sports writer for the New York Herald Tribune. His works have been made into two motion pictures.

He was the master of the brief human portrait as well as streetwise irony and piercing wit. He was fearless when revealing the abuse of power and eloquent when portraying the "little guy."

"I lived in the everyday excitement of meeting strangers who unfold in front of you and become people you cannot wait to tell others about," he wrote in his memoir, "I Want to Thank My Brain for Remembering Me."

Journalism should strive to be both truthful and entertaining, Breslin said. "With news and important facts you can entertain people too. Have a little humor. Life isn't all that deadly all the time, but while you're having fun, tell the truth."

What wisdom would he impart to young writers? "Go around with your eyes like a camera. Don't lose it by talking. Go and listen. And work!"

questions you will ask. If the goal is to gain information, the questions will be different than if you are seeking your source's experiences, feelings and thoughts.

The questions you write are for you. You will not read them word-for-word; that would make the conversation seem wooden and unnatural. Ask them naturally. If you are nervous or the interviewee changes the subject, your written questions will keep you on track. If the interview develops into a free-flowing and interesting conversation, the questions will remind you of what else you need to ask when the conversation abates.

You will change how you ask your questions based on the sort of conversation you are having. Ten minutes into your interview, "What is your strongest reaction to the new ruling affecting players who have been excluded from competition for a year because of a change in their school of attendance?" may sound much too formal. "What do you think of the new red-shirting rule?" may sound too casual. Glance at your notes, then ask the question as naturally as possible, as part of your conversation.

What Kinds of Questions?

Some questions can be answered with a simple yes or no. These have a place early in the interview when you are establishing the accuracy of what you already know, as you build rapport with a person whose feelings or experiences are important to your story, or when you may feature the person in an article. These questions are especially important as you interview people who may be shy, who may have experienced a trauma or who are young. That may include high school students.

Some questions are obvious. "So how does it feel to win your first game?" These should be used rarely, perhaps more rarely than yes/no questions and for the same reasons.

Avoid questions that are too complicated. They should not be longer than the interviewee's likely answer. Avoid questions that call attention to you instead of to the interviewee.

Avoid questions that box in your interviewee: "Do you like American schools better than Egyptian schools?" Such questions may make the person uncomfortable. He does not want to insult his new country, but he may like home better. The answer may really be "French schools," but you did not give him that option. You rarely get information that is helpful with such questions.

If it looks like a true-false question, you will probably get a one-word answer. If it looks like a multiple-choice question, you will probably get a brief, uninformative answer.

Better questions are often gentle commands and look like short-essay prompts. For instance, if you notice a football player taping a small digital watch face into the center of his helmet, you could—unwisely—use a multiple-choice question: "Are you putting that in there so you can time yourself doing something or to check your pulse?"

But if you instead say, "Explain what you are doing right now," he may answer, "I'm tucking my watch in here because we can't wear watches during practice. Coach runs practice over, all the time. It's supposed to be over at 11:30, so I just take off my helmet, look at my

And Now... Closer to Home

Using Your Reporter's Notebook

So far, there is no perfect digital replacement for a reporter's notebook. Write your interview questions in your reporter's notebook, leaving plenty of space between the questions to write the answers. That way you will not have to flip back to your question page while you interview, and you will have a record of what question prompted the reply: "Over my dead body. Not while I am working here." (Some experienced reporters write all their questions at the front, but that causes a great deal of page flipping, a distraction.)

Write on one side of the page from the front to the back of the notebook, then flip the notebook over and write on the still-bare backs of the pages, starting at the end of the book and moving to the front.

Label the cover of each reporter's notebook with the date and name of the person interviewed. On the inside cover, write all the contact information you have for your subject as well as the correct spelling of names and titles.

File these notebooks after you have submitted your story. Putting them in a shoebox or a drawer in chronological order, oldest in the front, is a good plan. You will be glad you have them.

watch, put the helmet back on and ask him if we can cool down for a minute. He looks at his watch, then tells us to take a break until 5:00."

Of course, you cannot quote the player when he has asked you not to reveal something, but you can watch what happens at 11:30. And you can ask the players about the most difficult time in their practice. And you may have found a great lead: *Around 11:30 each hot summer morning, the clock seems to stand still for Mariner football players.*

Other "short-essay" questions are also gentle commands (Figure 9.4).

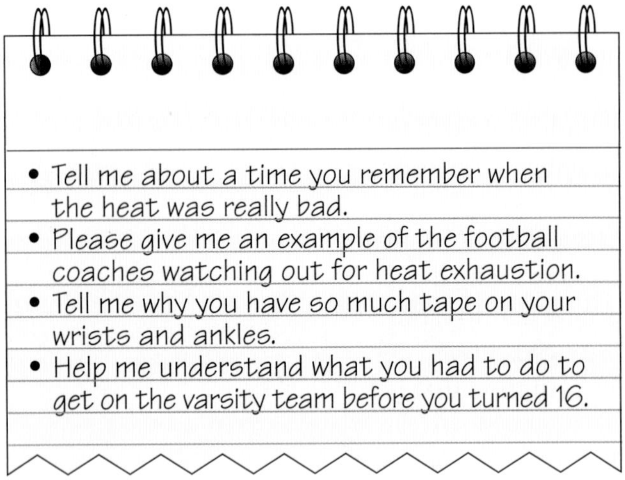
• Tell me about a time you remember when the heat was really bad.
• Please give me an example of the football coaches watching out for heat exhaustion.
• Tell me why you have so much tape on your wrists and ankles.
• Help me understand what you had to do to get on the varsity team before you turned 16.

Figure 9.4 "Short-essay" questions such as these encourage your subject to provide more information. *Can you think of other essay-type questions for the football story?*

- "Tell me about ..."
- "Please give me an example of ..."
- "Tell me why ..."
- "Help me understand ..."

If you need good sound files or are interviewing an expert who speaks at a high level, you may wish to help her simplify her explanation for your audience or provide more background. Change your question or your prompt:

- "How would you explain mitochondrial DNA variations to an intelligent 10-year-old?"
- "Help me visualize what a volcano in Antarctica would look like."
- Ask for an analogy: "If your body were a machine, what would heatstroke be like?"

David Kestenbaum, a reporter for National Public Radio, recalls spending half an hour in vain asking a scientist about a still-living 300-million-year-old bacterium. The scientist sounded like he was delivering a graduate lecture, even calling the bacterium by its scientific name. Kestenbaum finally asked, "Can we try looking at it from the bacterium's point of view?" The expert figuratively removed his professor's hat and moved away from the podium to tell a snappy tale of 300 million years of Earth's history from the perspective of "Harry the Bacterium."

Scheduling the Interview

Set up your interview well in advance of your deadline. Use whatever media are available to you to reach the people who can contribute to the story—a telephone, a knock on the door, a text message, microblogging, email, even social media.

But do not conduct an interview through any medium where you are not sure of your subject's identity. Do not quote anyone until you have contacted the person and verified his identity. More than one journalist has been "stung" by someone pretending to be a refugee or an abused teen when in fact the person was someone else entirely.

And Now... Closer to Home

Interviewing on the Fly

You may not have an opportunity to prepare for every interview. Sometimes a great opportunity comes up and you need to think quickly. You find yourself washing your hands in the ladies' room with the secretary of state's aide. Do not waste time being flustered or embarrassed. Be a journalist.

She will probably not give you an exclusive interview about classified information, but if you are quick, you can make good use of your opportunity. Identify yourself as a student journalist and ask her a question, one that can be answered in the time it takes to dry her hands. Ask the question your audience would most like to have answered.

You might ask

- how she got her job;
- how she travels when she is with the secretary;
- what she did during the summit in Iceland;
- how many countries she has visited;
- where she got that great handbag; or
- something entirely different.

Try asking a **follow-up question**, that is, a question based on the answer to the previous question. Be sure to ask her for her card and give her yours so that you can check facts as you write your story.

And look around to see if the secretary of state is emerging from another stall!

Sometimes you will need to interview on the fly because your subject has been unable or unwilling to talk with you. You may need to jog along with your reporter's notebook while your subject strides away. Ask your question—you are working in an old and honorable journalism tradition.

Most people honor persistence; so if you choose the right question, your subject may slow down and talk to you. If the administration has just announced that your principal will move to a junior high school next month, you probably will not get too much more information from the superintendent as you jog beside him. But you may get a response if you say, "It has been painful for us Oilers to have so many different leaders. Can you tell us what will come next for the school?" The superintendent, most likely an educator himself, may be willing to address your audience through you. He may reveal information that is important to your audience.

Use **ambush journalism** rarely and carefully. Ambush journalism involves an element of surprise. You hope your contact will reveal something when you surprise him. For instance, this would be an ambush: You catch the superintendent coming out of his office and ask, "Did you remove Principal Jones because of the lawsuit brought against the school by the former assistant principal?"

You *may* get an unguarded response: "That was part of it, but it was not the final straw." But you have now lost your access to the superintendent—and probably every other administrator. They will be on guard against another ambush. You have made it difficult for every other staff member to do his job. If you publish the information (which may result in another lawsuit for the district), you will interest some readers, but you may also lose the trust of others who read your work. They may avoid you and make it harder for you and your colleagues to get other interviews.

Ambush journalism has a place—and a cost. Consider carefully when to use it.

In-person interviews are generally the strongest and the safest, journalistically. You have an opportunity to observe body language, to rephrase questions to get the source to say more. You can ask follow-up questions in a natural way. Telephone interviews substitute for the face-to-face interview when distance is a problem or contact could be dangerous, but make sure you are talking to the person you wanted to reach.

Sharing Questions and Restrictions

Whatever medium you use to schedule an interview or to conduct it, it is fair to share with your sources the type of questions you will be asking. "I'm interested in your experiences qualifying for the Paralympics and the difficulties you face paying for your training and travel." You will be more likely to get that interview than if the athlete suspects you are trying to write another "inspirational cripple" story.

Extend

Some sources may tell you that they will welcome those questions but that they will not reply to questions about other issues, for instance, questions about athletes doping. If you were not seeking information about doping, then you can easily agree. If you had wanted to ask about doping, but the interview would still be valuable without questions about that topic, you should talk to your editor before you agree to the restrictions—your source could be using you.

If you choose to do the interview with the restrictions, you may leave open an opportunity at the end of the interview for the source to discuss the topic. If the subject has come to trust you, he may be willing to discuss the matter. An open-ended question, such as "Is there anything else I should have asked you, to better understand your situation?" may be an opportunity for the source to speak. But if he refuses to discuss the taboo topic, honor any promise you made before you started the interview.

Methods and Timing

Some expert sources may prefer to answer via email, but others will simply arrange a time for a phone conversation. It is rude to assume they will want to respond to your list of questions with a 700-word essay. However, some sources may prefer to comment on complex issues, such as statistics or legal matters, in writing to increase the probability that they will be quoted accurately.

Most experts will welcome the use of a voice recorder during phone interviews, but journalists ask before they record any conversation. Some states require that you seek permission from all parties in a conversation before you record it. This includes telephone interviews.

If possible, plan ahead in October for December. Talk to the man who runs the snowplow before the first snow, the football captain before the championship game, the candidates for student body president before the election, the homecoming nominees before the homecoming dance. You may not use four out of five interviews, but you will have strong coverage ready to go when the president, the king or the queen is announced.

If possible, interview the person where she is comfortable, perhaps in her home, car or work space. The details you notice may later help you paint a picture of your subject if you decide to feature the person in the story.

But always secure your own safety. Bring along a friend, another reporter or a photographer when you go to meet someone, especially a stranger, off-campus (Figure 9.5).

Try to schedule an interview for a time when something is happening, preferably a transitional moment. Ask a JV football player to describe how he feels, what he is thinking and—especially if you are recording sound files—what he sees as he comes to football practice at 6:00 a.m. on a hot August day, leaves for the midday break at 11:30 or returns at 5:00 for the sunset practice.

Interview the baker who makes your school's breakfast cinnamon rolls as she starts the dough after lunch and puts it in the walk-in refrigerator for the next day's breakfast. Or talk to her the next morning at 4:45 as she rolls out the dough. Ask her to describe what she is doing and why. Ask what that smell is or what sound you are hearing. Ask her to describe how she knows the rolls are done. See if she can make your audience's mouths water.

People may be more comfortable being interviewed while they are doing something—playing golf, giving you a tour, performing their jobs, driving, eating lunch, cooking dinner. Their answers may be more natural and less formal than when they are sitting across a desk from you.

Conducting the Interview

Come to the interview on time, neatly and appropriately dressed. Do not dress in a way that calls attention to yourself. When you interview the mayor, do not wear your "Suicidal Tendencies" hat, either backward or forward. Do not wear your best clothes to interview the custodian. In general, be subdued, respectful and less important than your subject, as if you were a minor player in your subject's world and your subject is more important than you are. That manner of dress and attitude will help you get the best sound recordings, the best information and the best insights into your subject's experiences and character.

Figure 9.5 Do not go alone to interview a stranger. Take someone with you and choose a public place.

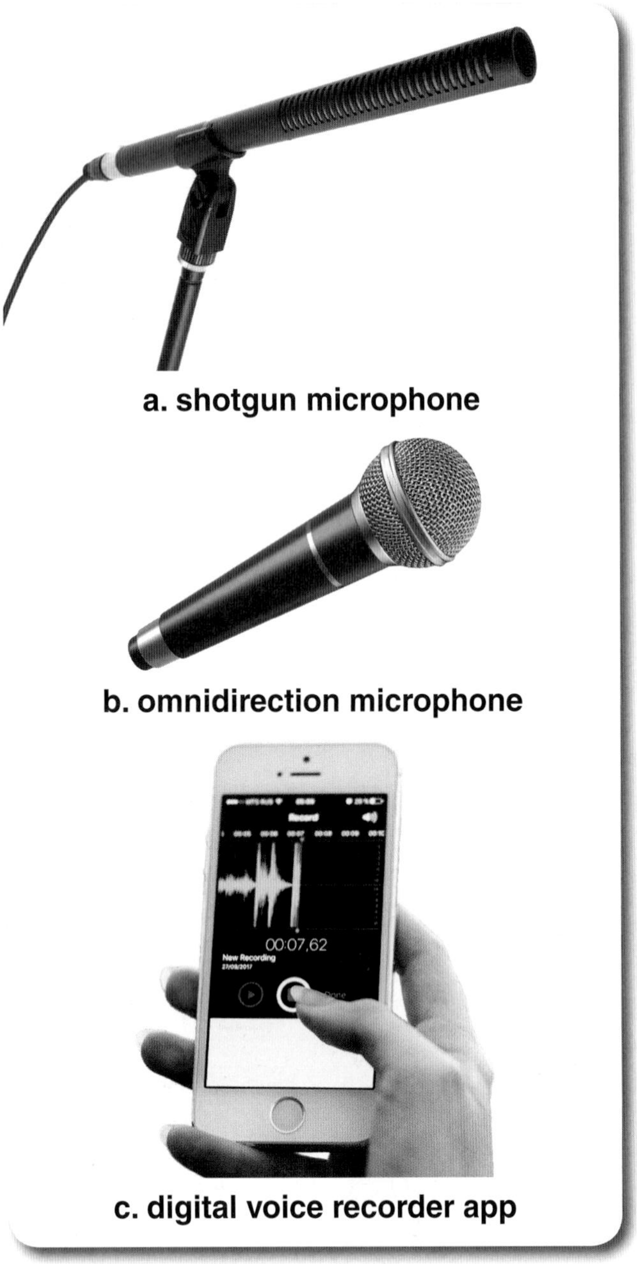

Figure 9.6 A shotgun microphone (a), omnidirection microphone (b), or digital voice recorder (c) may be used to record your interview. Choose the equipment you feel confident using and always ask your subject for permission to record the conversation.

Shake hands if that seems appropriate. Give the person your card. Chat briefly about the view, the nice day, the picture of his kids. Make notes, mentally or on paper, of what the setting looks like.

Ask permission to record the interview. If your subject seems reluctant, offer to use it only to verify your notes. At the end of the interview, the interviewee may be willing to give you permission to publish the sound files.

Do not let your equipment get in the way of your interview. You may get clearer sound with a shotgun mic, but it can be intimidating. If you use an omnidirectional mic, place it to the side of the speaker's mouth. It should be out of your subject's line of vision while you talk with each other. A simple sound recorder, such as the one on your cell phone, is a third choice. You can turn it on and then ignore it. Be sure your mic will pick up your questions as well as your subject's answers (Figure 9.6).

Beginning journalists often go to interviews in pairs. One conducts the interview while the other handles the mics and takes the notes.

Maintain eye contact during as much of the interview as possible, looking away only to glance at your reporter's notebook or make notes. Eye contact signals interest, and interest encourages conversation.

However, eye contact is rude in some cultures and inappropriate at other times. It may make some subjects uncomfortable, and it is not always appropriate when interviewing children. Children are geniuses at picking up the cues of adults and giving the answer the adult expects. Imagine instead interviewing a child who received Christmas presents from your school's toy drive. The child is coloring. You color and doodle alongside the child, occasionally asking him questions, some about his picture, some about his dog, and some about the Christmas surprises he found under his tree. It is potentially a great interview.

Start the interview by verifying the spelling of your interviewee's first and last names, his proper title and other bits of information you got from your preliminary research. "You've been with Edison School District for seven years after a career in law enforcement. Is that right?"

Do not be embarrassed about the time it takes to write this information down. This lets your subject know you are prepared and careful, diligent and not threatening. Your interview will be stronger if your subject believes you are fair and accurate. Too many officials feel they have been misquoted, misrepresented or even had their name and title reported incorrectly.

Though you want to show that you are prepared for the interview, it is not necessary for your subjects to be impressed with how much *you* know or how smart *you* are. You need to find a balance between being well-informed and being the eyes and ears of your public. The interview is never about you and your opinions or experiences.

For instance, if you are familiar with police radio codes, you may be comfortable asking an officer, "What was your 10-20 when you received the 10-72?" (What was your location when you heard there was a major crime in progress?) But your subject may respond with more codes and jargon. "The 10-11 came in about 22:50. We spotted an OC perp leaving the store. A few minutes later, we called in a 10-12." (Translation: The alarm was reported about 10:50 p.m. When we got there, we saw a gang member leaving the store. A few minutes later we called in that we were holding a suspect.)

That insider language is not very helpful to your audience—you will need to translate it—and you may not get a single usable quotation or sound bite. Your interview would be stronger if you played a little dumb and asked, "Tell me about what you did when you heard someone was breaking into the store." Remember, your job is to get information, not to impress the interviewee.

How you ask your questions may be as important as what you ask. Remember your goal for the interview. If you are seeking information from an expert source, be businesslike and respect the source's time. Be polite and informed, but proceed to your questions quickly.

If you are asking a witness or participant about feelings and experiences, lower your energy level and create a slower conversation. This is the time to throttle your own nervousness. The level of energy you give off is what you will get back. Start with easy questions. It is fair to ask questions you already know the answer to and that the subject can answer easily.

Listening and Asking Follow-Up Questions

Make it a conversation. They talk, you listen.

Interviews generally are not Q and A sessions; they are conversations that require real listening. Your questions are not bowling balls hurled down an alley, hoping to hit a few pins. An interview is more like a friendly game of catch. You toss a question and listen for the response. You catch the answer the interviewee tosses to you, and you toss another question back to her.

If you listen well, your interviewee will keep sending the ball back to you. If you do not listen, if you start looking away or at your next question, the interviewee will lose interest in returning the ball, like this:

Interviewer: How was practice today?

Player: Great! We turned over the coach's van and put 73 watermelons in the principal's Camry. Then we lead a cow into the athletic director's office.

Interviewer: OK. So what do you think about the Oilers' lineup for the first league game?

Player: Umm. Yeah. It will be challenging, but the team has really come together.

Your next question often comes not from your notes but from the answer your source tosses you. Your follow-up question may

- ask for clarification. "What do you mean when you say 'the body's thermostat gets stuck'?"
- repeat the interviewee's answer but with a question mark at the end. "American students are more casual?" Then wait.
- ask for details. "Please help me understand what you mean when you say, 'the dough needs to rest.'"

Follow-up questions may take you in a different direction than your original plan, but you will not get lost because you have your prewritten questions in your reporter's notebook, ready to bring you back to the original purpose of the interview.

Sometimes the best follow-up question is silence. Simply wait, looking expectantly at your interviewee. Discipline yourself to wait. You may be rewarded with additional information or great sound bites. Let your body language rather than your words indicate you are interested. You do not want your recording to be full of your vocalizations. "Uh huh." "I see." "Yeah."

Many times the best—and most challenging—questions are only one or two words long. How? Why? What? What kind?

Interviewee: After that, I started to get lazy about my schoolwork and take shortcuts.
You: What kind?

District Administrator: Mr. Black will be principal at Corrigan Junior High next year, and we will search for a new principal for Central Valley High School.
You: Why?

Mayor: To curtail crime, we will institute new police procedures.
You: What procedures?

Coach: We're losing two of our most promising freshman players because they are ineligible, because their grades are in the toilet. We're going to stop that from happening next semester.
You: How?

Save the challenging questions for late in the interview, after you have established rapport with your subject.

Your Turn

Interrupting is the opposite of listening. You may communicate that you think the other person has nothing important to say or that you are more interested in a confrontation than an interview. How long do you wait after a friend finishes his sentence before you respond?

(Continued)

YOUR TURN *(Continued)*

A longer wait time may indicate respect and interest—if your body language continues to indicate interest.

This exercise requires three people and a digital timer that records seconds. Person A asks the questions. Person B answers them. Person C records the time lapse between the end of B's answer and the beginning of A's next question on a chart like the one below. The questions really do not matter—you can change them. The silences between questions and answers are the important parts.

Time between B and A	A speaks	B speaks	Time between A and B
N/A	I see you are wearing/using ____.		
	Where did you get it?		
	Do you like it?		
	Would you buy one again?		

Now repeat the exercise but ask person A to wait three seconds after B's answer before asking the next question.

Repeat the exercise again, waiting five seconds before answering. Did person B have the urge to add more information?

Be Skeptical

Can you trust whatever people say in interviews? Of course not. All of us have points of view, blind spots and private interests.

- Some people have an agenda. They may have a political point of view or other strong opinions that color their judgment. To someone, problems in your community relate to illegal immigration. To someone else, problems relate to budget cuts. To another, problems relate to religious issues or to drug abuse or to lack of family planning.
- Others need to protect their careers. A new assistant principal may think your campus is overcrowded and unkempt and that your library is miserable, but it would be dangerous to her career to tell you that. She will say she is excited to be here and that everyone has been "so welcoming."
- Other people either want to or need to control information. Your school district's information officer may not want to disclose the number of students who are truant each day or the number who are sent to the county alternative school. These statistics might make the district look bad. His job is to help the district look good.

Case Study: A Newcomer to America

In this interview your purpose is to learn your interviewee's feelings and opinions about coming to America and what it is like to start at a new school in a new country. Because you want to encourage her to feel comfortable, you keep your energy level low and ask your questions patiently and simply. It is quite different from the interview with the expert on heat exhaustion.

You: May I ask you a few questions about your first days at Bull Head High School?

Fatima: Of course, but my English is not so good.

You: My Arabic is terrible.

(laughter)

You: Is Arabic your first language? *(an easy one, a yes/no question)*

Fatima: Yes.

You: *(three-second pause, looking interested)*

Fatima: Also Italian. My mother's father was Italian. We spoke a little Italian with him.

You: Your English is very good. Did you study English for a very long time before you came here? *(an easy one, with a possible numeric reply)*

Fatima: We study English in school. For three years. And French for four years.

You: So you speak Arabic, French, Italian and now English? That is remarkable. Where did you go to school? *(an easy one, with a possible one-word reply)*

Fatima: In Egypt. Near Cairo.

You: Was it a private school?

(This yes/no question does not work. The interviewee does not understand what you are asking.)

Fatima: I don't know what does that mean, private school.

You: Did you have to pay to go there?

Fatima: All schools charge money.

(You try another way to learn about her school and perhaps her social or economic status in Egypt.)

You: Did you go to a school with both boys and girls? *(yes/no)*

Fatima: No, no. Girls only. I never went to school with boys before.

You: Is it better to go to school with boys? *(a little harder question, but still yes/no)*

Fatima: I don't think so. It is better girls only. It is so hard to think only about school. And for the boys too. My brother, my little brother, 12 year old, he complain that the girls in his class bother him.

You: Are there parts of going to school with boys that you like?

Fatima: A little. Yes. I like it. *(giggle)*

You: What else is different here? *(a more demanding question)*

Fatima: You are so casual.

You: Tell me what you mean. *(This is a gentle command and requires a longer answer.)*

Fatima: You are so casual with your teachers!

You: *(You remain silent and in eye contact, waiting for her, letting her know you are interested.)*

Fatima: The way you talk to them. You talk while they are talking and you just go up and talk to them like you do to your friends.

You: What was it like in Egypt when you were around teachers?

Fatima: We stand up when they come into the room. We wait until they will talk to us. We are not, ah, impatient. And all our teachers are women.

You: Are we casual in other ways? *(This is an open-ended question. It also helps you construct a picture of her former school.)*

Fatima: With friends we are pretty much the same there and here. But not with boys.

You: *(silent, listening)*

Fatima: We don't have so many chance to talk with boys at home. Maybe our brothers or our cousins or something. Here the boys are in classes with us. At home we wear uniform. Everyone the same. Maybe a headband or a watch. But everyone the same. It's different here. Sometimes you dress some way because there are boys.

(Continued)

CASE STUDY A Newcomer to America (continued)

You: Tell me what you mean.

Fatima: You wear something because you will look older. Or makeup or something. It's not like when you wear a uniform for school.

You: When did you arrive in the United States?

Fatima: Tuesday, last week.

You: When was your first day of school?

Fatima: We go to the office on Wednesday. They say I need shots and paperwork. I start last Friday.

You: Tell me about what surprised you on your first day here. *(A gentle command, this comes close to the purpose of the interview.)*

Fatima: It was all so confusing.

You: Tell me about some things that were confusing.

Fatima: Mr. Loftis is very nice, but I did not know what was the bells. I did not know about lunch card or cafeteria.

You: What did you eat for lunch? *(follow-up question)*

Fatima: Nothing! The first day, nothing.

You: You must have really gotten hungry.

Fatima: I went to my home and ate and ate and then I went to sleep.

You: Did you eat lunch the next day?

Fatima: Maria, she showed me the vending machine. But now I have lunch card.

You: What foods are strange to you here? *(This question asks her for words that are not yet in her English vocabulary.)*

Fatima: I don't know how you call it ...

You: Which lunches do you like?

Fatima: Oh, the chicken box. Is so good. But greasy.

- Some people are just muddled. They may have told an old story so often, they think it is true. Many people, for instance, will tell you that their great-grandmother was half American Indian, often a princess. Research may not bear out this story, but the story has been told so often the speaker thinks it is true.
- Some people lie. Some just want to tell a good story. Another may want to project a more favorable image. Some are hiding information. Some just want to see if they can get away with it.

Remember, you are there as your audience's eyes and ears. You owe them a skeptical point of view.

You need to continually ask yourself: Why are my sources telling me this? Is that the whole story? How would this look from another point of view? What could this source be missing or misunderstanding? What part is he ignoring?

What to do? Check it out. Verify, verify, verify. Always seek a second, reliable source for every bit of information, and use a primary source, if possible. Three sources are better than two. The more interesting or controversial the news, the more sources you need and the higher quality the sources should be.

In an interview—perhaps at the end of the interview—you can ask for your source's help to verify what she said. For instance

- If your source offers you figures or facts—98 percent of your school's students graduate, for instance—do not publish them as fact. Ask her where you might find those numbers in print and then look to see how the numbers were derived. Is that 98 percent of the students still enrolled in May of their senior year? How many of the students who enrolled as freshmen graduate?

- At the end of the interview, ask for contact information for other people who can verify what she reports. Eyewitnesses are best.
- Ask who else you should talk to, who else has firsthand experience.

Remember, if your mother tells you she loves you, check it out. You personally may be convinced of her love and need no further confirmation, but you are not acting as a private citizen. You are acting as the eyes and ears of your audience, and they deserve verification (Figure 9.7).

You cannot always confirm all you hear, at least not on deadline. If you get contradictory points of view from two reliable sources, you may need to publish both, being careful to attribute the information to the source.

Several students report witnessing potential heat exhaustion.

> *"The coaches had to hustle this big, fat freshman over to the water cooler last week and pour water over his head," sophomore Joseph Smythe said. Alvin Diaz and Homer Nguyen report seeing the same thing.*

However, when you relate what Smythe said to head coach Devon Pedersen (you tell him "a student reports" or "several students report"), he says that there have been no heat-related emergencies.

> *"We have never poured water on a kid as part of first aid," Pederson said. "Kids sometimes do that at the end of practice, but they do it to themselves or each other. We've never done it as part of heat-related first aid."*

Photo by Chris Martin, Woodrow Wilson High School

Figure 9.7 Whether your interview results in a print piece, an online story or a broadcast, verify your source's assertions. Check out each statement before publishing or broadcasting. A second reliable source is essential. Two additional sources are better than one additional source.

Handling Quotations

Without quotations and attributions, your reporting would be as interesting as tepid 7UP. Strong journalists choose strong quotations—and use them often. Think of a chocolate chip cookie with only one chocolate chip. Now think of a cookie with 19 chocolate chips.

The reader's eye goes to quotations on the page. Quotations, with their white spaces, provide visual relief from gray lines of type. The little quotation marks say, "Something interesting here!"

The listener's ear is more attentive when a fresh voice, especially a distinct voice, begins to speak.

Quotations lend authority to your reporting. They say, "I was there, and this is what I heard."

But quotations bear a heavy burden. Only the strong should survive to be printed and read. Others become partial quotes, snippets or paraphrases.

- Quotations portray characters, sometimes with no description needed.

  What is 17-year-old Olympic swimmer Melissa Franklin like? This is how she describes her turn on the victory platform as she received an Olympic medal for the 100-meter backstroke.

"I was trying to sing, I was crying at the same time, I forgot the words, I didn't know what I was doing. I was a huge mess," Franklin said. (Bill Plaschke, Los Angeles Times)

- Quotations allow readers to judge for themselves the trustworthiness of the speaker.

  Jonah Lehrer is a disgraced journalist who had invented quotes and attributed them to singer Bob Dylan. After his fraud was revealed, in a statement released by his publisher, Lehrer explained that he had lied to a reporter, Michael Moynihan, who had contacted him to verify several of his quotes. Lehrer wrote:

"I told Mr. Moynihan that they were from archival interview footage provided to me by Dylan's representatives. This was a lie spoken in a moment of panic." (Hillel Italie, Christian Science Monitor)

- Quotations convey unique perspectives, or at least unique ways of speaking.

  In 1963 Clifton Pollard talked with his co-worker John Metzler as Pollard dug President John Fitzgerald Kennedy's grave.

"He was a good man," Pollard said. "Yes, he was," Metzler said. "Now they're going to come and put him right here in this grave I'm making up," Pollard said. "You know, it's an honor just for me to do this." (Jimmy Breslin, New York Herald Tribune)

- Quotations advance a story. In the example below, the quotations allow us to see and "hear" the conflict.

  A 2012 Senate Democrat report critical of for-profit colleges stated that over half of the students who enrolled in a for-profit college dropped out after about four months. The quotations in the paragraphs below, from an article by Jamie Goldberg of the Los Angeles Times, explain the controversy and pull the readers deeper into the story. The first paragraph explains the problem by quoting Senator Tom Harkin (D-Iowa). The next paragraph contains a rebuttal of sorts—an attack on the report and those who made it.

  "In this report, you will find overwhelming documentation of exorbitant tuition, aggressive recruiting practices, abysmal student outcomes, taxpayer dollars spent on marketing and pocketed as profit, and regulatory evasion and manipulation," Harkin said. "These practices are not the exception—they are the norm."

  But Steve Gunderson, president of the Assn. of Private Sector Colleges and Universities and a former Republican congressman, said the report, "twists the facts to fit a narrative, proving that this is nothing more than continued political attacks on private sector colleges and universities."

- Quotations let the audience get into the source's head. A journalist can only speculate on how someone else feels, and journalists should refrain from speculation.

  Michael Moynihan is the reporter who discovered and reported Jonah Lehrer's fraud. How does he feel, knowing that Lehrer's career is ruined? The only person who can say with certainty what Moynihan feels is Moynihan.

  "I don't want the scalp," Moynihan said in a phone interview. "It's not what I am interested in."

  Lehrer called Moynihan on Monday morning, shortly before the story was published, and told him he would resign [from The New Yorker]. "I felt horrible. I felt like s---," Moynihan said.

  "I knew—he knew—this was a situation of his own making," Moynihan said. He believes his story was "totally fair." Still, when the result of a story is that "somebody's life is going to be unalterably changed ... it is not a burden you want on yourself." (Steve Myers, Poynter.org)

How to Choose Strong Quotes

Weak quotations bog your story down, like sacks of wet laundry, while good quotes carry it forward. Not everything your sources say is concise, interesting and valuable. The same is true of press releases, reports and documents. The strongest, most interesting journalism contains frequent quotations, but the quotations are each strong (Figure 9.8).

Journalists watch for good quotations as they interview, at press conferences and in written sources. For instance, only a few things Fatima said in "Case Study: A Newcomer to America"—about 113 words out of 375—could be considered as quotations for an article about her:

"I never went to school with boys before."

"It is better girls only. It is so hard to think only about school."

"You are so casual with your teachers! The way you talk to them. You talk while they are talking and you just go up and talk to them like you do to your friends."

"It was all so confusing."

"Mr. Loftis is very nice, but I did not know what was the bells. I did not know about lunch card or cafeteria."

(In response to "What did you eat for lunch?") "Nothing! The first day, nothing."

"I went to my home and ate and ate and then I went to sleep."

"Oh, the chicken box. Is so good. But greasy."

When you quote sources who are working in their second language, avoid exposing them to ridicule for their non-standard English. Err on the side of generosity toward your sources. You may:

- embed their words into your journalistic sentence to avoid the non-standard usage: *Fatima said that at her all-girls school in Egypt they wore uniforms but that here, "sometimes you dress some way because there are boys."*
- fix minor errors that result because certain sounds in English are sometimes difficult to say, such as the final "s" sound. On your recording, a second language speaker may say, "He go to work every day after school at two job." You may decide to quote her as saying, "He goes to work every day after school at two jobs."

But hold the subjects of your story to a higher standard. If you are writing about the school's response to a prank and an assistant principal (a representative of the school) says, "Between you and I, that wasn't a smart move," print it as he said it. If the candidate for school board speaks non-standard English, either because English is her second language or for other reasons, quote her as she spoke. Your audience deserves to hear how she speaks.

Figure 9.8 Quotations with one or more of these characteristics will add interest and impact to your story.

Strong quotations

- say something better than you, the journalist, could;
- say something more forcefully than a fair and objective reporter could;
- say something in a way that reveals character;
- say something that your audience will remember long after they have forgotten the rest of the story;
- say something important, especially if the speaker is an important person; or
- say something your audience would not believe the speaker said, unless you have quotation marks around it and the attribution after it.

Your Turn

Return to the five stories you marked for the Your Turn activity on page 256 or choose five new, interesting, news, sports or feature stories. Choose two quotations from each to demonstrate five of the bullet characteristics of strong quotations in Figure 9.8. Mark and share them with your group or class. Rank them in order from strongest to least strong. Explain your reasoning to your group.

What to Avoid

Avoid long quotes. Quotations should be concise, interesting and informative. Your job is to find those concise bits in your notes. Do not expect the reader to do your job for you.

Avoid quotes with jargon. If the quotation includes technical jargon or insider language, consider removing the quotation marks and paraphrasing the quotation, although paraphrases lack the authority of quotations. Or front load enough information for the audience to understand the quotation or sound file. Front loading should be done shortly before you use the term in a story. It can be a simple sentence that includes some sort of definition, such as an appositive. This technique is used below for the term *load shedding*.

This is an excerpt from a National Public Radio story on electrical power shortages in India.

> *Regular localized outages, known as load shedding, are common throughout India, as power grid controllers are forced to make cuts to keep the system in balance. As a result, many businesses, hospitals and airports use generators to make up the temporary shortfalls.*
>
> *Massoud Amin, a senior member of the Institute of Electrical and Electronics Engineers and professor of electrical engineering at the University of Minnesota, has studied India's power system firsthand. "In a big city like Bangalore, you have a half-hour to 45 minutes of load shedding every day," he says.*

But if the audience needs help with more than one term, paraphrase the quotation.

Do you want to avoid jargon-filled quotes? Play a little dumb at the interview. Ask for clarification, or ask your expert to explain things so that an intelligent 10-year-old could understand them.

Avoid quotes that repeat what you said in the lead-in paragraph just above it. Journalists frequently set up quotations so that the reader understands who is speaking and why. But do not tell what is in the quotation before you give the quotation (Figure 9.9).

Do you want to avoid quotations that repeat your setup? Get more information. Interview better, interview more. After Principal Blackfoot said, "I don't expect any more trouble from the electrical system," the interviewer should have asked, "Why?"

Do not do this:

BFN High School Principal Orrin Blackfoot does not expect any more trouble from the electrical system.

"I don't expect any more trouble from the electrical system," Principal Blackfoot said.

This is better:

Principal Orrin Blackfoot thinks the school's electrical problems are in the past.

"The power company has changed out the main switching box not far from the school. It's down the road. You probably saw the backhoes and hard hats working. We think the switching box was what caused our blackouts. It took them three days of steady work, but we will have power for the school as usual next Monday.

"The district has also installed a new backup generator that will keep us going for 10 hours on reduced power if the main power goes out again. We will be able to complete the school day and back up all our computers before we really need to get on the grid again."

Figure 9.9 A lead-in paragraph should set up a quotation but not repeat it.

What to Do With Profanity

As a general rule, it is simplest to avoid quotes that are obscene or profane. In almost all cases, the quotes you use should follow the same standard of language that you use in your own writing for your publication or broadcast. It is important to have written guidelines in your staff manual to help decide what expressions are obscene or profane for your audience.

A reporter may make a compelling case for including a profanity or obscenity in a story: "The story is about the use of the word." "The story is about verbal sexual harassment." "That is how he talks. The reader needs to hear it to understand his character."

Editors should consult the publication's handbook for guidance if the usage may be controversial. The publication's editorial board may be convened to decide difficult cases where the strength of the quotation may justify publishing unusual language.

If it seems necessary to refer to an expression that does not meet standards—if the word is discussed in a story or if the quotation seems so compelling the story is damaged when you take it out—the Associated Press Stylebook offers several options.

- Try to find a way to give the reader a sense of what was said without using the specific word or phrase.
- Confine the offending language, in quotation marks, to a separate paragraph that can be deleted easily by editors who do not want to use it.
- If a full quote that contains an obscenity, profanity or vulgarity cannot be dropped but there is no compelling reason for the offensive language, replace the letters of the offensive word with hyphens, using only an initial letter. That is what was done in Steve Myers' interview of Michael Moynihan: *"I felt horrible. I felt like s---," Moynihan said.*

In some stories or broadcast scripts it may be better to replace the offensive word with a generic descriptive in parentheses, such as (vulgarity) or (obscenity).

Do not replace the profanity or vulgarity with a milder word. *Damn* should not be replaced with *darn*.

If you and your editorial board choose to allow profanity that includes the word *god*, it is not capitalized.

How Much to Use

Use strong quotations just as they are. Many sources, including the AP Stylebook, say never to alter a quotation. Some publications do allow for one—and only one—minor grammatical fix. For instance, an assistant principal announces that school will be closed for the rest of the day and for the weekend because of a fire in the nearby canyon.

> *"Each student should take their books and everything in their lockers home with them," assistant principal Joy Badger said.*

Considering the stress on the assistant principal of evacuating a school under threat of fire, you could make a two-word change to clean up a grammatical error.

> *"All students should take their books and everything in their lockers home with them," assistant principal Joy Badger said.*

If the source would recognize a grammatical mistake in print and would be embarrassed by it, you may have a solid reason to fix a single grammatical error.

Even the publications that allow one minor change also suggest that many quotes with grammatical irregularities should be left as they are for accuracy or to show emphasis, character, background or regional characteristics.

Partial Quotes

Long but strong quotes may be turned into partial quotes, also called embedded quotes. Remove complicated, unclear or cumbersome parts of the speaker's sentence and put the remaining strong and compelling words into your own. An ellipsis, three dots preceded and followed by a space, marks the place where a writer has taken something out of a quotation.

Ethical journalists are careful to preserve the speaker's meaning even as they edit his words and place them in their sentences.

Steve Myers has done this in his interview with Michael Moynihan, who wrote about Jonah Lehrer's fraud. The words in bold type are Moynihan's. Note the ellipsis:

> *Still, when the result of a story is that "somebody's life is going to be unalterably changed ... it is not a burden you want on yourself."*

Snippets

Strong words or phrases can be enclosed in quotation marks as a **snippet** to show that the words came from your source, not you. Avoid overusing this technique. Only important words or phrases deserve this treatment. Myers did this when he wrote:

> *He believes his story was "totally fair."*

Paraphrases

If not even one outstanding or unique phrase can be mined from your source's words, paraphrase them. Rewrite the quotation in your own words, removing the first-person pronouns and verbs but including an attribution. Myers did this in this paragraph:

> *That statement was the first time that Moynihan heard Lehrer admit that some of those quotations had been fabricated. Even Sunday, he said, Lehrer insisted that the quotations were real, but he couldn't find the sources.*

Full quotes, partial quotes, snippets and paraphrases may be inaccurate if you do not provide the original context for them. Is your source saying something with a shrug, a smile, a smirk? Let the audience know. Is he satirizing someone when he says something? Is he making air quotes with his fingers? Tell your audience. To quote the words without the context may be to misquote your source, even if you have the words right (Figure 9.10).

For appropriate punctuation of dialogue and quotations, please see the Journalism Style activities for Chapters 6 and 7.

Subject said. Subject said. Subject said.

The default language for attribution is to give the quotation and then to follow it by *he said*, or *she said* or *title and name said*. It gets boring to write, but it becomes invisible to your reader, attracting no more attention than a punctuation mark. In this chapter you have read numerous quotations and attributions, all done in this format: *Joseph Smythe said, Franklin said, Pollard said. Metzler said. Harkin said. Moynihan said. Principal Blackfoot said. He said.*

Did you notice any of them? Did they seem repetitive? See Journalism Style in Chapter 5 for more information about the language of attributions.

Figure 9.10 You have many options—full quotations, partial quotes, snippets, paraphrasing—as you incorporate quotations into your story. Strong quotations may be published exactly as spoken, while weaker quotations require editing or paraphrasing.

Photo by Forrest Czarnecki, Conifer High School

Chapter Nine

Review and Assessment

Recall

1. What are three sorts of information you may seek from interviewees?
2. List three kinds of interview questions. Which is usually most effective?
3. What factors should you consider when you arrange a place for an interview?
4. How should you handle requests to avoid certain topics in an interview?
5. What is a follow-up question?
6. How can you confirm what your source tells you?
7. What can you do with information that comes from two reliable sources that contradict each other?
8. When should you ask difficult questions or introduce controversial topics?
9. Describe five uses for quotations in a story, column or editorial.
10. Describe the characteristics that make a quotation strong.
11. What characteristics should you avoid in quotations?

Critical Thinking

1. Explain why you need both paper and sound files from interviews.
2. Besides participants, what sources might you interview for a story?
3. How would you present yourself when you interview the mayor of your city in his office? How would you present yourself when you interview evacuees from a brush fire who are housed in a school gymnasium? Are your answers different? Why?
4. When is it better to use a partial quote, snippet or paraphrase instead of a full quote?
5. What methods would you use in your publication or broadcast to handle offensive language in a quotation? Who would be part of the decision-making process? Who would make the final decision?
6. Under what conditions would you be allowed to alter a word in a quotation for your publication or broadcast? Who would make the decision?
7. Give an example of a quotation that is accurate but untrue because the reporter did not give a description of the context.

Application

1. Arrange to have a classmate videotape you as you conduct a five-minute interview with another student. The camera should be on you, the interviewer. You may wish to interview your source about familiar or unfamiliar experiences such as cooking or working with horses, sports, family vacations or music. The goal is not to learn something amazing but to capture your subject's experience and personality.

   Before the interview
   - Choose a purpose for the interview.
   - Write your interview questions in a reporter's notebook.
   - Schedule the interview and the videotaping.
   - Prepare and use equipment for sound recordings as well as written notes.

   During the interview
   - Start with easy questions. Save hard ones for the end.
   - Use eye contact. Ask at least three follow-up questions, including at least one for clarification.
   - Verify and spell the source's name, year in school and contact information on camera.
   - Videotape the whole interview, from the pre-interview chitchat to the closing, which should include, "Is there anything else I should have asked you about?"
2. Using any interview found in Chapter 8 or 9, or using written notes from another interview:
   A. Identify two strong quotes that should be included in a news or feature story.
   B. Create a lead-in paragraph for each quotation to identify the situation and speaker.
   C. Correctly attribute and punctuate the quotation.
   D. Present these in published form, ready to go onto your publication or broadcast's Web page.

Chapter Nine

Journalism Style

Names and Titles

You are mentioning your principal for the first time in a story. Which is the correct way?

1. After a long day, Principal Pamela Johnson sat at her desk to make a phone call.
2. After a long day, Principal Johnson sat at her desk to make a phone call.
3. After a long day, Pamela Johnson, Principal of West High School, sat at her desk to make a phone call.
4. After a long day, Pamela Johnson, principal of West High School, sat at her desk to make a phone call.

According to the AP Stylebook, two of these examples may be correct, depending on the following:

- Is *principal* an informal position or an official title?
- Does *principal* come before or after the person's name?

We will start with the first question: Is *principal* an informal position or an official title? Informal titles or positions are never capitalized. If you were to reference a science teacher, for example, you would not capitalize *science* or *teacher*. Here are a few other examples of informal positions that would not require capitalization.

- The first to arrive was freshman Bill Chu.
- Keeping with tradition, coach Leigh Simmons led the chant.
- After math teacher Joe Lundgren left, the department changed dramatically.

There are some exceptions. Names of languages are capitalized. Additionally, the formal name of a course is capitalized. Here are a few examples:

- *chemistry teacher Pat Locke* but *Advanced Placement Chemistry teacher Amedeo Avagadro*
- *language arts teacher Bob Wood* but *English teacher Barbara Drake*

Now look at the second question: Does *principal* come before or after the person's name? As a general rule, capitalization is only necessary for formal titles that appear before a name. When the title comes after the name, set off by commas, it does not need to be capitalized. For long titles, try to place the title after the name instead of before it.

Which two of the four sentences about Pamela Johnson would be correct?

The first sentence is correct, assuming *Principal* is an official title at the school. The last example is also correct, though, because the title follows the principal's name.

Once the principal has been introduced in the story, each subsequent reference should use only her last name. You do not need to repeat the title. However, if two or more people in the story share the same last name, use both the first and last names. See if you can spot the errors in the following example:

> *Last night, Senior Jacob Marks arrived late to the game. Jared Utley, Head Coach of the team, benched Jacob for the first quarter because of it.*

You should recognize that *senior*, not an official title, should not be capitalized and neither should *head coach*, which follows the coach's name. The second reference to senior Jacob Marks should refer to him just as Marks (*benched Marks for the first quarter*).

Try It!

Find the style errors in the following passage:

> *On December 2, Freshman Erica Taylor missed a message District Officials sent out to students canceling school for the day. Two feet of snow had fallen overnight, and Pamela Johnson, West High School Principal, decided traveling to school would be unsafe for students. Erica left for school early that day, missing that message and trudging through the snow to school, where Principal Johnson, the only person she encountered on the long walk, turned her around.*

Extend Your Knowledge Style Exercises

It is correct to write *This morning, Principal Pamela Johnson canceled school* but incorrect to write *This morning the Principal, Pamela Johnson, canceled school*. Find out why—and learn about other guidelines for capitalizing titles—on the *Journalism* website.

Chapter Nine

Writers' Workshop

In these Writers' Workshops you will:

- Find the right details to tell a story and make a point.
- Use dialogue to reveal character and advance the story.

Workshop 9.1

Finding the Specific That Shows the General

Mini-Lesson: Zooming In

Bill Plaschke's Los Angeles Times column a week before Super Bowl XLIX had a thesis, and the copy editor who wrote the headline knew exactly what is was. NFL's modern-day gladiators pay the price as the crowd roars. But Plaschke is a journalist, not a scholar, an activist or a politician arguing his point. He makes us see, smell, taste, feel and hear it. And because he is a journalist, every specific is accurately reported from the scene. Like a zoom lens, his writing focuses in on details that tell the story.

> *On a cloudless, gentle Sunday afternoon in America's newest football palace, fans gathered on a patio behind the San Francisco 49ers bench to compare jewelry and sip margaritas.*
>
> *Ten yards away, helmets collided with a sickening thwack and a giant body groaned in agony as it was flattened into the grass.*
>
> *Everyone cheered. Next play.*

Let's take apart what Plaschke did in 54 words. In the first paragraph, 27 words, he suggests:

- Fans are like royalty removed from the suffering of the commoners. The stadium is a "football palace."
- They are perfectly comfortable. The day is a cloudless and gentle Sunday.
- They are genteel as they "sip margaritas."
- They are wealthy and self-absorbed as they "compare jewelry." With the jewelry image, he suggests the presence of well-groomed socialites, perhaps decorated by their husbands' prosperity.
- They are only mildly interested in the game.

In the next 23 words he creates a jarring contrast with what is happening only 10 yards away: "sickening," "groaned in agony." ("Ten yards away" is much better than "a little ways away," isn't it?)

How does he suggest the aristocracy is indifferent to the players' suffering? Just four words: "Everyone cheered. Next play."

Try tallying the sensory imagery this short piece engages. Did you smell crushed grass? Hear the clink of the margarita glasses?

Throughout this text you have seen multiple examples of great journalistic writing, writing that relies on great reporting and has a zoom-lens focus on the image, the moment, the character, the dialogue that tells the story and stays in the audience's mind.

Roy Peter Clark called in specificity when he wrote about two dogs and the 9/11 attack on the World Trade Center (see Chapter 6). Do you remember the search and rescue dogs' names?

Apply It!

Please remember a journalist needs to observe and report genuine details. In this workshop, you are allowed to create them from your imagination, but when reporting news, never make up even the smallest detail.

1. Choose one of the settings below or create your own. Write a short (no more than 25 words) observation that zooms in on details that would suggest each of the following five scenarios:

   Someone is a bully; self-absorbed or vain; overprotective; wasteful; generous, kind, forgiving or empathetic.

   Read your work to a responding group, then revise, share or publish.

Settings—choose one or more

   The gym during a volleyball game; the waiting room of a hospital's emergency room; the scene of a minor automobile accident; an elementary school lunchroom during the last minutes of lunch; or a clothing store during back-to-school shopping time.

2. Examine your work in number one, above. How many of your observations appeal to the sense of sight? Sound? Touch? Taste? Hearing? If you do not have at least one observation that appeals to each sense, revise your observations or add more.

Workshop 9.2

When You Speak, You Reveal Yourself

Mini-Lesson: Capturing Dialogue

Reporter Jim Sheeler received a Pulitzer Prize for his 12-part series in the Rocky Mountain News on the return of a Marine's body from Iraq. Look at the role dialogue plays in sketching the characters and explaining the grief. Only once does Sheeler resort to adjectives, describing Major Steve Beck's voice as "soft, steady." Everywhere else the journalist writes some version of the standard "she said." The words the three characters speak carry all the weight and advance the action in this brief scene.

> Inside a limousine parked on the airport tarmac, Katherine Cathey looked out at the clear night sky and felt a kick.
>
> "He's moving," she said. "Come feel him. He's moving."
>
> Her two best friends leaned forward on the soft leather seats and put their hands on her stomach.
>
> "I felt it," one of them said. "I felt it."
>
> Outside, the whine of jet engines swelled.
>
> "Oh, sweetie," her friend said. "I think this is his plane."
>
> As the three young women peered through the tinted windows, Katherine squeezed a set of dog tags stamped with the same name as her unborn son:
>
> James J. Cathey.
>
> "He wasn't supposed to come home this way," she said, tightening her grip on the tags, which were linked by a necklace to her husband's wedding ring.
>
> The women looked through the back window. Then the 23-year-old placed her hand on her pregnant belly.
>
> "Everything that made me happy is on that plane," she said.
>
> They watched as airport workers rolled a conveyor belt to the rear of the plane, followed by six solemn Marines.
>
> Katherine turned from the window and closed her eyes.
>
> "I don't want it to be dark right now. I wish it was daytime," she said. "I wish it was daytime for the rest of my life. The night is just too hard."
>
> *(Continued)*

> Suddenly, the car door opened. A white-gloved hand reached into the limousine from outside—the same hand that had knocked on Katherine's door in Brighton five days earlier.
>
> The man in the deep blue uniform knelt down to meet her eyes, speaking in a soft, steady voice.
>
> "Katherine," said Maj. Steve Beck, "it's time."

Katherine Cathey's grief is beyond description, but it is not beyond portrayal. Sheeler chose carefully from hours of dialogue over more than a week to create a scene, describe character and engage the audience.

The more dialogue you have to choose from, the more likely you are to find the precious "right quote" to make your writing come alive.

Apply It!

1. In the next few days, until your next writers' workshop, use a cellphone or other device to record dialogue—the give and take between two or more people—in three of the following situations. (If you are in a public space where the people have no expectation of privacy, you may record without first asking for permission. Otherwise, ask before you record.)

   Someone giving advice, complaining, asking for a favor, gossiping, being nervous, distracted or in a hurry, bored, talking to a child or children, stressed, encouraging another, or expressing gratitude to another.
2. In your responding group, choose the recording that best reveals the speaker's character. Look for other storytelling elements, such as conflict, plot, irony, suspense and the revealed relationships. (Think what Sheeler revealed when the young woman, identified only as one of Cathey's best friends, said, "Oh, sweetie. I think this is his plane.")
3. Using your recording and no fictionalization, write the scene using dialogue. You do not need to use every word that was spoken. Choose only the strongest quotations. Describe the setting and action surrounding the quotations, as Sheeler did, but make nothing up and avoid adjectives and any attribution except "subject said." The dialogue should advance the action or conflict in the scene. Aim for 150 words.

Extend Your Knowledge

Extend

Visit the *Journalism* website for additional practice in using storytelling elements.

Chapter Ten

Feature Stories

When it's time to go deeper

Photo by Jake Crandall, The Harbinger, Shawnee Mission East High School

G-WLEARNING.COM

While studying, look for the activity icon to:

- **Build** vocabulary terms with e-flash cards and matching activities.
- **Extend** learning with further discussion of relevant topics.
- **Reinforce** what you learn by completing style exercises, worksheets and end-of-chapter questions.

Visit the Journalism website: www.g-wlearning.com/journalism/

Chapter Objectives

After reading this chapter, you will be able to:

- Explain the difference between feature, news and opinion stories.
- Describe several types of feature stories.
- Explain how the use of appropriate photos can enhance a feature story.
- Distinguish between a feature photo and a photo illustration and explain the limitations of photo illustrations.
- Explain the difference between a story angle and a topic.
- List several angles for feature stories based on a single topic.
- Explain the importance of effective leads in feature stories.
- Distinguish between hard and soft leads.
- Give examples of several kinds of weak feature leads that should be avoided.
- Describe several ways to organize feature stories.
- Explain The Wall Street Journal style of organizing feature stories.
- Discuss the appropriate use of conclusions in feature stories and how they differ from those in essays.

Key Terms Build Vocab

angle
circle kicker
first person
hard lead
mug shot
objective
poster child
soft lead
subjective
The Wall Street Journal formula
third person
wild art

Before You Read...

Working in small groups, assign each person a section of the chapter to read silently to him or herself. Starting at the beginning of the chapter and working your way to the end, take turns summarizing the material. Take notes as your classmates share what they learned. Ask questions about anything you did not understand.

Introduction

"People are hungry for stories. It's part of our very being. Storytelling is a form of history, of immortality too. It goes from one generation to another."

–Studs Terkel, noted interviewer and Pulitzer Prize winning author

Some journalists and scholars break journalistic stories into three categories: news, feature and opinion. Features are the most difficult to define. In fact, it is almost easier to say what feature writing is not, rather than what it is.

Feature stories are *not* news stories. News stories are based on timely events. The campus is locked down for three hours due to a hazardous substance scare. A dedication ceremony will name a newly remodeled building for a retired teacher. Standardized test scores are released. News stories are always connected to a specific, timely event.

Feature stories are based on solid reporting and they are rooted in one or more of the seven news values. But their importance does not stem primarily from their timeliness. Journalists write feature stories because something is interesting, not necessarily because something just happened. Since they usually are not trying to cover late-breaking news, feature writers may have time to report and write with more depth.

Feature stories are *not* opinion writing. The journalist's opinions do not belong in feature stories. Leave that for editorials, columns and reviews. An editorial praises the administration for its handling of the lockdown, a columnist writes about stresses she and her fellow seniors face applying for colleges and a reviewer evaluates a new gaming interface. People read opinion pieces to learn these writers' opinions.

Features *are* filled with opinions—just not yours. The opinions come from the people you interview. You are like a telescope, focused on the moon. Your audience should be so interested in the surface of the moon that they forget about the telescope, about you and your opinions. You want to show your audience the moon, not to distract them with the telescope.

Any time you inject your opinion, the focus shifts from the subject and the viewpoints of the people in your story, to what you think about the subject. When this happens in a feature story—or in a news story—it is editorializing, and it is not appropriate.

News and feature stories are generally **objective** in nature, meaning that the opinions of the writer do not appear in the story. Opinion pieces, on the other hand, are **subjective** in nature since they do contain the writer's opinions.

Like news stories, feature stories contain solid reporting, are based on at least one of the core news values and avoid editorializing. For instance

- Two boys in the English Language Learners program are avid rodeo riders. Their story would make a human-interest feature story with a touch of oddity, especially if rodeo riders are rare at your school.
- You analyze the nutritional value of cafeteria food. This feature is strong on proximity and impact. There may also be a conflict between what most students want to eat and what is available in the cafeteria line.

- A personality profile of your principal, even if she has not recently done or said anything newsworthy, will be interesting, but only if it is well done. Her prominence is the primary news value in this feature story.

Types of Features

Topics for features stories abound on your campus, but they are not always easy to recognize. (If they were easy to find, why would people need journalists?) They may be hiding in plain sight, but if you can give them names, they will be easier to find and easier to write.

Personality Profiles

A personality profile shows your audience how someone else thinks, looks, acts and talks. Sometimes it is a famous person. Sometimes it is an unusual person—that means someone with an unusual background or someone odd, wacky or eccentric. Sometimes it is a hero, either a well-known hero or an unsung hero. But not always.

Some of the best personality profiles involve familiar strangers—people you see frequently but do not really see. Almost always their lives are much broader and more interesting than what you see as you walk by. Bill Plaschke's profile of the water boy and mascot for University of Southern California's football team is a great example (see Chapter 2). Until Plaschke wrote about him, even journalism students thought "he was some weird kid who kept showing up."

Personality profiles lend themselves well to monthly student newspapers, daily broadcasts or a website. Quotations, sound bites and video footage help portray your subject.

The late Studs Terkel, a Pulitzer Prize winning author, radio host and historian, believed that everyone has a story (Figure 10.1). Not just those in power—the movers and shakers, the big men and women on campus—but everyday people, those who usually go unnoticed. They may have interesting stories to tell as well, if someone would take the time to talk with them.

Longtime television journalist Charles Kuralt spent a quarter of a century and wore out six motor homes travelling the back roads of America, where he sought out ordinary people and told their stories in feature pieces that aired regularly on CBS. Inspired by a 1985 meeting with Kuralt, newspaper columnist David Johnson spent decades writing about people he picked at random from the phone book and from cell phone

Figure 10.1 During his 45 years on the radio, Studs Terkel conducted over 5,000 interviews.

Chicago History Museum, ICHi-65439; Stephen Deutch, photographer

numbers submitted by readers. His weekly column, published in his Lewiston, Idaho paper, was called "Everyone Has a Story."

The bottom line is that a huge part of journalistic writing is about people. The people you find on and around your campus are the ones whose stories you can tell better than anyone else. Sometimes prominent people are the subjects of these stories—the graduate of your school who is serving on the school board or the student body president with an unusual hobby. However, the strongest features may be about the "ordinary" person with an extraordinary story to tell. A soft-spoken math teacher spends his weekends kayaking in class-five rapids. A foreign exchange student speaks six languages. A quiet junior boy has not missed a day of school since kindergarten. Stories that profile these people can make strong journalism.

Your Turn

1. Working with a partner or in a small group, brainstorm a list of people on your campus who would make interesting personality profiles.
2. For one person on your list, explain the one aspect of their life you believe would be most interesting to your audience.

When you interview people for personality profiles, you must cultivate two primary qualities: respect and curiosity. Take a genuine interest in the person you interview. Strive to find out everything you can about the things that they are passionate about. Do not be satisfied with surface answers to your questions. Be *insanely* curious. Keep digging. Ask follow-up questions to get your subject to talk about his underlying feelings and motivations. Wait patiently after you ask a question or give a gentle command. "Tell me about growing up then and there." Interviews with the subjects of personality profiles cannot be done effectively in just a few minutes.

And Now... Closer to Home

Ingredients for a Successful Personality Profile

- Background information from your preliminary research.
- Interview information from subject.
- Specific quotes from subject—your subject's words reveal him.
- Information provided by others.
- Specific quotes from others.
- Your detailed observations of the subject (physical appearance, mannerisms or details from their surroundings).
- A chronology that records their memorable turning points, moves, adventures and education.
- Your subject's plans, goals and dreams.

Ongoing Issues

Ongoing issues that affect your school make strong feature stories. Maybe students suffer in hot weather because the air conditioners don't work. Or the roof in the gym has leaked for years and nothing is being done about it. How about the continual increases in the costs of going to college? The ongoing problem of student lockers being broken into? The P.E. lockers you can open with a coat hanger?

Each of these issues could be the basis of a feature story because they impact your audience. Notice that they aren't necessarily connected to timely events. These stories are not written to answer "what happened?" or "what's about to happen?" They are written to provide insight, to increase understanding, to shed light on topics that affect people, to open your audience's eyes to issues that surround them.

You are the eyes and ears of your audience. They do not have the time or the skills to interview school officials and find out what's wrong with the air conditioning and why it's taking so long to get it fixed. As a journalist, you can get that information for your audience and present it in a balanced and understandable way.

Although identifying widespread problems can be a fruitful way to come up with feature story ideas, the issues that prompt feature stories are not all negative. A story on the pros and cons of military service as an alternative to college can make a strong feature story. Or how about a piece on how having a steady boyfriend or girlfriend affects one's schoolwork and post-high school plans?

Remember that when you write about issues, it's the people affected by those issues that bring life to your story. Some charitable organizations have used a promotional technique known as the **poster child**. In the past, people afflicted with a disease or debilitating condition, such as muscular dystrophy, were chosen to be part of campaigns to help fund research. Their pictures were used in advertisements and other media in order to put a face on the problem that might otherwise just be seen in statistics and reports. (Some observers considered this practice to be exploitation of the person living with the disability.) You can also put a face on an issue by finding a person who is impacted by the issue and make her the focal point of your story.

The French III student who swelters each fall because the foreign language wing has a broken air conditioner becomes the poster child for the larger story. While you certainly must give the facts on the number of classrooms affected, how long the problem has gone on, the causes of the problem, and what district officials say they plan to do about it, your poster child gives your audience a human face to the issue.

Your Turn

1. In a small group, discuss ongoing issues of specific interest to your campus.
2. Identify one or two people at your school who would make good "poster children" for each issue.

APRIL 2014

SENIOR ALL NIGHT PARTY GETS MOVED TO DAVE & BUSTERS

WHAT DO THE PEOPLE THINK?

BY AUBREY RITZ

Having looked forward to the Senior All-Night Party (SANP) for four years, senior Sabrina Hansen was disappointed when she heard it would take place at Dave and Buster's this year instead of at RHS, as it has in the past.

"In my opinion, the location of the senior all-night party really does make a difference," Hansen said. "It would have been really special to get to have the SANP at Rochester since to many of us, Rochester High has become a sort of home away from home, so where better to celebrate the last four years of our lives and the memories we've made than in the place where we made them."

Sindy Klonke, the Chairman of SANP for 2014, says there are many reasons for the change, including: difficulties with not enough funds for decorations, lack of volunteers and not enough entertainment for students.

"2013 was the worst for volunteers, and no one would help clean up at 5 a.m.," Mrs. Klonke said. "Only 1-2 families had to clean up and move everything to a storage unit. Another reason was that we heard that students had been bored in the past and there wasn't as much to do."

Since Adams had their All-Night Party at Dave and Buster's last year and they claim it was a smashing success, the RHS SANP committee decided to follow suit. Mrs. Klonke met with Student Council to tell them the pros and cons of the change in location and they decided to send out a survey for students and parents through Survey Monkey.

"Since I didn't think it was fair for me to make a decision, I decided to bring Dave and Buster's in for a SANP meeting and open it up for questions and answers," Mrs. Klonke said.

After opening the survey to seniors and their parents 102 people responded, and the majority results were in favor of a change in location. Senior Jed Macatula agrees that a change in venue could be advantageous due to more games, food, and a better atmosphere.

"I think at school it would be more of a hangout, but they wouldn't have much stuff to do here," senior Jed Macatula said. "Dave and Busters would provide more entertainment."

Even though the survey was in favor of the change in location, some students are upset by the change in tradition.

"I thought it was a shame to do away with such a tradition," senior Derek Xia said. "I believe that having it at RHS is a great way to remember our school and spend the last few days creating new memories here would be a great way to go."

All activities from years' past, including the highly anticipated Vegas-style games, will be there, plus games at Dave & Busters along with new activities.

"I think it so cool that D&B closes down for our entire school. Instead of spending money on decorations, we are putting more money into activities and prizes for the students," Mrs. Klonke said. "We have a lot of cool gifts that the students will be able to use off at college."

It's too soon to tell whether the change in location will increase participation in the SANP or not, but Hansen says she plans to attend either way.

"Despite the fact that the SANP will not be at Rochester this year, I have high hopes for how it will turn out," Hansen said. "I'm certain that the senior class will have a blast and make memories that they will always remember."

AT DAVE & BUSTERS

PROS:
- Less volunteers needed
-Limited set up and clean up time
-Higher security with onsite police officers
-Some activites from RHS plus more games
-RHS students only will be there
-Everything is hot and fresh from D&B including a sundae bar and breakfast bar
-Less money will be spent on decorations more on other activites or prizes

CONS:
- Must take buses since it is around 15 minutes away, which cost around $1200
-Change is difficult to accept for some

AT RHS

PROS:
-Tradition for atleast ten years
-Closer to Home bus not needed
-Get to stay over night at the school you are graduating from

CONS:
-Never enough volunteers which leads to longer set up time and decorations falling apart
-Need to invest in more decorations
-Parents helping had to leave commencement early
-Have to rely on Junior's parents for set up and clean up

WHAT DO YOU THINK OF THE CHANGE IN LOCATION?

"If they are going to have a senior all night party they better have it here. There's no point in supporting a restaurant corporation."
JOSEPH MANDWEE, SENIOR

"I party anywhere I go so the location doesn't really matter."
SCOTT DIFILIPO, SENIOR

"I've heard good things since Adams went last year, so it can't be that bad."
ALLISON FRIEBE, SENIOR

"I like it because I feel like if it was here we'd have nothing to do."
EMILY SMITH, SENIOR

DESIGN BY AUBREY RITZ

THE TALON

Courtesy of The Talon, Rochester High School

Figure 10.2 Sidebars can be used to share additional information or opinions related to the feature story.

Sidebars

Even though feature stories are not usually based on news events, sometimes news stories can provide feature ideas, and some news stories need a sidebar to be fully understood. A sidebar is a background story that enriches a news piece. It is related to the news story by a figurative news peg (Figure 10.2).

For example, if a student from your school is injured when a stolen car fleeing police jumps the curb and hits him, the news story will cover the who, what, when, where and why of the unfortunate event. The sidebar might focus on the broader issue of police vehicle chases, asking whether or not they are too dangerous in residential areas or near schools. You could interview school officials, a police department spokesperson and a criminology professor to get relevant opinions. The news story on the injured student is the news peg on which the sidebar story about the relative value of police chases hangs.

In another example, a feature explaining in detail how state officials arrive at those school-wide academic performance scores could accompany the news story on your school's latest scores. Or the news piece on the recently announced performing arts center to be built on your campus might run next to a sidebar that details the history of your campus buildings or a piece about other performing arts centers at schools in your community.

How-To Stories

Another type of feature story is the how-to story or an explainer, in which journalists give their audience a detailed understanding of the inner workings of a particular activity or function. A step-by-step description of how to get involved in the online role-playing game World of Warcraft could make a fascinating feature story. Students might also benefit from a story on how to find a community service opportunity that would fit their interests, how to pitch a softball or execute a particular competitive dive, or how to get an appointment with their counselor. They might be interested in why they sneeze when the school heaters first fire up in the fall.

Stories of this type may be accompanied by photo illustrations or graphics to make them more interesting and informative. Sometimes they appear as a sidebar published next to a news or feature story. For example, the how-to piece on how to play World of Warcraft might be presented alongside a personality profile on a student who spends hours participating in that hobby. Or the "how to get in to see your counselor" story could run next to a larger feature on the ongoing issue of key pieces of information a freshman needs to know to survive at your school.

Consumer Features

Consumer interest features guide your audience as they shop and use local services. Give them information about restaurants, clothing stores, limo rentals, tux rentals and florists near Prom or Winter Formal. Survey used and vintage clothing stores and entertainment venues like arcades, mini-golf courses, and paintball fields. Do not forget more ordinary establishments such as barbershops and beauty salons. Products students use also make good consumer interest features (Figure 10.3). Digital games, phones, skateboards and accessories, and backpacks are just a few ideas that could work here.

A&E

ALL IN ONE

All the objects the smartphone has come to replace

BY JYOTSNA NATARAJAN AND VANESSA QIN

1. Alarm clock

junior Navya Annam
iPhone 4s user for a month

Junior Navya Annam frequently takes naps and depends on her iPhone to keep on schedule with her work and her sleep. "I just think it is easier to have everything in one place so I don't need my laptop, alarm clock and camera all the time," Annam said. With the many choices of sounds for alarms, Annam chooses the most annoying one so she won't have a choice but to get up and turn it off. While she would be willing to get an alarm clock if, Annam believes that the smartphone is a convenient device to have.

2. Gaming

sophomore Joseph Kuo
iPhone 6 user for a month

Prior to the age of the smartphone, back when Nokias were standard, sophomore Joseph Kuo had been playing Bejeweled and other classic phone games. Now, Kuo is an avid iPhone user for its convenience of communication and access to social media and gaming. Kuo's favorite game on the iPhone is Puzzles and Dragons. "Without my iPhone, I would actually get work done and have more of a social life," Kuo said with a laugh. Though having an iPhone provides a distracting source of entertainment, Kuo feels that it is also a necessary device for communication.

3. Notes

junior Lily Spitzen
iPhone 5 user for over a year

Page 67, bottom of page 111. These are annotations of the literature book that junior Lily Spitzen is reading. She jots them down on the Notes application on her iPhone 5. Spitzen writes everything she needs, and makes it her screen cover to have that constant reminder. Occasionally, she also records moments of her day that she wants to remember. "I write all the inside jokes [my friends share] so I can remember it and put it in their birthday card," Spitzen said. Spitzen believes that the Notes application is more convenient than a physical planner.

4. Social media

junior Lucca Martins
iPhone 5s user for over a year

Junior Lucca Martins discreetly pulls out his phone during a movie in his World Literature class. He consults the photos of his textbook that he took the night before to finish up homework during class. The teacher doesn't notice him. Martins, like many other students on campus, constantly checks his iPhone, using it primarily as a source of entertainment and as a way of communicating with his friends. "I look at my phone almost every five minutes," he said. "I'm addicted to it." Martins feels that smartphones have combined various devices from the past all into one convenient little block.

j.natarajan@elestoque.org | v.qin@elestoque.org

18 EL ESTOQUE

Courtesy of El Estoque, Monta Vista High School

Figure 10.3 Unlike a review, which might try to sway someone into buying, or not buying the iPhone, this feature highlights the benefits of the smartphone in an objective manner.

Your Turn

1. During a class discussion, assign someone to list all the items the members of your class are carrying or wearing.
2. Discuss which of these items would make good consumer interest features.
3. **Going Deeper.** Pick one of these story ideas and, as a class, create a detailed plan for making the story happen.

Historical Features

Feature stories do not need to be timely. History features, if done well, can capture your audience. Take a field trip on your own campus and ask lots of questions about what you see.

- When did they put all the chain-link fences around the school? Were they there when the school opened?
- Who created the carved wooden pictures on the wall of the auditorium lobby? When were they done? What do the images in the pictures represent?
- What is behind those tiny windows high up on the back wall of the performing arts center?
- Why is there a black and yellow sign on the door to the basement with the words "Fallout Shelter"?

Many in your audience may have these same questions. As a journalist, you have the means to find and report on the answers.

Your Turn

1. As a class or by yourself, take the field trip on your own campus as suggested above.
2. Make notes when you see something you are curious about: a plaque, a piece of artwork, an unusual class gift, anything that leaves you wondering.
3. **Going Deeper.** Pick one item from your list and research it. Report your findings to your class.

Know enough of your campus history to know when an anniversary is coming. Maybe it has been exactly 50 years since your campus first opened, or exactly one year since a major tragedy rocked your school or 40 years since a veteran's memorial plaque was placed in your quad. Anniversaries are opportunities for your publication to remind its audience about these events and compare those times with the present. Do not write about the history of Valentine's Day, Christmas or St. Patrick's Day. If it is in Wikipedia, it is not news. Tell them interesting facts about your school and community. Localize your historical features to your campus.

And Now... Closer to Home

Save Subjective Writing for Reviews

This is probably a good place for a reminder that features are written objectively. The emphasis of your consumer interest feature is not your opinion about the products and services—you'll save that for reviews, where subjective writing is appropriate. The idea behind consumer interest features is to give the audience information they can use to help make their spending choices. So, focus on the facts and on helpful ways to group those facts. Describe 10 different video games at the local arcade, compare the menu offerings and prices at three nearby Mexican restaurants, or line up the prices and capabilities of three popular cell phone models side-by-side. Consider the Scripps media company motto: "Give light and the people will find their own way."

People associated with your school's past may make strong historical feature stories as well. In the "where are they now?" feature, reporters find out what has happened to their schools' alumni and former staff members. Members of the first graduating class, former student body presidents, principals, top athletes, musicians and artists make good subjects for these kinds of stories. But don't forget the former auto shop student who now runs his own racecar building business or the former cheerleader who owns a dance studio.

Firsthand Accounts

Even though features do not usually contain the opinions of the writer, a firsthand account is different. In these stories you, as a reporter, participate in an activity and then describe your experience. This sort of reporting is a powerful way to handle some topics. It adds variety to your publication or broadcast. A firsthand account provides a behind-the-scenes view of something your audience probably won't have the opportunity to experience for themselves.

For example, you might arrange to ride along with a local police officer or television news crew, or participate in a 24-hour fundraiser like Relay for Life, or switch gender roles and practice routines with the cheerleaders or work out with the football team.

In these stories, it is appropriate for you to write about your own experiences and include your own feelings and opinions on the subject. You should also interview and quote those you meet in the process—police officers, professional reporters, other walkers, cheerleaders and football players. This gives the audience an insider's perspective and lets them learn about the experience almost as if they were there with you.

Firsthand accounts differ from standard news and feature stories because they are written from the **first-person** point of view. **Third person** is the standard for most journalistic writing. When you write in the third person, you use pronouns like *he, him, she, her, they* and *them.* But writers of firsthand accounts use the first-person pronouns *I*, *me* and *mine* since these writers are writing about their own experiences and feelings.

In a typical feature on skateboarding you might write, "The skaters devote hours to perfecting *their* craft, often practicing *their* tricks until well past dark." But when you write about your experience on a skateboard in a half pipe, you write "*I* tried and fell, tried and fell, and then tried and fell again until long after the sun went down. By the time *I* dragged *myself* home, both of *my* knees were black and blue."

The firsthand account allows you to *show* rather than just *tell*. When you experience an event, you can describe it in vivid detail with stronger writing than if you merely talk with people and then tell your audience what they said. You write a story about your first job interview:

> *The "tick, tick, tick" of the clock on the wall seemed to slow almost to a stop as I waited in the lobby for my name to be called. My sweaty palms got worse despite all of my attempts to dry them on my pants before the inevitable handshake with the boss. I began to shake uncontrollably. How could I possibly get through this?*

This writing that *shows* is much more informative for your audience than merely *telling* them, as you would if the story was written in the third person: *She said she was really nervous before the interview* or even, *"I was so nervous before I met the boss," she said.*

Your Turn

1. In no less than one full page, describe an event that lasts six seconds or less, like a tumble down the stairs, that first kiss or the buzzer-beating free throw. Include detail of what happens, but also consider feelings, thoughts and sensory impressions. Only describe what happens physically and mentally during the six seconds of time—do not describe the whole day.
2. Read your writing aloud to your fellow staff members. While you read, your listeners will take notes on
   - what they experience most vividly from your description; and
   - what they would like to have heard more of.

Feature Photos

Visuals are an important part of journalism. They say a picture is worth a thousand words, and, like so many old sayings, this one is true.

Your audience will be more likely to read your story and will grasp information more quickly if it is accompanied by visuals (Figure 10.4). Some journalism staffs try to create something visual to go with every story. That's a tall order, but the principle behind it is a good one.

As you plan coverage ask, "Can we get a picture of someone doing something that will go along with this story?" Sometimes the answer is obvious. A personality profile on the new guidance counselor could include—at the very least—a picture of her meeting with a student. A sports feature on the senior who competes on a roller derby team cries out for a photo of her in action, or, better yet, a package (or grouping) of photos. Your piece on the nutritional value of the food available in the school cafeteria needs a picture of people eating—ideally in the cafeteria, or perhaps a tray full of food sliding into the trash can.

Other stories demand creativity when you look for a picture. Avoid boring shots—students just listening to a lecture at their desks or typing in front of computer screens. Instead, get a close-up of a pair of hands working a video game controller or texting on a smartphone, a head bent over a page or screen full of notes. A plate of food or a book jacket could accompany a consumer review.

Photo by Emily Cunningham, Arapahoe Herald, Arapahoe High School

Figure 10.4 Powerful feature illustrations spark the readers' interest and draw them into the story. *What questions or feelings does this strong image inspire in you?*

Stay alert for candid photo opportunities, those in which the subjects are not posing for the camera. Often the very best pictures are taken of people who are actively engaged in an activity and who don't even know they are being photographed.

Mug Shots

If you cannot get an action photo, at the very least, get a **mug shot** or two to show the key players. The term *mug shot* refers to the pictures the police take of people when they are arrested, but it has been generalized to mean any picture of the face. Dating from the 18th century, mug is

And Now... Closer to Home

Award-Winning Student Journalism

Go to the National Scholastic Press Association website to find examples of some of the finest student journalism in the country. In the contests/critiques section, the NSPA presents annual contest winners in a wide variety of categories, including feature stories. Check out the stories found under Individual Awards.

Courtesy of Jake Collins, Redondo Union High School

Figure 10.5 Wild art adds visual interest and helps catch the reader's eye.

an English slang term for face. Mug shots are small photos of individual faces cropped so little more than the face is in the picture. Faces should never be smaller than a dime. Try for a little personality in the mug shots—a grin, a raised chin, a solemn look. Yearbook photos are rarely a good source as they may be too posed.

Wild Art

Some feature photos are so strong they tell a story without much writing. A brief caption is sufficient. Photojournalists call these pictures **wild art** or *enterprise art* (Figures 10.5 and 10.6). Carry a camera around campus and in the neighborhood, alert to those "found" moments that capture an interesting slice of life. The security guard carrying yet another stray puppy to the impound area, a pair of lovebirds holding hands while engaged in a sweet conversation, or the gigantic football lineman walking with his mom and little sister. These could all work as wild art.

A word of caution is in order here: Feature photos should either show reality or what is obviously *not* reality. People who view your publication will assume that the activities they see in the pictures actually happened the way they appear to be happening. If you stage the photo, shoot it in a studio, use props or actors, or manipulate the photo, it should be clearly labeled a photo illustration. Your audience should never wonder if it is posed or real. Only pose people for photos as a last resort. A good rule of thumb: If the only thing the caption writer can say about the photo is *Seniors Bill Smith and Jane Jones pose for the camera*, you need a better photo.

Features stories are probably the only part of your publication where photo illustrations are ever acceptable. Photo illustrations are usually confined to consumer features and how-to features.

Your Turn

1. Think of one feature story idea from each of the following categories. Only list ideas that could run in your publication.
   - Personality profile
   - Ongoing issue
   - Firsthand account
   - Consumer review
   - Historical feature
   - How-to feature
2. For each of your story ideas, develop four options for accompanying visuals: two candid photos of people participating in activities and two photo illustrations that could be posed or staged.

Writing Feature Stories

Interviews, research and firsthand observations are important elements of a successful feature story. As you prepare to write your story, you talk with people and write down what they say. You read reliable information from several sources and save parts that may fit in your story. You show up in all the right places and take detailed notes, photos and sound recordings of what you see and hear—and maybe even things you smell, touch and taste. You have pages of notes and possibly many megabytes of recorded material.

Courtesy of Casey Simmons, Westlake High School

Figure 10.6 You never know when the opportunity for a powerful image will present itself. Wise journalists have their cameras ready so they can capture these exciting, unplanned moments.

But now what do you do with the information? How do you take all of this data and craft it into a well-written piece of journalism? The answer to that question may be different for every story but will involve some of the same steps.

Before You Write, Find an Angle

An **angle** is like the theme of an English essay—it is the point, the main idea or the peg on which everything else in the story hangs. Just as you should not confuse the topic of your English essay with the thesis, do not confuse the topic of your story with your angle on the topic. A topic is a subject, while an angle is a particular way of looking at that subject.

Your editor might assign a feature story on skateboarding, a very broad subject (Figure 10.7). You need to narrow it down to one angle. Try asking yourself: "What interesting aspect of this topic can I zero in on? What questions does my audience have about this topic that I can find answers to? How can I get beyond the obvious information that most people already know about this topic?" Some possible answers include

- the frequency, types and causes of skateboarding injuries;
- detailed descriptions of the most common skateboarding tricks;
- whether to wear a helmet;
- skateboard sizes and local board manufacturers;
- a firsthand account from observations at the local skateboarding park; or
- tension between property owners and skateboarders.

Figure 10.7 Suppose your editor asked you to write a story about skateboarding. *What steps might you take to pick an angle?*

Here's another example of a search for an angle. Your varsity football team hasn't won a game in three seasons. You've interviewed several players, the coach, and the athletic director. You've researched all the numbers

Exploring Possible Angles

What people are doing and talking about on your campus can generate thousands of story ideas. Any given topic can lend itself to a variety of angles. Here are some examples:

Topic: The school cafeteria is serving more nutritious food in response to government regulations.

Possible angles:

- Since students are now buying less cafeteria food and eating more junk food purchased elsewhere, the regulations might cause unintended consequences, like a drop in cafeteria income or a rise in student obesity.
- Discuss the conflict between those who appreciate government efforts to improve health and those who think government is meddling too much in our lives.
- Find out how the changes toward more nutritious food offerings are impacting the cafeteria workers. Is it more work for them? Do they prefer the new way or the old way?
- Discuss the relative costs associated with serving more nutritious food. How is it impacting the school budget?

Topic: The presidential election is next month.

Possible angles:

- Focus on what the two major candidates plan to do about education, if they are elected.
- Show students—many of whom are, or soon will be, voting age—how to register and vote.
- Report on the extent to which students are aware of the candidates and their positions on the issues.

Topic: A well-loved teacher has announced she is retiring at the end of the school year after 35 years in the job.

Possible angles:

- Report her views on the changes in education since she began.
- Focus on the comments of her current and past students, her colleagues and her supervisors.

so you can put this sad situation into historical context. You've been to practice and to the most recent game. As you agonize about how to write your feature, you're a bit jealous of the reporter who writes the news piece on that game. He has a much easier job than you do. He just has to report the final score, give some details about key plays, update the win-loss record and sprinkle in a few quotes from the coach and a key player or two. The main idea of this sports news story is fairly obvious: The varsity football team lost again on Friday night. But as a feature writer, you need to create the angle for this story. You must come up with the unifying idea that will hold the story together.

The key to your search is in your interview notes. The quarterback, who has played varsity in all three of these losing seasons, told you he thinks winning is nice, but he has learned to enjoy playing each week, even without wins. Another three-year player said he thinks he's a better person than he was before this losing streak started. The coach told you, "Any kid can show up and play his heart out when his team is winning, but it takes real men to do what my kids do. They sweat it out every day in practice, and they leave it all on the field every Friday night. That's character."

There is your angle: It really is not whether you win or lose. It's what kind of person you become while playing the game. Understanding this theme will drive everything you do as you put the story together. Your angle will affect how you start the piece—your lead, which will set the tone and hook your audience. It will also determine which quotes, facts and observations you choose to include. That angle will show up again in your conclusion.

Great! You have your angle. Now what? Like the essay we mentioned earlier, feature stories usually have a beginning, middle and end. Your English teacher calls those the introduction, body and conclusion. The lead is the beginning.

Write the Lead

In chapters 5 and 6 you learned about the importance of leads, especially five W's leads. This is the most common news lead and is also called a **hard lead**. A sports news preview story might open with

> *The league championship will be decided Friday night when two undefeated teams meet at Tiger Stadium. East High and South's Lions have perfect 9-0 records, and both coaches say their teams have no intention of losing this one.*

Your Turn

1. Brainstorm two or three potential angles for feature stories on each of the topics below.
   - Several houses near your school have been vacant for many months, and they are turning into eyesores, with graffiti on the fences, dead landscaping and broken windows. Police have reported that students have been caught holding parties in the homes.
   - Two prominent students on your campus have been suspended for cheating on a major test in their economics class.
   - It is the anniversary of the 9/11 attacks.
   - One of your classmates is being raised in a two-mother household.

This summary lead style can work for some feature stories as well as news stories. Make your first sentence or two sum up the main idea of the story. This lead from an eHow.com piece on shoe care makes it very clear what is coming next.

> *Odor-causing bacteria thrive in dark, damp spaces, which makes your sweaty tennies an ideal habitat. You'll need to wipe out the smelly bacterial population to achieve truly odor-free shoes.*

But in writing leads for feature stories, journalists often use the **soft lead**. Much like the author of a short story or novel, feature writers need to grab the audience's attention, not by summarizing the whole story, but by telling just a piece of it. They create suspense by delaying the answer to the question, "What is this story about?"

Student journalist Tessie Murphy (Ink, Georgiana Bruce Kirby Preparatory School) used this soft lead in her NSPA first-place story:

> *Junior Craig Petrocelli waltzes around Actors' Theatre's small stage, clutching a bottle of champagne and singing nonsensically to himself. Wearing a skirt, afro wig and fake moustache, he doesn't break character while multiple women flounce around him, wearing only lingerie and pumps.*

Like many soft leads, these opening sentences paint a vivid picture of an unusual scene, and they effectively raise the audience's interest. But they don't tell us much about what is to come in the story. That's why soft leads are usually followed by a nut graf.

Here's the next sentence in Murphy's story, its nut graf.

> *Such was the nature of Kirby's spring play, Lend Me a Tenor: lots of scantily-clad women, lots of singing, and lots of afro.*

Now we know we are reading a story about the spring play. This paragraph, like all nut grafs, does the job of the hard lead in a news story. It tells the reader what the story is all about and why they should read it. Staffers at The Philadelphia Inquirer referred to the nut graf as the "You may have wondered why we invited you to this party" section.

When writing a nut graf, you will want to ask yourself two questions: What is my story about and why should people read it? Type the answers to those questions in just a few sentences. But don't tell your readers too much at this point. You want to give them reasons to read on.

Here's another soft lead written by Tricia O'Neill, In-Depth Editor of the A-Blast, Annandale High School's online publication:

> *After finally finishing her homework around 11:30 the night before, and getting a less than satisfactory six hours of sleep, junior Kaitlyn To rolls over to shut off the loud*

> *beeping emitted by her alarm clock. She hesitates to get up, forcing herself to make her way downstairs toward the pantry to retrieve her favorite brand of cereal and a carton of 1% milk from the refrigerator.*

Is the angle of this story something about student sleep habits or is it about food? At this point we're not sure. But O'Neill's nut graf clears it up for us.

> *But, what she doesn't know is that her favorite type of sugary cereal not only contains little nutritional value, but also genetically modified ingredients. She couldn't know, as it is not required under U.S. law that products be labeled as containing these types of ingredients.*

So, while feature stories may open with hard leads, as most news stories do, they may also start with a soft lead followed by a nut graf. A creative soft lead followed by a nut graf hooks your audience into your story. Feature-style soft leads come in as many forms as there are people who publish lists of them.

Anecdotal Leads

An anecdote, or story, is a strong way to grab your audience's attention. The anecdotal lead starts with a brief story about a person or event. Here's a prize-winning example from Bob Young of the Seattle Times.

> *Melany Vorass called to say dinner was trapped in her front yard.*
>
> *A few hours later we were eating risotto di rodentia—eastern gray squirrel braised in Lopez Island white wine with mushrooms and Italian-style rice. It did not taste like chicken.*

Here is his nut graf.

> *As you might guess, Vorass is serious about eating locally. She teaches urban foraging. She raises goats, chickens, bees and worms at her Green Lake house. And she believes she's the only person in Seattle harvesting squirrels for protein.*

For the Record

Describing a Nut Graf

Ken Wells, a writer and editor at The Wall Street Journal, described the nut graf as "a paragraph that says what this whole story is about and why you should read it. It's a flag to the reader, high up in the story: You can decide to proceed or not, but if you read no farther, you know what that story's about."

Narrative Leads

Like the anecdotal lead, the narrative lead tells a story but typically by focusing on a dramatic moment, the high point of the action. The audience is drawn in as if they were seeing the event firsthand. Like the opening words of a good fiction piece, the narrative lead begins in the middle of the action. You do not need to set it up first. Just jump into the story.

> *As soon as he enters the senior lot after the 3:10 bell, he can tell something is wrong. His vintage Camaro looks crooked somehow. His heart falls when he sees his right front tire is flat. A closer look reveals it has been brutally slashed.*

You could follow this lead with a nut graf on the rise of vandalism at your school and then complete the story with details and quotes gathered from this victim and others, as well as school and law enforcement officials.

Notice that this and many other examples in this section are written in present tense, as if the action is happening now. Many writers prefer this to past tense, believing it is more powerful for the reader. What do you think? Compare the sample above to the past tense version below. The words that have been changed are underlined.

> *As soon as he entered the senior lot after the 3:10 bell, he could tell something was wrong. His vintage Camaro looked crooked somehow. His heart fell when he saw his right front tire was flat. A closer look revealed it had been brutally slashed.*

Your Turn

Marty Burleson of the Visalia Times-Delta opens a story about very young rodeo riders with this soft lead:

Rider No. 171 is a cowboy's cowboy, a dirty, skinny, word-shy rascal who's spent darn near half his life in places like this one, a sun-soaked arena near Woodlake.

As "Wild Thing" plays over the sound system, Judd Post, hidden behind a fence, secures the grip on his rope and digs rounded spurs into the animal between his boots. The public address announcer prepares the Woodlake Bull Bash audience for what's sure to be a treat, a ride by a local product who just happens to be the defending California State Champion.

"OK, Visalia. Get ready for one of your own. From Liberty School. ... "

The chute opens and out come two things that you, an urbanite with neither a John Deere cap nor ESPN 6, may never have seen:

- *A sheep doing 25 mph.*
- *A 5-year-old boy hanging onto that sheep like it was the last Tonka truck in a box full of Barbies.*

(Continued)

YOUR TURN *(Continued)*

1. With a partner or small group, discuss the effectiveness of Burleson's lead. Consider the writer's choice of present tense rather than past tense, his choice of details, and the element of suspense.
2. **Going Deeper.** What else makes this an effective lead? In what ways might you improve it?
3. Write a paragraph that discusses the strengths and weaknesses of this lead.

Descriptive Leads

Writing a descriptive lead is another strong way to begin a feature story, one that grabs your audience's attention. Journalists use their powers of observation—and their notes and recordings—to capture vivid details of scenes and people as they report. Then they draw on the details to create a descriptive lead.

Which is a better lead, *telling* your audience that the guidance counselor's office is cluttered, or *showing* them this?

> *Not a single square inch of wall space is visible. "A mind is a terrible thing to waste" and "Today is the first day of the rest of your life" shout encouragement from brightly colored posters. Eight-and-a-half-by-eleven bell schedules, the school attendance calendar, and a host of other duplicated announcements are stapled everywhere, but not one hangs straight. Covering up several other papers, a hot pink flyer urges you to run in or donate to the next 5K fundraiser. What seem like a thousand smiling former students beam down from snapshots that crowd an entire wall. A pile of winter coats fills one corner. And on the desk, peeking out from behind a huge, disastrous pile of papers, is a framed color photo of an attractive brunette and two grinning toddlers, the loving family waiting for him at home after each long day as a University High guidance counselor.*

By leading with these descriptive details, your audience can visualize the scene. They construct a picture of this man's personality, even before they read a single quote from your interview. Photos and video footage can help do some of the same things, but writing tells your audience what they are seeing. Words and images together are most powerful.

Your Turn

1. Pick a place where you can be alone for at least 15 minutes. Take detailed notes on everything you observe. Consider all of your senses, but for this exercise do not take your feelings into account.
2. Write a one-page description of your observations. Read your description to another student and listen while they read theirs to you.
3. S **Going Deeper.** Select one story you have written for publication or for a class assignment and add a section which includes detailed description.

Shocking Statement Leads

Another type of feature lead is sometimes called the shocking statement lead. In contrast to our previous examples, this one is just four words.

For sale: one town.

This time the interest grabber is the radical idea that a whole town could be for sale. In the shocking statement lead, the idea is to grab your audience's attention by giving them something they don't expect, an idea that challenges their assumptions. Then you follow up with a nut graf that answers the questions raised by your surprising lead.

Connie Carpenter, a film and television actress who bought a remote village in the Colorado Rockies, today put the town up for sale. Carpenter said she plans to sell Echo Cross Roads and buy an island in the South Pacific.

For the Record

Writing with Descriptive Details

Descriptive details are a big part of former New York Times reporter Rick Bragg's writing. The Pulitzer Prize winner started a story on the victims of the 1995 Oklahoma City bombing, which killed 168 people and injured nearly 700, this way:

After the explosion, people learned to write left-handed, to tie just one shoe. They learned to endure the pieces of metal and glass embedded in their flesh, to smile with faces that made them want to cry, to cry with glass eyes. They learned, in homes where children had played, to stand the quiet. They learned to sleep with pills, to sleep alone.

Here Bragg taps into his readers' emotions by listing challenges survivors face. If you look closely at this sample, you'll notice each element of Bragg's lead is a separate visual image. For him, the "aha" moments of writing were about connecting visual images to his words. "Usually it's just the image that sings out," Bragg told About.com.

YOUR TURN

What kinds of stories would benefit from each of these shocking statement leads?

- Sometimes you *can* judge a book by its cover.
- This wrestler is definitely not one of the guys.
- The last time he missed a day of school, Ronald Reagan was president.

Feature Leads to Avoid

When stuck for an idea, you might be tempted to write a question lead. *Do you know the most popular brand of cell phone?* is easy to come up with, but it's not a very effective way to begin a story. Your audience is looking for answers, not questions.

Starting your story with a quotation only works when you have just the right quote. That rarely happens. *"I had a wonderful time at the prom"* isn't going to grab your audience's attention. But *"I lay in the street with my leg bent behind my back and thought for sure I was going to die,"* just might.

Inexperienced reporters tend to begin stories with background leads. *Relay for Life is a program to raise money for cancer research and has been going on in Ourtown since 1985* is valuable information, but it belongs farther down in the story. It's way too boring for a lead.

Then there's the over-obvious lead. *Healthy eating is an important part of any wellness program.* Really? Healthy eating leads to wellness? Who knew? Or even worse: *Our town has many cultures, and each one has much to offer.* This one is both too obvious to mention and way too vague. Start with a specific example of culture, and describe it in vivid detail. Then generalize to the topic of varied cultures in your town if appropriate.

Finally, stay away from the cliché lead. Avoid them like the plague. Not even a mother could love these worn out expressions that are as old as the hills and twice as dusty. When you lead with a cliché, you tell your audience that this story wasn't worth the time to come up with a fresh idea. Be original.

Organize the Body

While breaking news stories often use the inverted pyramid (see Chapter 5), feature writers organize their stories in a wide variety of ways, depending on the style and purpose of the piece.

Chronological Order

Some stories work well when told in simple chronological order, beginning with what happened first, then second and so on. A first-hand account of your ride-along in a police car could be organized this way. After a brief summary lead or editor's note, begin at the beginning and tell the story step by step as you experienced it. Highlight the most interesting parts of the event and remember to include descriptive details of what you saw, heard and felt.

Parallel Narrative

One creative approach to organizing stories is the parallel narrative. In this form you tell two people's stories at the same time, alternating between one and the other. Used in many novels and movies, this organizational style ends with the two stories coming together. Think about the campaigns of two candidates for student body president, or a boy and a girl separately preparing for their big prom date.

Your Turn

1. Brainstorm a list of stories from your campus that would work well organized as parallel narratives.
2. **Going Deeper.** Can you think of a story that could be told effectively as three or more parallel narratives?

Sections

Many feature stories can be organized into logical sections. A feature highlighting students' reactions to a controversial assembly speaker could have a section for each differing point of view. Or one person's opinions on a variety of subjects could be divided into a section for each topic. Sometimes spaces provide the organizational structure, as in a room-by-room description of a new campus building under construction. You can logically organize historical features around years or decades, and your consumer pieces on products and businesses divide neatly into pros and cons. Sometimes a simple listing is the best way to organize your story, like the step-by-step instructions in a how-to piece.

And Now... Closer to Home

What Is an Editor's Note?

Sometimes publications precede a story with a brief note from the editor to put the story in context. Here's an example of an editor's note that might appear right above a firsthand account written by a reporter who rode along with police.

Reporter Jeremy Jones spent a recent evening riding in the back seat of a police patrol car. No, he hadn't been arrested. He obtained permission to ride along with officers so he could give readers of The Campus Times insight into what policemen experience on a typical night in Ourtown.

Question and Answer

A feature story focusing on just one person may use a question and answer format. It creates a conversational tone, and, if used sparingly, can provide welcome variety for your readers. It is easy to read and easy to write. You'll begin with a paragraph that sets up the story, giving your audience the facts they need to put the conversation in context. Then you will write your questions and your source's answers pretty much the way they occurred during the interview. Here's a sample.

> *Novelist Judy Jones will visit Campus High next week to promote her latest book The Longest Night. In a recent telephone interview, Jones told The Gazette staff about writing the novel and about her life as a writer.*

The Gazette: What gave you the idea to write this new book?
Judy Jones: When I was a little girl, I had a terrifying experience. I truly thought I was going to die.
TG: Without giving away too much and spoiling the book for your readers, can you tell us more about that experience?
JJ: Yes. It really was a dark and stormy night, and my parents had gone to the neighbors' house for a party.

Notice you do not need quotation marks since it's obvious you are using the exact words of the source and the reporter. It is perfectly acceptable to select some questions and answers from your interview while leaving out others, as long as what you publish accurately reflects the source's ideas.

The Wall Street Journal Formula

An organizing technique known as the *Wall Street Journal formula* first gained popularity in the 1940s when Barney Kilgore, then managing editor of The Wall Street Journal, declared, "It doesn't have to have happened today to be news." His paper would no longer use "today" and "yesterday" in its story leads and would adopt a more feature-oriented approach. A radical idea at the time, this was the beginning of what has also become known variously as the nut graf story, the news feature and the analytical feature.

Think of **The Wall Street Journal formula** story as a play in three acts. In Act I, you begin to tell the story of one person who is affected by the issue at hand. In Act II, you explain and discuss the main issue, and in Act III, you circle back to the person you introduced in Act I. Since this type of organization is a bit more complicated than the others, we'll discuss it in more detail, from beginning to end.

Worksheets

As we discussed in the section on feature leads, like the majority of feature stories, The Wall Street Journal formula begins with a soft lead—a brief story or piece of descriptive text that focuses on a person, a scene or an event. This gives your story a poster child, a specific example of someone who relates to your main idea. You might begin a story on the new tardy policy at your school by describing a freshman girl running down the hall as she tries to beat the late bell. Or you could start a feature on the increasing costs of higher education with the story of a senior boy whose parents just told him they can only afford to send him to the local junior college. The Wall Street Journal formula works especially well with stories about complex issues that might be rather dry if organized more traditionally. It also lends itself to stories featuring recent changes in issues that affect your audience, like school dress codes or graduation requirements.

In this type of story, writers go from the specific to the general. With photography in mind, think of the soft lead as a close-up shot. These first few sentences focus on a specific person, one who is affected by the issue. Immediately following the soft lead the camera zooms out to show the entire scene. This is the nut graf. As we discussed earlier, this paragraph or two explains what the story is about and why it is important. It follows up the specific example with general information on the focus of the story.

Here's an example of a soft lead followed by a nut graf in our story about the new tardy policy.

Soft lead:

Freshman Sally Smith has exactly 30 seconds to get to class. Knowing the consequences, she runs as fast as she can down the freshly waxed hallway. Her 25-pound backpack bounces crazily as she slides around the final corner. She can see her math teacher shaking hands with the last student to enter the classroom. The bell rings. The teacher steps inside. The door closes behind him.

Nut graf:

Campus High's new tardy policy has captured the attention of many students, with its tougher penalties on those who are late to class. Beginning this school year, teachers have been instructed to hand out detentions for every tardy.

But many wonder if the new policy is having the desired effect. Are more students showing up to class on time, or are they figuring out ways to beat the new system?

Now that you've written the soft lead and the nut graf, it's time to write the body of your story. In this section you will thoroughly discuss the issue, using what you've learned in interviews and other forms of research. You'll alternate between quotes from experts that support the story's thesis, statistics and other facts you have discovered that shed light on the issue, and reactions from others who are affected by the issue. In our tardy policy story, you would include comments from an administrator to explain the background and reasons for the new policy. Before and after statistics on tardiness as well as data on the number of students cutting class would be relevant. Quotes from teachers and students would help to round out the story.

The ending to a Wall Street Journal formula story is sometimes called a **circle kicker**. Here you return to the person you started with—the poster child. This provides balance and brings closure to your story. You've taken your audience from the specific to the general, and now you return to the specific. Since it is the last thing your audience sees, you will want to take as much care in writing it as you did with the lead.

Here's a circle kicker in our new policy story that opened with Sally Smith, the tardy freshman.

> *Smith is only a few seconds late when she opens the door to her math class. She writes her name and i.d. number on the tardy sheet clipboard near the door and slides quietly into her seat. Smith will join several dozen other students this afternoon for a full hour of after-school detention. "Maybe next time," she thinks, "I'll just ditch class and avoid all this hassle."*

Do Feature Stories Need Conclusions?

You might recall that, like essays you write for English class, features have a beginning, middle and end. So features need conclusions, right?

The answer to that question is "yes and no." Feature stories, like all journalistic stories, need to come to a satisfactory ending. If you raise questions, they should have been discussed. Your audiences should leave your story with a sense of completion, with the sense that all the important bases have been covered.

However, a feature story does not need a conclusion like the one you write in an essay. In English class you may have been taught to use different words to restate the thesis you introduced in your opening. The same technique may have applications in editorials or columns, where your opinions and conclusions are important. But in feature writing, the only opinions you include are the opinions of others.

Features end in ways that flow naturally from the organization of your story. The chronological story can end with the last event, the question and answer piece with the last answer, and the list story with the final item in the list. The Wall Street Journal formula calls for the story to return to a quote or situation involving the person introduced in the lead.

It is tempting to write a conclusion for every feature story, but the results may be forced—or contain editorializing. Most of the time, it's best to just finish telling your story and save the conclusions for your English class.

Analyzing a Wall Street Journal Formula Story

Chip Scanlan worked as a reporter for two decades at various newspapers around the country and has authored several books on journalistic writing. As a faculty affiliate at The Poynter Institute, a school for journalism in St. Petersburg, Florida, he published a section-by-section analysis of one of his own Wall Street Journal Formula stories. Visit www.poynter.org and search for "Too Young to Diet?," Scanlan's story on preteen dieting. Then, search for "Nut Graf, Part I" to read his insightful explanations of how the story fits together.

Chapter Ten

Review and Assessment

Recall

1. Explain the basic similarities and differences between feature, news and opinion stories.
2. What are seven types of feature stories?
3. What are five ways to organize feature stories?
4. How is an angle different from a topic?
5. What is the difference between a hard lead and a soft lead?
6. Which would be the most effective photo to accompany a feature story on the varsity football water girl?
   A. A shot of her posing for the camera.
   B. A picture of her pouring water from a bottle into a sweaty lineman's mouth during a time out.
   C. A photo of the entire football team posing with the water girl.

Critical Thinking

1. Explain why a photo taken of a student's face while she intently works on a painting in her art class might be more effective than a photo of her smiling at the camera holding her paintbrush.
2. Identify the person on your campus whose mug shot you would publish in each of the following stories.
   A. An ongoing issue story on the sorry state of your school's landscaping.
   B. A sidebar detailing the history of AP courses taught on your campus.
   C. A how-to story on applying for summer jobs.
3. Write one-sentence summaries of the angles you discover in five feature stories from student or professional publications.
4. The angle of your feature story on social media is that many students are becoming addicted to their digital devices, to the point where their face-to-face relationships are suffering. Write a soft lead of two to four sentences for each of these types: anecdotal, narrative, descriptive and shocking statement.
5. List two story ideas for each of the following organizational styles: chronological order, parallel narrative, sections, question and answer, and Wall Street Journal Formula.
6. Explain why this concluding paragraph is inappropriate for a feature story about your school's retiring volleyball coach and suggest a better way to end the story.

   So, here's wishing Coach Stevens many more successful years as City High School's head volleyball coach. We all love you.

Application

1. In a small group, choose a topic of interest to many people in your primary audience. Brainstorm at least three angles you could take in writing a feature story about this topic. Share your ideas with other small groups.
2. In a small group, look through past issues of your school's yearbook. Make note of significant events that would make for interesting historical features.
3. Using Standard English means your word choices, sentence structures, paragraphs and narrative follow the rules used by those who speak English. Well-written features are usually the product of editing. Write a personality profile, how-to story or firsthand account. Edit and revise your feature story until the ideas are polished and clear to the reader. Check that your writing follows Standard English grammar rules, such as subject-verb agreement, pronoun agreement and appropriate verb tenses.
4. Select a story from a student or professional publication that you think would be effectively told using the Wall Street Journal formula. Using the Wall Street Journal Formula Writing Map on the *Journalism* website, rewrite the story in that style, incorporating a "poster child" and adding a soft lead, nut graf and circle kicker.
5. Ask your adviser to put the names of random students, teachers and staff members in a hat. Then pull one out, find the person you drew, arrange interviews with them and at least two other people who know them. Then write a personality profile.

Chapter Ten

Journalism Style

Abbreviations and Acronyms

An *abbreviation* is a shortened form of a word or phrase. Examples include *N.Y.* for *New York* and *Mr.* for *Mister*. Sometimes abbreviations are pronounced as if the whole word were present. "Mr. Odinga spoke." Sometimes they are pronounced as separate letters. "He was interviewed by the FBI when he visited the U.S."

An *acronym* is a word formed from the first letter or letters of a series of words. *Scuba* is an acronym for **s**elf-**c**ontained **u**nderwater **b**reathing **a**pparatus. An acronym is pronounced as a single word.

Your stylebook may deal with local abbreviations and acronyms in its own way, but if you follow AP style, you should know these things:

AP style requires abbreviations for

- titles when used before a full name: *Dr. William Smith*, *Sen. Evelyn Jones*.
- some words after a person's name or a company name: *Martin Luther King Jr.* (no comma before the abbreviation), *John Snow, Ph.D.* (set off academic degrees with commas), *The Walt Disney Co.* (because *Co.* is part of Disney's official name).
- dates and numerals, but only when used with figures. **Correct**: *in 540 B.C., at 6:30 a.m., in room No. 7, on Sept. 15.* **Incorrect:** *Late in the a.m. on a cloudy Sept. day she asked for his room No.* Correct: *Late in the morning of a cloudy September day she asked for his room number.*
- months with more than five letters, but only when used with specific dates. **Correct**: *Jan. 16 and Sept. 11, 2001*. **Incorrect**: *Dec. 1941*. Never abbreviate March, April, May, June or July.
- *avenue*, *boulevard* and *street*, but only with numbered addresses. *The president lives on Pennsylvania Avenue. He lives at 1600 Pennsylvania Ave*. Spell out all other roadway designations: *His address is 2400 Barbary Road.*
- most state names in datelines when used with towns and military bases: *Reading, Pa., Fort Benning, Ga*. AP state abbreviations are not usually the same as the two-letter postal code abbreviations: *Ind.* vs. *IN*, *Conn.* vs. *CT*. Also, the two states not connected with any others (Alaska and Hawaii) and the six states with five or fewer letters (Idaho, Iowa, Maine, Ohio, Texas and Utah) are not abbreviated. Spell out all state names within the body of a story, whether used alone or with the name of a town or military base.

Some abbreviations are acceptable but not required.

You may use abbreviations your audience easily recognizes.

The CIA for *the Central Intelligence Agency* and *the U.N.* as *the United Nations* may be appropriate. If your audience recognizes *AP courses*, *the ASB* and *SAT tests*, use them; but if you are online, be sure you make things clear to everyone you hope to reach.

Use periods in most two-letter abbreviations.

For example, *U.S.* and B.A. are correct, but *AP* (for Associated Press) is written without periods. No periods are needed in longer abbreviations when the letters are pronounced: ASB, SAT, FBI, CBS. Note they are in all capitals.

If in doubt, look it up!

> Avoid alphabet soup. Use only abbreviations and acronyms that your audience will quickly recognize. When in doubt, spell it out.

Try It!

Which usage in each sentence is correct?

1. She was the best doctor/dr. he had ever visited.
2. Let me introduce you to Dr./Doctor Henry Green.
3. We refer to my dad as Robert Harris senior/Sr.
4. School starts this year on August/Aug. 25.
5. Last p.m./evening we had a great time.
6. I look forward to the picnic on Jul./July 4.
7. He grew up in a house on a major blvd./boulevard.
8. The address is 3346 Saginaw Road/Rd.
9. Camp Pendleton, California/CA/Calif./Ca. is near San Diego.
10. Davenport, IA/Iowa is on the Mississippi River.

Extend Your Knowledge

Style Exercises

Visit the *Journalism* website for additional information and practice in using abbreviations and acronyms.

Chapter Ten

Writers' Workshop

In these Writers' Workshops you will:

- Employ parallel construction for items in a series.
- Employ parallel construction in phrases, sentences and paragraphs.

Workshop 10.1

Parallels for Clarity

Mini-Lesson: Parallels All in a Row—Using Parallel Language with Items in a Series

Imagine a first draft of Julius Caesar's letter to Rome after the battle of Zela. "When I got here, after I had looked around, I smeared their faces in the dirt." Not nearly as effective as what he sent the Senate, "I came, I saw, I conquered."

The power of Caesar's message comes in part from its parallel structure. He uses parallel verbs—the same tense, voice and number—to indicate that the ideas are parallel. His parallels also suggest that for him conquering was just as easy as coming and seeing.

Parallels make for wonderful and easy reading, but they call for precise and skillful writing. Julius Caesar's first drafts may have been powerful, but ours may need revision—and a robust and supple vocabulary—to hone our parallels.

When you identify a series of people, use parallel language. If three people will speak at your baccalaureate, keep titles, names and descriptions in the same order for each speaker.

Not: *Linh Le, a senator from Santa Fe, a Navy chaplain from the hospital ship USNS Comfort, Lt. Cmdr. Jay Kersten, and the author of the bestselling novel "Ask," alumna Eileen Hammond, will speak.*

Better: *Sen. Linh Le, who represents the Santa Fe area, Lt. Cmdr. Jay Kersten, a Navy chaplain from the hospital ship USNS Comfort, and alumna Eileen Hammond, author of the bestseller "Ask," will speak.*

If you list verbs, stick with verbs. If you list nouns, stick with nouns. And if you list prepositional phrases, stick with prepositional phrases.

Not: *He writes poetry, is an actor and serves in Congress.*

Better: *He writes poetry, acts on stage and serves in Congress.*

Better: *He is a poet, an actor and a Congressman.*

Not: *He likes to fish from the pier, off a boat and surf fishing.*

Better: *He likes to fish from the pier, off a boat and in the surf.*

If you use gerunds and infinitives (such as *listening* and *to listen*), stick with one form or the other.

Not: *She likes to sketch with charcoal, to paint with watercolors and selling her work online.*

Better: *She likes to sketch with charcoal, to paint with watercolors and to sell her work online.*

Better: *She likes sketching with charcoal, painting with watercolors and selling her work online.*

Do not get lazy with the last item in a series.

Not: *The team plans to compete during Thanksgiving, to train during winter break and travel in the spring.*

Better: *The team plans to compete during Thanksgiving, to train during winter break and to travel in the spring.*

Parallel verbs are especially important. Follow Julius Caesar and use the simplest, clearest and most parallel form possible.

Don't turn verbs into nouns.

Not: *He learned code, designed infographics and made an analysis of how the human eye moved on the screen.*

Better: *He learned code, designed infographics and analyzed how the human eye moved on the screen.*

Don't turn verbs into adjectives, either.

Not: *She <u>took</u> online classes, <u>decided</u> to enroll in summer school and was <u>hopeful</u> she would graduate a semester early.*

Better: *She <u>took</u> online classes, <u>enrolled</u> in summer school and <u>hoped</u> to graduate a semester early.*

Apply It!

With a partner or in a small group, revise these two first-draft sentences from students who were writing about their portfolios.

1. Each photo that is taken gives more insight into what people think and how they are going to react and their feelings.
2. I do not go to my friends when I need response to my writing because they might not tell me the truth because they are afraid to hurt my feelings or that I will be mad at them.

Workshop 10.2
Parallels for Power
Mini-Lesson: Parallels Big and Small

Correlative conjunctions—*either/or, neither/nor, not only/but also, whether/or* and *both/and*—are most clear when they contain close parallels. They sometimes stretch our vocabularies and move us beyond our usual sentence patterns, but parallels can make our writing shorter and more powerful.

Not: *He either needs to study math right now, or they will assign him to math in summer school.*
Better: *Either he studies math tonight, or he studies math this summer.*
Not: *As finals approach, the twins are neither prepared, nor do the tests worry them much because they plan to join the circus.*
Better: *As finals approach, the twins are neither prepared nor concerned; they plan to join the circus.*
Not: *Not only is she pretty, but also everyone likes her and she gets good grades.*
Better: *She is not only pretty but also popular and academically talented.*
Not: *"Whether they give me an A or I just barely get by, I still get my diploma," the slacker wrote.*
Better: *"Whether I earn an A or a D, I still graduate," the slacker wrote.* (But then, slackers rarely revise their writing.)
Not: *John Randolph of Virginia said in 1820 that his Congressional colleague Henry Clay was both a very attractive and talented politician and very corrupt, so corrupt that he stank like a dead fish.*
Better: *John Randolph of Virginia said in 1820 that his Congressional colleague Henry Clay was "like a rotten mackerel in the moonlight, he both shines and stinks."*

Parallelism helps make relationships clear by repeating strategic words.

Ambiguous: *He wants to write programs that help children with disabilities access the Internet and study epileptic seizures.* (Will the children study seizures, or will he?)
Better: *He wants to write programs that help children with disabilities access the Internet and to study epileptic seizures.*
Ambiguous: *My brother annoys me by burping and laughing through his nose.* (Both at once?)
Better: *My brother annoys me by burping and by laughing through his nose.*

Powerful parallels may involve only a few parallel words, but they also may extend over several sentences or even multiple paragraphs.

Bill Plaschke used parallelism in the service of irony, in this case, to criticize a renowned golf club's lack of perspective. The parallels span four paragraphs, pivoting on *in honor of the ... anniversary* and *the club unveiled*. The first and third paragraphs of this excerpt are parallel but emphasize a contrast.

> *In honor of the first anniversary of the loss of the Eisenhower Tree, a famed 17th-hole landmark that was felled by an ice storm, the club unveiled a richly appointed memorial featuring a glass-encased slice of the actual tree trunk.*
>
> *"Many months in the making to mitigate against normal shrinking, cracking and twisting," he said proudly.*
>
> *However, in honor of the 40th anniversary of Lee Elder becoming the first African-American to play at the Masters, they did not unveil a memorial or throw a party or even invite Elder to play in Wednesday's par-three contest, much to his dismay.*
>
> *Instead, they threw him a few tickets.*

Apply It!

1. Look for effective parallelism in the following.
   A. The writing of professionals—find five examples.
   B. Your own work—as many examples as possible.
2. Look for three passages that would be improved by parallel construction, then revise them, seek response, revise again and publish them.
   A. In published writing by non-students.
   B. In your own work or the work of your peers.

Extend Your Knowledge

Extend

Visit the *Journalism* website for additional information and practice.

Chapter Eleven

Sports

Who won and why?

Photo by Allie Shorin, The Viking, Palo Alto High School

G-WLEARNING.com

While studying, look for the activity icon to:

- **Build** vocabulary terms with e-flash cards and matching activities.
- **Extend** learning with further discussion of relevant topics.
- **Reinforce** what you learn by completing style exercises, worksheets and end-of-chapter questions.

Visit the Journalism website: www.g-wlearning.com/journalism/

Chapter Objectives

After reading this chapter, you will be able to:

- Cover a game and write a recap of it.
- Use social media to provide in-game coverage of sports events.
- Shoot strong sports action photos.
- Write a player profile.
- Incorporate player, team and season stats in your sports writing.
- Create sports features that incorporate current issues, concerns and topics.
- Write a first-person sports column.

Key Terms Build Vocab

bullet time
decisive moment
game brief
live coverage
long-form feature
player profile
real-time updates
recap
sportrait
stats
Title IX

Before You Read...

Active listening is particularly important while conducting an interview. Practice active listening while your instructor presents a lesson. Focus on the main points and important details. Note any unfamiliar language and seek clarification when needed. How did you use prior knowledge to help you understand what was said?

Introduction

"I always turn to the sports section first. The sports section records people's accomplishments; the front page nothing but man's failures."

–Earl Warren, Chief Justice, Supreme Court

It is Monday morning before the first bell. Students in the halls talk excitedly, maybe even angrily, about a controversial call moments before the game-ending buzzer at Friday night's football game. As students pass the publications classroom, they pick up a copy of your publication, hot off the presses. Turning to the sports pages, they see ...

Freeze that moment. What *will* your readers see when they open the sports section and start reading? Coverage of Friday's game? A strong action photo of the key play? A sports column about the role of officiating and the impact of the new conference rules on Friday's game?

If you sent the paper to the printer before the Friday game, will your readers see a teaser that tells the audience to check online for the game summary? Online, will they find coverage posted Friday night? Did your staff's real-time updates via social media allow everyone to be well-informed and interested in the game, and its controversy?

Why Does the Sports Section Matter?

A high school publication has a daunting task: to keep tabs on everything about school for ten months every year. That would not be so hard if you did not also have homework, sports, community service, work, family obligations and a hundred other potential pressures and obligations.

Some may wonder why sports are allowed to occupy so much "real estate" in your print publications, so much space on your Web page, so much time in your broadcasts, so much data in your social media and so much energy from your staff. The seven news values hold the answer.

- **Proximity:** The sports section covers your school, the people you see every day. It covers the teams that may represent you and your community.
- **Timeliness:** Sports happen. A heat has just finished, the buzzer has sounded at the half, the season will begin in two days. While much of the school year may seem to unroll in slow motion, sports crackles and pops with timely events.
- **Impact:** Often 40 or 50 percent of a student body participate in sports. Those who do not participate have friends or relatives who do. For some, a team's success or failure represents the school's worthiness, power or heroic efforts. A sports team may be a proxy for the whole community, with alumni and local businesses following its fortunes.
- **Prominence:** Athletes can achieve a kind of visibility that is usually out of reach to all but a few students. The athletes may be the movie stars and supporting actors of your school, and what affects them affects their team, your school and perhaps the wider community.

- **Oddity:** Some of your most-read stories will be about traditions, people, places, objects and occurrences that never show up in the box scores. Sports is rich with these stories.
- **Conflict:** Where else can you find intense, even violent, conflict visible to the public from start to finish that begins and ends on a schedule?
- **Human interest:** Long-time UCLA basketball coach John Wooden said, "Sports do not build character. They reveal it." Your audience is interested in the people involved in and attached to sports.

With all these potential news values, sports can provide journalists with rich storytelling opportunities. Sports coverage can be bright, active, up-to-date and visually strong. Sports writing also provides a "lens" with which to look at issues that impact the lives of all students. A strong sports section might focus its lens on topics such as these:

- stress
- time management
- technology
- nutrition
- sleep
- head injuries and their impact on academic performance
- use of medical marijuana
- hazing
- racism
- drug addiction and recovery
- gender inequality
- homophobia
- physical rehabilitation and recovery from injuries

Your Turn

1. In a small group, brainstorm at least three specific sports stories from your school or community based on one of the topics listed above.
2. What other topics could be included in the list above? Add to the list.
3. **Going Deeper.** Describe how two of the topics or stories that you have discussed could serve as a lens for looking at topics that relate not just to sports but to your broader community as well.

Is It a Sport?

What should be covered in a high school sports section? That can be tricky. Is cheer a sport—or an activity? Is ballet a sport—or an art form? Is surfing a sport—or a hobby (Figure 11.1)? What about a student who

Figure 11.1 Some publications cover athletic activities, such as surfing, that may not traditionally be considered "sports."

Photo by Scotty Bara, The Viking, Palo Alto High School

has joined a local roller derby team—is she an athlete? Should your publication cover her and her team?

The simplest and most limiting policy, the policy that lists what your sports section cannot afford to ignore, is this, "If it is a school team, we cover it." If it is sanctioned by your school, has school-endorsed coach and school-based season schedule, it is a sport. Under this definition, cheer competitions should be included on your sports coverage list.

When you say you cover school teams, it means all teams and all the sports, not just the teams the staff *likes* or *wants* to cover, but *all* of the teams and sports.

Talk to athletes at your school about your coverage. Do not be surprised to hear students say some sports get all of the ink while other sports do not seem to exist. A strong sports section covers all sports

For the Record

Beyond Title IX: Girls Sports

Prior to the 1970s, many American high schools had strong boys sports programs that often featured the "big three": football, basketball and baseball, along with the other traditional boys sports of wrestling, track, tennis, swimming, water polo and hockey. Girls sports programs, however, offered fewer sports, included fewer athletes and were not supported at the same financial level as their male counterparts.

In 1972 federal legislation was passed to correct this gender disparity in scholastic sports programs. Collectively, this legislation became known as **Title IX**.

Since then, American high schools have seen tremendous expansions in the athletic opportunities available for female athletes and the recruiting of female athletes at the collegiate level. Not only are more girls playing sports, more sports are available to them. In the 2000s, for example, lacrosse became one of the fastest-growing U.S. girls sports.

during their seasons. Baseball belongs on the sports page, but so does badminton. Volleyball's win should be featured, but also girls cross-country competition.

But if you only cover sanctioned team sports at your school, you will miss students who participate at a high level in sports off campus. Surely they are athletes and deserve to be covered. Consider the California high school student who participated in the 2012 Summer Olympics in table tennis, though her school had no table tennis team. (Figure 11.2).

If your publication is to cover sports in your community, you need to broaden your coverage beyond just school teams. Having made that decision, you then need to decide what stories should be in sports and what stories should be covered in another part of your publication. For example, if a student participates in circus training, such as silks and trapeze, should that story be in the sports section or in the features section?

Consider these criteria: If it is an Olympic event, you are safe calling it a "sport." If it has appeared in the pages of Sports Illustrated or ESPN or on a broadcast sports segment, it is probably a sport. If it involves competition, physical ability, physical training, strategy and winners and losers, it is probably a sport.

Broadening coverage to include all your local athletes, not just those on school teams, can lead to vibrant story ideas. For example, one high school journalist spent an afternoon photographing fellow students who liked to participate in parkour (urban chase and obstacle competition). He came back with strong photos and a solid sports story that interested his audience.

Figure 11.2 Interesting sports stories, such as this story about an Olympic table tennis player, can be found outside of the school-sponsored teams.

LILY

started from the bottom

by AMI DREZ AND CHRIS SMITH

photo by Grant Shorin

Many Paly students recognize Lily Zhang ('14) as the girl who participated in the Olympics, met NBA superstar Kevin Durant and shook hands with President Obama. However, her road to glory is far more complicated than the posts we see on Facebook.

In an arena filled with hundreds of people at the U.S. Women's National Junior Championship, Palo Alto High School student Lily Zhang ('14) felt the pressure as her opponent was preparing to serve for match point. She recalls the sweat dripping down her face and her palms beginning to clam up. Holding a one-point lead, knew that everything she had sacrificed for was for this one play, this one moment.

"Everything was on the line," Lily said. " I had worked so hard to get here and it all came down to this."

Her opponent blasted the ball over the net. Without hesitation, she returned it back, feeling the rush of adrenaline spreading to her head. She had returned long-time rival Ariel Hsing's serve one last time to clinch the U.S. Women's National Junior Championship. This tournament marked a pivotal point in her career, but how did her journey begin?

As a wise man once said, "don't judge a book by its cover." On the surface, Lily may appear to live the perfect life, participating in the 2012 Summer Olympics in London at age 16, traveling, missing school, receiving sponsorships, gaining college attention and much more, but in reality, it is far from that. Between the lines, she has encountered many obstacles, making her road to glory more difficult than people might think.

When she was 12, while most children her age were attending Bar Mitzvahs and birthday parties in the summer, she traveled to China for intense table tennis training. At age 14, when other lads were spending time with their peers, she was practicing four hours of table tennis on a daily basis. At age 16, at the time many of her high school classmates pursued their drivers' licenses, she trained all summer and competed at the 2012 Summer Olympics in London. Starting from ground zero to now ranked sixth in the world for girls age 18 and under, Lily truly has never lived a normal life.

It all began for Lily at age seven when she went to the India Community Center (ICC) Table Tennis Program with childhood best friend and current Paly student Felicia Wang ('14).

"It started out as something just for fun and not serious," Lily said.

For the next two years, she practiced occasionally, playing every

30 | THE VIKING | www.vikingsportsmag.com

MARCH 2013

Story by Ami Drez and Chris Smith, Photo by Grant Shorin, The Viking, Palo Alto High School

If students at your school surf, race road bikes or dirt bikes, row crew, compete in ice skating, martial arts, curling, rock climbing, geocaching, gymnastics, ultimate Frisbee, skateboarding or skiing or snowboarding, they belong in your sports section (Figure 11.3). Talk to them and tell their stories.

Getting Started with Strong Sports Reporting

Strong, balanced sports coverage requires journalists to plan ahead and follow through on their commitments. Calendaring and scheduling help editors, reporters and photographers communicate with each other,

"Evergreen" Sports Story Ideas

An "evergreen" story is one written ahead of time, to be published as time, space and interest allow. It is not time sensitive but may be edited to become a timely story or a sidebar to a timely story. Evergreen stories allow your staff to invest significant time and resources in a story without the pressure of an immediate deadline. Strong publications and broadcasts keep a file of evergreen stories, to be published or adapted to changing circumstances.

Consider these topics for your evergreen file:

- *Concussions*. Young athletes sustain head injuries at least as often as do their older counterparts. Second impact syndrome, which can lead to death, also concerns athletes and your community. Watch for policies, laws, gear or practices that reflect an awareness of these issues.
- *Fitness routines*. How do different teams at your school work out for optimal strength, health and flexibility? This story has potential for visual storytelling.
- *The trainers.* A feature or profile on the trainers and others who keep the athletes in top playing condition can provide an interesting look behind the scenes.
- *Fields, pools, tracks.* The physical spaces where athletes train and perform vary considerably from school to school, or even within the same school. Athletes have strong opinions about the fastest pool in the conference or the best baseball field in the league. Try a feature on the turf, or the surfaces on the school track, or the divots in the soccer fields. Contrast the facilities two different teams use.
- *Research the best team at your school from 10 or 20 or 25 years ago.* Find the key players on a successful team from the past. Ask them to retell the story of their best season. Use school yearbook photos and pictures from those years to illustrate the piece.
- *Gear.* Choose any of the sports at your school, then do a piece on the gear required to do the sport, how the gear is put on and used, what it allows them to do, how the gear has changed over time, or how players feel about types and brands of gear. For soccer or cross-country, for example, the topic of cleats may provide good story material and great quotes. Research a sport for which rules and protection guidelines have changed over the past years and examine the impact of those changes on the game. Do improvements in safety make for a better game or a less interesting one?
- *"Where are they now?"* Look through yearbooks from the past decade. Which players had breakout seasons, or unusual seasons? Do you have athletes from your school who went on to play in university or semi-pro or professional teams? Do not ignore people who did not play after high school. Did athletics form—or damage—these people?

balance their schedules and still be present to cover their sports. Ideally editors help with this scheduling, but reporters also take responsibility to keep commitments and to enlist others to help when they cannot be where they promised to be.

Strong sports coverage requires that journalists attend many practices and games or matches during the season, not just a single game or event. It also can mean attending post-season activities if athletes and teams are highly successful.

Photo by Grant Shorin, The Viking, Palo Alto High School

Figure 11.3 Crew can be a school-sanctioned sport, but is more likely to be a club sport. Stories of students who participate in club sports can enrich a publication's sports section. *What athletic activities not sanctioned by the school are covered in your publications?*

Scheduling Sports Coverage

Most high school sports are held during three distinct seasons: fall, winter and spring, though the sports and their seasons will vary across regions of the country. At the beginning of the school year, journalists should create a master list of all school teams by season (Figure 11.4). This will help ensure that all are covered and allow you to begin planning your coverage.

As soon as possible, sports journalists create a master calendar that shows when and where each sport practices and competes and when post-season play may begin. Include the junior varsity and frosh-soph teams. They may become the strongest stories.

Your calendar allows sports writers and photographers to plan their coverage as well as their own busy schedules. With this type of advanced planning journalists may be able to arrange for someone else to help them when they cannot be at an important event. Planning ahead also allows editors to make sure everything is being covered and photographed as appropriate.

Good calendaring helps avoid bad coverage. Journalists know it may be hard to get a strong game story or a great photo on deadline in the

West High School's Master List of Sports

- Badminton
- Baseball
- Basketball (girls and boys)
- Cheer
- Cross-country
- Diving
- Football
- Hockey
- Golf (girls and boys)
- Lacrosse (girls and boys)
- Soccer (girls and boys)
- Softball
- Swimming
- Table tennis
- Tennis (girls and boys)
- Track and field (girls and boys)
- Volleyball (girls and boys)
- Water polo (girls and boys)
- Wrestling

Figure 11.4 A master list of your school's sports can help your staff create a sports calendar for every practice, game or other important sporting event for each team.

final week of the season. Rain happens, snow happens, injuries happen and life happens.

Good scheduling means that you have weeks, not days, to cover interesting games and take action photos that feature individual players. When the season ends, you can **recap** (summarize) the season based on solid reporting and a file of photos. It also means you will avoid competing with six other reporters covering six other sports for the good camera or the services of your best photographer.

Sports Events Are News Events

Scores and game recaps are breaking news. They need to be reported as swiftly as humanly, and electronically, possible. They also need to be reliable. If you rely on a buddy at the game to give you the score, you are reporting hearsay, not news. Reporters and photographers need to be physically present at a sports event. Phoning players and coaches for quotes about a game from the journalism room days after the event took place is *not* the way to report breaking news.

Journalists gather the five W's of the game, and possibly of the season, by having their cameras and their notebooks at the ready when the teams are playing. The reporters note scoreboard times when important plays take place and listen for key stats throughout the game. They may take a hundred photographs each game, but like or use only a dozen.

Journalists who are physically at the game can accurately report scores and recap the game afterward, but in addition, they are there to report newsworthy events. At the very least, their reporting can

Seven Guidelines to Keep in Mind About Sports Coverage

1. Provide balanced coverage of male and female teams and sports, including visual representation in photos and videos.
2. Cover all sports, not just the "big" sports. Badminton, cross-country and gymnastics take incredible amounts of time and commitment, and deserve to be covered.
3. Tell the story of the whole team, not just the stars.
4. Focus on the story, not just the score box, of a game or competition.
5. Keep it fair. The same ethics apply to sports coverage as to any other coverage. Do not let your publication be used to promote private agendas. Consult with your editor before publishing anonymous reports, such as player complaints about the coach or other players. Cover tough stories when the public has the right to know, but always with solid research, strong sources, and balance.
6. A season is not just one game. Provide scores and summaries throughout the season.
7. Make it easy for your audience to get accurate, updated sports stats from your publication.

contribute to a meaningful season recap. But if you publish online, you can publish a game story for each competition, including JV and frosh-soph games. If you report accurately and write well, your stories will be read and appreciated more often than you suspect, and you will develop a following as a sports writer.

Before You Begin Your Coverage

Once you know which sport you are going to cover, do some research. If you are not familiar with the goal of the game or how the game is scored, learn about it. Ask someone who plays the sport to explain the basics and the key strategies to you as if you were an interested 10-year-old. Never be afraid to ask about what you do not understand. Find out what abilities make a standout player.

Learn the technical terms and lingo specific to that sport. Each sport is like a little country with its own language. A good reporter will make sure she speaks the language and uses the lingo accurately in any sports articles. Use a term incorrectly, and you lose credibility.

The lingo itself can be fascinating. In hockey, for example, a "hat trick" has nothing at all to do with head gear. In basketball, "double doubles" sound like an ice cream sundae, but actually refer to a specific threshold a player reaches in scoring, rebounding and assist statistics.

While it is possible to look up the sport's terminology online, you may do better by talking with a player or coach in person. Ask him to describe the common terms that players of that sport use to describe

Tips for Planning Sports Coverage

- Ask your school's athletic director for a list of teams, coaches (with contact information) and the calendar of games in each level in each sport at the beginning of the year. Check for revisions at the start of each season.
- Post the game schedules in your publications room and make it available digitally to everyone on staff.
- Update the calendar monthly and cover—or arrange coverage—for every home game.
- Consider using beats for sports coverage, assigning specific reporters and photographers to cover each sport for the season.
- Plan ahead for the big games. Often reporters and photographers may require special credentials for big games or post-season play. Check on the availability and condition of your staff's cameras and other equipment. Check the lighting of the venue in advance, if possible.
- If you face any administrative or coaching staff restrictions for photographers or reporters wanting access to fields or players, request a *written* reason explaining the restrictions. You may want to get parents and players involved in requesting coverage of these events. This could help you get the access you need. School publications have a right to cover the events of the school community, and sports games are an important part of what is happening in a school.

scoring, statistics or specific moments in the action. Doing this in person allows you to get a better "feel" for the sport. In addition, you can ask for clarification when a term is confusing or odd.

Continue your background research on the sport by reading online or print sports news from professional media sources. You will learn how writers talk about that sport, and how they incorporate sports-specific terms into their reporting. It is hard to write sports if you do not read sports.

Learning to Cover Sports

The first game story you write will probably not be a strong one, but your second one will be better. How do you get past those first few weak stories?

For the Record

Colorful Sports Terms and Phrases

Sports has a language of its own. Here are just a few examples:

love (tennis): means "zero," and is thought to stem from a mispronunciation of l'oeuf ("egg" in French)

flea flicker (football): a quarterback hands the ball off to the running back, who quickly tosses the ball back to the quarterback, who throws it downfield (the play resembles a dog who uses a quick flick of his paw to get rid of fleas)

duffer (golf): a person who plays golf without much skill

pickle (baseball): situation in which a base runner gets caught between two bases

can of corn (baseball): a lazy fly ball

Lambeau Leap (football): a colorful and well-known move in which a Green Bay Packer player jumps into the stands (at Lambeau Field) after scoring a touchdown

suicide squeeze (baseball): a "squeeze play" occurs when there is a runner on third base, and the batter bunts the ball in the hope that the third base runner will make it to home plate while the batter is thrown out at first base. It's a "suicide" squeeze if the runner on third, rather than waiting to see if the batter successfully bunts the ball, heads for home as soon as the pitcher releases the ball.

dormy (match play golf): leading by as many holes as remain to be played

catching a crab (rowing): a blade error in which the rower doesn't get the oar out of the water in time, causing major drag as the momentum of the boat surges forward. If the boat is moving even at moderate speeds, the blade handle can strike the rower in the chest or face, go over the rower's head, or even eject the rower from the boat.

nutmeg (soccer): kicking a ball between the legs of an opponent

nickel back (football): the fifth defensive back brought in on more obvious passing downs, such as third and long (standard defense has four defensive backs)

put him in the popcorn machine (basketball): to confuse a defender with feints and gyrations while handling the ball, generally followed by scoring

charity stripe (basketball): the free throw line

slam dunk (basketball): a player leaps up and jams the ball through the basketball hoop in a showy display of athletic ability

ducks on the pond (baseball): runners on base

decleater (football): a powerful tackle that takes a runner right out of his cleats

After you have done your background research, watch a game, match or meet covered by the professional press. Write your game story first, *then* read what the professionals wrote. Make a list of the facts the professional press included that you left out. Scratch out anything you put in that was not needed. Were you inaccurate in any of your facts?

Another helpful technique is to follow a more experienced journalist as she covers a competition. Write your story, compare it to the other journalist's work and learn from the difference.

Your Turn

You can enjoy the experience and at the same time practice covering sports by conducting a mock sports event. Assemble the members of your class for a game of dodgeball or basketball. Determine who will serve as reporters and photographers, and who will be the players and referees. (If possible, the referee should be a student who has actually officiated games since referees are a key part of any sports event.) Photographers should take photos during the "game," while reporters record details. Make the game short (20 to 30 minutes) so there is enough time after the game for reporters to practice interviewing the players. Reporters should write a game brief for the next day's class.

Photo by Jonathan Dai, The Winged Post, The Harker School

Sports Coverage Work Plan

At some point after doing your research and practicing your reporting and writing, it will come time for you to do your actual sports reporting. Where do you start? As simple as it may seem, your first task will be to find the team, the coach and the team statistician (if there is one) wherever they hold their team practices.

For the sport that you are assigned, head to a scheduled practice in person and politely introduce yourself (at an appropriate time) to the head coach and assistant coaches. Ask for their names, official team titles, and also request their contact information in case you have questions or need a quote as the season goes on.

Find out who keeps the **stats** for the team and *where* they are kept. Sometimes team stats are kept only on paper, but more and more teams keep their stats in an online file, where team members can easily access the stats.

These first meetings are important to your success as a reporter. You want the coaches, players and statisticians to get to know you and become familiar with your face and your presence at practices and games. Tell the coaching staff that you will be covering the team at the next game (or for the season, if your staff elects to go with beat coverage).

Here is a basic work plan for covering a single sports event.

1. preparation
2. setup
3. live coverage during the game
4. game brief
5. comprehensive recap

Preparation

Before heading out to cover the event, you need to prepare. This means double-checking the starting time and location of the game a day in advance. Do not take it for granted that all games will be played exactly as indicated on the schedule. Sometimes there are changes due to field conditions, bus schedules, school conflicts or other situations.

Getting Comped

Check in with the athletic director or someone from the sports booster club to find out how to get your name added to the list of "comped" people who will attend that game for free. Standard practice in the media is that if a person is covering an athletic event for a publication, that person need not pay admission to the event. Press coverage provides a public service to the school community, and therefore, media should not be asked to pay. Reporters are not there as spectators. For postseason play, you may need to get additional press credentials depending on your league or conference policies. If you need help, talk to your athletic director well in advance of the event.

Doing It All

High school reporters often work alone as they cover regular season games or events. This means you will be doing all of the reporting, providing social media updates and shooting still and video photography by yourself. Do not worry. If you have prepared properly and developed your own game plan as you head out to the field, you can easily accomplish all of the tasks necessary to create great game coverage.

If you will be taking photographs of the event, be sure to talk with your editor or designer before the event to determine which shots you will need. Bring your shot list with you to the event.

Assembling Your Tools

After you know for certain where you need to be, and you have added your name to the media access list, collect your tools for the game.

- Bring a reporter's notebook and pens, as usual.
- Check out a camera with a fast shutter speed and telephoto or telephoto zoom lens, assuming your program has this photo equipment available. A fast shutter speed is a must for high-quality still photos of any sport.
- Pack an extra battery for the camera. The duration of many sporting events is longer than the life of some batteries. It is not uncommon to have the first battery die just as the game or match is heading into its final, crucial minutes.
- Add a shotgun mic, if you have one, for recording interviews and game highlights with better sound quality.
- Use a digital recorder for interviews. (A smartphone also works well.)
- If you don't have the ability to shoot video with your assigned camera, plan on using a smartphone. Smartphones now have built-in lenses and digital video options that will allow you to shoot, edit and post great footage. The earlier advice about battery life holds true for smartphones, so plan ahead. Many high school journalists who have covered sports have had their phones or other digital devices die in the middle of an interview or while shooting a clip of game action. Make sure your device is fully charged before you go to the event. If possible, bring an external, spare battery pack.

Checking the Weather Report

On game day, dress appropriately and allow yourself enough time to make sure you arrive before the action starts. It is usually acceptable practice to wear a sweatshirt or jacket in your school colors. For outdoor sports, it can feel chillier on the sidelines than it does on a crowded bleacher, so think about bringing gloves or a hat to keep warm.

Anticipate the possibility of rain, sleet or snow. The fans can leave if they are cold or wet, but you cannot. You must stay to cover the game for as long as the game goes on, and after the game. The good news is that games played in tough weather conditions often provide great opportunities for fabulous quotes and riveting sports photos.

Make sure you protect your equipment from the weather and wet conditions. For example, you can quickly re-purpose a plastic garbage bag to cover and protect your camera. Just cut or tear a small hole in the bag for the front of the lens to peek through.

Showing and Honoring Your Credentials

It is standard practice to wear a laminated press pass with your name, staff position, school name and year on it. It is personal preference whether you put your pass on a lanyard, on a clip or attached to a camera bag, but it must be easily visible on your person while you are near the field of play. It also is helpful to have the athletic director, principal or vice principal sign your press pass before it is laminated.

Press credentials serve several functions. They lend an air of official status (as press), calm game officials who may otherwise jog over and ask who you are and why you are on the sidelines, and tell people in the stands who are wondering why you are on the sidelines that *you* have press authorization to be there.

A quick word of caution: A code of ethics accompanies this kind of special access to athletic events. If you have press credentials and are attending the game for free, you have an implied contract with the schools and teams involved. This implied contract says that you are doing the job of reporting and photographing the event. You are *not* there to be a fan, or hang out in the stands with friends or to pal around with players on the sideline, in the dugout or on the bench. You are there to work.

Another aspect of this code of ethics is that you never "lend" your press pass to anyone simply to allow that person to get into the game for free or to provide that person access to the sidelines. On many staffs, loaning your credentials for non-journalism purposes is grounds for immediate dismissal from the staff or revocation of staff privileges.

Figure 11.5 Getting close to the action will improve your chances of getting a high-quality action shot.

Courtesy of Ellen Austin

Setup

As mentioned previously, well-prepared sports reporters show up before the game, prior to the first pitch or opening tip and preferably before the announcer calls the names of all of the starting players.

Situate yourself in a location with a good viewing angle of the action, which could be a spot on the sidelines or in the stands (Figure 11.5). Make sure that you have a good field of view for shooting photos and video.

In your notebook, record the basic facts before the game gets underway: date of the game, location, conditions (weather, lighting, heat and cold, rain or snow). This level of detail will help you report this single game and may also come in handy when writing a season recap, pulling up specific game highlights or memories.

How Big Was the Crowd?

If the crowd is too big to count, how do you give your audience a sense of the size of the crowd attending a sports event, or any other kind of event? You may attempt to verify actual attendance numbers from event sponsors, but be aware they may want their event to seem better attended, and therefore more successful, than it was.

Most of your readers or listeners do not want an exact number for large crowds, such as "the game attracted 477 people." They will be happy to know that "over 450 people" attended the game or "almost 500 people" attended.

One substitute for an attendance number is to show your audience the scene through whatever media are available to you. Shoot images from a high point, such as the press box of a football field or the top row of the gym. Recording ambient sound can give your audience an indication of the size of the crowd.

You can also use descriptions to indicate how large the crowd was. How far away did people have to park? How long were the lines to the entrance? Describe the area the crowd covered and where the overflow extended.

Sometimes only a number will give your audience a sense of the size of the gathering. Getting a rough count of a large group—such as the crowd at a basketball game—takes skill, practice and preparation.

Follow these instructions to estimate crowd size in your school's gym.

1. Go to the gym. Sketch the bleachers.
2. Count the rows in the bleachers.
3. On your sketch, divide the bleachers vertically into equal sections. The bleacher handrails and walkways or the supports under the stands may help, or you may rely on markings behind or under the stands.
4. Count the number of sections.
5. Note any large areas blocked off from public seating, such as an announcer's box. How many rows does it take up? How much of a section does it take up?
6. Next, find a picture of the gym when it is packed. Make sure the picture shows at least three rows of one of the sections you identified in step three.
7. Count the number of people sitting on three packed rows in that section.
8. Divide the number by three to get the average number of people sitting in one row of one section when it is packed. This is your key number, so count and multiply carefully.
9. Multiply this key number by the number of rows in a section.
10. Multiply by the number of sections.
11. If necessary, subtract for any unusable seats, such as the announcer's box.

You should now have a good estimate of the number of people in attendance if the stands are packed. If your gym has identical stands on two sides of the basketball court and both sides are packed, be sure to multiply the number by two.

Use the same technique with photos of three lightly filled rows. This will give you an estimate for a more lightly attended event.

Collaborate with other staff members to ensure accuracy. If possible, use several different pictures and compare your results with those of classmates.

Save a master copy of your sketch and your estimates for lightly filled and tightly packed rows. You will use this master document many times as you report events that take place in the gym. When a function has both packed and lightly packed rows, take a minute to highlight or shade the sections that are lightly packed. Use a different color or type of shading to mark the densely packed rows. It will be easy to estimate the attendance later.

You will find additional measuring tips, such as guidelines for estimating the density of a crowd and measuring without a tape measure, on the *Journalism* website. Extend

Include crowd size in your notes, even if you do not think you will include it in your story. Look around and count the people at a small event. Estimate or ask the ticket collectors if you are in a large stadium.

Jot notes as you survey the scene before the event starts. Who is in attendance? Is it mostly parents? Are many students at the game? Are there scouts in the stands? Are there any alums who are back to watch the game? Is there a "celebrity sighting" in the stands that might make a good secondary interview and sidebar for the game recap?

If one is available, grab a game program to use for additional info or stats later. Review the photo shot list of specific images needed for strong coverage of this game, especially any shots needed of key players in both offensive and defensive moments.

Pay attention to the other team's players and names. It is a mark of quality reporting to identify the *other* players by name, as well as your own. This can give your writing a professional touch since too often high school reporters overlook the other team in reporting specific details.

Live Coverage

Given the increasing participation in social media and the continuing transition to mobile devices, strong sports reporting should appear (literally) in the reader's hands, whether *during* a sports event or shortly after the final buzzer. As more and more schools take their publication programs online, the opportunity to provide cutting-edge, **live coverage** has never been easier, or faster.

Sports audiences are a devoted bunch. This means that if you provide **real-time updates**, you have an excellent chance of developing a loyal following. Of course those real-time updates are of no value unless you tell your audience in advance where to find them. If your audience knows ahead of time where you will be posting, they will be looking and waiting for your first post.

Whichever social media platform you use for your publication, the principles of reporting will be the same. As you take notes in preparation for your full story, you will also be posting quick reports on key plays in real time throughout the duration of the game (Figure 11.6).

Your live posts need to be concise, accurate and free of bias. Follow AP style and your publication's guideline for social media posts. Avoid passive voice in live posts. With so few words to work with, choosing action verbs will better communicate the essence of the game's movements and pacing.

Figure 11.6 Twitter can be a useful tool for posting live reports of key plays during a sporting event. *How does your publication utilize social media?*

Start your live coverage as the game gets underway. Provide the basics: Who is your school playing? What's their season record? Where is the game happening?

It helps to think about the score of a game and the actual game itself as a breaking news event. Your audience wants to hear about what's happening as it happens. They will "stay tuned" if you continue to provide in-game coverage.

Continue with live coverage, focusing on providing updates immediately as big plays happen. Keep the score updated as halftime, innings or periods end.

If possible, include a photo or short video clip with your key posts. Using your handheld smart device will usually be the fastest and easiest way to do this.

When the game ends, post immediately a closing to the "live" coverage. In the same post, tease the game brief that will be coming soon so that your audience knows to watch for more.

Game Brief

The bread and butter of basic sports coverage is the **game brief**, a thumbnail overview of the game. Your goal is to post the brief via social media or online almost immediately after the game. You can accomplish this faster than you might think because you will have already written much of the content for the brief in your earlier posts and notes.

But before you can begin writing your brief, you have one last reporting task. You need a quote. As soon as the game ends or after posting your closing to the live coverage, hustle over to the players and coaches as they head to the locker room or bus. Interview them to get their thoughts on the game. Include the strongest insights and comments in your brief.

The brief can be as short as 100 to 200 words. It starts with a summary news lead of up to 35 words, including the basic facts of who played, where, when and the final score (the season record and changes in the league standings could also be included). You will also need a captioned photo and a description of at least one key moment, highlight, or turning point

And Now... Closer to Home

Covering Club Sports

In increasing numbers, high school athletes play on both a school team and a club team (a private team with its own schedule, ranking, league). While coverage of the school's own teams is always the primary interest for your school community, the club teams do provide other options for story ideas and another way of looking at sports in off-campus venues. For example, you could question players about what it is like to have multiple coaches and how the players balance the different, possibly conflicting, suggestions and strategies from the different coaches.

in the game. Choose the most significant play or plays. You will either expand on your live coverage or write from your notes. You may not be able to decide until the game is over which plays should be included in your brief or which ones deserve expanded coverage.

Experienced reporters may write much of the brief during the game, in between taking notes, shooting photos and videos and doing their online updates. They write their summary lead after the game and place it at the head of what they have already written. In that way they can post a game brief before leaving the event. As a beginning reporter do not expect that you will be able to accomplish this so quickly and easily. You will become more efficient as you gain more experience.

Sometimes a game brief is all that your publication wants or needs. In other situations the game brief may be all that the reporter assigned to the game has time to complete. And that is OK, because if this were *"all"* that your audience had, they would still have a great deal: real-time game coverage informing them of key plays as they happen, plus a short recap and a photo that they could access shortly after the game ends.

Comprehensive Game Recap

The game brief is often an intermediate step on the way to a more comprehensive game recap to be published in a different medium, such as a print magazine. For other staffs, who may not be able to cover every game in a team's season, the comprehensive game recap is an option for covering one game (hopefully a key matchup or big game) and providing a longer (400–700 words), more complete story of the game for readers.

To write a comprehensive game recap, follow the steps outlined previously for preparation, setup and game coverage. Detailed notes on the stats and play-by-play are essential to making a good recap sound lively and in the moment.

Great quotes are vital to a quality recap. Get to the players and coaches before they leave the field or locker room, and make sure that

Writing Sports With a Voice

How do you develop your own voice for sports reporting? Here are some tips:

- Use strong, descriptive verbs.
- Interview your school's players, coaches and fans to get their perspective on the game. Their insights can add an extra dimension to your reporting.
- Also interview the opposing team's players and coaches. Their view of your team's players and performance can provide an interesting angle to a game recap or profile.
- Do not just interview the players and coaches, quote them. Quotes can become the "heart" of any good sports story.
- Do not include your opinions. Opinions belong in columns and commentary, not in game briefs, recaps and player profiles.

your questions are specific to that day's game, not just generic questions that an athlete or coach can answer with a stale sports cliché. Do not ask, "How did you think the game went?" Instead, ask the key player, "What were you thinking as you went diving for the ball in the third inning and you could see the runner rounding third?"

In general, the more players and coaches you interview, the stronger your story can become. Try for a minimum of three players, plus the coach. Also, head to the opponent's sideline and interview your rival's coaches and players. It can be illuminating to hear what the opposing player was thinking or planning as a key play got underway. These quotes may provide balance and an added dimension to your reporting.

When you have everything you need, it's time to go home and write your recap. Here is what you need to write a recap:

- Names of players
- Basic facts of the game, including the score, stats, key plays and the players' names who made the plays. It is a good idea to verify your stats with the team statistician before you leave the game.
- Season record (always a part of the recap, and goes into brackets when your team is mentioned the first time)
- Colorful details of moments in the game (sight, sound, color, smells, the crowd's vibe)
- An angle (What is the "story" of this game? What aspect of the game should you focus on to give the reader a sense of what made this game special?)
- Quotes (from home team, from opponents, from coaches, from parents, from people in the crowd)

In general, the sooner a comprehensive recap can be published, the better. Even if the recap is not seen until the next print edition, however, a well-written recap will provide your audience a much fuller and richer experience of the team and the game than they would have received from live posts and postgame recaps.

A good comprehensive recap is not a simple, chronological retelling of the game. Strong game recaps focus on the most important moments of the game and present them in a format very much like an inverted news-style story. The well-done recap shows the reader how certain moments and certain players in that particular game made the difference, whether for the better or the worse.

A strong recap also often has a colorful and attention-getting first graf that gives the reader a sense of what made the game unique. Writing with flair is one of the hallmarks of a strong sports writer.

Figure 11.7 on the next page is a mid-season game recap of a boys baseball game, written by a senior staff writer. This recap is about 500 words. The writer has found a "story" for this game—the standout performance of the centerfielder—and has built the comprehensive game summary around that core. Notice the use of strong, active verbs throughout the game summary and the use of quotes to provide a first-person sense of what the game felt like from the players' perspectives.

Along with strong writing and stats, the online recap works well when it includes slide shows of great photos from the game, as well as video clips. A full-game recap with video footage and accompanying voice-over is a powerful addition to your multimedia coverage of the game.

Figure 11.7 Active verbs, stats and quotes strengthen this game recap of a mid-season boys baseball game. The lead provides the story's angle.

THE VIKING

Palo Alto High School sports news

Fall Sports | Winter Sports | Spring Sports | Scores & Schedules | Visuals | Features | Columns | About

Foug's two-out, game-winning single lifts Vikings over Maria Carrillo

by Kevin Dukovic

James Foug may only stand a mere 5 feet 9 inches tall, but the senior centerfielder came up big Saturday afternoon.

In a game that was dominated by solid pitching, Foug had two hits, including a game-ending single in the bottom of the seventh inning, and Paly (2-3) rallied past visiting non-conference opponent Maria Carrillo (2-1) 2-1.

The Vikings entered the home half of the seventh inning trailing 1-0. A leadoff walk by clean-up man Rowan Thompson ('13) followed by a bloop single by designated hitter (DH) Danny Erlich ('14) set the table for catcher Alec Furrier ('13), who drove home Isaac Feldstein ('13) on an RBI groundout.

Two batters and two outs later, the Pumas then elected to intentionally walk Sean Harvey ('13) to face Paly's ninth hitter, Foug.

With the score knotted at 1-1 and runners on second and third, the lefty slapped a two-out, two-strike curveball into shallow left field to cap a late comeback victory for Paly.

"I was just trying to make contact," Foug said about his final at-bat. "And especially with two strikes I just wanted to put the ball in play and make the defense do something and luckily it found left field."

Rohit Ramkumar ('13), who started on the mound for Paly and tossed five scoreless innings before conceding a go-ahead RBI single in the sixth, was impressed with how his teammate handled himself in the at-bat.

"Some guys will get discouraged when they have two strikes," Ramkumar said. "But [Foug] battled and managed to get the hit and it was a big win."

Foug went two for three and received plenty of praise from his head coach Erick Raich for his performance and style of play.

"He's been a grinder all year," Raich said. "He's the kind of guy that you look at and say he'll beat you in multiple ways. You play back, he'll put a drag bunt down. You wanna play up? He'll hit the ball by you. He's great on the bases; he's smart and fast. He just plays hard and he attacks the game."

While Paly didn't overpower the Pumas offensively (the Vikes amassed seven hits, six of which were singles), Raich was very pleased with his team's overall effort.

"I thought we finally played our 'A' game today," Raich said. "We did all three aspects well. We threw strikes on the mound, we played great catch behind our guy and we were hitting the ball hard at guys. It was great to see us kind of scrap in the final inning there. We didn't do anything miraculous, but we played Palo Alto baseball by putting pressure on the other team. This is probably the happiest I've been all season from the standpoint not that we won, but that we played well finally. We played the way we're capable of playing."

The Vikings, who started their season with three straight losses, have now won two in a row and will look to build on this momentum Wednesday when they host league opponent Homestead High School.

Story by Kevin Dukovic, The Viking, Palo Alto High School

Your Turn

1. For the recap in Figure 11.7, write every verb the writer used on a separate sheet of paper. What is your evaluation of the writer's verb choices?
2. **Going Deeper.** Now, select one team practice or game event on your campus this week. Grab your notebook, go to that sport event and try writing a recap. When you are done with your first draft, circle all of your verbs. Are they vibrant and active? If not, start editing your recap by replacing them with specific, active "sports worthy" verbs.

If you are unable to achieve that level of multimedia presentation, try to include raw clips (shorter clips of 10 to 20 seconds) of several key moments in the game. For print-only publications, run the recap with a large photo (or several photos) to maximize the impact of the reporting.

Beyond the Game Recap

The backbone of strong sports reporting centers on providing well-written, consistent coverage of seasonal games and matches of all of the sports at your school. If, however, the sports segment of your publication consists of nothing but recaps of these games, you will have a flat, uninspiring sports section.

And Now... Closer to Home

Using Social Media to Reach Your Audience Immediately

As you become more experienced and establish a rhythm for your sports reporting, you will want to begin and then increase your live coverage on social media. More than almost any other activity on campus, sports events are the events that your audience wants to hear about as the action unfolds. They want to know who won (and how), as soon as the outcome is determined. The bigger the game—a postseason conference championship or the matchup against your historic rival for example—the more you should plan to post throughout the game.

The platform(s) your publication uses for social media will help determine what you need to upload during the game. At a minimum, consider doing an early post, a halftime post and a final score recap or key play post. While words can do the job, a photo or a video clip is also highly recommended for inclusion in the posts.

For short clips you may want to use a handheld device such as a smartphone, which is designed to seamlessly upload directly to social media platforms. A DSLR camera provides higher resolution video and allows you to benefit from using interchangeable lenses, but it also requires a more cumbersome uploading and editing process, which is not easy to do in the middle of covering the game.

If you only publish every month or so, use social media to provide micro bursts of sports coverage on game days. Then use the comprehensive recap or game feature for your regularly published coverage.

Readers come to the sports section to feel immersed in the action, drama, issues and emotions associated with competitive events. While game recaps are essential to strong sports coverage, they provide just one piece of the whole picture for a robust sports section.

Sports Features

Sports can focus a lens on topics beyond sports that interest and affect students. Sports features give sports writers the opportunity to write about players, gear, issues, light moments, old games and famous alumni, to name but a few topics that can enliven your sports section and engage your readers.

Player Profiles

A standard feature for any sports section is the **player profile**. Zooming in on a single player adds personality to the sports pages.

Pro sports rely heavily on player profiles. The covers of ESPN magazine and Sports Illustrated, for example, usually feature a profiled player because the editors know that fans will pick up those magazines to find out what is going on behind the scenes in their favorite sport.

A strong player profile begins with research. Know the player's stats and her strengths before you do the interview. Ask questions more interesting than "What do you like about your sport?" Look for a fresh angle; do not provide just another take on the games, scores and stats that has probably already been reported in your publication.

Although interviews with the subject of the profile produce much of the material for your piece, a well-written player profile will have multiple sources. Think of the player as the hub of a wheel. The spokes that radiate out from the player are sources (coach, teammates, parents, fans and friends) who can speak to different aspects of the player's life. Sometimes it is even appropriate to talk to opponents who have played against this player. With interviews from these sources, the profile can build a more interesting picture of the player.

Sometimes the key player on a team is not the dominant scorer, but rather the spirit leader of the team. If you watch baseball, for example, you will hear announcers talking about the "dugout leader" who keeps the team going and energized, no matter what. That player may not post the top stats or score the most runs, but he is vital to the team's synergy and success.

Find out who the "dugout leader" is at your school, whether in baseball or another sport, and write a profile of that player. Or profile the athlete who faced a tough injury a year or two ago yet is still playing the sport (or has transitioned to another sport). Or the athlete who has faced a life-threatening illness, such as cancer, yet continues to play the sport.

Where-Are-They-Now Profiles

The where-are-they-now profile is a type of player profile. Almost every school has alumni who were famous athletes in their high school days. Look through online resources, old yearbooks or old issues of your school paper to find those names. Then start making phone calls and sending emails to find out what has happened in that person's life since graduating from high school. Sometimes an athlete has continued his successful sports career; sometimes he has advanced in other careers that are equally interesting (Figure 11.8).

Alumni pieces can sometimes lead to surprisingly interesting and successful stories. At one high school, an Internet search by staff writers turned up the name of a former alumnus who had won Olympic gold medals in wrestling 30 years earlier. When the writers started researching, they found out that the Olympic wrestler's life had been tragically cut short by a wealthy sponsor who shot and killed the wrestler at the training facility where he was working out. That piece, which started as a simple where-are-they-now about a wrestler named Dave Schultz, turned into a compelling story of success and loss and won national recognition as a sports feature.

Story by Kevin Dukovic and Austin Poore, Photo by Scotty Bara, The Viking, Palo Alto High School

Figure 11.8 This story features an alumnus, Jeremy Lin, who went on to play in the NBA. *Where are your school's star athletes from three years ago? From five years? From ten or twenty?*

The Long-Form Profile

When writing a profile, try not to get pigeon-holed into a sunshine-and-glory look at a player. Instead, try to identify a theme of that player's career and life, then write with that angle in mind. A true **long-form feature** reveals to the reader the joys and challenges of that player's life experience.

Figure 11.9 on the next page shows the opening spread of a long-form feature that appeared in a student sports publication. This student-written feature about a campus athlete gained national honors for its look at a young man who stepped away from the sport he loved to have the life he wanted.

For online publications or news-feature, magazine-format publications, the long-form sports feature provides an opportunity to talk in-depth about topics broader than sports. A long-form feature usually begins at 2,000 words or so, and can run up to 5,000 words or more. Effective long-form features often require months to research, write, edit and publish.

In the online version of a long-form story, the feature can also include multimedia pieces such as video, slide shows, hyperlinks, audio clips and interactive graphics.

BACK
in the
BOX
A fallen athlete's journey back to the game
by Jacob Lauing and Sam Borsos *design by* Sam Borsos
Baseball is a game of adjustments. A flyout teaches a hitter to stay on top of the ball. A walk does not discourage a pitcher from pounding the strike zone on the next at-bat, it drives him to try even harder. A baseball player is considered great for getting a hit just thirty percent of the time. Even though perfection is unreachable, every athlete from a backyard Little-Leaguer to a Hall-of-Famer strives to have a perfect season, an undefeated record and to be the best on the squad.
So what happens when players step off the field? The same idea of perfection applies. The pressure to be right, the expectations to practice morality, the assumption that to be the best you can't make mistakes. Whether it's on or off the field, perfection is impossible.
Just as an baseball player can strike out during a game, he can strike out in life. What separates a good athlete from a great athlete is not the strike-out itself, but how he reacts to it.

Story by Jacob Lauing and Sam Borsos, Photo by Scotty Bara, The Viking, Palo Alto High School

Figure 11.9 A long-form feature provides an opportunity to take an in-depth look at a player's life and career. These features typically cover broader topics than just sports and require considerable research, writing and editing time.

Gear and Trend Features

Writing about the people in sports is always a strong play for the sports writer. But in addition to the players, your readers will enjoy reading and watching features about the gear that is popular at the moment. That can mean gear in a specific sport (soccer cleats), or it can be more universal in appeal, such as the five enhancements that you can add to your bike for a better ride. The "stuff" that goes with sports, especially individual, off-campus sports, such as golf, biking, hiking, flying, boating, hunting and laser tag will bring readers to the sports section who might not otherwise be interested.

Food can be another sports-related topic of interest. Sports drinks, snack bars, best pre-game dinners, five energy-building snacks or the top places to eat after the game are all feature topics to explore.

Trend stories in sports, whether local or national, can also be of great interest. For example, yoga was a hot sports trend for a while. Reporters could write about different styles of yoga, studios that offer yoga basics, or a sports and meditation piece that *includes* a look at a student who also is a yoga instructor. Depending on the big stories of the day, you might want to do a sports feature on race, gender equity, hazing, college recruiting, eating disorders or addiction. To write these pieces well, plan far ahead so that you have time to do thorough research and interviewing.

Your Turn

The following ethical dilemmas describe events that have actually happened to high school students covering sports. What would you do if you or your staff members were involved in these events?

1. Your staff has heard that the varsity basketball players have been hazing the new players at one of the player's houses. Supposedly the hazing involves punching the new players as hard as possible in the stomach. Many believe that this team has the potential to make it all the way to the state finals this year, but if this story is true, and it is reported, the team could be sanctioned, or star players could be removed from the team and possibly suspended or expelled. What will you do: investigate and cover the story, or avoid chasing what sound like wild rumors? If you do cover it, what protections or agreements would you offer players who agree to talk to your reporter? Are there legal issues to consider, such as potential criminal investigations that might be underway? What boundaries do you have to consider in your reporting?
2. You go to the athletic director to obtain field passes for a staff photographer and reporter. You cannot always send two staffers to these games, but you get two passes just in case. The next week, a friend of yours who is not on the publications staff asks you if both staffers will be covering the game. You tell him that you are the only one who will be at the game (and using one of the passes). He then asks you if he can "borrow" the extra press pass you have to get into the game for free and hang out on the sidelines with you, watching the game near his buddies who are on the team. How will you handle your friend's request?
3. A school photographer is on the sidelines during a key football game. Three minutes before the first half ends, the star wide receiver goes up for a catch and comes down with the ball, then collapses in agony. The photographer, who was covering the play, has photos of the entire sequence and brings the photos to you (the sports editor). Your team will go on to play the second half of the key game without this star receiver, and they will lose by a wide margin. You have to decide whether or not the photos of the play involving the injury should be published with the game recap of the big loss. Explain your reasoning.
4. Halfway through the season, a player on the soccer team dies in a car accident. What will you do, both in terms of covering the student's death and in terms of talking about the team, which will play the remainder of the season without their friend and teammate?
5. On Monday morning, you hear a rumor that over the weekend several players on the softball team were at an off-campus party to which police were called. The rumor is that several of the team members were caught drinking and that they will be suspended for several days. According to the rumor, they will also be prohibited from playing the next three games. Will you cover this story? If so, how will you do it and what ethical concerns or legal issues will you need to consider in your reporting?

Visual Journalism and Sports

Visuals matter deeply in all aspects of strong journalism, but in sports, photos and video are essential. Great sports writing makes the sports section a delight for readers, but without strong images and video, the audience will not see the slam dunk on senior night or the 90-yard kickoff return for a touchdown at the homecoming game. Strong visuals bring your audience's eyes to your written story.

The pioneering photographer Henri Cartier-Bresson coined the term **decisive moment** more than a century ago. The term was Cartier-Bresson's

Images for Sports Profiles

Every profile needs great images of the featured player. Too often, the shortcut choice for reporters on deadline is to take a fast photo of the player between classes, standing in a random spot in the school, and often not even with his jersey on. That is not OK because it does not give the reader any sense of context for the photo. Often the lighting is poor, the photo is posed, and you end up with an unflattering photo that negatively impacts the profile.

Only slightly better than the type of photo described above is another photo shortcut too often used in player profiles. This shortcut consists of using the team-supplied or archive photo. These photos provide a face to go with the story, but they will not add creativity, personality or an emotional key to the tone of the profile.

So what visuals should be included in a player profile? The basic standard for a player profile is a solid, tightly cropped action shot of the player in uniform at a game, with the player's face clearly visible. You may want to pair the action shot with the team mugshot photo. Inset the mugshot somewhere in the piece since action photos are often full of intense emotions, grimaces, squints or other expressions that add to the emotion of the photo but distort the features of the player in the photo.

If you want to raise the profile imagery to a higher level, on par with the ESPNs and Sports Illustrateds, you can create a "**sportrait,**" or sports portrait. With a little advance planning and cooperation from the subject of the profile, a sportrait can move a profile from "it's OK" to "amazing."

Photo by Grant Shorin, The Viking, Palo Alto High School

Sportraits are a subcategory of a type of photo formally known as environmental portraits, which means that a person is photographed in his environment, connecting the face of the person to the work he does. These photos are also posed to take advantage of portrait lighting. For a piano player, for example, an environmental portrait might be taken by a photographer standing on a ladder almost directly over the head of the pianist, looking down at the keyboard, with the pianist looking up with hands on the keyboard.

way of identifying the particular instant that captures the emotion and importance of an event. It is at that instant that the photographer should snap the shutter.

Sports photography provides endless opportunities for capturing these decisive moments. It can be the exact moment that a bat connects with a pitched ball. It can be the softball player reaching to tag out a runner as she slides to the plate, raising a cloud of dust in the air (Figure 11.10). It can be the greatly extended body position of the running back as he plants his foot to make a sharp change of direction.

Sports events are full of action and emotion. But getting quality sports photos can be a tricky challenge. Shooting great sports photos means being able to freeze the peak action (high shutter speeds) and being able to get great action and reaction shots. Several limiting factors can make this a tough task.

Lighting Challenges

Sometimes you will shoot sports outside during daylight hours, and you will have very few difficulties with the light. But most of the time you will need to adapt to difficult lighting situations. For example, schools rarely light their night games well enough for clear, fast shots with simple cameras.

The lighting that makes playing a night football or soccer game possible can also wreak havoc for a photographer. Stadium lights can cast a ghoulish tint on players' skin. Harsh overhead lights in the indoor volleyball or basketball gym can create dark, unattractive shadows on players' faces. Swimming pools may have little effective lighting in the lanes. To overcome these challenges and produce strong sports photography, you must be aware of the specific circumstances of each facility. You must be prepared ahead of time to deal with any potential challenges or limitations.

Photo by Allie Shorin, The Viking, Palo Alto High School

Figure 11.10 This photo captures the decisive moment when the runner is tagged out.

Remember that light has color, whether the "normal" cast of sunlight or the green, red, yellow, or blue-tinted hues of artificial lighting. Those artificial lights act like a paintbrush on the uniforms and skin tones of the people you are photographing.

Before photographing any event involving artificial light, check and adjust your white balance. This is a technical term that means you are telling the camera to automatically correct the weird lighting hues that may be occurring with the artificial light. The result of adjusting the white balance is that your photos are already color-corrected as much as possible when you go to upload them. On a digital or video camera, this step is easy. Check your camera manual or find directions online.

"Bullet Time": A Short Sports Feature of a Single Moment

If your publication comes out only every six weeks or so, a standard game recap will not be of much help to your school community. The game will be old news by the time the recap is published. But by getting creative, you can find other ways to tell the story of that event.

One technique is to retell a defining moment in a game, match or solo competition by capturing the moment in present tense so that the reader feels as if he is in that moment, as it happened. The technique for re-creating such moments is called **bullet time**. Notice in the rodeo example below that this can be accomplished in a short piece of just over 200 words. This technique could be used just as effectively to tell the story of a fourth-and-one goal line stand or the last 10 meters of a neck-and-neck race.

Tall in the Saddle: Five Seconds in an Afternoon of Roping

by Katie Kressin (Cannon Falls High School, Minnesota)

The chute doors fly open. The horses on either side rock back on their haunches and dig into the arena sand, exploding forward only moments behind a red-and-white steer. Their ears lie flat against their headstalls, and above their heads, hissing lassos beat the horizon.

Three seconds later, the left rider has secured his rope around the steer's horns, and his horse swerves away, taking the steer off his path. Now the right horse closes in, the rider aims, and the steer suddenly stretches out, heels and horns roped, dust settling.

The horses' sides heave. Sweat and lather gather around their breastplates and the cinches around their bellies. The support boots strapped around their legs are lined with dust. The saddles are tooled and braided, the curb bits curve gently past the horses' chins. Riders squint against the sunlight.

Now the pinto comes forward and backs into the box on the left of the chute. He is taut, his chin against his chest, knees high, forelock falling over his eyes. The tightness of the reins shows in the raised veins along his neck as he presses against the rider's hold. Horse and steer eye each other through the bars, counting down the seconds.

Go.

You may be thinking, "Why don't I just use a flash?" In non-sports situations, using a flash might be a great solution. In sports, however, a flash could create a distraction to the players, and in many schools flash photography in the gym or on the sidelines is prohibited.

Check with your school's athletic director or the coach of the team you want to photograph to see whether flash photography is permitted. Sometimes a flash can be used during team practice but not during games. Some coaches never allow flash photos. So check it out. And keep in mind that your own school's policy might be different from the policy at the school where your team is playing an away game.

Access Challenges

One of the rules of strong photography emphasizes shooting closely cropped, tightly framed photos. In a perfect situation, that means that the photographer is able to get close to the subject of the photo.

In most sports, however, photographers are restricted to a certain distance from the field of play, which means shooting photos from a vantage point that is less than ideal. Shooting from the sidelines or behind home plate is not easy. Still, thinking ahead and preparing makes getting a good photo possible.

One of the best tools for sports photography is a "fast" telephoto lens (Figure 11.11). For most field sports, a lens that goes to 200 mm or 300 mm is very helpful in bringing the action closer. Although professional photographers use lenses that are even longer (400 mm or longer), few schools can afford such lenses.

In shooting sports, freezing the action is usually the desired effect. To do that requires keeping a relatively high shutter speed. For quick-moving action (swinging a bat, diving into water, serving the ball), keep the shutter speed above 1/500th as a general rule. For casual shots of the dugout or of players at rest, a shutter speed above 1/125th should provide crisp results. A "fast" lens means that the lens is built to be able to shoot under lower-light conditions while still keeping a relatively high shutter speed (essential for crisp sports action photos). An f/1.8 lens (for a normal lens) or an f/2.8 lens (for a telephoto) provides a bright lens that is more likely to allow faster shutter speeds.

Figure 11.11 Using the proper equipment, including a telephoto lens, will help you shoot strong photos, even if you cannot get close to the subject.

Photo by Forrest Czarnecki, Conifer High School

Sports Columns

Ask a die-hard sports fan to identify his favorite part of the sports pages and his answer is likely to be the columns. Sports columns are meant to entertain and engage the reader. Professional sports columnists have devoted followers. High school publications can create the same interest and impact with a strong columnist.

A high school sports column works best when the writer covers sports on his or her campus. It is a mistake for a high school columnist to cover only the professional teams in the area. Those teams are already being covered, and covered well, by professional media. But sports on your own campus are likely being overlooked.

It is possible to produce an interesting, entertaining sports column even if you lack a strong writer with lots of good ideas for sports columns. One way to do this is to instigate a first-person column in which an athlete describes a crucial moment or a significant event from that athlete's perspective. The column could rotate among the school's athletes, or the same person could interview and write the accounts for each publication.

Figure 11.12 shows a repeating column in a sports magazine. The columnist, Michael Cullen, often used a light, humorous approach, which his readers found entertaining. But for the final appearance on his home turf, he stepped back and took a more serious look at the game he had loved his whole life.

Your Turn

Sit down with a notebook. Think about the hardest-fought, most dramatic game you ever played in; or if you have not participated in such a game, imagine what a challenging game might feel like. List five key details from that game. Did you or your team win or lose? What is the "takeaway" you carry inside you from that game today?

Now, set a timer for 30 minutes. Once you start, you will not stop. Just jump in and begin writing about the event. Focus, be brave and remember strongly. Use your notes. Write three long grafs (about 100–150 words each):

Graf 1: Describe (in present tense) three key moments in the game.

Graf 2: Describe what happened and how you felt after the game, when you (and team, if appropriate) left the playing field.

Graf 3: Now skip to this moment. Sitting here, looking back, write one long graf about how that game has changed you, or why it mattered to you and your friends.

Did the timer just go off? Take a look at what you wrote. Does it sound like a sports column?

The Last Game

Michael Cullen, Columnist
March 11, 2011

If you take close look at the helmet of a member of the 2010 Palo Alto Vikings football team, you will get a glimpse into the life of a warrior who by day hammers out essays and math worksheets, and by night hammers opposing players to the turf. A helmet that started off in August as a smooth, spotless, gleaming white headpiece has progressed into a mangled and chipped orb that looks like it served a term as a bengal tiger's scratching post.

A ding in a helmet is more than just evidence of a past collision. Each chip, scar, or chunk of sticker missing from a helmet has a story behind it. I could pick up my helmet and point out individual gashes and streaks of paint, then tell you the story of how such an imperfection in the uniformity of my bonnet was acquired. But to me, the scars that criss-cross the front of a player's helmet are as far from imperfections as Davante Adams' ('11) vertical jump is from mine. A 'stick mark' on a Paly Vike helmet is art: art acquired in the pursuit of perfection.

From the moment I strapped on a helmet in 4th grade and had my first taste of contact, I was hooked. I fell in love with every aspect of the game and the culture that surrounds it. There is no feeling in the world like stepping onto the gridiron and awaiting the opening kickoff of a football game. On that field, mind and body are in sync, senses razor sharp, heart pounding, with the sights, sounds, and smells surrounding you blending together and magnifying. You feel untouchable. It's the feeling I get any time I step out under the lights in the green and white with my brothers. It started in the Pop Warner days; Weighing less than 100 pounds, I would run around in bulky pads with the coordination of a baby deer. I distinctly remember being blocked into a gigantic puddle of mud during my first month of practice. I thought it was the coolest thing ever. I emerged from the muck and walked home covered in mud, to the horror of my mother.

I can tell you all about the time my Palo Alto Knights team (which included many players from this year's team), placed third in the country at Nationals, defeating a team from Pennsylvania in the final seconds of the game on a pass from TJ Braff ('11) to Miles Anderson ('11). Or I could tell you about how my Freshman year, during the second game of the season while playing on JV, I broke my left hand in a contest against Burlingame. All good, I thought, because I was allowed to play with the cast padded, until two weeks later when I broke the other wrist. I could even tell you about how Kevin Anderson('11) and I, as young freshman used to work out at lunch, for fear of letting the seniors see our pathetic bench press. Needless to say Kevin is doing just fine on the bench now, but looking at us then you might not have pinned us for future State Champions. I can tell you any number of moments from my football career, but none will ever compare to my senior season.

Throughout the 2010 CCS playoffs every time I left the locker room and headed toward the field, I felt weighing on my shoulders the possibility that it could be my last time, and that no matter how far we had come, or how well we had done up to that point, it could all come to a screeching halt in one game. That feeling just makes you want it more. In three games, we squashed out the looming possibility of elimination. The Mitty game tested us like nothing before. I can't say I wasn't scared that my high school career was going to end right there, in the torrential downpour that soaked Hod Ray Field to the core. But even lining up for that fateful 4th and goal from the 24, I believed, like I did every time we stepped onto the gridiron this season, that we could do it.

Four weeks after Christoph Bono's ('11) pass floated in the rain and found its way into Adams' arms in the corner of the endzone, we exited the locker room of the Home Depot Center and began the walk to the tunnel leading onto the field. After defeating Valley Christian in the CCS Finals, we had a pretty good idea of who we would be facing. When it was announced officially that we would be taking on Centennial High School of Corona, few gave us a chance at holding Centennial under 40 points. We stepped onto the field against an opponent who outsized us, both by physical size and sheer numbers. Before kickoff, as the rain drifted down and coated our helmets, I told my teammates: "This is David and Goliath…and we've got the rock."

The game was a battle from the beginning, but when the clock wound down to zero, it was us alone who stood as champions. Everyone had overlooked the underdogs from Palo Alto.

My helmet sits in my room now, grass from the Home Depot Center still plastered to the white shell, along with the fresh red streaks left from impact with Centennial helmets, which blend in seamlessly with the gashes attained during battles won on the road to perfection. One of the first things my dad taught me when we would play catch in my youth was how to hold the ball. You tuck the pigskin hard into your elbow, squeezing with your forearm against your rib cage, and lacing your fingers over the exposed tip of the ball. It's known as the 'four points of pressure', and it makes it nearly impossible for defenders to rip the ball away from you. My dad, whether he knew it or not, added a fifth point: a love for football that I will hold on to forever. I'm never letting this game go.

Column by Michael Cullen, The Viking, Palo Alto High School

Figure 11.12 A sports columnist says a heartfelt goodbye to his regular column in this farewell piece.

Chapter Eleven

Review and Assessment

Recall

1. For each of the seven news value, create a specific hypothetical example, using your school's players and teams, that shows how the sports section can reflect that particular news value.
2. How does an evergreen story differ from a breaking news story?
3. Assume your publication adviser limits sports coverage to the school-sanctioned teams. Give reasons why the coverage should be expanded to additional sports.
4. Explain how Title IX changed high school sports.
5. List at least three potential problems that can occur if sports reporters fail to prepare properly.
6. Why is it a good idea to read sports if you will be writing about sports?
7. What does it mean to be "comped"?
8. Why is location an important part of setting up for your game coverage?
9. List several live game coverage strategies.
10. Describe the elements of a strong sports photo.
11. Who should be interviewed for a player profile?
12. What kind of sports stories can you write, beyond the game recaps?
13. List the reasons that you should consider including a sports column in your publication.

Critical Thinking

1. Why is it important to cover sports regularly and in a timely manner on your campus?
2. What are the sports at your school that should be included when planning the year's sports coverage? Of those, which sports do you think will require more reporters due to the number of games or the importance of that sport on your campus? Explain.
3. How will you ensure that the photos on the sports page are quality action photos? How will you make sure that you have photographers on site and credentialed to cover games for each sport during the season?
4. You are the first sports editor for your school's new weekly online news publication. Describe for an audience of school administrators and parents your plans for making the sports section a "must read" for your school community. What will you do beyond reporting the game facts?

Application

1. Look at the past two years' issues of your publication, and also grab the past two yearbooks. Make a list of how many sports are covered, and how often. Look back at the list you made in Question 2 in Critical Thinking. What sports are not present at all, or barely covered right now at your school? Of the sports that get top coverage, count the actual number of games that have been covered—what is that number? How many total games were there in that season? Calculate the "stat" for your reporting coverage. If you are hitting more than half (batting .500 or better), then you are awesome. If your coverage is less than .100, it may be time to do a better job in this part of your coverage.
2. Using the same publications as above, look at the sports photos in your publication. Review all of them. Find three photos (three different sports, please) that you think are strong. What do you like about those photos? Now look at the photos that you think are not as strong. What exactly is weak in the not-great photos? How could the photo have been improved?
3. One of the guidelines on page 322 for strong sports coverage recommends telling the story of the whole team, rather than the standard focus on an individual star player. Another guideline suggests doing stories on the season as a whole rather than a single game. In groups, brainstorm angles for stories on a team and for stories on either part of or the whole season. Review suggestions for writing effective features in chapter 10 and in this chapter, then work in pairs to develop and write a team story and a season story intended to both inform and entertain your audience. Share and critique the stories in class.

Chapter Eleven

Journalism Style

Using Numerals

If you are writing about your baseball team's recent win, how should you write the headline?

1. *The home team squeaked past Windy River 11-9 Friday.*
2. *The home team squeaked past Windy River 11 to 9 Friday.*
3. *The home team squeaked past Windy River eleven to nine Friday.*
4. *The home team squeaked past Windy River 11 to nine Friday.*

If you are not sure which is right, you are not alone. According to the AP Stylebook, sports scores are written in numerals (not words) with a hyphen, with no space between the hyphen and scores. This is true for large scores, *77-73*, as well as smaller scores, *1-0*. So the headline is correct in option #1 above. Here are some additional examples of AP style:

- *The Reds defeated the Red Sox 4-3.*
- *The golfer had a 5 on the first hole but finished with a 2-under-par score.*
- Use a comma in this format: *Boston 6, Baltimore 5*.

If you are writing a caption for a photo of the winning pitcher and her little brother, which of these is correct?

1. *High-fives: Pitcher Angie Garcia, 16, celebrates her 11-9 win over Windy River with her five-year-old brother, Jaime.*
2. *High Fives: Pitcher Angie Garcia, sixteen, celebrates her 11-9 win over Windy River with her five-year-old brother, Jaime.*
3. *High-Fives: Junior Pitcher Angie Garcia celebrates her 11-9 win over Windy River with her 5 year old brother, Jaime.*
4. None of the above.

The AP Stylebook recommends using ages only when they are important to the story. In the high school press, it is more common to identify the student by her class in school. A large school may contain more than one Angie Garcia. So *Junior Pitcher Angie Garcia* is the preferred form.

But Jaime's age is important in this instance because it highlights the bond that sports creates between the brother and sister, especially since they were born more than a decade apart. If you use *5-year-old* as an adjective modifying *Jaime*, it should be hyphenated: *5-year-old Jaime Garcia*.

Which version of *high five* is correct? If you looked in the AP Stylebook, you would see *high-five* (*n.*) and *high-fived* (*v.*) for the noun and verb forms. Since you should capitalize only the first word of a hyphenated pair (unless the second word is a proper noun), only the H should be capitalized: *High-fives*. So none of the original examples were correct. The sentence should read: *High-fives: Junior Angie Garcia celebrates her 11-9 win with her 5-year-old brother, Jaime.*

Other notes about ages:

- Always use figures; do not spell out the age. *The 5-year-old loves baseball*.
- If you use age as a compound noun (*the 5-year-old comes to all his sister's games*), you should also hyphenate it, just as you do for the adjective form.
- You could also write *Jaime, 5, comes to all his sister's games* but not if you are writing for broadcast. For broadcast, craft two sentences. *Jaime comes to all his sister's games. He is five years old*.
- If you write *He is five years old* (either for print or broadcast), do not use hyphens.

Try It!

Copy edit the following sentences for numeral use, writing the correct sentences on a separate sheet of paper.

1. Boston defeated the Yankees 14 to two.
2. Brigham Young University scored 55 and Stanford scored 54.
3. After four outstanding years playing football at Home High, Tiny Tafua, 18, will don Buckeye red in the fall.
4. Title 9 will be forty-five years old this June.
5. The forty five year old law requires schools that take federal money to give equal opportunities to female and male athletes.
6. The nine year old was thrown from the car by the force of the collision. His four year old sister Huynh was extracted from her car seat by the fire department using the jaws of life. (Look up "jaws of life.")

Extend Your Knowledge

Style Exercises

Visit the *Journalism* website for additional examples and practice in using numerals.

Chapter Eleven

Writers' Workshop

In these Writers' Workshops you will:

- Eliminate the phrases *a lot* and *a lot of* and replace them with specific details.
- Modify nouns to provide accurate numbers.

Workshop 11.1

A Lot Is a Place to Park Cars

Write notes about the appearance of your building and classroom from the outside and the inside as if you needed to describe it for a feature or news story. Include what the students are doing as they wait for class to begin and as class begins. You may use sentences or just phrases, but not single words. Be as observant as possible.

Remember, when writing a story, it is easier for a journalist to leave out details listed in her notes than it is for her to go back and look for information she forgot to write down.

Mini-Lesson: A Lot Is a Noun, Not a Modifier

A lot can be used as a noun to indicate the place where you park your car, a parking lot, or the place where you can build a house, an empty lot, or the batch of yarn or cloth colored at the same time, a dye lot, or Purim, the Jewish Feast of Lots. All of these are good, solid nouns.

In the casual language of everyday speech, *a lot* is used frequently as a modifier. We use it

- for emphasis: *She is in a lot of trouble*.
- as a filler: *Her locker is full of a lot of garbage*.
- to indicate we did something often: *I swam there a lot when I was little*.
- with count nouns when we do not know how many there are: *She has a lot of shoes*.
- with noncount nouns when we do not know how much of something there is: *There is a lot of water in the swimming pool.*

But *a lot* has almost no place in written journalism except in direct quotations and should be used rarely if ever in broadcast copy. Its use suggests that the reporter did not investigate thoroughly before writing the story or that he is a weak writer. *A lot* communicates almost nothing to the audience. Their minds skid over the words like a car turning on loose gravel, and your sentence loses both direction and drive.

This workshop will help you eradicate *a lot* from the first three uses: for emphasis, as a filler and to indicate frequency.

Apply It!

Look in the notes you wrote about the appearance of your building and classroom, or look in your other writing for the phrases *a lot* and *a lot of.* Did you use them? If so, how?

Mini-Lesson: A Lot for Emphasis

When we have used *a lot* for emphasis, simply removing it will shorten and strengthen the sentence. *She is in a lot of trouble* does not tell us any more than *She is in trouble*. *A lot* did not tell your audience how much trouble she is in. Is her mother going to yell at her for 15 minutes? Is her father going to take away her cellphone? Is she going to be expelled from school? Is she going to be arrested or lose her admission to the college she wanted to attend?

If the sentence deserves more force, then tell the audience how much trouble she is in. *She will lose her athletic eligibility. The judge will decide on Tuesday whether to suspend her license.*

Apply It!

Find in your own writing, or write a sentence now, where *a lot* is used for emphasis. Rewrite the sentence first without *a lot* and then give it more force by adding important information.

Mini-Lesson: A Lot as a Filler

In casual speech we add filler words to take up time while we think of what we want to say. Something like this:

> *In casual speech we throw in filler words, a lot, to kinda take up a little bit of time and stuff while we, like, think of what we want to say.*

Otherwise people a lot of the time think we are done talking, and they interrupt us a lot while we are thinking. A lot is used a lot to fill up time.

The language we use in broadcast and in writing should be much more respectful of our audience's time. When *a lot* is being used as filler, just eliminating it will improve the sentence. *Her locker is full of a lot of garbage* (nine words) becomes *Her locker is full of garbage* (six words) or *Her garbage-filled locker is just below mine* (eight words, with added information). The shorter sentences devoid of *a lot* have more punch and perhaps more information.

If the sentence deserves more force, you can describe the garbage. *Her locker is a landfill of old lunch sacks, empty water bottles and six months of handouts and unfinished homework.*

Apply It!

Find in your own writing, or write a sentence now, where *a lot* is used as a filler. Rewrite it first without *a lot* and then give it more force by adding description or additional information.

Mini-Lesson: A Lot to Tell How Often

A third way we use *a lot* in our casual speech is to indicate how often we do or did something. *I swam there a lot when I was little*. In addition to deleting *a lot*, we could replace it with other adverbs such as *often* or *regularly* or *frequently*; but these also do not convey much information, and the sentence may be better off without any adverb at all, since the simple past tense can imply regular activity.

In the negative, *a lot* can be replaced by *seldom* or *hardly ever*.

I hardly ever swam there when I was little.

My brothers swam in the Slough behind The Oaks Park, but I seldom went there.

Avoid *almost never* when using AP style.

If the sentence needs more force, provide an appropriate adverb or adverbial phrase that carries additional meaning.

I swam there almost every day when I spent summers with my grandparents.

I swam Huntington Beach Pier at least once each summer from the time I was nine until I left for college.

I swim twice daily on school days, once at 6 a.m. for early morning workouts and once after school.

Apply It!

Find in your own writing, or write a sentence now, where *a lot* is used to indicate how often you did something. Rewrite it first without *a lot* and then give it more force by adding description or additional information. Try it in the negative, too.

Workshop 11.2

Let Me Count the Ways

In casual speech, we use *a lot* and its more formal brother *many* to modify nouns that can be counted rather than measured.

Though *many* is more formal than *a lot*, both expressions tell us only that we mean "more than one." Whether you say, "She has a lot of shoes" or "She has many pairs of shoes," your audience does not have a clear idea of what you mean. Try asking several classmates how many shoes are meant by "a lot of shoes" or "many pairs of shoes."

Mini-Lesson: Modifying Count Nouns

Specific, accurate numbers can provide valuable details. Look at these descriptions of one high school journalism room by Matt Welch, a professional journalist writing in Teacher Magazine.

Three students are at their desks 15 minutes early ...

Room 502 is a pleasantly ramshackle cross between a newsroom and a classroom.

Thirty desks, a half-dozen mismatched computers, and a jury-rigged overhead projector fill the large space.

Thirty desks, six mismatched computers, three students, room 502, 15 minutes early. You can see the precision in Welch's reporting. He does not use *some*, *a lot of* or *many*.

Apply It!

Add to your notes from Workshop 11.1, concentrating on accurate counts. Write about the appearance of your classroom as if you needed to describe it for a feature or news story. Include what a number of students are doing as they wait for class to begin and as class begins. You may use sentences or just phrases, but not single words. Be as observant as possible. Avoid *a lot*!

Extend Your Knowledge

Extend

Visit the *Journalism* website to learn more about describing quantities in your writing, including how to measure without a ruler.

Chapter Twelve

Editorials, Opinion Pieces, Columns, Blogs and Cartoons

What do you think?

Image courtesy of National Scholastic Press Association (nspa.studentpress.org); cartoon by Joel Greenspan, Eastside, Cherry Hill High School East

Courtesy of Rachel Fung, The Broadview, Convent of the Sacred Heart High School

Image courtesy of National Scholastic Press Association (nspa.studentpress.org); cartoon by Garrett Wilson, Epic, Shawnee Mission West High School

G-WLEARNING.com

While studying, look for the activity icon to:

- **Build** vocabulary terms with e-flash cards and matching activities.
- **Extend** learning with further discussion of relevant topics.
- **Reinforce** what you learn by completing style exercises, worksheets and end-of-chapter questions.

Visit the Journalism website: www.g-wlearning.com/journalism/

Chapter Objectives

After reading this chapter, you will be able to:

- Describe how publications and broadcasts identify editorial and opinion content so that it will not be confused with news.
- Describe the similarities and differences among staff editorials, op-eds and columns.
- Tell what shape the staff editorial generally takes.
- Identify and explain the use of hyperbole, irony and repetition in an op-ed.
- Describe a columnist's role as a reporter, op-ed writer and storyteller.
- Explain why it is important for a columnist to develop a voice for his column.
- Explain advantages of journalistic opinion blogs.
- Explain concerns a journalist should have when expressing opinions in a blog.
- Tell the difference between an editorial illustration and an editorial cartoon.
- Explain the role of symbols, labels, caricatures and allusions in editorial artwork.

Key Terms

Build Vocab

column
editorial board
editorial cartoon
editorial illustration
exposition
fictionalize
journalistic blog
narrative
rhetorical device
rhetorical question

Before You Read...

Make a KWL chart like the one shown here. Fill in the chart, listing what you know about editorials, opinion pieces, columns, blogs or cartoons; what you want to know; and, after reading the chapter and listening to your instructor's discussion, what you learned.

K	W	L
What I Know	What I Want to Know	What I Learned

Introduction

"The greatest threat to freedom is the absence of criticism."

–Wole Soyinka, Nigerian playwright and poet

You have been told your opinions should not appear in your news or feature stories or color your reporting or writing. But like most people, you do have opinions and insights. Yours may have special value because you, as a journalist, have access to places, people and information your audience rarely sees. You read widely, including the professional press, and research the background of current issues, including sports, the arts and politics. You are able to evaluate sources, and you are a keen observer.

If your writing is informative, insightful and perhaps entertaining, your opinions will matter and your audience will want to read or hear what you write. They may even come to rely on your judgment.

Journalists Wear Two Hats

Your writing should clearly indicate whether you are expressing opinions or reporting the news. Commentary should never be inserted into news or feature stories. Your audience should know at once which hat you are wearing, the objective journalist's or the commentator's.

The editorial or opinion section of your publication should be clearly marked. Even casual observers should know this is the place set aside for informed opinions. Opinion podcasts should be labeled as such. Your audience should never wonder whether they are receiving news or commentary.

Columns—regularly occurring articles—may appear in almost every section of your publication or broadcast, but your audience should not easily confuse them with news. Design elements such as bumper music (short music clips), a different backdrop or set, a different typeface, a drop capital, a different byline style or a label such as *Commentary* or *Review* should identify columns that appear in your publication or broadcast (Figure 12.1). (See Chapter 13 for review writing.)

The line between news and commentary is important, but the types of commentary will probably evolve as media evolve. Publications may adopt styles for their opinion pieces that blur the differences between the traditional forms of staff editorials and opinion pieces and the newer, online journalistic blogs and columns, but ethical journalists and their publications will never blur the lines between reporting and commentary.

Figure 12.1 Set in a column identified as "Opinion" with "Our View" beneath, it's hard to confuse this staff editorial with news. *How does your school publication distinguish between news articles and opinion pieces?*

Opinion

Our View

Saturday school is not so bad

Our school supports you six days a week, and this is an awesome thing.

Twice a month, teachers, staff, and deans dedicate their time to the unique program that is Wildkit Academy. Few schools have a support system as strong as this one that "provides their students the extra boost they need to succeed."

The typical Saturday session starts with a free breakfast from Le Peep at 8:15 a.m. and continues with support sessions from 9 a.m. to noon. Along with help in core classes, Wildkit Academy offers other free support services such

Affordable lo

BY ALEX HAAB
Opinion Writer

Education is more thar
name.

Many believe that thes
only schools that churn ou
ful graduates are those wi
recognizable names. How
recognizability of a big na
that a lot of people have h
does not lead to immediat

In addition, while man
that degrees from recogni
schools are the only path
many underestimate the f
that a high-GPA degree fr
school carries. A high GP
any school still reflects ha
and dedication that emplo
respect.

The same principle ap
the cost of a college's tuit
college's price tag does n
the quality of the degree,
opting to go to an afforda
institution are not at a dis
because of it.

Some argue that colleg
prestigious reputations fo
due to their level of rigor
sors. Sure, some colleges
professors than others. Ho
lege is more about what y
it rather than factors such
which you cannot control

Not only that, but an u
graduate degree for many
a launching pad into high
tion, such as graduate or l
Those institutions are the

Courtesy of The Evanstonian, Evanston Township High School

And Now... Closer to Home

Who Will Read Your Work?

Three kinds of people may follow your work as an opinion writer. You need to write for all three audiences at once.

1. Those who already agree with you. You provide these readers with evidence, anecdotes, insights and language that express their position better than they could say it themselves. They should read or listen all the way to the end of your work and say, "Yes! That's exactly what I think, too!"
2. Those who hold a different, even opposing, opinion. You predict their objections and discuss them, perhaps showing them the limitations of their position. Your goal is to be fair to them and help them see the strengths of your position, though they still may not agree. They should want to read or listen to your entire piece and say, "I still think you're wrong, but I see your point."
3. Those who do not yet know or care about the issue. You help them to care and to make up their minds. Warning your audience and alerting your audience are two of your most powerful functions as an editorial writer. They should read or listen to your work and say, "Oh my gosh. I never thought of that."

The Staff Editorial

The staff editorial is unsigned—there is no byline—and is the voice of the publication. Traditionally, it is one of the most formal elements of your publication and should be one of the best-researched and best-written pieces you publish. Your publication's reputation is behind your opinion. It may rise or fall on how honestly and clearly you support and express your publication's opinion.

Figure 12.2 At the website shown below the reader can choose Opinion/The Review from tabs such as News, Sports and A&E. The reader can then choose tabs such as Columnists, editorials and cartoons. The distinction between news and commentary is clear.

Courtesy of Trib Total Media

The staff editorial should be the opinion of a majority of the **editorial board**, the student leaders, usually the editors, of your publication. An editor will bring up an issue at an editorial board meeting. The board will discuss the issue and develop an opinion that a majority of the board members can support. One member of the board or a skillful staff journalist is assigned to research and write the editorial. The editorial board will review it before it is published. Though board members' opinions are rarely unanimous, the board will publish only one opinion. It will not write a point-counterpoint pair of staff editorials. The editorial board speaks with one voice. (Op-ed pieces may express different opinions on a topic.)

Professional publications may have separate tabs on their websites for "Editorial" and "Op-ed" (Figure 12.2). When the readers want the opinion of the paper, they go to "Editorial." When they want the opinions of informed individuals, they go to "Op-ed," where they will find signed opinion pieces.

In print publications, editorials are set apart by their layout. They often are printed in wider "legs" than opinion pieces; that is, they are two columns wide but stretched across the space usually given to three columns of text, with wider gutters between the columns. They may be surrounded by more white space or given wider leading, that is more space between lines. The section may also be marked "Editorial."

Your Turn

1. Go to the print and online editions of two professional publications. Clip, print or download pages from each. Identify the design elements or navigational tools that identify staff editorials.
2. **Going Deeper.** Read an editorial and an opinion piece from the same publication. Observe how they differ in
   - organization—watch the opening and closing closely.
   - tone—how formal is the word choice? Any humor?
   - purpose—describe the purpose of each. How does the writer hope to change the reader?
   - length—which is longer? Can you tell why?

What to Write for a Staff Editorial

The staff editorial should be timely in one of these ways:

- It may take a position on an issue that has been covered objectively in the current edition or in a recent edition of your publication. If you have just covered a fight at a volleyball game, it is appropriate to comment on the level of security at your away games.
- It may take a position on a topic of national or international interest that has been covered in the professional press and is of interest to your audience. If child soldiers have been in the news—and on the minds and social media pages of your audience—it is fair to point out bogus charities that claim to rescue them, and then point out meaningful ways to contribute.
- It may be proactive, pointing out a potential problem that your audience should care about. If a reporter has noticed that surrounding districts offer junior high school students two choices of foreign language and your district offers none, you may both inform your audience and take a position. (However, if the last junior high school foreign language class is about to be cut, it is generally better to cover the cut in news before you take a position on your opinion page.)

- It may come from your knowledge of a pending lawsuit. It could come from an item on the agenda of the school board, the police commission, the town council or planning commission. A law being considered in the state or national legislature is another possibility. Good reporting comes before strong editorials.

If the topic is not timely, no matter how passionately you may feel about it, consider carefully before you write a staff editorial on the topic. Editorials call for action or change. If there is no possibility for change, there is no need for an editorial.

Five Things You Need to Know About Opinion Writing

Opinion Writing Criticizes and Suggests Solutions

Be positive, even when you are pointing out a problem. Whining is easy. Your audience does not need journalism for that.

If for example, new security measures at your school cause long lines before first period, cover the story in news. Photos or video work well. In your opinion writing, suggest a solution. After researching possible fixes, you may suggest that the bus schedule be adjusted so that students arrive at staggered times. Your opinion piece should describe the problem, describe possible solutions and tell why your suggestion is the best solution.

Opinion Writing Advocates

You give voice to the voiceless. You see problems others do not. If you cover the life of a single mother for a feature story, you may decide your campus needs a quality day care program. Research what is done in other districts, how it is financed and how it could serve the needs of teachers and staff as well as students. Then advocate for it in your opinion writing.

Opinion Writing Appreciates

Point out something good that is happening, something that is working well, someone who deserves notice. For example, if the school has worked well since the bell system broke, point that out. If your campus has responded generously to help after a recent disaster, praise the effort. If you want more of something, praise it.

Opinion Writing Observes

Great writing grows from keen observation. Los Angeles Times columnist Steve Lopez heard a homeless man playing beautifully on a two-stringed violin near an outdoor statue of Beethoven. In time Lopez discovered Nathaniel Anthony Ayers had studied at Juilliard before schizophrenia overtook him. Lopez's observation helped him write over a dozen columns and a book, "The Soloist," which was made into a movie. He also gained a friend, helped him, and helped millions of readers better understand the nature of mental illness and the power of music. It started because he observed well and did not look away.

Opinion Writing Connects the Dots

You see meaningful connections between events that your audience sees every day but may barely notice. It may be common to see people at a football game taking selfies, texting during pep assemblies and watching movies on the game bus, each time ignoring the drama that is unfolding a few feet or a few hundred yards away. Although everyone may see these things, you as an observer may connect the dots and point out a trend, criticize, praise, advocate or warn in your writing or your editorial cartoon.

How to Write a Staff Editorial

The staff editorial should be as brief and direct as possible, though some topics demand extended explanation. The Los Angeles Times often keeps its editorials under 450 words; The New York Times, 350 words.

It should handle only one issue at a time. If you are proposing a change to the school dress code, do not comment on the city's curfew or the fabric in the PE shorts. An editorial is not a gripe session but an opportunity to focus with laser precision on one issue and one action.

A staff editorial rarely uses a first-person pronoun because it concentrates on what is happening and what others are doing and saying, not what the editorial board is doing. If it does use a first-person pronoun, it is the formal editorial "we" because the writer is speaking for the paper. The editorial "we" includes "our" and "us."

For instance, when the Chicago Tribune wrote in favor of news cameras in the courtroom, the opening read, "In January, when the Illinois Supreme Court announced plans to experiment with allowing news cameras in circuit courtrooms, our first response was this: What's left to figure out?" The editorial later quotes the judge as not wanting "to turn the courtroom into a circus." The next paragraph starts, "Neither do we." It ends "Like it or not, a growing number of people get their news from their smartphones. Let's make this work."

Staff editorials also avoid from-the-scene reporting, anecdotes and quotations from participants in the controversy. Use those in a balanced news story, a column, a blog or an op-ed. In the staff editorial, the editorial board, having already evaluated these sources, is communicating its informed position to the audience. Your publication's reputation for intelligence and fairness stands in the place of anecdotes, observations and quotations.

And Not *You*

Because the staff editorial is rather formal, it generally avoids addressing the audience as "you." One way to avoid this construction is to refer to members of your community by the name of your school's mascot: Vaqueros, Cavaliers, Mariners, Oilers, Fighting Fishermen, Galloping Ghosts, Unicorns, Nimrods, Atom Smashers, Pretzels or Honkers.

Instead of writing:

~~*If you worry about us driving in snow, you should write the school board and tell it not to cancel school on snowy days but to give us late-start days.*~~

Write:

Minutemen who worry about students driving in snow should write the school board and tell it not to cancel school on snowy days but to use the late-start schedule.

Both sentences are about the same length and both contain the same information, but by avoiding "you," the writing is more appropriate for a staff editorial.

Your staff editorial may quote experts and authoritative sources such as the Centers for Disease Control and Prevention to support your position and to emphasize the importance of the issue. Because the reputation of your publication is behind all claims made in the editorial, use your experts carefully. If you write that "teenage birthrates have been going down, according to the CDC," you had better be right, accurate and fair.

The staff editorial uses facts and logic, not emotion. It assumes the audience is interested in the topic but does not yet have all the appropriate information to take a stand on the issue—or even to care about it.

Staff editorials avoid satire and humor. Keep the editorial short and clear. Save humor and satire for columns and for editorial cartoons.

Staff editorials end with a clear call to action on one issue. It is not enough to create a flutter of emotion about how students need physical activity to cope with the stress of school. The voice of the paper knows what is needed. It says it clearly. *The principal needs to rethink her position on intramural basketball and reopen the courts during the lunch period.*

The Shape of a Staff Editorial

The staff editorial follows a set form. It begins with background information and concludes with a call to action. It should be so well-written and clear that people will read your conclusion to learn your position even when the body of the piece requires you to communicate dull-seeming technical, legal or policy information. Clear, tight writing will help your audience through the dry parts.

The Opening

The opening includes the background information your audience needs to understand the issue, as in this lead from the Los Angeles Times editorial "Occupy L.A.: Free speech is free" (Figure 12.3 on the next page).

> *With the Occupy L.A. encampment dismantled, the city is left with the task of refurbishing the battered grounds of City Hall and tallying up the costs of the occupation.*

It identifies why the issue is timely and the opportunity for action. Opportunities for action may include pending policy decisions, legal actions, laws being considered or an urgent problem you want your audience to consider. The anniversary of a landmark event may provide an opportunity for change.

It indicates the editorial board's position or suggests it, if the position requires a great deal of explanation.

The Body

The body includes a fair statement of the opposing point of view and a respectful statement of why it is wrong. It may include a different

Los Angeles Times LOCAL | CALIFORNIA | SPORTS | ENTERTAINMENT | BUSINESS | OPINION | NATION | WORLD | MORE

YOU ARE HERE: LAT Home → Collections → **Opinion**

FROM THE ARCHIVES

Some Occupy L.A. protesters may get a lesson in free speech
December 22, 2011

L.A. drops charges against Westwood protesters who...
March 4, 2011

Not fit to be tried
February 12, 2011

Los Angeles gets tough with political protesters
February 11, 2011

Editorial

Occupy L.A.: Free speech is free

City Hall embraced Occupy L.A. Trying to make protesters foot the bill now is wrong.

December 29, 2011

With the Occupy L.A. encampment dismantled, the city is left with the task of refurbishing the battered grounds of City Hall and tallying up the costs of the occupation. Officials estimate the city spend $1.7 million in overtime for police enforcement. Graffiti must be removed from three monuments. And it could cost $400,000 to repair the irrigation system and replace the lawn (if the city upgrades to desertscaping). These are not insignificant figures, but suing the Occupy L.A. protesters to foot the bill – an option, according to City Atty. Carmen Trutanich – is wrong.

From a practical perspective, it seems impossible to pinpoint who is responsible for what damage. From a legal standpoint, the city seems unlikely to recoup its police overtime costs. And as a matter of plain fairness, it is contradictory given the city's own actions. The City Council passed a resolution supporting the "continuation of the peaceful and vibrant exercise in 1st Amendment rights" by the occupiers; Council President Eric Garcetti told them to stay as long as they liked; and Mayor Antonio Villaraigosa passed out ponchos during the first rains. Given all that, how can Trutanich turn around and present them with a bill?

The protesters did sue first, notes William Carter, Trutanich's chief deputy. In three lawsuits, groups representing the occupiers alleged civil rights violations before they were evicted, asking the courts for an injunction against eviction and for costs associated with their suits as well as any other relief deemed appropriate. Any time the city is sued, its attorneys consider countersuing, according to Carter.

Still, there is something unseemly about charging people for exercising their 1st Amendment rights on public property, even if that protest was confrontational or illegal. Would we have expected the federal government to charge Martin Luther King Jr. and the Southern Christian Leadership Conference for trampling the grass on the National Mall during the 1963 March on Washington?

On balance, the Occupy L.A. demonstration was carried out by a nonviolent group that did not seriously damage City Hall itself. The protesters broke no windows, stormed no doors – and when they were forced out, they either left or surrendered to arrest with little resistance. They had their say, and now the city has its frontyard back. At this point, there appears to be scant need for legal action from either side. But whether or not the protestors drop their lawsuits, the City Council should drop any thought of trying to get its money back. That's one cost a city must bear for being open to all.

Courtesy of the Los Angeles Times

Figure 12.3 The opening of a strong staff editorial indicates the editorial board's position on the issue discussed.

way to look at the problem, provide historical perspective or examine the action from a different ethical perspective.

The Los Angeles Times' position is clear from the headline—the protesters should not have to pay to clean up after their protest. However, the paper is fair to those who disagree, in this case the city, which is suing for the cost of cleanup. Fairly, and without sarcasm, the paper states the city's position. The protestors are being sued because they first sued the city for civil rights violations. Cities often countersue when they are sued. The editorial is discussing the countersuit by the city, both explaining it and saying why it is not right.

> *The protesters did sue first ... In three lawsuits, groups representing the occupiers alleged civil rights violations before they were evicted, asking the courts for an injunction against eviction and for costs associated with their suits as well as any other relief deemed appropriate. Any time the city is sued, its attorneys consider countersuing, according to Carter.*
>
> *Still, there is something unseemly about charging people for exercising their 1st Amendment rights on public property, even if that protest was confrontational or illegal.*

The transitions between paragraphs are especially important in editorials. Clear transitions help your audience know when you are acknowledging the opposing position, adding information, giving an example to clarify your position, or asking a question for effect, that is, a **rhetorical question**.

The Los Angeles Times editorial uses a rhetorical question combined with another rhetorical device, *reductio ad absurdum*, Latin for "reduce to the absurd." **Rhetorical devices** are classical methods of persuading an audience. *Reductio ad absurdum* shows the fallacy of a position by taking it to an extreme.

> *Would we have expected the federal government to charge Martin Luther King Jr. and the Southern Christian Leadership Conference for trampling the grass on the National Mall during the 1963 March on Washington?*

Your Turn

1. As a careful reader, what do you expect these transition statements to introduce?
    - For instance ...
    - From a practical perspective ...
    - Still ...
    - On balance ...
    - On the other hand ...
    - Nonetheless ...
2. **Going Deeper.** Locate and print out three editorials and highlight the transitions used. What does each signal?

The Closing

The closing includes a call to specific action on a timely matter: abolish the bells, establish a day care center, allow late starts on snow days, write your legislature, rearrange the bus schedule.

"Free speech is free" finishes by clearly opposing the city's lawsuit:

That's one cost a city must bear for being open to all.

Signed Opinion Pieces

The signed editorial, opinion piece or opinion column, often called an op-ed, is the work of one writer, generally a member of your staff or, more rarely, a well-informed member of your community whose work you have carefully edited so it conforms to journalistic standards of honesty and accuracy. In print media, it appears in the editorial section. The piece bears the writer's name and may be read on-air by the writer. Opinion podcasts should be clearly labeled as opinion.

Opinion pieces are almost always followed by contact information for the writer. If the writer is a member of your staff, then a staff e-mail address is included.

If you accept submissions from people who are not on your publication's staff, their affiliations and contact information should also be provided: *Sophomore Bishoy Tawfik is an exchange student from Egypt. He can be reached at BHTawfik@xnet.com.* Remember to hold all contributors to the same standards of accuracy and fairness, whether they are on your staff or not. Fact check everything. Ask the writer for his sources. Check them!

What to Write for an Op-Ed

An op-ed is timely. It adds perspective to an issue that currently concerns your community, perhaps as revealed by the comments and links on the social media sites of your audience. It may inform the audience about a timely issue as well as persuade it. The op-ed provides a unique perspective on an issue that has been covered or discussed in previous editions, your publication's social media site, or in blogging and micro-blogging sites. It may also comment on issues being discussed in the national or regional media when you can provide local perspective on the problem.

Do not publish an op-ed on a topic that is unrelated to something covered in your publication or broadcast, or that has not been a current and important story in the professional press or of great concern to your audience. By doing so you would risk seeming both irrelevant and selfish—the editorial page is not a personal soapbox.

Consider covering the issue first as news or a feature. Think about your core news values of proximity, timeliness, impact, prominence, oddity, conflict and human interest. If it does not have news value, perhaps the topic does not belong in an op-ed. Publishing fair and balanced news or feature coverage of an issue before you editorialize about it may blunt criticism that otherwise would be aimed at your publication. When you do take a strong, and perhaps unpopular, stand in your opinion section, you will be able to contrast your balanced and objective coverage of the issue with your clearly labeled and signed opinion. This practice provides some protection against claims that your publication is slanted, biased, overly critical or unfair.

How to Write an Op-Ed

Op-eds should be no longer than necessary to make a significant comment. Opinion pages in professional papers often limit contributions to 1,000 words. Student publications should consider carefully before allowing a writer more space. Broadcast op-eds are shorter, usually fewer than 500 words—about three minutes.

Op-eds may be less formal than unsigned staff editorials, but they are usually about serious issues and are presented in a dignified, though sometimes playful, manner. Topics can be varied: the media's silliness during a political campaign; brain damage to professional football players; the death of a friend, classmate or family member.

An op-ed generally uses relatively formal language. It may address the audience as "you" but will use "I" sparingly. When "I" is used, it is usually to relate what the writer saw or did, not how the writer felt.

Personal Reactions

An op-ed often concentrates on the topic and the facts, but it may include the writer's personal reaction or changes to the writer's point of view: "But as a fan, I'm finding it a little harder to cheer ..." (Figure 12.4).

Well-written personal reactions, such as reactions to serious events like a disaster or death, may make a strong op-ed. When your listeners or readers finish such an op-ed, they should say, "Oh my gosh. I never thought of it that way" or "I feel the same way, but she said it better than I could" or "I wonder how I would feel if that happened to me?" However, the emotional impact of the story should come from what the writer shows the audience, not from a discussion of the writer's emotions.

Taking a Stance

An op-ed may quote expert sources, statistics and facts. The writer's reputation for honesty and solid research should stand behind each fact. The op-ed uses from-the-scene reporting only as anecdotes to illustrate or persuade, not to create balance, as in a news story. After looking at both sides, you are reporting your conclusions and your reasons and attempting to persuade or enlighten your audience.

Two op-eds may be presented together as point-counterpoint. Another writer with a different, though not necessarily opposite opinion, writes an op-ed that is roughly the same length.

An op-ed, like an editorial, may call for a specific action, but it may also seek to change attitudes or point out inconsistencies. It may be less direct than a staff editorial, but its message should be clear to the audience. The writer should be able to tell an editor, "The point of this op-ed is that ..." even if such a statement never appears in the op-ed.

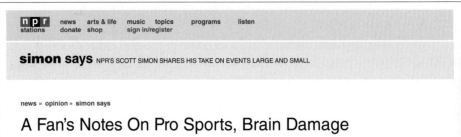

Figure 12.4 Although op-eds are fact based, writers may include a personal reaction in their op-ed, which can strengthen the piece.

npr stations news donate arts & life shop music sign in/register topics programs listen

simon says NPR'S SCOTT SIMON SHARES HIS TAKE ON EVENTS LARGE AND SMALL

news » opinion » simon says

A Fan's Notes On Pro Sports, Brain Damage

JANUARY 28, 2012 7:40 AM ET

SCOTT SIMON

I will watch the Super Bowl next weekend, along with several billion other people. I expect to cheer, shout and have some guacamole.

But as a fan, I'm finding it a little harder to cheer, especially for my favorite football and hockey players, without thinking: They're hurting themselves.

Not just breaks and sprains but dangerous, disabling brain damage.

Case studies have mounted over the past year. Dave Duerson of the 1985 Super Bowl-winning Bears shot himself in the chest just after the last Super Bowl and left a note: "Please, see that my brain is given to the NFL's brain bank."

That's Boston University's Center for the Study of Traumatic Encephalopathy, which determined that Mr. Duerson's brain had been battered by at least 10 concussions and countless other football hits that may have caused dementia, addiction and depression that led to his death.

Jim McMahon, once the team's brash quarterback, confided at a 25th reunion that his memory is "pretty much gone."

"It's unfortunate what the game does to you," he said.

The dazzling Walter Payton of that same famous team died of liver disease. But a biography published last year achingly depicts the depression and addictions Mr. Payton suffered during decades of hits: thousands in games, tens of thousands in practice.

Sidney Crosby of the Pittsburgh Penguins is hockey's greatest star — the skater who scored Canada's goal over the U.S. to win a gold medal at the 2010 Olympic Games.

But Sid the Kid suffered a concussion last January. Who knows when, or if, he'll play again?

Just a few weeks ago, John Branch of *The New York Times* wrote a heart-piercing series after three NHL "enforcers" — paid brawlers — died within four months last year. He focused on Derek Boogaard of the New York Rangers, who accidentally overdosed on booze and oxycodone at the age of 28.

Boston University's Center opened Derek Boogaard's brain and found profound damage.

Chris Nowinski, a center co-director, is a former pro-wrestler who loves contact sports. But he went to a Boston Bruins hockey game shortly thereafter and says that when a routine brawl broke out, fans stood and cheered. He couldn't.

Several former players have filed lawsuits. Sports writers and pundits have called for new rules and equipment, although most studies show new rules and equipment may do little to limit injury while players grow larger, faster and risk more to sign million-dollar contracts.

I'll watch the Super Bowl next week with my children and wonder how comfortable we fans can be, sitting and snacking while too many of the players we cheer entertain us and get rich at such terrible cost to themselves.

Courtesy of NPR

Rhetorical Devices

An op-ed may use analogies and rhetorical devices such as irony, hyperbole and repetition, but it does not assume everyone is a friend or like-minded buddy. It uses irony sparingly, and only when the irony is made clear to the audience or when it is used in such small doses that even if the reader misses the irony, the meaning is still clear. For instance, an opinion writer wrote that one presidential candidate was "colorless and charisma-free." If the reader only understood "colorless" but missed the humor in "charisma-free," the passage would still mean the candidate was bland and uninteresting.

Humor

An op-ed may use humor to comment positively about lighthearted or positive events. For instance, in politics, "baggage" often means

And Now... Closer to Home

Rhetorical Devices in Op-Eds

- Hyperbole—deliberate overstatement, such as calling a month "an eternity." *It's been a month since President Obama announced his support for same-sex marriage and was declared, on the cover of Newsweek, "the first gay president." **That's an eternity in politics**.* (Meghan Daum, "Really? First gay president?" Los Angeles Times)
- Irony—tension created by the contrast between appearances and reality. ***There are some nice deals to be had** in the income tax code these days, but most wealth accumulates and passes from generation to generation with no tax at all.* (Michael Kinsley, "The wealth gap" Los Angeles Times) "Nice deals" usually refers to shopping for cars, not working an unfair tax code.
- Repetition. ***How bad is it?** Bad enough that references to the 1930s have begun gingerly creeping into Italians' conversations … **How bad is it?** Bad enough that to many Italians, President Obama's economic policies look like a success story.* (Doyle McManus, "All pain, no gain in southern Europe" Los Angeles Times)

previous errors and mistakes, and "dirty laundry" means moral, ethical or legal infractions in the person's past. At the end of a signed editorial about a presidential candidate's dog, which had traveled atop the family car in a dog carrier, Meghan Daum wrote, "... if this is the extent of his personal baggage, he's traveling light." She ends by saying, "It's even been said that [the candidate] shared his bed with [the dog] when his wife was away. Now there's some dirty laundry for you."

The humor pokes fun at the amount of attention the dog was receiving from the media while other candidates had more serious moral failings. The candidate would probably have been pleased to see the "dog-carrier" issue lampooned.

Self-deprecating humor, humor that pokes fun at the writer or the writer's group, also may be part of an op-ed, but not the main point of the piece. For instance, conservative—that is, "right wing"—columnist William F. Buckley once commented that he would appear on a television show if the producer would agree to fly him on a plane with "two right wings." He laughed at his own politics.

An op-ed writer should consider carefully before attempting satire. If your satire leads you to use hyperbole—to exaggerate or say anything that is not literally true—your audience, especially those who disagree with you, may condemn you for journalistic inaccuracy even though *you* know you are being satirical. Many people—including adults—should read and respond to your satire before you publish it to see if the satire is clear to all parts of your audience and is well-aimed. Each of your responders should see immediately that the piece is meant to be satire, and they should be able to identify what is being satirized.

The Shape of an Op-Ed

Op-eds do not follow a set formula as do staff editorials, so journalists have more room for powerful language, narrative and creativity but also more potential to lose their audience or to bore them. Every word must count. It is good discipline to write your op-ed, then edit it down by 20 percent. A 1,000-word op-ed should be tightened to say the same thing in 800 words.

The Opening

Opening sentences in op-eds require strong writing. After all, you are not offering information but rather your opinion. If the opening is not strong, you will lose your audience in the first inch or the first 20 seconds. If your opening implies a problem, your audience should want to read to the end to see your insight or your solution.

The opening needs to engage the audience and establish the subject and tone of the op-ed—serious, satiric, self-mocking, critical or reflective. Scott Simon's op-ed in Figure 12.4 engages the audience by contrasting the pleasant anticipation of a football game with the specter of serious injury to the players.

> *I will watch the Super Bowl next weekend ... I expect to cheer, shout and have some guacamole.*
>
> *But as a fan, I'm finding it a little harder to cheer, especially for my favorite football and hockey players, without thinking: They're hurting themselves.*
>
> *Not just breaks and sprains but dangerous, disabling brain damage.*

The Body

The body of an op-ed may contain **exposition**—language that conveys information or provides an explanation—such as arguments, evidence, rebuttals of the opposing side, timelines and even bulleted lists. Note Scott Simon's use of exposition in his op-ed on sports injuries.

> *... Boston University's Center for the Study of Traumatic Encephalopathy ... determined that Mr. Duerson's brain had been battered by at least 10 concussions and countless other football hits that may have caused dementia, addiction and depression that led to his death.*

The op-ed may also contain **narrative** (story) elements, such as the writer's own experience or well-told (and well-verified) stories from others.

The narrative elements should be as tightly written and fast-paced as any piece of fiction, with strong settings and real (not just real-seeming) characters. The dialogue needs to be both realistic and truthful.

Narrative journalism has its own special dangers. Of course, stories should not be made up. But even true stories should not be **fictionalized**.

Ethical journalists do not create details, nor do they change them. If a conversation happened before school, do not say it happened at lunch. If one short person reports being hit in the face by a tall person's backpack in the hallway, do not say *people* have complained. Do not say you saw the assault by the swinging backpack if you only heard about it. Do not say you saw the bruise if you did not.

The Closing

The closing of an op-ed, whether it is primarily narrative or primarily expositive, should make the writer's position clear. It may be a call to action, or it may be a clearly stated conclusion or a summary of an

Seven Ways to Make Your Audience Cranky: How *Not* to Start an Op-Ed

Don't:

1. Make a claim without verifying it.
   - *More and more teenagers are smoking.* Nope. Teen smoking has been going down.
   - *The entire student body expected huge changes for this school year.* Really? Did you ask everyone?
2. Use *most* or *all* without statistical evidence. "Most" is over 50 percent. "All" is 100 percent.
   - *Every student has tried to get onto his favorite website while at school and has been upset when Facebook or Twitter was blocked."* Really? How about the kids with smartphones?
   - *We all have opinions on everything.* Even about eyebrow waxing in Albania?
3. State the obvious. Your audience's first reaction should not be "Well, duh!"
   - *The holiday season is upon us.*
   - *Many of us take the bus to get to school and back home.*
4. Ask questions that cannot be answered in fewer than 1,000 words.
   - *Is the Christmas season too commercial?*
   - *What does it mean to be a Cantwell Indian?*
5. Start with the time element when the time is not the focus in the op-ed. Better to start with a subject and a verb.
   - *On Friday, November 28, students involved with the larger "occupy" were pepper-sprayed.* Would it have been OK on Saturday, November 29?
   - *Every year there is a huge story about nutrition in American schools.* Only once a year?
6. Make your audience wade through a swamp of empty words to get to the noun and verb. *Whether it be in the form of Tumblr posts, music videos or ubiquitous YouTube advertisements, it's certain that something is brewing in mainstream American culture, something that's been bubbling underneath the surface for centuries. Feminism.*

   Without the confusing swamp of words, the writer seems to mean, "Aren't we about ready to outgrow our gender biases?"
7. Fragments! Gawwkkkk! Save the single words for the headline, or better yet, the slammer in the headline.
   - *Lockers. In almost every high school movie ever made ...*
   - *Homework. College applications. SATs. What more can a senior ...*
   - *Spirit week. Five craze-filled school days ...*

important insight. The closing may seek to motivate the audience's actions or to change their attitudes.

> *I'll watch the Super Bowl next week with my children and wonder how comfortable we fans can be, sitting and snacking while too many of the players we cheer entertain us and get rich at such terrible cost to themselves.*

Columns

Columns are regularly occurring articles published in the same section—and often the same position on the page or in the broadcast—in each edition, broadcast or post. A column is written by the same person—or a series of people—each time it appears. At most major papers, columnists write two or three times a week. Two or three columnists trade off throughout the week, so readers know where to look for a column in each edition. In papers that publish less often, the column appears in every edition. Broadcasts establish a set schedule for columns—and columnists—to appear.

Figure 12.1 shows how design elements can mark an opinion column as different from news and feature content. These design elements will draw your audience's eye and ear to your work. They also signal that the column is the opinion of one person.

Columns may appear in almost any section of your publication, but columnists usually focus on their specialties, their beats. That is, they specialize in a limited number of topics. For example, one columnist may write about state politics, laws and policies, another about local governments and the people affected by local government decisions, and a third about education.

Your columns will become stronger over time as you learn more about the topics you cover. Though columnists may branch out to write about a variety of topics, your readers should expect them to be highly knowledgeable about a limited number of beats. Your electronic media columnist would not be expected to provide expert commentary on the cheerleading finals. Your fashion columnist is not expected to provide expert coverage of religion in his column. The sports section often divides the column-writing responsibilities so that two or more columnists follow different sports in fall, winter and spring.

A columnist is a combination of a beat reporter, an op-ed writer and a narrative author who shares his informed opinions with his audience over and over again. His is one of the most prized jobs in journalism. If you do this job well, people will look for your writing no matter what your topic. They will stop you in the halls to agree with you or argue with you about what you have written. If you do it poorly, only your mother will read it.

What Does It Take to Be a Good Columnist?

Columnists need the strengths of an experienced reporter and the skills of an op-ed writer. They also need many of the talents of a short story writer, though of course columnists—like other ethical journalists—do not create or misrepresent facts. An effective columnist needs to create a unique voice and appropriate tone to bring readers back, column after column.

The Columnist as Reporter

Like a good reporter, a columnist needs to know her beat and her sources well so that she can continue to find interesting story ideas and not miss important developments. She needs a broad base of knowledge and good reporting and interviewing skills. She needs a firm grasp of the core news values as well as the knack of finding the unsung hero or the out-of-the-way event. She needs a nose for news, for almost all columns are built around a news peg.

Show Me What You See Before You Tell Me What You Think

Yvette Cabrera is an award-winning investigative journalist. As a columnist for the Orange County Register, she wrote about beer and the Latino community in a column headlined "Brewing: Latinos are the most targeted by the beer industry. How much are we missing because we're too drunk to remember it?" The column both reports and comments on the issue. The news pegs—there are two—are the release of a Latino-themed commercial for Miller beer and one local nonprofit's efforts to fight alcoholism in the community. In her column she reports:

Photo by Daniel A. Anderson, Courtesy of Yvette Cabrera

... America Bracho and her Santa Ana nonprofit Latino Health Access launched a campaign of their own. But not with slick television commercials or thousands of dollars.

Instead, America comes live and direct on the kind of sweaty August afternoon that makes you want to retreat to a shady, air-conditioned corner. She and her team of health workers advance into the heat of Santa Ana's streets.

You can see signs of their door-knocking, pavement-pounding work all over the tree-lined neighborhood near Garfield Elementary. Sarapes, bright rainbow-colored blankets that symbolize nurturing and caring, are draped from apartment balconies, chain-link fences and doorways. These sarapes show solidarity for alcohol awareness and compassion for families affected by alcohol.

Though Cabrera has a strong, even impassioned, message, the work of Latino Health Access and the release of the Latino-themed advertising campaign provide the news pegs. Her column was timely and sprung from her knowledge of her beat.

The Columnist as Op-Ed Writer

A columnist's job may begin as a reporter's job, but it goes beyond it. A columnist needs to discover the meaning in the events. Like an editorial or op-ed writer, a columnist may criticize and suggest solutions, advocate, appreciate and point out when an incident is becoming a trend. He needs to be master of the op-ed form because columns are also opinion pieces. Like op-eds, they include facts, interviews, anecdotes, or characters and conflicts that illuminate the point the columnist wants to make or the insight the columnist wants to share. In a column, characters or events often figure more prominently than in an op-ed.

Like the op-ed writer, the columnist needs to be able to identify the point; for instance, "The point of this column is that mentally ill people love and are loved, even if they cannot function in families." That sentence will probably not appear in the column, but the columnist needs to be able to tell an editor or responder what the point is. The copy editor who creates the headline should be able to recognize this point. The copy editor may even use it as the headline.

For instance, in Cabrera's story the headline *says* what the column *shows*.

> *Brewing: Latinos are the most targeted by the beer industry. How much are we missing because we're too drunk to remember it?*

The Columnist as Storyteller

Columnists report real settings, such as the hot August streets of Santa Ana, California. They portray real people—columnists never create events or characters, but they portray them as deftly as any short story writer and in just as few words.

Cabrera begins her column by describing the beer company's advertising campaign, which is aimed at Latinos. The lead is

> *I don't know his name, but he's brown-skinned like me. I don't know who he is, but he tells me in that voice—that played out, pachuco-style East L.A. drawl—that beer is part of our lives.*
>
> *Our lives being Latino. The beer being Miller.*
>
> *"People talk with friends over this beer. They spend time with family over this beer," the man says into the camera and directly into my living room via the only connection we have: my television.*

Columnists sketch real conflicts. Cabrera reports on an Alcoholics Anonymous meeting in Anaheim.

> *... when a Mexican father told the group that even after 3 1/2 years of being sober it was hard to win back his family.*
>
> *"My 18-year-old still rejects me. I hurt her the most," he said.*

Columnists may pace the action, sometimes breaking from the action at a crucial point to provide statistics and quotes, then return to finish their story. A story often frames the column, beginning with the lead and not ending until the final line. Well-told stories keep audiences interested. They make the columnist's point.

The Voice of the Column

A columnist needs to develop and sustain a voice—a characteristic way of expressing herself—that her audience recognizes and enjoys. A voice helps maintain a regular following, that is, repeat readers and viewers. Finding your voice is as much art as science—voice is made up of thousands of choices—but finding it is an essential part of column writing.

Sandy Banks, who wrote a twice-weekly column for the Los Angeles Times for over 36 years, tells how she developed her voice:

> *I try to follow the advice I offer to young women: Be true to yourself. I don't always have the answers, but I am always willing to ask the questions. I try to follow my own heart in pursuit of columns, and that means owning up to confusion, conflict, indecision, anger, awe. I try to be intellectually curious and emotionally vulnerable. If you are reliably authentic, people may disagree, but they will trust you enough to at least listen.*

Courtesy of the Los Angeles Times

MEET THE PROFESSIONALS:

Sandy Banks

Sandy Banks grew up in Cleveland, Ohio, with an after-school routine: On cold days, she'd lie on the floor, put her feet on a heating vent and read Ann Landers and Dear Abby. Then she'd clip out her favorite columns and stick them in her journal. She still has a few. They remind her of the power of the written word to comfort, challenge, teach and inspire.

She worked on her college paper at Ohio State University, but when her mother was diagnosed with cancer during her sophomore year, she moved home to help care for her. Sandy's mother died a few months later.

The next year Sandy graduated *cum laude* from Cleveland State University and took a job as a sports writer at a black weekly newspaper while trying to decide between law school and teaching. She had so much fun—and learned so much from the people she wrote about—that she found herself hooked on journalism. She spent two years as a reporter at the Cleveland Press before moving to California in 1979 to join the staff of the Los Angeles Times.

She worked for the Los Angeles Times as an education reporter, the religion and education editor, assistant metropolitan editor, a features columnist, an editorial writer and as the director of the newspaper's internship program. She was on the team awarded a Pulitzer Prize for coverage of the Los Angeles riots in 1992.

Her twice-a-week columns on events and issues in the news offered her personal perspective as an African-American woman and a single mother—her husband died when her three girls were small.

It's *Not* How You Talk!

Record yourself in conversation with others, especially when you think you are being witty or persuasive. Then type out a transcript of your words. Are you witty and persuasive in print?

Very few people seem intelligent or interesting when they transfer their speaking voices directly to print or broadcast. Skillful columnists appear to be using "everyday language" and a casual voice, but their job is rarely as simple as "writing the way you speak." A columnist needs to develop a written voice through careful choices and careful rewriting. Columnists know that their everyday speaking voice will not necessarily make an appropriate and enjoyable voice in a column.

Columnists frequently create a persona—a personality—for their columns that they may not use in their other writing. The persona is not fictional—it is rather an attitude toward himself or his reader and his topic that the columnist puts on or takes off like work clothes, different clothes for different writing tasks. When the audience and the purpose vary, so does the persona and therefore the voice.

Chris Erskine (Figure 12.5), a Los Angeles Times columnist and editor, has used several voices during his career, contributing four types of reoccurring works for the paper.

1. Travel Ticker, a weekly feature for the paper's travel section.
2. Fan of the House, a column for the sports section.
3. Man About Town, a column in the home & garden section.
4. Book reviews.

For each task, each with a different audience and purpose, he assumes a different persona.

As he wrote "Travel Ticker," Erskine is a journalist, almost always in the background, collecting and prioritizing travel opportunities and events, then crafting the 5 W's into brief mentions, each separated by four dots. Erskine says, "I try to keep it a little jaunty, but most of the work goes into collecting the info."

Figure 12.5 Los Angeles Times columnist Chris Erskine.

Courtesy of the Los Angeles Times

A "Pirates of the Caribbean" movie marathon, plus a question-and-answer session with some members of the cast and production team, will be part of the ParkFilm Fest on May 5 at Paramount Studios. Proceeds will help offset cuts to California state parks. Info: www.calparks.org/.... Big Bear Lake is offering special deals for cycling fans at this year's Amgen Tour of California Stage 6 Finish, May 18.

In the Fan of the House sports columns, Erskine *talked* to his audience, usually as one fan to another, often with some fan-to-fan ribbing. He writes, "I'm constantly fighting against the forces who take it (sports) all too seriously, even though for those involved, it's a big and serious business. The fans shouldn't see it that way though, which is where I come in."

> *While you were sleeping, L.A. has become America's most-accomplished sports town—three teams in the playoffs, a first-place baseball club, a championship soccer franchise and a college football team that will probably contend for a title this fall.*
>
> *At one point, it looked as if the Lakers and the Clippers would be squaring off against each other at the Big Staple at the same time the Kings would be in the Stanley Cup finals.*
>
> *OK, get a grip.*

In his earlier Man About Town columns and in his current column, The Middle Ages, Erskine often writes about his own family's experiences in Los Angeles. Here, his voice is the most distinctive. Erskine writes, "I mock myself to make up for my mocking of everything else."

He is a clueless, large-sized child surrounded by—and at the mercy of—a competent wife (he refers to her as "Posh" or "Poshy"), sons (he refers to the youngest as "the little guy") and competent daughters. He refers to one as "the lovely and patient older daughter." As for the younger, he writes:

> *Took the daughters surfing the other day. I've noticed lately that most of the activities they like have dollar signs in front of them. In fact, one of them just legally changed her name to Vi$a. Tough decision. It was either that or Cha-Ching.*

But when Erskine reviews comedian and actor Paul Reiser's book "Familyhood," he discusses the author's voice as ably as would any professor of literature.

> *As a performer, Reiser's particular gift seems to give words a percussive emphasis, almost a rim shot. They are reactive, these jabs, to other people in the show.*
>
> *In his writing, it takes a while to hear that voice again, to find the beats of his sentences. But if you like Reiser the comic, you're likely to enjoy Reiser the writer ...*
>
> *Point of view is everything with Reiser, not to mention an eye for the little things in a father's life. Reiser doesn't so much pick the right word as accentuate the right emotion.*

> *Next to the computer on my desk is a black-and-white photograph of my mother and father on their wedding day," he writes. "They look impossibly young; he in his Army uniform, looking like a cross between John Garfield and Glenn Miller; she, beautiful and sparkly, a Jewish Donna Reed. Stare at it long enough and you can almost make out the sound of their thoughts."*
>
> *Fine passage, particularly that "sound of their thoughts" line. It captures Reiser at his best ...*

Who better than a columnist to appreciate a writer's voice?

Journalistic Blogs

A blog is a publishing format—online, updated frequently. A **journalistic blog**—unlike a personal blog—follows journalism ethics and standards and may contain the same sorts of content that are in the rest of the journalistic publication, including reviews, op-eds, columns and editorial cartoons (Figure 12.6).

One of the beauties of the blog format is its freedom. This applies to editorial content as well as all other journalistic content.

It can be shorter than a column, or longer. It can be more timely than a column, or it can be evergreen; that is, without a strong time element and therefore fresh—"green"—for a long time. It can include sound, photos or video. It can be full of links to evidence and background—documents,

Figure 12.6 Journalistic blogs can report news or express informed opinions. They can embed links to further reading and sources and they can be as long or short at the topic requires. *How does a journalist's blog need to differ from that of a private citizen?*

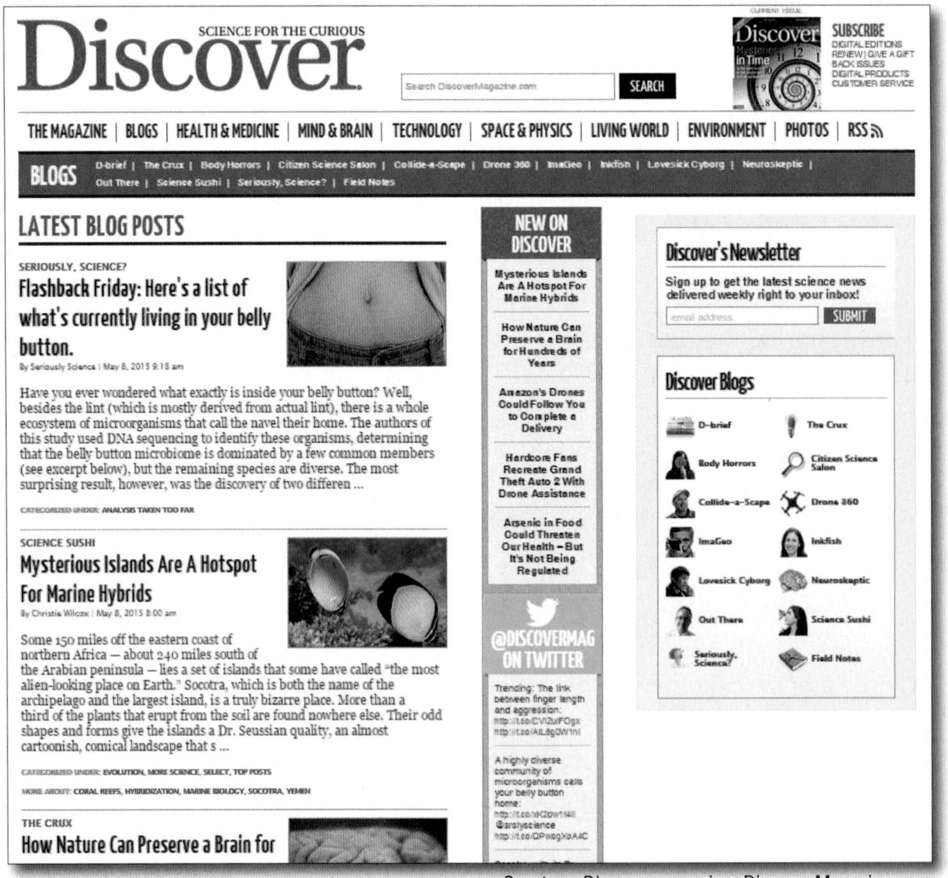

Courtesy *Discover* magazine, DiscoverMagazine.com

websites and audio and video elements as well as other stories your publication has covered.

A blog can be one observation, or it can follow a story as it unfolds, adding new entries several times during a day. Adding new posts requires some skill. The newest blog generally will appear on top, with older ones available below. The new posts need to be clear even to those readers who have not read the earlier entries.

Blog Advantages

Journalistic blogs allow you to exchange ideas and information with your audience. The number of responses may indicate your audience's interest in the topic and suggest which stories deserve more coverage. Readers may suggest additional story ideas, tell you more facts and stories about the positions you take and correct you when you are wrong either in fact or in perspective. They will remind you if there is another side that has not been represented or point out that you have ignored important background information.

Journalistic blogs allow you to grow as a multimedia storyteller using sound, interactive elements, and still and video images on short entries.

They allow you to develop your voice as a columnist, to develop your ability to find column-worthy, newsworthy stories and to grow as an interviewer, a researcher and an opinion writer.

Standards Are the Same

Journalist blogs should adhere to the same ethical and journalistic standards as the rest of your publication or broadcast.

- Opinion blogs should be separated from news blogs. Your readers should know whether the blog is news or commentary.
- Good headlines and your byline should pull readers and viewers to your blog.
- Opinions need to be backed by facts and examples.
- Facts need to be backed by solid reporting.
- Blogs should be checked for libel, slander, invasion of privacy and copyright infringement. Links embedded in your blog are a strong way to share content without breaking copyright laws.
- Blogs should adhere to the same standards of language use and appropriateness as the rest of your publication.
- Blogs should be fact checked for accuracy and proofread for your publication's style.
- At least two sets of eyes should see a blog before it is posted. One is usually an online editor.

Journalistic blogs are not the correct forum for all your private opinions. As a journalist you need to guard against expressing any opinion that would make you appear incapable of covering news in a fair and balanced manner. Be careful to remain a journalist.

YOUR TURN

With a small group, make a list of 10 topics about which you have opinions or about which you have made complaints or comments. For each of the opinions, complaints or comments, describe research or perspectives that would turn the topic into a journalistic blog.

Example (so far this is a personal complaint): *Why do all of our teachers have to assign big projects due the last week before Christmas break? I have papers or projects in five classes, all due in the last three days!*

To make it a topic for a journalistic blog, you would need to talk with teachers who make such assignments. If you find that they assign such projects because Christmas break gives them time to correct them, you could write a humorous piece about how all of you stress out to submit the projects before the holiday but the teachers go home with their rolling luggage full of essays to grade during the holiday.

In professional publications, bloggers are often limited to one range of topics. In your publication, your viewers should know whose blog to read for commentary on softball, the academic decathlon, the child care class or the culinary arts class. For successful journalistic blogging, remember these guidelines.

- Post commentary regularly so that the audience keeps looking to your blog for new material. Stale blogs should be archived, usually with a link on the blogger's page to the older stories.
- Good writing garners readers. Bad writing bores.
- The same is true for photos and videos. Do not waste your audience's time.
- Develop a voice for your blog.
- Sound, slide shows and videos also may have a distinct voice.

Editorial Illustrations and Cartoons

Though photographs are relatively rare in editorial and opinion sections, these sections are not visually uninteresting columns of text. Editorial illustrations and editorial cartoons add visual interest and depth to the writing and to the section. Both types of editorial work cause the viewer to think. They both need to be clearly and cleanly drawn, whether by hand or by computer.

Technically, an editorial illustration and an editorial cartoon are different. An **editorial illustration** enriches an op-ed piece and is meant to draw the readers or viewers into the article and to emphasize its point (Figure 12.7).

An **editorial cartoon,** on the other hand, may be about a new topic not already discussed in writing or provide a new viewpoint on a topic that has been discussed. An editorial cartoon is frequently critical of the subjects it portrays and almost always attempts to make a single, pointed comment about the issue being discussed (Figure 12.8 on page 378).

ECONOMIC ▶ HOLIDAY

Black Friday shopping overshadows time with family

Amanda Livingston
Opinions Editor

Black Friday. The day when companies prepare their stores for a massive crowd of aggressive, sale seeking customers.

My dad has worked retail pretty much all his life with the exception of one year he was unemployed. As a kid, my dad wasn't gone too much to work for Black Friday -- or at least, it seemed that way.

As the years have gone on, I've become more aware of the gap left by the absence of his presence.

My dad worked for a number of years at Target, where they would have to be at the store at 4 a.m., to open at 6 in the morning. They would then work a 12 hour shift.

When he worked at the Sony Outlet store in San Marcos, my dad would have to eat an early dinner on Thanksgiving, and take a nap before leaving for work at 9 p.m. They would then work until midnight prepping the store, and would open at midnight.

Black Friday is a ludicrous excuse for businesses to boost profits by making people work obscenely scheduled hours so that consumers can go out and spend all their money on things they don't need.

Occasionally there's some insane customer who pulls a knife or a gun on someone, just because they called dibs on a shirt that someone else tried to grab at the same time. Last year a woman took a knife from the home accessories section of a Wal-Mart, only to use it to stab a man several times to prevent him from taking the last Xbox 360.

Some would argue, that Black Friday saves money on holiday presents and that the deals are great. I won't deny that. You can get all your Christmas shopping out of the way, for much less than you would spend on a normal shopping excursion. Others would argue that when someone applies for a job in retail, they should know what they're signing up for.

However the amount of hours the employees are asked to work has increased greatly over the years and the dangerous crowds make it difficult to support. Before, retail stores would open the Friday following Thanksgiving, but now some like Kmart, aren't closing at all.

Alright mom, I'm going off to work!
But Sweety, what about Thanksgiving dinner?
Save me some! The store opens in 5hours, and I need to help prep!
Johanna Dakay

Corporations need to set a boundary, and stop taking away from something as special as Thanksgiving.

The Thanksgiving season is about being thankful and taking advantage of what you are given, and what you have. Having a shopping day right after Thanksgiving where people spend their money to buy a bunch of new stuff takes away the meaning of the holiday.

Article by Amanda Livingston, Illustration by Johanna Dakay, The Eagle's Eye, W. Charles Akins High School

Figure 12.7 An editorial illustration accompanies and supports an op-ed piece, while also adding visual interest.

YOUR TURN

Clip or print two editorial illustrations and two editorial cartoons that communicate to you. Describe to your group or class what each piece of editorial art means to you.

Symbols, labels, caricatures, and references to common sayings and stories all help make the meaning of the art clear. These communication tools are especially important if the artwork is an editorial cartoon not associated with a story.

Symbols

Editorial illustrations and cartoons go beyond mere decoration. Good editorial page artwork invites thoughtful consideration of the issues raised in the op-ed. It often does this by communicating through symbols—concrete objects that represent an abstract idea.

Your school mascot is a ready-made symbol for your entire school and school community. You probably do not need to label him. When a graduate of your school is killed in military action, your Viking or Fighting Fisherman or Atom Smasher can hold his headgear in his hand and bow his head in respect before a military grave.

Institutions and public figures are also frequently represented in editorial cartoons by symbols that most readers and viewers easily recognize, thus avoiding the need for labels. Political cartoonist Thomas Nast created the elephant as the Republican Party symbol and popularized the donkey as the Democrats' symbol and Uncle Sam as

Courtesy of David Horsey

Figure 12.8 The wealthy who increase their worth by "down-sizing" companies are targeted in this editorial cartoon using two familiar tropes, the saying, "A mother's work is never done," and the image of Uncle Scrooge McDuck who had so much excess money he took daily swims in his money pile. Uncle Scrooge is a reference to Ebenezer Scrooge in Dickens' "A Christmas Carol."

a symbol for America. These stock symbols allow cartoonists to make critical comments in a simple drawing because these abstract ideas—the parties and the country—can be shown performing symbolic actions (Figure 12.9).

Labels

The test of a good editorial illustration or editorial cartoon is how easily it communicates to the viewer or reader. Labels may be needed to make your illustration or cartoon clear to your audience. If in doubt, get responses from others on your staff and from several diverse readers to see if your meaning is clear.

Labels may be necessary on several parts of your cartoon (Figure 12.10). If you show your mascot cowering behind the post of a school building's porch, wiping his forehead, weak with relief, while a runaway school bus careens away, you may need to label the bus to explain the disaster that your school has just avoided. "State School Budget" or "Drastic Budget Cuts" or "School Closures" makes clear the danger the mascot—and your community—has just escaped.

Figure 12.9 Debuting in an editorial cartoon by Thomas Nast in the late 1800s, the elephant and donkey have represented the political parties in the United States ever since.

Caricatures

Political leaders, entertainers and other public figures are often drawn as caricatures

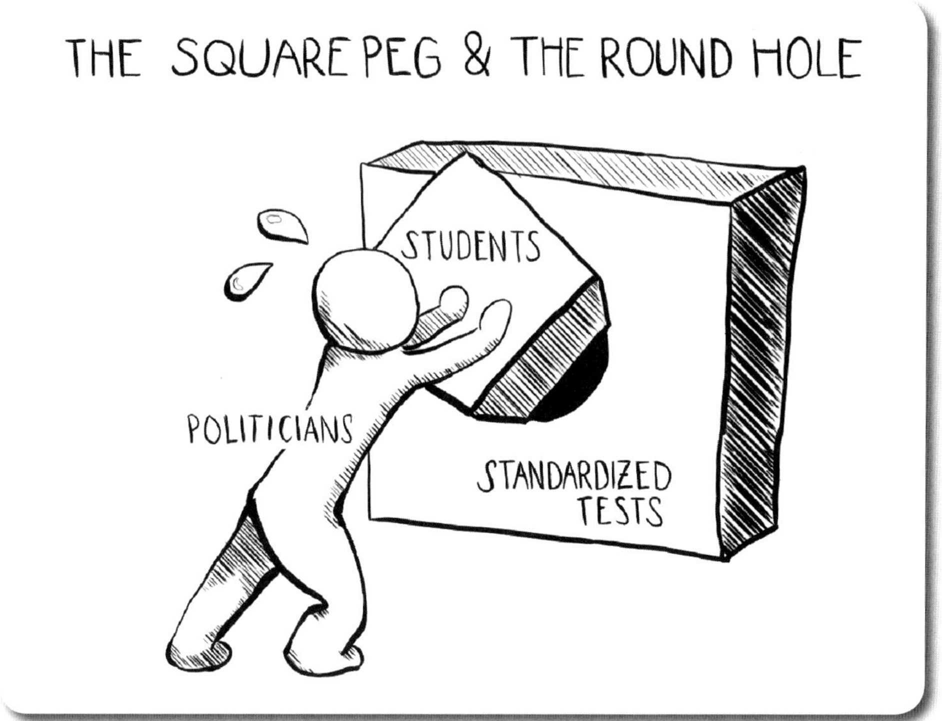

Alexandra Fernholz, Lakota East Spark, Lakota East High School, Cincinnati, Ohio

Figure 12.10 Labels make this common phrase, "a square peg in a round hole," take on a new meaning, and they make the meaning clear to your audience.

(Figure 12.11). A distinctive feature—such as large ears, a prominent jaw or an extreme hairdo—is exaggerated. Public figures are fair game for an editorial cartoonist to criticize. The audience usually understands that when the governor's caricature is shown throwing a grandma under a bus, especially if the grandma is labeled "Senior Citizens Programs," the reference is to funding cuts. The cartoonist is not accusing the governor of murder. Figure 12.12 on the next page is an example of how to criticize without using caricatures.

Figure 12.11 A caricature exaggerates features for a comical or satirical effect.

Figure 12.12 Labels and dialogue in this editorial cartoon make clear to the audience what the symbols stand for. The school administration is criticized without being caricatured.

Image courtesy of National Scholastic Press Association (nspa.studentpress.org); cartoon by Anita Hodge, The Register, Central High School

However, private citizens are entitled to greater protection under libel laws, and a caricature may be a form of libel if the recognizable figure is shown doing something the person has not done—eating babies, for instance, even if the babies are labeled "campus day care" and the reference is to the principal's closure of the child care class and the on-campus day care.

Metaphors and Allusions

Editorial cartoons and illustrations often use metaphors and allusions, relying on the audience's familiarity with common stories, sayings and traditions to communicate abstract ideas.

A metaphor may use a concrete object or experience to illuminate an abstract idea. (The word *illuminate* in the previous sentence is an example. The "concrete object or experience" has become a lamp or a flashlight. The "abstract idea" has become a dark cave or room. Because of the concrete object or experience, the abstract idea is illuminated. The verb *illuminate* creates this implied metaphor.)

An allusion draws on your audience's knowledge of another story or event. The reference to the story becomes a sort of shorthand for all the events, characters, emotions and morals associated with the story or event.

If a federal agency is about to limit access to an environmental zone where your cross-country team trains, a cartoon about it—perhaps titled "Snake in the Grass"—could show the legs of a runner in the tall grass of the environmental zone. A snake labeled with the federal agency's name, coiled to strike at the runner's legs, would be an allusion to the common saying "a snake in the grass." The proposed federal action will injure the runner.

Figure 12.13 Get opinions, as many as you think necessary, to make sure that the majority of your audience will "get" your metaphors and allusions. The point of these references is to clarify and strengthen your message, not show off your vast knowledge.

Suppose a local community college offers your football team something that seems too good to be true—college credit for off-season weight training. But your publication has discovered that the summer weight training program will deplete most of your football budget if the players sign up.

In such a case, your editorial cartoon can portray the situation with a reference to Little Red Riding Hood. Most of your audience will recognize the story. A burly football player dressed like Little Red and the wolf in Grandma's bed labeled with the name of the community college would make an allusion to a well-known fairy tale. (This allusion works even better if one of your school colors is red.) Or the weight training could be a Trojan horse, community college officials the Greeks and the high school football fund could be the city of Troy about to be raided.

Song lyrics, movies and books all help editorial artists communicate, but the artist and the section editors should use multiple responders to make sure most of the audience understands the references. An editorial cartoon is no place for an inside joke. Be sure to use a variety of responders to see what your cartoon communicates (Figure 12.13 above).

Your Turn

Clip or print three editorial cartoons or editorial illustrations: one that relies on labels, one that relies on symbols and one that relies on an allusion to a commonly known story or saying.

Chapter Twelve

Review and Assessment

Recall

1. How do publications and broadcasts identify their editorial and opinion content so it will not be confused with news content?
2. How do staff editorials differ from op-eds?
3. What is the traditional shape of a staff editorial?
4. In what way is a columnist's job like that of a beat reporter?
5. How is a columnist's work similar to the work of a storyteller?
6. What is meant by a columnist's voice and why is it important?
7. Do columnists create their voice by writing how they speak? Support your answer.
8. Name at least three advantages a journalistic blog has over a printed publication.
9. True or False: Blogs do not require an editor. Support your answer.
10. Why are labels important in editorial cartoons?

Critical Thinking

1. Create a Venn diagram comparing and contrasting a staff editorial with an op-ed.
2. Locate and print or clip two editorials about topics that interest you. Number the paragraphs for convenience as you discuss the work.
   A. Explain how you know each is a staff editorial.
   B. How long is each?
   C. Identify the issue each is discussing.
   D. What makes the issue timely?
   E. What pronouns do the editorials use?
   F. What background do the editorials provide?
   G. How do they identify and rebut the opposition's argument?
   H. What expert facts do they use?
   I. What transitions do they use?
   J. What is each editorial's position?
3. Locate and print or clip two op-ed pieces. Number the paragraphs for convenience as you discuss the work.
   A. How long is each?
   B. Identify the issue each is discussing.
   C. What makes the issue timely?
   D. What pronouns do the op-eds use?
   E. What background do the op-eds provide? Where?
   F. Do the op-eds identify and rebut the opposition's argument? Where?
   G. Do the op-eds use facts? Conflicts? Characters? Settings? Quotations or dialogue? Where?
   H. Do the op-eds use hyperbole, irony, satire or repetition? Where?
   I. What does each writer hope to accomplish with the op-ed?
4. Create a Venn diagram comparing a column and an op-ed. What is the most significant difference?
5. Create a Venn diagram comparing a journalistic blog and a personal blog. What are the most important differences?

Application

Choose a campus issue of concern to you. Use the topic of your choice for exercises 1 through 8.

1. Take a position on the issue you have chosen and write an outline of a staff editorial. Explain the content of the editorial to a response group.
2. Take the same issue and create a rough draft of an op-ed arguing for the same position. Share the draft with a response group.
3. Draft an opening for the op-ed using a strong subject-verb sentence.
4. Write a *reductio ad absurdum* argument suitable for the staff editorial.
5. Write hyperbole suitable for the op-ed.
6. Use irony or satire suitable for your op-ed.
7. Use repetition (at least three) suitable for your op-ed.
8. Sketch an editorial cartoon on an issue important to you. Use labels as necessary. Share your cartoon with your response group. Ask how you can improve your cartoon.

Chapter Twelve

Journalism Style

Plurals of Letters and Abbreviations

High schools are full of abbreviations and letters:

- I got an A!
- The AP (assistant principal) broke up the fight.
- ASB (Associated Student Body) ran the assembly.
- I will have an AP (advanced placement) class next fall.
- I'm taking the SAT (Scholastic Aptitude Test) and the ACT (originally, American College Testing) in March.
- They are abolishing SSR (Sustained Silent Reading).
- Harry Potter passed an OWL (Ordinary Wizarding Level).
- That was his best IM (Individual Medley) of the season.

We also use numbers as nouns.

- He ran the 440 (the 440-yard dash) in record time.
- Title IX (Title IX of the Education Amendments of 1972) requires that female athletes be given more opportunities.

What happens when we use these letters, abbreviations and numbers as plurals?

If you are writing the plural of a single letter, add an apostrophe and a lowercase *s*.

Examples:

- He loves the Oakland A's.
- He received seven A's and two C's.
- He learned his three R's: reading, writing and 'rithmetic.
- Any U's in citizenship will hurt your chance of admission to the honor society.
- He received O's in work habits and D's for grades.

> When type was set by hand, printers could easily confuse the letters *p* and *q* because they were arranging type to print the mirror image of what they saw. This is possibly the origin of the saying, "*Mind your p's and q's.*"

To express the plural of multiple letters, just add an *s* without the apostrophe.

Examples:

- The APs broke up the fight.
- ASBs met in Santa Barbara.
- Do you know the ABCs of journalism?

Numbers are also made plural by adding an *s*.

Examples:

- His closet floor is littered with shoes he has outgrown—three pairs of 12s, two pairs of 13s and one pair of 14s.
- His grandparents started a store in the 1950s.

Try It!

Which is correct?

1. I will have two APs/AP's/APS in the fall: chemistry and world history.
2. I am planning on getting 4s/4's or 5s/5's on both tests.
3. I'm sitting for two SATs/SAT's/SATS before the application deadline.
4. I like the University of California, and I'm applying at two UCs/UC's/UCS: UCLA and UC Berkeley.
5. I hope colleges will overlook the two Ns/N's/NS I received my freshman year.
6. Harry Potter passed all his OWL's/OWLs/ OWLS except astronomy.
7. Those were his two best IMs/IM's/IMS of the season.
8. He ran three league-record-breaking 440s/440's.
9. We do not look for other Title IXs/IX's to even the playing field for other disadvantaged groups.

Extend Your Knowledge

Style Exercises

Visit the *Journalism* website to find out the following:

1. How to make the plural of proper names.

Example: *They are spending too much money trying to keep up with the Jones'/Joneses/Jones's.*

2. How to make the plural of words used as words.

Example: *Her note of apology was filled with* sorrys/ sorry's/sorries.

Chapter Twelve

Writers' Workshop

In these Writers' Workshops you will:

- Create a chart to discover a pattern in a favorite columnist's work.
- Analyze the balance of first-person observations, interviews (including interviews with experts), other reporting, the columnist's personal experiences and the columnist's statements of opinion.
- Create a chart to discover the patterns in a strong opinion piece.
- Analyze the balance of first-person observations, interviews (including interviews with experts), other reporting, the writer's personal experiences and the writer's statements of opinion.

Workshop 12.1

How Do They Do That?

Mini-Lesson: Following Your Leader

You've seen and perhaps used writing maps for breaking news, general news, features editorials, reviews and sports. Wouldn't it be great if there were a map to write a really great column?

Too bad. You probably won't find one because columns follow many patterns and extend too many different lengths. Two columns by one journalist may vary from each other almost as much as they do from the work of another columnist. The freedom is part of the joy—and terror—of writing a regular column.

But you can learn from columnists you enjoy or admire. In this workshop you will chart one or more columns. After you have analyzed your results, you will know more about what goes into a strong column, and you will be able to use your chart as a map for writing your own column.

Charting a Column

1. Print out or clip a column 20 to 30 paragraphs long—about 50 sentences.
2. Create a chart similar to the one on the next page, but skip the last column. (Yours will be only three columns wide, not four.)
3. Number each paragraph and put the numbers in column one.
4. In column two write a statement of the paragraph's mission, that is, what the columnist wants to accomplish in the paragraph or what point is made.
5. In column three mark the source of the information in the paragraph: **OB** = observation; **QI** = quotation from interview; **R** = reporting; **Ex** = expert source; **Col** = columnist's opinion; **PE** = personal experience (apart from the columnist's reporting). Discuss with your group any other sources—or abbreviations—you need and adjust the categories. (You do *not* need to copy the words of the column as in the example on the next page. Quotations from the column, by Sandy Banks of the Los Angeles Times, are included on this chart only to show you how to identify the paragraph's mission.)

Tallying and Analyzing the Results

1. In the chart you have created, count the number of paragraphs that come from each source. For example, your chart might list Observation: 12; Reporting: 5; and so on.
2. What can you conclude about how columns are reported? What percent of your column could have been written without leaving the newsroom?
3. What can you conclude from your tally about the way columnists communicate their opinions? How often does the columnist tell you what to think?

Comparing Results

Compare your results with those of others in your group.

1. Do you see a pattern in the mix of observations, quotations, expert sources, the columnist's personal experience and statements of the columnist's opinion?
2. Do columns share certain patterns about what comes first, second, third and at the end?
3. What advice would you, as a group, give to someone who wants to write a column for your publication or broadcast?

Apply It!

S On an appropriate topic of your choice, write a 500- to 1,000-word column using what you learned from this mini-lesson.

Paragraph's Number	Paragraph's Mission	Source	Columnist's Text (optional)
1	Sets the scene, introduces the van.	OB	The giant brightly colored van has become a familiar sight on the street outside Florence Griffith Joyner Elementary School, just across from the Jordan Downs housing project in Watts.
2	Introduces two opposing sides, each trying to influence families.	OB	It's not as popular a destination as the roving *paletero* selling ice cream or the display of fluffy pink batches of cotton candy peddled on the street corner. But a medical team from Cedars-Sinai is working to change that.
3	Introduces the health care team in the van.	OB	
4	Gives background about van's services.	R	The van is part of a mobile program that provides free health services to low-income families from Skid Row south to Inglewood. A pair of vans makes regular rounds to more than two dozen schools, parks and social services centers. Children get their eyes checked, ear infections treated and immunizations updated.
5	Heart of story, nutritional advice is key to improving long-term health.	R	But in an area where 55 percent of teenagers are overweight or obese, its most important product may be health and nutrition advice, clearly explained and gently delivered.
23	Girl sullenly studies snacks, nurse urges water.	OB	
24	Girl pockets $1, leaves.	OB	
25	Columnist calls it a standoff.	Col	I considered it more a standoff than a victory for the forces of good health. That dollar was likely burning a hole in Dafne's pocket. And there was another mother pushing another snack cart just around the block.

Workshop 12.2

How Did the Op-Ed Writer Do That?

Mini-Lesson: Charting an Op-Ed

Opinion pieces are usually limited in length by editorial policy. Some publications keep them below 700 words; others, below 1,000. They always require strong, efficient writing and close editing.

They also tend to follow several patterns. You and your group will discover a few of these in this workshop.

Though they need not be as timely as a staff editorial, they address timely issues or concerns.

Compared to the freedom and wide open spaces available to a columnist, opinion pieces may feel confining, but they possess a power granted to few other types of writing. A strong op-ed piece may be "picked up" and reprinted in publications across the country and discussed in public forums and private meetings.

1. Choose an opinion piece from a professional publication that impresses you.
2. Chart the opinion piece as you did the column in Workshop 12.1.
3. Perform the analysis, paying particular attention to how narrative elements, that is, storytelling elements from personal experience or observation, are mixed with expert sources and statements of the writer's opinions.
4. Working with your group, discuss your findings:
   A. What elements are common in opinion pieces but rare in columns?
   B. What elements tend to start an opinion piece?
   C. What elements tend to end an opinion piece?
   D. If you colored in the narrative elements in the opinion pieces you charted, what parts of the pieces would be colored?
   E. What percent of an opinion piece could be written (if you had a good research library) without leaving the newsroom?
   F. What advice would you, as a group, give to someone who wants to write an opinion piece for your publication or broadcast?

Apply It!

S On an appropriate topic of your choice, write a 700- to 1,000-word op-ed. Use the chart you created for this mini-lesson as a writing map.

Extend Your Knowledge Extend

The writer's tone, his attitude toward his subject, his audience and himself, also shapes op-eds and opinion columns. For a Writers' Workshop on handling tone, visit the *Journalism* website.

Chapter Thirteen

Reviews—of Everything

If you want my expert opinion ...

G-WLEARNING.COM

While studying, look for the activity icon to:

- **Build** vocabulary terms with e-flash cards and matching activities.
- **Extend** learning with further discussion of relevant topics.
- **Reinforce** what you learn by completing style exercises, worksheets and end-of-chapter questions.

Visit the Journalism website: www.g-wlearning.com/journalism/

Photo by Kyle Farrell, Lee County High School

Chapter Objectives

After reading this chapter, you will be able to:

- Explain the importance of labeling reviews as reviews.
- Describe how to make reviews unbiased, transparent, ethical and fair.
- Describe behaviors or affiliations that could lead to a conflict of interest or ethical breaches, and discuss language appropriate to disclose possible conflicts of interest.
- Explain special considerations when reviewing student work.
- Describe the tools used to analyze a product or experience.
- Describe the form most reviews follow.
- Identify various tones a reviewer might use.
- Explain the importance of writing a closing that mirrors the opening.
- Identify transitions that help your audience move from one idea to the next.
- Identify and avoid clichés and superlatives.

Key Terms

Build Vocab

advance story
analyze
cliché
conflict of interest
critic
full disclosure
genre
quick take
review
reviewer

Before You Read...

Using what you have learned thus far, create a Venn diagram comparing the qualities of print, broadcast and online media. What qualities do these media share? How are these three media different? Keep your Venn diagram nearby and add to it as you learn more.

Introduction

"No good movie is too long and no bad movie is short enough."

–Film critic Roger Ebert

We all have opinions, and most of us can publish them. We "like" things on social media, microblog as we leave restaurants, rate our transactions, review our purchases, leave feedback about our experiences and post comments about almost everything. People assign stars, diamonds, thumbs, letter grades, golden keys, percentages or rotten tomatoes to all kinds of products and experiences. They label things "awesome" or "not awesome," "wired" or "tired," "rated" or "hated."

With all those opinions on paper and in cyberspace, why would your audience read or listen to your journalistic reviews? For three reasons:

1. They respect your opinion. You strive to be trustworthy, which means that you are unbiased, transparent, ethical and fair.
2. You are well-informed and give the product or experience a meaningful context.
3. You write well; people enjoy reading your work.

A **reviewer** is a person who experiences and evaluates a creative work or a product for an audience. Reviewers report on literary works, music, art, theater and dance, television and movies, fashion, computer games, restaurants and travel. In addition, they may review consumer products and services.

The audience may use the **review**, the journalistic piece in which the reviewer shares her experience, to decide how to spend their money or time, or they may simply be interested in learning about the subject of the review (Figure 13.1). If they have already experienced the product or creative work, they may read the review to look for additional insight into their own experiences or to see if the reviewer's opinion agrees with theirs. They may also read the review for entertainment.

Audiences do not always agree with reviewers. People may call you names but still read your reviews. They may rebut you online but still read your reviews. They may complain in letters to the editor but still read your reviews. They may shout at their radios, their computers or their television screens, but they may still seek out your reviews. They may argue with you in person but still look for your byline. But they will *not* read your reviews if you lose their trust, if you fail to provide useful information or if you write poorly.

Figure 13.1 These moviegoers might have decided which movie to see based on a review. *How often do you rely on reviews to determine which shows or concerts to attend? Do your reactions to the event usually coincide with those of the reviewer?*

How does a reviewer do her job? The answer, of course, is carefully. Part of it is done swiftly *but* carefully, and much more is done slowly *and* carefully.

The *swift* part is the first impression. Since the reviewer stands in for the audience and describes the experience for the audience, an informed first impression is important. It should not be dismissed, no matter what judgments you make later. Were you frustrated, bored, delighted, transported, satisfied, excited, entranced, mildly amused or rolling on the floor? Hold that thought. It becomes one of the tools you will use to develop your position and then write your review.

The *careful* part of "swiftly but carefully" comes as you guard against making judgments based on irrelevant factors that could, but should not, color your judgment. Was it a wonderful movie because your date was great company? Was it a boring game because your computer screen was too small or because you needed more RAM? These factors are not relevant to the quality of the item you are reviewing. To be a trustworthy reviewer, you must overcome them.

The *swiftly and carefully* part of creating reviews comes about as you provide your audience with meaningful, accessible, and well-organized information and commentary.

Earning Your Audience's Respect

Your audience's trust is your most valuable asset. Your audience must know when your publication or broadcast is presenting news or features and when you are offering your opinions. Like op-eds, columns and editorials, reviews should be clearly labeled (Figure 13.2). Some online and print publications use the words "Movie Review" or "Book Review" in half-height capitals as a hammer before the headline. Broadcasts often introduce the reviewer with language like this: "Here is Juan Alcantara, University High School's theater reviewer, giving us his take on the latest Marvel movie, which opens this Friday in theaters. Juan, what did you think of it?" Some online publications exist primarily to review products. Such sites may not need to label articles as reviews, but sites that provide both news and opinion should make clear which is which.

In addition to trusting your publication to separate opinion from news and features, the audience should trust you as an individual reviewer. But what is it they trust you to do or be? They trust you to be unbiased, transparent, ethical and fair.

Avoiding Biases and Prejudices

Reviewers, including high school reviewers, have the power to damage or help, maybe even make or break, the people, events and places they review. Use this power carefully.

One way to do this is to focus on what is being reviewed, not on yourself—not on what you personally like, where you have traveled or how you dance. You and your tastes are not the subject of the review. You may use the first-person pronoun *I* and share your experiences and your informed opinion in a review, but the review must focus on the topic being reviewed and on the needs of your audience, not on you, the reviewer. Many reviewers avoid using first-person pronouns completely.

Figure 13.2 Reviews should be clearly labeled so your audience does not confuse them with a feature, news story or op-ed.

REVIEWS

Infinity War breaks box office

MARVEL INSTAGRAM

Bsy Zoe Graves
MANAGING EDITOR

One of the most anticipated movies to come out of Marvel Studios, "Avengers: Infinity War," is a rollercoaster of emotions. The last film in phase two of the Marvel Cinematic Universe, the two-hour, 40-minute movie kept viewers on the edges of their seats the entire time.

"Infinity War" raked in over $630 million dollars worldwide its opening weekend, even though it hasn't been released in China, which currently boasts the second-highest movie market. The opening shattered the box office record for highest global opening weekend of all time, passing 2017's "Fate of the Furious," which held the record with $541.9 million.

The underlying plot is simple — the cast of superheroes have to stop Thanos (Josh Brolin) from getting all six infinity stones and destroying half of the universe's population. That, of course, turns out easier to be said than done, as everyone is spread out across the universe.

"Infinity War" is the first team-up of the Avengers and Guardians of the Galaxy, along with appearances from Dr. Strange (Benedict Cumberbatch) and the Black Panther entourage. Most of the Avengers remain on Earth — specifically in Wakanda — defending against Thanos's army, while the Guardians, Tony Stark (Robert Downey Jr.), Peter Parker (Tom Holland) and Dr. Strange confront Thanos directly in space. Continuing from the end of 2017's "Thor: Ragnarok," the film starts off in space. Here, Thanos is introduced, and the tone for the rest of the movie is set, as in the first five minutes of the movie it's made painfully clear to viewers that no character is safe.

As seen in trailers, Thor (Chris Hemsworth) finds himself with the Guardians, where Thanos's plan is first figured out. There, an unlikely partnership between Thor and Rocket (Bradley Cooper) forms, as the two, along with Groot (Vin Diesel), separate from the rest of the group. The pair is one of the highlights of the otherwise emotionally draining movie. Hemsworth's character retains the comedic attributes that were revealed in "Ragnarok," which when paired with the snarky humor of Rocket, brought a lot of the comedic relief "Infinity War" desperately needed. Banter among the characters is an essential piece of a Marvel movie and has been a staple in the otherwise action-packed films since 2008's "Iron Man." The larger-than-normal cast in "Infinity War" manages to create hilarious dynamics between characters — such as Rocket and Thor — that audiences wouldn't have seen coming.

The standout characters in the film were not expected, with many of the original Avengers pushed to the back burner while performances by Dr. Strange, Gamora (Zoe Saldana) and Peter Quill/Starlord (Chris Pratt) were especially memorable, as the three were essential to Thanos getting certain infinity stones and increasing his power. Holland also gave a stellar performance as Spiderman, with a larger role than initially expected as he teamed up with Iron Man and Dr. Strange. The trio provided their fair share of comedic relief, with constant banter between Stark and Strange and pop culture references from Parker.

Although the movie was good, it wasn't much more than that. It wasn't great, it wasn't fantastic — it was just good. Maybe that's because it was hyped up so much by fans and producers alike, but the film itself was a bit of a let down. It featured a lot of surprising twists and turns and moments that left fans shocked in their seats, but nothing overwhelming happened that was able to make up for the emotional distress it caused fans.

w2wwThanos and the rest of the Avengers will return to the big screen in the fourth Avenger film, which is currently untitled. All of the stars from "Infinity War," along with a few new faces, are confirmed to be in the second part of the film, set for a May 2019 release.

★★★★

"Avengers Infinity War" 2018

GAME

NANO GOLF

★★★★

YOUTUBE

Performing as a quick, compact version of golf, mini-golf parks have maintained their status as attractions for decades. Revamping the casual design, the game "Nano Golf" transforms the concept into an assortment of puzzling levels, featuring innovative hazards to evade along the way.

At its core, the simple objective of the game is akin to mini-golf: strike the ball to reach the hole. Each time the ball is struck, the number of strokes increases, dwindling one's score. More or less, the concept is unchanged.

Unlike its traditional counterparts, the levels of the game are designed similarly to that of a labyrinth, as to lead the ball to the hole via linearly connecting corridors and a multitude of close corners. There are hazards beyond the typical golf elements, such as conveyor belts to push the ball away or golf carts which, when touched, destroy the ball and force the player to restart.

Due to its grand adjustments to the basic formula of mini-golf, the aging concept is adapted for mobile systems. There is greater emphasis on fast-paced action through the ability to repeat levels multiple times over, especially with the dangerous obstacles overall. In future levels, the option to bounce off of walls is hindered, as to force the player to rethink previous plans, for the walls begin to have spikes peppered around, forcing a restart if impacted.

For controls, the power and direction of a swing is manufactured via pulling a joystick around on the screen. Since the control is radial, the player has greater effects upon the destination of the ball.

Oddly enough, the only possible downfall of "Nano Golf" is its limit on the number of strokes per level. While it necessitates the strategization of levels by emphasizing where the ball is to bounce, it harms player freedom. As an alternative, it would be better to allow players to have unlimited strokes at the risk of worse rankings per level.

"Nano Golf; 2017; Free on Google Play

By Colin Haroutunion

GAME

BMX 2

★★★

GOOGLE PLAY

"BMX 2" is designed to get users to steady their movements and react to the rapid pace of the game. Players use a bike and have to steer past bumps and jump over barriers to the finish line of the course to complete the game. Once completed, they start to gain access to different arenas as they advance. As a user comprehends the components of the game, they start to improve their technique.

Players are also able to view their strategy after they play. Replay mode is a very beneficial aspect of this game since it lets players view their mistakes. They can either view the replay from the driver's seat or have a long outer-range angle, which allows the gamer to view the place that they could improve their skill pattern.

Another perk of this game is that there are specific tasks to complete. For example, a certain number of flips need to happen or a higher score needs to be achieved before the user can move on. It is dictating a list that has to be checked off to help the user build on their gaming skills.

However, while players can gain access to different arenas, only one is given to them when they start the game. This takes away a sense of variety from users who play. They don't get to test out other options before deciding whether or not this would be a game that they could excel in or not. Offering a bit more variety before making the users work for it would enhance their understanding and make them feel more driven for the entire experience.

This app offers a challenge that tests quickness, but also tests how users react to mistakes. With "BMX 2," it isn't about your gaming skills, but how you can build upon previous challenges you've had throughout the game. If you want an app that gives you a little bit of everything, then BMX 2 is the app for you.

"BMX 2" 2017; Free on Google Play

By Adam Schwartz

ALBUM

MY DEAR MELANCHOLY

★★★★

ITUNES.COM

"My Dear Melancholy," the newest extended play (EP) from The Weeknd, tells the story of a painful heartbreak in the duration of 21 minutes, while expressing the vulnerability that we're exposed to through love.

The first track, "Call Out My Name," makes listeners feel the sting of the ultimate devastation — unrequited love — setting the mood for the rest of the tracks. In this piece, along with five other songs, The Weeknd uses passionate rhythms and verses to elicit emotional responses drenched in pity from listeners.

After an emotionally charged performance of "Call Out My Name" at Coachella, listeners were hit with how much the song really meant to The Weeknd, and the performance cemented the idea the song was about his ex-girlfriend, Selena Gomez.

Here, and throughout the EP, The Weeknd's transparent lyrics portray heartbreak and sorrow due to a lost romance. However, some songs such as "Try Me," although heartbreaking in content, have more aggressive undertones while still maintaining that same feeling of emptiness.

The EP itself has a variety of intricate sounds. Whether they be slow and mournful or steady and meaningful, each song sheds light on a different angle of a breakup with the help of purposeful lyrics and passionate vocals.

Although each song sounds different, they seem to fit together like puzzle pieces, allowing the audience to create the image of a broken man and what he's going through.

The story that's being told is also relatable because of the different viewpoints exhibited in each of the songs. In the fifth track, "Hurt You," the focus is centralized around the purpose of a rebound, while the sixth, "Privilege," is about being able to move on and say goodbye

Overall, "My Dear Melancholy," is an emotional rollercoaster both for listeners and the artist. It's solemn lyrics accompanied by engaging beats tell an overwhelming, yet relatable story that much of the audience has experienced for themselves."

"My Dear Melancholy," 2018; Available to download for $5.99

By Amelia Nowicki

MOVIE

CANDY JAR

★★★★

IMDB.COM

"When two seniors are experts in arguing all the time, opposites can really attract, and in the movie "Candy Jar" that is depicted quite clearly.

With winning constantly on their minds, two enemies from the start have been on the debate team, competing against each other since middle school. But here comes Lona (Sami Gayle) and Bennett's (Jacob Latimore) senior year of high school — where they have to debate on the same team. The two not only hate getting along but have two very different backgrounds. One comes from a rich family and the other from a working-class family, adding in more to be defensive about.

With weeks on end, the two try to figure out how to debate together as arch enemies. Their cycle revolves around studying, staying up all night and fighting, while romance sneaks in to debate too. Spending so much time together brings them closer and closer until they realize they actually have a shot at winning state championships.

Besides learning how to work with people you disagree with the most, there was another moral to the story — that even a lot of hard work can result in an important lesson, not always being what you hope for. Both Lona and Bennett portrayed hard working students in high school, trying get into their dream college — which for them was Harvard and Yale respectively. With all of their hard work, they realized that they missed out on normal high school events such as football games, parties and regular human connections.

This movie is perfect for any high school student or hard worker in general. It conveys that sometimes missing out on the fun things in life or the opportunity to be able to love someone is not worth all the hard work, and that working too hard or focusing too much on winning can result in failure or an outcome you weren't hoping for. The movie combines elements of romance with hard truths, unexpected plotlines and good laughs, making it undebatable that "Candy Jar" is a must-watch.

"Candy Jar;" 201/8; Netflix

By Mariah Loper

Courtesy of North Pointe, Grosse Pointe North High School

Objectivity is not just about the pronouns you use. It is also about how you approach your work as a reviewer. You need to be aware of your own biases or prejudices so they do not affect your review. If you have already decided before you review an item that you dislike all fantasy books or chic flicks or bluegrass banjos, you are not capable of being an unbiased reviewer of such books, movies or music.

A reviewer needs to guard against such personal prejudice. Prejudice is literally *pre-judging*. If you cannot put aside your prejudice, let someone else write the review.

In addition to avoiding bias in your writing, you must avoid *appearing* biased. An offhand comment on a social media site or sent over your phone may make it seem that you—and by implication your publication—cannot be trusted about what you will review. If you tweet "Off to review yet another pretty-boy band," your audience will assume you went to the performance planning to be bored. Reviewers, like all other journalists, need to avoid publishing their personal opinions on topics they may cover as journalists (Figure 13.3 on the next page). Almost all forms of electronic communication are forms of publishing. Many publications have guidelines that prohibit their employees from expressing opinions about matters they might possibly cover as journalists. The Austin American-Statesman code of ethics includes this discussion of social media use amongst its employees.

> *Staff members should be cognizant that use of social media – Twitter, Facebook, blogs or other online interactions – is covered under the newsroom ethics policy. Staff members should assume that all blogging, Twittering and commenting on Facebook or elsewhere is public. Newsroom staff should avoid posting opinions that will reflect partiality or create perceptions of bias that undermine the credibility of the newspaper. This includes joining political causes or listing party affiliations on social media sites.*

Your Turn

1. Make a list of the products, arts or services you feel you could review intelligently without a great deal of background research. For instance, have you eaten enough Vietnamese food to review a Vietnamese restaurant? Do you know enough about rap music to review local artists battle rapping? Do you know enough about motocross—and movies—to review a recently released motocross movie?

(Continued)

YOUR TURN *(Continued)*

2. **Going Deeper.** Discuss with a small group or your class this dilemma. If you are knowledgeable enough to review something, you probably already have opinions. For instance, if you are a fan of traditional or old-time music, you know a great deal about the musicians, the instruments, the venues, the traditions and the style. Perhaps you are a musician yourself. This knowledge can help you write strong reviews. But does this knowledge also make you prejudiced? Can your editor or producer trust you to review a traditional music performance or recording fairly, without bias? Can your audience trust you to do so? What is the difference between informed opinions and prejudice?

Transparency

Transparency is a lack of secrets or secret agendas. Just as a reader can look through transparent (clear) glass, your audience can see who you are and who has your loyalty. They can see all your connections and your potential prejudices. Your audience knows your real identity and the identity of your producers and editors.

When you review something, you sign your name to it. Your audience knows whose opinion they are reading or hearing—yours. Your publication is not like the online movie and TV distribution website that recommended movies to customers based on ratings *supposedly* provided by their viewers. When the identities of these online "reviewers" were revealed, the audience learned that a few hundred anonymous people had written the reviews for over 50,000 titles.

If a company has not been transparent about who has been writing reviews—and why—it risks losing the audience's trust. When you recommend

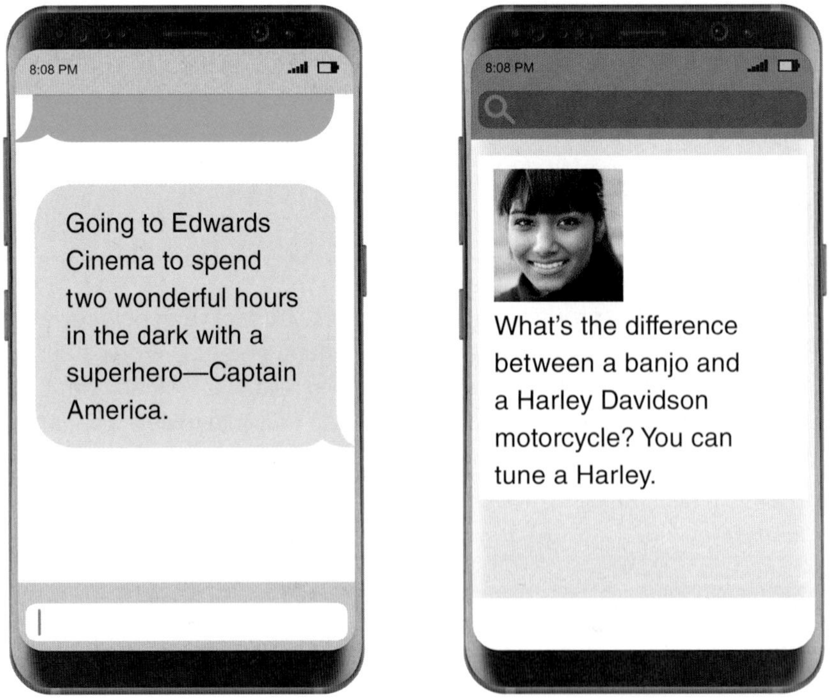
8:08 PM
Going to Edwards Cinema to spend two wonderful hours in the dark with a superhero—Captain America.
8:08 PM
What's the difference between a banjo and a Harley Davidson motorcycle? You can tune a Harley.

Figure 13.3 Be mindful of your reputation as a journalist when you post personal opinions on social media. These posts could make both you and your publication appear biased.

or pan (criticize) a movie, your audience must know who you are, how you work and whom you work for. That should be your audience.

Ethics

Maintaining your audience's trust means being ethical. An ethical journalist is never paid in any way by the people, events, products or places she covers. Your readers must trust that your only loyalties are to them and to your publication. You represent an organization with clearly stated standards, standards that should be in your staff manual.

You never accept gifts, money or favors from anyone or anything you cover. You or your publication pays your way to restaurants. You come and go as anonymously as possible, as would any other patron. You buy the track shoes you review, as would any other customer. You may accept review copies of books or music, but you must not resell them. You may accept two properly issued press passes to events (one for you and one for a guest), but you generally will not accept food or travel or discounts on food or travel.

Your audience must also know if you are friends with the artists or related to them. This is in contrast to the reviewers on the website of one major retailer. When the identities of its Canadian online book reviewers were accidentally released, the public learned that many of the reviews and ratings were written by the authors themselves, their publicists, and their friends and families.

If you are connected in any way to the item you are reviewing or even to its competitors, talk with your editor or producer and your adviser to see if this connection creates a **conflict of interest**, a connection that might make it difficult for you to report objectively. For instance, if your mother works at Disneyland, your mother's job probably depends on the company's financial health. You may appear to have an interest in the success of a Disney movie you are reviewing. Your editor may choose to assign the review to someone else. The New York Times Company's policy on ethics in journalism has this to say about staff members covering entertainment and the arts.

> *Staff members covering entertainment and the arts have a special duty to guard against conflicts of interest, real or apparent. Arts coverage, whether national or local, can often make or break reputations and commercial success. In theater, movies, music, art, dance, publishing, fashion and restaurants, critics and reviewers have an obligation to exert our newsrooms' influence ethically and prudently.*

Another option would be to inform your audience what your connection is and suggest how this connection will not unduly influence your review. Informing your audience of any possible conflict of interest is called **full disclosure** and is an essential element in your organization's transparency.

The usual language is something like this: "In the interest of full disclosure, I should mention here that my brother is an intern in the accounting department of XYZ music distributors." What could have turned into a personal attack on you, "You cannot trust her—her brother works for the competition," has been defused. Your readers will then know that you and your publication are committed to transparency and to following strong ethical guidelines.

You need to avoid even the appearance of conflict of interest. If your last name is Le and you are reviewing a work choreographed by a young dancer named Suzann Le, you will insert a disclaimer, a parenthetical "*(no relation)*" after the first mention of her name to avoid an apparent conflict of interest. If you are working in nonprint media where your audience hears the names but does not see them, you may need to advise your audience that there is no relationship, even if the dancer's name is Suzann *Lee*: "The original choreography, built around flame-red skirts that become capes or umbrellas or fans or Frisbee discs, is by Suzann Lee (no relation)."

Fairness

Your audience must know that you will be fair. Though you may be inventive with invective (strong criticism) and funny with sarcasm, you

And Now... Closer to Home

Reviewing Student Plays

Reviewing the work of your peers can be an ethical and journalistic minefield. On one hand, we are told:

- We should not hold students to the same standards we hold professionals.
- The Society of Professional Journalists Code of Ethics tells us to "Show compassion for those who may be affected by news coverage. Use heightened sensitivity when dealing with juveniles ..."
- Your mother told you, "If you can't say something nice, don't say anything at all."
- The play or show may be over by the time you publish, so why praise—or criticize—it?

On the other hand, journalists are committed to building a sense of community:

- Your audience wants to see local faces and local names in the news, and the more names and faces, the better.
- As a journalist, you should not ignore a major campus event such as a student production or show. To ignore the production or a person performing a major role in the production implies that you have judged the work and found it is not worthy of notice.
- If the show is over, your audience needs to know what it missed, so they can decide whether to attend future productions.
- Reviewing live theater or music or a local art show is an educational opportunity for the performers, the writers and the readers.

Some publications or broadcasts avoid the minefield entirely by covering the play as news. They may cover rehearsal, preferably a dress rehearsal, or report audience reaction after the play.

Others write reviews as well as news stories. Publications with access to several media may cover the play as a news or feature story before the play opens, using the appropriate media and including audio, visual, and spoken or written elements. Soon after the reviewer has seen the production, she may publish her review online.

For instance, you might do an **advance story**, a story published before the event, being careful to avoid seeming like the production's publicist or as if you are making a public service announcement. Publish the five W's for the production as well as photos, interviews, sound files or video of the rehearsal. In addition, you can also look beyond timeliness and proximity for conflict or oddity, do not skewer your subject just because you can be funny. You serve as the eyes, ears and taste buds for your audience. Your job is to bring them information they want. The review should not be about how clever or intelligent or sophisticated you are. It is about the item you are reviewing and what your audience wants or needs to know.

Fairness also demands that you do not hold student work up to the same standard you hold professional efforts, even though you may be familiar with the work of professionals. Student productions, fashion shows, culinary creations, pep assemblies, cheerleading, half-time entertainment and art shows should be compared to professional work only when the comparison is positive, such as "professional quality" or "near-professional quality."

Fairness demands balance. Though you must make a clear judgment about the overall value of what you are reviewing, give praise where it is due, even in a generally negative review. You should

prominence or human interest. For example, you might:

- focus on the understudy who takes the lead only on Thursday night and plays a small silent role the other nights. What does she get out of the experience?
- focus on the costume designer's work. How hard was it to find all the costume parts?
- focus on the student director, or the accompanist, or the sound and light technician.
- ask about the budget and funding.
- find out who is doing the posters and programs and how these will look.
- take notice of the many volunteers who never appear on stage. Theirs may be the best story of all.

If you publish online, you may add to your strong advance story by publishing a short, informal review as soon as you have seen the show:

> **GW Times Reviewer** @gwtimes — Follow
>
> Arsenic & Old L. starts slow, hard to understand, but when criminal brother shows up with a corpse, it is roll-on-the-floor funny. Josh P's Uncle Teddy is great. Charge!
>
> 8:40 PM – 5 April 2020

But this does not mean that you are writing during the performance. Remember, common courtesy requires that you darken and silence all electronic devices during the show.

You may encourage your audience to microblog to your publication after they have seen the performance. After you have screened the comments and identified the submitters, you may publish their messages on your website. Remember, to keep your audience's trust, you need to know who the comments are from, even if you do not publish the submitters' actual names.

If the production will continue for at least another show, write and publish a well-developed online review quickly. Write to enrich the audience's experience when they attend. Point out the setting or time period or technical expertise they will see. Summarize the central conflict, characters and setting of the play, but do not give away the climax of the story or the most powerful scenes. Provide interesting background information.

Use as many local names as possible, focusing in large part on what is done well. Sometimes balanced comments may be appropriate, recognizing both the weakness and the strength of the actors: "After a shaky start, sophomore Mario Ortez made a believably creepy Dr. Einstein to senior Tuan Huynh's psychotic murderer, the aptly named Mortimer."

also give criticism where appropriate, even in a generally positive review. You comment on the *work* of artists, entertainers, chefs or game designers, not on their personal lives, beliefs or appearance—unless those personal details directly and obviously affect what you are reviewing. You know the difference between factors the actors and director cannot control (the heat in your school's Little Theater, the bad sound system, the lead vocalist's laryngitis) and those they can control (pacing, projection, characterization, body language and the energy of the performance).

Providing Meaningful Information

Your audience will value your opinions if you give them useful information in addition to your informed judgment about the product or creative work. The purpose of a review is to help the audience make their own decisions or to help them understand their own experiences better. It is not merely to tell them what you have decided. You are often more like a host inviting your audience into a world where you are comfortable, as opposed to being a referee, blowing a whistle at every weakness and determining winners and losers.

Worksheets

As with any work you do as a journalist, you should never try to "fake it" when writing a review. That means you must prepare yourself well before you see the play, try the product, read the book, attend the concert, eat at the restaurant or watch the movie so that you will be an intelligent observer. (Completing a prewriting chart will help you prepare for your review.) It also means you never pretend to have seen a play, tried a product, read a book, attended a concert, eaten at the restaurant or watched the movie if you have not actually done so.

Reviewers try to experience what they are reviewing more than once, if it is possible. They go to a restaurant at least three times (and never until it has been open at least a month), see a movie twice, spend hours on a computer game, read a book more than once, use a snowboard in several types of snow, listen to recorded music multiple times. They also listen to the band's recorded music when preparing to review a live performance.

Because you are well-informed and share your knowledge with your audience, your judgment is worth more than that of the "average man on the street" who might post comments. A reviewer will give the context for what he is reviewing and provide an overview of the item. He will compare it with other similar products or experiences and mention its positive and negative aspects. This running shoe review from Wired magazine is a good example (Figure 13.4).

Contrast Billy Brown's review with the following comment left by a reader, Bwiley. His comment received 15 "likes" and two comments in response, so it may be a valuable comment, but it is different from Brown's informative review.

> *I'm 47. I started running in them about a year ago, have two pairs of the model this article is based*

WIRED | Review: Vibram FiveFinger Bikila LS | SUBSCRIBE

BUSINESS | DESIGN | ENTERTAINMENT | GEAR | SCIENCE | SECURITY

BILLY BROWN 04.21.11 9:00 PM

REVIEW: VIBRAM FIVEFINGER BIKILA LS

VIBRAM'S NEWEST FIVEFINGERS FIT BETTER, STILL LOOK FUNNY

Courtesy of Vibram USA

FiveFinger shoes made by Vibram, the poster children of the barefoot-running movement, are as close as you can get to running in your bare feet without having to worry about hookworms and broken glass.

One of the company's newest offerings, the Bikila LS, is designed specifically for the barefoot runner. Named after Abebe Bikila, who ran barefoot and took the gold medal in the marathon in the 1960 Olympics, the Bikila LS sports a few features added specifically for distance runners.

The outsole is beefed up with extra padding on high-impact areas like the heel and forefoot to soften the impact of running on concrete, and Vibram has added cushioning in the cuff and the shoe's topline to reduce irritation and pressure on longer runs.

A drawstring closure secures the shoe, which is a distinct departure from the Velcro closures on every other FiveFinger shoe. It makes a big difference — the shoe's cuff opens up wider for easier entry, and the lacing draws the middle of the shoe up around the midfoot. It makes the shoe fit even more snugly than previous FiveFinger shoes I've worn. It's easily the most glovelike iteration of the Five Fingers family. They're also the most comfortable — the soft interior lining and padding make them feel great for just walking around town, as long as you don't mind the occasional pointing and staring.

Purists may balk at the phrase "more padding," but believe me, it's incremental. While the padding does a bit to absorb the shock from running in what amounts to your bare feet, the modular pod design of the outsole ensures a full range of motion in the sole, and you still feel every bit of each step. During test runs on pavement, I could feel the contours of the road as my toes splayed out and I felt every single rock that I stepped on.

There's little margin for error. The occasional heel strike was a jarring event, and after about half a mile, I had settled into a proper forefoot strike. Running up hills actually felt much better than doing so in regular running shoes, as the neutral heel made it easier to stay up on my toes and charge uphill.

The padding takes some of the sting out of pounding pavement in your bare feet, but don't go all out if you're not used to running in barefoot-style shoes. It's best to start with short distances and work your way up into longer distances. Be prepared for some sore calves and arches.

Usually, if you're wearing toe shoes, subtlety isn't high on your list of priorities, but the Bikila LS's styling is about as subtle as toe shoes get. My pair's black body with gray details drew much less attention than, say the blue camouflage styling of the last pair of Vibrams we tested. That said, you're still going to draw some stares during your run. I mean, come on — they're toe shoes.

Billy Brown/Wired; © Condé Nast

Figure 13.4 Provide meaningful information and answer the questions you think your audience might ask in your review.

on - one for running and one for gym - because they are absolutely the best of the 4 models I've now owned. When I took to them, I hadn't been able to run due to knee and back problems in over 10 years. Couldn't even stand on a hard surface for 20 minutes before back pain. Now I'm running 30-50 miles a week. My calves have grown about 1.5 inches, my feet are totally reshaped (my arch has risen unbelievably). It took about 4 months of running, honestly, to get used to them - I started out at maybe 200 yards but was up to about 3 miles by the end of 4 months. 8 months later and I can hit 20 miles. I have half a dozen friends I've turned onto them - all with similar stories to mine now. Maybe not for everyone - but for some people these things are an absolute godsend. Reinvigorated my life.

Both the review and the comment are very favorable, and both writers clearly have used the shoes, but Billy Brown's unbiased point of view (the review is about the shoes, not about his health and his feet) provides us with more information and may draw our trust more than Bwiley's enthusiastic and very personal endorsement. If Bwiley were a journalist, he would have needed to verify the statement that barefoot running can change the shape of an arch before he published. In addition, Bwiley's comments, which are appropriate for a readers' forum, are more about Bwiley than about the shoes, something journalistic reviewers should avoid.

Billy Brown's review contains elements that are essential to a strong review:

- *Context.* Brown begins his review with the context for the shoe. He explains the barefoot running movement and the origin of the shoe's name—the Olympic gold medalist from Ethiopia who ran barefoot. He tells us about the manufacturer's history of providing shoes for barefoot runners. He identifies the audience for the product: distance runners.
- *Overview.* He tells us the shoe is odd-looking and glovelike. We learn the shoe is as close to running barefoot as possible. The picture helps give the overview.
- *Comparisons.* Brown mentions other barefoot running shoes he has worn and writes that this model has new padding and a drawstring rather than a Velcro closure.
- *The negative as well as the positive.* Though the review is basically positive, the writer mentions that the shoes look funny. People point and stare at you. Purists may worry that the padding will limit foot motion. Brown could feel every rock he stepped on, and the heel strike was jarring. Be prepared for sore calves and arches, he warns. Don't go all out at first.

Your Turn

Worksheets

1. Choose an item you have used in the last 24 hours. Avoid expensive or highly complex items such as computers or cars. Using the Writer's Map for a Review, available on the *Journalism* website, record the information you accumulate about *context*, *overview*, *comparisons*, and *negatives and positives* to help you prepare to write a review. Check the Internet for the information you need to write your context entry. When you write your review, you will not necessarily use all the information you included in your chart, but the more you know, the stronger you can make your review. Below is an example—a review of a pencil.

Context	*For over 400 years, people have written with sticks of greasy graphite held in wooden cases. Henry David Thoreau mixed the graphite with clay to create a smear-free pencil. (As a messy writer, I'm grateful.) The clay also controls the hardness of the pencil. In 1858, my personal hero, Hymen Lipman, attached an eraser to the end of the pencil. Now expensive "writing implements" (and matching pens) as well as inexpensive plastic retractable pencils take a large share of the pencil market, but traditionalists still think of slender wooden sticks when someone says "pencil."* *Pencil graphite, sometimes called lead, comes in different hardness ratings. The harder the graphite, the lighter the mark it will leave. A 9B (the B is for black), the softest rating, will leave a very intense black mark. A 9H (the H is for hard) will leave the lightest mark.*
Overview	*These wood-cased pencils are hexagonal, painted bright yellow and capped by a pink eraser held on by a metal band.*
Comparisons	*Mechanical pencils. $70 writing implements. Graphite-encased in plastic to look like a pencil. Plastic retractable pencils.*
Balance (Negatives and Positives)	*Need to be sharpened, which can be disruptive, noisy or messy.* *If you lose one, you will not be heartbroken, as you would be if you lost a $70 writing implement.* *Feel better in the hand than plastic.* *Plastic uses petroleum.* *Pencils are made from incense cedar. Pleasant smell when sharpened. Company website does not say if it is harvested from sustainable forests.* *The 2.5 hardness is too hard to use on Scantron-style tests that require a number 2.0 pencil for machine grading. Using a 2.5 pencil could be risky.* *Better to buy a 2.0 hardness pencil. Dixon makes them.*

(Continued)

YOUR TURN *(Continued)*

Remember, you are not selling the product, you are reviewing it. The review's purpose is to provide valuable information for your audience and help them decide if they want to spend time or money on the product themselves.

2. **Going Deeper.** Present your review to your group or class. Critique each other's reviews on these criteria, giving them one, two or three cheeseburgers:
   - The reviewer gave me a useful context for the product. (This may be a history of its development or our use of it.)
   - The reviewer gave me a useful overview of the product, including what it looks like or how it works and who might benefit from it.
   - The reviewer compared it to similar products, so I could make informed choices.
   - The reviewer mentioned or explained both strengths and weaknesses.
   - The reviewer was clearly reviewing the product for me, not selling it.

Using the Right Tools for the Job

Reviews go beyond first impressions. Reviewers **analyze**, or mentally take apart, what they review, and in doing so they make use of a wide array of tools.

Reviewers use different tools to evaluate different **genres**—that is, the different kinds—of art and entertainment and different kinds of products or experiences. Before you begin reporting, you need to know the appropriate analysis tools for the particular kind of review you will be doing. You need to choose the right tools for each review. Just as you would not think of taking apart a watch with an overhead crane or a boat with a Q-tip, you would not want to review a product such as a pencil with a movie reviewer's tools.

By compiling a list of tools before you report, you will be a better-informed reviewer and a more organized writer. This can make the difference between writing a personal response and writing a review that will be useful to your audience.

How do you know which tools to use for different kinds of reviews? Reading reviews of related products or creative works will give you examples of what tools other reviewers use. In some cases you may need to create your own set of tools for a new and different product or experience.

Reviewing Books and Other Literature

The analysis tools you probably know best are the ones you use in your language arts classes, the tools of literary analysis. These tools will help you review any narrative, such as fiction, biography, a poem or a short story, and they also will help you review movies, theater, computer games and songs.

And Now... Closer to Home

The 10 Tools of Literary Analysis

1. Some knowledge of the author and the period in which the work was written.
2. The situation: the setting, which includes time and place, and the problem that creates the conflicts.
3. The characters and their relationships.
4. The plot or action.
5. The point of view. Is it first person? Second person? Third?
6. The structure of the work.
7. Any imagery, including symbols, metaphors and allusions.
8. Irony, if any.
9. The intended audience and the desired effect on the audience.
10. The theme.

Extend

Book reviewers choose the tools of literary analysis that best illuminate the work they are reviewing and ignore those that are less important. But before reviewers write, they use these standard tools to analyze the work. Experienced reviewers use these tools fluently, often without consciously thinking about them. Young reviewers may use the 10 tools as a guide as they take notes, form their opinions and organize their reviews. The specific strengths and weaknesses they mention in their reviews are based on the tools they use for analysis. They often compare one product or production to another using those tools of analysis.

Reviewing Movies

A movie review uses the tools of literary analysis as well as tools that apply to movies—the tools of movie analysis. Because many people are responsible for a movie's success or failure, the reviewer may mention the screenwriter, director, cinematographer and the actors, as well as the author of the story from which the movie was made. She may comment on the quality of the characterization and acting. She might discuss the

Your Turn

1. Find two journalistic book reviews and identify the tools the reviewers used to support their positions.
2. **Going Deeper.** What tools do the reviewers use beyond the 10 tools of literary analysis? Collaborate with others to see if the tool is important to the reader of the review. Discuss whether the added tool is part of one of the 10 tools. For instance, if the reviewer talks about how predictable or unpredictable the story is, you may add that to your list. Then talk with classmates to see if *predictability* is part of one of the 10 tools, such as plot.

cinematography. The movie reviewer needs to be familiar with the genre she is reviewing, such as musical, action-adventure, comedy, horror, documentary or war movie.

In his review of "Mia and the Migoo," Shawn Levy uses tools of literary analysis (Figure 13.5). He briefly describes the *situation, plot* and the *characters and their relationships*. He tells us the story has an ecological *theme*.

But Levy also uses tools of movie analysis. He informs us that "Mia and the Migoo" is an animated film, and he comments on the "eye-popping color and motion and dreamscapes." He mentions the director, who also co-wrote the story.

This review appeared online, and it is search engine optimized. Search engines will find the review through keywords such as *review, Mia and the Migoo* and *ecologically-oriented*, as will readers.

Figure 13.5 Some of the ten tools of literary analysis are applicable when you review movies, but reviews of animated films use additional tools.

Menu Set Weather OREGONLIVE The Oregonian Subscribe Sign In Search

'Mia and the Migoo' review: ecologically-oriented animated film is lovely but daft

By Shawn Levy, The Oregonian
Follow on Twitter
on May 12, 2011 at 12:00 PM

If it were just a series of animated frames and sequences, "Mia and the Migoo" would nearly be a must-see. A hand-painted film that draws inspiration from Van Gogh and Cezanne, it's genuinely beautiful, with eye-popping color and motion and dreamscapes: really inspired stuff.

But director Jacques-Rémy Girerd and his three co-writers have a fairly insipid tale on their hands, slathered with a clumsy ecological message, and after a while even the fairy tale quality of the thing feels forced and arbitrary. You shift from wonder at the real beauty of the film to wondering what Girerd and company were thinking when they wrote it.

The film weaves together a few stories: orphan girl Mia sets out to find her daddy; daddy is trapped in a cave after a construction accident; the evil boss for whom he works is intent on eradicating the obstacles in completing his environmentally-harmful development; the boss's son tries to teach his father some gentleness; and the Migoo, a fanciful but dumb forest creature, strives to keep the balance of the ecosystem intact.

It's lovely, truly, but so heavy-handed and slipshod that it's probably best enjoyed with the sound off -- an option they're not likely to offer at the movie theater.

(88 min., PG, Fox Tower) **Grade: C-plus**

Your Turn

1. Read three or more movie reviews and note the tools the reviewers use. Collaborate with other students and create a list of the tools of movie analysis, beyond the tools of literary analysis.
2. **Going Deeper.** Group the tools of movie analysis logically. For instance, camera angles, lighting, color and use of wide or close shots might be grouped as cinematography, while special effects might be its own category with its own vocabulary, such as *3D* or *CGI*.

Reviewing Digital Games

As digital games evolve, so will the tools you need to review them. But the tools of literary analysis serve as a starting point because games are at heart works of fiction. The reviewer describes the setting, characters and conflict. He identifies genre and point of view.

In addition, he employs tools of digital game analysis: the scoring and how to win; the weapons, protections and vehicles; the game play features and number of players; the offensive and defensive modes.

He may mention the developer of the game or talk about the graphics and hours of play the game provides or the difficulty of the game.

Video game reviewers might use the same tools as an art reviewer, describing the colors, images, depth of field, perspective and realism of the game.

Your Turn

1. Read three or more game reviews and note the tools the reviewers use. Collaborate with other students and create a more extended list of tools of game analysis for your staff or class.
2. **Going Deeper.** Group the tools logically and give a name to each group.

Reviewing Products

Each time you review a new sort of product, you will change the tools you use to review it. Reading reviews of similar products will help you create your own list of tools, as will your experience with the product.

However, when something is truly new, you will need to develop your own set of tools to analyze it. Basic questions will help you develop your tools of analysis for the new product.

- What does this product try to do?
- Who is the audience for this product?
- What is the new or improved function of this product that sets it apart from similar ones?
- How well did the product achieve its goals?

Organizing Your Review

Reviews usually take a predictable form. This form is one that you can use for a scholarly book review; a paper of literary analysis in your language arts class; or a journalistic review in print, online or in a broadcast. Your audience expects this form. It is not set in stone, but unless a reviewer can articulate a strong reason to vary from it, it is the best shape for a review. The three major parts of this form are

- opening. May be in the first paragraphs, or it could be included in the teaser or headline.
- body. Uses the appropriate tools to analyze the product. Includes context, overview, comparisons, negatives and positives.
- closing. Mirrors the opening.

The opening, and the closing, of a review are especially important. Many readers will only see the opening.

The Opening

Your opening should include two elements:

1. A statement of the item you are reviewing, what kind of thing it is and usually, who is responsible for it. You probably know TAG—title, author, genre—for papers of literary analysis that you have done in your language arts class. A similar form works for other items you review.
2. A strong, clear indication of your informed opinion. It is important to let your audience know your position in the opening paragraph, the sooner the better. Consider how most people read your review—swiftly:
    - First they read the headline and your opening paragraph.
    - If they are still interested, they read the closing paragraph.
    - Over half stop there. In print, the majority probably read only about 20 percent of what you write. Online, the majority read even less, about 18 percent.

So, what does that mean for you, the reviewer? It means that you should

- use a clear, searchable headline that includes the name of the item you are reviewing and a suggestion of your opinion. For instance, the headline for a review of Taylor Swift's "Reputation" tour, according to the Detroit Free Press, *Review: Taylor Swift earns her 'Reputation' during Ford Field stunner*. A search engine looking for the artist's name and the album or tour would find it. A human would know the product was stunning.
- make your opening and closing so interesting and informative your audience wants to read more. For instance, the opening of a review of the movie "11 A.M." begins: *That old space-time conundrum—can we change the past or future without unforeseen consequences in the present?—receives an effective workout in "11 A.M."* (Sheri Linden, Los Angeles Times)

- write to draw your reader from one paragraph to the next. Transitions and a strong organization will help do that. Vivid, clear language will keep the audience reading.

You only have a few seconds to capture your readers' attention. Do not make them wonder what you think. Your position is communicated both by what you say and by the tone—your attitude toward what you are reviewing and toward your audience. Your tone will be revealed by your word choice and in the shape of your sentences.

Your Turn

1. For each of the following openings, identify the TAG (the title, author and genre). For products, identify the name of the product, who makes it and what sort of product it is. One of the TAG elements is missing from three of the following openings. Tell which element is missing. Why do you think it is missing?
   - *FiveFinger shoes made by Vibram ... are as close as you can get to running in your bare feet ...* (Billy Brown, Wired)
   - *If it were just a series of animated frames and sequences, "Mia and the Migoo" would nearly be a must-see. A hand-painted film that draws inspiration from Van Gogh and Cezanne, it's genuinely beautiful, with eye-popping color and motion and dreamscapes: really inspired stuff. But director Jacques-Rémy Girerd and his three co-writers have a fairly insipid tale on their hands ...* (Shawn Levy, The Oregonian)
   - *I did not see the "original" version of "Spider-Man: Turn Off the Dark," the new Broadway musical and cultural dartboard many critics attended (and trashed) this past March after multiple cancellations of official openings left them frustrated. But I found something innately decadent and off-putting about both the serious stage accidents that triggered a ghoulish frenzy during previews, and the show's $70 million budget. But now the "new and improved" version of the show will open Tuesday at the Foxwoods Theatre in Times Square. And a visit to the musical this weekend left me with one question: If this is what the final edition of "Spider-Man" looks like—after months of reworking overseen by "show doctors," and a three-week suspension of performances to institute changes—just how stupefyingly bad must the first edition have been?* (Hedy Weiss, Chicago Sun-Times)
   - *Gangster clichés fly like submachine gun bullets in the Italian crime biopic "Angel of Evil"* ... (Robert Abele, Los Angeles Times). Note: A biopic is a film biography.
   - *A few months ago, I reviewed Sherwood Smith's fantasy novel "Inda," the first volume of a projected trilogy, and I believe I said very positive things. I recently read volume two, "Fox," and the achievement of this writer is only getting more remarkable.* (Orson Scott Card in his blog "Uncle Orson Reviews Everything")

(Continued)

YOUR TURN *(Continued)*

- *"Terri," starring newcomer Jacob Wysocki and John C. Reilly, is a lovely lyrical ode to high school misfits and the adults they grow into by director Azazel Jacobs and screenwriter Patrick deWitt ...* (Betsy Sharkey, Los Angeles Times)
- *Headed out for a weeklong or longer trek through bear country? The voluminous BearVault (the largest of four we tested) is the canister to carry.* (Jason Kauffman, Backpacker.com)

2. **Going Deeper.** For each of the seven openings above, write a statement that begins "This reviewer thinks ..." and attempt to summarize the reviewer's opinion. Discuss your statements with your group. Did you all come to similar conclusions? Discuss each writer's word choices that reveal his or her opinions.

The Closing

The closing of a review should mirror the opening and reflect your analysis of the product or experience. The closing may be the only part of the review your audience reads after scanning the opening. You should present the same position and the same tone in both the opening and the closing. The language of the closing should remind the reader of the language of the opening.

Look again at the beginning of the "Mia and the Migoo" review. What tone do you expect at the end? And what position do you expect the reviewer to take?

This is what he wrote:

> *It's lovely, truly, but so heavy-handed and slipshod that it's probably best enjoyed with the sound off—an option they're not likely to offer at the movie theater.*

His tone of regret and his conflicted feelings about the beauty of the animation and the weakness of the story match his opening.

YOUR TURN

Try matching the openings of the reviews on the next page with the endings. Concentrate on the reviewer's position and tone—that is, the reviewer's attitude toward the work.

(Continued)

YOUR TURN *(Continued)*

Openings

1. *Director Willa Smith has a knack. A creative and fresh voice, she's taken a subject that's been beaten to death and brought it amazingly to life in her clever and amusing debut feature "Sailboat."*
2. *I'm afraid that no amount of counseling could cure what ails "Love and Marriage." The romantic comedy ... is an emotional disaster of gigantic proportions.*
3. *"Boo," the story of the real dog trainer Jane Jacobsen, presents itself with the understated eloquence of the woman herself ... an unsuspecting hero who never claims to be anything special.*
4. *There's not a lot for the brain but more than enough for the eyes. There's no doubt about it: "Scrooge: The Musical," now at the Wiltern, is a sumptuous package, a feast for the eyes.*
5. *Gangster clichés fly like submachine gun bullets in the Italian crime biopic "Angel of Evil," a restless and hollow rundown of '70s criminal Renato Vallanzasca.*

Closings

A. *Thanks to the just as gentle touch of the director, they take us to a better place, if only briefly.*

B. *Although there's no shortage of mustache-quivering energy and wide-collared strutting, ____ can't separate itself enough from the pack as a character piece to be memorable as anything other than a blood-spattered timeline.*

C. *Debut films come and go, but ____ is one to remember.*

D. *Moments of inspired whimsy are genuinely moving, and Fenwick's wildly inventive characters are a must-see.*

E. *You will have stopped caring about the characters long ago. You will just want to exit the theatre.*

Writing Well: People Want to Read Your Work

It is nice to imagine one of our readers sitting in a comfortable chair, perhaps in fuzzy slippers with a cup of hot cocoa nearby, reading every wonderful word we write. Perhaps she smiles or chuckles from time to time at our insight and wit. When she has read all the way to our conclusion, she highlights the best parts and saves the review in a favorites folder. Then she blogs about our writing, links to it and forwards it because it is so good.

We can imagine all we want, but chances are the only people who will read our reviews in that manner are our grandmothers.

People do read reviews all the way through to the end, but only if nothing derails them. Readers are more like swiftly moving sports cars on a mountain road than they are like our grandmothers. At the first slick spot, they leave us, never to return.

How do you keep your audience engaged, pulling them from paragraph to paragraph? Clear, tight writing is important. Great content is key. But even great content will not retain the audience's interest unless you use clear transitions, avoid unsupported superlatives and clichés, write the appropriate amount, and write the review for the medium you are using.

Using Clear Transitions

Reviewers tend to switch frequently between comparisons and contrasts, between praises and pans. Such sudden switches can cause audience whiplash (Figure 13.6). You lose your audience's attention at these turns unless you use clear transitions, so the audience can recognize your new direction and the relationships between each part of the review. In addition to valuable but common transitions such as *but, yet, on the other hand, however, also, consequently, clearly, then, furthermore* and *in addition,* reviewers draw on a hoard of other phrases and words to indicate transitions. These include:

- *Unfortunately ...*
- *There is nothing wrong with ... But ...*
- *Indeed, X does Y ...* (to dismiss its importance)
- *In fact ...*
- *At times ...*
- *At its best ... At its worst ...*
- *Just as it does not ..., neither does ...*
- *For some readers* (or gamers, viewers or diners), *that will be enough. For others ...*
- *His voice conjures ...* (to indicate a comparison)
- *Naturally ...* (to indicate something predictable)
- *For all its X, it is not untouched by Y ...*

Avoiding Superlatives

Superlatives are dangerous, slick spots in a review. How does your audience react when they read or hear you say

- *the greatest action film of the year;*
- *arguably the best Chicago-style slide guitar player in the business;*
- *the most amazing screen interface*; or
- *one of the worst action games of the last 10 years?*

It depends on your credibility, your ability to appear as an expert. Does your audience believe you have played all the action games of the last 10 years? Or tested every screen interface on the market? Listened to the majority of Chicago-style slide guitar players still performing? Watched all the action movies released this year?

Figure 13.6 A review without effective transitions is like a roller coaster with sharp, unexpected turns.

If not, the use of superlatives suggests you are pretending to have knowledge and experience that you do not have—or that you are selling something. If your review sounds like you are endorsing a product or pretending to be more expert than you are, you diminish your credibility as a journalist.

In addition, your audience may stop reading or listening after the first superlative. You have had your say. They know your opinion. Why should they read more?

Which of these online reviews of the game "The Legend of Zelda: Ocarina of Time" would you click on to read in full?

1. *This game is, hands down the best game ever.*
2. *From the date it was released to present day, this game is none other than the best game of all time.*
3. *A game that will forever withstand the test of time.*
4. *The greatest video game ever created. Period.*
5. *This game is a one-of-a-kind classic.*
6. *One of the best games ever!!!!*
7. *Breathtaking for its time, "Ocarina of Time" is a wonderful, spiritual experience.*
8. *"Ocarina of Time" will go down in history as one of the best games of all time.*

If opening number seven appealed to you more than the others, you may have been drawn into the review by one of two enticements, either to find out how it is a spiritual experience or to learn about the development of computer games over time. The writer promises you information as well as opinion.

Well-established critics may be entitled to use superlatives. But a reviewer is not the same as a critic. A reviewer is a well-informed journalist who provides her readers with the information they need before they spend their money or time. A **critic** is an expert in a field, usually with university training or significant professional experience, who interprets a work and ponders its social significance. Of course good reviews may also contain these elements, but reviewers who have more limited experience should leave superlatives to the writers with the credentials to say that something is the greatest or worst.

Avoiding Clichés

Reviewers keep the audience's interest by using clear, fresh and interesting language. **Clichés**, familiar and much-used descriptions and other tired expressions, are not clear, not fresh and not interesting. Your audience's attention slips away from the review when you resort to clichés because they communicate very little. Writers' Workshop 13.1 explores avoiding clichés.

Acknowledging Your Audience's Attention Span

What you say, how you say it, and how long you take to say it will vary according to your audience and your media. Journalists strive to use the full potential of each medium in which they publish, though some media may be more appropriate than others to well-developed and thoughtful reviews.

Quick takes are graphics that contain a rating and several key pieces of information. Though not reviews in themselves, they often accompany reviews. These may appear in print as graphics, as a crawl on a screen, and in microblogs and on websites (Figure 13.7).

Some reviewers think quick takes dumb-down the review, insult the audience and diminish the publication they appear in. Some worry that the readers will read the graphic and not their carefully written review. Other reviewers like quick takes, saying people are busy and need information quickly. These reviewers add that the quick takes bring traffic to a Web page or section of a print publication. Once you have your audience's attention, they may read, watch or listen to your longer, more nuanced work.

Making Your Review Appropriate for Your Medium

Each medium provides a reviewer with different opportunities to communicate, perhaps with different audiences. Each medium demands different content, organization, visuals, story lengths and styles. Each medium has different strengths and weaknesses. Though a journalist may review items or performances for several media, it would be foolhardy to try to move the same review from one platform to another.

For instance, Larry Mantle, a Public Radio talk show host at KPCC in Southern California, hosts a half-hour segment each Friday called FilmWeek where two film critics and he converse about at least four

Courtesy of Goodreads

Figure 13.7 This quick take summarizes Maxwell King's biography of Fred Rogers while also allowing readers to rate it by selecting anywhere from one to five stars.

films that were released that week. The critics' opinions are in content like their written reviews, but in style, they seem to be talking with each other about the films. They do not simply read their written reviews on the air.

FilmWeek Marquee is the quick-take version of FilmWeek, where each critic records one or two sentences to summarize his view of each film. The critics have no opportunity for analysis, but interested listeners can look for the longer show or just trust a reviewer's conclusion.

Mantle's show retains many aspects of print reviews, while other broadcasters comment on notable creative works in a format similar to a feature story or arts reporting. Since they are covering a creative work, and perhaps the people behind it, they suggest the work and its creators are noteworthy.

Online music reviews draw on the strength of their medium, perhaps linking to sound files and showing album covers or live performances. In each case, the format controls the length and depth of the reviewer's work.

Chapter Thirteen

Review and Assessment

Recall

1. Why is it important to label reviews as reviews?
2. Describe one way a journalistic review can maintain transparency.
3. Name one of the ethical standards a reviewer must adhere to.
4. What special considerations should be given when reviewing student work?
5. Describe how a journalist's review is different from a user's comments.
6. Name four tools of literary analysis that might be helpful in writing book reviews.
7. What are four tools that might be helpful in writing movie reviews?
8. What are four tools that might be helpful in writing a game review?
9. What questions would you ask if you were about to review a product or creative work that has not been reviewed before?
10. What are the major parts of a review? Which parts are read the most often?
11. What is meant by the *tone* of a review? How is tone conveyed?
12. How similar should the opening and closing of a review be?
13. Name five transitions that are helpful to reviewers.

Critical Thinking

1. *Impromptu speaking* is talking without advance notice to plan what will be said. This skill is especially valuable when asking follow-up questions during an interview. Ask a classmate to explain why it is important to be unbiased and transparent when writing a review. Ask for clarification if necessary. Were you able to hold an impromptu conversation on this topic?
2. Imagine you have been asked to respond to or edit another journalism student's review. Unfortunately, it sounds like the journalist is advertising the work, not reviewing it. What would you suggest the young writer look for and change in her review?
3. Look at ads, book jackets or publicity websites for entertainment products such as books, music CDs, movies, theater productions or concerts. Find three unsupported superlatives.
4. List clichés you find in reviews published in the media you consume.

Application

1. In Writers' Workshops 3.1 and 3.2, you learned about the benefits of writing short and cutting unnecessary words. Find an example of a review online and analyze the writers' sayings and expressions. Are there any short words you feel could be eliminated?
2. Return to the chart you created for Your Turn on page 399, in which you identified the context, overview, comparisons, and the negative and positive features of your simple product. (If you'd rather, you may choose a different product and create another chart.) Write the opening paragraphs and the concluding paragraphs of a review for this product. Make it a generally positive review, but avoid sounding like you are selling the product.
3. Use the chart you created and the opening and closing you wrote in answer to question 2 above. List the tools you will use to analyze the product, then write the complete review. Rate your own work from 1 (poor) to 4 (good enough for The New York Times) for each of the qualities listed below.
   - A. Does your review have one defensible position that is held consistently throughout?
   - B. Have you used the tools you listed?
   - C. Have you included both negatives and positives?
   - D. Have you included an overview of the product?
   - E. Have you included comparisons?
   - F. Do the paragraphs you wrote for this exercise support the position you stated in your opening and closing?
   - G. Is your tone consistent throughout?

Chapter Thirteen

Journalism Style

Comma Usage

Commas are the lightest of the dividers a writer can use. They do the least to interrupt the flow of thought. Inexperienced writers tend to over-use commas. Journalists, who resent every space, letter or punctuation mark that takes room away from their stories, use fewer marks than are expected in formal essays. Journalists use as few commas as possible, and they use them to make writing clear to their readers. **If the comma does not help the reader, leave it out.**

Several uses of commas are of special interest to journalists, either because journalists use these rules with great frequency or because journalism usage differs slightly from usage in formal writing. The rules of most interest to journalists are discussed in Journalism Style for Chapters 13 and 14. Other uses and additional information are on the *Journalism* website.

Separate Attributions from Quoted Matter

When the quotation comes before the attribution, commas always go inside the quotation marks and replace the period, but not a question mark or an exclamation mark. Those marks go outside the quotes.

Coach Arlan Smythe said, "We'll do it again."
"We'll do it again," coach Arlan Smythe said.
White-nose syndrome has affected bats across the eastern United States, according to the U.S. Geological Survey.

Separate Items in a Series

Use a comma to separate items in a series. In formal essays a comma before *and* is required, but in journalism, it is generally not used. The comma can separate nouns (and noun phrases), adjectives of equal rank, adverbs, phrases or even clauses.

- Nouns: *Please bring sandwiches, chips, apple slices, cookies and something to drink.* (Apple slices and something to drink are noun phrases.)
- Equal adjectives: *She was a mean-spirited, yellow-bellied, sneaky, manipulative dog.* In this case, all the adjectives modify dog and so are equal. Do not use a comma before the last adjective if it is part of a noun phrase: *She was a mean-spirited, manipulative hound dog.* (Hound dog is a noun phrase.)
- Adverbs: *He sighed loudly, passionately, pathetically and not very convincingly.*
- Phrases: *I searched for my lost keys in my gym bag, on the hall tree, under my homework and in the front door.*
- Clauses: *I came, I saw, I conquered.* Periods between these parallel clauses would create choppy prose. Conjunctions would weaken the impact.

Set Off an Individual's Age, Class and Hometown

If you mention a person's age, class in school or hometown, use commas to set off the information. Technically, these are nonessential appositives, but many journalistic publications routinely include this information in news stories.

Andrea Perez, 24, of Aurora, Missouri, received first prize.

Try It!

1. Use commas correctly as you write three sentences in which commas are used with attribution. Feel free to have fun as you compose.
   A. one sentence with the attribution before a quotation
   B. one sentence with the attribution after the quotation
   C. one sentence attributing the content to a written source
2. Create sentences in which commas are used to separate the following items.
   A. nouns or noun phrases in a series
   B. adjectives in a series
   C. adverbs in a series
   D. parallel phrases in a series
   E. parallel clauses in a series
3. Look in journalistic publications and find five examples in which an individual's age, hometown or graduation year is set of with commas.

Extend Your Knowledge

Style Exercises

Consult the table above to see what is available on the *Journalism* website and in Chapter 14's Journalism Style.

Chapter Thirteen

Writers' Workshop

In these Writers' Workshops you will:

- Learn to recognize and avoid clichés.
- Seek fresh and interesting expressions to replace clichés.
- Use a writing map to structure reviews.

Workshop 13.1

Avoid Clichés Like the Plague

Mini-Lesson: Recognizing Clichés in Reviews

If you use clichés, you are lazy, either too lazy to observe and think well or too lazy to use your own words to express your unique ideas. Clichés are mental cut-and-paste.

Reviews seem to invite clichés. Do any of these sound familiar? Try to describe precisely what each means:

- *beautifully realized*
- *tour-de-force*
- *riveting*
- *readable*
- *deeply felt*
- *fright fest*
- *haunting images*
- *crowd pleaser*
- *great chemistry*
- *steamy*
- *a three-hankie climax*
- *chick flick*
- *over-the-top*

The following list of clichés was compiled by film critics who detest the expressions that some reviewers use when they have little new to say:

- anything political or dramatic: *charged*, *taut*, *woven*, *layered*
- anything romantic or happy: *heart-warming*, *life-affirming*, *feel-good*
- anything containing crime: *seamy*, *gritty*, *underworld*

Reviewers who want to keep their audience do the real work of a writer. They find clear, fresh and interesting descriptions and avoid clichés.

Apply It!

1. In a small group read at least three reviews from student or local publications. Highlight anything you suspect is a cliché.
2. Look at a review you wrote, perhaps for this chapter. Search for clichés and invite your group to look for clichés in your work. Do the same for the work of your partners.
3. Rewrite the offending passages to say what you should have said, something that is clear, fresh and interesting. Do not be surprised if you need to re-examine the item you are reviewing to remind yourself of what is important.

Mini-Lesson: Recognizing Clichés in Other Writing

Editorials and columns also attract clichés, as do sports and feature stories and almost every other form of journalism. Sometimes they creep in when an inexperienced journalist wants the comfort of sounding like someone else. Sometimes they are a relic left over from English class assignments where students were told to "write a 500-word essay." But any editor would rather have 120 solid words than 500 words of froth.

Clichés may be as simple, such as "we head back to school" or "nowadays" or "in this day and age." Or they may show up in analogies.

In 1699 the analogy "avoid like the plague" was fresh and interesting. When the plague came to your densely packed 17th century city, a city with a sketchy water supply and no sewer system, your life was in danger. If you had the means or ability, you would barricade yourself in your house or flee to the country. You certainly avoided sick people. So when William Penn, the founder of Pennsylvania, wanted a forceful way to say "Choose your friends carefully," he wrote "An able bad Man, is an ill Instrument, and to be shunned as the Plague."

The expression was probably fresh and interesting for the next 101 times it was used. But three centuries later, it is not.

A *blockbuster* was the largest World War II British bomb, capable of destroying an entire urban block. By 1957 *blockbuster* had made the leap from bomb to adjective for a wildly successful play, movie or game. A producer wrote, "One day I had what seemed to me like a blockbuster of an idea for a musical play."

This was an original and clever way to describe an important production, one that a large number of people would view, one that would influence the industry and the larger society.

Fifty-five years later, an Internet search found 53 million uses of the word. It probably has lost its freshness and originality. So avoid this cliché—and all other clichés—like the plague.

Apply It!

Examine your written work for clichés, then rewrite the offending passage with what you really should have said.

Workshop 13.2

The Hardest Part Comes Before You Write

Mini-Lesson: Using a Writing Map to Write a Review

Robert Frost wrote, "The only thing that can backbone an essay is thought." If you do prewriting, that is, gathering your information and establishing your opinion and tone before you begin to type, your writing will have meat. If you have mastered the basic form of a review, much of the precomposing, that is, finding a shape for your ideas, will already be done and you will be on your way to writing swiftly and well.

Experienced journalists prewrite and precompose in their heads, perhaps not even realizing what they are doing. They know all the elements of a review. They know its basic shape, a shape the audience expects, a shape that frees them to write swiftly.

A writing map allows you to do—slowly and on paper—what you will learn to do in your head after you have written 15 or 20 solid reviews.

Apply It! Worksheet

S Below is an abbreviated example of a writing map for reviews. Use the full version of this writing map, found on the *Journalism* website, to write a review of a product, art or entertainment presentation, or book. Be sure to use the appropriate tools of analysis, describe positives and negatives, and write a strong lead and closing. Save your work in your stringbook.

Extend Your Knowledge Extend

Visit the *Journalism* website for additional information and practice for avoiding clichés and writing strong reviews.

Sample Writing Map for a Review

What you need to know before you write your review: What is the item being reviewed? What tools are appropriate to review this item? (Using the ten tools of literary analysis might be a good place to start. Other tools exist for reviewing a video game, movie, or product.) What should I compare the item to? What are the negatives? What are the positives? What tone do I want to take?

Sections of Review	Factors to Consider	Your Prewriting
1 Opening	• Tone suggests your evaluation • Context (genre, definition) • Overview	
2 Opening	• Comparisons to similar products or experiences. • Share your *informed* experience	
3 Body Analysis	• Analysis using tool • If appropriate, tell both positives and negatives	
4 Body Analysis	• Analysis using tool • If appropriate, tell both positives and negatives	
5 Body Analysis	• Analysis using tool • If appropriate, tell both positives and negatives	

Chapter Fourteen

Letters to the Editor, Online Responses and Community Forums

Is it good if they talk back to you?

Photo by Forrest Czarnecki, Conifer High School

G-WLEARNING.COM

While studying, look for the activity icon to:

- **Build** vocabulary terms with e-flash cards and matching activities.
- **Extend** learning with further discussion of relevant topics.
- **Reinforce** what you learn by completing style exercises, worksheets and end-of-chapter questions.

Visit the Journalism website: www.g-wlearning.com/journalism/

Chapter Objectives

After reading this chapter, you will be able to:

- Describe ways that an audience may shape news coverage.
- List ways to draw your audience's attention to your publication or broadcast.
- List ways to encourage your audience's comments and discussions of the news.
- Discuss how to make news stories local.
- List ways of including multiple perspectives in your publication or broadcast.
- Identify legal, ethical and journalistic concerns involved in publishing or broadcasting vertical exchanges between the audience and the press.
- Tell how legal and ethical issues for online publication of audience comments differ from those for traditional print or broadcast media.
- Discuss policies and procedures for creating an online forum appropriate for your publication.
- Distinguish between personal and journalistic communication on blogs, social media, microblogging sites and other digital media.
- Identify legal, ethical and journalistic concerns in allowing your audience to provide content as citizen journalists.

Key Terms Build Vocab

cyberbullying
external links
focus groups
horizontal exchange
narrowcast
online forum
troll
vertical exchange

Before You Read...

Journalists must be able to adapt spoken language for both formal and informal purposes. Ask a classmate what they did last weekend. Take notes during your conversation so you do not forget the details shared with you. Write a brief story inspired by what you learned during your conversation.

Introduction

"The Press is at once the eye and the ear and the tongue of the people. It is the visible speech, if not the voice, of the democracy."

–Pioneering investigative journalist W.T. Stead

You know that as a journalist you frequently act as the eye and ear of your audience, going where they may not go, hearing what they may not have heard, even asking the question they do not have the opportunity to ask. But how is journalism the voice of democracy? When are the audience's voices heard?

This chapter is about ways journalism listens to its audience and listens as they talk to each other in the forum that journalism can provide. Journalism can unite communities and actually be the voice of democracy.

The Audience and the News

Imagine you lived three thousand years ago in a busy seaside town. A stranger, washed up on your shore, becomes the king's guest, protected and honored as guests are. One evening a bard sings of the Trojan War. (You can think of the bard as an ancient Greek documentary filmmaker.) The bard's song brings tears to the stranger's eyes, so the king asks the stranger:

- Where have your wanderings taken you?
- What countries of men have you seen?
- Who were the people in the crowded cities; which were savage and violent, and which were good to strangers?
- Why do you weep?

You may have guessed that the stranger is Odysseus (Figure 14.1), the ancient Greek hero from Homer's "The Odyssey," who spent ten years battling nature, men and gods to return home after the Trojan War. At this point in his story, he has survived shipwreck and been washed up on the island of Scheria in King Alcinous's kingdom. You have also probably noticed that King Alcinous' questions look a great deal like four of journalism's five W's (the *when* is missing). You may also recall that Odysseus considered what his audience wanted to hear as he told of his adventures.

Do you imagine just one or two people listening to the bard and Odysseus in some small, dark room? Or do you imagine a large hall with many people sitting in rows at banquet tables as a steward pours wine from bowls and carries it around and fills the cups?

Of course it was in the large and well-filled hall. To the ancient Greeks, receiving news and entertainment was a communal activity, and the more people the better. Odysseus says that "all the people feel this joy. ... It seems the loveliest thing of all to me."

They did not sit silently while Odysseus told his tale, either. They talked among themselves about what they heard. Homer tells the readers that only when Odysseus had finished his amazing tale did the people, spellbound, fall silent in the darkened hall.

Figure 14.1 Painted early in the 19th century, Francesco Hayez's painting imagines the scene in which Odysseus (standing, center left, covering his face as he cries) tells his tale at King Alcinous' court.

Fast-forward a few thousand years to medieval Europe. The town crier, a public employee, comes into the town center at a busy time of the day and the week (Figure 14.2 on the next page). He rings a bell (in England), hits a gong (in Holland), beats a drum or sounds a hunting horn (in France) to attract attention. Once the crier has the public's attention, he—or she, for town criers included women—delivers the news. He announces deaths and funerals, market days, the close of fishing season, laws and proclamations by the mayor. He reports who was convicted of night fishing with illegal nets and the reward offered for the return of a lost pig. He reads advertisements, telling where sugar is for sale in broken packets from a wrecked barge.

Do you imagine the townspeople receiving these announcements in stony silence and then returning to their work without comment? Or do you imagine discussions, disagreements, comments? Something like this:

"Vic the cooper died? Well, God rest his soul. He made fine barrels, but that wife of his will have a hard time without him. And four children, just babies."

"Five."

"Five children? Who's going to help her? Does she have family nearby?"

For the Record

Communities Shaped and Received News

- Historically, the audience's questions and interests shaped the reporting of events.
- Historically, people received news in communities, not in isolation, and only in extraordinary situations did they receive the news in silence.

"I don't know. But the oldest girl could be let out to work. She must be 12 or so. Do you think the baker'll hire her?"

"I think I saw Rowley's pig rooting in the parson's garden."

"Naw. The parson's got his own pig. He's never had the sense to pen it in properly and keep it away from his parsnips."

"I don't think it was the parson's. His is black and white. This one was pink and brown. I'm going to fetch a rope and see if I can get the reward."

"Parson'll be pretty mad if you take his pig."

"Will Gibson shouldn't be fishing at night. That's not fair."

"And with those nets. He'll catch the little fish, and the rest of us will have nothing left to catch next year, when they could have grown to legal size."

"There's nothing in that river that is legal size anymore. He's got a family to feed. I say they should let him alone. Let him take what he needs."

"We've all got families to feed. And I say he doesn't have a right to take small fry. He got what he deserved."

Forward another 400 years to the 1930s in the American South, as portrayed in Harper Lee's "To Kill a Mockingbird." Atticus Finch, the book's hero, reads the paper aloud to his already literate children, "Alabama might go to the Rose Bowl again this year." He reads them Windy Seaton's column. For Atticus' family receiving the news is still a communal activity, even among literate people (Figure 14.3).

Figure 14.2 The hustle and bustle of a medieval town square was interrupted by the announcements of the town crier—a public employee paid to deliver news.

Illustration by Laura Klepfer

Atticus Finch reads The Mobile Register, The Birmingham News and The Montgomery Advertiser, all real papers, as well as the fictional Maycomb Tribune, whose editor, Braxton Bragg Underwood, knows Atticus well enough to call him by his first name and is known by almost everyone in town. He silently guards Atticus' life with a shotgun the night of the near-lynching.

Harper Lee wrote, "He rarely gathered news; people brought it to him. It was said that he made up every edition of *The Maycomb Tribune* out of his own head and wrote it down on the linotype."

After Tom Robinson's death, B.B. Underwood, generally as prejudiced as many other citizens of Maycomb, wrote Tom's obituary in a section called "Colored News" but then wrote a bitter editorial, saying "it was a sin to kill cripples. ... He likened Tom's death to the senseless slaughter of songbirds."

Lee wrote, "Mr. B.B. Underwood was at his most bitter, and he couldn't have cared less who canceled advertising and subscriptions. (But Maycomb didn't play that way: Mr. Underwood could holler till he sweated and write whatever

For the Record

News Was Local and Shared

- Historically, journalists went to their audience and requested the public's attention when they had something to report.
- Historically, news was intensely local. People in France did not hear about a lost English pig or a cooper's death in a little village in Prussia. The people in the next Prussian village probably did not hear about the death either.
- Historically, people discussed the news as they received it. And then they discussed the comments of others about the news. They added to each other's understanding. They disagreed with each other and talked through issues.

he wanted to, he'd still get his advertising and subscriptions. If he wanted to make a fool of himself in his paper that was his business.)"

Each town had its paper, perhaps more than one, each one independent, each one loyal to its own community. The editors knew their communities and were involved in them. Each paper had a different point of view.

Somewhere in the last century, the nature of news shifted. The distance between the audience and the journalists increased. Though small, local newspapers still exist and are even enjoying a renaissance, many disappeared or became part of larger media groups during the 20th century. Cities with two or three daily newspapers in 1950 had only one by 2000 as large news corporations bought up or ran out the competition, well before the Internet decreased paper circulation.

Figure 14.3 Atticus Finch, played by Gregory Peck in the 1962 film "To Kill a Mockingbird," is shown holding the local newspaper in this movie still. Reading and discussing the local news was a communal activity during Atticus' time.

Technology in the early 20th century brought faraway voices into our homes. News was still communal; members of the household often listened together. But we listened inside our homes, in isolation from our community (Figure 14.4 on the next page).

By the second half of the 20th century, more and more people got their news from people they did not know personally and who knew them only as demographics and consumer statistics. Local news and local perspectives were often ignored, or if they were covered at all, were mentioned briefly in articles that did so to maintain balance and fairness.

News became less a dialogue between journalists and their audience and more a lecture—a lecture with pictures and sound, but still a lecture—delivered from a remote podium to a faceless and generally voiceless crowd.

As the country became more prosperous and radios and televisions shrank and became

For the Record

Perspective Was Limited

- Historically, news was by and about the community it served.
- Historically, each paper reported and commented on news from its own perspective—the perspective of the locale and audience and the perspective of the editor.
- Historically, it was often necessary to read several papers to form well-reasoned opinions and learn what others were thinking.

more affordable, receiving news became more of a solitary and silent event with fewer opportunities for discussion (Figure 14.5).

With the advent of individual data devices, more people received the news from distant authority figures while they were alone, separated not only from their immediate household but also from their larger communities (Figure 14.6). In the absence of the Greek banquet in the *megaron*, the medieval town square and the local journalist, people had fewer opportunities to discuss the news, to talk through the issues the news raised, to add to others' perspectives or to argue against them.

Using Journalism to Create Community

We no longer sit together in a Greek *megaron* or gather in a town square with a variety of our peers. Many people can go days without having a meaningful interaction with anyone except a small group of like-minded friends and family members. Yet journalism, if done thoughtfully and skillfully, still has the capacity to create bonds among widely diverse people.

Figure 14.4 In the 1930s, families gathered around the radio to hear the latest news report.

Figure 14.5 By the late 20th century, many people received their news via television broadcast.

Your Audience Can Shape Your Content

Good print journalists and their editors watch the number of letters to the editor that result from a story. The letters may be submitted on paper or electronically. Stories that provoke many comments may be stories that deserve more coverage. If a three-inch story about a lost Chihuahua found on campus brings nine letters to the editor, it may be time to do an investigative story on the school district's animal control policy and how it is implemented. You may want to do a feature story on one four-footed campus visitor, from his arrival on campus to his successful return to his owner or his trip to the pound, to be adopted or destroyed. Perhaps doing these stories will provide an opportunity for an opinion piece or a staff editorial.

Knowing your audience's concerns can inform your coverage, but unfortunately, students rarely take the time to write letters to the editor and only do so when they are strongly moved. The time lag between publication of a print story and the publication of the letters in print is long. Print publications may find themselves trailing their audience's interest and publishing on topics that have already become stale.

Focus groups can help publications with long news cycles be more proactive. In **focus groups**, journalists request the opinions of a diverse group of readers on what topics need to be covered that have been ignored, what topics they would like to read or hear about, what topics have been covered too much (Figure 14.7 on the next page). The people you invite into a focus

Figure 14.6 Today, up-to-the-minute news coverage is available on smartphones, tablets and other devices.

Figure 14.7 Successful focus groups are comprised of a diverse group of people—not just the most popular or outspoken students. *How would you assemble focus groups at your school?*

group need to represent as many different segments of your campus as possible. They should not be drawn primarily from campus leaders, and they should be continually changing, with each participant serving only for a few meetings. A pizza lunch one Friday each month can provide a good forum for focus groups.

Online publications have the ability to see how many times each of their stories is read, usually by counting the times a reader clicks beyond the teaser to the full story. Often the most popular stories are listed on the home page under a heading, such as Most Read or Most Popular (Figure 14.8).

But these methods that allow the audience to shape content are indirect. Digital media provide many opportunities for the audience to shape coverage directly.

Journalists can follow their community's digital communications. What are the most common topics on the microblogging services that your audience uses? What questions or comments are showing up on social media sites? Follow whatever platforms and services people in your audience use when they talk to each other. Their discussions can shape your coverage.

You can also directly request audience contributions through your publication's site or its social media accounts. "If you are going to the cheer competition, please contact us." "If you are going to a concert this weekend, send us your pictures." "Have you experienced or observed hunger and homelessness in our city? Please contact us." "What public service do you do? What does your club or organization do?" "What are you shopping for?" The most open-ended question is this: "Do you know of a story we are not covering? Contact us." Make certain the invitation to "Contact us" is a live link, so you will get their message.

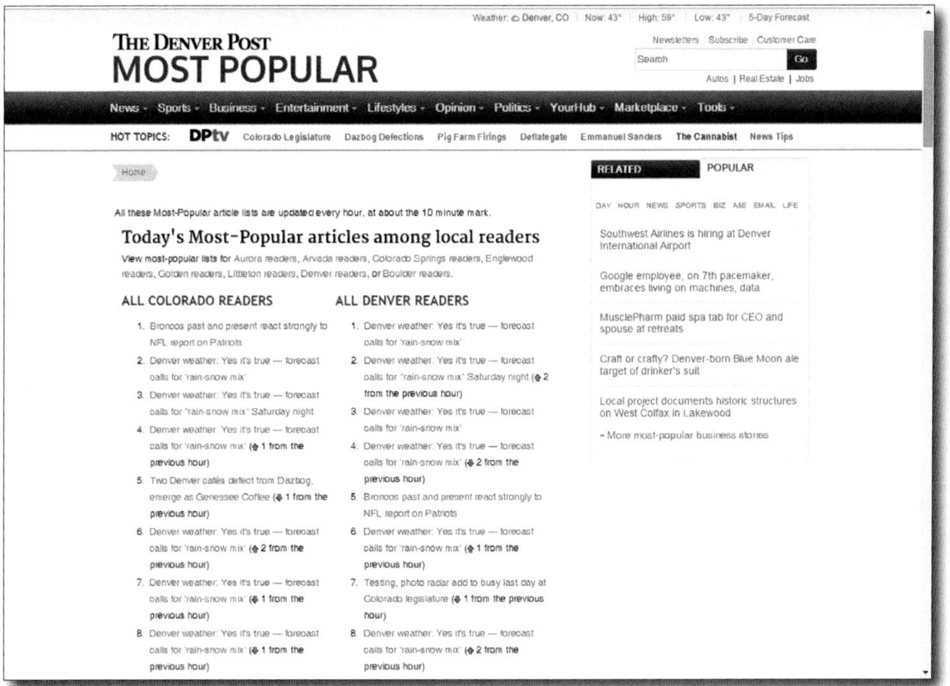

Courtesy of The Denver Post and denverpost.com

Figure 14.8 By tracking how many times a story is opened, digital publications are able to create a Most Popular list of stories. *How might your publications benefit from tracking their most popular stories?*

The BBC, the British Broadcasting Corporation, asks its viewers, listeners and readers to submit questions and comments on current topics for experts, then uses those questions and comments to shape its audio shows, including podcasts. Their opening line is, "You've heard the news from the BBC. Now it is your turn."

The program features a moderator, a number of experts, many of them in remote locations, and the invitation for listeners to post questions and comments on the BBC's Facebook page, on Twitter, via email or in text messages or phone messages.

The show you design can be about whatever is currently being discussed by your audience. If your football team is being plagued by injuries, your show and your audience's questions will be about football injuries, recovery time, the likelihood someone will need surgery and the dangers of contact sports. Your guests, most of them connected by phone, may include a sports medicine specialist (someone who is not involved in the treatment of your athletes, so he will not violate professional confidentiality), a professional journalist who has written about the joy and danger of football, an alumnus who is playing college ball and your athletic director, who can discuss the safety precautions you already use.

If your campus has experienced a tragic death, invite a grief specialist (they are usually psychologists) as well as members of the clergy (who may themselves be grief specialists) from your local community. Include an alumnus—not too much older than your audience—who experienced the death of someone close when he was in high school, and a school counselor to answer the audience's questions.

Your Turn

1. What does your publication currently do so that the audience's questions and interests shape the news in your publication?
2. **Going Deeper.** What more can you do with your available technology and your news formats?

Invite Viewers, Listeners and Readers to Your Publication or Broadcast

Once it was the town crier's gong, bell, hunting horn or drum that announced the news in a busy medieval town square. Later, it was a newsboy selling papers on city streets, calling out the headlines and shouting, "Read all about it" (Figure 14.9). Both newsboys and town criers went where their audience was and requested the audience's attention.

Today the audience for student journalism is not generally on the streets or in the town square. They are on Twitter, Facebook, Snapchat and Instagram. Though we have few town squares, the same principle holds: The place to announce updates to your publication or broadcast is still wherever the students are. If they are on Twitter, then announce your stories on Twitter. Before this book is more than a few years old, your audience will use other sites and other media. Wherever your audience is, you should go there and request their attention.

Figure 14.9 Newsboys in the late 19th and early 20th century attracted customers by shouting out the headlines at street corners, prompting people to buy the newest edition of the newspaper.

Send out a teaser, enough information to bring eyes and ears to the platform where your story is published. How much of your story do you send out to invite your audience to your site? More than just *Come learn the name of the new student body president*, but less than a complete recap of the election. Do not give away your whole story. You want people to be drawn to your site for more information.

Determining the right amount to post is a delicate balance. You may tell who won the game and by how much and perhaps mention the name of a standout player, but always leave the audience wanting more information. A good tease on a microblogging site following student body (ASB) elections might be *Newly elected ASB president: Toni Huynh, runoff elections for two other seats.* Include a link or a reference to your publication or broadcast.

Make sure your audience will find more depth of coverage if they follow the links. One or two dead links, or links that lead to a story that says little more than the teaser said, will destroy your credibility. If you report ASB elections, include a graphic with the actual number of votes for each candidate, photos of the candidates learning there will be a runoff, the dates and times of the runoff, and statements from the elected leaders. If you announced who won the game, include the actual game score, perhaps broken down by player or by quarter. Your audience should find game highlights, photos or video and further details of the game soon after you send out your tease.

If you do not have more information or images, do not include a link. If you are covering the league finals for cross-country, you can keep your audience informed by tweeting, "Light rain at noon making the course slick." That may be enough to keep your audience informed—and interested.

Since you already know your audience's interests and you have a clear understanding of basic news values, you can decide which stories deserve extended coverage. Then provide it and let your audience know when you have posted photos, video, stats and interviews from the cross-country finals.

You also will draw eyes and ears to your publication if you **narrowcast** as well as broadcast (Figure 14.10). As you report, collect contact information for the people you interview and their organizations, including off-campus sources. When you post, broadcast or publish the story that mentions a person or campus group, narrowcast on whatever media your interviewees regularly see and let them know they are in the news. If you cover the Spanish Club beach cleanup day, post a notice on the club's wall. You will generate traffic to your site, bringing in viewers, readers and listeners and creating valuable contacts for the future.

Your Turn

1. What does your publication currently do to announce news stories, broadcasts or issues to your audience? How do you narrowcast to people who have a stake in a news story?
2. **Going Deeper.** Where else should you go to communicate with your audience?

a. Broadcasting b. Narrowcasting

Figure 14.10 Broadcasting the news is much like a gardener widely scattering the seeds for a wildflower meadow (a)—the message is sent far and wide, to reach a large audience. Narrowcasting is a more thoughtful, careful process similar to planting a row of seeds in a garden (b)—narrowcasting targets a specific audience. *Does your publication practice narrowcasting in addition to broadcasting? Why or why not?*

Encourage Comments and Discussions of the News

Journalism has an opportunity to recreate the vanished town square, a place where people talk about the news and respond to each other's comments. The Letters to the Editor section, especially in papers that are published frequently, serves that purpose. For instance, a letter to the editor from a teacher, printed in the Orange County Register, opined that some of her brightest students could not fulfill their dreams to be licensed as nurses, pharmacists or teachers because they had entered the country illegally as small children. Three days later, another reader wrote that there was a bill to fix the problem, the federal DREAM Act, and that it needed citizen support. The Letters to the Editor served as a forum for an exchange of ideas among readers.

Unfortunately, few student print publications come out frequently enough to sustain a conversation among readers, a **horizontal exchange**, though there may be exchanges between the publication and the reader, **vertical exchanges**. But these vertical exchanges between the publication and its audience may result in a sort of conversation. A reader may challenge a statement in the paper in a letter to the editor:

"You printed that no female team from Roxy High has ever made it to state-level competition. You neglected to mention that the 1968 softball team was defeated in the final round of playoffs for the state championship."

The editor may write back, usually in italic type just below the reader's letter:

> *While it is technically true that the 1968 softball team did go to state, the team was declared ineligible to compete because of three illegal players who lived out of the Roxy attendance area. The team was stripped of all league records as well as its standing at state.*

Of course if the reader was right, the paper would have issued a correction in the next issue rather than merely publishing the letter to the editor.

Journalistic radio shows also may allow for listener comments, submitted in print and read by the radio journalists or recorded by phone and broadcast as "Talkback," as the Canadian Broadcasting Corporation's "As It Happens" does. But these also tend to be vertical exchanges,

And Now... Closer to Home

Invite Corrections

Publications should invite corrections, usually much shorter notes than actual letters to the editor, which are intended for both the editor and the publication or broadcast.

The usual language is *Report an error in the Roxy High School Reveille. Send an email to* LetterstoReveille@XXmail.com, *call XXX-XXX-XXXX or leave a note in the Reveille's box in the mailroom.*

between the publication and the audience, not horizontal ones between members of the audience.

Digital publishing, however, has the capacity to create a virtual town square where people comment on the news you produce or write. They may comment to you or to others and then respond to comments other people post. They may refute what has been posted before, or add further examples or insights. (You will read later about moderating these discussions so they do not turn into brawls.)

Most online publications create live links in the reporter's byline so that her name is linked to her journalistic email account. By answering emails with patience and civility, reporters form additional bonds with the community and increase their contacts list. Someone who criticized your article on the security at SATs may be a good source when you want to write about crowd control at school dances. Be sure to respond to what people say to you, not how they say it or how they make you feel.

Just as all comments in the medieval town square were not insightful and well-informed, some audience reactions will be less than inspiring. The comments are not journalism. What your publication produces is. The comments help people process the developments you report, give your audience a voice, let them receive feedback from their peers and increase their engagement with the news and with your website. Just as the town square built a sense of community, providing your audience with the opportunity to comment can do the same.

YOUR TURN

1. How successful is your paper at evoking letters to the editor, giving your audience access to your journalists, providing opportunities for online comments and inviting other audience responses?
2. **Going Deeper.** What factors limit your success? What avenues are available to you to increase discussion of the news and features you produce?

Keep It Local

In many ways, high school publications are the heirs of the small-town paper. Your coverage and your story ideas reflect local activities, people and perspectives and you unabashedly cheer for your school's teams. You make national and state stories local. You may not cover a crash at an airshow in another state, but you will cover the local students who witnessed the crash.

But to be a part of the community you cover, you may need to leave the soft chair in the journalism classroom, at least long enough to pick up your phone and publish microblogs, such as tweets, to the members of your community that follow you. Share stories as they develop, being careful not to give away all the details. You want to draw the audience to your publication or website. Let them know when you get an interview with the student whose car was vandalized or when someone is named student of the month. Express your frustration if the school's server blocks your research. Microblog when you reach the district's Internet administrator, then write a story about Internet freedom movements, what your server blocks and does not block and who makes the decisions. Your audience will be waiting for it.

The more involved you are in your school and community, the stronger your journalism will be. You need to post updates on your publication's or broadcast's wall and follow the posts and messages on social media sites in your community. These communications will bring stories to you and whet your audience's interest in your publication or broadcast.

If you are successful in becoming part of your local community on social media, your publication will become an essential means of communication, not just a place where announcements are made. People will turn to you to share information, to ask questions, to receive information and also to distribute it.

Include Multiple Perspectives

Atticus Finch read several papers to learn what others were thinking, knowing that The Maycomb Tribune had a relatively narrow view. But our communities are not as homogeneous as Mr. B.B. Underwood thought Maycomb was, and good journalism suggests our publications and broadcasts need to represent as many voices in our community as possible.

Traditional print or broadcast news is constrained by space or time. Stories may mention opposing points of view, but not have room or time to explore them and let diverse voices be heard. Online publishing, on the other hand, allows student journalists to explore multiple perspectives in some detail. The BBC's podcasts (mentioned previously in "Your Audience Can Shape Your Content") are examples of an audio presentation featuring experts representing divergent opinions and taking questions and comments from an even more diverse audience.

Journalistic blogs are one way of exploring multiple points of view, as is an in-depth coverage of an issue, which can include links to many perspectives. For instance, the DREAM Act, which offers undocumented students a path to legal status, would at first glance seem to be favored by all minority students and perhaps opposed by another segment of your audience. But a journalist might find that a minority student who is here legally is worried that if the DREAM Act passes, there will be more students applying for needs-based grants and therefore less money available for those here legally. There are multiple sides to every story.

In addition, you can provide links to other stories you have published on related topics, as well as clearly labeled outside links to sites mentioned in your blog or article. Your audience will choose which points of view they wish to explore further.

Online publishing provides opportunities for multiple local perspectives to be heard and viewed. Though good journalism may not be able to solve all the issues it covers, it can decrease the isolation that many people feel in a diverse student body by recognizing their positions and concerns.

Links to Inside and Outside Sources

Strong journalistic sites have many internal links. You link to earlier stories. When your second baseman returns after a knee injury, link to the story about the game where he was injured. You also link to related stories. Perhaps you have written seven stories in the last two years about athletic injuries. If you write about another injury, link to the earlier ones.

External links, links that take the reader away from your site, are more problematic. First, they do take your readers off your site, so they are no longer reading and viewing your content or your ads. Second, you may appear to be recommending the information that they find there, information over which you have no control. Third, a small typing error in the link can misdirect your reader to a site that is not appropriate for your audience. Fourth, if a link goes dead, it may reflect poorly on your publication.

Some publications include a statement on their home page that indicates they are not responsible for material on these links. Some create a message to let the audience know when they are leaving their site. Some avoid links altogether in their news and feature content, though they may allow them in blogs.

Gate-Keeping: Protecting Your Publication's Journalistic Integrity

A gatekeeper positioned himself near the door of a lord's castle and controlled who gained access to the lord and who stayed out; so serving as a gatekeeper may not sound like a good job for a journalist in a democracy. However, journalists act as gatekeepers in at least two senses, and both are heavy responsibilities.

As a journalist you sift through a great deal of "noise," inconsequential details, to find news. Every charming dog-and-baby video, every complaint about a coach, every fashion trend is not newsworthy, but you find the issues and trends that are. You bring to your audience's attention the things that matter, the things that you have let through the gate and into your coverage.

In a second sense, you guard the gate to the forum your publication has established, so that your publication's journalistic integrity remains strong.

Print and Broadcast Letters to the Editor

You are the Letters editor for a publication or broadcast. Your job is to choose which letters or emails will be published, broadcast or posted online in your Letters to the Editor section.

You have provided your audience with several methods of contacting you, as well as guidelines for the submission of letters to the editor (Figure 14.11 on the next page).

As the Letters editor, you hope to be very busy. You want to foster the healthy, informed debate that is essential to democracy, and you want to publish as many points of view and diverse and divergent voices as

Figure 14.11 Your submission guidelines will contain some version of these statements. *Which of these guidelines would be different for your publications?*

Submission Guidelines for Letters to the Editor

- Include your full name, mailing address, phone number and email address. This information will be seen only by the Letters editor and not published or used for commercial purposes.
- Letters without full contact information will not be published.
- You will be contacted if your letter is a candidate for publication.
- Letters to the editor should be sent only to our publication, not to any other. We do not publish duplicates.
- Letters should be brief and to the point. Letters under _____ words will be given preference. (*Most major publications request under 150 words; others, under 200. Some publications simply ask for brevity and publish well-written letters that may be 450 words long.*)
- Consider submitting longer opinion pieces to the Opinion editor. (*Include Op-Ed contact information.*)
- If you know of something we should be covering but are not, please contact our News editor. (*Include News contact information.*)
- We cannot return or acknowledge unpublished letters.
- Letters should refer to an article that has been published or broadcast by this organization within the last _____ days.
- We generally do not publish more than one letter from an individual in 60 days.
- Letters may be edited for length, civility, style and clarity. We will send you a printed copy of the edited version before we publish it.

possible. The robust debate and diverse comments are good for your publication.

When you consider a letter for publication you always

- Fact check the letter. Your publication's reputation will suffer if you print errors or, worse yet, lies. Not every letter writer speaks the truth. (Print a retraction if something does get by you.)
- Verify the identity of the letter writer. Call the person and ask her if she wrote the letter. Verify the contents. You may do an Internet search to further verify the writer's identity and perhaps her credentials, if the writer represents herself as an expert.
- Ask about the writer's connections with the topic. Readers should be able to judge the writer's credibility and motivation.
- Look for any possible copyright infringements in the letter. Your organization will be responsible for what you print.
- Look for any possible libel or slander. If you reprint a libelous comment or broadcast a slanderous statement, your organization is responsible for it.

Your Turn

Your publication just covered the closure of a local community center. In addition, you ran a feature story about the 47-year-old women's basketball league that will be displaced by the closure. The next day you receive a letter to the editor concerning the league and the woman who runs it, Alma Abbott, who is African-American.

Part of the letter reads:

> *I played basketball in that community center for almost 20 years. That league is about more than just sports. It's given girls and women a place to learn competition in a good way and to relieve stress.*
>
> *And I wouldn't count out Coach Abbott. She always gets her way, no matter what it takes. There's a kind of strength that is almost frightening in black women. It's as if a steel rod runs right through the head down to the feet.*

Using the bulleted list in Figure 14.11, what ethical or journalistic concerns do you have about this letter? What will you do before you consider printing this letter?

Hint: Pulitzer Prize-winning American poet Maya Angelou said, "There is a kind of strength that is almost frightening in black women. It's as if a steel rod runs right through the head down to the feet" in a 1973 interview, which was reprinted in the book "Conversations with Maya Angelou." (See Chapters 3 and 4 for more information on copyright issues.)

Online Comments and Forums

Clearly the town crier bore little responsibility for what the townspeople said and did in the town square after they heard her news. Nor was the bard who sang of the Trojan War responsible for the truth of the tales Odysseus told in King Alcinous' banquet hall. When NBC radio journalist Max Jordan reported from Vienna that Nazi Germany had invaded Austria, he was not responsible for the arguments and anger around family radios.

But the bard, the town crier, and Max Jordan and NBC did not own the banquet hall, the town square or the living rooms where the audience reacted. If your publication, on the other hand, creates an **online forum** (an electronic public square) or allows audience comments on its website, are you responsible legally, ethically and journalistically for your audience's reactions?

There are no simple answers to these questions. Libel and copyright laws vary from state to state. The courts will be refining and adjusting their rulings on such issues for the next several decades at least. Each new medium of expression will invite new challenges. In addition, cases specifically involving online student expression may be heard and decided long after the precedents are set for the larger population.

Nonetheless, because of your publication's role as an electronic town square, you will need to know the law and establish policies and procedures that protect your publication, your community and yourselves as journalists.

Copyright

In general, online publications have slightly greater privileges than print publications concerning copyright when such material is submitted by commenters. Your publication will be subject to a lawsuit under copyright law only if you continue to host copyrighted content submitted by an online commenter after you have been told to take the material down by the legal holder of the copyright.

Libel

In general, if a statement is libelous in print, it is libelous online, but when someone else posts it on your site, you are probably shielded from charges of libel. (See Chapter 3 for a fuller discussion of libel and how it differs from slander.)

Ironically, you are more likely to be legally responsible for libel if you or your publication has screened or edited the online comments that have been submitted to your publication than if you allow all comments from members of your online community. The legal argument is that if you actively allowed the libel to get past your screening and editing processes, you are more responsible than if you passively provided the forum where libel was committed.

Protecting Minors

Since your audience is principally made up of minors, additional issues may shape your policies and practices. Laws and policies designed to curtail **cyberbullying**, that is, online harassment, may further complicate issues concerning students' free expression. Though the courts have held that school districts are not legally liable for the content of student-produced media, the protection of minors concerns your community and your school, as well as your publication and its reputation.

In addition, since your audience may include students as young as 13 or 14, many hold it is in society's interest to protect them from inappropriate interactions and comments, including online interactions and online communications.

Policies and Procedures for Online Comments

Some professional news organizations have discontinued audience comments, while others have never allowed such comments. They cite profanity, racist and sexist comments, personal attacks, libel, insensitivity and threats, as well as spam. Some publications note that, while most commenters used their ability to make online comments responsibly, a small number of online **trolls**—crude or insensitive people—have forced them to discontinue comments. Some of these news organizations intend to restore comments when they can require commenters to register. Some will require the use of a commenter's full name instead of allowing use of a screen name. They have found that anonymity attracts trolls.

Other professional news organizations have outsourced the moderating of online comments to free up journalists for more appropriate tasks. Moderating and removing inappropriate comments is time-consuming.

If your publication or broadcast has decided to host online comments, you will need to establish policies about who may comment, what sorts of comments are appropriate and how you will moderate the comments.

And Now... Closer to Home

Where to Go for Legal Advice

If you are not sure about a legal issue affecting your student publication, go to http://www.splc.org, the website of the Student Press Law Center. The SPLC is a nonprofit public service organization providing information on student press law to student journalists. You may find the answer to your questions in the resources on the site. If not, you may contact the SPLC for advice.

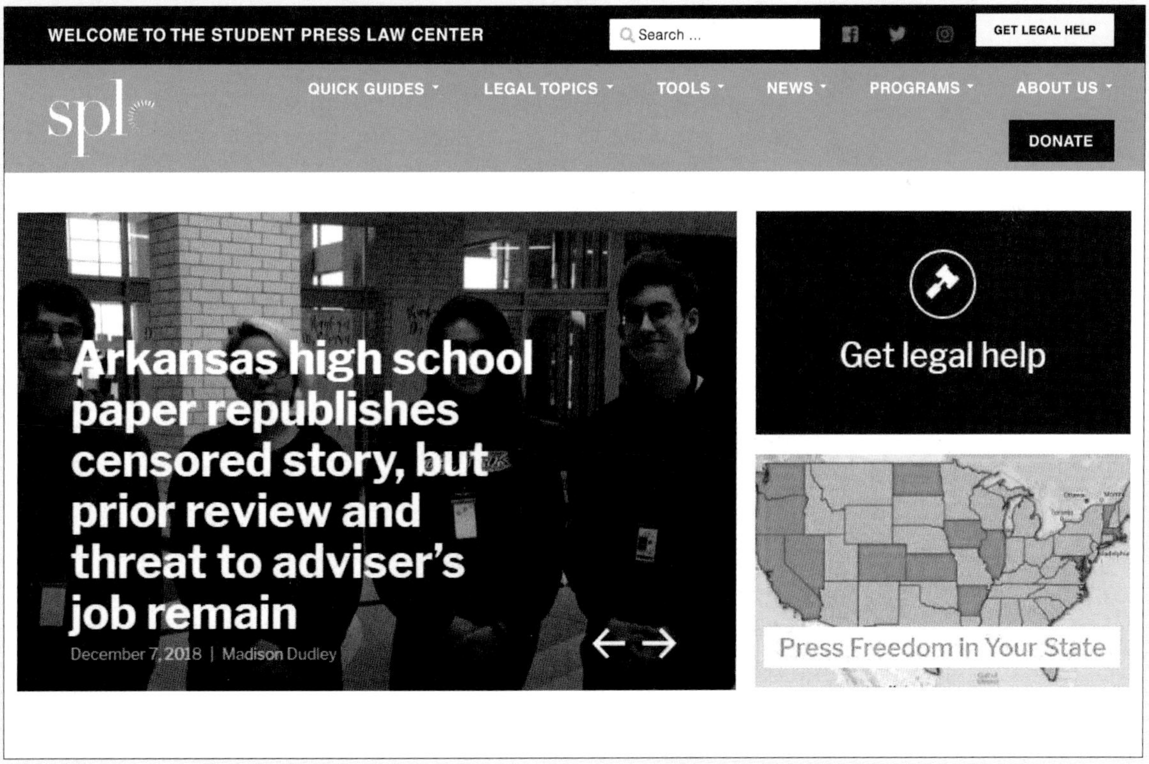

Courtesy of the Student Press Law Center

Some publications treat online comments much as they do letters to the editor. Like letters to the editor, the comments are placed in a queue, waiting for an editor to screen them for inappropriate content and to verify identities. Some also fact check comments before they are released onto the website. This imposes a lag from the time a comment is submitted until it is published.

The advantage of this practice is that your publication will be less likely to publish libel, host cyberbullying or commit a copyright infringement. You can refuse to publish comments that contain inappropriate language and content. All the comments will be appropriate for all of your audience. Your under-age commenters will not become involved in inappropriate electronic exchanges with people from outside your community.

But there are also disadvantages:

- Your audience is likely to post comments somewhere else where they can see their views published immediately. You will be unable to filter those comments.
- Your audience members who do post on your site will be less likely to have a horizontal conversation—a conversation with other members of your audience—and less likely to have a robust discussion.
- If libel or copyright issues do slip by your editor into print, you will be more likely to be liable for them.
- You will need to devote considerable time to fact checking and verifying information in the comments and screening for libel and copyright issues.
- If you do not publish comments from underrepresented groups, you could be accused of censoring their free speech rights and perhaps racism. (The courts have held that print and broadcast publications, because their space and time are limited, have greater protection from such accusations.)

Student publications and broadcasts utilize a variety of policies and procedures which affect the nature of their online forum and comments. Most limit who can comment on their site, and they restrict anonymity (Figure 14.12).

Your goal is to make the level of discussion on your site better and more interesting than elsewhere in the community. Your policies may influence the quality and depth of the discussion. Your statement of policy should be clear and be prominently posted on your website. Audience members should acknowledge these standards when they register to comment and understand they will lose their ability to comment if they violate your site's standards. Consider including some version of these policies:

- Comments should pertain to a published or broadcast story. If you know of something we should be covering but are not, click here. If you wish to submit a comment on a subject we have not covered, consider submitting an opinion piece to the Opinion editor.

Registration Guidelines for Online Comments and Forums

- Registration is required to comment on this site. Registration information is kept confidential and not used for commercial purposes.
- Commenters are required to create a password.
- Registration is open to ____. (*Only to students, staff and administration? Alumni? Who else?*)
- Screen names will (*or will not*) be allowed.
- The registration process requires a real name, a physical address, an email address, phone number, year in school and student number.
- Nonstudents who wish to register will be required to give the following information: ____.

Figure 14.12 Your registration procedures will contain some version of these requirements.

- Personal attacks or breaches of civility, including profanity and obscenity, may result in your comment being removed. Repeated infractions may result in your access to the website being disabled.
- Comments should be limited to ____ *(you name the number)* in a 24-hour period *(or 48-hour period).*
- Comments should be limited to ____ words. *(You decide the number.)*
- This is not a forum for personal communication. Private jokes, abbreviations and allusions to private matters are not appropriate.
- Sexist or racist comments are not appropriate.
- Threats are not appropriate.
- Advertisements for commercial products are not appropriate.
- Do not include links to inappropriate sites in your comments.
- Consider before you push Send. Do you want to be associated with the comments you have just written?

A member of your journalism staff can monitor the comments and the commenters in a variety of ways. Consider using some version of these methods:

- The identity of each commenter is verified before he is allowed to post.
- Inappropriate comments are removed as soon as they are seen.
- Extra moderation is provided when a controversial story is being aired or published.
- Members of your online community may flag inappropriate comments, bringing them to the attention of your monitor, who may remove them.

- Some stories you publish or broadcast may allow comments, while others may not.
- You may close down the comments section on a story when it is appropriate to do so.

But remember, your staff should not edit the comments in any way. Either allow the comment or remove it.

Blogs and Other Communications with Your Audience

Journalistic blogs are a log of the reporter's research and journalistic activities. They allow journalists to publish a great deal of information that might be cut from news or feature stories because of length or time constraints. Blogs on the publication's website and on microblogging sites, such as Twitter, also allow journalists to update followers as they report stories, thereby creating interest in the publication or broadcast. They often allow two-way communication between the audience and the journalist as the journalist researches a story, enriching the coverage and correcting misinformation before it is published as news or feature content. Blogs may provide the audience with a "behind-the-scenes" view of how journalists gather and verify the news.

Journalistic blogs can either damage or build your publication's greatest asset—your audience's trust. They should adhere to the same standards of transparency, accuracy and fairness as the rest of your publication or broadcast.

Journalistic blogs are an interesting hybrid of standard journalism and personal communication.

- The writer takes an objective point of view as does any other journalist, but she may appear in the story to show the audience how the news was gathered.
- The style is less formal than is usual for journalism, but not as informal as personal communication.
- The writer strives for journalistic accuracy, but may have less time to verify everything in the story.
- The writer has the luxury of offering informed speculation as events unfold.

Objective Point of View

Use an objective point of view in journalistic communication. In a blog you may report what you saw and heard as you approached a motorcycle accident. You may even include what you did, if it was to provide a blanket from the trunk of your car. But you will concentrate on others' actions and reactions, not on your own.

If the story is news for your audience, do not give away the story in a blog or other electronic communication before you write it as news, though you should share a teaser directing your audience to the website, publication or broadcast.

And Now...
Closer to Home

Telling a Good Story

If the story has local news value, publish or broadcast it as soon as possible and use your blog or other electronic communication to bring the audience to your news site. But what can you do with the blog, and the experience, if the accident was distant from your school and does not have news value for your community?

Write well. If you do, people will read your work. A good writer can make her reader care about her characters: *Beside the Kawasaki was a thin 17-year-old in a Rams jacket whose leg was pinned under the indifferent, idling bike, his jeans ripped and damp with blood.* Tell your readers how you learned his name and his hometown. Let them see the scene you saw and follow the action you witnessed. They will want to know which hospital receives him and how badly he is hurt. Tell them. A week later they will still care, whether you have good news or not, and they will read your journalistic blog to find out how he is, even though he is a stranger who was injured many miles from your school.

Blogging Style

Blogging style is slightly less formal than what you may use in your broadcasts and published work. Contractions are acceptable, as well as widely known abbreviations for places, organizations and events. The key is to know your audience. If you blog for the Roxy Reveille at Roxy High School, your audience will probably understand RHS. If your teams compete in the California Invitational Finals, CIF will be understood. Will they know ASB is Associated Student Body? If so, then you may use it.

But blogging style is not as informal as most personal communication. Do not use emoticons or emojis. Avoid abbreviations that only a small segment of your audience will understand. Avoid vulgar language and casual expressions that may be acceptable in private communication to some members of your community, but not all. Remember, you represent your publication and are writing for all the members of your audience—and everyone is not exactly like you!

Accuracy and Corrections

Ideally, accuracy should never be compromised in the interest of speedy electronic communication, for inaccuracy destroys trust. Make sure the most essential information is completely accurate before you push Send. If you blog or tweet about the motorcycle accident, you must give the correct name of the victim. Imagine how his sister would feel if you post that Thanh Nguyen, 17, was injured when in fact it was Danh Nguyen, 17. Or how the family will feel if you send them to Long Beach Community Hospital when Danh has been taken to Long Beach Memorial. It will take you months to build up the trust and goodwill that such errors have destroyed. Indeed, you may never restore the public's trust.

However, errors will appear in almost any hastily posted communication. Your audience may be the first to notice errors and let you know you have made a mistake. All errors should be quickly acknowledged and updated information published quickly in their place. If you wrote that the accident took place at the corner of Dale and Chapman but it was actually closer to Dale and Lampson, let the audience know. One way to do this is to correct the blog on your site but put an asterisk by "Lampson," the correct street name, and a note below that says, *Earlier posts incorrectly reported the name of the cross street.*

Informed Speculation

If you have followed a story for some time, you may be a credible expert on it. If so, you can indulge in a little speculation on your blog, knowing that in a few hours or days you will be proved right or wrong. But right or wrong, leave your blog up. As a journalist, you will live with your words and speculation.

If you have written about the negotiations between your district and the teachers union, you may be in a position to speculate on the outcome of the crucial meeting that will decide how to cut money from the budget. Will the participants agree to shorten the school year by two more days, or will the teachers simply take a pay cut? If they shorten the school year, will you get out two days earlier in June or have a longer spring recess or have two more nonschool days at Memorial Day?

A journalist may blog on the morning of the crucial meeting what he thinks the outcome will be.

> *The union will not agree to do the same work for less pay. Why should they? And the district will not want to reschedule all the graduations and baccalaureate exercises in June, let alone reschedule the start of summer school. So the days will be cut from inside the year. But they'll postpone the budget-cut days until after we've taken all the standardized tests in the spring because cutting instruction before the tests would hurt the test scores. I predict we will get a five-day weekend for Memorial Day.*

The Audience as the Eyes and Ears of Your Publication or Broadcast

Your audience will be more likely to follow you if you listen to them as well as talk to them. In addition, they can be a valuable source of information and images for your broadcast. If they have the opportunity to suggest stories and to contribute their sound, videos and photographs to your site and share their experiences with you and with others in the audience, their loyalty to your publication or broadcast will grow. However, audience contributions may not adhere to journalistic standards, and your journalistic organization can be damaged by these contributions. Libel or copyright infringement in your news and feature content is not protected in the same way it is protected in your listeners' comments sections.

You should treat your digital audience as you would treat sources you contacted face-to-face. Confirm their identities. Verify what they say with a second and third source. A groundswell of anonymous posts suggesting you cover the gambling in the wrestling room during lunch may be only one anonymous person posting 49 times. Do not assume 49 people have witnessed the activity. Know who is reporting from cheer tryouts and yearbook camp and what their affiliations and loyalties are.

Educate your audience about journalistic standards, but do not assume they are following them. A few may maliciously falsify information. More will simply make assumptions or commit errors innocently. Make your expectations clear for those who will contribute photos or videos. You may wish to specify that all images should be fresh from the camera and unedited. Let them know your standards for images and sound. Examine all contributions carefully for signs of inappropriate editing.

Citizen journalists should not have the same access to your site as do your editors and writers (Figure 14.13). An editor should clear all microblogs, photos, sound and video before they are posted to your site. He should not post citizen microblogs without verifying who is sending the blog. It is better to hold a post until you can verify the information in it than to post an inaccurate or just plain false report. There is no better time and place to remember the old adage from the Chicago City News Bureau: If your mother says she loves you, check it out.

Photo by Amber Primus, Woodrow Wilson High School

Figure 14.13 Most student publications review audience contributions before they are posted on a publication's website.

Chapter Fourteen

Review and Assessment

Recall

1. Describe three forms of journalism used before the digital age. Name a strength of each one.
2. How can the audience help shape news coverage? Give examples from both traditional and digital media.
3. List three ways journalists have invited their audiences. Include both historical and contemporary examples.
4. How can your audience comment on or discuss the news you have produced or published?
5. List three ways a journalist can become part of the local community and increase the strength of local coverage.
6. How can you include multiple perspectives in a news publication?
7. What should you do when deciding whether to publish or broadcast a letter to the editor?
8. In what ways are the laws concerning copyright and libel different for online comments than for letters to the editor in a print publication?
9. What additional concerns for the safety of students affect the way a high school online forum may be managed?
10. What policies and procedures may be used to create an online forum for a high school publication or broadcast?
11. What are the advantages and disadvantages of screening online comments before posting them?
12. In what ways do blogs differ from news and feature coverage? In what ways are they the same?
13. In what ways do blogs differ from personal communication?

Critical Thinking

1. Compare digital media with print or broadcast media. Why is digital media able to cover more perspectives and include more divergent voices?
2. What dangers are involved in allowing your audience to help shape your content?
3. Your understanding of the core news values indicates that a story deserves very little coverage, for instance, gossip about two anonymous seniors. But the topic is being discussed frequently by members of your audience. What questions would you ask before you cover the topic, and what are ways of covering the topic in a professional manner? What additional concerns would you have about covering the topic?
4. Follow at least five blog entries from a professional journalist. Discuss the following with a partner:
   A. How formal is the style?
   B. What additional information is given in the blogs but not in the news?
   C. How objective is the writer? Does the writer appear as a character in the blog?

Application

1. On a podcast forum hosted by your publication, whom would you ask to discuss this topic: "Does caffeine help or hurt your grades?" What would you write or say to request audience questions or comments? Where would you place this request for information?
2. Choose a topic covered in a recent edition or broadcast. What additional voices could have been included in the story?
3. Look at your most recent publication. Choose a story and create a teaser you could have sent to your followers or friends.
4. S Create a journalistic blog. Make at least three entries as you produce your next broadcast or publication.
5. Create a paragraph or bulleted list for members of your audience who want to submit digital images and video for your publication or broadcast. Explain what content is appropriate (or inappropriate), what editing or processing is acceptable (or forbidden) and any other information you feel they need so that their work will be useful.

Chapter Fourteen

Journalism Style

Using Commas to Set Off Introductory and Nonessential Matter

Also see Chapter 13 Journalism Style and the website for information about comma usage.

Set Off Introductory Matter

- When subordinate clauses are introductory, they require a comma. When they come after the main clause, they do not require a comma. *When he came, I was not there*. BUT *I was not there when he came*.
- When you introduce a sentence with two of more prepositional phrases, use a comma after the final introductory phrase but not between the phrases. *In the dim glow of the streetlamp, he looked even more menacing*.
- Participial phrases used as introductory elements require a comma. *Soaked by the rain, they left the football game. Handing the policeman her license, she broke down and cried*. Do not write *Handing the policeman her license, tears came to her eyes*. Tears do not have hands or licenses. In this case, *handing* is a dangling participle.

Set Off Nonessential Matter

If you take out nonessential matter, you do not substantially change the meaning of the sentence. Nonessential matter is set apart from the rest of the sentence with commas (or sometimes with dashes or parentheses).

- Parenthetical expressions are words or phrases used to explain or qualify a statement, such as *for example, on the other hand* or *however*. In journalism, parenthetical expressions most often appear in oral interviews and in writing that attempts to seem casual. *The mayor had, however, met with the demonstrators earlier in the day.*
- Nonessential appositives. An appositive follows a noun or noun phrase and explains or identifies it. *Kennedy, the 35th president of the United States, was also the youngest to be elected*. Essential appositives are NOT set apart with commas. *Assistant volleyball coach Randall Scott also spoke at the funeral*. Without the appositive *Randall Scott*, the sentence fails to identify which one of perhaps several assistant coaches spoke and therefore falls below journalistic standards.
- Nonessential phrases. *The man, running toward the light, felt happier than he had for days*. (He just happened to be running toward the light when he started to feel happy.) But if there are 15 depressed men, and only the man running toward the light is happy, then *running toward the light* is essential to the meaning of the sentence and is NOT set off with commas. *The man running toward the light felt happier than he had for days*.
- Nonessential clauses. If a clause is essential to the meaning of the sentence, it does not take commas. *The river that empties into the Gulf of Mexico is the Mississippi*. But if a clause is not essential to the meaning of the sentence, commas set it off. *The Mississippi River, which empties into the Gulf of Mexico, is the setting of the musical "Show Boat."*

Try It!

1. Write two sentences that begin with a participial phrase. Use commas appropriately.
2. Write three sentences using the following constructions. Use commas correctly.
   A. Write a sentence from an interview using a parenthetical expression.
   B. Write a sentence from a restaurant review using an essential appositive.
   C. Describe an expert source for an article on trained fleas using a nonessential appositive.
3. Use these phrases in your own sentences. Use commas correctly.
   A. which he bought last year
   B. that he made himself (as an essential element)
   C. that he made himself (as a nonessential element)

Extend Your Knowledge

Style Exercises

Visit the *Journalism* website for more detailed information about setting off introductory and nonessential matter.

Chapter Fourteen

Writers' Workshop

In this Writers' Workshop you will:

- Recognize your usual sentence lengths and consciously vary them.
- Use varying sentence length effectively.

Workshop 14.1

Varying Sentence Length

Mini-Lesson: The Long and the Short of It

> *Usually we don't think about how long our sentences are, any more than we think about how often we breathe, but our sentence length says a great deal about who we think we are and who we think our audience is.*

That one sentence has 41 words. Here is the same information in five sentences.

> *Usually we don't think about how long our sentences are. Our sentence length is usually automatic, like breathing. We don't count our breaths. But our sentence length communicates who we think we are. It also communicates who we think our audience is.*

Those 42 words are divided into 10-word, 8-word, 5-word, 10-word and 9-word sentences for an average of 8.4 words per sentence.

Here is the same information in eight sentences.

> *Do you know how long your sentences are? Most of us don't think about that. Sentence length is like breathing. We do not count our breaths. But sentence length is important. Longer sentences may suggest we are smart. Shorter sentences may suggest we think our audience is young. They may also suggest we think our audience is stupid.*

Those 58 words are divided into 8-word, 7-word, 5-word, 6-word, 5-word, 7-word and two 10-word sentences for an average sentence length of 7.25 words.

Clearly, shorter sentences require more total words. Which version appeals most to you? If you dislike one version, why do you dislike it?

Gary Provost, a renowned writing coach, offered this advice in his book "100 Ways to Improve Your Writing."

> *VARY SENTENCE LENGTH*
>
> *This sentence has five words. Here are five more words. Five-word sentences are fine. But several together become monotonous. Listen to what is happening. The writing is getting boring. The sound of it drones. It's like a stuck record. The ear demands some variety. Now listen. I vary the sentence length, and I create music. Music. The writing sings. It has a pleasant rhythm, a lilt, a harmony. I use short sentences. And I use sentences of medium length. And sometimes when I am certain the reader is rested, I will engage him with a sentence of considerable length, a sentence that burns with energy and builds with all the impetus of a crescendo, the roll of the drums, the crash of the cymbals—sounds that say listen to this, it is important.*
>
> *So write with a combination of short, medium, and long sentences. Create a sound that pleases the reader's ear. Don't just write words. Write music.*

If you have developed the habit of reading your work aloud to yourself or your response group, you may have already learned to write music with your words. Good writers move their lips when they read!

Short sentences slow down the reader. Or rather, the frequent periods do. Semicolons, colons and dashes marking the ends of sentences can also stop the reader. In formal written English, you may use a semicolon to join two independent clauses, but as a journalist you would write two sentences.

Short sentences jab. They crash. They twitch. They grapple. They come to a halt.

The last three sentences (joined by semicolons) in Brian Phillips' ESPN article about the Iditarod sled dog race slow the reader down, just as the sleds are slowed in a hellish stretch of the trail through an old burn.

> *Sleds intended for snow and ice had to be dragged across hardened mud and gravel. Runners broke; tree shards snagged tug lines; speeds dropped to 3 or 4 miles per hour.*

Short sentences make the reader pause before moving on to the next idea. They explain complicated ideas in simple parts.

Short sentences emphasize emotional truth. *Jesus wept.*

They create suspense. *Long ago the door was locked. The key is lost. That's all I know.*

Longer sentences carry the reader further on. They express longer motions, such as the time spent waiting to be helped at the Department of Motor Vehicles and the length of the lines. They carry the reader across longer expanses of time and space.

Willa Cather in "My Ántonia" writes about the grave of Mr. Shimerda, whose wife and son had insisted that he should be buried "on the southwest corner of their own land; indeed, under the very stake that marked the corner," despite warnings that in the future two roads would follow the section lines and cross over his grave. The narrator carries us forward many years in three sentences, two quite long.

> *Years afterward, when the open-grazing days were over, and the red grass had been ploughed under and under until it had almost disappeared from the prairie; when all the fields were under fence, and the roads no longer ran about like wild things, but followed the survey section-lines, Mr. Shimerda's grave was still there, with a sagging wire fence around it, an unpainted wooden cross. As grandfather had predicted, Mrs. Shimerda never saw the roads going over his head. The road from the north curved a little to the east just there, and the road from the west swung out a little to the south; so that the grave, with its tall red grass that was never mowed, was like a little island; and in the twilight, under a new moon or the clear evening star, the dusty roads used to look like soft grey rivers flowing past it.*

Longer sentences carry the reader to deeper understanding.

Apply It

1. Choose three passages of about 100 words from writing you admire from three different modern writers. Make them as diverse as possible. One might be a journalistic sports story; another might come from a novel. The third might be from interesting informational reading. Consider the work of columnists you enjoy.
   A. For each passage, count the total number of words. Then count the number of sentences. Divide the number of words by the number of sentences to determine the average sentence length. What is the average sentence length in each of your three passages?
   B. For each passage, list the number of words in each sentence and note the variations from the average. How much longer than the average are the longest sentences? How much shorter than average are the shortest sentences? Do your writers vary their sentence lengths?
2. Choose about 150 words from your writing. Choose pieces you like. Use several if you wish.
   A. What is your average sentence length?
   B. List the number of words in each sentence. How many are within one or two words of the average length? How do your longest and shortest sentences compare with the average? Does your writing display much variety?
   C. Rewrite at least one of your pieces, consciously varying sentence length. Locate or create several short sentences, then edit them to become as parallel as possible. Punctuate them first as separate sentences, then with semicolons between the short sentences to create one longer one. Do not allow any sentences to be within one word of the previous average length. Share your work aloud with your response group, revise and publish.
3. Describe a real or imaginary struggle to its conclusion in at least 250 words. You may describe a physical, mental or moral struggle. Consciously vary your sentence length to carry your readers forward or to slow them down. Share your work aloud with your response group, revise and publish.

Extend Your Knowledge Extend

Visit the *Journalism* website for additional information and practice.

Chapter Fifteen

Designing with Purpose

How do we pull the reader in with design?

Photo by Mary Brown, Woodrow Wilson High School

G-WLEARNING.COM

While studying, look for the activity icon to:

- **Build** vocabulary terms with e-flash cards and matching activities.
- **Extend** learning with further discussion of relevant topics.
- **Reinforce** what you learn by completing style exercises, worksheets and end-of-chapter questions.

Visit the Journalism website: www.g-wlearning.com/journalism/

Chapter Objectives

After reading this chapter, you will be able to:

- Explain what news designers learned from eye-tracking studies.
- Give examples of strategies designers use to show what is most important on a page.
- Understand the difference between a design topic and a design concept.
- Identify the elements of design.
- Define the basic principles of page design.
- Check a design for verbal-visual unity.
- Plan a story package with alternative story forms.

Key Terms Build Vocab

alignment
alternative story forms
balance
bleed
center of visual interest
design concept
direction
display headline
emphasis
eye-tracking research
grid
gutter
kerning
leading
line
modular design
packaged story
points of entry
proportion
proximity
rhythm
scale
subheadlines
type
value
verbal-visual unity
visual hierarchy
white space

Before You Read...

Sight words are those you know just by seeing them. Skim this chapter and identify five to ten sight words with which you are familiar. Where do you usually see or hear these words? Next, identify five unfamiliar words used in the chapter. Use context clues, such as defining words you understand nearby to help you understand what the unfamiliar word means. Then, look up the term in your glossary or a dictionary. Did you correctly define the word using context clues? How did the formal definition change your understanding of the word?

Introduction

"There are three responses to a piece of design—yes, no, and WOW! Wow is the one to aim for."

–Milton Glaser, graphic designer

"Why did you choose that image for your story?"

"I didn't. Maria did."

"But it doesn't make sense with your story. Did you talk to Maria first?"

"No. I'm just writing the story. She's designing the page."

Why spend hours reporting, writing and editing your story only to plop it down on a page with a bad photograph and boring headline? Though it may seem like writers write and designers design, the two processes should be intertwined, with each one dependent upon the other.

The key to strong design is communication. When writers, photographers, editors and designers meet to plan concept-driven designs, the result can be stunning.

Strong design has become increasingly important to news media in recent decades. Take a look at your parents' yearbook or old newspapers from your school. You will probably see students posed, smiling at the camera, pages filled with uniformly sized images, and headlines like "Band" and "Chess Club wins match." You may see clever drawings or themed borders, and if you are lucky, you may see the hottest design trend of decades ago: a collage.

Professional newspapers and magazines have changed enormously as well (Figure 15.1). Advanced graphic design software has raised the ceiling on what is possible for page designers. In addition, research has given journalists a deeper understanding of how people view stories in print and online.

Figure 15.1 A New York Times telegraph operator transcribes the front page news from this 1942 edition of the paper. Page design was much simpler at that time.

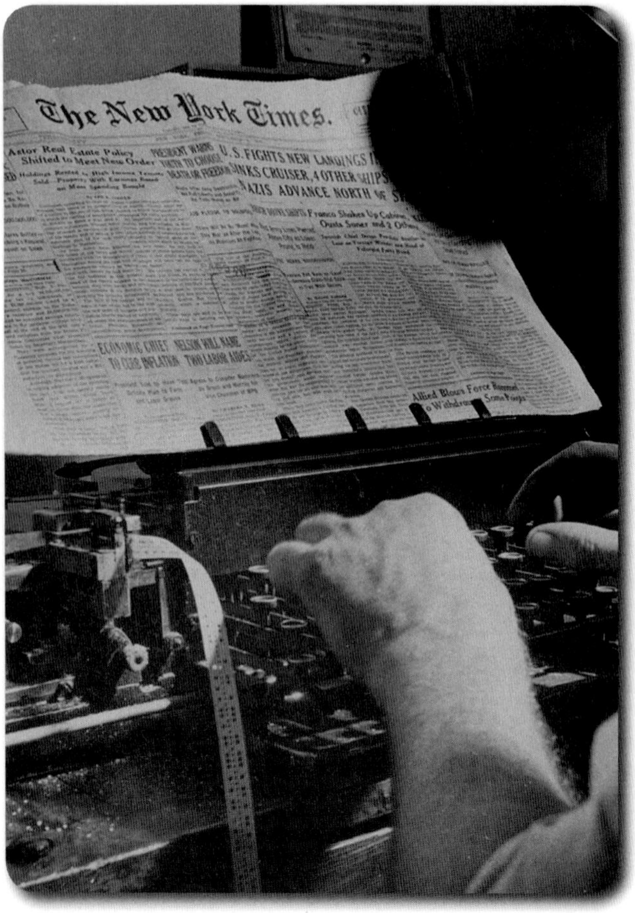

Eye-Tracking Research

The Poynter Institute used **eye-tracking research** in the 1990s to learn how we read print publications. Do most people read a newspaper like a book—left to right and top to bottom? Do they read headlines first? Do their eyes bounce from photo to photo? Do they read the entire article before they move on to the next story? More recently, they conducted even more extensive research to see how we read on the Internet. Participants in the studies wore glasses equipped with cameras that tracked their eye movement as they viewed a page of a newspaper or news stories on a website. After the participants finished reading, researchers quizzed them to see how much information they had retained. All participants received the same facts and information, but the designs of the pages they read varied. From the study, researchers and designers gained new understandings of how design influences what the audience reads and how much of the page content they absorbed. From this study they learned

- Your audience is made up of two types of readers: methodical readers, who read full stories; and scanners, who read headlines, parts of stories, captions and lists.
- **Alternative story forms** (such as fact boxes, lists, Q & As and charts) draw the readers' attention and help the reader remember facts from the story.
- Participants read print headlines and look at photos first. They read large headlines before small ones. **Packaged stories** (those with large headlines, a dominant image and at least one alternative story form) attract more attention than other stories.
- Large, action photos draw more attention than small or staged photos or mug shots.

The Poynter eye-tracking research showed newsrooms they could not afford to ignore how their audience consumes the news. They realized they needed to reinvent the way they planned and designed pages and to use design to help deliver the news. Page design needed to become purposeful.

Smart *and* Pretty Design

To design with purpose, you must first understand your purpose. Some student journalists think the purpose of design is to make "pretty" pages. While it is true that well-designed pages are also visually appealing, they do much more than please the eye. They guide the audiences' eyes and minds into the stories. Design guru and author Tim Harrower believes that newspapers do two things best:

> *You know what newspapers do best? Two things: teaching and storytelling. In a way, that's our sacred mission—giving people data they need to lead better lives, and capturing the drama of life in the 21st century. Teaching and storytelling. Data and drama. Good teaching conveys data; good storytelling conveys drama.*

According to Harrower's philosophy, our pages should be designed to either teach or tell the story. This means tossing out traditional layouts to make room for designs that are not just pretty, but pretty smart.

What makes a design "smart"? Some designers call this the **verbal-visual unity** of a page design. The story itself, all of the words on the page and all graphic elements, work together to send one clear message to the audience. Imagine shopping for a book. Most people use the cover of the book—its images, color scheme, title font and back cover book summary—to decide whether or not to pick up the book, to open the book or to begin reading. Before they have read more than a few pages, they have a good idea what to expect. In the same way, your audience relies on smart page design, including your well-planned headline, dominant image, alternative

Design by Colleen O'Brien, The Communicator, Community High School

Figure 15.2 The cover design of this student newsmagazine exemplifies conceptual design that is not just pretty, but smart.

story forms, captions and subheadlines, to tell them about your story and to entice them into reading it.

The cover of one student newsmagazine on technology shows this concept at work (Figure 15.2). On one level, plugs and wires suggest technology. Twitter's signature blue bird logo is an allusion to social media. On another level, the lowercase "i" in the headline evokes Apple's line of i-devices. The shades of blue create a feeling of sterility or disconnect, one of the issues tackled by stories inside. The designer of this cover left little room for confusion about the theme of the issue.

A designer's most important job is to bring order to chaos. Your audience wants to be told what is most important on each page and within packaged stories. Strong page designers can do that without the reader ever noticing. In the graphic design world, experts say good design is invisible.

While design may be invisible to your audience, it will not be invisible to you once you learn to use the elements and principles of design. Not only will you be able to recognize good design when you see it, you will also be able to create powerful designs.

Planning Your Design

Most new designers are surprised to learn that the design process does not begin at the computer with an open blank page. It does not even begin with a sketchpad. Instead, design planning begins with words. Remember that you are aiming for smart design, not just pretty design, so you first need to figure out the **design concept** for your page.

Design "concepts" may be best defined by what they are not. Concepts are not topics. Chess club is a topic. Topics are too broad to make meaningful design decisions. They lead to page designs that seem childish and one-dimensional, often incorporating stock images or clip art. If you have done a good job writing a story with a clear and specific angle, the last thing you want is a design that does not support the story (Figure 15.3).

A design concept also is not the story angle, which may be too narrow or too literal to allow design creativity. In a simple story package with only a headline, photo, caption and story, a story angle should help you write the headline and the cutlines, but more creative packages need a strong concept.

The concept is what you want the audience to take away—to feel—from the story and its design. Your concept is the driving force behind your design. Every aspect of the page design—headlines, photos or art, graphics—stem from the concept you select.

Chess club wins championship

by Victor Knight

The Centerville High Chess Club brought home the Lake County Chess trophy in a come-from-behind defeat of the Valley Union High team, the reigning champions, Thursday.

Centerville had slipped to third place at the end of play Wednesday night, but stunning—and swift—wins by Trojan sophomore Damaris Andreica and junior Son Kim put the championship back within reach.

Figure 15.3 This one-dimensional story package was based on the topic, chess club, rather than created from a design concept.

In the chess club example mentioned above, you know that "chess club" is the topic, which is too broad to be a design concept. But the story angle, "chess club wins championship in come-from-behind win" is too narrow to serve as a concept for a well-executed creative package. You need to discover the concept that will unify all the design elements and written content on the page. To do this, begin by trying an activity called word association.

1. Gather together everyone who has a stake in the page, including the writer, page designer, photographer, artist and editor. Explain the angle and direction of the story.
2. Begin by listing all the words each person associates with the story's angle. In the case of the chess club story, your list may include words and phrases like *surprise*, *underdogs*, *come from behind* or *underestimated*.
3. At this point, no one should evaluate or dismiss any of the ideas. Accept all ideas without judgment. The goal at this point is to collect many ideas. Focus on quantity and encourage everyone to contribute.
4. Next evaluate all of the words and phrases that you listed. Look at each potential concept for connotations that do not align with the story. This process will narrow down your list. You may also notice that some of your concept ideas listed, such as *surprise* for the chess club example, do not exactly capture the full story. Eliminate these words and phrases as well.
5. Continue examining the remaining potential concept ideas until your group agrees on a word or phrase to use as your design concept.

Aiming for Smart Design

The Maestro Concept, introduced in Chapter 6, is a powerful way to achieve smart, effective designs. The Maestro Concept is a process by which a maestro, or leader, uses teamwork between writers, editors, designers, artists and photographers to build an effective story package. The maestro coordinates the planning of a story's design, keeps track of assignments and due dates and helps everyone follow through. By coordinating their efforts and managing their time effectively, smart design can be achieved.

Just as the members of the team must come together, all of the elements that make up a story package (your written story, headline, dominant visual elements and graphics) should come together to send a unified message to your audience. The process of collaboration is essential to achieving verbal-visual unity, a unity that all great designs exhibit when words and visual elements project a unified message.

Packages that clearly and swiftly convey one design concept require planning and preparation. Together your team will find a headline, plan and then create a center of visual interest, and consider what alternative story forms (timelines, graphs or fast fact boxes, for instance) will support smart *and* pretty page design.

In the world of graphic design, "content is king." That means all of the visual elements are intended to do one thing—get the audience to read the story. The headline, the visuals and the informational graphics all serve as different **points of entry** for a story. Think of them as a door the audience can open into the story. As a designer, you want to make sure you provide enough points of entry in your package to draw your audience into the written story.

Making Headlines

The headline is the most important point of entry into a story. To create headlines for a package, consider two factors, content and form. Though both are important, content (the words of the headline), comes first. Chapter 7 describes how to do this. However, packaged stories, features and bigger projects may allow for more creativity with the content.

Finding the words of a headline is very similar to finding a design concept. The process involves brainstorming and is most successful when done in a team, which may include writers, designers, editors, photographers or artists. Sometimes in the search for the concept you will also stumble upon the headline.

Learn to Improvise

Graphic designers need to be flexible. What may look like a good design plan on paper may be flawed when all the elements of the design come together on the computer.

For example, you may plan a spread for a written text of 400 words, but the writer submits 700 words. The editor may ask the writer to cut down the story, but the story may simply need to be that long, in which case you need to modify your design.

A good designer knows that long blocks of text need subheads, or small, bold headings, to provide the audience with multiple points of entry. Also, long texts may appear in print or on a screen as big gray walls, so designers make text more inviting by breaking it up with pull quotes, teasers and fast fact boxes.

Strong designers learn how to improvise and adapt to serve the content. This adaptability is an essential skill in design and in life.

Headline writers play with words and look for plays on words. Use your audience's prior knowledge, perhaps a movie or song title or common saying, and spin it into something new that supports your concept. Use word associations. The goal is to create a headline that has layers of meaning that support the story.

The brainstorming and word association session for the chess club story might list these ideas:

- Chess champs
- We are the champions
- Come from behind
- Unexpected champs
- Kings of the board
- Check mate
- Chess mate
- Unlikely win
- Unlikely kings
- Comeback win
- Comeback kid
- *Comeback kings*

Notice how the final headline has several layers of meaning. First, it plays off the well-known phrase "comeback kid." The term "kings" refers to the chess piece but also to their ultimate championship title. Rather than simply focusing on the win, the headline hints at the story's angle: that the championship was unlikely because the team was behind. To top it off, *Comeback kings* rolls nicely off the tongue because the words alliterate, repeating the *k* sound.

Once you have a headline, do not throw out the other ideas that led to your headline. They may be used as **subheadlines** or as headlines for sidebar stories and graphics.

Your Turn

1. Working in small groups, determine a design concept for each of the three stories. Follow the word association and brainstorming process.
   - The soccer team began the season 0-7. After a close game in which the team won on a penalty kick against a higher ranked team, they turned the season around, making it to the playoffs. Your story will be published right before the first playoff game.
   - A new student teacher on campus is working under a mentor who was her English teacher when she attended the school several years before. Your feature story will delve into their relationship.
   - A reporter on your publication staff has noticed a trend: fewer students are selecting arts electives and are instead moving in the direction of computer science courses. This feature package will explore the reasons behind the shift.

(Continued)

YOUR TURN (Continued)

2. **Going Deeper.** Take one of those three concepts a step further. Using the process for generating headlines, word associate and brainstorm to find a headline for the package. Evaluate the headline for accuracy, both in content and in connotation. Ask yourself these questions:
   - Does this headline have the right tone?
   - What are the layers of meaning? Do they make sense with this story?
   - How does the selected headline support the concept?
   - Would any of our rejected ideas be appropriate for subheads or as titles for sidebar stories or alternative story forms?

Creating Visual Interest

Once you have a design concept and a creative headline, plan the **center of visual interest**, the main image or art for the package. After reading the headline, this is the image your audience should look at first. It is essential the photographer or illustrator be part of the planning. The meeting should be collaborative, with everyone involved as you marry the content and the visual elements.

Eye-tracking studies found that readers are drawn to the largest visual on the page, so both the image and its placement are crucial. This is not something you want to leave to the last minute, as the best visuals may require time, special materials or a particular skill to execute.

You also do not want to "design from the sky;" that is, you do not want to cast your eyes upward and hope a great idea falls from the sky onto your computer or sketchpad. Designers frequently scour printed magazines and the Internet for examples, or models, they like. They become great observers of design and have many examples that inspire their own ideas. Just like riffing on language leads to great headlines, riffing on the visual designs of professionals will lead you to smart designs.

The most common choices for dominant visuals fall into six categories: candid photos, environmental portraits, photo illustrations, illustrations, infographics and typography (Figure 15.4 on page 456).

Candid Photos

In a news page based on an event or in a yearbook spread, news or candid photos can serve your design concept. Once you have chosen photos that work with your concept, you need to decide how to present the photos. Do you want one dominant photo or a photo essay consisting of a collection of related photos? Should the photos have frames? Should a photo be fully contained within the margins or allowed to bleed, or run off the edges? Do you need to adjust the composition of the photo by cropping it before you place it on your page?

Environmental Portraits

In feature stories or profiles, the photographer, and perhaps the writer or editor, meet with the subject in his natural environment to create an environmental portrait. In these portraits, the subject may look directly into the camera lens, and he does not necessarily smile. In fact, some of the most powerful environmental portraits in history have expressed emotions other than happiness.

Photo Illustrations

The title "photo illustration" implies that a photograph has been altered for artistic effect or it has been staged. Cutting out an image, coloring an image unnaturally or blending artistic modes, such as photography and hand illustration, are all examples of this technique. Creative photographs

And Now... Closer to Home

Finding Inspiration

Rookies in a design bind, hoping for an idea to fall from the sky, research the topic on the Internet, typing in related terms and clicking on Images. While this is not inherently bad—sometimes the Internet can be a source of inspiration—it can lead designers to very literal, simplistic interpretations of the concept. Instead, try these sources of inspiration:

- **Magazines and newspapers.** Skim through the magazines or newspapers available at the library or in bookstores. Sketch or photograph designs. Then create files of interesting designs and design elements you might want to use someday. Do not limit your search to publications about topics you think are relevant. Esquire, a popular men's magazine, may give you design inspiration for a prom spread. Sunset, a home and gardening magazine, may inspire the design of a summer travel feature.
- **Design annuals.** Two organizations, the Society of Publication Designers and the Society for News Design, each produce an annual, thick, hardbound book featuring the winners of their international design contests. While the books are pricey, your school or local library may have them available for you to browse. If you have the funds, they are a good newsroom investment and helpful during design planning meetings. Current editions also keep your designs fresh.
- **Online image boards.** Many online tools allow you to search for a term or phrase then add the images you like to a digital pin board. These inspiration boards can usually be shared with collaborators, so your staff can all contribute to one collection of inspirational images. If you know you may need to create a timeline, for example, try searching the term *timeline* and see what turns up. Though the content will probably be unrelated to your topic, an inspirational design may be modified to fit your content.
- **Everyday life.** Your smartphone camera is a design tool. Snap photos of design inspirations when you encounter them in everyday life. Product packaging, menu boards, commercials, street art or architecture can inspire a design. Whenever you see something that moves you, capture it and organize it into a collection. You may not have a specific project in mind as you take the picture, but when the time comes, you will be able to say, "What about this?" instead of trying to describe what you remember and hoping you can find the original. This also trains you to think like a designer wherever you go.

shot in a studio, staged in an artistic way or influenced (for example, with props) are photo illustrations and should be labeled as such. Photo illustrations never pretend to be real photos. Rather, they use photography as a starting point for artistic interpretation of the design concept.

Illustrations

Sometimes the best visual is an illustration, either drawn by hand or created using computer illustration software, but use illustrations only when you have a compelling reason to do so, not because you failed to send out a photographer. The illustration must align with the design concept for the page. Illustrations, if used, should match the tone of the story. Opinion columns may include an editorial illustration or be placed near an editorial cartoon, both of which are types of illustration. Icons are a type of illustration that are helpful in infographics. On occasion, a photograph may not be appropriate for a feature story but an illustration can be powerful.

Figure 15.4 The six main categories of dominant visuals include candid photos, environmental portraits, photo illustrations, illustrations, infographics, and typography. The selection and placement of the image are critical in creating a center of visual interest.

a. Candid photo

c. Photo illustration

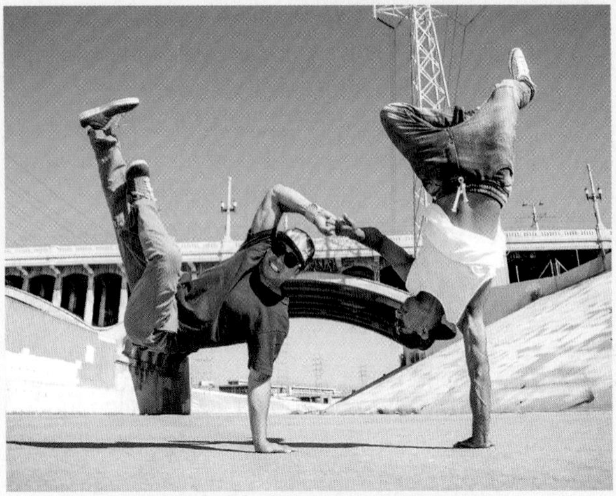

b. Environmental photo

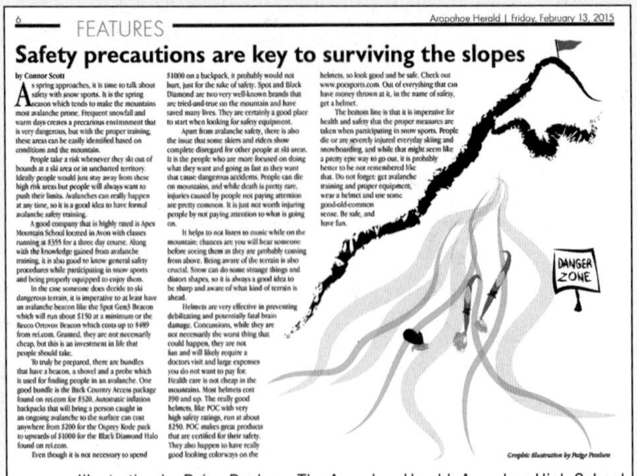

6 FEATURES Arapahoe Herald | Friday, February 13, 2015

Safety precautions are key to surviving the slopes

by Connor Scott

As spring approaches, it is time to talk about safety with snow sports. It is the spring season which tends to make the mountains most avalanche prone. Frequent snowfall and warm days creates a precarious environment that is very dangerous, but with the proper training, these areas can be easily identified based on conditions and the mountain.

People take a risk whenever they ski out of bounds at a ski area or in uncharted territory. Ideally people would just stay away from these high risk areas but people will always want to push their limits. Avalanches can really happen at any time, so it is a good idea to have formal avalanche safety training.

A good company that is highly rated is Apex Mountain School located in Avon with classes running at $355 for a three day course. Along with the knowledge gained from avalanche training, it is also good to know general safety procedures while participating in snow sports and being properly equipped to enjoy them.

In the case someone does decide to ski dangerous terrain, it is imperative to at least have an avalanche beacon like the Spot Gen3 Beacon which will run about $150 at a minimum or the Recco Ortovox Beacon which costs up to $489 from rei.com. Granted, they are not necessarily cheap, but this is an investment in life that people should take.

To truly be prepared, there are bundles that have a beacon, a shovel and a probe which is used for finding people in an avalanche. One good bundle is the Back Country Access package found on rei.com for $320. Automatic inflation backpacks that will bring a person caught in an ongoing avalanche to the surface can cost anywhere from $200 for the Osprey Kode pack to upwards of $1000 for the Black Diamond Halo found on rei.com.

Even though it is not necessary to spend $1000 on a backpack, it probably would not hurt, just for the sake of safety. Spot and Black Diamond are two very well-known brands that are tried-and-true on the mountain and have saved many lives. They are certainly a good place to start when looking for safety equipment.

Apart from avalanche safety, there is also the issue that some skiers and riders show complete disregard for other people at ski areas. It is the people who are more focused on doing what they want and going as fast as they want that cause dangerous accidents. People can die on mountains, and while death is pretty rare, injuries caused by people not paying attention are pretty common. It is just not worth injuring people by not paying attention to what is going on.

It helps to not listen to music while on the mountain; chances are you will hear someone before seeing them as they are probably coming from above. Being aware of the terrain is also crucial. Snow can do some strange things and distort shapes, so it is always a good idea to be sharp and aware of what kind of terrain is ahead.

Helmets are very effective in preventing debilitating and potentially fatal brain damage. Concussions, while they are not necessarily the worst thing that could happen, they are not fun and will likely require a doctors visit and large expenses you do not want to pay for. Health care is not cheap in the mountains. Most helmets cost $90 and up. The really good helmets, like POC with very high safety ratings, run at about $250. POC makes great products that are certified for their safety. They also happen to have really good looking colorways on the helmets, so look good and be safe. Check out www.pocsports.com. Out of everything that can have money thrown at it, in the name of safety, get a helmet.

The bottom line is that it is imperative for health and safety that the proper measures are taken when participating in snow sports. People die or are severely injured everyday skiing and snowboarding, and while that might seem like a pretty epic way to go out, it is probably better to be not remembered like that. Do not forget: get avalanche training and proper equipment, wear a helmet and use some good-old-common sense. Be safe, and have fun.

Illustration by Paige Paulsen, The Arapahoe Herald, Arapahoe High School

d. Illustration

Infographics

Informational graphics, or infographics, once were only used as sidebars but now may take center stage as the center of visual interest on a page. Publications like Wired magazine create graphics that convey dense data in artistic ways. This can be done by creating one large graphic or a collection of smaller graphics grouped closely together. Use repeating design elements to ensure multiple graphics are cohesive visually.

Typography

Typography can make a bold statement. It always contributes to the visual impact of a design, but sometimes a powerful headline, phrase or quotation is the star of a design and the center of visual interest. When typography is a visual, focus not only on the words, but the appearance of the words. Font selection, font weight, size and arrangement can all work together to turn a collection of words into an artful visual.

Once you have determined your main headline and your dominant visual for a design, you are well on your way to creating an eye-catching package for your audience.

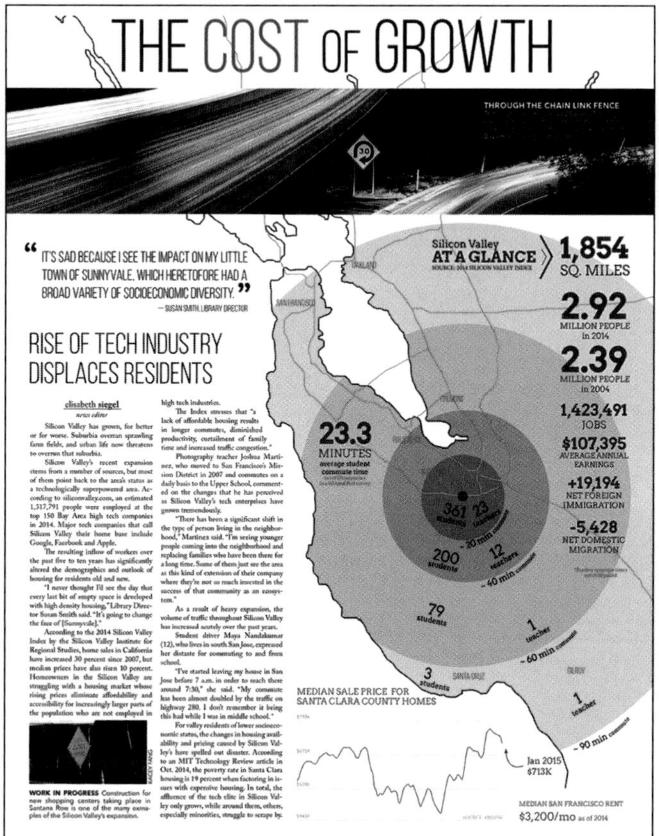

Design by Kacey Fang, The Winged Post, The Harker School

e. Infographic

Design by Christophe Haubursin, El Estoque, Monta Vista High School

f. Typography

Your Turn

1. Student designers need to transition from passive consumers of media to savvy media critics. Start by completing a scavenger hunt searching for examples of each of the six types of dominant visuals. Cut and paste, sketch or photograph these, and place them in your notebook or create a digital collection.
2. **Going Deeper.** You know how to spot each of the dominant visuals, but what about planning a design with them? Using the story ideas below, choose which type of dominant visual makes the most sense for that story. Justify your selection.
   - A story about a cheerleading coach who, trying to debunk the "dumb cheerleader" myth, has been encouraging and rewarding her team members for academic excellence.
   - A feature story about a girl who is the lead singer in a local folk band. She is the only teenager in the band, but they schedule practices and performances around her school schedule to accommodate her.
   - A story about the school board's recent decision to cut back on spending because of budget cuts at the state level.

Alternative Story Forms

You now have developed a concept to unify your design, a headline with layers of meaning, and a center of visual interest that will draw in your reader to your text. The next step is to brainstorm alternative story forms to add interest and additional points-of-entry to your design.

An alternative story form (also referred to as an alt copy) is basically what the title implies—an alternative to a traditional, written story. Infographics are sometimes considered alternative story forms. The best alternative story forms add to the written story and usually require additional reporting. Take a look at the catalog of examples from student publications featured in Figure 15.5 on pages 460–463.

While alternative story forms are visually interesting, they do not add much to your story package if they simply repeat the content found within your story. In fact, if your reader begins reading the story and realizes that it repeats information already found in the sidebars, infographics or other alternative story forms, she may assume the rest of the story is redundant and stop reading. Plan alternative story forms that add value to the package.

Different stories invite different infographics. If you write about the school's 50th anniversary, then a timeline may support your design concept. If you write about frozen yogurt, then a map of nearby yogurt sources might best support your design. If you publish online, make that map interactive, allowing your audience to learn about prices, flavors and store hours by clicking on the icons on the map. If you are explaining something complex, a diagram might help.

The idea is to ensure that you are choosing the alternative story form that supplements the text and complements the design concept. If you plan well, the package will feel not like a box filled with unrelated pieces but one that feels complete.

Bringing the Design Concept to Life

It is not uncommon for designers and their team to create a design concept, write a creative headline, choose a center of visual interest and sketch an alternative story form all before anyone has imported anything

And Now... Closer to Home

Making Images Look Their Best

There is nothing more disappointing than getting your publication back from the printer, only to find your powerful images printed too dark or light, off color or pixelated. To prevent that disappointment, make sure you fully understand how color processing and printing work. Familiarizing yourself with these acronyms is a good start:

- *DPI*: An image's resolution, or sharpness, is measured in DPI, or dots per inch. Much like it sounds, every image you process digitally is a collection of colored dots or pixels. The more dots there are per inch, the smaller those dots are and the sharper the image will appear. The fewer dots there are per inch, the larger those dots are and the blurrier the image will appear. In most print publications, images should be at least 300 dpi. Images published online may be as low as 72 dpi, which allows them to load faster in your Web browser.
- *CMYK*: The acronym CMYK stands for cyan, magenta, yellow and key (black). This four-color process is used when printing in color.
- *RGB*: The color process used to display images online is RGB, which mixes red, green and blue to make various shades of color.
- *HEX*: When working on digital publications, you may see the six-digit hex codes, which are used to control color on the Web. The hex code is a universal code that can be read by Web browsers to display an exact color. It tells the computer how much red, green and blue to put together to display the exact color you choose.

Resolution is an important factor in image clarity, but it is not the only factor to consider. Imagine the resolution of your image is appropriate for your media, but your image is still pixilated. There could be a few reasons this is happening. If you take an image from the Web and attempt to use it in a print design, chances are the image resolution will be too low and the image will be pixelated. (Remember: Low resolution means larger pixels.)

Another possibility is that your print image is not correctly linked in your document. When working with most design programs like Adobe InDesign, placing an image in the document actually puts a low-resolution placeholder version in the document. This allows the document to load faster, which allows you to work faster. When you export the document, the full resolution image is pulled from the source and embedded into the document. If you export and the source file is no longer where you originally placed it from, your document will embed the low-resolution image and notify you that a link is missing. If left uncorrected, the low-res image will be printed and will likely appear pixelated.

Also, remember that all monitors display differently, so the only way to know what your images will look like when printed is to calibrate your monitor to display colors as accurately as possible. Once you have done that, you are well on your way to becoming a professional graphic designer.

Alternative Story Forms

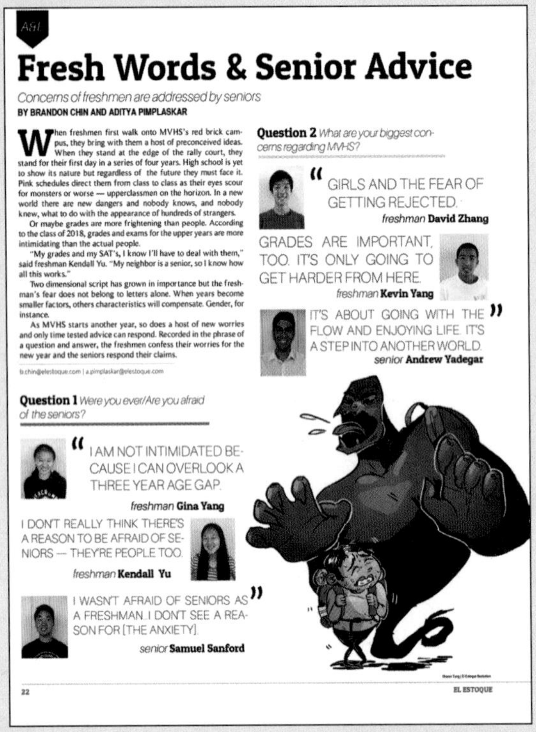

Quote reel: a collection of quotes, usually expressing different opinions in response to the same question or prompt

Fast fact box: a few key facts related to the story presented in a concise, visually engaging format that is easy to understand at a glance

Bio box: facts and information about one subject or group, usually used in profile or feature stories

Quiz: questions for the reader, usually used to convey data or factual information in a teaching way

Figure 15.5 Strong alternative story forms can strengthen your story by creating visual interest and adding additional points of entry. *Have you used any of these story forms in your publications? If not, choose one you have not used and incorporate it into your next story.*

Courtesy of El Estoque, Monta Vista High School

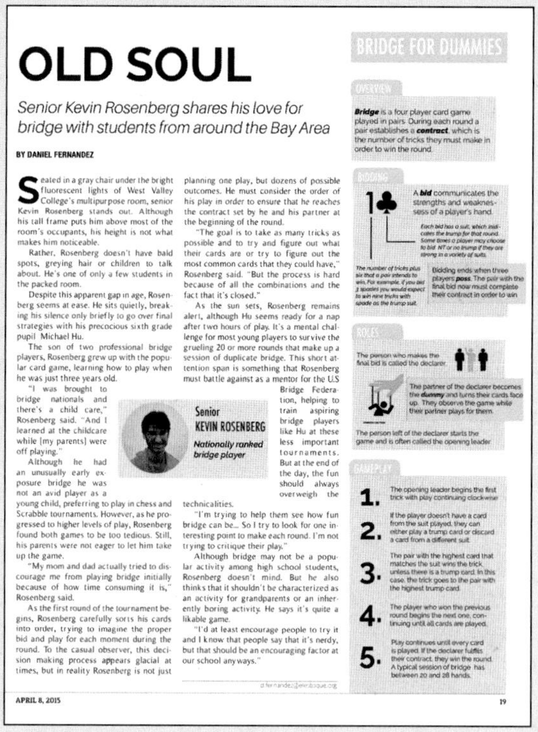

Glossary: key terms related to the story presented with their definitions

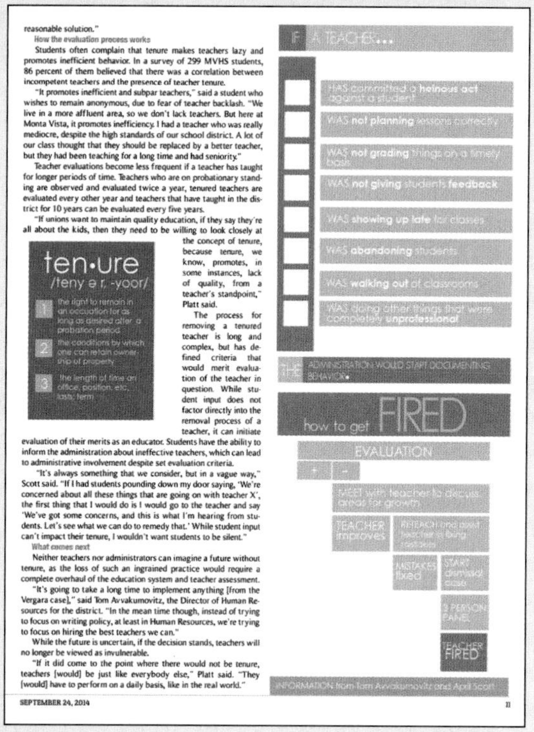

Checklist: a list of items related to the story, particularly helpful in stories that inform the reader of a process or set of requirements

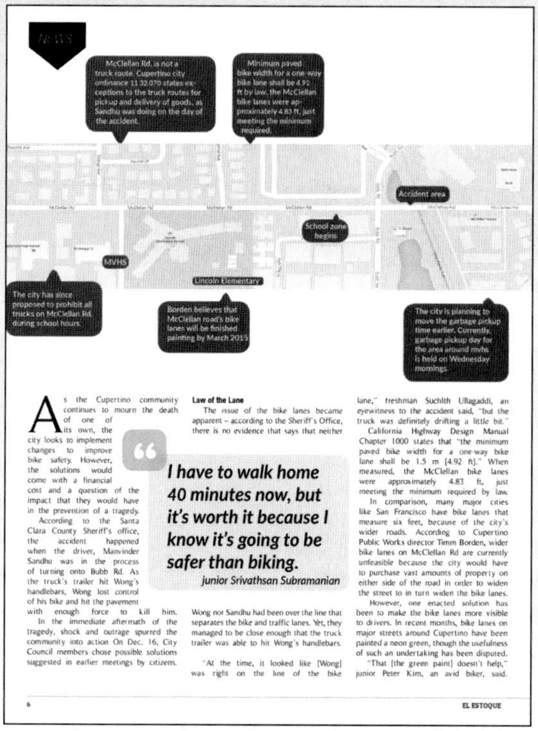

Map: small and simple or more complex, used in stories with a geographic element; appropriate in stories in which place plays a significant part in the storytelling

Diagram: paired images and information to explain something to the reader by illustrating the component parts of a whole

Alternative Story Forms

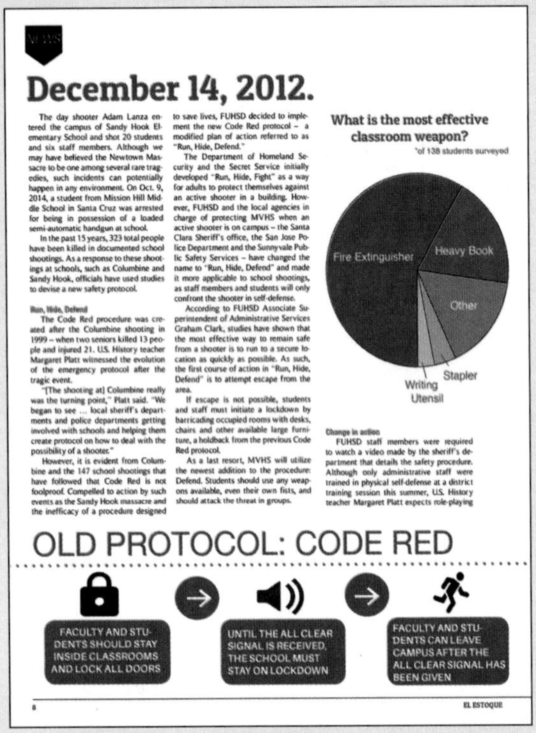

Step-by-step: a listing of steps used to demonstrate a process or to simplify something complicated by breaking it down into parts

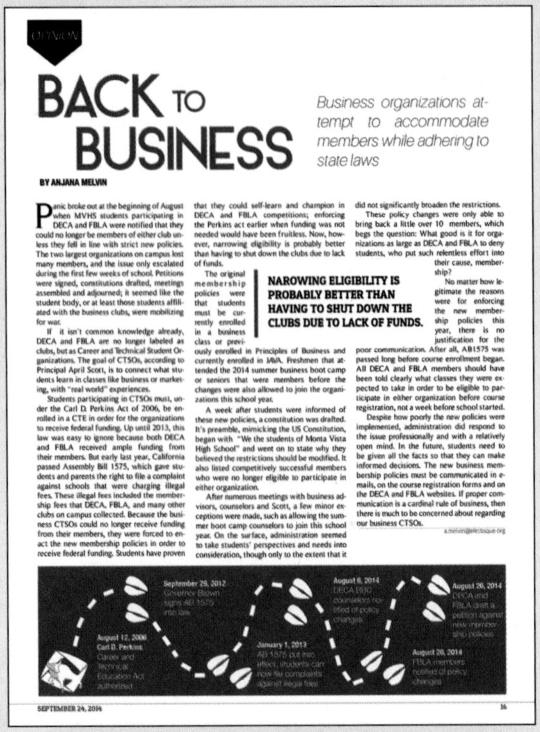

Timeline: a chronological graphic can be marked by years, days, hours or even minutes; used when you want to show the development or evolution of something

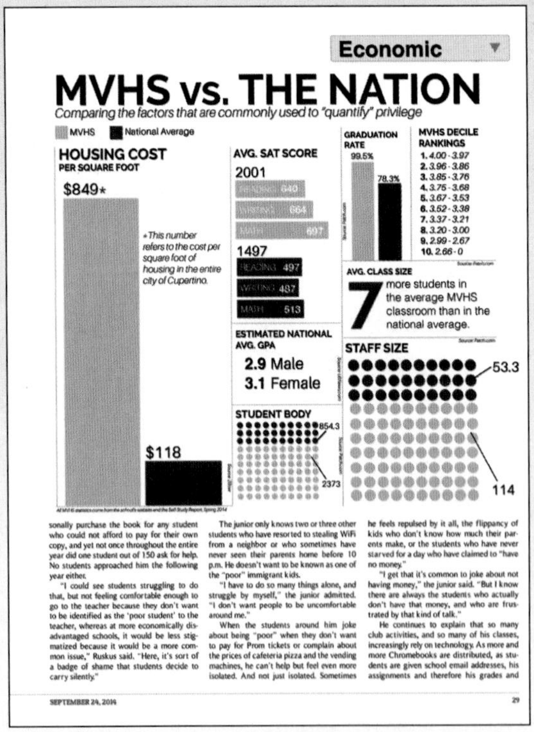

Chart or table: graphics particularly helpful in stories that call for comparison and large amounts of data and facts

Figure 15.5 *Continued*

Courtesy of El Estoque, Monta Vista High School

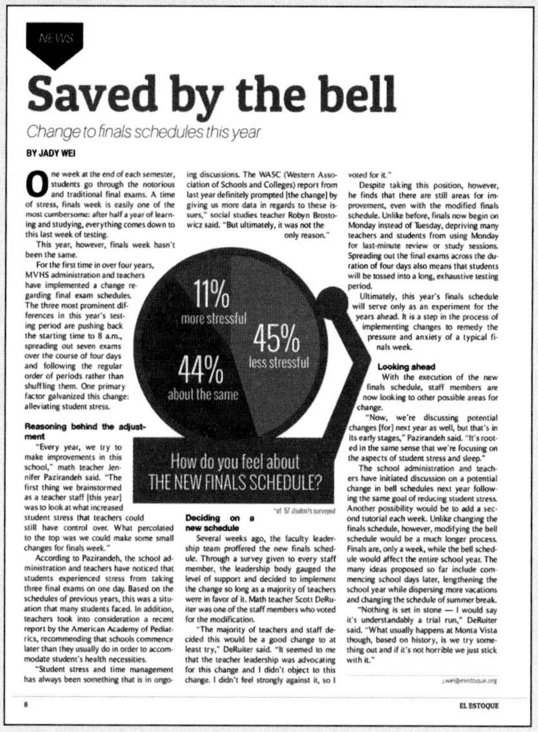

Bar or pie chart: a visual representation of statistics relevant to the story

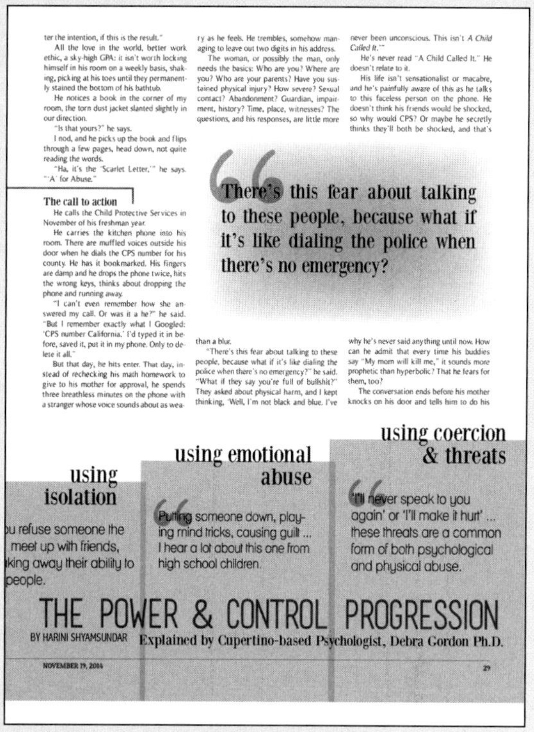

Pull quote: quotes pulled from the story work best when you use a poignant, powerful quotation that creates a bit of mystery for the reader

Teaser: typically a small graphic, teasers can be used to lead readers to related content in another part of the publication or online

Photo by Jody Rogac, Courtesy of Caleb Bennett

Meet the Professionals:
Caleb Bennett

The August 2014 cover of Wired magazine explodes in color. Like a mosaic, tiny, artistic objects arranged by color, burst from the center of the page, where the headline "Smart Phone" is centered. A thick line, an unexpected dark gray, stands out against the rainbow behind it, strikes through the *sm* in *smart*, making it read *art phone* at second glance. The final touch to the visual feast? The *o* in *phone* takes the shape—boxy, larger than it would be, rounded at the corners—of a smartphone.

"How perfect was it that the 'o' is in the middle of 'phone'?" Caleb Bennett, freelance designer and former design director at the magazine said.

Bennett, who previously designed for The New York Times Magazine, Texas Monthly and his own high school yearbook at Del Rio High School in Texas, says the electric cover, which he designed in collaboration with an outside artist, was one of his earliest influences in his role directing design at Wired. It is an example of a philosophy of design that drives Bennett's work—simplicity.

Designs should attempt to convey a message in the fastest way possible, Bennett says, and to do that, you have to boil something down to its simplest form. It is possible to over-design something, so Bennett advises using familiar images as a reference point, then peeling back layers until you reach something subtle but immediately recognizable.

Getting to that point can be difficult, though, and Bennett encourages young designers to risk failure with their designs as a method to find that perfect product.

"There are lots of things I've done that my first versions are awful," Bennett said. "You find so many ideas in mistakes. You have to fail to achieve."

A regular part of the design process for Bennett is seeking guidance from editors. The editor is closer to the story, and maintaining a dialogue with her may inform design choices. As stories change from their original concept, so must the accompanying design. If Bennett comes up with an idea he thinks is great, he will still take it to the editor to gauge her response.

"I may set out on some art direction path that, in the end, may not be the right one," Bennett said. "You have to stay informed to pursue the right angle or develop the right concept. One thing I love about magazines is that the editor is sort of like my partner *and* my client."

Though many think that the job of design is to get out of the way, Bennett doesn't. He believes that design is a tool that can actually further the content, pushing the story or enhancing it in some way. He prides himself in having a reason for design choices, not leaving anything to chance or for purely aesthetic reasons.

That explains the color palette, the dark gray strikethrough, the phone-shaped *o* of the August 2014 Wired cover. More than just design elements, each is a *choice*.

"One of the hot words right now is *storytelling*," Bennett said. "Design is communication. You have to use it as a vehicle. Our job is to help tell those stories."

Sara Cwynar/Wired; © Condé Nast

into a computer document. Each step in the preparation is essential to strong design. Before you design, you need a clear vision of the story package in your mind and on your sketchpad.

With the preparation done, you are ready to map out how each design element will work on the page. To do that, you first need a firm grasp of the difference between elements, the parts of your design you just envisioned, and the principles, or rules, that guide your decision making.

New designers may confuse design elements and design principles because they sound similar. Think of the elements and principles of page design in terms of a board game. To play, you need to understand the elements of the game, the board and the pieces, and how they each work. The elements can be as simple as Candyland and as complex as chess, but they each can exist in physical space.

The principles, on the other hand, are the rules that guide your game play and help you develop strategies. Principles are ideas, and while they influence the way you play, they are not tangible parts of the game, as are the elements. Design principles are the intangible parts that guide where and how we place design elements.

Elements of Page Design

When you look at a well-designed page in a magazine, newspaper or yearbook, you quickly see photographs, headlines and the body text. What you may not see are the hundreds of decisions that led to that final, published page. Each of the elements of page design listed here represents at least one decision you must make as a designer. The choices you make as you design will shape how the audience interprets your story.

Figure 15.6 The lime green type—reminiscent of neon lights often found in a casino—practically leaps off the black background.

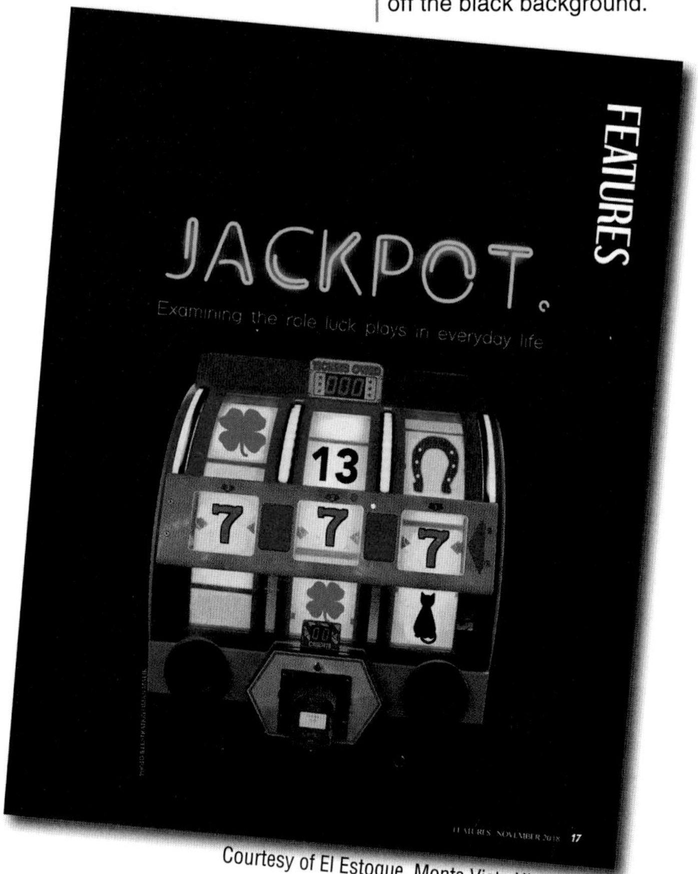

Courtesy of El Estoque, Monta Vista High School

Type

Consider the font, weight (thickness of the font), color and arrangement (Figure 15.6). In headlines, vary those four factors to create dramatically different headline packages.

Space

Where you place the elements on the page is also important. New designers tend to fill every open space on a page, making it seem crowded or cramped. Such designs risk drawing the audience's attention away from the center of visual interest. Skillful use of **white space**, also called negative space, can give your page greater impact. White space can be an important element of design when used wisely (Figure 15.7). Consider how it contributes to your design

Switched
Junior Katie Byrne leaves a childhood dream behind for a new passion
by Rachel Beyda and Megan Jones

Courtesy of El Estoque, Monta Vista High School

Figure 15.7 When used properly, white space on your page can be a powerful design element.

concept. A concept communicating loneliness and alienation would use white space differently than would a design concept communicating exciting plans. Also consider how white space helps maintain visual balance on the page. Too much white space can make a page feel incomplete, or out of balance. Yet white space, when used intentionally, can make a powerful statement.

Scale

Scale is the size of elements. Graphic elements that are all the same size feel parallel, but a designer's job is usually to help the audience prioritize information. Design will emphasize one element, the center of visual interest, and suggest to the audience it is most significant or interesting. The center of visual interest should be significantly larger than other, less significant elements on the page.

Color and Shade

Even if you publish in black and white, you should consider color in your design. Strong designers use shades of gray to set elements apart in the design. When you can work with color, choose colors carefully and work with a limited color palette. By repeating these colors, you will suggest to your audience that the colors were chosen for a reason and that they communicate something about your design concept.

By creating a color palette and custom color swatches in your computer design program, you can ensure a cohesive design within a spread or across several pages, even if several people are working with you. Create your color palette by referring to your files of inspirational ideas. You can pull colors directly from an image or photograph using an eyedropper tool or similar function. Alternatively, you can also use an online website that offers color inspiration. Simply search the phrase "online color scheme" and you will see several tools that allow users to find, create, share and save color palettes.

Line

Actual **lines**—referred to as a stroke in most graphic design programs—and invisible lines, or implied lines, will play an important role in your designs. Use them to guide the reader's eye in a specific direction, to divide content and to emphasize certain elements.

Value

Designers use the term **value** to describe how light or dark a design element is. Take a look at the design of the newsmagazine spread titled

"Just Breathe" (Figure 15.8). The image itself—its value—is very dark. To offset that darkness, the text of the overlaid headline is white. The result is a page that is still dark, which supports the design concept and fits the story, but is now more balanced.

JUST
BREATHE
One teen learns the power of steady, deep breathing to calm anxiety and reduce stress
By Emily Johnson and Claire Anderson

Figure 15.8 The white headline offsets the dark value of the image. *How might value influence the tone of a design?*

Designing a Display Headline

In Chapter 7, you learned about three different types of headlines: summary, narrative and descriptive. While summary headlines usually accompany news stories and follow the publication's standard style, narrative and descriptive headlines offer designers a bit more flexibility in creating designs that will attract your audience's attention. Creatively designed headlines that support a specific story and its design concept are called **display headlines**. Figure 15.9 on the next page shows how you would design a display headline using the following steps:

1. Begin with the words of the headline, placing words or phrases that go together in their own separate text frames. This will allow you to apply different styles to each word or phrase and to move them around easily.
2. Decide if each of those words or phrases should be parallel or if one word or phrase should be emphasized. In the headline *Comeback kings*, for example, you may decide to emphasize the word *kings*.
3. To create emphasis, vary
   - font;
   - size;
   - weight; and
   - arrangement.
4. Design a drop head, or a smaller and more descriptive headline, to accompany the display headline to explain the display head or add significant information.

Understanding Type

Effective designers understand **type**. There is much to know beyond what you learned from the drop-down menus of fonts in Microsoft Word. Behind each one of those default fonts is a designer (or team of designers) who made careful decisions and took great pains to make the O the right width for his font, to construct the mid-line in the Z at the most appropriate angle and to choose the best length below the line for the tail of the q.

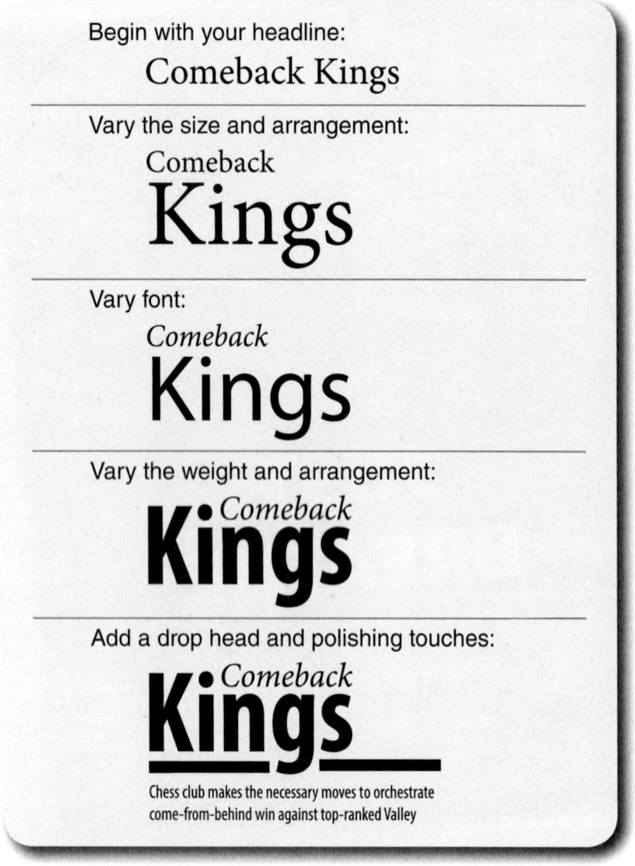
Begin with your headline:
Comeback Kings
Vary the size and arrangement:
Comeback
Kings
Vary font:
Comeback
Kings
Vary the weight and arrangement:
Comeback
Kings
Add a drop head and polishing touches:
Comeback
Kings
Chess club makes the necessary moves to orchestrate
come-from-behind win against top-ranked Valley

Figure 15.9 When designing a display headline, experiment with various treatments before deciding on the design you like best.

By understanding type, you can exercise the greatest possible control over your designs, experimenting with variations, and perhaps even developing your own, original font. (Yes, that is possible.) Begin by reviewing the font types discussed in Chapter 7, then learn the key terminology related to type.

Leading

Leading is the spacing between lines. If you have ever increased the spacing to produce an essay (double spacing, for example), you have altered the leading within a block of text. Increasing the leading moves lines farther apart (Figure 15.10a), while decreasing it moves them closer together (Figure 15.10b). Be careful, though, because decreasing the leading too much may give you unwanted effects, like pushing some lowercase letters into the lines below them (Figure 15.10c).

Kerning

The spacing between letters in a block of text is known as **kerning**. While the designer of a font sets the default kerning, at times adjusting the kerning of a word, phrase or block of text can help achieve a distinctive look. It is also the mark of a designer who pays attention to details because in every font, there are a few letters that, when paired together, could benefit from manual kerning (Figure 15.11).

Figure 15.10 Experiment with the leading, or space between lines, when designing your page.

a. Increased leading

It started as a peaceful Saturday, according to Redda S. Beete, 56, who had been soaking in her backyard Jacuzzi eating Oreos and milk. Just inside the door, in her family room, a Xeroxed copy of her late husband's obituary was Scotch-taped to the table by each chair, and a box of Kleenex lay next to her Ouija board in preparation for a séance planned for that evening.

b. Decreased leading

It started as a peaceful Saturday, according to Redda S. Beete, 56, who had been soaking in her backyard Jacuzzi eating Oreos and milk. Just inside the door, in her family room, a Xeroxed copy of her late husband's obituary was Scotch-taped to the table by each chair, and a box of Kleenex lay next to her Ouija board in preparation for a séance planned for that evening.

c. Decreased leading causing line overlap

It started as a peaceful Saturday, according to Redda S. Beete, 56, who had been soaking in her backyard Jacuzzi eating Oreos and milk. Just inside the door, in her family room, a Xeroxed copy of her late husband's obituary was Scotch-taped to the table by each chair, and a box of Kleenex lay next to her Ouija board in preparation for a séance planned for that evening.

a. Standard kerning

It started as a peaceful Saturday, according to Redda S. Beete, 56, who had been soaking in her backyard Jacuzzi eating Oreos and milk. Just inside the door, in her family room, a Xeroxed copy of her late husband's obituary was Scotch-taped to the table by each chair, and a box of Kleenex lay next to her Ouija board in preparation for a séance planned for that evening.

b. Decreased kerning

It started as a peaceful Saturday, according to Redda S. Beete, 56, who had been soaking in her backyard Jacuzzi eating Oreos and milk. Just inside the door, in her family room, a Xeroxed copy of her late husband's obituary was Scotch-taped to the table by each chair, and a box of Kleenex lay next to her Ouija board in preparation for a séance planned for that evening.

c. Increased kerning

It started as a peaceful Saturday, according to Redda S. Beete, 56, who had been soaking in her backyard Jacuzzi eating Oreos and milk. Just inside the door, in her family room, a Xeroxed copy of her late husband's obituary was Scotch-taped to the table by each chair, and a box of Kleenex lay next to her Ouija board in preparation for a séance planned for that evening.

Figure 15.11 Kerning, the space between characters, can be adjusted to create a tight or loose appearance in the type.

Ascenders and Descenders

Ascenders and descenders can work as design elements if you understand them. Some lowercase letters have ascenders, which extend upward to meet the top of the line. Other lowercase letters have descenders, which extend below the baseline (Figure 15.12). These ascenders and descenders may allow for creative arrangement in display headlines. Other times, though, they get in the way of your design. You can avoid them by working with capital letters. But be careful because text printed in all caps is not a neutral design element. The headline seems to shout at you. Think about what it is like to receive a text from someone in all caps.

Principles of Page Design

Where should each of your design elements go on your page? That depends on your purpose, but these principles will help you make decisions that reinforce and support your page design concept.

Emphasis

Rookie designers may be tempted to treat all elements on a page equally. For example, if your news page contains three stories by three different reporters, a tender-hearted designer may give them all equal space and parallel visuals with headlines of the same size. But your well-intentioned

Figure 15.12 Always consider the ascenders and descenders in your text as you design a display headline.

attempt at fairness (*But they all worked so hard!*), can confuse your readers, who look to you, the designer, to tell them what to read first. They may read none of it. In essence, if everything is important, nothing is important (Figure 15.13).

You need to create a **visual hierarchy** on the page, by adding **emphasis** to the most important story on the page—the one your audience should see first. Emphasis comes from several design techniques:

- *Move it up.* When you read a book and turn the page, where does your eye go first? The top left of the page, perhaps because in English, we read top to bottom, left to right. This means that the top left corner of a page is prime real estate, as eyes will naturally be drawn there. Placement can add emphasis no matter the medium you are working with. In a newspaper, placing a story "above the fold," on the top half of the page, gives the story prominence. The online equivalent of this is to put a story at the top of the landing page, the page where readers are likely to go first before clicking any links. Design elements near the top of a story package attract more attention than similar elements placed lower down.
- *Make it bigger.* The largest image on a page will draw the reader's eye first, so to emphasize a particular story or design element, increase the size of the element or the size of the image you are pairing it with (Figure 15.14). The most significant story package occupies the most space on the page. Your dominant image or graphic should be at least twice as large as the next largest image on the page.
- *Utilize color.* Have you ever seen black-and-white photos with one element colored? Director Steven Spielberg did this very memorably in the film "Schindler's List" when a young girl in a red coat walks

The Goodheart Times

Earth Day
Getting up early for mother Earth
by Sybil Respons

What gets high school students out of bed before 5:30 a.m? That would be trash.

Ten members of the West High Conservation Club cleaned Silver Creek Park Wednesday morning in

Sutterfield steps up
LHS assistant principle Jarrid Sutterfield to serve as interim principal
by Piper Muñez

When health issues caused Principal Steven Jones's retirement in May, Lincoln was temporarily left without a leader. That gap was filled Tuesday when the

Promenade dining
Prom tickets to include coupon for Promenade dining
by Nolo Contendre

Prom goers will find a coupon for the prix fixe menu at Hector's on their prom tickets this May, according to Junior Class President Emanuela Fuentes. The upscale restaurant, managed by Lincoln alum Charlie Dufek, is paying for

Weak Design

Figure 15.13 If all three stories are treated equally, your reader will not know what to look at first if you fail to create emphasis on the page. *Compare this page to the one in Figure 15.14. How has the designer created emphasis and a visual hierarchy in that page design?*

The Goodheart Times

Earth Day

Getting up early for mother Earth

by Sybil Respons

What gets high school students out of bed before 5:30 a.m? That would be trash.

Ten members of the West High Conservation Club cleaned Silver Creek Park Wednesday morning in honor of Earth Day before racing to first period.

Club President Jill Barnes' crew picked up almost a dozen trash sacks of micro trash and other litter and deposited them in a dumpster the city provided during their hour and a half service.

"Micro trash is actually much more dangerous to the environment than larger bits," club member Ansel Washington

Sutterfield steps up

LHS assistant principle Jarrid Sutterfield to serve as interim principal

by Piper Muñez

When health issues caused Principal Steven Jones's retirement in May, Lincoln was temporarily left without a leader.

Promenade dining

Prom tickets to include coupon for Promenade dining

by Nolo Contendre

Prom goers will find a coupon for the prix fixe menu at Hector's on their prom

Better Design

Figure 15.14 The most significant story package should occupy the most space on the page, creating a visual hierarchy and adding emphasis.

through a black-and-white sea of adults. The viewer's eye is drawn immediately to the one isolated child by the power of color. Page designers may pull colors out of their dominant visual and create a color palette that visually marries all the elements in the spread (Figure 15.15).

- *Give it shape.* The shape of a visual can also attract the reader's eye, especially when the shape contrasts other shapes on the page. Many designers cut out the subject of a photo from its background to eliminate distracting background. The natural shape of the cut out image draws attention as it contrasts with other, more geometric shapes on the page (Figure 15.16 on the next page). This contrast makes the image more dominant visually.
- *Break a pattern.* When you create a pattern, then intentionally break it,

Courtesy of The Lancer, Thousand Oaks High School

Figure 15.15 The use of color on the players' jerseys makes them stand out from the otherwise black-and-white image.

Courtesy of El Estoque, Monta Vista High School

Figure 15.16 The clever use of cutouts in this story about a competitive diver eliminates the image's distracting background and draws the reader's eye to the page.

Figure 15.17 The high heels break the pattern established by the row of kettle balls and emphasize the theme of the feature.

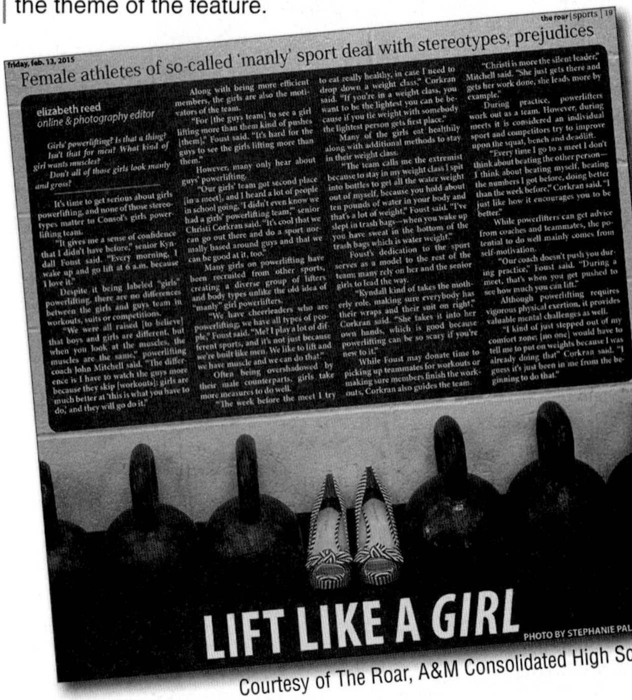

Courtesy of The Roar, A&M Consolidated High School

you create emphasis (Figure 15.17). The contrast between rhythm or symmetry elsewhere on the page and the disruptive element draws the audience's eye and creates emphasis.

Proportion

Proportion is the relative size of elements on a page and how well they work together (Figure 15.18). If you are not sure what proportion is, think of a toddler drawing the figure of a person. We immediately recognize if the head is too small for the body or the hands too large for the arms. Most designers do not think of proportion until two or more elements in a design are noticeably out of proportion. This could be a sidebar story that is too small in relation to the main story on a page, or a secondary image that is dwarfed by the dominant image. You can train yourself to recognize disproportion with practice.

Contrast

Contrast creates emphasis. In Figure 15.19, your attention is drawn to the word that differs from the rest of the headline in size or style. This use of contrast allows the designer to emphasize a significant word or phrase within the larger headline. In addition, contrast captures the audience's attention in photos, graphics and illustrations. To create contrast, take your best photo on the yearbook spread and run it big—at least twice as large as the next largest image on the page. Another method is to use color, such as a pop of bright yellow on a black or white page, to draw the reader's attention to a specific element.

The biggest mistake that rookie designers make with contrast is not creating enough contrast. Be brave when designing a page and experiment with dramatic contrast.

Proximity

Like things on a page should be grouped together. We call this **proximity**. Rather than placing your image of three injured athletes in the far corners of your story package, group them together (Figure 15.20 on page 474). If they have captions, those captions should be near the photos as well. Proximity is what designers use to give a design a sense of

The Goodheart Times

Earth Day

Getting up early for mother Earth

by Sybil Respons

What gets high school students out of bed before 5:30 a.m? That would be trash.

Ten members of the West High Conservation Club cleaned Silver Creek Park Wednesday morning in honor of Earth Day before racing to first period.

Club President Jill Barnes' crew picked up almost a dozen trash sacks of micro trash and other litter and deposited them in a dumpster the city provided during their hour and a half service.

"Micro trash is actually much more dangerous to the environment than larger bits"

"Micro trash is actually much more dangerous to the environment than larger bits," club member Ansel Washington said as he cleaned near the park's water fountain.

"Birds eat little things. So cigarette butts and the little plastic sleeves from around the top of sealed bottles end up in their stomachs and in their babies' stomach's. It poisons them. Or the micro trash washes out to sea and floats and fish ingest it, then die," Washington said.

Neighbor Irving Schmidt, who was walking his beagle Dulcy in the park, was surprised to see the students at work so early. "That's great. I didn't think kids knew how to get up this early. I love seeing them here, working away. These kids are great," Schmidt said.

Weak Design

The Goodheart Times

Earth Day

Getting up early for mother Earth

by Sybil Respons

What gets high school students out of bed before 5:30 a.m? That would be trash.

Ten members of the West High Conservation Club cleaned Silver Creek Park Wednesday morning in honor of Earth Day before racing to first period.

Club President Jill Barnes' crew picked up almost a dozen trash sacks of micro trash and other litter and deposited them in a dumpster the city provided during their hour and a half service.

"Micro trash is actually much more dangerous to the environment than larger bits," club member Ansel Washington said as he cleaned near the park's water fountain.

"Birds eat little things. So cigarette butts and the little plastic sleeves from around the top of sealed bottles end up in their stomachs and in their babies' stomach's. It poisons them. Or the micro trash washes out to sea and floats and fish ingest it, then die," Washington said.

"Micro trash is actually much more dangerous to the environment than larger bits"

Neighbor Irving Schmidt, who was walking his beagle Dulcy in the park, was surprised to see the students at work so early. "That's great. I didn't think kids knew how to get up this early. I love seeing them here, working away. These kids are great," Schmidt said.

Better Design

Figure 15.18 The proportions of different design elements affect the balance of a page. *What changes were made to improve the Weak Design example on the left?*

order and organization, to tell the reader that these elements relate closely to each other.

Alignment

Once you have taken proximity into consideration and grouped like things together, you can then focus on the **alignment** of elements on the page. Aligning elements on the page is another way to show their relationship and guide the audience's eye to design elements in the order you want them to be seen. Rookie designers may begin their design by typing a headline, increasing the font size, then centering it on the page or spread. While this approach may work for a book report, it is not likely to add anything to your design or communicate anything to your readers.

Instead, look at the edges of the elements on your page—your text boxes, images, captions and graphics. Using alignment (left, right and center), create an invisible line for the reader's eye by aligning related elements along their strongest edges (Figure 15.21 on page 474). If the text in your headline is aligned to the right, consider aligning the right edge of the body text box along the same line, with the right edge of an image and the right aligned image caption on the same invisible line. Those aligned edges will guide your audience's eyes and help them make sense of the content on the page.

Figure 15.19 Contrast is used here to draw attention to the repeated word, *Evil*, which also alludes to the theme of the story.

LIFE
PAGE 5

Left: Michal Ruprecht rides an elephant in South Africa. Right: Ruprecht gives a doll to Norma, a Peruvian girl, at Lares Valley Trek.

NORTH POINTE

GROSSE POINTE NORTH HIGH SCHOOL

SINCE 1968

FRIDAY, OCT. 31, 2014

END OF FIRST QUARTER
Today at 3:05 p.m.

POPS & PASTRIES CONCERT
Saturday, Nov. 1 at 7:30 p.m. in the gym (see page 2 for details)

NO SCHOOL
Tuesday, Nov. 4 due to elections and staff development

SAT TESTING
Saturday, Nov. 8 at 8 a.m. at North

MICHIGAN COLLEGE APPLICATION WEEK
Begins the week of Nov. 3, ends Nov. 7

Contents

1-2 News
3 Ideas
4 On Campus
5 Life
6 Reviews
7 Sports
8 In-Depth

IDEAS

"HER IMPACT ON MY LIFE HAS

Phones linked to poor health

By Anu Subramaniam & Jennifer Kusch

It's in your hand when you walk into school, in your pocket at dinner and on your side table while you sleep. Modern dependency on phones is apparent, but the negative health effects are not. Sophomore Luke Muschong is among many cell phone users who are unaware of the possible consequences.

"I am not aware of any health issues my phone causes, except for occasional headaches," Mus-

While most studies that link phones' electromagnetic radiation to tumors are inconclusive, there have been some cases where cell phone use correlates with tumor development.

"It's been demonstrated by some studies that a few types of cancer, especially tumors related to the brain, increase in percentage," Dr. Zyad Kafri, a specialist in hematology and medical oncology said. "That's not yet, however, concrete. The only one that found to really increase in a statistically significant

After sophomore Katie Lesha's mother read about possible health consequences, she encouraged Lesha to keep the phone away from her when she sleeps.

"I can't sleep with my phone near me or anything. I usually just charge my phone in a different room than where I sleep. I just put it in a different spot in my room so it's not near my head," Lesha said.

Lesha not only sees the possibility of a phone disrupting sleep, but also sees the psychological effect it can have on people when they use

Courtesy of North Pointe, Grosse Pointe North High School

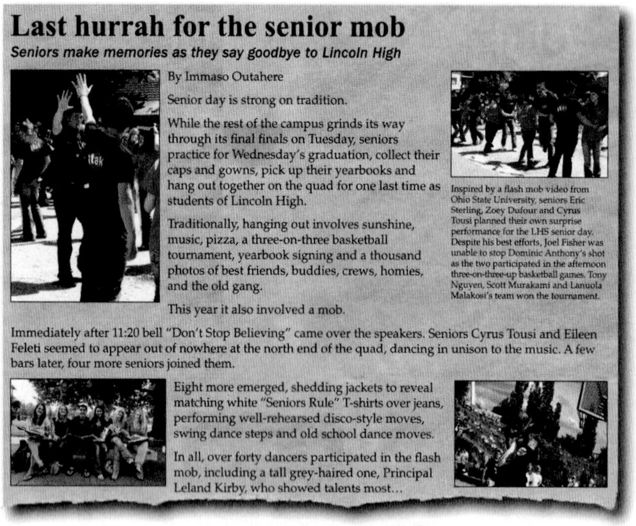

Last hurrah for the senior mob

Seniors make memories as they say goodbye to Lincoln High

By Immaso Outahere

Senior day is strong on tradition.

While the rest of the campus grinds its way through its final finals on Tuesday, seniors practice for Wednesday's graduation, collect their caps and gowns, pick up their yearbooks and hang out together on the quad for one last time as students of Lincoln High.

Traditionally, hanging out involves sunshine, music, pizza, a three-on-three basketball tournament, yearbook signing and a thousand photos of best friends, buddies, crews, homies, and the old gang.

This year it also involved a mob.

Inspired by a flash mob video from Ohio State University, seniors Eric Sterling, Zoey Dufour and Cyrus Tousi planned their own surprise performance for the LHS senior day. Despite his best efforts, Joel Fisher was unable to stop Dominic Anthony's shot as the two participated in the afternoon three-on-three-up basketball games. Tony Nguyen, Scott Murakami and Lanuola Malakosi's team won the tournament.

Immediately after 11:20 bell "Don't Stop Believing" came over the speakers. Seniors Cyrus Tousi and Eileen Feleti seemed to appear out of nowhere at the north end of the quad, dancing in unison to the music. A few bars later, four more seniors joined them.

Eight more emerged, shedding jackets to reveal matching white "Seniors Rule" T-shirts over jeans, performing well-rehearsed disco-style moves, swing dance steps and old school dance moves.

In all, over forty dancers participated in the flash mob, including a tall grey-haired one, Principal Leland Kirby, who showed talents most…

Weak Design

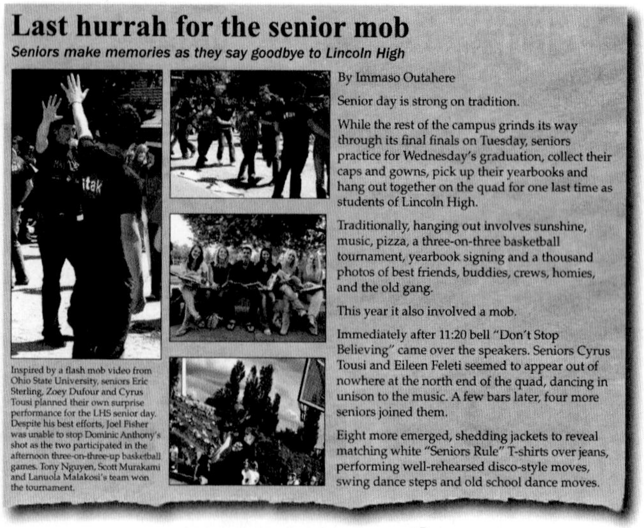

Last hurrah for the senior mob

Seniors make memories as they say goodbye to Lincoln High

By Immaso Outahere

Senior day is strong on tradition.

While the rest of the campus grinds its way through its final finals on Tuesday, seniors practice for Wednesday's graduation, collect their caps and gowns, pick up their yearbooks and hang out together on the quad for one last time as students of Lincoln High.

Traditionally, hanging out involves sunshine, music, pizza, a three-on-three basketball tournament, yearbook signing and a thousand photos of best friends, buddies, crews, homies, and the old gang.

This year it also involved a mob.

Immediately after 11:20 bell "Don't Stop Believing" came over the speakers. Seniors Cyrus Tousi and Eileen Feleti seemed to appear out of nowhere at the north end of the quad, dancing in unison to the music. A few bars later, four more seniors joined them.

Eight more emerged, shedding jackets to reveal matching white "Seniors Rule" T-shirts over jeans, performing well-rehearsed disco-style moves, swing dance steps and old school dance moves.

Inspired by a flash mob video from Ohio State University, seniors Eric Sterling, Zoey Dufour and Cyrus Tousi planned their own surprise performance for the LHS senior day. Despite his best efforts, Joel Fisher was unable to stop Dominic Anthony's shot as the two participated in the afternoon three-on-three-up basketball games. Tony Nguyen, Scott Murakami and Lanuola Malakosi's team won the tournament.

Better Design

Figure 15.20 Images that are scattered across a page make a design look unorganized. By grouping like items together, you create order.

Repetition

Professionals recommend student designers follow the rule of three. Design elements best support your design concept when they are repeated at least three times. If you are using red as a design element in a package about breaking a law, repeat that red in three key places on the page. If you are using a circular shape in your dominant visual, utilize circles at least two other places on the page.

Repetition makes the design concept of a page clearer and makes the design choices feel intentional (Figure 15.22). As with most design rules, there is an exception. Sometimes, to make a powerful statement, you will use a bold design element only once, just one circle amid contrasting linear shapes, just one spot of red set amid monochrome.

Figure 15.21 By aligning elements on the page, you guide your reader's eye from one design element to the next in the order you choose.

Rhythm, Direction and Balance

When a page design has great **rhythm**, it is typically because the designer has paid careful attention to the way the elements on the page

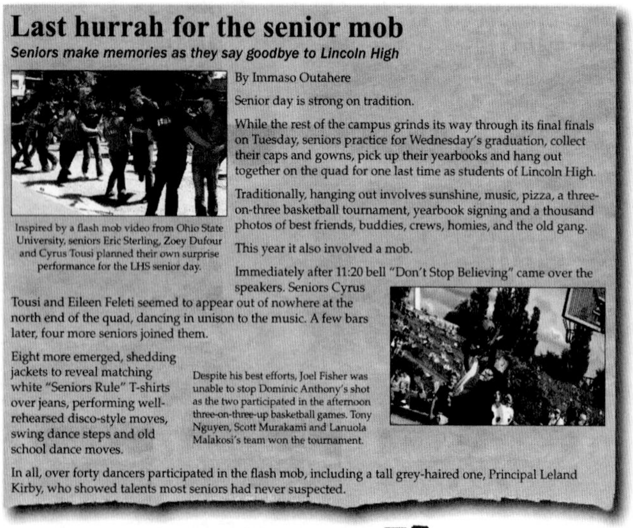

Last hurrah for the senior mob

Seniors make memories as they say goodbye to Lincoln High

By Immaso Outahere

Senior day is strong on tradition.

While the rest of the campus grinds its way through its final finals on Tuesday, seniors practice for Wednesday's graduation, collect their caps and gowns, pick up their yearbooks and hang out together on the quad for one last time as students of Lincoln High.

Traditionally, hanging out involves sunshine, music, pizza, a three-on-three basketball tournament, yearbook signing and a thousand photos of best friends, buddies, crews, homies, and the old gang.

Inspired by a flash mob video from Ohio State University, seniors Eric Sterling, Zoey Dufour and Cyrus Tousi planned their own surprise performance for the LHS senior day.

This year it also involved a mob.

Immediately after 11:20 bell "Don't Stop Believing" came over the speakers. Seniors Cyrus Tousi and Eileen Feleti seemed to appear out of nowhere at the north end of the quad, dancing in unison to the music. A few bars later, four more seniors joined them.

Eight more emerged, shedding jackets to reveal matching white "Seniors Rule" T-shirts over jeans, performing well-rehearsed disco-style moves, swing dance steps and old school dance moves.

Despite his best efforts, Joel Fisher was unable to stop Dominic Anthony's shot as the two participated in the afternoon three-on-three-up basketball games. Tony Nguyen, Scott Murakami and Lanuola Malakosi's team won the tournament.

In all, over forty dancers participated in the flash mob, including a tall grey-haired one, Principal Leland Kirby, who showed talents most seniors had never suspected.

Weak Design

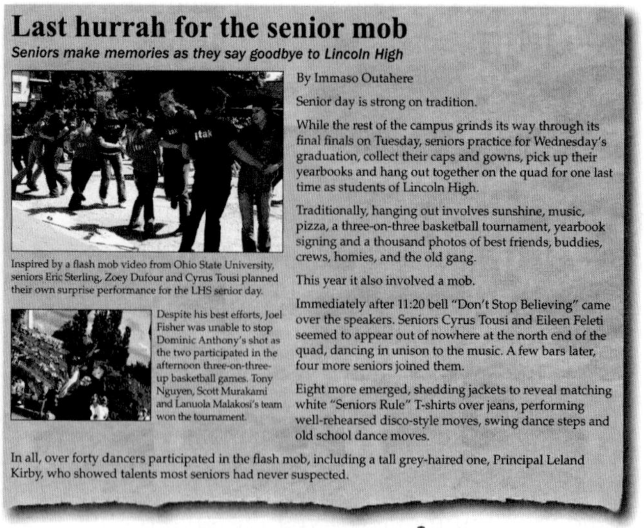

Last hurrah for the senior mob

Seniors make memories as they say goodbye to Lincoln High

By Immaso Outahere

Senior day is strong on tradition.

While the rest of the campus grinds its way through its final finals on Tuesday, seniors practice for Wednesday's graduation, collect their caps and gowns, pick up their yearbooks and hang out together on the quad for one last time as students of Lincoln High.

Traditionally, hanging out involves sunshine, music, pizza, a three-on-three basketball tournament, yearbook signing and a thousand photos of best friends, buddies, crews, homies, and the old gang.

Inspired by a flash mob video from Ohio State University, seniors Eric Sterling, Zoey Dufour and Cyrus Tousi planned their own surprise performance for the LHS senior day.

This year it also involved a mob.

Immediately after 11:20 bell "Don't Stop Believing" came over the speakers. Seniors Cyrus Tousi and Eileen Feleti seemed to appear out of nowhere at the north end of the quad, dancing in unison to the music. A few bars later, four more seniors joined them.

Despite his best efforts, Joel Fisher was unable to stop Dominic Anthony's shot as the two participated in the afternoon three-on-three-up basketball games. Tony Nguyen, Scott Murakami and Lanuola Malakosi's team won the tournament.

Eight more emerged, shedding jackets to reveal matching white "Seniors Rule" T-shirts over jeans, performing well-rehearsed disco-style moves, swing dance steps and old school dance moves.

In all, over forty dancers participated in the flash mob, including a tall grey-haired one, Principal Leland Kirby, who showed talents most seniors had never suspected.

Better Design

OFF CAMPUS

OFF CAMPUS

is it BLAZE, or is it BLAST?

UNIQUE FACTORS

"The s'mores pie tasted really good. I think it's really cool that they offered such a unique desert for a pizza place."
– ABI BROOKS

"It was just like any s'more: gooey sweet goodness. It was an interesting compliment to the rest of the food."
– KACIE NICHOLSON

PIZZA

"The pizza at Blaze was definitely a lot thinner and easier to eat. It was a little greasier but tasted better."
– CARSEN VAN DER LINDEN

" I'm usually not a fan of thin crust pizza, but I ended up really liking it."
– SARAH MARTINEZ

ATMOSPHERE

"The first thing I noticed walking in was the lit up sign in the back corner. It read 'Non-Conformists,' and I loved it."
– OLIVIA GRAHL

"Not only were the people at Blaze friendly, but it was so open and inviting. An exciting atmosphere."
– J.T. SCOTT

& BLAZE: BLAST:

WHERE:
10325 Fairway Dr
Roseville, CA 95678
www.blazepizza.com

THE ROAR | ISSUE 5 22

ATMOSPHERE

"Way smaller. The music was louder, and there were less people but [it was] brighter."
– SIERRA YOUNG

"Bright and open and more family-friendly, it was more of a place to go with family, not friends."
– SARAH MARTINEZ

PIZZA

"Lots of random toppings, like ones you wouldn't even think to put on a pizza."
– DESIREE STONE

"The crust was particularly good, really fluffy. The larger toppings made for a pizza that felt more filling."
– CARSEN VAN DER LINDEN

UNIQUE FACTORS

"Lots of different kinds of lemonade. The blood orange was particularly good."
– LILY JONES

"Blast's gluten-free pizza was really good. There are many bad tasting gluten-free pizzas. Blast made it taste like a regular pizza."
– ARIELLA APPLEBY

Check out a video of Blaze and Blast restaurants

PRICE BLAZE: BLAST:

WHERE:
1132 Galleria Blvd
Roseville, CA 95678
www.blast825pizza.com

23 WHITNEYUPDATE.COM

Courtesy of The Roar, Whitney High School

Figure 15.22 Repeating the circle elements on this spread creates a unified design.

work with each other. Where does the reader's eye go first, second and third? Are there natural lines in the dominant visual that draw the reader's eye from one element to the next? A design with strong rhythm leads the reader on a complete journey, with each element working with, not against, other elements on the page.

Some elements of your design will move the reader's eye in a certain **direction**. The neck of a guitar, for example, may point in the direction of a headline, which leads your reader's eye from the image (the guitar) to the words (the headline). If you are using a dominant image that has an obvious direction, for example a runner facing left or right or the side profile of a person sitting at a computer, place the image so that the subject is looking or moving into the content. The reader's eye will follow the direction of the image, and the last thing you want is to lead the reader off the page.

Though some students mistake it for symmetry, **balance** is something you should seek when designing any spread (Figure 15.23 on the next page). A dominant visual on one side of the spread may be balanced out by a collection of smaller visuals on the right. White space in the top right corner may balance out white space in the lower left. Balance is closely related to proportion, in that when elements on the page are proportionate to one another, you are likely to achieve balance.

Executing the Design

Once you have completed the creative work of planning your design and mapping out the spread, the "dirty work" of placing and arranging

The Goodheart Times

Earth Day

Getting up early for mother Earth

by Sybil Respons

What gets high school students out of bed before 5:30 a.m? That would be trash.

Ten members of the West High Conservation Club cleaned Silver Creek Park Wednesday morning in honor of Earth Day before racing to first period.

Club President Jill Barnes' crew picked up almost a dozen trash sacks of micro trash and other litter and deposited them in a dumpster the city provided

Sutterfield steps up

LHS assistant principle Jarrid Sutterfield to serve as interim principal

by Piper Muñez

When health issues caused Principal Steven Jones's retirement in May, Lincoln was temporarily left without a leader. That gap was

Promenade dining

Prom tickets to include coupon for Promenade dining

by Nolo Contendre

Prom goers will find a coupon for the prix fixe menu at Hector's

The Goodheart Times

Earth Day

Getting up early for mother Earth

by Sybil Respons

What gets high school students out of bed before 5:30 a.m? That would be trash.

Ten members of the West High Conservation Club cleaned Silver Creek Park Wednesday morning in honor of Earth Day before racing to first period.

Club President Jill Barnes' crew picked up almost a dozen trash sacks of micro trash and other litter and deposited them in a dumpster the city provided during their hour and a half service.

"Micro trash is actually much more dangerous to the

Sutterfield steps up

LHS assistant principle Jarrid Sutterfield to serve as interim principal

by Piper Muñez

When health issues caused Principal Steven Jones's retirement in May, Lincoln was temporarily left without a leader. That gap was filled Tuesday

Promenade dining

Prom tickets to include coupon for Promenade dining

by Nolo Contendre

Prom goers will find a coupon for the prix fixe menu at Hector's on their prom

Figure 15.23 An unbalanced page can affect the way readers perceive your design. Balance is achieved when white space and design elements are properly balanced across the page.

content on a page begins. Some of the work can be frustrating or difficult, especially at first, but it is rewarding to turn a vision into reality.

Executing your design may require you to gain new computer skills or become more efficient with the ones you have. However, tutorials and how-to articles abound on the Internet, and you can even find a wealth of learning material provided by the makers of design software such as Adobe. The more pages you design, the easier it will become.

As you progress as a designer, you may notice that professional designers break some of the rules and principles discussed in this chapter. Remember, you must know the rules before you can break the rules to serve a good cause. Smart design is intentional. It is purposeful. Whatever you choose to do with design, do it for a reason.

Controlling the Chaos

As you begin placing the elements of your design on the page, things may initially feel jumbled and chaotic. There are a few key concepts and guiding principles that will help you to reign in the chaos and put the design in order.

The grid is an essential concept and the basic structure of the page. You will need to make a decision about it when you first open a new document. The **grid** includes the margins on all sides and number of columns. You may also use horizontal guidelines, which, like the grid and the margins, are invisible to your audience. These all help you organize elements on the page. At the same time you set the margins and columns, you will also set the **gutter** (the space between columns) and the page **bleed** (the space between your margin and the line where the printer will trim the page).

Publications use **modular design** most of the time. Content is organized into modules, almost always rectangles, of various sizes (Figure 15.24). The rectangular modules that show up on your computer screen are like the columns and grids, invisible to your audience, but important to you as you place content. By skillfully using alignment, proximity and lines, both visible and implied, you will create unified and cohesive modules that everyone can see.

As you look at professional examples, you may see where the modular design of a page is broken. This unexpected element may pull the reader into the story, but it only works with *one* element on the page. If multiple elements on the page break modular design, the page will feel chaotic and incoherent.

Caution: What to Avoid When Executing Your Design

Sometimes designers make poor decisions that can lead to weak design or even embarrassing mistakes. The following list of rules and tips will help you avoid some of the more common design mistakes.

- *Armpits and doglegs.* Though occasionally a break in modular design may be justifiable, an armpit is rarely enticing to the audience. An armpit occurs where the headline of a story is wider than the story's module and so extends above an adjoining, unrelated story and its headline. It confuses the reader, and confused readers turn the page or click elsewhere. Like armpits, doglegs also break a module, this time by wrapping an L-shaped column of text around art, ads or other stories.
- *Dollar bill rule.* To break up big blocks of gray text that intimidate readers, use graphics or subheadlines, that is, mini headlines within the story, to chunk information for the reader. Follow the dollar bill rule: You should not be able to place a dollar bill anywhere on the page without touching a design element.
- *Dime rule.* In photos, no subject's face should be smaller than a dime. This is true even for mug shots. Though there may be some smaller faces in a crowd in the background of the photo, any main subject's face should be larger than a dime.
- *Orphans and widows.* The term *widow* refers to a single word that ends up at the top of a new column or page. *Orphans* are single words at the end of a paragraph that are forced onto a new line. These both create awkward white space that may visually distract the reader. Edit and kern the text to avoid these.

B8

VOLUME 16 · ISSUE 5
MARCH 13, 2015

BACK PAGE

IN THE SPOTLIGHT

HALL OF FAME

PREVIEW

tara parimi & lauren russell
Aquila copy editor & reporter

The Upper School's annual talent show, dubbed HOSCARS, will be held on March 25 and will feature performances from students across all grade levels.

Student council invited all students to sign up to audition for a spot in this year's HOSCARS via a google form. The audition process is currently ongoing for both performers and the MCs, and student council hopes to incorporate an increased number of acts into the show to match the influx of audition sign-ups.

Maya Rai (10) and her friends will be continuing the Bollywood tradition in an all-sophomore number.

"I am mostly looking forward to seeing people's reactions to our routine, because it is really funny," Maya said. "I thought it would a great way to spend time with my friends."

Another act this year includes students from across grade levels, with freshmen Darren Gu, Marcus Chen, and Maxwell Woehrmann, junior Lev Sepetov and seniors Alex Thomas, Vivek Sriram and Jai Ahuja. They will be dancing to the K-pop song "Roly Poly," by the all-girl group T-ara.

"I am most excited to show all my friends how much heart I have put into this dance, as I have been working on this for a long time already," Darren Gu said. "I definitely would like to participate next year; it's really exciting to prepare for, and a nice way to hang out with your friends when you're practicing."

Student council has formed three committees to prepare for HOSCARS: tech, auditions and decorations/publicity.

5 years of HOSCARS

~17 final acts

30 auditions this year

LASTING GLORY

raveena kapatkar
Aquila copy editor

"THE FACULTY DANCE LAST YEAR WAS REALLY FUNNY AND IT WAS MY FAVORITE ACT IN THE SHOW."
HALEY TRAN (10)

"ERIC ANDERSON'S JUGGLING WAS AMAZING."
LEON CHIN (12)

"THE K-POP GROUP, WHEN THEY DANCED TO A BUNCH OF K-POP SONGS. THAT WAS MY FAVORITE HOSCARS MOMENT."
KRISTEN KO (10)

ALL PHOTOS - WINGED POST ARCHIVES

LOOKING BACK (1) Varun Cherukuri ('14) dances to Michael Jackson's "Smooth Criminal." (2) Lydia Werthen ('13) sings a Simon & Garfunkel song while accompanying herself on the guitar during Hoscars 2013. (3) Riya Godbole (12) beats out a rhythm with a plastic cup while singing a medley of pop tunes, including "Thrift Shop" by Macklemore. (4) Andrew Zhang (12) busts out flips and dance moves, showcasing his agility during Hoscars 2013. (5) Erik Andersen ('13) juggles his way to a Hoscars prize in 2013. (6) Vincent Lin ('14) bobs up and down to a k-pop song during Hoscars 2013.

KACEY FANG - WINGED POST

AUDITIONS (Top Left) Hannah Bollar (12) and Leeza Kuo (12) sing as Glinda and Elphaba from the musical *Wicked* for their audition. (Bottom Left) Thyne Boonmark (12) accompanies the act on piano. (Middle) Vivian Jou (12) and Harry Xu (12) play violin and clarinet to Wicked's "Popular." (Right) Lev Sepetov (11), Alex Thomas (12), Vivek Sriram (12), Darren Gu (9), Maxwell Woehrmann (9) and Marcus Chen (9) dance to "Roly-Poly," a K-pop song.

Courtesy of The Winged Post, The Harker School

Figure 15.24 The use of modules organizes the content and brings order to the page. *Can you detect the invisible grid lines that organize this page?*

- *Tombstoned headlines.* Newspaper designers who fail to create a visual hierarchy on the page may tombstone headlines. Two headlines are placed side-by-side on the same line (like tombstones in a cemetery) over two stories with very little significant contrast between one headline and its neighbor. The two headlines appear to run into each other. In addition to being boring, these headlines confuse the reader.
- *Trapped white space.* Sometimes the edges of two design elements, when placed next to each other, create a distracting gap or white space. Though white space can be beneficial on the perimeter of your design, white space that is too small or "trapped" between elements can be awkward. The only trapped white space in your design should be the white space you decided to put there to further your design concept.
- *Square photos.* Though square photographs have become more popular on handheld devices with photo-sharing apps, most photos are best cropped horizontally or vertically. Only use square photos when you have a compelling reason to do so.
- *Eyeline.* When the subject of a photograph is looking or moving in a clear direction, such as an athlete running to the left, the reader's eye will move in the same direction. Place photos so you lead your audience's eye toward your text and avoid placing photos in a way that will lead the reader's eye off the page.
- *Screened images.* Use care when you place text over an image or graphic. It will never be as easy to read as text on a plain background. The color of the text should contrast markedly with the colors in the image. If it is difficult to read, your audience will not.
- *Decoration.* Never add design elements to the page because you think it needs more decoration. Clipart, borders and stock images are amateurish and indicate that a design was not well planned.
- *Display fonts.* While on some occasions display fonts (fancy, decorative fonts) may be appropriate, use them sparingly. Save the display font for one word or phrase in the main headline, and surround it with text in other, more neutral fonts.

Your Turn

1. Take a look at the disastrous page design on the next page. Can you identify what went wrong? Using the list of what to avoid in page design that begins on page 477 and continues above, examine the numbered design elements on page 479. Number a separate sheet of paper and identify the poor design decisions.
2. **Going Deeper.** Using the same words and phrases in the list of decisions to avoid, write a short note explaining to the designer how to fix the poorly designed page. Use information from earlier in the chapter to coach her to a stronger page design.

What Went Wrong?

The Goodheart Times

1

Last hurrah for the senior mob

Seniors make memories as they say goodbye to Lincoln High

Inspired by a flash mob video from Ohio State University, seniors Eric Sterling and Cyrus Tousi planned their own surprise performance for the LHS senior day.

By Immaso Outahere

Senior day is strong on tradition.

While the rest of the campus grinds its way through its final finals on Tuesday, seniors practice for Wednesday's graduation, collect their caps and gowns, pick up their yearbooks and hang out together on the quad for one last time as students of Lincoln High.

Traditionally, hanging out involves sunshine, music, pizza, a three-on-three basketball tournament, yearbook signing and a thousand photos of best friends, buddies, crews, homies, and the old gang.

This year it also involved a mob.

Immediately after 11:20 bell "Don't Stop Believing" came over the speakers. Seniors Cyrus Tousi and Eileen Feleti seemed to appear out of nowhere at the north end of the quad, dancing in unison to the music. A few bars later, four more seniors joined them. 5

Eight more emerged, shedding jackets to reveal matching white "Seniors Rule" T-shirts over jeans, performing well-rehearsed disco-style moves, swing dance steps and old school dance moves.

In all, over forty dancers participated in the flash mob, including a tall grey-haired one, Principal Leland Kirby, who showed talents most seniors had never suspected.

The crowd of seniors cheered and clapped for almost two minutes as the flash mob melted back into the rest of their class.

Most of the seniors returned to their yearbooks, flipping through pages, checking the index to find names and exchanging books for signatures.

Many students seemed impressed with the yearbook staff's accomplishments.

"I can't believe they got pictures of the forensics competition!" said senior Hazel Crawley, pointing to a two-page spread.

Lissa Chow was taken by yearbook designer Miriam Ibrahim's cover design. "The lion just seems to be leaping off the cover at your. I don't know how they did that, but it is a great cover, the best I've seen. I like the colors, too."

Pizza and three-on-three basketball tournament filled the afternoon with Tony Nguyen, Scott Murakami and Lanuola Malakosi's team emerging as the champions.

At the conclusion on the senior's last day as students, senior Hannah Schmitz said, "Ten years from now, we won't remember all the drama of high school or the bad test scores. We'll remember days like today."

6

7

Despite his best efforts, Joel Fisher was unable to stop Dominic Anthony's shot as the two participated in the afternoon pick-up basketball games. Anthony and Steve Barton came out on top over Fisher and his teammate, Jordi Andres.

2

Sutterfield steps up

LHS assistant principle Jarrid Sutterfield to serve as interim principal

3

by Piper Muñez

When health issues caused Principal Steven Jones's retirement in May, Lincoln was temporarily left without a leader. That gap was filled Tuesday when the district announced Jarrid Sutterfield will serve as interim principal while the district searches for a permanent leader, the district public information officer said in a prepared statement.

Superintendent Marshal Law said, "Sutterfield was an easy choice for interim principal. He knows and cares about Lincoln and its students."

Student reaction on social media was generally positive. "So excited for Sutterfield to be in charge," Karly Koch tweeted.. "Wish he could be principal forever!" 4

"Who is going to handle all the detentions, Saturday schools, truants and tardies now?" junior Amalga Mate asked on Facebook.

Sutterfield is looking forward to the challenge. "I'm honored that they chose me," he said.

Earth Day

8

Getting up early for mother Earth

by Sybil Respons

What gets high school students out of bed before 5:30 a.m? That would be trash.

Ten members of the West High Conservation Club cleaned Silver Creek Park Wednesday morning in honor of Earth Day before racing to first period.

Club President Jill Barnes' crew picked up almost a dozen trash sacks of micro trash and other litter and deposited them in a dumpster the city provided during their hour and a half service.

"Micro trash is actually much more dangerous to the environment than larger bits," club member Ansel Washington said as he cleaned near the park's water fountain.

"Birds eat little things. So cigarette butts and the little plastic sleeves from around the top of sealed bottles end up in their stomachs and in their babies' stomach's. It poisons them. Or the micro trash washes out to sea and floats and fish ingest it, then die," Washington said. 9

Chapter Fifteen

Review and Assessment

Recall

1. List three key findings from the Poynter eye-tracking study.
2. Explain the idea of verbal-visual connection.
3. What are three common points of entry in a story?
4. Identify and describe the six categories of dominant visuals.
5. Identify and explain five alternative story forms.
6. Explain the pros and cons of incorporating white space into your design.
7. What is the difference between leading and kerning?
8. What are two ways to establish a visual hierarchy in your page design?
9. Explain the concept of modular design.
10. Identify and explain three practices to avoid when executing your design.

Critical Thinking

1. Try conducting your own simple eye-tracking study. With a pen in hand, look at a professional newspaper page or magazine spread and track where your eyes go in the order that they move around the page. Circle anything that you read (only circle the parts that you read, not the whole article). From your informal study, what would you say about the page design? Did it lead you to the most important parts of the page first? If so, how? If not, explain which elements may have led you astray.
2. Repeat the exercise above with a student publication, preferably your own. Describe what you learned about the students' design.
3. Look at the front page of your local newspaper. Using sticky notes, mark each place where you can see specific page design elements and principles. On each sticky note, name the element or principle. Decide which story is dominant, and explain how the designer of that page has used the design elements and principles to send readers that message.
4. Find an example of a story package with a dominant visual, a display headline and at least one alternative story form. In a short paragraph, evaluate how well the elements work together to convey the concept. Pay attention to the story's angle, the words of the headline, any subheadlines and the dominant visual, as well as any of the page design elements (such as color, if applicable).
5. Go on a scavenger hunt through magazines and newspapers looking for examples of alternative story forms. When you find one, snap a digital photo of it and post it to a pinboard shared online. Alternatively, you could cut out the example and paste it into your notebook, creating a visual glossary.

Application

1. Using the "Comeback kings" example, brainstorm three to five alternative story forms that could accompany the main story, and sketch a plan for a double-page spread.
2. Review the front page of an inner section, such as sports, from a print edition of a professional publication. Think about how the same information could be presented differently by incorporating alternative story forms, changing the dominant visual and using a display headline. Sketch a redesign of the section's front page using those components.
3. In a small group, conduct a design planning meeting for a story related to your school or community. Brainstorm a concept, a headline, the dominant visual and alternative story forms. Sketch the layout of the spread, making sure you can justify your choices using your understanding of the elements and principles of page design. Use this spread as you prepare your layout for publication.
4. Building off the spread you prepared in question 3, create a new edition of your publication. Manage your time wisely and work together to meet your deadline.

Chapter Fifteen

Journalism Style

Possessives and Apostrophes

Is it *Oiler softball*, *Oiler's softball*, or *Oilers' softball*? (Try it with the name of your mascot.) Should you write *Mr. Jones's car* or *Mr. Jones' car*? *The measles' effect* or *the measle's effect*?

Possessives are highly useful and great space savers when you are writing for tight spaces. *Smythe's role in scandal revealed* reads better in a headline than *Role of Smythe in scandal revealed*. The possessive also may read better in a lead or elsewhere in news stories. But how do you know when to use an apostrophe alone and when to use an apostrophe s?

Try It!

Use either an apostrophe or an apostrophe s, as appropriate. Refer to the tables as necessary.

1. Write a sentence using *dog* as a possessive. Now write a similar sentence using *dogs* as a possessive.
2. Write a sentence using *horse* as a possessive. Now write a similar sentence using *horses* as a possessive.
3. Write a sentence using *United Auto Workers* (the name of a union) as a possessive.
4. Write a sentence about the excitement of robotics. Use *robotics* as a possessive.
5. Write a sentence about the leadership of Moses (an Old Testament prophet). Use a possessive.
6. Write a sentence about a clinic for children. Use *children* as a possessive.

Extend Your Knowledge — Style Exercises

Visit the *Journalism* website to find out:

1. Why you should avoid using possessives with inanimate (nonliving) objects.
2. Where to use an apostrophe when two or more people possess the same thing.
3. What exceptions are made for certain familiar, and old, expressions.

To form the possessive of a word ending in s, add only the apostrophe	Examples
Plural nouns ending in *s*	*the cats' food* *others' wishes*
Plural names for singular entities ending in *s*	*the United Nations' mandate* *General Motors' profits*
Nouns plural in form but singular in meaning. (These do not have a commonly used plural; we say "cases of measles," not "measleses." Words ending in *ics*, meaning roughly "study of," avoid plurals. We say "types of physics" or "schools of politics.")	*the measles' effect* *mathematics' beginnings* *politics' challenge*
Nouns ending in *s* that are the same in the singular and plural	*one corps' location* *two corps' location*
Singular proper nouns ending in *s*	*Jesus' teachings* *Mr. Jones' car*

Exception	
Singular common nouns ending in s do take an apostrophe s	**UNLESS the next word begins with s**
the class's gift *the witness's testimony* *the press's power* *the lens's focal point*	*the class' swan song* *the witness' sobbing* *the press' system* *the lens' safety catch*
To form the possessive of a word ending in any letter but s, add 's	**Examples**
Singular nouns not ending in *s* (even words that sound like they end in *s*)	*cat's food* *prince's wedding* *justice's delay*
Plural nouns not ending in *s*	*alumni's visit* *women's meeting*
Nouns that are the same in the singular and the plural	*One moose's bellow* *Six moose's answers*

Chapter Fifteen
Writers' Workshop

In this Writers' Workshop you will:

- Recognize right- and left-branching sentences and the uses of each in journalistic writing.
- Create journalistic sentences that branch primarily to the right.

Workshop 15.1
Controlling Long Sentences
Mini-Lesson: The Tree to the Right of the Wall

In Writers' Workshop 14 you were challenged to vary your sentence lengths. You also read clear, interesting sentences that were long—as long as 91 words. But younger readers may lose interest in long sentences if they are not perfectly clear, and younger writers may struggle to write clearly when they write longer sentences. Your job, writing to your peers, may be tougher than the job of Wall Street Journal reporters whose readers regularly take in sentences with 50 words or more.

Perhaps you found that your average sentence length is relatively short.

This Writers' Workshop examines how professionals put longer sentences together while still remaining clear and interesting to their readers.

To do this, we are going to talk about a tree growing just to the right of a wall. Its sturdy trunk is made of two elements, a subject and a verb. The tree does not have much room to grow toward the wall on its left. Likewise, good journalistic sentences avoid putting sentence elements to the left of the subject and verb, the trunk.

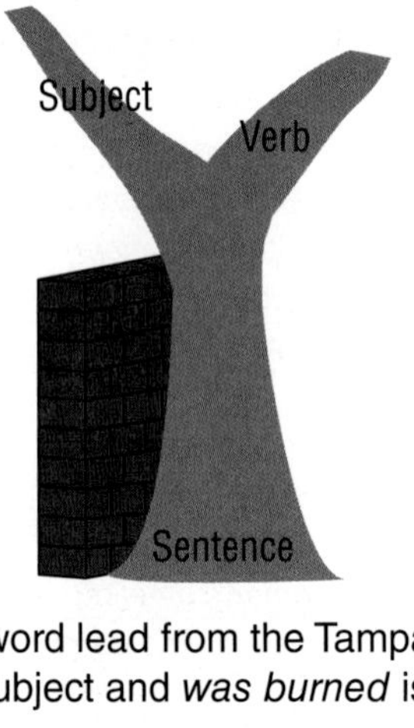

In this 25-word lead from the Tampa Bay Times, *woman* is the subject and *was burned* is the verb.

ST. PETERSBURG — A 90-year-old woman was badly burned on her face and upper body by a fire in a home on 19th Avenue South overnight, authorities said.

The adjectives *a 90-year-old* come before the noun and verb, like leaves growing on the left side of the subject-trunk. If you count *a 90-year-old* as four words, that leaves 19 or 20 words growing out of the right side of the tree. In this case nothing is growing between the subject-trunk and the verb-trunk.

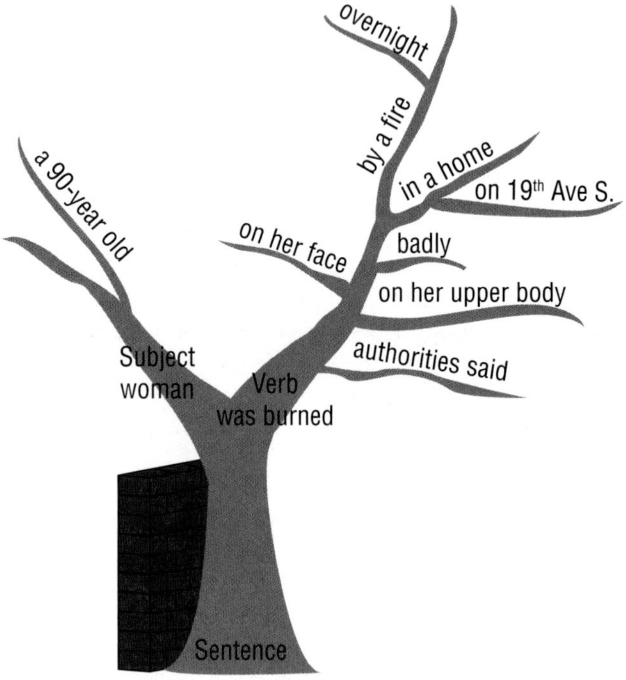

Journalistic sentences generally grow to the right, with only very little branches to the left. Right-branching sentences increase clarity and engage the reader. Most readers of journalism want to get to the *who* and the *what* as swiftly and clearly as possible.

In the 35-word lead sentence from the Austin American-Statesman at the top of the next page, one element branches to the left: *In another sign of its expanding Austin presence*. Such left-branching elements as these two prepositional phrases are used to give the reader context for the rest of the lead, set a scene or explain the event's significance. Sometimes an element branches left only because the right side of the tree is already too full.

The adjectives *technology giant* also grow leftward from the trunk that represents the subject.

But a full 21 words of the 35-word lead branch to the right. Once again nothing grows between the subject-trunk and the verb-trunk.

> *In another sign of its expanding Austin presence, technology giant Apple Inc. has signed a lease for an entire 215,000-square foot Capital Ridge office building under construction in Southwest Austin, local real estate sources say.*

The previous two examples were leads, but this 54-word sentence comes from within a Boston Globe news report on the Boston Marathon. Lelisa Desisa of Ethiopia had just won the race for the second time.

> *On Monday afternoon the man from Ethiopia earned himself another medal in a most satisfying reprise, running away from countryman Yemane Adhane Tsegay in the final few miles to win the 119th Boston Marathon in 2 hours, 9 minutes, and 17 seconds, a most creditable clocking on a raw day with a stiff headwind.*

The brief phrase *from Ethiopia* comes after the subject *the man* and before the verb *earned*, so this sentence has two words branching inward.

Notice what the reporter did NOT do. He did not put many branches between his subject and his verb. For instance, though this information was later in his article, he did NOT write:

> *On Monday afternoon Lelisa Desisa from Ethiopia, who won the Boston Marathon two years ago and gave his first-place medal back to the city as a tribute to the victims of the bombing and their families, running against countryman Yemane Adhane Tsegay, earned another medal in a most satisfying reprise ...*

The 37 words placed to the right of Desisa's name but to the left of the verb *earned* are like branches that grow in the center of the tree. They interrupt the flow of the sentence and make it harder to follow. It is hard to find the trunks for all the branches. Though academic writing may accept such sentences, journalism uses modifiers between the subject and the verb sparingly. Generally the information in those 37 words would become adjectives before the noun, as in *Ethiopian Lelisa Desisa* or *2013 winner Ethiopian Lelisa Desisa*, or that information would be moved to the right of the verb or to another paragraph.

Apply It!

1. Sketch a tree by the wall for the Austin American-Statesman's sentence about Apple leasing an office building.
2. Sketch a tree by the wall for The Boston Globe's news report about the Boston Marathon. The reporter has elected to start with the time element *On Monday afternoon*. Do you think this was justified or just done to keep the sentence from leaning too far to the right?
3. Choose a longer sentence, 20 to 30 words, from a student publication. Sketch a tree by the wall for that sentence. Could it be revised to be clearer by pruning left-branching elements or elements that grow between the subject and the verb? Revise the sentence if it can be improved.
4. Sketch a tree (it will not be by a wall; readers of literature may have the patience for branches to the left) for Willa Cather's description of Mr. Shimerda's grave, quoted in Writers' Workshop 14. What effects do her left-branching sentences have on the reader?
5. Choose one of the longer sentences you have written. Sketch a tree for it. Could it be revised to be clearer by pruning left-branching elements or elements that grow between the subject and the verb? Revise the sentence if it can be improved.
6. The following information was in one 33-word sentence in the body of an Oregonian article about high school senior Ted Morissette's service-learning project, building a tiny house for a city-authorized homeless encampment. Recombine this information into one or two sentences, limiting the number of left-branching elements and elements that would separate the subject-trunk and the verb-trunk.
   - Morissette is from Oregon Episcopal School.
   - Morrissette worked with a crew.
   - The crew were volunteers from the school.
   - They built a house.
   - The house has 85 square feet of space.
   - The house has a pitched roof.
   - They will deliver it on May 13.
   - They will deliver it to a city.
   - The city was a tent city.
   - The residents needed housing and employment.
   - The city has helped residents since 2000.

Extend Your Knowledge

Extend

Visit the *Journalism* website for additional practice.

Chapter Sixteen

Visual and Multimedia Storytelling

How do we show them the story?

Courtesy of Sean Ziebarth, Fountain Valley High School

G-WLEARNING.com

While studying, look for the activity icon to:

- **Build** vocabulary terms with e-flash cards and matching activities.
- **Extend** learning with further discussion of relevant topics.
- **Reinforce** what you learn by completing style exercises, worksheets and end-of-chapter questions.

Visit the Journalism website: www.g-wlearning.com/journalism/

Chapter Objectives

After reading this chapter, you will be able to:

- Explain why photography is an important part of journalism.
- Utilize basic principles of photojournalism and photographic composition to shoot powerful photos.
- Make a plan for a photography assignment.
- Identify the qualities of a strong video story.
- Prepare a shot list and interview questions before shooting a video story.
- Record and edit a basic news story, using interviews and b-roll in a meaningful way.
- Explain how traditional alternative story forms can be used and expanded on the Web.
- Plan the structure and multimedia elements for an online story package.

Key Terms

Build Vocab

axis line	lead room	pre-production
b-roll	leading lines	production
backpack journalism	low angle	rule of thirds
depth of field	lower-thirds titles	screen
eyeline matching	motion sequence	shot list
high angle	natural sound	storyboard
interactive graphics	pan	three-point lighting
Ken Burns effect	post-production	tilt

Before You Read...

Skim the headings of this chapter and look at each figure. After analyzing this information, write three predictions for what you think you will learn on a blank sheet of paper. Then, when you have finished reading, write a brief summary of the chapter. How do your predictions compare to your summary?

Introduction

"Try to be conspicuously accurate in everything, pictures as well as text. Truth is not only stranger than fiction, it is more interesting."

–William Randolph Hearst, American publisher

"This is a great story, Max. What kind of visual are you planning?"

"Can't we just use her yearbook portrait? I don't have a very good camera."

"It's not the camera, silly. It's what you do with it.

"That's like saying, 'I can't do math because I don't have a very good calculator.' The simplest equipment can create powerful multimedia stories, if you have the skills."

Scroll through your social media news feeds and count the number of photos and videos posted. Some are personal, some are political, some are funny or celebratory or sad. At least a few are selfies. Our lives are rich in images. They appear on billboards, on the sides of buses, in advertisements, through television, in your textbooks and in your teachers' PowerPoint presentations.

We seem to trust pictures. We say: *A picture is worth a thousand words. The eyes do not lie. I have to see it to believe it.* These clichés show the extent to which we trust our eyes to tell us the truth. This makes visual journalism powerful. Visual journalists can take their audience to a unique place and a unique time, to a specific moment. With a simple image they show, rather than tell, a story.

But do photos and audio recordings give us the pure truth? Not exactly. Al Tompkins, a veteran TV broadcaster and broadcast news instructor, explains that what our eyes see and how we perceive what we are seeing are two different things. "While vision goes on between the eye and the brain," Tompkins writes in his book *Aim for the Heart: Write, Shoot, Report and Produce for TV and Multimedia*, "perception is a process entirely within the mind."

Tompkins explains our perception is shaped by our previous personal experiences and our ideas and values. This makes multimedia storytelling more complicated than simply pulling out a cell phone and releasing a shutter or pushing *record*. It requires thoughtful, thorough preparation to decide when, where and how to shoot or record.

To craft an experience for your audience, focus less on the equipment you have—or do not have—and more on the skills and knowledge you need as you choose your media and create journalism that transports them. Photos, audio, videos or interactive graphics, when carefully collected and edited, have the power to engage your audience's emotions. It is not that *seeing* is believing, but that *feeling* is believing. When we feel something, we are more likely to be convinced.

Photojournalism

The job of the photojournalist is to transport the viewer, to take him to places he cannot or will not go. Photojournalists around the world risk their lives and sacrifice a great deal to allow viewers to see things that enlighten and uplift them, that anger and move them, that compel them to action. Though some freelance photojournalists work for themselves, more are employed by news organizations, which rely on them for images that tell a story in a glance.

The Photojournalist's Duty

The Supreme Court made a monumental ruling in 1954 meant to end school segregation. That ruling was tested three years later in Little Rock, Arkansas, where a group of African-American high school students, now known as the Little Rock 9, attempted to integrate all-white Central High School in the face of strong opposition from the white community and local government officials.

One of the nine, Elizabeth Eckford, did not know that the other eight were gathering to travel to school together, so Elizabeth journeyed to Central High School alone. She found herself face-to-face with an angry mob blocking the entrance to the school. But Elizabeth and the mob were not the only ones present. Photojournalist Will Counts also was there on assignment from The Arkansas Democrat. Wielding a 35mm camera that allowed him to shoot 36 frames before reloading, Counts' camera allowed everyone in America to witness what Elizabeth faced (Figure 16.1).

A 2007 Vanity Fair article titled "Through a Lens, Darkly" describes the power of Counts' photo

> *Few pictures capture an epoch. But in the contorted, hate-filled face of a young white girl named Hazel Bryan standing behind Elizabeth, screaming epithets at her, Counts encapsulated the rage of the Jim Crow South. And even behind her large sunglasses—her eyes were as sensitive as the rest of her—Elizabeth embodied something else: the dignity, and determination, and wisdom, and stoicism, with which black Americans tried to change their lot. It's all there in one picture, in a way white America could readily understand when it landed on its front stoops.*

What if Counts had not photographed that moment? Would Americans have understood the anger and determination present in Little Rock? Would the president have sent federal troops to protect the Little Rock 9? We will never know. But we do know that Elizabeth Eckford's tall, straight stance

Figure 16.1 Strong photojournalism transports the viewer to another place and time, helping them to understand and feel what the moment was like.

Will Counts Collection: Indiana University Archives (P0026600)

and dignified stride was photographed beside the contorted, screaming face of Hazel Bryan, and that photograph told a story that moved a nation.

That is the power of photojournalism—to show in clear images the experiences of others who are distant from us. Photojournalists, video journalists and audio journalists have the power to tap into our senses and make us feel. In some cases they change our minds, in other cases, they change our hearts. In rare cases, they change the world.

How to "Be There"

Rookie multimedia journalists miss opportunities because they worry they may be conspicuous or offend others. While there are important ethical and legal considerations (see Chapters 3 and 4), more often rookies miss shots because they are simply uncomfortable. Here are four signs that a photojournalist is uncomfortable shooting an event:

- She relies on a zoom lens rather than getting close to the action.
- He stops to review the shots he has taken instead of shooting continuously.
- She stops shooting during breaks and pauses.
- He never turns his back to the action, which means he does not take any reaction shots.

You may feel awkward at first, but the more you photograph or record sound, the more comfortable you and those around you will become with your presence. You will be conspicuous for only a few moments and then become no more noticeable than wallpaper. When that happens, you will begin to get powerful, candid shots and important sound.

So how do you become that all-but-invisible journalist in the right spot at the right time? Research, pause, interview, get close and back up.

Research

Do your homework before you shoot. Talk to the subjects you will be photographing, learn about the event and try to predict possible shots. Scout the location, taking note of angles, lighting and obstacles, such as goal posts. Review others' shots from the same venue. If you cannot visit the site in advance, look it up online.

Pause

Try to arrive early, but pause for a moment before you pull out your camera and start shooting. Walk around looking for the best places to position yourself. Think about the lighting as it will be during the event, so you can choose the best settings for your camera and so you will not be shooting into bright lights. If you are shooting at an event where special authorization is required to access certain areas, request press credentials and wear a press pass.

Interview

The best photographers talk to the people they are photographing. They ask them questions about what they are doing and why. This information may allow you to be in the right place at the right time. It also will help you write stronger captions.

Get Close

Get even closer. Where you are is more important than your equipment, your zoom lens or your boom microphone. Rookies try to shoot basketball *from the bleachers!* You need to be in the action to capture the action. That will only happen if you muster the courage to get as close as you can without getting yelled at. And if you do get yelled at, that is a sign you are in the right place.

Back Up

"OK, do I get close or do I step back?" Both. Darren Durlach, 2009 National Press Photographers Association photographer of the year, says that on every assignment he chants to himself "Tight, medium, wide, action, reaction, get the moment." Photographers need

- tight shots, or close up shots that reveal details;
- medium shots, or standard distance shots that duplicate how most people see the world most of the time;
- wide shots that capture a complete scene and give a sense of the scope or scale of a location;
- action shots that focus on what is happening; and
- reaction shots that show the emotions of those at the scene and convey its impact.

Take a look at Los Angeles Times photographer Marcus Yam's set of photographs for a story about the crew of the Coast Guard boat Blackfin, who search the coastal waters for smugglers (Figure 16.2 on the next page). The story follows the crew through a two-day excursion. Each photo tells a different part of the story. The wide shots give the viewer context and help to set the scene, while the tight shots bring the viewer close, turning the crew into individual characters and highlighting the feeling of anticipation. Together, the photos allow the reader to ride along with the crew, giving them access that they would not otherwise have.

With a clear idea of where you need to be, you are ready for the basics of photo composition and editing.

YOUR TURN

1. You are planning to shoot photographs backstage during a drama performance. What shots could you plan? Develop a shot list of wide, medium, tight, action and reaction shots you might get during the performance.
2. **Going Deeper.** What kind of research would help you to prepare for this shoot? Who should you speak with in advance?

Figure 16.2 Using a variety of shot distances and techniques, Marcus Yam gives the viewer an inside look as members of the Coast Guard perform their duties.

Courtesy of Marcus Yam, the Los Angeles Times

Working with Photos: Composition

Great design requires great photos, composed well, shot well and edited well. These basic principles apply equally to photography and videography.

Rule of Thirds

Artists, architects and designers have long known the power of thirds and that our eye is attracted to images arranged according to this principle. Look at Figure 16.3. Imagine that the image is split into three equal parts horizontally and three parts vertically. When the center of interest in your photo, or in art, architecture or design, is placed at one of the points where those imaginary lines intersect, the eye is drawn to the image and the image is more pleasing. That is the power of the **rule of thirds.**

Figure 16.3 Using the rule of thirds can make an already strong photo even more powerful.

Photo by Tori Caudill, The Crimson Crier, Sparkman High School

Leading Lines

The world around us is filled with lines—the lines of a road, the line of the horizon, the line of an arm pointing at something. Skillful photographers consciously look for the lines within a potential image, then use them to draw their audience's eye to what the photographer wants them to see (Figure 16.4). These are **leading lines** because they naturally lead the eye. In addition, lines inside of photos can be used to lead the reader's eye to another element on the page, for instance the headline or the text.

Photo by Ashley Potts, Legend, Centreville High School

Figure 16.4 The lines of the bookcase lead the reader's eye to the subject.

Grounds

Photographers pay attention to the foreground, what is toward the front of the photo or in front of the subject, and the background, what is at the back of the photo or behind the subject. Many award-winning photos use both the foreground and the background to tell parts of the story (Figure 16.5). But if the background does not contribute to the story, shoot so you minimize its power to distract your viewer's eye. For instance, you can move right or left so a pole behind your subject's head is out of the frame.

Lighting

Generally the light, either sunlight or artificial light, should come from behind you, the photographer, as you shoot. The light will

Photo by Chris Bull, El Paisano, Westlake High School

Figure 16.5 Both the background and foreground of this image help tell the story of an athlete and his dedicated, solitary workouts in the football stadium.

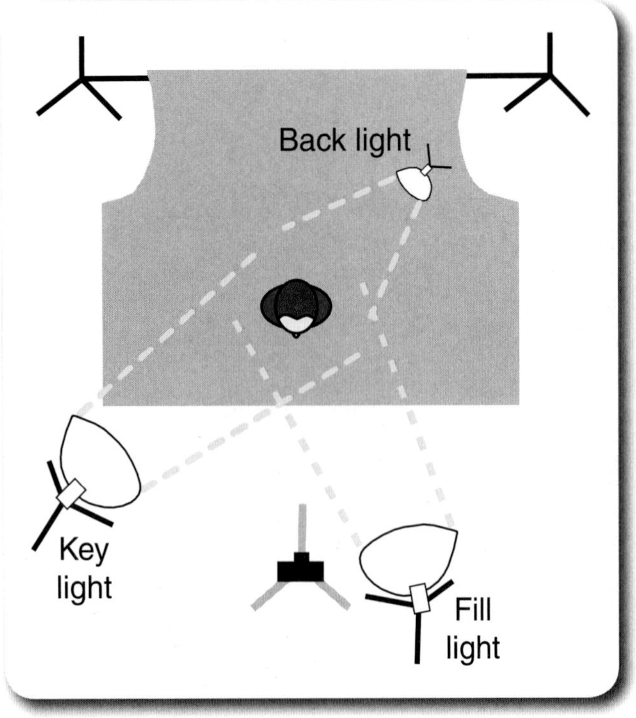

Figure 16.6 Together, the key, fill and back lights form a three-point lighting setup. *When might you use a three-point lighting setup?*

illuminate your subject and not create harsh shadows or turn her into a silhouette as light from the side or the back will. When you cannot control the direction of the light on your subject, for instance in a classroom with overhead lighting or outside at high noon, you can bounce light back onto your source with reflectors or use fill lights, less powerful lights, to fill in the shadows. Sometimes harsh shadows cast by just one light coming from above or at the side can create dramatic effects and make strong portraits.

If you have the luxury of shooting a still subject, for instance in a formal interview, try using **three-point lighting** (Figure 16.6). The key light, the main and brightest light, is used to illuminate your subject's face and should be placed in front and slightly to the side of your interviewee. Use a less-powerful fill light on the opposite side to illuminate some of the shadows so that you do not lose all of the subject's facial details on the side away from the main light. The back light, usually the smallest of the three lights, goes behind your subject and toward him. It tends to separate him from the background, giving the video or photo a three-dimensional appearance.

Angle

Rookies tend to shoot every photo from the same angle, usually by standing and pointing the camera at eye level. These become visually boring over time. Vary your shots by shooting from a **high angle**, from above your subject or a **low angle**, from below your subject (Figure 16.7). Be aware each angle can carry meaning. High angle shots can make the

Figure 16.7 Varying the angle of your shots creates visually interesting photographs and a new perspective.

Photo by Valorie King, Buffalo, Haltom High School

Photo by Hannah Kunz, The Featherduster, Westlake High School

Photo by Stefano Byer, The Harbinger, Shawnee Mission East High School

Figure 16.8 Keep your eyes open for opportunities to frame your subjects within the photograph. *What are other common objects that could be used to frame subjects?*

subject seem powerless or struggling. Low angle shots can make them seem daunting, imposing or threatening. Experiment with angles to give your audience fresh perspectives.

Framing

Skilled photographers frame shots using elements within the environment. Shooting through a window, through a barbed wire fence or into a mirror can provide drama to your image. The frame focuses your viewer's eye where you want it to go (Figure 16.8).

Patterns and Symmetry

You are surrounded by symmetry—man-made symmetry, such as a house with two identical windows flanking a centered door, and natural symmetry, such as the walls of a narrow canyon. This repetition of shapes can make strong, interesting shots. Patterns surround us in similar ways, sometimes in obvious places like fabric curtains or brick walkways, and sometimes in more surprising places, like people waiting in line who coincidentally wear alternating colors.

The journalistic power of symmetry and pattern comes when the pattern is broken by an unexpected element (Figure 16.9). Our eye is drawn to a singular red coat in a sea of gray, or the pink-haired student in a cafeteria mob of neutral colors, or when all the adults are saluting to the left and a child kneels to the right watching ladybugs.

Photo by Danielle Norton, Hauberk, Shawnee Mission East High School

Figure 16.9 Santa's red suit stands out in the sea of black and blue choral outfits and draws the eye to him.

Depth of Field

Which do you find to be more emotionally powerful—Figure 16.10a or 16.10b? If you like b, your attention may have been drawn to the face of the main subject because the photographer used a shallow **depth of field**. Focusing sharply on the face leaves the background, with all of its distractions, blurry. This technique works well in portraits and helps to eliminate irrelevant elements in the foreground or background.

YOUR TURN

1. Look around the space you are currently in, and think like a photographer. Where do you see lines you could use as leading lines? What could you use to frame a shot? Where are the patterns or symmetry within your space?
2. **Going Deeper.** Choose an object small enough to easily move and take a series of photos of the object to demonstrate your understanding of each of the concepts in the composition section, above.

Working with Photos: Editing

While we strive for crisp, perfectly framed shots, most photos benefit from editing. (See Chapter 4 to learn about ethical concerns involved with editing photos.) Whenever possible, photographers should edit their own photos so they can keep them true to what they witnessed at the scene. The following tools and principles should be considered as you edit your photos.

Cropping

All but the most exceptional photos become more powerful through cropping. Cropping allows you to adjust the borders so your center of

Figure 16.10 The eye tends to wander from the subject to the background when a greater depth of field is used (a). A shallow depth of field helps focus on the subject and blurs the background (b). *When might a shallow depth of field be used to create a strong photograph? A greater depth of field?*

a b

interest is at the thirds. You can eliminate distractions from the edges of the image, reduce its size, change its orientation and communicate or emphasize a topic. If the photo is clearly focused, cropping may allow you to zoom in on a detail, such as the expression on a subject's face (Figure 16.11).

Cutting Out

The lasso or selection tools in Photoshop give photographers and designers the ability to cut away the background of an object or person in a photo (Figure 16.12 on the next page). This process requires incredible attention to detail, so designers zoom in on the computer screen to see small details when they use this tool. For this tool to work well, the edges of the image need to be clearly distinguishable from the background. If you expect to create a cutout from a photo, shoot the image on a contrasting, solid-colored background to make it easier to lasso.

Lead Room

In a photograph that depicts motion, such as a sports photo, crop the photo to include what photographers call **lead room**, or open space in front of the subject. In a photograph of a running lacrosse player, leave room in front of the player for the player to "run." Do not run her off the

Figure 16.11 Cropping the original photo (a) eliminates the distractions and follows the rule of thirds, allowing the subject of the photograph to shine (b).

a. Original photo

Cropping tool

b. Cropped

Figure 16.12 The lasso tool can be used to remove the background, creating an interesting cutout image. *How might you incorporate cutouts into your publication?*

Lasso tool

edge of the photo (Figure 16.13). Lead room will give the photograph balance and direct the reader's eye in the direction the subject is running. In strong designs, the text of the story is often placed in that direction.

Screens

Combining images and text can make for a powerful design. Placing a headline, the text of a story or a caption on top of an image may draw the reader into the text. A **screen** is an image or other design element used as the background for text (Figure 16.14). The readability of the text must be your first concern when you place it over a screen. To make text easier to read, apply effects, like a drop shadow or a transparent shape behind the text.

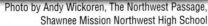

Photo by Andy Wickoren, The Northwest Passage, Shawnee Mission Northwest High School

Figure 16.13 Leaving an appropriate amount of lead room (a) makes the image feel balanced and avoids running the subject off the edge of the photo (b).

NEWS

3.78 inches.

BY BRIAN FAN AND JADY WEI

3.78 inches is the level of rain Cupertino received from the most recent series of showers, in late November and early December. The violent downpour prompted many to inquire whether the national drought could have been ameliorated, or possibly even remedied. Yet, according to the National Weather Service Forecast, a healthy level of rain for the November-December season is an average of 5.94 inches.

We're nowhere close.

While a handful of MVHS students believe that the recent lengthy period of rain has remedied the national drought, evidence actually proves otherwise.

"The drought was pretty severe, and it has been going on for three years. We're just starting to head out of a three-year drought," AP Environmental Science teacher Andrew Goldenkranz said. "The simplest way to think about it is that right now, the recent rains have resolved about one-sixth of our water needs."

A common misconception is that the drought is measured by the depth of the reservoir. However, because people can easily move water in and out of the reservoir at any time, this is not an adequate tool for gauging the severity of national drought.

Instead, climatologists measure the drought by the height of the snowpack, which is, in some ways, similar to an actual reservoir. Snow sits up on the ground and slowly percolates into the earth. Therefore, for drought and water conservation purposes, snow would be the most beneficial source because it moves more slowly than water into the aquifer.

"When it rains hard, like it did in late November, early December, the rain starts to run off and therefore runs quickly down into the bay, where we can't use it anymore," Goldenkranz said. "So heavy rain is actually not as useful to us in terms of drought as moderate amounts of rain over a long period of time."

Geographical impacts of the drought

So far, the amount of precipitation the district has garnered with the rain season is not sufficient to pull our nation from the drought.

"We have some parts of the state which are more affected than others," Goldenkranz said. "There are wetter and drier areas, and areas where literally the water has been turned off. Here, they may just say, 'Remember to conserve your water' or 'Please don't wash your car.'"

Drawing from historical evidence, wet and dry season are cyclical. According to a prognosis issued by the Weather Channel, the United States is possibly moving into an El Niño year, though prospects may wane in the February to April period.

"Typically, droughts happen in around three-year cycles," Goldenkranz said. "So we can see that we may be moving into a short-term wetter cycle."

DID YOU KNOW? *CALIFORNIA HAD ITS WORST DROUGHT IN THE 1980s*

According to Goldenkranz, California — at its origins — was settled over a geologically wetter area of land during a comparatively wetter period, which explains why the regions is relatively less parched compared to neighboring states. In Northern California, household water supply comes solely from the Sierra Nevada. In Southern California, people getting a large proportion of water from the Colorado River, along with areas of Nevada and Arizona, thus amplifying the competition and exacerbating water shortage.

In other regions like Las Vegas, Sacramento, Phoenix and Los Angeles, the municipal governments have already begun to pay residents to replace their lawn with more natural landscaping or a fake lawn. In addition, the Santa Clara Valley Water District sanctioned a high-efficiency toilet rebate program, which offers refunds for individuals that install premium model high efficiency toilets in their homes.

The drought was 'preventable'

California's history has been one littered with droughts at intervals, and the last notable drought was in the 1980s.

"It's a natural drought. If you want to blame anyone, blame Mother Nature," Information Officer, Doug Carlson said, from the Public Affair Office of the CA Department of Water Resources.

Many people point to the fact that we are only utilizing around 50 percent of the total water available from rainfall. This water, which gradually drains into groundwater and the bay, is called environmental water. Some contend that had districts used this environmental water, we would have prevented much of the negative effects of the drought.

"Environmental water is used for maintaining the ecosystem. There are animals that can only survive in a specific pH or salinity of water and environmental water is nature's way of maintaining that balance. If we don't let water naturally flow into waterways, we will kill the fish."

'We aren't doing all we can to help'

The focus of California's water management is to increase transportation of water.

"There are places where there is literally no water, and we're trying to transport water into those area," Carlson said. "We're also trying to increase the efficient use of water rather than preventing its use altogether."

The California Water Management Department is also requiring their own facilities to cut back on their use of water.

"We want the to put in place a plan to reduce their usage of water. If they can't do that, then the department comes in and does it for them," Carlson said.

DID YOU KNOW? *MORE THAN HALF THE STATE DEPENDS ON OUTSIDE SOURCES OF WATER*

Data on the California Water Management's website have shown that we need to achieve at least 150 percent of the average rainfall in order to remedy the drought. Rainfall collection stations reveal that while the rainfall has been doing well earlier in the rainfall season, a month long period of dry weather means that we may actually fall below the mean rainfall line. The only subsequent conclusion is that, as a state, we are still severely parched.

The phrase "ridiculously resilient ridge", coined by the California Weather Blog, comes into play when discussing how the drought appeared. The phrase describes natural circumstances of California's location prevents clouds from dumping rainwater into the mountains, resulting in snow

Which is why our water usage needs to change.

"Imagine if you had a bathroom sink where when you finish brushing your teeth, it says 'You used 31 ounces of water just now,'" Goldenkranz said. "Were you aware of that? The minute you start getting into that feedback cycle, that's when we'll finally start using less."

The drought seems to be far from over, but recent changes in attitude towards water usuage may help alleviate what may be one of the worst droughts in California's history.

b.fan@elestoque.org | j.wei@elestoque.org

STEVENS CREEK AND BLACKBERRY FARM *Bottom: The water levels under the bridge show a dramatic decrease. Left: The bottom of the creek and the local underwater flora has been revealed for most of the drought. Right: The water levels at Blackberry farm under the bridge show a dramatic decrease.*

8 EL ESTOQUE FEBRUARY 4, 2015 9

Courtesy of El Estoque, Monta Vista High School

Figure 16.14 The screen used here helps solidify the "where" lead used in the story.

Captions

Photos, especially news photos and candid shots, require captions. Captions are important points of entry into your story for your reader. Eye-tracking studies found that the audience's eye goes first to the largest image on the page and second to the caption. Captions answer the questions that develop as readers view the image: Who is this person? What is she doing? What meaning should I take from this? Your caption's job is to answer those questions while also pulling your audience into the accompanying story.

Most captions follow a simple two-sentence format, with room for creativity in the second sentence (see Chapter 7). A caption can introduce intriguing details, create suspense or give a face to issues being explored in the accompanying article. Remember that the reader is likely to read the caption *before* she reads the story.

Video Journalism

Even the simplest video capturing device allows videographers to capture high-definition video that can look professional as long as you follow principles of journalism, visual composition and video editing. Video journalism overlaps photojournalism. Everything you have learned about photo composition applies to video, and it is possible to create high-quality films with even the simplest of tools. Independent film writer and director Sean Baker premiered a full-length feature film at the Sundance Film Festival in 2015 shot entirely on iPhones.

What Makes a Good Video Story?

Is a story a good candidate for video storytelling? Ask:

1. Is there anything to see?
2. Is there action?
3. Will there be good natural sounds?
4. Are there interesting "characters" to serve as the face of the story?

A school board meeting might be an important news event, but unless a parade of people shows up to protest, it will be difficult to make it into a compelling *visual* story. An actual parade, however, is a different matter. A water balloon fight? A robotics competition? These would each make compelling video stories.

Your Turn

1. Look through your school's announcements or bulletin and search for stories that would make good video stories based on the answers to the four questions above.
2. **Going Deeper.** In your search through the announcements, look for stories that do not initially seem like good video stories, then brainstorm ways to make them better candidates for video. Who might be a good face for the story? What action that relates to the story could you capture? Is there a compelling setting? Strong natural sound?

Once you have determined that a story is worth covering using video, plan your video. Production involves three stages:

1. **Pre-production**: This is the planning stage. Contact sources, conduct preliminary research, storyboard and plan shots.
2. **Production**: Time to pack up your equipment and go out to shoot. Collect interviews, b-roll, ambient sound and produce any graphics you might need.
3. **Post-production**: The stage when you will put it all together. Import video into an editing program, find or produce music and package the story in a compelling way.

Depending on the length and complexity of the video project, this process may take several weeks or just a few hours. In fact, most television news stations will go through this complete process multiple times each day, with stories filmed in the afternoon appearing on the evening news.

Getting Ready: Pre-Production

Rookie broadcast journalists often use their pre-production time to prepare and pack equipment, check batteries and grab lights. These are important, even crucial, tasks, but the best video journalists do these tasks and also prepare in other important ways.

Before filming

1. **Scout the location or predict relevant circumstances.** If you are doing a story about the football team's interesting pregame rituals, which include singing on the bus, you may not be able to climb on the exact bus they will take to their next game, but another bus will help you decide where you should sit, what you should shoot and what angles work well. If possible, consider the natural light at that time of day.
2. **Make a shot list.** A **shot list** is a checklist of shots you want. Make sure your list includes at least one tight, medium, wide, action and reaction shot.
3. **Write open-ended interview questions.** You may not use these exact questions, but well-phrased queries invite full responses from people as you are filming. Avoid questions that bring a yes or no answer. They make for boring video. For the football rituals story, ask the coach or players what they thought when they first heard the singing, what the players get out of the ritual, how the rituals prepare them for the game or why they chose specific songs.
4. **Develop a storyboard.** You cannot predict exactly what you will shoot or what people will say as you film, but you will be able to predict at least a few motion sequences, for instance the players boarding the bus. Use a **storyboard** (Figure 16.15 on the next page) to plan the shots you need to make to complete a sequence: wide shot of the line of players entering, closeup on the players' feet stepping up from the curb into the bus, an over-the-shoulder of the players as they load in from the driver's perspective, the back of the players at the back of the line as they take their seats and bus door closing from the inside. That is one complete action sequence that is guaranteed to happen, will set the scene for your audience and can be planned in advance.
5. **Charge, pack and check off your equipment.** Charge all batteries and all spares well in advance. Create a master list of all equipment you use for shoots, including cameras, batteries, lights and reflectors, memory cards, microphones, headphones, rechargers and whatever else you ever use. Keep a copy of your list in your camera bag and highlight the items you will need on this particular shoot. Before you leave, check off each item on your list. When you come back from a shoot, add to the master list anything you wished you had brought so you can consider bringing it on the next shoot.

Production: Getting the Shots

Whatever the story, you are likely to have four basic components:

- Stand-ups or voiceovers: a reporter, either in front of the camera or by narrating written copy off camera, directly addresses the viewer
- Interviews: subjects respond to questions from the reporter, usually presenting different perspectives
- **B-roll**: any footage that is not of an interview but illustrates the story, such as detail shots, establishing shots and action sequences

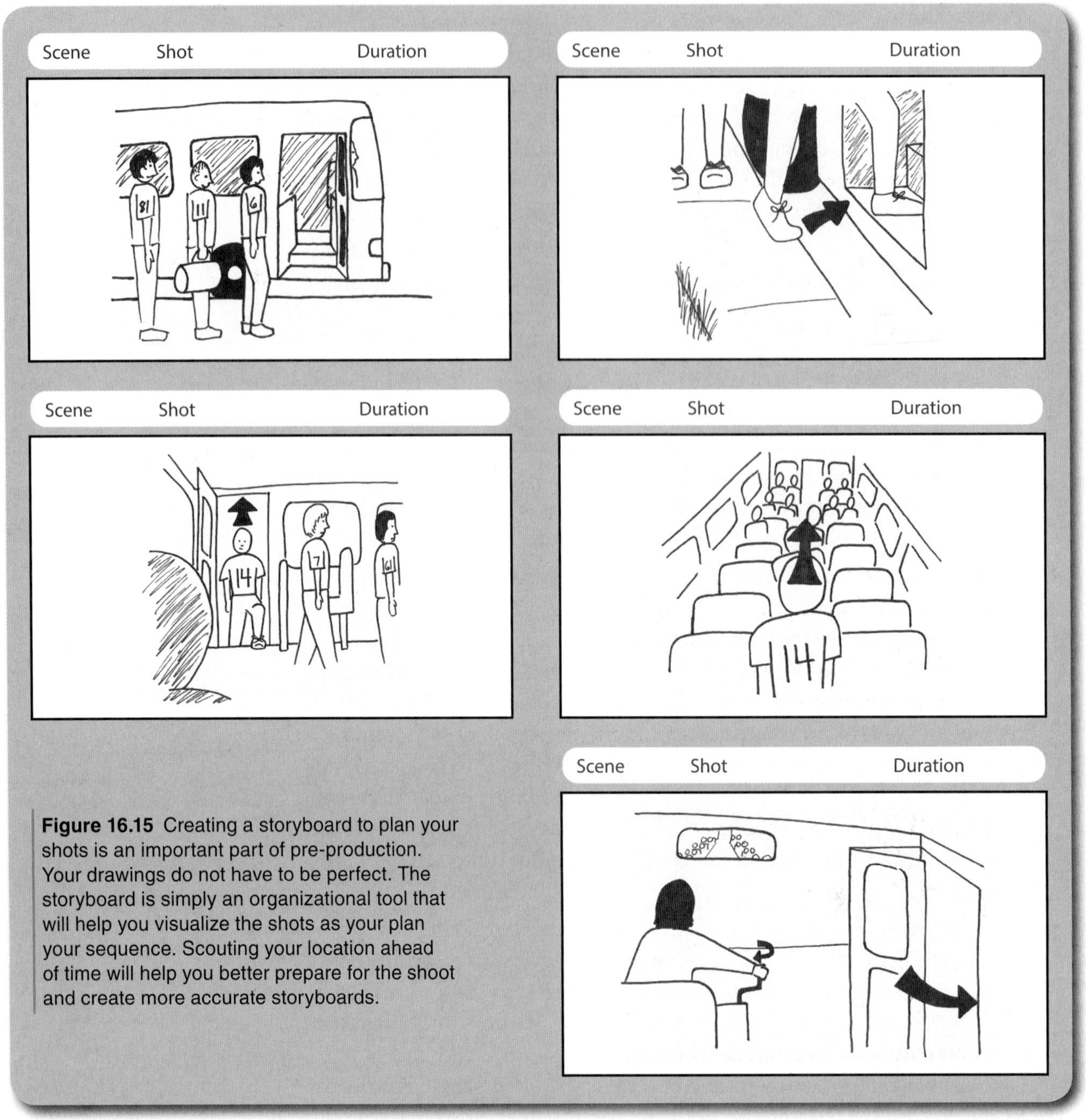

Figure 16.15 Creating a storyboard to plan your shots is an important part of pre-production. Your drawings do not have to be perfect. The storyboard is simply an organizational tool that will help you visualize the shots as your plan your sequence. Scouting your location ahead of time will help you better prepare for the shoot and create more accurate storyboards.

- **Motion sequences**: a subcategory of b-roll; a series of shots that, when combined in logical order, convey a complete action in compressed time

To make sense of these four components, consider the football team story. Here is one possible outline for the video:

- Opening sequence of the players loading on to the bus while the reporter narrates a lead that creates interest or suspense.
- Cut to team singing loudly.
- Cut to player interview explaining how they began the tradition.
- Cut away during interview to show tight, medium and wide shots of players singing.

- Cut back to the player, who finishes the interview by saying, "I just feel a little sorry for our driver!"
- Cut to shot of driver looking into bus' rearview mirror and laughing. Audio of interview with driver begins.
- Cut to driver interview (with driver sitting in bus seat, but bus is parked and empty).
- Cut away to b-roll of driver on the full bus, interactions with players.
- Cut to interview with coach.
- Cut away to b-roll of the coach interacting with players on the bus. Interview with the coach continues as coach talks about how the rituals affect their game mentality.
- Cut to b-roll of the coach interacting with players on the sideline of a game.
- Cut back to players singing on the bus after the game as the reporter narrates the ending.
- Cut to a motion sequence of players exiting and walking away from the bus.

This is just one of thousands of sequences a reporter could create, but in this example, the story begins and ends with the bus because the ritual—singing before games—happens on the bus.

Production: Working with Video

Nearly everything you have learned about shooting photographs—lighting, leading lines, framing, grounds, angle, rule of thirds—applies to composing video as well. Yet beyond that, videographers must also capture motion and collect audio as well. The following concepts will help you to do this successfully.

And Now... Closer to Home

Why Make Lists?

Video stories involve risk. If a reporter who is writing a story misses a key scene or moment, she can ask someone who was present to describe it and then recreate the scene using quotes from the witnesses. A broadcast journalist who misses that moment, though, has no second chance. It is unethical to ask participants to recreate the original moment. That is why planning during pre-production, and especially lists, are essential.

Your staff should develop a series of checklists to use for all video journalists, but especially for new ones who are heading out into the field for the first time. An equipment checklist may keep them from forgetting batteries or the headphones they need to monitor audio. A basic shot checklist will ensure that they do not come back from an assignment without establishing shots of each location or without detail shots for the b-roll to use to hide jump cuts.

Shot Distance

You have already learned the basics of shot distance—tight, medium and wide. Tight shots are closeups, and extreme closeups bring the viewer very close and focus on details. Medium shots are just as they sound—shots taken at a medium distance. This is how most of us see the world. Wide shots include not just the subject or your center of interest, but the surroundings as well. Figure 16.16 depicts the difference between the three shot distances.

Establishing Shot

The establishing shots play an important role in video stories; they tell the reader where, and sometimes when, the action takes place. If you are doing a story about a drama performance, you may want to have several shots of the exterior of the theater, which may include wide shots of the whole building and tight shots of the marquee.

Head Room and Lead Room

Head and lead room refer to the space you leave above a subject's head and in front of a moving subject, respectively. Unless you want to bring the viewer very close to your subject as in an emotional moment, you should leave some space above the interviewee's head (Figure 16.17).

Figure 16.16 Varying your shot distance will help create visual interest and focus on both the subject and her surroundings.

Photo by Grant Shorin, The Viking, Palo Alto High School

a. Wide

b. Medium

c. Tight

Photo by Josie Pringle, Bryant High School Hornet Yearbook

Figure 16.17 Creating head room above your subject helps prevent the shot from feeling cramped or off-balance.

When you have a subject in motion, or if your subject is faced at an angle to the camera, leave space in the direction the subject is moving or looking. This prevents the shot from feeling cramped and off-balance.

Shot Movement

On occasion you may need to move your camera to capture an action or create a specific effect. You can zoom in or out on your subject, **tilt** the camera, move it vertically up or down, or **pan** the camera, moving it horizontally left or right. To track, move the camera alongside a moving subject using a wheeled device such as a bike, skateboard or car. Be aware that too much camera movement is jarring to your viewer. Try to move the camera no more than once and in only one direction during any sequence or clip.

Ken Burns Effect

This technique, named for renowned documentary filmmaker Ken Burns, creates the illusion of movement with still images. Burns uses historic images and documents in his films, slowing zooming in or out to focus the viewer's attention on specific details. After his groundbreaking use, the technique became known as the **Ken Burns effect**.

Natural Sound

Natural sound, also called nat sound, is the soundtrack of our daily lives. Think about what you hear in your school halls: lockers shutting, students talking and laughing, the floor squeaking under hundreds of sneakers hurrying to class. These are the natural sounds, and every story needs natural sounds to bring video or audio recordings to life. Every space in which you record will have its own natural sound, including every park, stadium, store or gym. Sometimes it is enough to simply capture the silence of a place, remembering that places are never really silent. To capture other natural sounds, you will need to get your microphone close—*very close*, within five or six inches—of the source. This may mean capturing audio separately from your video, then using your video editing program to layer over the video on a separate audio track.

Axis Line

Videographers maintain the **axis line** when they film action. Also called the 180 degree rule or the line of action, it ensures that the camera consistently films from one side of the principle subject, so that a character on the camera's right is always on the camera's right in every shot (Figure 16.18). The dotted line is an imaginary line the videographer will not cross. If she does, she risks capturing shots that, when edited together, will confuse her audience. Figure 16.19 shows two shots of the same scene that break this rule. The audience will probably wonder if the subjects have switched places and will be confused because the videographer has crossed the axis line, or line of action.

Eyeline Matching

Eyeline matching is an editing technique that assumes your audience will want to see what your subject is pointing to, looking at or talking to, if it is out of the frame, and they will want to see it in the next shot. If you shoot a cheerleader with wide eyes and her hands to her mouth, the next shot should show the end-zone fumble that caused her so much anxiety. Delaying the eyeline match risks confusing or frustrating your audience. However, a slight delay may be used to create suspense.

Figure 16.18 Observe the axis line when filming a subject to ensure the camera consistently films from one side of the main subjects. Imagine you are filming two people having a conversation. If you cross the axis line, it will look like the two people have traded places, creating a confusing shot.

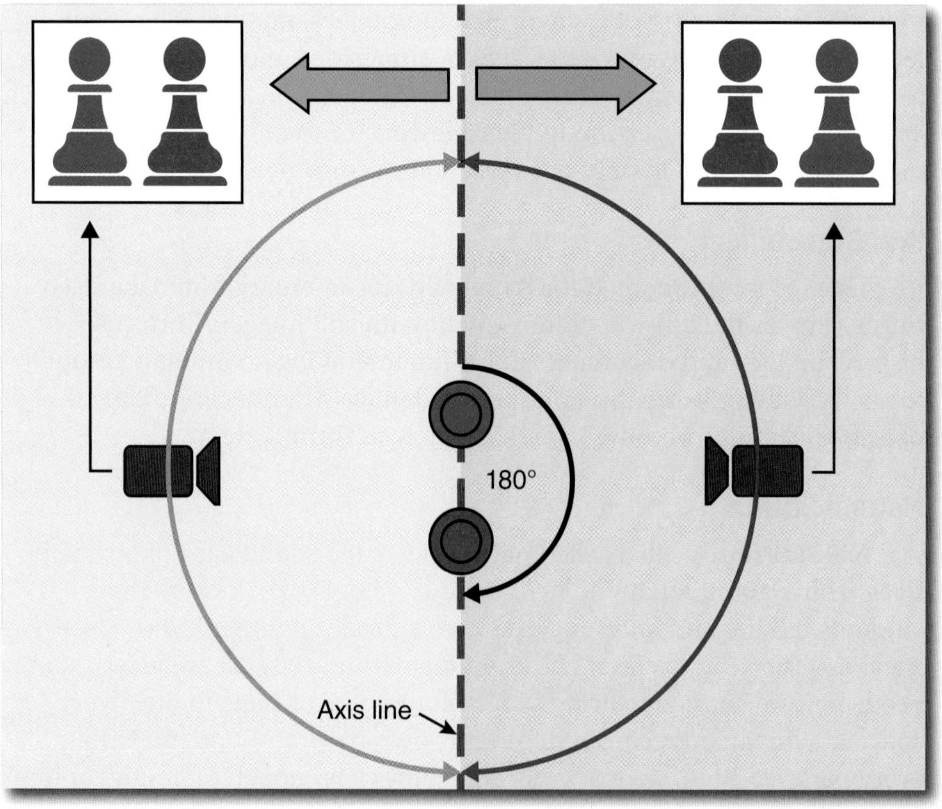

a. Camera position one

b. Camera position two

Figure 16.19 You might think that the student with the backpack moved from the right side of the shot to the left. However, it was the videographer who moved, not the students. As he moved, he crossed the axis line, leaving him with two shots that feel disjointed.

Your Turn

1. Watch a short video segment on your local news or a news-style package on ESPN or another specialized network. As you watch, search for the production strategies such as the Ken Burns effect, eyeline matching or an establishing shot used in the package and list them in your notebook, deconstructing the video package as you watch.
2. **Going Deeper.** Take a look at the list of shots from the video segment above. Which shot choices are the most interesting or surprising? Suggest why the video producers and editors made those choices.

Interviewing for Video or Radio

Interviews are the heart of video or radio journalism. As in journalism created for other media, they are the major source for your reporting, they put a face on news and issues, and they reach to the heart of the audience.

When you report on school district budget cuts, you put a face on the story by interviewing the saxophone player who feels his senior year is ruined because Jazz Band was canceled. If teachers' salaries are cut, interview a first-year teacher who is struggling to support a family and pay off student loan debt. Is standardized testing in the news? Find the mom who opted out of the tests for her children because she feels testing hurts students and is a misuse of their time.

Great interviews come from great questions. Here are seven tips to help you prepare broadcast interview questions:

1. Always, always begin with, "What is your name, and how do you spell it?"
2. Stick to open-ended questions that can lead to more thorough responses. Avoid yes-no and either-or questions. Questions that begin with "why" and "how" will lead interviewees to give explanations.

3. Ask sources to describe, remember or recreate scenes for you. For example, it is better to ask, "Can you describe what you saw when you arrived?" rather than "Did you see the fire when you arrived?"
4. When you report on technical subjects, in science or economics for instance, ask experts how they would explain the topic to an intelligent 10 year old. Ask them to use analogies and to minimize their use of technical terms.
5. Ask only one question at a time, and ask questions that are important to the story, even if you already know the answer. Your audience might not, and as an interviewer, you represent your audience.
6. Stay quiet. A great sound bite can be ruined if your own "ums," "uh-huhs" and chuckles can be heard in the interview. Smile and nod, but stay silent.
7. If you are shooting video, interview the source while he is demonstrating something for the story. The interview will be more engaging because it accompanies illustrative action, plus the interviewee is likely to be comfortable in his own element. If you are shooting audio, ask the source to describe what he is doing.

Filming great interviews is rewarding, but do not forget b-roll. Note the topics your interviewee discussed and capture b-roll to pair with those parts of the interview. If you interview the class president about the carnival fundraiser, she might mention the dunk tank, cotton candy machine and inflatable slide. Be sure to get shots of those things after your interview to use as b-roll.

Tech Tips

Videographers and sound reporters rarely get a "do-over" if they miss a vital moment. The following tips will help you get usable material on your first and only chance.

Monitor Your Audio

Journalists monitor their audio as they shoot. Otherwise they risk returning with unusable audio or no audio at all. If your camera has a headphone jack, always, *always* wear headphones to monitor your audio. However, some older DSLR cameras and most smartphones do not offer this option, so test your audio by recording a few minutes on the scene of your shoot. Play it back, listening for quality before you record your actual footage.

Stabilize the Camera

Whenever possible, use a tripod. This is especially true when shooting with a light device such as a smartphone, in which case you will need both a tripod adapter and a tripod. If a tripod is not available, look for other ways to stabilize your camera. Is there a ledge on which you can rest your elbow? A stack of books you can place under your camera? Any support is better than no support when you record.

Get the Details

Remember how to begin your interviews? Always ask this question: "What is your name, and how do you spell it?" It may seem simple or obvious, but getting the correct spelling and pronunciation on tape will reduce the potential for errors and ensure that you know how to pronounce your sources' names.

Leave Handles

As you edit you will need to cut and merge video and audio clips, transition between them and sometimes fade into or out of clips. To do that without cutting into your recorded audio, record a few seconds before and after the action. Hit record and slowly (and silently) count to three before asking your first question or capturing the action. This will give you or your editor room to edit without compromising the recording's quality.

Wait and Hold

Each clip you collect should be at least 10 seconds. That is 10 *real* seconds, a long time if you are more familiar with still photography. Count silently "one Mississippi, two Mississippi, three Mississippi ..." Frame the action in the most ideal composition, and hold the shot without moving the camera for 10 seconds. If you want three shots—for example, a wide, medium and tight shot of the same action—set each of the three shots and hold each for at least for 10 seconds or through the complete action. And remember, while you are waiting, stay silent so that you can cleanly capture the natural sound of the shot.

Anticipate Action

Skillful video journalists anticipate action and they prepare for it. Multimedia journalist Colin Mulvany writes on his blog, "When I'm shooting, I'm always running scenarios through my mind. I'm asking myself: Where's the action headed? Where do I need to position myself to be in the right spot? What shots do I need to get me from point A to point B?" If you are recording a student cooking competition, you anticipate that students will be bringing plates of food to the judges, so you move behind the judges, using their backs or shoulders to frame a shot of the student chefs approaching their table with colorful plates of food.

Action, then Reaction

In *Aim for the Heart*, Al Tompkins reminds journalists to "shoot what will go away first." If there is a flash mob in the middle of the cafeteria, make sure you capture it first because it will end first. If you miss it, the opportunity is lost. Once you have several great shots, turn around and look for the reaction shot that shows what the others in the cafeteria say and do while the flash mob appears. You will probably record students laughing and pointing, dancing or standing open-mouthed in surprise. Without their reaction, you have an incomplete picture of the event. Reaction shots are not limited to crowd shots. In sports, player reactions after a big play, a devastating loss or an upset victory may tell the story

Photos by Amol Pande, El Estoque, Monta Vista High School

a. Action **b. Reaction**

Figure 16.20 It is not enough to record the action of a key play. Continue recording to capture the player's reaction—you may find that these are your most powerful shots.

in a way action shots cannot (Figure 16.20). If you stop filming when the play ends, you will miss those emotional moments. As Tompkins writes, "An action without a reaction is only half of an action."

Shoot to Edit

Rookie video journalists tend to film too much or too little. Remember that video storytelling compresses time. If you are covering the Honors Spanish class's taco party, do not film the entire party from beginning to end in one continuous shot. Instead, shoot in manageable clips of no less than 10 seconds each that will be easy to edit together. Collect at least six minutes of footage for each one minute you expect to have in the finished video but no more than 10 minutes of footage per minute of finished video. One guideline to follow is that a three-minute video is best made from at least 18 minutes of footage but generally no more than 30 minutes.

Post-Production: Putting It Together

If pre-production is preparing the ingredients, production is cooking and post-production is plating and serving the meal. Like a gourmet chef, you combine elements that complement each other and arrange the parts in a logical order to create a satisfying experience for your audience.

You may need to write a short introduction, a few transitions, or a conclusion to tell a complete story. These may be recorded as stand-ups, filming yourself or another reporter reading the lines in front of the camera. More likely, you will record the lines separately and layer that audio over the video footage as a voiceover.

Writing for video differs from writing for print. This sentence is from a New York Times story discussing airbag recalls.

> *Lawmakers were also sharply critical of the performance of federal regulators overseeing auto safety, citing government investigations that found the National Highway Traffic Safety Administration had mishandled inquiries about Takata airbags, as well as the long-delayed recall at General Motors last year of defective cars tied to at least 117 deaths.*

And Now... Closer to Home

The Five-Shot Method

Just as still photographers memorize "Tight, medium, wide, action, reaction, get the moment," videographers memorize "Hands, face, wide, over the shoulder, creative." Remember to hold each of these shots for at least 10 seconds or through the completed action.

1. **Hands**. Get close and shoot what the hands are doing. For example, a school administrator is checking off names as students enter a dance. Show the administrator's hands flipping through the printed pages, using a finger to scan down the page and find a name, then using a highlighter to mark the name on the list.
2. **Face**. Now the viewer wants to know, "Whose hands are those?" The next shot in the sequence is of the administrator's face, a close shot, so the individual's full body is not seen. Make sure both eyes are in the shot.
3. **Wide**. Show the reader where and when the action takes place. Show the administrators sitting at a table at the entrance, and show part of the line of students waiting to be checked in. Follow the 180 degree rule and do not cross the axis line you established, so if the administrator is photographed from his left in the previous shots, he should still be facing left in your wider shot.
4. **Over-the-shoulder**. Use the administrator's shoulder as a frame and give the viewer a shot of the action from the point of view of your subject, the administrator. Capture part of the administrator's shoulder and the back of her head in the foreground, with the check-in list and his hands in the middle ground and students lined up in the background.
5. **Creative**. Potentially the best shot in the sequence, this shot may use lines, angles, lighting or framing. Capture a visually unique part of the story. If you are shooting a dance check-in sequence, use the long, winding line as a leading line to the administrator who is at the top-right center of interest, using the rule of thirds.

Hands

Face

Wide

Over-the-shoulder

Creative

Courtesy of Amy Ding, Monta Vista High School

In print, the sentence is not too difficult to understand, but it would not be a good broadcast sentence because

- It is too long for most people to read aloud in one breath.
- It is a complex sentence with multiple subordinate clauses that make it hard for a listener to grasp.
- It contains too much information for the listener to take in all at once, and listeners do not have the luxury of re-reading.

When you construct broadcast sentences

1. Use short, simple sentences.
2. Lead with the subject and verb.
3. Do not use words you would not use in conversation. Eliminate jargon as much as possible.
4. Read it aloud and edit it using your ear.

Rewritten for video, the same passage is much easier to read.

Lawmakers criticized federal regulators tasked with overseeing auto safety. They pointed to investigations that showed Takata airbag inquiries were mishandled by the National Highway Traffic Safety Administration. They also cited delays in recalls of defective cars by General Motors. Those cars, recalled last year, were tied to at least 117 deaths.

The same principles apply in writing for radio. National Public Radio's Jonathan Kern says, "Remember: when you are on the air, you are communicating with one person at a time." Audio journalists should write as though they are talking to a friend.

Once you have gathered footage, recorded voiceovers and secured copyright-free music or still images, it is time to put it all together. This stage of post-production requires judgment and careful decision making. You may also need to go back to an earlier stage of the process to collect more footage, record another voiceover to use as a transition, or to grab

YOUR TURN

1. Rewrite these print sentences for broadcast.

   Principal Wendy Scott announced yesterday that this year will be the first in which juniors, who have gone untested in the areas of social studies and science for the past four years, will be required to take the state standardized test, and their test scores will be used by colleges and universities to determine their eligibility for admission, though the scores will not be the sole admission criteria.

2. **Going Deeper.** Now try writing the introductory script for an event happening at your school. Remember to follow the four tips for writing for broadcast.

another interview the story needs. You will also decide how to pair the visual (what the viewer sees) with the verbal (what she hears).

Visual-verbal pairing can be difficult for beginning video journalists. Instinctually, you try to "match" audio to video. In *Aim for the Heart*, Tompkins reminds video journalists that "words should explain pictures."

> *The words should tell viewers something they would not know about the pictures, even if they were standing next to the photojournalist when the pictures were taken. When words and pictures compete, the pictures win. But when they work together… the words make the pictures even more powerful and meaningful.*

Just as photo captions should not state the obvious, the reporter's words over video should add significant or interesting information. If you show football players singing on the bus and the reporter cuts in to say, "The players have made a ritual of singing before games. Here they are, singing Aretha Franklin's 'Respect,'" the viewer learns next to nothing.

Instead add information from your interviews and observations:

- *Senior Cody Jones acts as DJ, beat boxing in the background to keep them together.*
- *The captains' create a song list before the ride, but sometimes they improvise if the mood calls for it.*
- *Juniors Juan Gomez and Darryl Shaw can hit the high, long notes.*

With those details written into the narrative, the viewer gets value from both the words and the picture, and that multisensory experience increases engagement. That is how you hook your viewers.

Post-Production: Editing

Video editing software allows you to assemble all your clips, sound, stills, voiceovers and stand-ups into compressed time, so your audience understands the story and feels its impact.

Rough Cut

Create a rough cut by arranging collected clips in a logical order that is about as long as you intend your finished piece to be. This is something like copying chunks of your notes into a rough outline. It is not yet time to worry about specific transitions.

Tracks

Most video editing software allows you to use at least two tracks, so you can layer content. Each track may contain audio, such as music or recorded voiceovers, video clips or graphics. Content placed on different tracks at the same point in the video will play simultaneously. While voiceover on one track and video clips on a second track may work well together, guard against overwhelming your audience with a cluttered visual frame or too much competing audio.

Cutaways

A cutaway allows you to continue the audio from one clip while moving to the video of another clip. For instance, you can break up a long interview with a softball coach by cutting away to game footage that shows the player she is discussing. The audience continues to hear the coach while it watches the player. Cutaways visually break up long interview clips and hide jump cuts.

Jump Cuts

When two similar video clips that portray the same subject in the same setting are cut together, the effect can be jarring to the audience. Think of cutting out part of an interview and butting the two remaining clips up against each other. The clips are clearly not continuous and so they draw the audience's attention to your editing. The audience may wonder what was cut out or how the person was able to shift instantaneously from his right hip to his left. Video journalists avoid abrupt jump cuts by cutting away from the interview to b-roll or, if you have more than one camera, by cutting to another angle. If neither of those options is available, utilize an obvious transition like a cross dissolve, in which one clip fades out while the other fades in.

Transitions

Transitions are used between clips to move from one to another. The simplest transition is a cut, in which one clip ends just as another begins. You do not need to do anything to create this transition other than place two video clips next to each other on the editing program's timeline. Other simple transitions include fade out/in or cross dissolve. Usually the simplest transition is the best choice.

Shot-Reverse-Shot

Shot-reverse-shot is a method of eyeline matching often used to portray a conversation between two people. The first shot shows the subject facing one direction, the next shot shows a second subject facing the opposite direction, and the following shot returns to the first subject. The viewer assumes the two subjects are facing each other in conversation (Figure 16.21).

a b c

Figure 16.21 The shot-reverse-shot method can be used to record an interviewer's question, the subject's response and then any reaction or follow-up questions the interviewer may have.

Figure 16.22 Getting the details right, such as the player and team names, will help prevent any embarrassment when lower-thirds titles are utilized in your broadcast.

Cross Cuts

Cross cutting is cutting back and forth between two unrelated shots, which makes the viewer feel as though the two actions (usually for the point of comparison) are occurring simultaneously. For example, cross cutting between shots of a boy and girl both getting ready for prom in their respective homes will give the viewer the impression the actions are happening simultaneously.

Titles

Used often in news, **lower-thirds titles** are lines of text that appear overlaid on a video in the lower third of the frame, identify the person appearing on screen and often including the person's title or other identifying information (Figure 16.22). You asked "What is your name and how do you spell it?" as your very first interview question. Here the information will be indispensable. You can ensure you are spelling your interviewee's name correctly.

And Now... Closer to Home

Editing like a Pro

Rookie high school journalists often do not use a sufficient number of cuts when they edit. Watch a professionally edited package, and you will notice that shots are changed every few seconds. In the opening segment of one 45-minute show, students counted more than 35 different shots in less than two minutes. To make your video projects look more professional, begin by capturing enough footage and a great enough variety of footage so that you can cut between many shots in a short span of time. This also means having enough clips available to break up long interviews.

Effects

Sound and visual effects are available in most video editing applications, but professional journalists rarely use them and only when there is a compelling reason to do so. Audio and video effects should never be used to mislead or "trick" the viewer or to falsify a scene you recorded.

Ethical Visual Journalism

Photo and video journalists in the age of digital photography hold unique powers and face complicated ethical decisions. Like most journalists, they consult the Society of Professional Journalists Code of Ethics, but in addition they use the National Press Photographers Association code of ethics to address issues that concern visual journalists in particular. Here are two important points from that code.

Journalists are observers, not actors. They should not alter or influence events as they record them. This means no staged photos or recreated scenes to compensate for shots you missed. Make sure that your work accurately represents the situation and your subjects, including the context in which they appear.

As you edit, do not alter your photos or video in a way that misleads the viewer. Use only editing tools that make your work as close to reality as possible. Adjusting the image for brightness or contrast, cropping, color correcting and sharpening are all generally acceptable, unless they mislead the viewer. For instance, cropping that removes an angry crowd that surrounded a violent subject could mislead the viewer to think the subject was acting alone or without provocation. It is not ethical to remove distracting elements from within the frame or flip or merge photos. The resulting image is not an accurate nor a true representation of what the journalist saw.

In addition, visual journalists, like all other journalists, should take special care with subjects who may be young, vulnerable or who may be victims.

Online Multimedia

The modern journalist is becoming a master of many forms of storytelling. Veteran video journalist Michael Rosenblum predicted in 2010 that the future of journalism was "**backpack journalism**." The new journalist, Rosenblum and many others say, is fluent with photo, video, audio and text using high-powered devices they carry around with them in the field. The best journalists, then, are not print or video or online journalists. They are all of the above, proficient storytellers across all media.

The Internet has given journalists lower-cost to publish and almost infinite space for their stories compared to the print, radio or TV journalism of a few decades earlier. It has led old-school print publications, like The New York Times, to rethink visual and audio communication. Instead of one photo that is run on top of one story in the print edition, they now can run galleries of photos, a video or both online. Audio tracks narrate visuals. Instead of static graphics and alternative story forms run as part of print stories, they can invite their audience to contribute information or participate in a more immersive experience through **interactive graphics**.

You will recall from the discussion of alternative story forms in Chapter 15 that stories can come in many forms. Web-based publications can use those same forms in rich and interactive ways (Figure 16.23).

Recent interactive graphics and other multimedia stories include the following:

- In "Up Close on Baseball's Borders," The New York Times created an interactive map of the density of fan loyalty to each major league baseball team. The data was based on how many Facebook users in each ZIP code "liked" each team. Users scrolling over areas of the map could determine the precise ZIP code where Astros fans gave way to Rangers fans and where White Sox fans gave way to Cubs fans.
- In "Plunge in Kindergarteners' Vaccination Rates Worries Health Officials," The Los Angeles Times allows readers to explore a searchable database of vaccination rates by school or city.
- In "How Much Is Your Arm Worth? Depends on Where You Work," ProPublica presents an interactive graphic that allows users to view state-by-state comparisons of the worker's compensation maximum benefit amounts for individual body parts. It illustrated the disparity in worker's compensation benefits across the nation.

Though these publications have Web developers and designers to create their interactive graphics, you can create and embed interactive graphics in your stories using programs and applications available online, many of which are free for limited use. Search the Web for the function you want, using terms such as: *interactive timeline, interactive map, data visualization tool, photo slideshow* or *interactive image*. You may need to create an account to use the tool, and you will probably develop your content inside their website, but once your graphic is complete, you will be able to embed a link to it on your site. To do so, you will need to find the share button, which will lead you to a paragraph of computer code called the "embed code." Copy that snippet of code and paste it into your online story using the HTML or source editor (Figure 16.24).

Figure 16.23 *How might you use interactive alternative story forms in your work?*

Making Alternative Story Forms Interactive

In a print newspaper or yearbook the reader sees:	In an online story the audience can:
three students' mug shots and quotations in a *quote reel*	click on a mug shot and hear an audio clip of that person stating his opinion
a *timeline*, including text and graphics, running across the bottom of a story package	click through an interactive timeline to view photos, text, social media posts, audio and video
statistics presented as *graphs* and *charts*	click on graphs and charts to view an explanation of the data or scroll over the charts to view specific information, interviews, case studies or the sources of the data

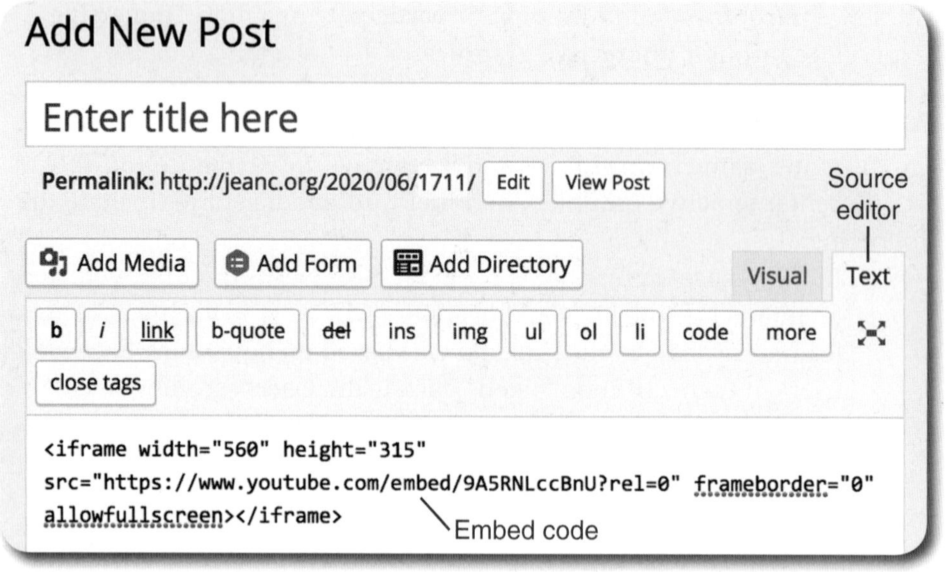

Figure 16.24 Interactive graphics can be created with online programs and then embedded in your site using the source editor.

Developing Story Packages for the Web

Your publication's staff may have the ability to write solid journalistic stories, shoot and edit compelling video, and tell stories through still photography, audio storytelling, interactive elements and alternative story forms. But just because you *can* do something does not mean you *should* do something, and not every story is best told through each of these storytelling tools. As you plan your online story, ask these key questions:

1. *How much time, and how much help, do I have?* If you are covering breaking news, your priority is to gather and publish news swiftly. Interactive graphics or video may come later. Focus on tools that allow you to collect and publish information from multiple sources as the story unfolds, possibly embedding social media posts into your story.
2. *Does this story "have legs"?* In Chapter 8 you learned some stories "have legs" and are worth pursuing, while others are not. This is doubly true as you consider online stories. Multimedia storytelling can take a great deal of time or require that you develop new digital skills. Do not invest time and resources in a project that will be old news by the time your package is ready to publish.
3. *Is my main goal to inform the reader or is it to make the reader experience something?* If the purpose is to inform, you will probably include data visualizations such as charts and graphs, explanatory diagrams or step-by-step slideshows to clarify and illustrate the information in your text. However, stories focused on conveying an experience will probably include video, audio or immersive storytelling modes that blend text and visuals.
4. *Are any of the following particularly relevant to the story: sound, time or chronology, sequence, data, geographic location?* If the answer to any of those is yes, you may want to include a relevant alternative story form for the story.
   - sound: embedded audio clips
   - time or chronology: interactive timeline

- sequence: sequence slideshow, step-by-step
- data: interactive charts, graphs or other infographic
- geography: interactive map

One more question will influence the forms your story takes. *Is there one single narrative, or are there multiple angles?* Your answer will suggest one of three basic models for online story packages:

- Story-plus: In this model, the journalist writes one basic story and all other elements supplement that story. The additional content adds value, but these elements are not additional stories in and of themselves.
- Guided narrative: There may be one story or multiple stories, but the elements are presented to the reader in a specific order, with one element leading to the next. The story may have parts (or chapters), and those parts may be text, video or other forms of storytelling. Each part is like a mini-story, and together they build up to a larger story.
- Menu of stories: If there are multiple stories to tell, and they do not need to be read or viewed in a specific order to make sense, the reader may be presented with a menu of stories to choose from. Each reader will create a different, individually customized experience. Developing news stories often are presented in this way. The audience can choose to see flood damage, view an interactive map of the inundation, hear the weather report for upstream areas, listen to interviews with survivors, read about disaster recovery plans and participate in discussions of the area's emergency response plan.

Study the professionals. The Online News Association honors the best stories presented on the Web that year. The work of ONA award finalists can serve as a study guide, showing you ways to package stories for the Web. Just as skillful designers do not "design from the sky," but collect examples, online journalists watch how others are innovating Web storytelling.

Your Turn

1. Each year, the Online News Association recognizes the best online news stories and coverage from around the world. Find the most recent list of award winners, and look through them for examples of each of the three types of online story packages listed above.
2. **Going Deeper.** Study one story package more closely. Why do you think the reporters, editors and designers decided to package the story in each of these ways? What do you suppose their answers would be to the questions that guide online and multimedia decisions?

Chapter Sixteen

Review and Assessment

Recall Assess

1. Explain what a photojournalist should do to prepare for photographing an event. Explain what the photojournalist should *avoid* doing while photographing the event.
2. How can varying the angle of your shots make a difference when photographing a subject?
3. Which photo editing technique is used to prevent moving subjects in an image from being cramped? What is the term used for the video equivalent of this technique?
4. By what measures should you judge a story idea to determine if it will make a good *video* story?
5. Describe what happens during each phase of video production.
6. Which video shots should you capture before leaving any scene as you shoot a video story?
7. What important guideline will ensure that your video shot is long enough to successfully use in editing?

Critical Thinking

1. What are the benefits of cropping?
2. Find a Pulitzer prize winning photograph online and research the story behind it. Evaluate the composition of the photograph, and explain its significance. Which elements make it a powerful photograph? What journalistic purpose does it serve?
3. Take a look at the following issues that plague a rookie video journalist returning from a shoot. What went wrong, and what should he have done differently to prevent the issue?
   A. The video he produced is shaky.
   B. There is video footage but no audio.
   C. The footage is captured in one, long shot, so it is difficult to search for usable clips.
   D. There are interviews with individuals, but he does not know who the individuals are.
   E. All of his shots are of the action.
4. Someone on your news publication staff complains that she should not be expected to take photographs of her subjects because she is a staff writer, not a photographer. How might you explain the concept of "backpack journalism" to convince her that she can, and should, explore a variety of media?
5. Effective speaking requires proper pronunciation of English words, particularly as a broadcast journalist. Practice pronouncing the key terms by saying them aloud to yourself. Then, say the words aloud to a classmate by using them in a sentence. Practice your pronunciation until it is correct.

Application

1. Take the following information and turn it into a two-sentence caption:
   - Subject: junior Megan Scott
   - Action: taking a standardized test
   - Date and Location: April 7 in the library
   - Significance: first group of students to participate in the newly computerized state standardized test for English
2. Find a photograph in a professional publication and name each of the elements of composition you can identify. Share your photograph and discuss your findings with the class.
3. Using a digital camera or a camera on a mobile device, practice the techniques related to photo composition with a single subject. Try to tell a story about the subject through a set of 5–8 photographs that vary in distance and composition.
4. Work with a small group to practice filming a video sequence. Have one group member do a complete action repeatedly (opening up a locker and removing books, braiding hair, making a free throw shot, etc.). Capture a tight shot, medium shot, wide shot, an action shot and a reaction shot that you can piece together to compress time and relay the action sequence visually.

Chapter Sixteen

Journalism Style

Spelling

In this Journalism Style, you will review and practice writing words that often are misspelled. If you have been keeping a "demon list" of terms that give you trouble, you may already have some of these words in your list. In addition, your publication may already have a list of class demons posted on a wall, words that bedevil many members of the class or make it into your publication and embarrass all of you.

Clean copy is everyone's job. Publishing well-reported, thoughtful and well-written journalism with spelling errors is like dressing in your best clothing, then spilling ketchup down your front.

You might think: "My spell-checkers will catch any mistakes I make."

No, they will not. Spell-checkers cannot read your mind. They do not know whether you mean *teeth* or *teethes*.

And spell-checkers are not everywhere. They are not on manual devices such as pens and paintbrushes. They are not on many programs used to microblog, post to the Web, create a design or perform engineering functions.

Why Do People Misspell?

Some people are born dyslexic; they have a language processing disorder that makes spelling—among other things—extremely difficult. However, people with dyslexia do become successful journalists and produce clean copy for publication. They learn strategies that allow them to do the work they love.

Some people have poor visual memory or poor memory for details. They need to concentrate to overcome these weaknesses, but they also can become successful journalists and produce clean copy.

Some people are careless and do not reread their copy. They need to get over it. There are almost no satisfying jobs or professions open to people who are careless with details. (Try naming three.) Journalism is a good place to get over being careless.

Many people who struggle with spelling have much more experience with spoken language than they do with written language. They need to read more. Everything a journalist reads becomes a resource for later work.

We all have four vocabularies. Which is your biggest vocabulary?

Receptive vocabulary—you can understand the word in someone else's sentence	**Generative vocabulary**—you can use the word well in your own sentences
A. Oral—words you hear and understand	C. Oral—words you use when speaking
B. Written—words you read and understand	D. Written—words you use in writing

Most people's receptive vocabularies are bigger than their generative vocabularies. If your oral receptive vocabulary, A, is larger than your written receptive vocabulary, B, you probably struggle to spell well because you spell words and phrases as you think they sound. If your written vocabulary is bigger, you may occasionally mispronounce words you know only from reading.

Try It!

Working in a group, take turns reading each set of often misspelled words while the others write them. Read the words in a natural voice, not emphasizing the spelling. Alternate readers so that everyone has an opportunity to spell each set of words.

At the end of each set, check your words against the list. Add any words you misspelled to your list of spelling demons. Study this list often and add to it whenever you make a spelling error. As you master the spelling, draw a thin line through the words you are now confident you can spell correctly.

1. accommodate	beginning	limousine
2. a lot of	surprised	thoroughly
3. probably	business	possess
4. calendar	definitely	exaggerate
5. decathlon	disappoint	absence
6. sophomore	descriptive	dumbbell
7. perform	occasion	ubiquitous
8. committee	truly	rhythm
9. boutonniere	recommend	rhyme
10. corsage	embarrass	souvenir
11. opponent	necessary	temperature
12. receive	occurred	sabotage
13. separate	noticeable	vignette
14. admissible	appropriate	weird
15. privilege	committed	siege
16. finally	guarantee	diploma

Extend Your Knowledge

Style Exercises

Visit the *Journalism* website to see these words used in a context sentence and to practice spelling additional words.

Chapter Sixteen

Writers' Workshop

In this Writers' Workshop you will:

- Use SEE format to build on a simile.
- Communicate abstract ideas with metaphoric verbs.

Workshop 16.1

Using Comparisons for Clarity

Similes, metaphors and allusions allow our audience to understand something new by comparing it to something familiar. A simile uses the word *like* or *as* to make the comparison. *His anger was like a boiling kettle*. A metaphor implies a comparison by using language normally applied to something else. *His anger boiled over*. An allusion is an indirect reference to some body of knowledge, such as literature or history, which is understood by the audience. *My former boss was an Ebenezer Scrooge clone*. (The writer assumes the reader is familiar with the miserly character in Charles Dickens' story "A Christmas Carol.")

Mini-Lesson: Do You SEE It?

You usually hear about similes, metaphors and allusions as you study poetry, but journalists also use these tools to communicate complex or abstract ideas in a small space.

Journalists, however, use these tools in the service of clarity, with an eye to their audience's previous experience, while poets may use them to create depth of meaning, beauty or new insight.

A poet might say, as Scottish poet Robert Burns did, "O my Luve's like a red, red rose ..." and leave us to ponder whether the *girl* he loves is like a red, red rose, or the *love* he has for the girl is like a red, red rose. And *how* is it like a red, red rose?

A journalist, on the other hand, uses something familiar to make clear something that is new, strange or abstract. How does Deepak Singh of Public Radio International describe the end-of-winter festival of Holi in northern India to an American radio audience? He does it in similes, drawing on what the audience knows to communicate something unfamiliar. He writes that 10-year-old boys are

> *dyed blue and purple from head to toe, with bandanas on their heads, and water guns in their hands ... <u>like a mob of hooligans out to make mischief</u>.*

Some cities celebrate for a week.

> *It's almost like one gigantic frat party or a pregame tailgate party in America.*

The city of Lucknow celebrates in a more controlled way.

> *There's an unspoken rule that the color playing begins around 8 a.m. and comes to a full stop around noon, as if someone flicked a switch.*

Often journalists follow an SEE pattern when describing something unknown. They present a simile—or sometimes a metaphor—then explain it, then give examples of it. Reeves Wiedeman does this repeatedly in his Popular Mechanics article "How the New York Times Works: This is how the Gray Lady gets made in 2015."

SAY the comparison	*Ernie Booth, the operations manager, glides through the* [plant] *like a small-town mayor,*
EXPLAIN the comparison (How is Booth like a small-town mayor?)	*jabbing the noisy air with quick chin nods, offering ritual greetings to some of the 350 employees who work here each night.*
EVIDENCE or EXAMPLES	*"What's happening, Tom?"* *"Hey, Andy."* *"All quiet, Dennis?"*

Booth himself describes the production plant's control room with a comparison, and Weideman builds on it.

SAY the comparison	Booth ... *scans the control room, a glass-walled office he compares to an indoor air traffic control tower,*
EXPLAIN the comparison (How is the control room like a traffic control tower?)	*overlooking the floor.*
EVIDENCE or EXAMPLES	*"You see all these flashing things?" he says, pointing to one of several screens displaying different parts of the plant. "Flashing things are bad. Flashing things mean we have a problem."*

Weideman describes the paper on which The New York Times is printed as ...

SAY the comparison	*rolls large enough to serve as the business end of a steamroller:*
EXPLAIN the comparison (How are the rolls like the roller of heavy equipment?)	*2,200 pounds each and fifty inches in diameter.*
EVIDENCE or EXAMPLES (of their size)	Eighteen-wheelers carried them to a Times storage facility in the Bronx, then to the production plant in Queens, where they *sit stocked in eight rows on nine shelves, four deep, like soup cans in a grocery store for giants.*

Apply It!

Use SEE format and a comparison such as a simile to explain or describe a process or technique that may be unfamiliar to others in your group or class but which you understand. Pick only a small part of a larger process; for instance, removing a clay pot from a wheel, signing (using American Sign Language) an abstract or religious idea, or a technique from hairstyling, cooking or sports.

Create your comparison using a chart such as this one:

SAY the comparison	
EXPLAIN the comparison	
EVIDENCE or EXAMPLES	

From the chart, create a paragraph that identifies the process and includes this sentence: "This is how it works." Read your work aloud to your group, receive responses, revise and publish.

Mini-Lesson: The Verbs Have It

More common than similes are implied comparisons such as metaphors. You use them to bring your audience's previous experience to the new or abstract thing. The most powerful way to do this is through a verb.

The business section often deals in abstractions, but look at the deck and lead of this Los Angeles Times story about gas price increases. (The metaphoric language is in bold. *Squeeze* is actually a verbal—a verb acting as a noun.)

> *"**Squeeze** on supply follows a refinery explosion and other facility closures.*
>
> *California gas prices have **shot up** about $1 a gallon in the last month ..."*

And in this crime report:

> *"Trouble **had been brewing** before closing time ..."*

And this report about Detroit's financial crisis:

> *"The groups say several things beyond homeowners' control have **dragged** tens of thousands of them **into financial holes** ..."*
>
> *"The problem has **festered** for years, but it is under a **spotlight** now because of the positive changes **being trumpeted** post-bankruptcy.*

Nothing is physically being squeezed, shooting up, brewing (like coffee or beer), being dragged into holes, festering (like an infected wound), illuminated by a spotlight or announced with the sound of trumpets. The audience may not even register that the sentences contain metaphors, but the power is there. The language, especially the verbs, is strong and active and creates mental images.

Try rewriting each of the examples without the metaphoric language. For instance, replace *squeeze on* with *problems with* or *shortages of*. Read your metaphor-free version aloud, then read the example as written. Which is stronger and more interesting?

Apply It!

Search through your own writing or the writing of others for sentences that would be stronger with metaphoric verbs. Look for stories that include abstractions, such as stories about economics, law, science and sports. Rewrite at least four paragraphs from a variety of stories using strong, metaphoric verbs. Read your work aloud to your group, receive responses, revise and publish both the original and your improved version.

Extend Your Knowledge Extend

Visit the *Journalism* website to learn how journalists use allusions to make their writing more powerful.

Chapter Seventeen

Advertising

How do we pay the bills?

Photo by Forrest Czarnecki, Conifer High School

G-WLEARNING.COM

While studying, look for the activity icon to:

- **Build** vocabulary terms with e-flash cards and matching activities.
- **Extend** learning with further discussion of relevant topics.
- **Reinforce** what you learn by completing style exercises, worksheets and end-of-chapter questions.

Visit the Journalism website: www.g-wlearning.com/journalism/

Chapter Objectives

After reading this chapter, you will be able to:

- Create a budget for your publication.
- Assemble a list of potential advertisers.
- Discuss ethical considerations involved in selling and placing ads.
- Assemble a sales kit.
- Make sales calls.
- Describe ways to respond when a potential advertiser says no.
- Place ads in your publication so they do little or nothing to limit your readers' access to your content.
- Explain the goals of radio, video and print advertising.
- Explain the goal of most online ads.
- Discuss the difference between static and interstitial online ads.
- Use text, sound, images and other elements to design radio, print and online ads.

Key Terms Build Vocab

ad server
banner ad
billboard ad (radio)
brand awareness
bumper music
button ad
camera-ready art
circulation figures
click through
expandable ad
hyperlinked
insert
interstitial ad
logo
pop-up ad
proof
public service ad (PSA)
rate sheet
royalty
static ad
streaming video
up-front payment

Before You Read...

Environmental print is the print of everyday life—logos, signs or labels, for example. Find three examples of environmental print in your school. Explain the meaning of each.

Introduction

"We have always said that advertising is just the icing on the cake. It is not the cake."

–Meg Whitman, American business executive

American journalist and critic A.J. Liebling wrote in The New Yorker, "Freedom of the press is guaranteed only to those who own one." He may have meant that the owners of newspapers controlled what news is printed. There was at least some truth in that statement. More than a half century later, the statement is both more and less true than it was in 1960.

On one hand, a dozen large, for-profit corporations control much of the media in the United States and the free world. Many smaller print publications have been swallowed up by large corporations or gone out of business, silencing a variety of voices. In many other parts of the world, governments control media. And in many countries, journalists are silenced, exiled or even killed for doing their work.

On the other hand, digital communication and the Internet make it possible for anyone who owns a computer or a handheld device with a reliable and uncensored Internet connection to own the modern equivalent of a printing press.

Journalism requires an audience, that is, subscribers, listeners, viewers, followers or readers. It requires ethical and effective reporting and commentary to earn and keep the respect of the audience. And it requires money: money to gather the news; money to buy cameras and recorders, software and hardware, cellphones and business cards; money to pay for hosting a website; money to travel to the scene of events; money to print a publication; money to enrich and empower the staff through training, conferences and conventions.

This chapter is about how to get the money.

Selling Ads

Some high school journalism programs raise money by selling subscriptions to alumni or members of their extended community, but most publications and broadcasts get money in the traditional way, by selling advertising to appear in their media (Figure 17.1).

How Much Money Do You Need?

Only a budget can give you that answer. Budgets may be more or less formal, tracked in account books or computer software, long-term, short-term or both. However, certain principles underlie all budgeting.

The first step in making a budget is to set a time frame. Most publications work on a 12-month cycle, though your organization may decide to look at longer range planning, perhaps to purchase new equipment or to add more media, such as video on your website or a DVD with your literary magazine. Or you may want money for your staff to attend workshops, summer camps or conventions at a date in the future. If you have long-range plans, you need to budget so that you will have enough funds left over at the end of the year, after all the bills are paid.

The second step is to survey your resources. Assets may include

- equipment, computers, cameras and software provided by your school;
- service and maintenance on school equipment provided by the school now and in the future;
- school funds budgeted for publications;
- funds left over from previous years;
- donations, prize money and grants;

Figure 17.1 Local businesses might be interested in advertising in your publication. Some will have ads ready-made, while others will have your staff design the ads. *What locally owned businesses might be interested in advertising in your publications?*

BIGGEST BURRITOS ON THE PLANET
At El Burrito Loco, our specialty is impossibly big burritos. From meat-filled to vegan, our enormous burritos are designed to please carnivores and herbivores alike. Conveniently located three blocks from Egan College Prep, our casual-dining restaurant is the perfect place to enjoy supreme Mexican cuisine with your friends and family.
El Burrito Loco
6415 W. 63rd Street

Open Monday – Sunday
11:00 a.m. – 10:00 p.m.

The Book Nook
From term-paper research to SAT prep to reading for pure pleasure, the Book Nook has you covered. Stop by to immerse yourself in centuries of knowledge stored within the shelves at the Book Nook.
The Book Nook
750 Cassel Parkway

9:00 a.m. – 8:00 p.m.

The Roman Forum
At the Roman Forum, you don't need to know Latin to appreciate our authentic Italian cuisine, served by a friendly staff in a casual setting among stone arches and Tuscan columns. Located just two blocks from Neil Armstrong High School, the Roman Forum offers a variety of delectable dishes at student-friendly prices. Stop in today with your friends or family for a hearty Italian meal!
The Roman Forum Restaurant
1375 Colosseum Drive
555-1400
Monday – Thursday
3:00 p.m. – 11:00 p.m.
Friday – Sunday
4:00 p.m. – midnight

- predicted income from reliable advertisers, which may include seasonal advertisements, such as those that usually come around the time of prom and at graduation;
- subscription income that exceeds the costs involved in delivery or mailing;
- funds and other types of support from boosters and parents;
- money expected from any fundraisers; or
- money from other sources, such as the sale of photos or videos, online or in person.

The third step is to identify your expenses. These should include the cost of printing one issue, multiplied by the number of issues you print, or the cost of Web hosting. Include money you should set aside to repair or replace lost or damaged equipment, money to purchase fonts or software, money for those who write reviews to purchase books, meals and tickets, and other expenses. Look at previous years' expenses to predict how much to include this year, but add 10 percent to last year's costs.

You should identify each expense as either a need or a want. Expect some disagreement as you discuss whether a purchase is a need or a want. How we spend our money—and how we spend our time—shows what is really important to us.

Is maintaining a surplus each year for future expenses a want, or is it a need? How much should be saved? Is a high-quality video camera a need or a want? How much will it cost? What about publishing more often? How much will each additional issue cost? (And how much additional ad revenue will it generate?) Publishing via a new medium? How much will it cost? Will it raise more money than it costs? Want food in the classroom for late-night and Saturday work sessions? Submitting work for competitions? (They often charge a fee for critiquing your work.) Travel expenses to conventions?

The difference between your resources and your needs is the amount of money you *must* raise through advertising to stay in business.

The difference between your resources and your wants is the amount of money you would *like* to make through ads.

Your Turn

1. Make a list of expenses for your publication. Estimate the cost for each. Then discuss with your group whether they are wants or needs.
2. **Going Deeper.** Research the cost of adding something that interests you—a significant want—to your budget, such as additional equipment or training at a convention or journalism camp. Include the cost of transportation or shipping and taxes in your estimates. Report your findings to your class or group.

Who Will Buy Your Ads?

You have a valuable commodity to offer. You can give your advertisers the eyes and ears of a group with money to spend. Teenagers and their families spend a great deal of it. Teenagers patronize malls, movie theaters, events, driving schools, nail salons, test prep courses, party planners, tuxedo rentals, gyms, yoga studios and florists. They get their teeth straightened, their eyebrows threaded and their complexions improved. Teens spend money skiing and snowboarding, skating, surfing and shooting each other with paintballs. They buy huge amounts of prepared and fast food and hours of music, films, games and videos. They or their parents may buy insurance, cellphone service or more expensive items such as cars.

Each place teenagers, or their parents, spend their money should be a potential advertiser in your publication. Some will be local, a nearby restaurant for instance. Others will be regional. Surfboards get more teen money in Huntington Beach, California; rodeo equipment, more teen money in Butte, Montana.

Do not ignore businesses that cater to ethnic groups at your school. They are part of your community and do business with your students and their families, and therefore are potential advertisers.

Do not ignore home-based or part-time businesses, especially those run by parents and alumni of your school. A small ad may bring large returns for these small businesses. These may include photographers, mobile auto mechanics, seamstresses, hairdressers, cosmeticians, auto detailers, musicians, DJs, caterers, Web designers, computer service technicians and people who sell cosmetics or other products.

In addition, you may decide to accept personal ads from parents and others congratulating students for their successes or cheering them on before important contests or events (Figure 17.2). If your advertising policy includes personal ads, you should make it easy for people to place an ad through your website. Consider running a small notice telling your audience about the design services you offer and how to place an ad. Run one or two such ads for free or for a very low introductory price to show their potential and your ability as an ad designer.

Figure 17.2 Personal ads can help earn money for the paper and give people an opportunity to congratulate a student on an achievement or cheer on a sports team for a big game.

Congrats, Maya!
We're so proud of you and we love you very much. We know you'll do well in college!
Love, Mom, Dad and Marco.

Your Turn

1. Make a list of potential advertisers. Include all the businesses you or your friends and their families patronize, including home-based and ethnic businesses. Large chain stores such as drugstores and big-box retailers may have local advertising budgets, so put them on the list, too.
2. **Going Deeper.** Make a list of regional, state or national advertisers who might consider advertising on your Web page. Examine other online student publications for examples.
3. Investigate the costs and benefits of online plug-ins such as Google Ads, which track your audience's browsing history.
4. Investigate the costs and benefits of online ads that may come with the service which houses your online publication.

Who Sees Your Work?

Your audience members are potential advertisers. If you distribute no further than your school, you limit your income. Consider placing copies of print publications

- in libraries;
- at clinics and the offices of doctors and dentists, including orthodontists;
- at cafes or donut and coffee shops;
- anywhere people sit, wait and read—hospital lobbies, bus stations, pharmacies;
- school libraries; and
- in the reception area of the school and district office.

Of course all your current advertisers get a copy, as do potential advertisers you have identified as likely supporters.

Offer mailed subscriptions to alumni and parents at a reduced price, just slightly more than what it costs you to mail the publication to them.

Make sure all the booster club parents—the football boosters, the drama club boosters, the cheer parents—see copies at their meetings.

If a local paper distributes in your area, ask the publishers if they would like to include copies of your paper with theirs. (The local paper may be willing to cover the extra printing costs.)

Even if you do not publish online, use social media and microblogging to alert members of your audience, including your extended audience, to articles that will soon be available in print.

If you are online, embed links to your publication or online version of your broadcasts in social media sites, on blogs published off your site, and in articles from your site that are placed on other sites. Be sure to invite the audience to link back to your site for further coverage. Use feeds or email to bring eyes and ears to your site. Microblog, but do not give away all your content in your tease or headline.

Even better than *seeing* your publication in print or online, is *interacting* with it. If your potential advertisers have interacted with your site or publication, they are more likely to consider advertising in it.

Consider interactive elements such as a series of "What do you know about teenagers?" surveys. Ask a series of questions, then invite students to submit their answers. Also ask adults in your community to predict what teens will answer. The results may not be scientific, but they will engage and perhaps inform your audience, both teen and adult.

Publish the results of the teens' answers and the adults' predictions in bar graphs or other charts (Figure 17.3).

How Do You Sell Ads?

Do not wait for ads to come to you—few will. Most ads result from personal contacts.

A few staffs have a business team that handles advertising contacts, but more often, everyone needs to help. Sooner or later, almost everyone needs to learn to sell ads.

The basic steps of ad selling follow.

Make a Plan

Coordinate with your business manager so you do not contact people who have already been contacted. Under her guidance, choose the businesses you will contact. (Managers often use a spreadsheet to keep track of who is contacting each business and when the contact is made.) If you are bilingual or have other assets, such as membership in a religious congregation or other organization, you may ask to contact businesses where you have that advantage. Consider going in teams of two for moral support and for safety.

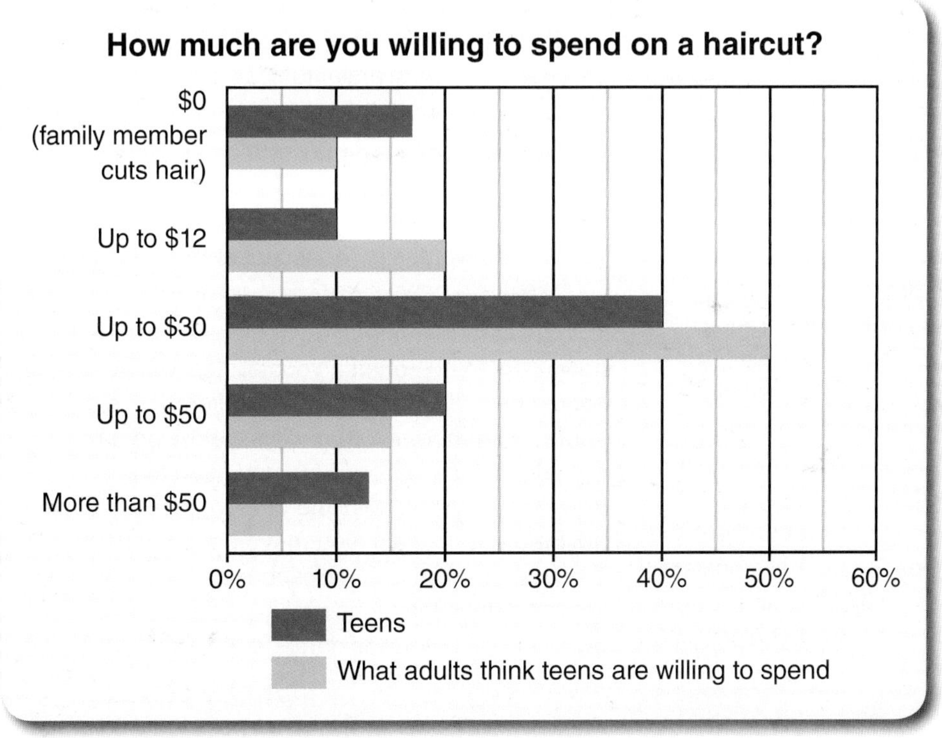

Figure 17.3 Survey results can be displayed in graphs or charts. *What survey questions would engage the adults and the students in your audience?*

Make Contact

Make personal contact with the business. The first step is often a phone call. Ask for the name of the person you should speak with about advertising. Find out when this person will be available.

Your Turn

1. With a partner, rehearse what you will say when contacting a business by phone and how you will say it. Do this in front of the class. Remember, you will be speaking to an adult. Use good telephone manners—and get rid of the chewing gum.
2. **Going Deeper.** Imagine the responses you will get, knowing that the person on the phone may not be the person with the power to place an ad in your publication, or that the business owner may have reservations about dealing with someone your age or that she may have questions about the services you offer. How will you respond to each of these situations?

And Now... Closer to Home

Three Ethical Questions

1. Should we alter our coverage to attract potential advertisers?

"We could cover the football boosters. Then maybe a booster would advertise with us."

"If we had an article about Ramadan, maybe we could get advertising from Arab-American businesses."

It's tempting, but it is also unethical. Journalists strive to keep a firewall between the business side and the journalism side of the broadcast or publication. Breaching that firewall caused a publisher of the Los Angeles Times to lose his job and the paper to issue multiple apologies to regain the public's trust. You should not alter your coverage to please advertisers.

Coverage decisions should be made on the basis of the core news values, your duty to your audience and your knowledge of your audience. If your editorial board decides the football boosters club or Ramadan is newsworthy, then find your focus and cover the story in a fair and balanced manner, not with an eye toward flattering potential advertisers.

2. What types of ads may we accept? What should we reject? Tanning salons? Political candidates? Advocacy for or against controversial topics? Tattoo or piercing parlors?

A clear advertising policy in your staff handbook will help you make these decisions when you are offered an ad that raises concerns.

3. Should we design or accept an ad that looks like it is a news story?

Be certain that ads do not look enough like news content to confuse your audience. They should use different fonts, have different designs, sound different or in other ways clearly be paid content, not journalism. You may need to put "Advertising" in the folio line or in the corner of an ad. Before a podcast, you may need to announce, "And now, a word from our sponsor." "Tricking" your audience into consuming an ad as news is a breach of faith and will damage your publication.

Assemble Your Sales Kit

Your sales kit will include

A. Business cards with your name and contact information for your publication. Include the business manager's contact information as well.

B. Copies of your publication. Show your website on a handheld device or bring printouts. Show how many pages you print or how big your website is.

C. A fact sheet with

- Your **circulation figures**—how many copies you distribute, how many visitors come to your site, how many viewers or listeners you have. The bigger your circulation, the more you can charge for ads.
- Awards and honors your publication has earned.
- Your publication dates if you are in print. Your broadcast schedule. How often you update your site if you are digital.
- Copy of the school calendar showing when students are on break, preparing for Prom or Winter Formal, or buying graduation flowers and hosting grad parties.

D. Your **rate sheet**, a page that shows the dimensions of potential ads and their costs (Figure 17.4 on the next page). If your paper uses **inserts** (their ads on their paper, inserted into your print publications), include those costs as well. Also include costs for online advertising. Specify the design services you offer and the cost for these services, if there is any. Specify any discounts for **up-front payment**, that is, payment received before the ad is published. (Some publications require up-front payment for all ads.) Offer discounts for repeat advertisers: "Buy nine ads, get the 10th free."

If you publish or broadcast in more than one medium, invite businesses to advertise with you wherever your content appears, including social media and image-sharing sites. Have a package price for advertising both in print and online.

E. Samples of ads you have designed. Let your potential advertisers see your best work. Offer to design an ad aimed at your students, perhaps with a coupon or special offer.

F. Contract forms (Figure 17.5 on page 533). The completed contract should include

- the name and contact information for the business or person buying the ad;
- the exact size of the ad and anything else you agreed upon; if the ad is an insert, whether you will pick it up or they will deliver it to the school;
- the place or time in the publication where the ad will run;
- cost of the ad; and
- how payment will be made.

G. A pen or two. It is embarrassing to have to borrow one when you are clinching a sale.

Make the Visit

Call on the business when the person who can decide to buy an ad is there (Figure 17.6 on page 534). This call is an in-person, flesh-and-blood visit. Phone or digital communications are rarely as successful as an in-the-flesh visit.

Groom yourself as a young adult. Be clean, neat and professional—even if you are going to sell an ad to a skateboard shop. Get rid of the gum.

Ask for the person by name and introduce yourself with your full name and the name of your publication. Shake hands, if appropriate. Present your business card and tell him why you are there.

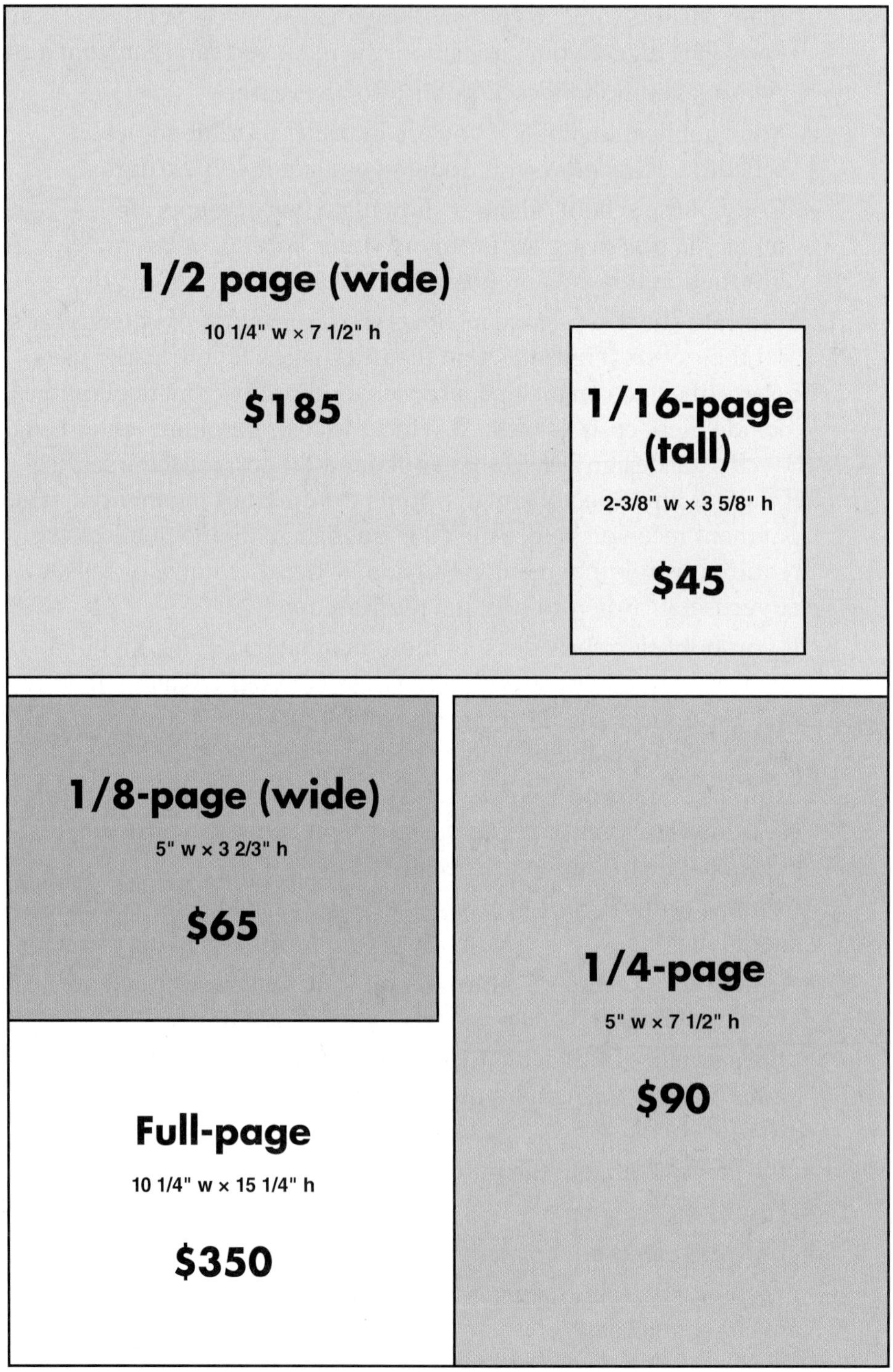

Figure 17.4 This sample rate sheet details the cost of each size ad offered at a publication. A rate sheet might also include prices for online ads, insert ads or any discounts for repeat customers. The measurements should match the width of the columns your publication uses.

CONTRACT STATEMENT

BUSINESS NAME ______________________________

Street address ______________________________

City ____________ State ________ ZIP Code ________

Telephone number with area code ____________________

Student selling ad ______________________________

Person purchasing ad and position ____________________

Signature of person purchasing ad ____________________

Date of contract signing ______________________________

LIST OF ADS COVERED BY THIS CONTRACT

Salesperson must fill in size and cost of EACH ad BEFORE contract is signed.

#1 September 17, 2020	Size of ad ______	Cost of ad ______
#2 October 8, 2020	Size of ad ______	Cost of ad ______
#3 November 5, 2020	Size of ad ______	Cost of ad ______
#4 December 10, 2020	Size of ad ______	Cost of ad ______
#5 January 28, 2021	Size of ad ______	Cost of ad ______
#6 February 25, 2021	Size of ad ______	Cost of ad ______
#7 April 8, 2021	Size of ad ______	Cost of ad ______
#8 May 6, 2021	Size of ad ______	Cost of ad ______
#9 June 10, 2021	Size of ad ______	Cost of ad ______

All checks must be made out to The Centerville Voice

Please mail payment to:
Ms. Camille Reynaud
Centerville High School
Centerville, USA

Figure 17.5 Contract forms include all the details regarding the purchase of an ad.

Speak briefly about the store and the products teens or their families use from such businesses. Establish rapport with the business person. Some cultures place a high value on small talk. In many countries it is rude to do business before you get to know each other a little. Be culturally and socially sensitive before you begin your sales pitch.

Show the manager your publication and the sizes and types of ads you are selling. Talk about the good things an ad in your publication or on your website can do for her business.

Ask which ad she would like to purchase. (That is different from asking *if* she wants to purchase one.)

If she agrees to buy an ad, fill out the contract completely, leaving no blanks, before you go. Have her sign it. If possible, leave a copy with her.

Tell her you will deliver a copy of your publication, or send her a link to the online ad, as soon as it is available. Then be sure you do so.

If you are designing an ad for her, tell her when she will see the proof before publication. A **proof** is a trial printout of the ad as it will look in your publication. The customer should have an opportunity to check the

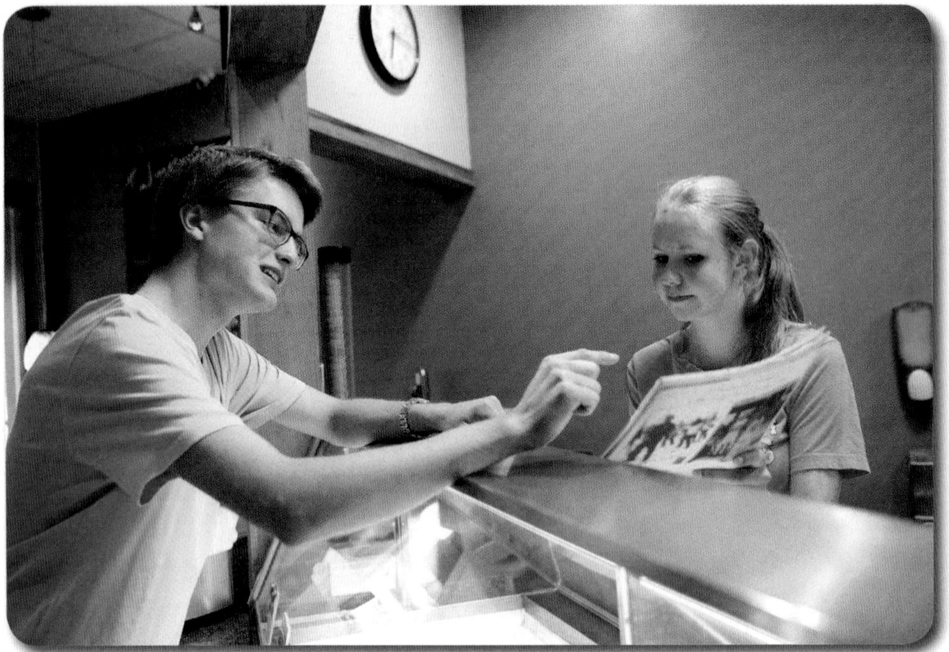

Figure 17.6 Be prepared and professional when calling on potential advertisers.

Photo by Forrest Czarnecki, Conifer High School

proof for accuracy and design. (You don't want to offer a limousine ride for $8.00 an hour when your customer wanted to offer a ride for $80.00 an hour.) Secure her signature approving the proof copy.

Report back to your business manager as soon as possible after your call, whether you sold an ad or not, so she can keep records. Give your business manager the contract and tell her any dates she should be aware of.

Your Turn

1. With a partner, practice calling on a potential advertiser. Practice both the words and the actions, such as handing the business card, shaking hands and showing the paper or website. When you have practiced several times, switch roles. Feel free to be a difficult customer or a hard sell when it is your turn to be the potential customer. Then switch with a neighboring pair of partners. Practice both successful sales and being rejected.
2. **Going Deeper.** Investigate various services for online advertising. Find out how they pay, how often they pay and if your publication can control the types of ads that appear on your site.

Where Do You Put the Ads, Now That You Have Them?

The money from ads is great, but ads have at least three downsides.

- Ads may annoy readers who are looking for news and commentary. They may lose interest in your site or broadcast or set aside your publication if they have to plow through too many ads to get to your content.

- Ads take up valuable real estate. They take space away from content in your printed publication. On your website, they push more of your content to inside pages. They take up your audience's time before they get to your broadcasts. If you run pop-up ads or ads before podcasts and other multimedia elements, viewers may click on something else in disgust. Fifteen seconds seems like a long time to wait when you are looking at a Web page.
- On websites, a reader who clicks through to an advertiser's Web page may never return to yours.

Editors and designers have to maintain a delicate balance between the needs of the readers and the needs of their advertisers. Where you place your ads is important.

Print Publications

In print publications, ads are usually kept off the front page and editorial section to avoid the appearance of a conflict of interest. However, some papers place removable stickers with advertising messages on the front page (Figure 17.7 on the next page). Others print ad sleeves that encase a third of the front and back pages (Figure 17.8 on page 537).

And Now... Closer to Home

Selling Online Ads

Some online ads are sold very much like traditional print ads. The advertisers pay a set price for an ad based on its location and the screen size, measured in pixels, which are single points on a computer screen. Ads placed in your header just below the navigation bar attract the most attention from your audience and usually are the most expensive. Your rate sheet may show an example of a 468 x 60 pixels ad, for instance, and the price. (This ad is almost eight times as wide as it is high.) Banner ads in sidebars—almost always the right sidebar—may measure 125 x 125 pixels or 125 x 60 pixels and be less expensive.

Other ads run at the start of a video embedded in your site. Your audience is captive, so you need to make these short, no longer than 30 seconds. If the ad is too long, or too boring, your audience may click away before your journalistic content begins.

Some advertisers pay each time their ad is viewed, so the more people who view your site, the more money you make. Others pay only when you bring traffic to their site. That is, they pay by the number of click-throughs on their ad. Some advertisers pay on a commission basis. They pay only when your viewers buy something on their site.

The good news is that these ads require very little work from you or other members of your staff. You can join an affiliate network that places ads on your site and not have to worry about ad design. Or you can join an organization such as Google AdSense that tracks your audience's interests by watching their keystrokes—the sites they view and the topics they search. When someone comes to your site, he finds an ad waiting for him that is tailored to his interests.

The bad news is that the money comes very slowly. You may earn only a half cent for each view of an ad. In addition, the affiliate, which does not like writing very small checks, may not send you any money until you have earned at least $25. Weigh the possible profit against the annoyance visitors to your website may experience.

Figure 17.7 Removable sticker ads easily peel off the page to avoid blocking the publication content.

Ads are placed inside news and other sections, such as sports or lifestyle, sometimes covering whole pages. Complete sections in the professional press may be devoted to advertising a certain type of product, such as real estate or cars.

Ads are generally placed so that they do not interfere with the flow of stories. Less expensive ads go toward the back of a section. (The very last page, however, is a very desirable place for an ad.) Half-page ads are placed on the lower half of an inside page. Smaller ads, such as quarter-page or one-eighth page ads, nestle in the bottom outside corner of most pages. If you have several small ads for the inside pages, stack them like the steps of a pre-Columbian pyramid, higher at the outer edge of a page and lower toward the center, leaving the rest of the page open for content (Figure 17.9 on page 538).

Magazines may cluster ads before or after the content, on the outside edges, or on pages reserved for advertising.

Any print publication may accept inserts, which are usually printed at the advertiser's expense and delivered to your school. These bring in revenue without taking space away from your content, but they need to be stuffed into the publication just before it is distributed. They frequently end up as litter on campus, so be sure to thank the custodial staff for all their extra work.

Your Turn

1. Locate and clip examples of ad placement or advertising sections in a newspaper and a newsmagazine. Analyze how and where ads are placed.
2. **Going Deeper.** Examine a professional publication with many ads. Are competing ads for similar products or services placed near each other? What methods, if any, does the publication use to keep ads for similar products or services separate from each other? Create a policy for your publication about ads for similar products or services. Be prepared to explain this policy to an advertiser.

Make sure you're getting our best side.
Oakvale Nature Reserve
• Lodge
• Restaurant
• Walking Trails
• Scenic Views
Special rates for overnight stays in October and November
Gazette
Oakvale fire department receives new fire engine for fleet
Now the Oakvale Fire Department will be doing their duty in style. A new fire engine was donated to the station from the Volunteer Firemen's fund. I was just waiting for them to get a new engine," said local resident Faye Buckley. "Their old one was so beat up!" Many town residents had noticed the dings and scratches on Oakvale's old fire engine. Now the shiny, red engine
(continued on p. 5)
Largest rainfall in 2020 leaves Oakvale flooded
Basements were underwater last weekend when nearly ten inches of rain fell in just three hours. The stormy afternoon left Oakvale residents reeling. Many spent their Monday mornings bailing out their own homes. "Because of the large amount of rain that fell in a short space of time," said local weatherman Todd Nash. "The accumulated water caused the river to overflow, leading to these flooded conditions." Nash said that this is the worst storm he's seen in Oakvale since 1968, when
(continued on p. 8)
Picking up the park
On Wednesday, ten students from West High School participated in a special cleanup event at Silver Creek Park. The cleanup effort, spearheaded by senior Jill Barnes, began bright and early at 5:30.
"We have to start early if we want to finish before school starts," says Jill.
The high school
(continued on p. 9)

Figure 17.8 Advertising sleeves wrap around a newspaper page and cover about a third of the front page. They can easily be removed to read the publication's content.

Figure 17.9 This newspaper page shows ads laid out in "pyramid" style. This arrangement helps avoid disrupting the flow of the stories on the page.

2 The Oakvale Gazette November 20, 2020

Falcons protest UC tuition increase

Three recent Ocean Vista alumni joined walkouts at University of California campuses Monday protesting proposed tuition hikes while seniors express worry.

Suzanne Jacobian helped occupy UC Berkeley's Wheeler Hall, while Sunny Huynh and Charlie Washington demonstrated at UC Riverside and UC Santa Barbara. All three students graduated in 2020.

The UC Board of Regents voted Wednesday to raise tuition by 5 percent each year for the next five years. Students who applied this fall expecting to pay $12,192 a year in tuition would pay $15,564 by 2019 under the plan.

Jacobean, 2020–2021 ASB president, tweeted, "Tuition hike is insane. We're taken hostage by the Regents."

Huynh, who entered UC Riverside as a sophomore because of AP credits, posted Instagram photos of herself among other students flashing the three-finger Hunger Games salute, while Washington, last June's Ocean Vista co-valedictorian, reports chalking protest messages and art on the UCSB sidewalk.

OV seniors also reacted negatively to the Regent's decisions. Ana Sanchez-Morales and her twin brother Hugo both applied to UC schools. "My parents are teachers. How could they afford $31,000 in tuition for us, plus books, fees and living expenses?

"The UC's were supposed to provied a world class education for students who prepared themselves. We kept our *(continued on p. 4)*

Largest rainfall in 2020 leaves Oakvale flooded

Basements were underwater last weekend when nearly ten inches of rain fell in just three hours. The stormy afternoon left Oakvale residents reeling. Many spent their Monday mornings bailing out their own homes.

"Because of the large amount of rain that fell in a short space of time," said local weatherman Todd Nash. "The accumulated water caused the *(continued on p. 8)*

Come to Oakvale

The crowd applauded when the candidates mentioned tax breaks. For years now, the residents of Oakvale have felt the crunch under high property taxes in the region. These candidates *(continued on page 10)*

Radio Broadcasts

On the radio, ads may be interspersed throughout the broadcast in sets of two, three or more ads. Thirty-second ads and 60-second ads are the most common. (Studies show that listeners remember 60-second ads better than shorter ones and the first and second ad in a set better than the third or fourth.) That means that a set of ads may take two or three minutes.

About eight percent of listeners switch stations or turn off the radio to avoid ads, a rather small percentage. Perhaps radio listeners are already multitasking, doing something else, such as driving or cooking as they listen. Waiting several minutes for more content does not frustrate them as much as a 15-second wait may frustrate someone focusing on a Web page. Nonetheless, radio announcers frequently tease stories that will come after the ads; that is, they read a headline or promotional announcement to entice the listener to stay tuned through the ads.

Ten-second ads called **billboard ads**, usually 30 words or fewer, run just before regular features, such as the traffic report. In your broadcast, you may say, "The lunch menu is brought to you by Westfork Urgent Care. No appointment necessary, most insurance accepted." Or before the sports wrap-up: "The sports wrap-up is brought to you by Bill's Electronics, where you can find 55" TVs for less." Before a movie review: "Marquee reviews are brought to you by C.F. Eye Care. Your vision is safe in the hands of our board-certified optometrists. Designer frames and colored contact lenses available."

Websites

When you design your website, leave space for online advertising. If you do not plan for advertising, you may be forced to place ads where

And Now... Closer to Home

Five Things to Do When They Say No

You will hear "No" more often than you hear "Yes." Remember, Babe Ruth was not only the home run king, he also led the world in strikeouts. You will strike out, too.

1. Thank the person politely for her time and ask if you may check back with her later. Very few business people will refuse to let you come back. The initial "No" may really mean "Not now. I cannot make up my mind." You may do better on your next visit. Sometimes she will advertise with you later just because she admires your persistence.
2. Bring the business person a copy of your next publication. "I just wanted to show the newest Daily Bugle." He may have told you no initially because he doubted you would publish on schedule. Prove to him you are trustworthy.
3. Point out what his business is missing out on. He may have said no because he did not think your advertising was a good value. If you distribute 2,000 copies of your paper (and they do not just sit unread in the back of classrooms) or get 2,000 hits on your site, point out that you can deliver 2,000 sets of eyes to his ad.
4. Offer your design services and show examples. The business person may have said no because she did not know how to design an ad herself.
5. Keep smiling. The business people did not reject you, they rejected a great business opportunity, silly them. Act as if they were a pleasure to meet, even if they were not. Perhaps they will buy an ad later, but whether or not they do, you have earned good will for your school and your publication.

Think of selling ads like shooting baskets or scoring a solid kick to the upper right side of the net. All the practice—and the missed shots—seem worthwhile when you score an ad.

they interrupt the flow of your journalism content. Or you may not have space to run ads where they will be most effective.

You need to leave space for ads where they will attract attention but do not distract from your content. Design your site to leave room for **banner ads**, usually rectangular ads that appear above, below or on the side of your content. For instance, you may leave room for a banner just below your header. Banner ads here can be as little as 60 pixels high but extend 486 pixels—or more—across the top of your page. You may also dedicate the right-hand margin of your home page to ads that are 125 by 125 pixels. If you placed ads on the left-hand margin, you would interrupt the readers' scan of your page. Readers usually scan the top of the page and then scan down the left side until they find something that interests them. Then they read across the page. They read in the shape of a capital F or E. If the left-hand column is full of ads, readers will be more likely to miss your stories (Figure 17.10).

Some sites place ads below the headline, read-out and lead, but just before a story, hoping the reader will be interested enough to continue reading the news content below the ad (Figure 17.11 on page 542). These ads may be 300 by 250 pixels, so the reader will need to either click on the ad, scroll past the ad or give up and go to another story—or site. These ads receive more clicks than ads placed in any other position on a website; so while they may be good for business—if you are being paid per click—they may be bad for your content.

Banner ads are most common on a home page, but they also can be placed on inside pages, such as the sports page.

Interstitial ads, ads that open a separate browser window, can show larger graphics or contain streaming presentations without slowing down your Web pages. These ads require that a great deal of data be transferred very quickly, so they are housed on an ad server instead of your publication's server. An **ad server** is a computer or system of computers that stores the ads and uploads them to your website.

These ads are activated when a user clicks on your content, such as a podcast or interactive feature. Your audience may not be expecting them. Too many of these ads, or dull ads or ads that are too long, may distract or annoy your audience before they get to your content. Some may leave your website entirely.

Think about advertising when you choose the colors for your site. If your website is royal blue and deep red, a couple of animated banner ads in magenta and green or in yellow and puce may clash with your page and make it as easy to read as a flock of excited tropical parrots.

Designing Ads

Many businesses will give you **camera-ready art**, ads ready to be scanned into your publication, or they may submit digital files ready to be imported. At other times you will be asked to create an ad for a client from the images, text and information the client gives you.

Figure 17.10 The arrangement of these web ads does not disrupt the readers' scan of the page. Keeping ads on the right side of a webpage helps readers from being distracted, since people scan down the left hand side, then read from left to right.

Figure 17.11 Readers are forced to scroll past an interrupter ad before reading the rest of the story.

Winter storm hammers Oakvale residents

Mon Feb 8, 2020 10:45am EST

By Angela Schreff

A winter storm blew into Oakvale on Thursday, causing school closures and traffic problems.

The storm, which was strong even for this time of year, swept through Oakvale and surrounding areas to the southeast on Thursday.

RETIREMENT PLANS ADVERTISEMENT

Financial Advice Available

retire-at-thirty.com

Test your financial health. Learn more today

"Folks just didn't know it would get this bad," said Dorothy Twain, 66, who spent much of the weekend stranded in her home. "We always get snowstorms, but nothing like this."

The storm carried frozen rain and high winds in addition to eight inches of snow. Some are blaming weatherman Todd Nash for failing to predict the power of this storm.

"The weather isn't always knowable," said Nash. "Sometimes we're working with data only six hours in the future."

The basic principles of design you learned in Chapter 15 all hold true for designing advertising. In addition, you should design ads to meet a specific goal.

What Is the Goal of the Ad?

The purpose of all advertising is to change the person who hears or sees it. Sometimes the desired change is in attitude. Advertisements are meant to attract attention in an effort to sell a product or service. Advertisements are sometimes confused with *propaganda*, which also seeks to influence people's opinions. However, propaganda generally promotes a political cause or idea. The goal of a **public service ad (PSA)**, an ad run without charge, might be to make students aware of an important value or program, such as the importance of the First Amendment or a coming blood drive. Public service ads can be run to fill in awkward spaces. In addition, designing public service ads is good practice for designing paying ads (Figure 17.12).

Sometimes advertisers just want students to be aware of their business. Radio billboard ads, such as "The weather is brought to you by New York Fog umbrellas. We're up when the rain comes down," tend to do this, as do business card ads such as the one in Figure 17.13.

Some ads are meant to create **brand awareness**, that is, recognition of a brand name, which may appear on different products sold by the same company, such as pants, sweatshirts, sunglasses and hats. These ads also are meant to change an attitude. The viewers should leave the ad sensing that anything with that brand carries with it a certain style—and they want that style.

"This grass is so much

shelter floor."

Adopted 7-15-19
All shelter dogs deserve a
person to call their own.

Best Friend Animal Rescue

Figure 17.12 PSAs can be used to promote worthy issues and programs. Consider including a PSA such as this in your October edition to promote adopt-a-shelter-dog month. *Why might this ad catch the readers' attention?*

But many other ads want the listener or viewer to *do* something. Click here. Order a pizza. Buy a Lexus. Order a yearbook before the prices go up. Take an SAT prep class. Clip this coupon, come to the shop and get half off on eyebrow waxing with a manicure.

Figure 17.13 A business card-sized ad, usually 1/16th of a page, should promote a company's service and be easy to read.

Your dog is not just a pet, but a member of your family.
It's Pawty Time!
Honor your canine companion's special day with a birthday party. We offer specially baked "doggy cakes," party invitations, balloons, party favors and more.
Office: 555.6200 • Mobile: 555-7640 • Fax: 555-6226
E-mail: pawty-time@dogsrule.com

Once you and your client agree on the purpose of the ad you are to design and the message you are to deliver, you can use the design elements of your media to meet that goal. Design elements are the "stuff" from which messages are created, the pieces and characteristics you can manipulate to create an impression, communicate information to your audience and motivate them to do what your advertiser wants. Mastering each of the design elements used in your media—radio, TV, print and online—allows you to create compelling ads.

Creating Radio Ads

Radio ads have only a few elements to work with. You have a text, a voice, music and sound effects, and thirty seconds to fill. Or maybe 60 seconds. Or only 10 seconds to reach your audience.

Crafting the Text

Talk with your client to learn what his goal is for the ad and what message he wants you to deliver. Ask him what benefit his product offers or how it is better than the competition's.

Write down the advertising version of the five W's: *who* the client is, *what* the product or service is that he is advertising, *where* it is available, *when* it is available and *why* the customer should spend money on the product or service. You will not necessarily include all these in your ad, but you need to know them to create the ad.

- *Who*: Crestline Dance Club
- *What*: alcohol-free dance club
- *When*: teens welcome until 11:00 p.m. on Saturday nights (alcohol served after 11:00 p.m. to legal drinkers)
- *Where*: Beach Road at Pacific Coast Highway
- *Why*: live music, dancing, beverages and appetizers in an alcohol-free, teen-friendly atmosphere

There is a second *why* in advertising, a crucial one, because it defines the message your advertiser wants you to deliver: *Why should you go or buy or do what is advertised?* In this case, the answer is that this is the only place an underage person in your area can go to dance outside of school or church dances, especially to live music, and it is more sophisticated than the other opportunities.

To refine your message, think about your audience. You have an advantage over most radio copy writers because you know your audience well—you see them at least five days a week. If you keep your audience and the product or service in mind, you will have an easier time deciding how to deliver the message, *why* they should do what the ad suggests.

You can choose the tone and style of the ad to appeal to your audience. You will also have a great advantage when you choose the music.

You will know what emotions and desires motivate them. Perhaps you know they are anxious to grow up, or need an opportunity to hang out with friends, or need an idea for a special date. You appeal to their desire to be more sophisticated than they are at school. You know they want to meet new people, to have an adventure, and you may appeal to these desires in your ad.

Your copy needs to fit inside the time your client purchased, so count your words as you write the copy. If you talk steadily for a minute, you can fit in 125 to 150 words, but you need to leave time for **bumper music**, the music that signals the beginning and end of your ad. You may need to leave two seconds before you start talking for background sounds to create a mood. If you are writing for a 30-second ad, you may have time for only 60 words.

You should mention the name of your client or his business at least three times in the ad. This repetition helps your audience remember what you are advertising.

Create engaging copy for the product or service. Imagine your listeners driving in a car. If the music or the show stops and a dreary or obnoxious ad comes on the radio, they can easily punch another station.

Speak to your audience. Do not talk down to them like this: "So kids, don't worry if you don't have ID. Underage is OK at Crestline on Saturday!"

Do not talk up to your audience, as if you were addressing Congress: "Because no alcohol will be served, you do not need to show proof of age to be admitted."

Simply talk to the people you know, your audience: "You won't be carded, so you can enjoy..."

Your first draft looks like this:

Crestline, the dance club by the sea, has alcohol-free dancing to live music on Saturday nights until 11:00 p.m. You won't be carded, so you can enjoy the beats, the friends and the atmosphere on Saturdays at Crestline. A 15 dollar cover charge lets you dance and mingle from 7 to 11, every Saturday at Crestline, where Beach Road meets PCH. Alcohol available after 11:00 p.m. to the legal-age drinkers.

Time your ad copy. This 70-word copy takes almost exactly 30 seconds, the length of the ad, but you need a few seconds for music and sound effects at the beginning and perhaps the end, so trim out unnecessary words.

Crestline~~, the~~ dance club by the sea has alcohol-free dancing to live music ~~on~~ Saturday nights ~~un~~til 11:00 p.m. You won't be carded, so ~~you can~~ enjoy the beats, the friends and the atmosphere ~~on Saturdays~~ at Crestline. A 15 dollar cover charge lets you dance and mingle from 7 to 11, ~~every~~ Saturday at Crestline, where Beach ~~Road~~ meets PCH. ~~Alcohol available after 11:00 pm to the legal age drinkers.~~ Legal drinkers may purchase alcohol after 11.

The copy is now 60 words long, 15 percent shorter than before, and it can be read in about 25 seconds.

Finding the Voice

The best voice for the ad may not be the best voice. That is, your announcer may have the best pronunciation and best sounding voice on your staff, but that may not be the voice you want to read this ad.

You will probably want someone who sounds only slightly older than your audience—the sophistication of the club is one of its draws, so someone who sounds about 18 or 20 would work well. (The person could be 40 or 14, so long as he or she sounds 20.)

Now you need to choose a male or a female voice. Think of your audience. Which do you most need to sell on the club, boys or girls? Will they respond better to a male or a female voice? Should the voice be sophisticated? Cute? Enthusiastic? A little raspy?

In radio advertising, the narrator's voice may add more than information. The narrator may become a character in the story you are telling with your sound and words. Some of the best voices are not perfect and golden but are interesting.

If you do not have a studio in which to record, you can get clean sound without background noise by sitting in a quiet room, such as a bedroom, with a quilt or comforter pulled over you like a tepee as you record.

Choosing the Sound—Music and Sound Effects

Your words tell the audience when and where and why to go to Crestline. The music should make your audience want to come and dance. Music has power to create impressions and desire. It should be interesting enough that no one is tempted to change radio stations when your ad comes on. It should represent the atmosphere at the club.

But most important, it should be royalty free. A **royalty** is money that goes to composers and performers whenever their work is used for commercial purposes. The CD, DVD or download you own allows you to use the music for private, noncommercial purposes. It does not give you the right to use it in your ad. If you search online for royalty-free music, you may find something appropriate, or you may create your own music.

A soundtrack of young men and women laughing socially, perhaps clinking glasses, and talking would work well with this ad. The sound will set a scene, tell a story and engage your audience's imagination.

Consider starting the ad with the volume up on the music, bringing it down after a little more than a second, bringing up the track of sociable laughter and then fading them both out while you read your copy.

Video Advertising

If you are crafting an ad to be both seen and heard—as an advertising podcast, an interstitial ad or an animated banner ad, or if you are preparing an ad for a televised broadcast—you add one more element, the visual element. But the visual element is so dominant that you will need to rethink the music, the sound effects, and possibly the voice that you used in your radio ad.

Visuals and Emotion

Visual elements can create strong emotional impressions, a powerful selling tool. The right impression will help sell your product. Should the emotion be romantic? If you think your potential customers are couples and it is near Valentine's Day, then romance might be the right emotion. If the customers are teens who are anxious to meet new people, then the emotion you want to portray would be excitement.

You may take still and video shots from across the highway with the sunset silhouetting the club and then shots with the lights coming on in the club. You might stage a group of 20 upperclassmen and recent grads (each with signed model releases) coming into the club in the twilight, a little too far away to be easily recognized. If you are targeting both couples and individuals, portray a few couples and other people in groups of three or four friends.

Inside, in the low light of the club—there are candles in bowls on the tables—you shoot a crowded booth with a mix of males and females, reaching out to help themselves to appetizers, glasses on the table. People are talking and laughing. You get a shot of a couple clinking clear glasses. No alcohol in the scene, but no 7UP either.

Details count. Do you use clear, bulb-shaped Coke glasses? Bottles? What kind? Champagne flutes? Plain bar glasses? Wine glasses? Even these small choices should be made based on your knowledge of your audience. How much do you want the pictures to emphasize the alcohol-free nature of the club? How much do you want the pictures to emphasize the sophistication?

The last shot is of a crowded dance floor. What should the dancers be wearing? How should they be dancing? If you make the scene look too safe, will some stay away? Will more stay away if you make it look too sophisticated? Too dangerous?

You still only have 30 seconds to tell all you can about Crestline and to entice your audience to come. How much time to spend on each scene? You experiment and decide you can begin with two seconds of sunset and the silhouette of Crestline's roofline, to suggest romance. At the third second, you fade to a shot of the lights coming on at Crestline and people coming in—the mood becomes more one of anticipation. You cut quickly to the booth. The last cut is also quick, to the dance floor, where the excitement is at a high point.

You want to create emotions from romance to excitement, all in 30 seconds. You decide the first four seconds should be without voice-over, so you cut the last sentence (seven words) from the text you used for radio and replace it with "Crestline!" The voice-over starts as the people go through the door. The sounds of couples talking and glasses clinking run during the first seconds but fade as the voice-over begins.

Crestline dance club by the sea has alcohol-free dancing to live music Saturday nights til 11:00 p.m. You won't be carded, so enjoy the beats, the friends and the atmosphere at Crestline. A 15 dollar cover charge lets you dance and mingle from 7 to 11, Saturday at Crestline, where Beach meets PCH.

Crestline!

The Voice

Video is a less intimate medium than radio, so you rethink your choice for the voice-over. In the radio ad, the voice you used created a character, someone who belonged in the scene. But videos already have characters, the people in the scenes. You may choose a different voice, one that is less of a character in the scene. You may consider a young adult voice to provide the voice-over.

Music and Sound Effects

You need royalty-free or low-cost music. If you want a romantic mood, you can start with a recording of friends playing a flute and violin duet. You use about three seconds of the 10 seconds they recorded, which is in the same key as the computer-generated dance music that follows. The dance music starts over the top of the flute and violin, as if in the distance, when the actors open the door to go inside. You avoid royalty problems because everyone composes or arranges her own music. You use the same soundtrack of sophisticated laughter and glasses clinking as in the radio spot. The volume and tempo of the music increase during the shot on the dance floor. After 27 seconds the voice-over is done and there is just music. At second 29, the announcer finishes with "Crestline!"

Print Advertising

The design elements of print advertising are the same as those for news and feature stories. (See Chapter 15 for a review of design elements.) For example, type is needed to create the written language of ads—the headlines, subheads and body copy. But type is a visual component as well. The font you choose affects the impression the words make: bold or subtle, formal or casual, elegant or edgy.

To design print ads, you will use

- headlines;
- subheads;
- body copy;
- fonts;
- color;
- layout;
- white space;
- logos; and
- drawings or photographs.

Headlines

The headline is in the largest, brightest font, one that is easy to read. In the absence of dominant art, it is often placed at the optical center of the ad, usually one-third of the way down from the top, sometimes one-third of the way up from the bottom. The headline should make the audience want to read more (Figure 17.14).

How do you decide what is most important? In advertising, it is all about the audience. It is what will be most compelling to your audience and make them want to click, buy, go, call today or order the product or services—or at least read the rest of the ad. Until you sell them on coming to Crestline, you do not need to tell them details, the address or the cover charge, no matter how important that may be.

Strong advertising headlines are not easy to write. Along with graphic elements, they need to do at least three things, all in very few words:

- communicate information
- create desire
- establish a brand

You may need many drafts to get the headline right. And you will know you have it right when you discuss it with your response group on your publication staff, or better yet, with focus groups, students who are potential customers. Focus groups will help you decide on the strongest, shortest language to communicate your message.

Knowing what to leave out is important as you keep the ad short. Since you are putting the ad in a high school publication, do you need to mention in the headline that Crestline is meant for teenagers during the early hours? Or mention the types of drinks available later?

Figure 17.14 In the absence of dominant art, place the headline of your ad one-third of the way down from the top and use an eye-catching font and type size. *What information seems to be most important in this ad?*

These are draft headlines you consider for Crestline:

1. Crestline Dance Club
2. Underage Dance Club
3. Come dance Saturdays at Crestline
4. Alcohol-free dancing on Saturdays
5. A Dance Club for You
6. Teen Dance Club
7. Mingle and dance at Crestline
8. Mingle and dance in alcohol-free Crestline
9. Crestline. The beat, the friends, the dancing
10. The beat, the friends, the dancing, alcohol-free
11. Wanna Dance?
12. You think you can dance?
13. Dance by the sea
14. Teen night at Crestline

YOUR TURN

1. Choose the three headlines with the most promise for your school community. Discuss their strengths and weaknesses with your group.
2. **Going Deeper.** Rewrite the best one, if necessary. Or create a new headline. Keep the headline at seven or fewer words.

Subheads

The next most important information will go into the subheads. These often are indented so the reader's eye is lead naturally to them after he has read the headline. When the ideas in subheads are parallel, the subheads look parallel. When one idea supports another, the subheads look like an inverted step pyramid.

Body Copy

The body copy is the "meat" of the ad. It should be as short and easy to read as possible. Edit out all unnecessary words. Use active verbs and interesting adjectives and nouns.

Body copy should be in smaller type than headlines and subheads. It may include a call to action, an imperative statement that tells the audience what they should do, such as "Come dance on Saturdays."

Other information may include coupons, discounts, prices and services or other selling points. Group similar items together and present them in parallel ways. (See the discussions of proximity and alignment in Chapter 15.) Use white space to indicate which items go together.

The size of the ad dictates how much information will fit. Be careful not to sacrifice white space to content. Who will read all that fine print? See Figure 17.15.

For smaller ads, edit out much of the information in the body copy to preserve white space. Your body copy may include only the bold text from Figure 17.15:

- **Live Music**
- **Dance inside and outside**
- **Alcohol-free bar**
- **Appetizers**
- **No ID required**

Send your audience to Crestline's website for the rest of the information.

You have one more piece of information to add, but it is more important than the live music and menu: a discount or coupon. You sold the ad to Crestline by convincing the manager you can deliver customers with a discount or coupon. "No cover charge for the first 40 guests with this ad on 1/22." You also include a QR code, so customers' cellphones can present the ad at the door.

If you create a coupon, it needs to attract the viewer's eye, so box it to look like a traditional coupon. Use a different font, edge or color. Put it two-thirds of the way down the ad, at the secondary center of visual interest. If the discount information is not boxed, set the text out to the left margin below your body copy, but in a heavier or larger typeface. It should be small enough not to compete with the headline, but it should get the second most attention. (If you publish in print, be careful not to put two coupons back-to-back, which would force your reader to decide which one to save.)

The least important information will go in small type near the bottom of the ad. If you have hooked your readers, they will look for the details: the address, the hours, the website, the QR code to scan. If you have not hooked them, they have no use for that information.

Come dance Saturday—at Crestline

Live music:

Karate in the Garage, November 6 and 13 ◆ Evolved, November 20 and 27
RabbitHole, December 4 only.

Dance inside and out:

Wooden dance floor inside ◆ enclosed patio outside—overlooking the Pacific

Alcohol-free bar:

Alcohol-free beers—Superbock ◆ Becks Blue ◆ Virgin Mixed
drinks—Virgin Mary ◆ Star of India ◆ Hair of the Dog ◆ Bench Warmers.
Soft drinks.

Appetizers:

Stuffed potato skins ◆ jalapeno poppers ◆ buffalo wings ◆ onion rings
sweet potato fries ◆ sampler plates ◆ shrimp quesadilla ◆ crab cakes

No ID required:

From 7 until 11 Saturdays no ID is required at Crestline. After 11, underage patrons will be admitted only with a parent or guardian and alcohol will be available to legal-aged drinkers only.

Figure 17.15 Poorly designed ads may overwhelm the reader causing them to skip the ad entirely.

Your Turn

1. How would you edit the information in Figure 17.15, based on the headline you chose for the ad? What would you like to add, rearrange or delete for your audience? What does *your* audience want to know first, second, or third? What additional information does your audience still want?
2. Is any information aimed at the parents rather than your high school audience? Should there be?

Fonts

Generally, limit your ad to three font families, fewer if the ad is small. (A fourth font may be added as a graphic element, for instance, to look like a handwritten note on the printed ad.) Make sure the headline font is easily read and dominant. Choose fonts that help convey the message of the ad: fun, romantic, exciting, important, serious, awesome. (See Chapter 15 for more information about fonts.)

And Now... Closer to Home

Color in Advertising

People react predictably to colors, and ad designers use their knowledge of color psychology to influence their audience. Match the color with the psychological response usually associated with it. The colors are red, blue, orange, black, white, yellow, purple, pink and green.

1. This color symbolizes nature, health, nurturing, tranquility, harmony and freshness, especially in the lighter shades. It means "Yes" and "Go" and the right answer, as well as money.
2. This cool color suggests serenity, clarity, intellect, precision, formality and elegance, especially in the darker shades. It is not a good color for food—it suppresses appetite.
3. This color is cool and airy and symbolizes purity. It can be modern and abstract. A room in this color looks calm.
4. This is a luxury color and very attractive to women. It conveys elegance and expense. Teenage girls are often fans of this color.
5. This is the number one feminine color, so it is used for "girl" things, for lotions, for anything that needs to seem silky or smooth. It sometimes symbolizes sweetness, and when used in foods, it entices sugar-lovers. It is vaguely irritating to some men.
6. This color symbolizes exclusivity and formality. When it is shiny, it suggests excellence. It says class and tradition.
7. This is a powerful color, full of energy. It says excitement and desire. Babies love it. It makes the viewer's pulse and respiration rate go up. It stimulates appetite, so restaurants use it. It symbolizes both love and hate.
8. This color is eye-catching but also fatiguing if used too much. It is happy, cheerful and energetic, and it goes with rich, buttery food. It is sometimes distasteful to men because it seems "cheap."
9. This color is warm and goes with energy—energy drinks, fruit flavoring and children's products. On the downside, it seems to go with cheap things, so do not use it for luxury products. It goes well with fast food and bargains.

Color

Are you advertising a warm, family-oriented product? A bright childhood item? A novelty? The newest style? Something formal and exclusive? Unless you create ads only for black-and-white publications, you use color. Make sure the colors you use help convey the message of your ad.

Layout

The ad needs a focal point where the viewer's eye will first land, generally a headline, art such as a logo, or a photograph. White space, graphics such as leading lines, photography and the way the text is arranged should lead your viewer through the copy all the way down to the contact information in the small print at the bottom.

YOUR TURN

Redesign the Crestline ad for your publication, using the skills you learned in Chapter 15. Choose a size that you are likely to sell in your publication. You may use your work in the Your Turn on page 552 to create the headline, or you may imagine that the audience will be excited to learn Karate in the Garage is coming to their area or that some other piece of information is the most important to your audience. That information should not only be included, but given a prominent position in the ad. It may even be the headline.

- Create a strong headline.
- Choose appropriate fonts and sizes to direct your reader's eye.
- Group like items together.
- Include a call to action.
- Choose appropriate colors for the fonts and background.
- Try redesigning the ad for a smaller or larger ad.

White Space

White space, also called negative space, helps your reader prioritize information. The more white space surrounding something, the more important the idea seems. Larger ads can include more information while preserving white space. If you are designing a small ad, edit the text to allow for the white space that helps the reader navigate the ad. An ad with too little white space, such as the one in Figure 17.15, feels like someone is talking too fast.

YOUR TURN

1. Clip two ads that use white space well. Clip two ads that use white space poorly. What would you tell the advertiser who uses white space poorly?
2. **Going Deeper.** Redesign the two poor ads so that the white space points the reader to the most important information.

Left, Right or Both?

Great ads appeal to both logic and emotion. Logic is often attributed to the left side of the brain, while emotion is attributed to the right. The text of the radio and video ads provides the information the left brain needs to decide whether to go to Crestline: the cost, how and when to get there. But the text also appeals to the right brain, setting a scene, engaging the audience's imagination and creating a desire: *Alcohol-free dancing, live music. Enjoy the beats, the friends, the atmosphere. Mingle. You won't be carded at Crestline*.

The background sounds, sounds that set a scene and suggest a story, appeal to the right brain. So do the visuals and music that provide characters, settings, even a glimpse of plot. Music especially reaches out to the right brain. All the right-brain approaches are meant to involve the audience's imagination and create desire for the product.

Some advertising designers start with a right-brained approach, a great creative idea, and add the left-brained information to it. The strength of these ads is their appeal. The potential weakness is that the audience may not remember the product, just the great image. One beer company showed teams of Clydesdale horses pulling a traditional beer wagon (the television ad included the rhythmic sound of clopping feet), and a tire company used a blimp to advertise both locally and nationally. Both ads were well received. But many viewers could not tell afterwards which beer or which tire company was featured in the ad.

Other designers start with the information and then add images and other visual effects if there is room. The potential weakness of these left-brained ads is that they may not create a desire for the product. Information may not be enough to make a sale.

When right-brain and left-brain approaches meet, an ad can be both informative and enticing—informing in the briefest possible manner and enticing through image, color and graphics.

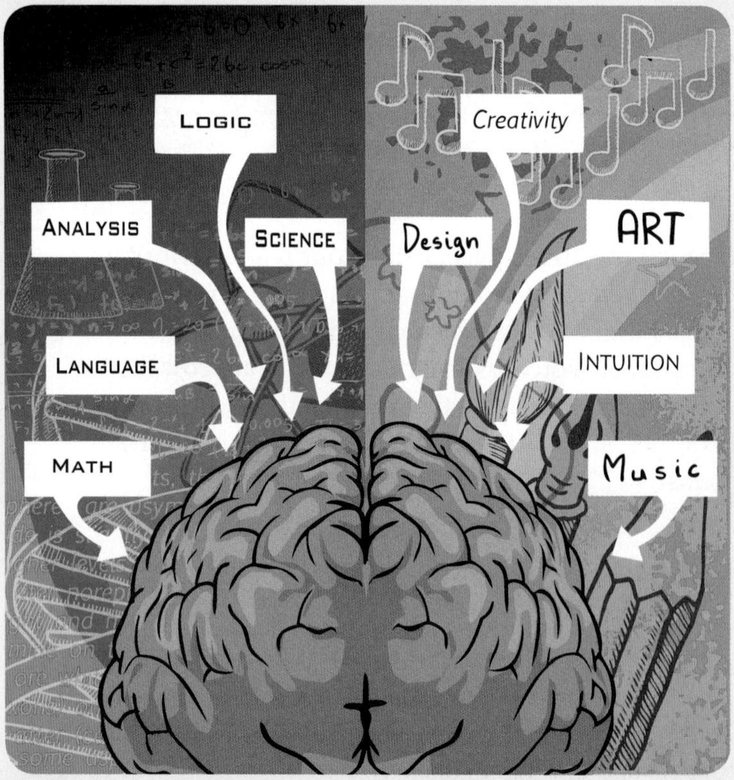

Logos

A **logo** is a visual representation of a company or idea, a sort of shorthand for who it is, where it is and what it stands for or provides. Your advertiser may provide you with a logo. Be aware that most logos are trademarked and should be used only by authorized dealers. Many companies have logo usage guidelines that specify color, size and other characteristics, such as requiring the company name to accompany the logo.

Drawings and Photographs

Drawings should convey a message and create an emotion in addition to illustrating a product or event. They should be simple enough to reproduce well and not too detailed to be instantly understood in the size in which they will be printed.

Photographs in advertising should create desire for the product or service you are advertising. They may tell a story the viewers would like to experience for themselves. They may create an image, or give a detailed and enticing view of a product. Close-up, well-lighted and carefully staged photos of products and experiences are powerful advertising tools.

Your Turn

1. Clip or download four ads that appeal to both sides of your brain. For each, identify which elements are more right-brained, which are more left-brained. Which ads do you enjoy more? Which are more likely to move you to action? Which ad best helps you remember the name of the product or cause?
2. **Going Deeper.** Find a left-brain, information-only ad that has run in your publication or in other media. Suggest elements to engage the audience's right brain and make them want the product. Design the improved ad.

Web Advertising

If you design advertising for a website for very long, you will eventually use every design element used in radio, TV and print advertising. But when you create ads for the Web, you will need to capture your audience's attention even while they are being enticed away by ten—or fifty—other choices.

You also need to make your ads so good that your viewer will read or view and respond to them in a matter of seconds. Web users expect speed, and their cursors flee to the Back button at the first whiff of boredom. Radio listeners will stay tuned through a two- or three-minute set of ads. Some TV viewers will do the same, but Web users may be frustrated by a 10- or 15-second delay when an interstitial ad appears before the content they wanted.

You also need to capture a Web user's interest with a small amount of information. Though print ads may take up whole pages in a newspaper or magazine, online ads often are only a few inches wide on a computer screen, smaller on mobile devices. Even the largest ads can be no bigger than the screen in the customer's hand, yet they must be powerful.

Print, TV and radio ads want to change people's attitudes or actions. They want the audience to think differently, clip a coupon, order something, shop somewhere, buy something, take a course, fall in love with a brand, plan a trip or vote.

Web advertising has a simpler goal. Almost always the goal is to get the viewer to click on something. More rarely, the goal is to get the audience *not* to click on the button that says Close or Skip This Ad.

Your Turn

Go to the home page of two major news organizations that publish on the Web. Find the Advertise link. (It may be on the bottom of the home page.) Find the types of ads, sometimes called the specs, offered for a platform you use or your journalism program uses.

1. List and describe the kinds of ads in which the viewer can choose to expand the ad to get more information.
2. List and describe the kinds of ads in which the viewer needs to opt out of the ad by clicking on a Skip This Ad or Close button.

Static Ads

The simplest ads are **static ads**—they just sit there, almost like print ads, with no animation or interactive elements except for a single hyperlink that lets the viewer **click through**, or click on the hyperlink to go to another site. Sometimes all the words or images in the ad are live, meaning that everything is a hyperlink; so wherever the viewer clicks, it links to the other site. Sometimes just a small section of the text will take the viewer to the site with more information.

These static ads can be quite small in two ways. A **button ad** may be as small as 120 pixels wide by 60 pixels high, extending one-eighth to one-fifth of the way across the width of the page. In addition to their small width and height, these ads are small in terms of the data they use. A button ad may use 10 kilobytes of data. Static banner ads using less than about 20 kilobytes of data can be housed completely on your site.

You cannot fit much into such a small ad. Some button ads allow only 40 text characters. A larger banner ad may allow a 50-character headline, including spaces, a 90-character text and 50 **hyperlinked** characters (characters that will take the viewer to another site that houses more information). That site can belong to your advertiser, but the copy, images and animation can also be housed on an ad server.

To write compelling copy in a very short form, revisit the process you used to create a radio ad or the headline for a print ad earlier in this chapter. After learning about your advertiser and the product, you write this headline, which is just under 50 characters:

Teen dance club Saturday—Live music at Crestline

You get 90 more characters of text. Your goal is to entice your viewer to click through and learn more about your advertiser. What information would be most likely to do that? You decide your viewers want to know the type of band that will play there. And that they need to know the club is nearby.

Karate in the Garage Nov 6 & 13
Beach Rd at PCH, Manhattan Beach

YOUR TURN

You still may use roughly 25 characters more in the body copy of your Crestline ad. What is the next most enticing piece of information you could add? Or would white space be better, to increase the readability of the ad?

Like print ads, online ads may use distinctive fonts and background colors to suggest excitement and a teen-friendly atmosphere. As you do when you design a print ad, you need to balance the exciting image you want to create against readability—how easily the font on the background color can be read (Figure 17.16).

Online ads have an additional restriction you do not face in print ads—the size of the file. An unusual font may require more file space than you have available.

Your advertisers may be able to buy extra storage space for their banner ad, storage that may allow them to include a logo or simple picture on a static banner ad. But the bigger the file, the more slowly your Web page will load.

Larger Ad Files

Larger ads need to be housed on a third-party server, an ad server. The ads housed there can load almost immediately and not slow down

Figure 17.16 *Do you find this ad easy to read? Why or why not?*

your site. The bandwidth—the rate at which a person's connection and device can receive and transmit information—will control how swiftly the ads come up.

Ads housed on ad servers require all your talents as a videographer and everything you learned as you designed ads for print publications.

These ads can be many pixels tall and wide. As with print ads, the headline and graphics, including art, photography, logos, color schemes and layout, need to engage your reader. If they do not, she will scroll past them to continue reading your journalistic content or perhaps never see the rest of your content.

Online advertising adds other dimensions. For instance, inside the leaderboard's 728 x 90 pixels, you may insert animation (a series of still images that change frequently) or text that crawls or appears from any direction or fades in and out, in effect creating a silent PowerPoint presentation.

Frequently these ads are **expandable ads** when the viewer accepts an invitation to "click here to expand." A 300 x 250 pixel ad may open to one that is 970 pixels wide, the total width of many Web pages, including margins.

In addition to banners, which remain on the screen once it is opened, your site may have interstitial ads that appear unexpectedly when a viewer or reader is seeking your content. These ads can open above your content or on top of your page. They need to capture the viewer's interest quickly before his mouse can find—and scamper to—the "Close this" X in the corner.

Pop-up ads are more than interstitial ads. They usually are new browser windows that appear on top of the window the viewer has selected (the active window). Pop-up ads block the content the viewer has requested—the viewer cannot simply scroll past the ad. A variation, the pop-under ad, appears behind the active window and therefore is not seen until the active window is closed. These sites often harvest the viewer's information, such as his computer address and his interests as shown by what he has researched and the windows on which he paused. Pop-ups and pop-unders have become so unpopular with Internet users that many programs allow users to block them unless the viewer specifically chooses to see them. Because they are so often blocked, they are a less efficient way to advertise a product.

Other online ads may be not much larger than a banner ad or even a button and contain very little information. The image is meant to create such curiosity, admiration or even envy that the viewer will mouse over the image. The viewer may be invited to "mouse over to explore" then invited to "Click here to explore." The ad will then expand.

Though the enlarged ad needs to be well-designed and well-written, the initial small ad requires the best of graphic design. If it does not engage the viewer, no one will see the expanded ad. It must be something beautiful, such as the hood and wheel well of an attractive car, or it must promise humor or enticing information.

Your Turn

1. Find and print out two small banner ads or buttons that open up to larger ads.
   - How many words are on the banner?
   - Discuss why the smaller ad entices a viewer to click for more information.
2. **Going Deeper.** Choose a static ad from your publication or another. Design a button or banner to entice the audience into the ad. Redesign the ad that opens up, if necessary.

Your skills as a videographer also support web advertising through **streaming video**, a traditional video compressed to be transferred over the Web.

Some streaming video ads are interstitial and run when a viewer clicks on a journalistic video. They are often just 15 seconds long, rarely more than 30 seconds, and must interest the viewer so much he does not find and click the Skip This Ad button, or worse, close your website.

Other video ads open when the viewer clicks the Watch Video link on the ad. Because the viewer has already shown interest in the subject and has chosen to see the video, it can be longer than the ones that run when a viewer is looking for something else. These may be over a minute long, but they still must be well-planned, controlling the viewer's emotional response with music, video, voice-over and interviews, as with any video ad.

For the Record

Three Legal Questions

1. Are we violating the First Amendment or other laws if we reject an ad?

If an employee of a public school district rejects an ad, the district may be sued for violating the advertiser's free speech, which includes commercial speech. A public school district is an arm of government.

But if the student leadership of a publication or broadcast rejects an ad, they are not the government and are not limiting someone else's First Amendment rights. (Remember, the First Amendment keeps the government from limiting those five freedoms. It does not restrain nongovernmental groups from having—and acting on—opinions.) It is important that the students create their own advertising policy and that the students—not the adults—decide what ads they will and will not accept.

2. Can the public school tell us what ads to reject?

A public school probably can forbid advertising for products that are harmful to minors or illegal for minors. That would include alcohol, cigarettes and other controlled substances. If tanning salons or tattoo parlors are not allowed to serve high-school-age students in your area, it is probably legal for the school to forbid ads for these services.

3. Can we use pictures of students or alumni in ads we design?

Only with written permission. You need a signed model release form for every person who is recognizable in the ad. People have the right to control their image and what it may appear they are endorsing. That means shots of pep rallies could be used in an ad only if you got permission from every student in the picture who may be recognizable.

Chapter Seventeen

Review and Assessment

Recall

1. Once you have established the time frame for your budget, you need to determine two other crucial pieces of information. What are they?
2. Who are potential advertisers in your school community?
3. Describe five things to do when potential advertisers say no.
4. Sketch how print ads are usually arranged on inside pages of a newspaper.
5. How is the goal of online advertising different from the goals of print, radio and TV advertising?
6. How does a static online ad differ from an interstitial ad?
7. What design elements can be manipulated in a radio ad?
8. What design elements can be manipulated in a video ad?
9. What design elements can be manipulated in a print ad?
10. What design elements can be manipulated in larger online ads, housed on ad servers?

Critical Thinking

1. How can your publication's fact sheet positively or negatively influence a potential advertiser?
2. How can you cover a controversy regarding the football team and still ask football boosters to advertise with you?
3. Why would you want a different voice to narrate a radio ad than you would for a video ad?
4. Explain the difference between advertising and propaganda.
5. Choose an imaginary product or service and design a color scheme for an ad. Explain why you chose the colors based on advertising psychology.

Application

1. Assemble a sales kit for your publication.
2. Make three ad calls, remembering to coordinate with your business manager. Make phone contact first and then make the personal call. Report in writing to your business manager.
3. You have been asked to create an advertising campaign for a new amusement center in your area. It will have a paintball area, an adults' ball pit, trampolines, courts for basketball, volleyball and dodge ball, and zip lines, among other features. You interview the manager who wants you to create the ads. (You may use your imagination and add features that you would like to see in an amusement center.) Write the five W's plus the *why* that defines the message of the ad.
   A. Design a 30-second radio ad. Write the text. Explain the sound effects, voice and music you would use. Use the name of the business at least three times.
   B. Design a video ad for broadcast or your website. It may be as long as one minute. Describe the mood or emotional reaction you wish to create.

   Describe
   - what you will video;
   - how long you will stay on each video section;
   - the music you will use;
   - the background sound;
   - whom you will interview on the video; and
   - whether you will use a narrator—and, if so, what sort of voice you would like to use.

   C. Sketch a half-page print ad for the amusement center. Write the headline and subhead (but you may use nonsense words for the body copy), design a logo, select dominant art and/or photographs.
   D. Sketch a static banner ad to run horizontally at the top of your website's home page. You may use one simple image and up to fifty characters in the headline (including spaces) and up to 90 text characters in the rest of the ad.
   E. Sketch an expandable ad that covers half a page. Be sure to include a focal point, art, text and animated or interactive elements.

Chapter Seventeen

Journalism Style

Oft-Confused Words

Rare tarantula found in dessert

Was there a spider in the banana cream pie or in a dry, sandy region? Using the wrong word, even one that is wrong by only a letter, can create embarrassing or misleading headlines and stories. In this Journalism Style, you will learn to distinguish between words that are often confused.

Write the correct word for the context provided by each sentence below. After identifying the correct word, check your answers at the *Journalism* website.

Record each error on the "demon list" that you started earlier for spelling errors. Then research the difference between the words you have confused and devise a way to avoid the error in the future. For example, suppose you missed this:

> *The new double-cinnamon bun has fewer/less calories than the old version.*

Reference sources, such as the AP Stylebook, will tell you to use *less* with mass nouns—butter, outrage, trouble, class spirit—and *fewer* with count nouns, things you can count—calories, days until spring break, graduates, buses.

You could make an entry like this in your list of personal demons:

> *Fewer calories. Count noun—I can count calories. (Not less, which is for mass nouns.)*

As with spelling errors, when you are sure you have mastered the uses of *fewer* and *less*, you can put a thin line through that entry.

Try It!

On a separate sheet of paper, write the correct word.

1. If you are not sure what to do, follow your conscience/conscious.
2. The principal/principle has plans for the school.
3. Weather/Wether/Whether or not you like it, the test is Friday.
4. The hole/whole class participated in the drill.
5. I want the bare/bear truth.
6. She barely/bearly passed PE.
7. I have the trophy, and its/it's huge.
8. What will he do than/then?
9. The Foreign Affairs Council/Counsel will meet next Thursday.
10. I'll read the first three verses/versus.
11. After three weeks in a coma, she is now conscience/conscious again.
12. Please accept/except this award.
13. Their/There/They're is no hope!
14. She has to/too/two pairs of twins.
15. Her dream of escaping poverty by playing in the NBA is probably just an allusion/illusion.
16. "This is Max Headroom, reporting from the briefing room of the Capital/Capitol."
17. The interview did not elicit/illicit any new information.
18. Her out-of-control spending put her finances in a hole/whole.
19. The migrant emigrated/immigrated from New Zealand.
20. He is taller than/then his mother.
21. Washington, D.C., is the nation's capital/capitol.
22. His song contained allusions/illusions to "The Lord of the Rings" and "Harry Potter."
23. The eagle flexed its/it's wings.
24. How can you bare/bear to face her?
25. Grab their/there/they're guns!
26. Please use a capital/capitol letter to begin a quotation.
27. The fight was Lopez verses/versus Tran.
28. It was to/too/two late.
29. Please sit/set at the front of the class.
30. Most of the class was there accept/except for Joao.
31. She gave him wise council/counsel.
32. Your/You're not safe here.
33. Their/There/They're going to lose.
34. He lost his title because his blood test showed an elicit/illicit substance.

Extend Your Knowledge

Style Exercises

Visit the *Journalism* website for additional practice in choosing the correct word.

Chapter Seventeen

Writers' Workshop

In this Writers' Workshop you will:

- Identify vocabulary items that allow you to write clearly and briefly.
- Learn how to make them part of your generative vocabulary.

Workshop 17.1

It's Not Really Yours Until You Use It Four Times

Manifest destiny, *judicial activism*, *sine and coefficient*, *tone*, *hue*, *intensity*, *iambic pentameter*, *pathetic fallacy*, *symbiosis*, *mitochondrial DNA*, *subjunctive*, *ablative*: you are given new vocabulary in almost every class. But journalists write simply and make complicated ideas clear. The news should not sound like an SAT vocabulary list. Why worry about vocabulary in a journalism class?

Journalists need powerful generative vocabularies. You have both a receptive vocabulary, words you understand when you see or hear them (especially when they are used in a meaningful context), and a generative vocabulary, words you use. For most of us, our receptive vocabulary is much larger than our generative vocabulary—we understand many more words than we use.

Journalists, on the other hand, should be able to use all or almost all of the words they—and presumably their audience—understand. Journalists choose among all these words to find the most powerful and clear methods of expression. They strive to use the fewest words and, when possible, the shortest ones that will do the job. They use advanced vocabulary and constructions only when nothing else will do as well.

Mini-Lesson: Identifying Words in Your Receptive Vocabulary

Look at this USA Today article. USA Today writes at a basic level about half the time. Note words that are in your receptive vocabulary but perhaps not in your generative vocabulary. (Suggestions are highlighted.)

Wastewater disposal tied to surge in Oklahoma earthquakes

Hoai-Tran Bui, USATODAY 2:40 p.m. EDT July 3, 2014

In 2014, it was not California that had the highest number of earthquakes over the magnitude of 3. It was Oklahoma.

Researchers say the rise in earthquakes may be a byproduct of wastewater disposal from hydraulic fracturing—also known as fracking. A study released Thursday in the journal Science found that the injection of subsurface wastewater from hydraulic fracturing into disposal wells is linked to the dramatic rise of earthquakes in central Oklahoma since 2009.

The chances are good that you already understood *tied to*, *surge*, *byproduct*, *linked to* and *dramatic rise*. You did not need a dictionary—or an encyclopedia—for these terms. But you may not have these words available for use in your own writing.

Why are these words powerful?

Both *tied to* and *linked to* avoid more obvious words such as *causes*, which would be inaccurate. The study in Science shows one thing follows another—they are linked or tied together—but respectable scientists, like journalists, have a very high standard of proof before they assert one thing causes another. *Byproduct* also suggests a weaker cause-effect link than *causes* and certainly does not imply that anyone is knowingly causing earthquakes.

Bigger than 3 is a tempting substitute *for over the magnitude of 3*. After all, it is shorter, but it loses out on two counts. *Magnitude* is the appropriate term for measuring earthquakes. In addition, a magnitude 3 earthquake is not just larger than a 2, it is 10 times larger, and it releases more than 31.6 times the amount of energy a magnitude 2 releases. *Magnitude* is both more appropriate and more accurate.

Surge is a more compelling word than *increase*, *uptick*, or simply *more earthquakes*. It probably accurately reflects the large upswing in earthquakes in Oklahoma—the *dramatic rise*.

Apply It!

Print out an interesting news or opinion article from each of the five largest newspapers in the U.S. (Wall Street Journal, USA Today, New York Times, Los Angeles Times and Washington Post). Highlight words that you understand but rarely use. Copy at least 10 words, and the sentences in which you found them, into a document. Save it for the next mini-lesson.

Mini-Lesson: Transferring Words From Your Receptive to Your Generative Vocabulary

A powerful generative vocabulary allows you to write briefly, freeing your reader from long trips through muddy undergrowth. Short is best for headlines, leads and using your audience's time wisely—in short, all journalism. In "How to Write Short," Roy Peter Clark tells writers to collect great short writing. He quotes fortune cookies, "Bread today is better than cake tomorrow," "A feeling is an idea with roots." He quotes cereal boxes, baseball cards, Valentine hearts and signs.

The prize for effective short writing may go to the National Park Service at Grand Canyon. Most casual hikers are accustomed to going up before they go down, so the first part of their hike is usually the hardest. When they get tired, they turn around and come back down.

But that may spell trouble in the Grand Canyon, where the first five miles take hikers down over 3,000 feet. By the time they are tired, they can be miles from water, exhausted by weather, wind and altitude, and have a long, steep climb in front of them. The Park Service rescues almost one person a day from the canyon.

So the Park Service posts warning signs and publishes literature explaining heat exhaustion, dehydration, wintertime ice on the trail and the effects of altitude—the canyon rims are between 6,800 and 8,200 feet high. But their most convincing publication is six words long, a clear sign posted beside the trail:

Down is optional. Up is mandatory.

Optional and *mandatory* are in almost every high school student's receptive vocabulary. But not everyone uses them to write something so compact, with such a compelling turn of phrase. How do you move such words and phrases into your generative vocabulary? In three easy steps, and you may be able to skip the first one:

1. Make sure you understand the word's meaning. If you are unsure, do the following:
   - Search for it in an online dictionary.
   - If you are unsure how to use the word or expression, capture three or four intelligent uses of the word from well-written Internet sites. (These should never be more than two sentences long.) Paste them into a document, read each one and then (without looking at the model) type each sentence from memory. If you do so accurately, you know how to use the word or expression. Go to step 2.
2. Use the vocabulary item in a sentence that is a ghost of the original, changing only a few words. For instance, a ghost sentence for *Down is optional. Up is mandatory.* might be *Group work is mandatory. Being a martyr is optional.*
3. Write three more sentences using the vocabulary item, but move away from the shape of your original model. For instance:
   - The TSA has made the removal of shoes *optional* for travelers over 75 years of age. For the rest of us, it is *mandatory*.
   - The fire department ordered a *mandatory* evacuation of residents in low-lying areas, but for those living on the bluffs, the evacuation was *optional*, though they could be isolated by surging stormwaters.
   - Foreign language study is *optional* unless you intend to apply to a university. Then it is *mandatory*.

Four uses of the vocabulary item is a magic number. Read your sentences aloud to a response partner. Edit as needed. The words should now be yours to use.

Apply It!

Choose five words you found during the Apply It for the first mini-lesson, above. Follow steps 1, 2, and 3. Time how long this exercise takes you for each word. Compare with your group members how long it takes to move each vocabulary item from your receptive to your generative vocabularies. Read the sentences aloud to a response partner or group.

Watch during the next few weeks to see which words have moved into your generative vocabulary.

Extend Your Knowledge Extend

Visit the *Journalism* website for additional practice.

Photo Credits

Front Cover

Student reporter conducting interview: Forrest Czarnecki, Conifer High School
Student reading newspaper: Nora Parisi, Woodrow Wilson High School
Videographer on football field: Kyle Farrell, Lee County High School
Student editing video at computer: Ana Perez, Daniel Pearl Magnet School
Photographer behind fence: Forrest Czarnecki, Conifer High School
Student working on laptop: Ellen Austin, The Winged Post, The Harker School

Back Cover

Photo by Forrest Czarnecki, Conifer High School

Chapter 1

Figure 1.0 Courtesy of Ellen Austin
Figure 1.1 Goodheart-Willcox Publisher
Figure 1.2 Goodheart-Willcox Publisher
Are You Already a Journalist? Monkey Business Images/Shutterstock.com, Ermolaev Alexander/Shutterstock.com, Fuse/Thinkstock, sirtravelalot/Shutterstock.com
Figure 1.3 Monkey Business Images/Shutterstock.com
Figure 1.4 Wavebreakmedia Ltd/Wavebreak Media/Thinkstock
Figure 1.5 Syda Productions/Shutterstock.com, Fulcanelli/Shutterstock.com
Your Turn, pg. 11 Goodheart-Willcox Publisher
Figure 1.6 Cybermama/iStock/Thinkstock, Fuse/Thinkstock
Figure 1.7 Jack Hollingsworth/Photodisc/Thinkstock
Meet the Professionals Ball State University
Figure 1.8 Kratky/Shutterstock.com
Figure 1.9 Chris Clinton/Photodisc/Thinkstock.com
Figure 1.10 Monkey Business Images/Shutterstock.com
Figure 1.11 United States Census Bureau
Figure 1.12 Rawpixel.com/Shutterstock.com
Figure 1.13 Mega_Pixel/iStock/Thinkstock
Figure 1.14 SimmiSimons/iStock/Thinkstock

Chapter 2

Figure 2.0 Photo by Forrest Czarnecki, Conifer High School
Figure 2.1 Jonah Charlton and Trinity Collins, The Evanstonian, Evanston Township High School
Figure 2.2 Courtesy of The Broadview, Convent of the Sacred Heart High School
Figure 2.3 Courtesy of The Paly Voice, Palo Alto High School
For the Record, pg. 38 Comstock/Stockbyte/Thinkstock, Photos.com/PHOTOS.com/Thinkstock
Figure 2.4 Goodheart-Willcox Publisher
Figure 2.5 Courtesy of The Villager, Westport High School
Figure 2.6 FashionStock.com/Shutterstock.com
Figure 2.7 Courtesy of The Flyer, Lewis University
Figure 2.8 Courtesy of The Eagle's Eye, W. Charles Akins High School
Figure 2.9 Jirayu13/iStock/Thinkstock
Meet the Professionals Courtesy of the Los Angeles Times
Figure 2.10 Cameron Whitman/iStock/Thinkstock, Diego Cervo/Shutterstock.com, UfaBizPhoto/Shutterstock.com, Monkey Business Images/Shutterstock.com
Figure 2.11 Goodheart-Willcox Publisher, photo courtesy of EKSO Bionics, article courtesy of the Los Angeles Times
Figure 2.12 Amir Ridhwan/Shutterstock.com
Figure 2.13 GaudiLab/Shutterstock.com

Chapter 3

Figure 3.0 Courtesy of Ellen Austin
Figure 3.1 Library of Congress, Prints & Photographs Division, LC-USZC2-3154
Figure 3.2 GRANGER
Figure 3.3 Courtesy of the Student Press Law Center
Figure 3.4 Goodheart-Willcox Publisher
Your Turn, pg. 71 Digital Vision./Digital Vision/Thinkstock
Meet the Professionals Courtesy of Kent State University School of Journalism and Mass Communication
For the Record, pg. 77 Everett Historical/Shutterstock.com
Figure 3.5 tommaso79/iStock/Thinkstock
Figure 3.6 360b/Shutterstock.com
Writers' Workshop 3.1 Courtesy of the National Archives

Chapter 4

Figure 4.0 Courtesy of Ellen Austin
Figure 4.1 otnaydur/Shutterstock.com
Figure 4.2 Courtesy of the Society of Professional Journalists
Meet the Professionals Handout via REUTERS
Figure 4.3 Courtesy of Matthew LaPorte
Figure 4.4 Monkey Business Images/Shutterstock.com
Figure 4.5 Courtesy of Ellen Austin
Figure 4.6 Denis Raev/iStock/Thinkstock
For the Record, pg. 115 Neville Elder/Corbis Historical/Getty Images
Figure 4.7 Library of Congress, Prints & Photographs Division, FSA/OWI Collection, [LC-DIG-fsa-8d22685]

Chapter 5

Figure 5.0 Farknot Architect/Shutterstock.com, Suzanne Tucker/Shutterstock.com
Figure 5.1 s_bukley/Shutterstock.com
For the Record, pg. 126 Everett Historical/Shutterstock.com
Figure 5.2 MarinaMariya/iStock/Thinkstock
Figure 5.3 Goodheart-Willcox Publisher
Figure 5.4 Goodheart-Willcox Publisher, drawing by lilmallugirl/Shutterstock.com
Figure 5.5 Goodheart-Willcox Publisher, photo by Michael Mitchell/Shutterstock.com
Figure 5.6 Goodheart-Willcox Publisher
Figure 5.7 Goodheart-Willcox Publisher
For the Record, pg. 144 hamdan/Shutterstock.com
Figure 5.8 Everett Collection/Shutterstock.com

Chapter 6

Figure 6.0 Courtesy of Ellen Austin
Figure 6.1 Courtesy of Before I Die - Louisville
Figure 6.2 moodboard/moodboard/Thinkstock
Figure 6.3 Courtesy of ProPublica/propublica.org
Figure 6.4 Bui Santisouk/Shutterstock.com
Figure 6.5 krutikof/Shutterstock.com
Figure 6.6 Goodluz/Shutterstock.com
And Now…Closer to Home, pg. 164 Goodheart-Willcox Publisher
And Now…Closer to Home, pg. 165 Smitt/iStock/Thinkstock.com
Figure 6.7 Neale Cousland/Shutterstock.com
Figure 6.8 HitToon.com/Shutterstock.com
And Now…Closer to Home, pg. 173 Noppadol_Anaporn/iStock/Thinkstock, Macrovector/Shutterstock.com, Twin Design/Shutterstock.com
Figure 6.9 Monkey Business Images/Shutterstock.com
Meet the Professionals Courtesy of Roy Peter Clark, ©Kenny Irby
Figure 6.10 AntonioDiaz/Shutterstock.com

Chapter 7

Figure 7.0 ©iStock.com/EyeJoy
Figure 7.1 Goodheart-Willcox Publisher
Figure 7.3 Danomyte/Shutterstock.com
Figure 7.4 Courtesy of North Pointe, Grosse Pointe North High School
Figure 7.5 Goodheart-Willcox Publisher
Figure 7.6 Courtesy of Anchorage Daily News
Figure 7.7 Goodheart-Willcox Publisher
Figure 7.9 GetCoffee Font by Cruzine Design & Dealjumbo, Gipsiero Font by Bumbayo Font Fabrik
Figure 7.12 Courtesy of El Estoque, Monta Vista High School
Figure 7.13 Courtesy of Poynter News University's e-learning course: Writing Online Headlines: SEO and Beyond [http://www.newsu.org/courses/writing-headlines-web-seo]

Figure 7.14 Goodheart-Willcox Publisher
Figure 7.15 Goodheart-Willcox Publisher, photo courtesy of Menemsha Films, Inc.
Figure 7.16 Goodheart-Willcox Publisher, photo by Kobby Dagan/Shutterstock.com
Figure 7.17 Goodheart-Willcox Publisher, photo by Studio One Photography, Stephanie Thune
Figure 7.18 Photo by Allie Shorin, Palo Alto High School
Figure 7.19 Courtesy of the Los Angeles Times
Figure 7.20 Photo by Christina House for the Los Angeles Times
Figure 7.21 Courtesy of the Los Angeles Times

Chapter 8

Figure 8.0 Photo by Forrest Czarnecki, Conifer High School
Figure 8.1 Brian Rome/iStock/Thinkstock.com
Figure 8.2 Elena Elisseeva/Shutterstock.com
Figure 8.3 Chimpinski/Shutterstock.com, Coprid/Shutterstock.com
Figure 8.4 Monkey Business Images/Shutterstock.com
Case Study, pg. 232 wavebreakmedia/Shutterstock.com, Blacqbook/Shutterstock.com
Figure 8.5 Goodheart-Willcox Publisher, photo by Brian A Jackson/Shutterstock.com
Figure 8.6 Courtesy of the Society of Professional Journalists
Figure 8.7 Courtesy of the National Freedom of Information Coalition
Figure 8.8 jabkitticha/Shutterstock.com
Case Study, pg. 239 Courtesy of the National Oceanic and Atmospheric Administration
Figure 8.9 Goodheart-Willcox Publisher
Figure 8.10 Erika J Mitchell/Shutterstock.com, Keith A Frith/Shutterstock.com
Meet the Professionals Courtesy of Morgan Jones
Case Study, pg. 244 Marine's/Shutterstock.com
And Now…Closer to Home, pg. 248 PathDoc/Shutterstock.com
Journalism Style Sheila_Fitzgerald/Shutterstock.com

Chapter 9

Figure 9.0 Photo by Kellen Ochi, Courtesy of Michelle Min, Sage Hill High School
Figure 9.1 Mark Herreid/Shutterstock.com
Figure 9.2 SpeedKingz/Shutterstock.com
Figure 9.3 Courtesy of University of Florida Media Relations
Case Study, pg. 260 Jeremy R. Smith Sr./Shutterstock.com
Meet the Professionals ©Christopher Felver/CORBIS
And Now…Closer to Home, pg. 263 Mega_Pixel/iStock/Thinkstock
Figure 9.4 Goodheart-Willcox Publisher
And Now…Closer to Home, pg. 265 Cameron Whitman/Shutterstock.com
Figure 9.5 Zurijeta/Shutterstock.com
Figure 9.6 nikkytok/Shutterstock.com, Slavoljub Pantelic/Shutterstock.com, XanderSt/Shutterstock.com
Case Study, pg. 272 A and N photography/Shutterstock.com
Figure 9.7 Photo by Chris Martin, Woodrow Wilson High School
Figure 9.8 ©iStock.com/johavel
Figure 9.9 Goodheart-Willcox Publisher
Figure 9.10 Photo by Forrest Czarnecki, Conifer High School

Chapter 10

Figure 10.0 Photo by Jake Crandall, The Harbinger, Shawnee Mission East High School
Figure 10.1 Chicago History Museum, ICHi-65439; Stephen Deutch, photographer
Figure 10.2 Courtesy of The Talon, Rochester High School
Figure 10.3 Courtesy of El Estoque, Monta Vista High School
Figure 10.4 Photo by Emily Cunningham, Arapahoe Herald, Arapahoe High School
Figure 10.5 Courtesy of Jake Collins, Redondo Union High School
Figure 10.6 Courtesy of Casey Simmons, Westlake High School
Figure 10.7 Maxim Blinkov/Shutterstock.com
And Now…Closer to Home, pg. 300 Volt Collection/Shutterstock.com

Chapter 11

Figure 11.0 Photo by Allie Shorin, The Viking, Palo Alto High School
Figure 11.1 Photo by Scotty Bara, The Viking, Palo Alto High School
Figure 11.2 Story by Ami Drez and Chris Smith, Photo by Grant Shorin, The Viking, Palo Alto High School
Figure 11.3 Photo by Grant Shorin, The Viking, Palo Alto High School
Figure 11.4 Goodheart-Willcox Publisher
Your Turn, pg. 327 Photo by Jonathan Dai, The Winged Post, The Harker School
Figure 11.5 Courtesy of Ellen Austin
Figure 11.6 Goodheart-Willcox Publisher, photos by murphy81/Shutterstock.com, eurobanks/Shutterstock.com
Figure 11.7 Story by Kevin Dukovic, The Viking, Palo Alto High School
Figure 11.8 Story by Kevin Dukovic and Austin Poore, Photo by Scotty Bara, The Viking, Palo Alto High School
Figure 11.9 Story by Jacob Lauing and Sam Borsos, Photo by Scotty Bara, The Viking, Palo Alto High School
And Now…Closer to Home, pg. 342 Photo by Grant Shorin, The Viking, Palo Alto High School
Figure 11.10 Photo by Allie Shorin, The Viking, Palo Alto High School
Figure 11.11 Photo by Forrest Czarnecki, Conifer High School
Figure 11.12 Column by Michael Cullen, The Viking, Palo Alto High School

Chapter 12

Figure 12.0 Image courtesy of National Scholastic Press Association (nspa.studentpress.org), cartoon by Joel Greenspan, Eastside, Cherry Hill High School East; Image courtesy of National Scholastic Press Association (nspa.studentpress.org), cartoon by Garrett Wilson, Epic, Shawnee Mission West High School; Courtesy of Rachel Fung, The Broadview, Convent of the Sacred Heart High School
Figure 12.1 Courtesy of The Evanstonian, Evanston Township High School
Figure 12.2 Courtesy of Trib Total Media
Figure 12.3 Courtesy of the Los Angeles Times
Figure 12.4 Courtesy of NPR
And Now…Closer to Home, pg. 369 Photo by Daniel A. Anderson, Courtesy of Yvette Cabrera
Meet the Professionals Courtesy of the Los Angeles Times
Figure 12.5 Courtesy of the Los Angeles Times
Figure 12.6 Courtesy Discover Magazine, DiscoverMagazine.com
Figure 12.7 Article by Amanda Livingston, Illustration by Johanna Dakay, The Eagle's Eye, W. Charles Akins High School
Figure 12.8 Courtesy of David Horsey
Figure 12.9 Courtesy of the National Archives and Records Administration, U.S. Senate Collection, Center for Legislative Archives
Figure 12.10 Alexandra Fernholz, Lakota East Spark, Lakota East High School, Cincinnati, Ohio
Figure 12.11 Library of Congress, Prints & Photographs Division, Miscellaneous Items in High Demand, LC-USZ62-60242, AVA Bitter/Shutterstock.com
Figure 12.12 Image courtesy of National Scholastic Press Association (nspa.studentpress.org); cartoon by Anita Hodge, The Register, Central High School
Figure 12.13 Mila Supinskaya/Shutterstock.com

Chapter 13

Figure 13.0 Photo by Kyle Farrell, Lee County High School
Figure 13.1 StockLite/Shutterstock.com
Figure 13.2 Courtesy of North Pointe, Grosse Pointe North High School
Figure 13.3 Lemberg Vector studio/Shutterstock.com, michaeljung/Shutterstock.com
And Now…Closer to Home, pg. 394 Goodheart-Willcox Publisher
Figure 13.4 Billy Brown/Wired; ©Condé Nast, photo courtesy of Vibram USA
Your Turn, pg. 399 Goodheart-Willcox Publisher
Figure 13.5 The Oregonian by Oregonian Media Group. Reproduced with permission of Oregonian Media Group in the format Republish in a book via Copyright Clearance Center.
Figure 13.6 mahout/Shutterstock.com
Figure 13.7 Courtesy of Goodreads
Writers' Workshop 13.1 lynea/Shutterstock.com

Chapter 14

Figure 14.0 Photo by Forrest Czarnecki, Conifer High School
Figure 14.1 commons.wikimedia.org/ The Yorck Project
Figure 14.2 Illustration by Laura Klepfer
Figure 14.3 ©Reuters/CORBIS
Figure 14.4 VladisChern/Shutterstock.com
Figure 14.5 ©iStock.com/coloroftime
Figure 14.6 WAYHOME studio/ Shutterstock.com
Figure 14.7 Monkey Business Images/ Shutterstock.com
Figure 14.8 Courtesy of The Denver Post and denverpost.com
Figure 14.9 Library of Congress, Prints & Photograph Division, LC-DIG-npcc-20259
Figure 14.10 Elena Elisseeva/Shutterstock.com, DUSAN ZIDAR/Shutterstock.com
Figure 14.11 Goodheart-Willcox Publisher
And Now…Closer to Home, pg. 435 Courtesy of the Student Press Law Center
Figure 14.12 Goodheart-Willcox Publisher
Figure 14.13 Photo by Amber Primus, Woodrow Wilson High School

Chapter 15

Figure 15.0 Photo by Mary Brown, Woodrow Wilson High School
Figure 15.1 Library of Congress, Prints & Photographs Division, Miscellaneous Items in High Demand, LC-DIG-ds-02122
Figure 15.2 Design by Colleen O'Brien, The Communicator, Community High School
Figure 15.3 Goodheart-Willcox, photo by Africa Studio/Shutterstock.com
Figure 15.4 Steve Buckley/Shutterstock.com, oneinchpunch/Shutterstock.com, ©iStock.com/ 4774344sean, Illustration by Paige Paulsen, The Arapahoe Herald, Arapahoe High School, Design by Kacey Fang, The Winged Post, The Harker School, Design by Christophe Haubursin, El Estoque, Monta Vista High School
Figure 15.5 Courtesy of El Estoque, Monta Vista High School
Meet the Professionals Photo by Jody Rogac, Courtesy of Caleb Bennett, cover by Sara Cwynar/Wired; ©Condé Nast
Figure 15.6 Courtesy of El Estoque, Monta Vista High School
Figure 15.7 Courtesy of El Estoque, Monta Vista High School
Figure 15.8 Goodheart-Willcox Publisher, photo by luxorphoto/Shutterstock.com
Figure 15.9 Goodheart-Willcox Publisher
Figure 15.10 Goodheart-Willcox Publisher
Figure 15.11 Goodheart-Willcox Publisher
Figure 15.12 Goodheart-Willcox Publisher
Figure 15.13 Goodheart-Willcox Publisher, photos by wavebreakmedia/Shutterstock.com, Mona Makela/Shutterstock.com, ©iStock.com/ gdagys, illustration by Valentina Razumova/ Shutterstock.com
Figure 15.14 Goodheart-Willcox Publisher, photos by wavebreakmedia/Shutterstock.com, ©iStock.com/gdagys, Mona Makela/ Shutterstock.com, illustration by Valentina Razumova/Shutterstock.com
Figure 15.15 Courtesy of The Lancer, Thousand Oaks High School
Figure 15.16 Courtesy of El Estoque, Monta Vista High School
Figure 15.17 Courtesy of The Roar, A&M Consolidated High School
Figure 15.18 Goodheart-Willcox Publisher, photo by wavebreakmedia/Shutterstock.com, illustration by Valentina Razumova/ Shutterstock.com
Figure 15.19 Courtesy of North Pointe, Grosse Pointe North High School
Figure 15.20 Goodheart-Willcox Publisher, photos by katja kodba/Shutterstock.com, katja kodba/Shutterstock.com, Orange Line Media/Shutterstock.com, Eldad Carin/ Shutterstock.com, illustration by Valentina Razumova/Shutterstock.com
Figure 15.21 Goodheart-Willcox Publisher, photos by katja kodba/Shutterstock.com, Eldad Carin/Shutterstock.com, illustration by Valentina Razumova/Shutterstock.com
Figure 15.22 Courtesy of The Roar, Whitney High School

Figure 15.23 Goodheart-Willcox Publisher, photos by wavebreakmedia/Shutterstock.com, ©iStock.com/gdagys, Mona Makela/Shutterstock.com, illustration by Valentina Razumova/Shutterstock.com
Figure 15.24 Courtesy of The Winged Post, The Harker School
Your Turn example, pg. 479 Goodheart-Willcox Publisher, photos by katja kodba/Shutterstock.com, Mona Makela/Shutterstock.com, Eldad Carin/Shutterstock.com, wavebreakmedia/Shutterstock.com
Writers' Workshop 15.1 Goodheart-Willcox Publisher, Julianka/Shutterstock.com

Chapter 16

Figure 16.0 Courtesy of Sean Ziebarth, Fountain Valley High School
Figure 16.1 Will Counts Collection: Indiana University Archives (P0026600)
Figure 16.2 Courtesy of Marcus Yam/Los Angeles Times
Figure 16.3 Photo by Tori Caudill, The Crimson Crier, Sparkman High School
Figure 16.4 Photo by Ashley Potts, Legend, Centreville High School
Figure 16.5 Photo by Chris Bull, El Paisano, Westlake High School
Figure 16.6 Goodheart-Willcox Publisher
Figure 16.7 Photo by Valorie King, Buffalo, Haltom High School, photo by Hannah Kunz, The Featherduster, Westlake High School
Figure 16.8 Photo by Stefano Byer, The Harbinger, Shawnee Mission East High School
Figure 16.9 Photo by Danielle Norton, Hauberk, Shawnee Mission East High School
Figure 16.10 Monkey Business Images/Shutterstock.com, Nagel Photography/Shutterstock.com
Figure 16.11 Courtesy of Rachael and Tom Woznick, tool icon George Toubalis/Shutterstock.com
Figure 16.12 Jamie Roach/Shutterstock.com, tool icon George Toubalis/Shutterstock.com
Figure 16.13 Photo by Andy Wickoren, The Northwest Passage, Shawnee Mission Northwest High School, Larry St. Pierre/Shutterstock.com
Figure 16.14 Courtesy of El Estoque, Monta Vista High School
Figure 16.15 Goodheart-Willcox Publisher, RealCG Animation Studio
Figure 16.16 Photo by Grant Shorin, The Viking, Palo Alto High School; Roberto Galan/Shutterstock.com; Jose Gil/Shutterstock.com
Figure 16.17 Photo by Josie Pringle, Bryant High School Hornet Yearbook
Figure 16.18 Goodheart-Willcox Publisher, kuroksta/Shutterstock.com
Figure 16.19 Goodheart-Willcox Publisher
Figure 16.20 Photos by Amol Pande, El Estoque, Monta Vista High School
And Now…Closer to Home, pg. 509 Courtesy of Amy Ding, Monta Vista High School
Figure 16.21 Goodheart-Willcox Publisher
Figure 16.22 Christian Bertrand/Shutterstock.com
Figure 16.24 Courtesy of Michelle Balmeo

Chapter 17

Figure 17.0 Photo by Forrest Czarnecki, Conifer High School
Figure 17.1 Goodheart-Willcox Publisher, photos by Nany New York/Shutterstock.com, Radiokafka/Shutterstock.com, stockcreations/Shutterstock.com
Figure 17.2 Goodheart-Willcox Publisher, photo by Blend Images/Shutterstock.com
Figure 17.3 Goodheart-Willcox Publisher
Figure 17.4 Goodheart-Willcox Publisher
Figure 17.5 Goodheart-Willcox Publisher
Figure 17.6 Photo by Forrest Czarnecki, Conifer High School
Figure 17.7 Goodheart-Willcox Publisher, photo by B. and E. Dudzinscy/Shutterstock.com
Figure 17.8 Goodheart-Willcox Publisher, photos by vvoe/Shutterstock.com, aerogondo2/Shutterstock.com, Nagel Photography/Shutterstock.com

Figure 17.9 Goodheart-Willcox Publisher, photos by B. and E. Dudzinscy/Shutterstock.com, tobkatrina/Shutterstock.com, ducu59us/Shutterstock.com, bikeriderlondon/Shutterstock.com, Nopporn Chainate/Shutterstock.com, aerogondo2/Shutterstock.com, stockcreations/Shutterstock.com
Figure 17.10 Goodheart-Willcox Publisher, photos by bonchan/Shutterstock.com, Nancy Kennedy/Shutterstock.com, Mark Herreid/Shutterstock.com, bikeriderlondon/Shutterstock.com, ducu59us/Shutterstock.com, Nopporn Chainate/Shutterstock.com
Figure 17.11 Goodheart-Willcox Publisher
Figure 17.12 Goodheart-Willcox Publisher, photo by Mallory Dufek
Figure 17.13 Goodheart-Willcox Publisher, photo by tobkatrina/Shutterstock.com
Figure 17.14 Goodheart-Willcox Publisher, photo by Dorottya Mathe/Shutterstock.com
Figure 17.15 Goodheart-Willcox Publisher
And Now…Closer to Home, pg. 554 MarijaPiliponyte/Shutterstock.com
Figure 17.16 Goodheart-Willcox Publisher

Glossary

A

accountable A term that means journalists and the organizations they represent are answerable for the accuracy, fairness and balance of what they publish. They strive to avoid errors and inaccuracy and to provide balanced coverage before publication. They admit publicly to errors and lapses, and they provide corrected information. (1)

across the wire Coming from a wire service, such as Reuters, Associated Press (AP) or United Press International (UPI), that originally used the telegraph wires to transmit news. (2)

add value To provide an additional benefit. (5)

ad server A computer or system of computers that stores ads and uploads them to a website. (17)

advance story A story that is published before the event it discusses takes place. (13)

advocacy site An Internet site devoted to gaining support, business or votes. (8)

affiliation Membership in, or connection with, an organization or movement. (8)

alignment The design technique that arranges elements on a page in an invisible line to guide the reader's eye. (15)

alternative story forms Parts of a story that offer different ways to tell a story or communicate information, draw the readers' attention and help the readers remember facts from the story; examples include fact boxes, lists, Q & As and charts. (15)

ambush journalism Intercepting and questioning a source by surprise in hopes of acquiring an unguarded response. (9)

analyze To mentally take something apart. (13)

angle The point, the main idea or the peg on which everything else in a story hangs. (10)

attribution Naming the source of information that does not come from personal observation. (4)

axis line The invisible line that the videographer should not cross when filming to ensure that the camera consistently films from one side of the principle subject, so that a character on the camera's right stays on the camera's right in every shot; also called the *180 degree rule* or the *line of action*. (16)

B

b-roll Any footage that is not of an interview but illustrates the story, such as detail shots, establishing shots and action sequences. (16)

backpack journalism A form of journalism in which journalists are fluent with photo, video, audio and text using high-tech devices that they can carry around with them. (16)

balance The visual distribution of design elements on a page, such as color, white space, objects and texture. (15)

balanced reporting Telling more than one side of a story and being fair to each side. (4)

banner ad An ad, usually rectangular, that appears above, below or on the side of the content on a website. (17)

beat A topic or news area, such as city politics or sports, covered regularly by a journalist. (2)

billboard ad In radio, a ten-second ad, usually 30 words or fewer, that runs just before a regular feature. (17)

Note: The number in parentheses following each definition indicates the chapter in which the term can be found.

bleed The space between your margin and the line where the printer will trim the page. (15)

brand awareness Recognition of a brand name. (17)

breaking news story A news story that communicates new information about unexpected events as they occur or shortly afterward. (5)

brights Short, humorous stories whose primary news value is oddity. (6)

bullet time The technique for re-creating or retelling a defining moment in a game, match or solo competition by capturing the moment in present tense so that the reader feels as if he is in that moment, as it happened. (11)

bumper music A short music clip that signals a change, such as the beginning or end of an ad. (17)

button ad A small online ad. (17)

C

camera-ready art Art that is ready to be scanned into a publication. (17)

catch line A word or phrase set off graphically from the beginning of a caption and meant to capture the audience's attention. (7)

center of visual interest The main image or art for the package. (15)

circle kicker The ending to a Wall Street Journal formula story that returns to the poster child to provide balance and bring closure to the story. (10)

circulation figures Statistics on the audience for a production, such as the number of print copies distributed, the number of visitors to a website, or the number of viewers or listeners who tune in to a TV or radio show. (17)

cliché A familiar and much-used description or other trite expression. (13)

click through To click on a hyperlink that leads to another website. (17)

code of ethics A written set of guidelines for ethical behavior established by the group they guide. (4)

column One of a series of regularly occurring articles published in the same section in each edition, broadcast or post; written by the same person—or a series of people—each time it appears. (12)

conflict One of the seven news values. Discord between people or ideas. (2)

conflict of interest A connection to someone or something in a story that might make it difficult for a journalist to report objectively. (13)

content Information and ideas reported in journalistic reporting; may be delivered to a cellphone from a news feed; published in a newspaper, magazine or book; posted on the Internet; broadcast on the radio or television; or delivered in any number of other ways. (1)

context Background and setting surrounding an event. (1)

copyright The exclusive right to reproduce, adapt, distribute, display or perform a creative work. (3)

copyright infringement Improper use of a copyrighted work; the theft of intellectual property. (3)

court-recognized privileges Privileges recognized by the courts and usually based on the First Amendment; vary from state to state and from situation to situation. (3)

credentials Academic degrees or professional experience or honors. Also, documents (such as press credentials) that provide proof of a person's position. (8)

credibility The quality of being believable and reliable. (4)

critic An expert in a field, usually with university training or significant professional experience, who interprets a work and ponders its social significance. (13)

cyberbullying Online harassment. (14)

D

dateline A contrasting line of type at the beginning of a story that names the place from which the story was filed; sometimes the date is also included. (5)

deadline The time or date by which a story must be completed and submitted. (2)

decisive moment The particular instant that captures the emotion and importance of an event. (11)

defamation Damage to someone's reputation brought about by libel or slander. (3)

depth of field A technique in which the object in the foreground is in sharp focus, creating distance between it and the unfocused, or blurry, items in the background. (16)

descriptive headline A headline that may use creative writing tools to provoke interest or controversy; might contain multiple layers of meaning, wordplay, a variation on a quotation or a vivid scene from the story. (7)

design concept The driving force behind a design from which all aspects of a design stem. (15)

developing story A news story that adds information to previously reported stories; also called *folo stories*. (5)

direct quotation A quotation that consists of the source's actual words, plus an attribution. (9)

direction A concept of design in which a design element can guide the readers' eyes to a certain spot on the page. (15)

display font A large font that adds graphic interest to the design of the letters. (7)

display headline A creatively designed headline that supports a specific story and its design concept. (15)

dominant story The story that receives the most prominent treatment in a broadcast or on a Web page or in a section of the paper; usually comes first in a broadcast or attracts the eye first through its placement, the size and style of font used in its headline and the graphic elements related to it. (2)

drop head A subsidiary headline that adds information below the main deck and is usually in a different font than the main head; also called a *read-out*. (7)

E

editorial board The group of people who determine a publication's or broadcast's editorial policy; usually includes the editorial page editor and editorial writers. (12)

editorial cartoon A drawing that makes a comment about events or people in the news; frequently critical of the subjects it portrays; may be about a new topic not already discussed in writing, or it may provide a new viewpoint on a topic that has been discussed; sometimes called a *political cartoon*. (12)

editorial illustration A drawing that accompanies and illustrates an op-ed piece; meant to draw the readers or viewers into the article and to emphasize its point. (12)

editorializing Inserting one's opinions into news coverage. (5)

emphasis A design technique that draws attention to the most important story or element on the page. (15)

enterprise stories Stories that a reporter finds or develops in addition to regular assignments from an editor. (2)

expandable ad An ad that enlarges when the viewer accepts an invitation to "click here to expand." (17)

exposition Language that conveys information or provides an explanation. (12)

external links On-screen links that takes the reader to different websites. (14)

eyeline matching A video editing technique that assumes your audience will want to see what your subject is pointing to, looking at or talking to, if it is out of the frame, and they will want to see it in the next shot. (16)

eye-tracking research Research studies in which participants wear glasses equipped with cameras that track their eye movement as they view a page of a newspaper or news stories on a website; designed to learn more about how people read publications. (15)

F

fair use The doctrine that there are some circumstances in which copyrighted material may be used without acquiring permission from the copyright holder. (3)

fictionalize To add imaginary details, such as events, characters or dialogue, to a true story; not acceptable in journalism. (12)

firewall A figurative wall that protects journalists from influences that would harm their ability to act independently, usually between the business department and the news and editorial parts of a journalistic organization. (4)

first person A point of view in which the speaker or writer refers to himself or a group including himself. (10)

first-person observation The eyewitness account from a reporter at the scene of a news event. (8)

five W's The five questions that every news story should answer: who, what, when, where and why. (5)

five W's lead A news story lead that includes answers to the five W's: who, what, when, where and why; also called a *summary lead*. (5)

focus group In journalism, a diverse group of individuals who are brought together to give their opinions about what topics need to be covered and the extent of the coverage. (14)

follow-up question A question based on the answer to the previous question. (9)

folo story A news story that adds information to previously reported stories; also called a *developing story*. (5)

freedom of information laws Laws requiring that all records generated by a public body are open to the public unless they are specifically exempted by law. (3)

full disclosure Informing the audience of any possible conflict of interest. (13)

G

game brief A basic sports report that provides the audience with a thumbnail overview of a game. (11)

gatekeeper A newsroom leader with direct responsibility to guard the integrity of a news publication or broadcast; has the power to send a story back for additional work, to alter it before it is broadcast or published, or to kill it. (4)

general news News stories that have timeliness and impact but do not necessarily involve an unexpected or immediate event. (6)

genre The family or type to which a creative work belongs. (13)

grid A design concept and the basic structure of a page; includes the margins on all sides and number of columns. (15)

gutter The white space formed by the margins of two adjoining pages. (15)

H

hammer head A subsidiary headline set in large, bold type above the main deck; often descriptive headlines with multiple layers of meaning, meant to intrigue the reader rather than communicate the most important or breaking news; used with news analysis and feature stories more than with breaking news stories; also called a *barker*. (7)

hard lead A news lead that immediately addresses the most important aspects of the story and summarizes the main idea of the story within the first few sentences. The most common news lead. (10)

hard news News stories about serious topics such as politics, economics, war, fires, earthquakes and murders. (5)

has legs A journalistic expression meaning that a story has sources and information to make it potentially reliable, interesting and significant. (8)

headlinese An abbreviated writing style used in summary headlines to convey the most important elements of a story in a small amount of space. (7)

hearsay Rumor, gossip or other unverified information. (8)

high angle A shot taken from above a subject. (16)

horizontal exchange Communication among a publication's or broadcast's audience members. (14)

human interest One of the seven news values. The aspect of a news story that deals with a person's problems, concerns, interests, backgrounds and achievements so that the reader's interest and perhaps emotion become involved. The subjects of these stories are "ordinary people," not prominent figures. (2)

hyperlinked An electronic link that joins a related document or image. (17)

I

impact One of the seven news values. The extent to which a story will affect the audience's lives. (2)

impartiality Not favoring one side over another; unbiased. (8)

implicit bias Attitudes and stereotypes we hold unconsciously, which affect our actions, understanding and decisions without conscious knowledge. (1)

indirect quotation A quotation that uses some of the source's words, but the words are embedded in the reporter's sentence. (9)

insert A separate ad, usually printed on heavy paper, that is placed into a print publication. (17)

intellectual property The result of creative work; for example, a novel, a song or artwork. (3)

intended audience The people you hope will view, listen to or read your work. (1)

interactive graphics Visual components of a web-based story that invite the audience to contribute information or participate in a more immersive experience. (16)

interstitial ad In online advertising, an ad that opens a separate browser window. (17)

inverted pyramid The structure used for many news stories in which the most important information is placed first, and succeeding paragraphs contain increasingly less crucial information. (5)

J

journalism The discipline of collecting, verifying, reporting and analyzing information regarding current events, including trends, issues and people, for a broad audience. (1)

journalistic blog An online publishing format that follows journalism ethics and standards and may contain the same sorts of content that are in the rest of the journalistic publication, including reviews, op-eds, columns and editorial cartoons, but sometimes less formal or written with a first person perspective on the events discussed. (12)

jump line In a printed story, a line of type that directs the reader to the page where the story is continued. (5)

K

Ken Burns effect Creating the illusion of movement by slowly zooming into or out of still images to focus the viewer's attention on specific details. (16)

kerning The spacing between letters in a block of text. (15)

kicker A subsidiary headline that adds information to the main deck; goes above the main deck and is usually half the point size of the main deck. (7)

L

lead The opening sentences of a news story. The lead is often a summary of the story's essential points; also spelled *lede*. (5)

lead room Open space in front of a moving subject in a photograph or video. (16)

lead story The most prominent story on a news page or in a broadcast. (2)

leading The spacing between lines in a block of text. (15)

leading lines Lines within an image that draw the audience's eye to a specific subject or feature of the image. (16)

liability Legal responsibility. The idea that any person who could have and should have prevented an injury can be held responsible for it. (3)

libel Knowingly publishing untrue or misleading words, pictures or symbols—that harms another person's reputation or harms an organization's ability to conduct its affairs in a community. This includes the reputation of corporations, churches, schools and businesses, as well as individuals. (3)

line Design elements, both visible and invisible, that guide readers eyes, divide content and emphasize certain elements. (15)

live coverage Sports reporting that occurs during a game or event. (11)

local angle The focus of a national or international story that features the story's impact on a journalist's community or connections the story has to a journalist's community. (2)

logo A visual representation of a company or idea, a sort of shorthand for who it is, where it is and what it stands for or provides. (17)

long-form feature A sports profile in which a reporter tries to identify a theme of a player's career and life and writes with that angle in mind; should reveal to the reader the joys and challenges of that player's life experience. (11)

low angle A shot taken from below a subject. (16)

lower-thirds titles Text that is overlaid on the lower third of the video frame that identifies the person appearing on screen; often includes the person's title or other identifying information. (16)

M

main deck The primary headline of a news story. (7)

media The plural of medium, a tool used to store or deliver information; include hard drives, oil paints and canvas, cellphones, paper and ink or pencil, skywriting, the Internet, DVDs and thousands of tools that have not yet been invented; also refers to organizations and their employees and contributors that intend to deliver content publicly to a large number of people. In this case, the media is short for *mass media*. (1)

metasite A website that is a directory to other websites. (8)

modular design Design approach in which content is organized into modules. (15)

motion sequence A series of video shots that, when combined in logical order, convey a complete action in compressed time; a sub-category of b-roll. (16)

mug shot Any picture of the face. (10)

N

narrative A story, either true or fictional; includes characters, conflict and action. (12)

narrative headline A headline written as a complete sentence in standard, sometimes conversational English; suggests that the reporting will include anecdotes and storytelling, as well as facts and breaking news. (7)

narrative lead A lead that begins with storytelling elements such as a vivid scene, an anecdote, an interesting character or a detailed account of an exciting moment and ends with a nut graf, providing the five W's and perhaps the *so what* of the story. (6)

narrowcast To transmit to a selected audience. (14)

natural sound The soundtrack of a particular space; also called *nat sound*. (16)

news aggregator A person, agency or website that collects and publishes news from other sources but does not do its own reporting or create original content. (2)

news cycle The time period between editions, broadcasts or digital posting of stories. (2)

news peg A connection to a timely event that justifies a feature or soft news story. (2)

In a sidebar: a reference to something in the main story. (6)

news value Something that makes a story newsworthy; one of the seven news values. (2)

nut graf The paragraph that tells the story in a nutshell; follows a narrative lead and provides a transition from the lead to the body of the story; provides any of the five W's plus the how and perhaps the so what that were not already included in the main and subsidiary headlines and in the narrative lead. (6)

O

objective Impartial; not influenced by the writer's opinions. (10)

oddity One of the seven news values. The quality of being unusual. (2)

online forum The electronic version of a town square, in which people are invited to participate in discussions and exchange ideas. (14)

P

packaged story A story with a large headline, dominant image and at least one alternative story form. (15)

pan To move a camera horizontally left or right. (16)

paraphrase A rewording of the source's words. A paraphrase should accurately represent the speaker's meaning. (9)

photo illustration A staged photograph. (4)

pitch To describe a potential story to persuade the editor or producer that the story is worth reporting. (2)

player profile A sports story that focuses on a single player and adds personality to the sports pages. (11)

points of entry Design elements that are intended to draw the audience into the written story. (15)

pop-up ad A new browser window that displays an ad and appears on top of the window the viewer has selected. (17)

post-production The video production stage in which the video story is edited and put together. (16)

poster child A person who gives a human face to the issue a journalist is covering. (10)

pre-production The planning stage in video production. (16)

press credentials A document—usually a card with a reporter's picture and name and the name of his or her publication—that identifies an individual as a member of the press; gives a reporter access to people, events and legal or governmental proceedings that may be off-limits to the general public. (3)

press package Material that a company has prepared for the use of the press; also called a *press kit*. (3)

primary source Someone who experiences an event firsthand or has firsthand knowledge in other ways. (8)

prior restraint Prohibiting the inclusion of certain elements in a publication or broadcast. (3)

prior review Review of a publication by officials before the publication is printed, broadcast or posted online. (3)

production The video production stage in which the raw elements of a video story are gathered, shot and produced. (16)

prominence One of the seven news values. The quality of being widely known. People in the public eye, such as politicians, sports figures and entertainment figures, have this quality. Their opinions or events in their lives are of greater interest than the same events in the life of a private, less widely known or "ordinary" person. (2)

proof A copy or sample ad (or other printed product); created to check for accuracy and design. (17)

proportion The relative size of elements on a page and how well they work together. (15)

proximity One of the seven news values. A term that means that an event occurred close to a journalist's geographic location. (2)

Grouping like things together on a page to signal to the reader that these elements relate closely to each other and to give the design a sense of order and organization. (15)

public forum A place for public assembly or public expression. (3)

public service ad (PSA) An ad run without charge, with the goal of making the audience aware of an important value or program; also called a *public service announcement*. (17)

punch list A to-do list of the most important points to include in a story. (6)

put to bed Sent to the printer or published online. At this stage, a story is beyond revision. (2)

Q

quick take A graphic that contains a rating and several key pieces of information about a product or experience; often accompanies a review. (13)

R

rate sheet A page in a sales kit that shows the dimensions of potential ads and their costs. (17)

read-out A subsidiary headline that adds information below the main deck and is usually in a different font than the main head; also called a *drop head*. (7)

real-time updates Quick, live reports on key plays throughout the duration of the game. (11)

recap To summarize, especially a sports season or event. (11)

retraction A correction that identifies an error and provides correct information. (4)

review The journalistic piece in which a reviewer shares her experience of a creative work or a product. (13)

reviewer A person who experiences and evaluates a creative work or a product for an audience. (13)

rhetorical device Any of the classical methods using words or speech to persuade an audience. (12)

rhetorical question A question that is asked for effect. The person asking the question is not expecting the reader or listener to reply. (12)

rhythm A concept of design in which all of the design elements work with each other to lead the reader on a journey across the page. (15)

royalty Money that goes to composers and performers whenever their work is used for commercial purposes. (17)

rule of thirds A principle of composition in which the center of interest in a photo, art, architecture or design, is placed at one of the points where the imaginary lines that divide an image into three equal parts horizontally, and three parts vertically, intersect. (16)

S

scale The size of elements on the page. (15)

scoop To report a story before a competing publication. (2)

screen An image or other design element used as the background for text. (16)

scrutiny Close examination. (4)

search engine optimized (SEO) A headline that has been crafted to capture the attention of search engines' spiders. (7)

secondary source A person or document that interprets the evidence from primary sources. (8)

shield laws Laws that protect journalists from official demands to surrender their journalistic research and images; vary from state to state. (3)

shot list A checklist of shots that a photographer wants in a particular photo or video shoot. (16)

sidebar A story set outside the main news story that goes along with the main story but does not belong in it. (6)

signature line In broadcasts, the identification that reporters give at the end of their report; also called a *tag*. (5)

slander Untrue spoken words that harm another person's reputation or harm an organization's ability to conduct its affairs in a community. The spoken version of libel. (3)

snippet A word or phrase extracted from a longer quotation. (9)

soft lead A lead that grabs the audience's attentions and tells just a piece of the story. (10)

soft news News stories about entertainment, fashion, celebrities, human interest stories, tourism and unusual or odd events. (5)

spider A program that crawls through millions of Web pages to provide data to a search engine. (7)

spike To kill a story, that is, withhold it from publication or broadcast. (2)

sportrait A sports photographic portrait. (11)

stale A term used to describe a news story that is out of date or no longer interesting. (2)

static ad An online ad that has no animation or interactive elements except for a hyperlink that lets the viewer click through to another site. (17)

stats The facts or data for a team. (11)

storyboard A sequence of drawings that a photographer can use to plan his or her shots in a video shoot. (16)

story flow The process for creating and editing stories. (4)

streaming video A traditional video that has been compressed to be transferred over the Web. (17)

subheadlines Headlines for sidebar stories and graphics. (15)

subjective Based on or influenced by the writer's opinions. (10)

subpoena A legal written order to appear in court to present documents, to testify, etc. (3)

summary headline A headline that briefly summarizes the five W's of a news story; consists of complete, compact sentences, often written in headlinese. (7)

summary lead A news story lead that includes answers to the five W's: who, what, when, where and why; also called a *five W's lead*. (5)

sunshine laws Laws that require meetings and actions of public officials to be visible to the public. (3)

T

tag In broadcasts, the identification that reporters give at the end of their report; also called a *signature line*. (5)

teaser A broadcast headline meant to attract and hold the audience's attention; brief summary, usually under 48 words and usually in complete sentences; also called *tease* or *taster*. (7)

A small graphic that can be used to lead readers to related content in another part of the publication or online. (15)

The Wall Street Journal formula A feature-story-organizing technique in which a piece begins with the story of one person who is affected by the issue at hand, the main issue is explained and discussed, and then the story circles back to the person introduced at the beginning. (10)

third person A point of view in which the writer avoids directly addressing the audience or using the first person point of view (10)

three-point lighting A lighting technique that consists of a key light, a fill light and a back light. (16)

tilt To move a camera vertically up or down. (16)

timeliness One of the seven news values. Describes stories that are currently happening, have just happened or are about to happen. (2)

Title IX The federal legislation that was passed to correct gender disparity in scholastic sports programs and helped improve the athletic opportunities available for female athletes. (11)

transparent Being open in one's news reporting, not concealing anything. (4)

troll In online forums, a person who disrupts normal discussion by making rude or insensitive comments. (14)

type The general term for all letterforms. (15)

U

unbiased Impartial. (4)

underground publication A student publication that does not use school resources and is not affiliated with the school. (3)

unintended audience People you did not necessarily expect to read or view your publication but who may do so now or in the future. (1)

unreliable source A source that you cannot trust enough to quote in a story. (8)

up-front payment Payment received before an ad is published. (17)

V

value A term that describes how light or dark a design element is. (15)

verbal-visual unity A concept of design in which the story itself, all of the words on the page and all graphic elements, work together to send one clear message to the audience. (15)

vertical exchange Communication between a publication and the audience; contrasts with horizontal exchange. (14)

visual hierarchy The arrangement or presentation of elements in a way that emphasizes the most important story on the page. (15)

W

white space Space in a design that is empty of text or graphics; also called *negative space*. (15)

wild art Feature photos that are so strong they tell a story without accompanying story also called *enterprise art*. (10)

Index

A

B

C

D

E

F

G

Q

R

S

W

Z